Human Development

A Life Span Approach   Second Edition

Human
Development

A Life Span Approach

John P. Dworetzky

Western Washington University

Second Edition

West Publishing Company

Saint Paul/Minneapolis • New York • Los Angeles • San Francisco

COPY EDITOR   Janet Greenblatt
COMPOSITION   Parkwood Composition Service
PHOTO CREDITS   Photo credits and acknowledgments appear following index.

WEST'S COMMITMENT TO THE ENVIRONMENT

In 1906, West Publishing Company began recycling materials left over from the production of books. This began a tradition of efficient and responsible use of resources. Today, up to 95 percent of our legal books and 70 percent of our college and school texts are printed on recycled, acid-free stock. West also recycles nearly 22 million pounds of scrap paper annually—the equivalent of 181,717 trees. Since the 1960s, West has devised ways to capture and recycle waste inks, solvents, oils, and vapors created in the printing process. We also recycle plastics of all kinds, wood, glass, corrugated cardboard, and batteries, and have eliminated the use of Styrofoam book packaging. We at West are proud of the longevity and the scope of our commitment to the environment.

Production, Prepress, Printing and Binding by West Publishing Company.

British Library Cataloguing-in-Publication Data. A catalogue record for this book is available from the British Library.

COPYRIGHT ©1989   By WEST PUBLISHING COMPANY
COPYRIGHT ©1995   By WEST PUBLISHING COMPANY
                     610 Opperman Drive
                     P.O. Box 64526
                     St. Paul, MN 55164-0526

Library of Congress Cataloging-in-Publication Data

Dworetzky, John.
    Human development / John P. Dworetzky.--2nd ed.
      p.   cm.
    Includes bibliographical references and indexes.
    ISBN 0–314–04533–3
    1. Developmental psychology.   I. Title
BF713.D89   1995   94-41823
155--dc20   CIP

TO VIVIAN

WITH ALL OUR LOVE

CONTENTS IN BRIEF

CONTENTS

Unit Two
Beginnings (0–1 Year of Age)   49

UNIT THREE

Early Childhood: Toddlers and Preschool Children (1–6 Years of Age)   145

CHAPTER 6

Early Childhood: Physical, Cognitive, and Gender Role Development   147

AT ISSUE
Reexamining Piaget's Assertions   159

APPLICATIONS
Overcoming Gender Stereotypes   170

CHAPTER 7

Language Development   177

AT ISSUE
Children and the Origins of
Language 193

APPLICATIONS
Strike When the Iron
Is Hot 196

CHAPTER 8

Early Childhood: Personality and Social-Emotional Development 201

AT ISSUE
Born to Be Wild: An
Evolutionary Theory of
Social-Emotional
Development 205

APPLICATIONS
Overcoming Childhood
Fears: "Things that Go
Bump in the Night" 226

UNIT FOUR
Middle Childhood (6–12 Years of Age)   231

UNIT FIVE
Adolescence (12–18 Years of Age)   315

CHAPTER 12
Adolescent Physical and Cognitive Development   317

CHAPTER 13

Adolescent Social and Personality Development   337

UNIT SIX

Early Adulthood (18–40 Years of Age)   355

CHAPTER 14

Early Adulthood: Physical, Cognitive, and Personality Development   357

CHAPTER 15

Early Adulthood: Loving and Working   387

UNIT SEVEN
Middle Adulthood (40–65 Years of Age)   415

CHAPTER 16
Middle Adulthood: Physical, Cognitive, and Personality Development   417

CHAPTER 17
Middle Adulthood: Relationships and Occupational Development   443

UNIT EIGHT
Late Adulthood (65+ Years of Age)   469

PREFACE

I began writing textbooks 15 years ago with the publication of Introduction to Child Development. I enjoyed writing that book because it was based on the pedagogy incorporated in Dennis Coon's highly successful introductory psychology text. In fact, I had come to writing because I had been using Dennis' text in my own classes and was so impressed with the response from my students that one day I wished aloud in front of Clyde Perlee Jr., editor-in-chief of West Publishing Company's college division, that it would be nice if such a text were available for child development. The next thing I knew, I was given a chance to write one. With the support of Clyde's friendship and confidence, it was published in 1981. The child text was successful and is now in its fifth edition (1993).

Following the success of the child text, a number of students and colleagues asked if I had plans to write a human development text. The hope was that I would write a text to cover the entire life span and that it would incorporate the same successful pedagogy, content rigor, and writing style found in the child text. I had often considered writing a life span book, but found that my time was limited, especially because I was also writing Psychology, an introductory text which is now in its fifth edition.

Then, in 1986, I had the great fortune to meet Nancy Davis. Nancy is a gifted and talented writer and, at that time, was a psychologist at the Charles River Hospital in Wellesley, Massachusetts. Her knowledge, good humor, intelligence, and hard work made a collaboration both a delight and a challenge. I believe we brought out the best in each other. When these efforts were combined with Clyde Perlee's skill and suggestions, the result was the first edition of Human Development: A Life Span Approach, a text we all took pride in producing.

By 1992, the first edition was becoming dated because so much had changed in the field. However, the hope of doing a new edition with Nancy was prohibited by the fact that she had built a private practice and was too committed to her clients to take the time to write a second edition. For a time I considered not revising the text and just letting it go. But so many of those who had used the first edition were asking for a revision that I decided to do the second edition on my own. Even though I wrote the second edition without the benefit of Nancy's skill and knowledge I still owe her a debt of gratitude. Those who have used the first edition will notice that some of Nancy's work is carried over to the second edition. The flavor of her writing and many of her interesting and timeless anecdotes are found in the pages of this book.

Of course, there are a number of fine texts in the field of human development, but I believe you will discover that the approach taken by this text offers readers something special in both content and style. Whether you are a professor adopting this text for your students, or are a student exploring the human life span, I hope you find this text enjoyable and informative.

ACKNOWLEDGMENTS

It would be impossible to write a textbook without the help and cooperation of many others. I would like to thank those who kindly and generously gave their time to review this book and to provide criticism, encouragement, suggestions, and ideas. I wish to express our personal appreciation to the following members of our academic community who assisted in the preparation of our textbooks. For the first edition:

Dana H. Davidson
University of Hawaii at Manoa

Jim Hail
McLennan Community College,
California

Dianne Irwin
Glendale College, California

Mary Kalymun
University of Rhode Island

Richard Marius
Harvard University, Massachusetts

William and Mary Perry
Harvard University, Massachusetts

Peg Hull Smith
University of Toledo, Ohio

Theodore Spielberg
Tufts University School of Medicine,
Massachusetts

Lee Springer
Glendale College, Arizona

And for the second edition:

Aline M. Garrett
The University of Southwestern
Louisiana

Janet R. Matthews
Loyola University, New Orleans

Rosellen Rosich
The University of Alaska, Anchorage

Lisa L. Weyandt
Central Washington University

Ruth Gynther
Auburn University

Francis J. Short
Broome Community College

Shirley R. Shular
Everett Community College

I'd also like to express my deepest gratitude to Clyde Perlee Jr., editor-in-chief of West's college division, for his inspiration, concern, and talent. Without Clyde there simply wouldn't have been a book. I value his friendship more than I can say. I also want to express special thanks to Bill Stryker for the design of the text and for his always speedy work under pressing time constraints. Thanks also to Janet Greenblatt for her fast and excellent copyediting, and to all others at West Publishing who have had a part in preparing this textbook.

John P. Dworetzky

UNIT ONE

FOUNDATIONS OF DEVELOPMENT

CHAPTER 1

History, Issues, and Research

Is It Fact or Fiction?

- *In the halls of Congress, concerned parents implore their elected representatives to ban violence from children's television programs. Testimony is given, and parents describe how their children have imitated the aggression they have seen on TV. Television producers argue, on the other hand, that the effect is overestimated and that many children are aggressive from time to time even if they haven't been watching television.*

- *In a high school health center in a disadvantaged neighborhood, a program is started to help eliminate unwanted pregnancies and sexually transmitted diseases among students. Sex education programs are conducted, and condoms are given to students without parental knowledge. Some parents and religious groups argue that such programs encourage sexual activity among teenagers and therefore lead to an increase in pregnancies and sexually transmitted diseases.*

- *In a cheerfully decorated room, a terminally ill patient waits with his family through his last hours. Many people who work with those patients in the final stages of life believe that having the family close helps to ease the patient's burden. They argue that death is a natural part of life and it is healthy for other family members to learn to deal with it. Other people, however, believe that the negative effects of this vigil, especially on young children, may be greater than the positive ones.*

Who is correct in these situations, and how can you tell?

How many debates can you think of that involve the development or welfare of people? For example, is it wrong for parents or teachers to spank children? What do babies think about? Do our intellectual abilities decline as we age? When should children be expected to walk? How do we acquire a sense of right and wrong? What are the effects of divorce on children and on the divorcing spouses themselves? Should there be a mandatory retirement age? On questions such as these, unlike questions about nuclear physics or molecular chemistry, for instance, almost everyone has an opinion.

Try it. Ask friends or relatives, "Should I mix sodium ferricyanide with ferric ammonium sulfate?* See what they say. Then ask, "Is it wrong for parents to spank their children?" The first question is not likely to bring ready responses, except from chemists, while the second will usually provoke comment and advice. The reason for this is that people think they should know about children because they've been around them, raised a few, or can recall their own childhood, while almost no one expects to be knowledgeable about complex chemical reactions.

There are thousands of commonly held and discussed opinions and beliefs about human development—and many of them are contradictory. In this chapter, we'll take a look at the first thing that any good psychologist, chemist, researcher, or student needs to know—how to separate fact from fiction. We'll also look at some of the important issues that developmental researchers have debated for years. But first, let's examine the emergence of scientific interest in the human life span and the history of research in this area.

WHY STUDY THE DEVELOPING HUMAN?

> In our society, as in most others, age is a major dimension of social organization . . . to a greater or lesser extent, families, corporations, even whole communities are organized by age. Age also plays an important part in how people relate to one another across the whole range of everyday experience. . . . Age is also a major touchstone by which individuals organize and interpret their own lives. Both children and adults continually ask of themselves, "How well am I doing for my age?" (Neugarten & Neugarten, 1987, p. 29)

From the time we are born, our position in society is determined to a large degree by our age. As we grow older, we change. These changes are most noticeable during the early years of infancy and childhood. As each month passes, an infant grows larger and shows dramatic gains in intellectual and social competence. Children undergo great changes from one year to the next. As they approach adolescence, their physical changes bring them closer to adulthood. Yet, for the adolescent, there are new developmental tasks to work out and new competencies to acquire. Even when adolescents have reached physical maturity as adults, there are still common developmental changes they must go through. As they approach old age and death, they will face yet more changes. Any study of human behavior must consider the common developmental changes that occur as humans are born, age, and die.

All societies are composed of groups of people who are at different stages in their lives—who are different ages. Any attempt to understand or change a society must take into account the ages and the levels of developmental competence of that society's members. A typical growing population consists of more young people than old. When plotted on a graph, this pattern is known as a **population pyramid**. In such a population, it is typically the group of people who have reached maturity, in the middle of the pyramid, that must provide support for *both* the very young and the very old.

---

*Answer: Only if you want to make a blue dye.

Figure 1.1 shows a typical population pyramid for the United States from the census years 1950 and 1980. It also projects what the pyramid will be like in the years 2000 and 2030. As the population stabilizes around 290 million in 2030, the pyramid is projected to square off; that is, there will be a proportionally much larger group of older people. A smaller group of middle-aged people will still have to provide support for both the very young and the very old. As you can imagine, such changes could have wide-ranging effects on society as a whole. It is therefore important that developmental researchers be aware of both the individual changes that take place during a lifespan as well as developmental changes within whole societies. Such knowledge is essential if we are to be prepared for the problems that could be created by these changes.

POPULATION PYRAMID

A graphic depiction of the number of individuals within given age ranges. Each age range is stacked from the youngest to oldest; in the normal population, the graph typically forms a pyramid shape.

THE HISTORY OF DEVELOPMENT

> Go to school, stand before your teacher, recite your assignment, open your schoolbag, write your tablet, let the teacher's assistant write your new lesson for you. . . . Don't stand about in the public square. . . . Be humble and show fear before your superiors. (Sommerville, 1982, p. 21)

In this letter, you can hear a father's concern as he writes to his son. In terms of its content, the letter might have been written yesterday, but it wasn't. It was found in the dry sands of Egypt, where it had been undisturbed by the elements. The date: 1800 B.C.!

After reading the ancient letter, you may think that things haven't changed much in the last 3,800 years. Yet our view of childhood as a special time of development, a time when foundations are built, is quite a recent development. In fact, it is difficult to find our current perspective if we go back more than about 400 years. For example, in the Middle Ages, most social interest concerning children was centered on family ambition. More children, especially sons, meant more power and wealth for the family or at least a surviving heir who could inherit. Concepts of children during this time generally cen-

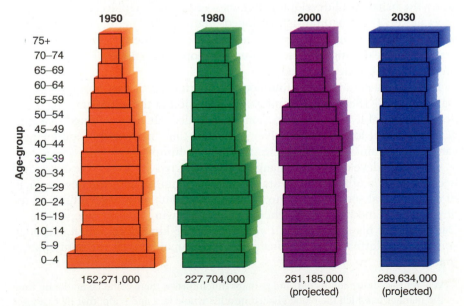

FIGURE 1.1

Population pyramids for the United States for 1950 and 1980, with projections for 2000 and 2030. (SOURCE: U.S. Bureau of the Census and the World Bank, as reported by Horn & Meer, 1987, p. 84)

EMPIRICAL
Relying or based solely on experiments or objective observation.

NATURALIST
A person who studies natural history, especially zoology and botany.

DEVELOPMENTAL PSYCHOLOGY
The study of age-related differences in behavior. It is a branch of psychology. Psychology is the study of behavior and mental processes.

EVOLUTION
The process by which plants or animals change from earlier existing forms. Darwin understood evolution to occur primarily through the processes of diversification and natural selection.

tered on the view that they were simply miniature, imperfectly formed adults (Aries, 1962).

People haven't always thought of childhood as something special or qualitatively different from adulthood. Although early Greek, Hebrew, and Roman cultures understood childhood (in males only) as a special time during which to educate a person, ideas about childhood as being a unique and special time of development began during the Renaissance. The English philosopher John Locke (1632–1704) wondered if children were born *tabula rasa* (as a blank slate). According to this view, a child would be born neither "guilty" nor "good" nor any particular way at birth but rather unshaped and unmolded, and every behavior and manner that the child would come to possess would be acquired through interaction with the environment. In this way, the culture would determine what was written on the "blank slate."

A little later, support for the *tabula rasa* idea (that children were the product of their environment) grew when Captain James Cook (1728–1779) became the first Westerner to discover Tahiti. He and his sailors found Tahitian children to be very different from European children. For instance, no one in that culture, including the children, equated sex with guilt (as the Christian Europeans did). In the Rites of Venus, for example, young Tahitian boys and girls who had just reached puberty were brought together by the older women and taught the most enjoyable ways to have sexual intercourse. The French philosopher Jean Jacques Rousseau (1712–1778) reacted to these observations by writing in praise of "natural man." He argued that the aim of education should be to offset the corrupting influence of institutions, allowing children to develop without any interference, especially from the church or state.

Throughout the eighteenth century, interest in child development grew, and speculation about how children might best develop became a topic of general interest. By the middle of the nineteenth century, however, many of the philosophical speculations about the nature of children that were common to earlier times were being replaced by a new approach.

The Nineteenth Century

The first **empirical** efforts by British **naturalists** to record and scientifically study the behavior of developing organisms eventually replaced philosophical speculation. These naturalists developed methods for carefully observing and recording nature. Their attempts to document observations systematically also marked the beginning of contemporary **developmental psychology** (as it, too, incorporates empirical methods).

The famous naturalist and founder of modern evolutionary biology, Charles Darwin (1809–1882), made a unique contribution to the understanding of the development of living creatures, humans included. He demonstrated that time was a powerful force and that given sufficient time, many important changes can occur within any given species through **evolution**.

Once the developmental changes that occurred in living creatures had become an area of interest, naturalists, already familiar with the development of other animal species, began to compare their data with observations of the development and behavior of children. The following passage was written by Darwin about his own son. In it you can see the kind of thorough, although sometimes informal, observational method common among the naturalists at that time:

> When nearly four months old, and perhaps much earlier, there could be no doubt, from the manner in which the blood gushed into his whole face and scalp, that he easily got

Charles Darwin (1809–1882), whose concept of evolution through natural selection became the cornerstone of modern evolutionary biology.

into a violent passion. When eleven months old, if a wrong plaything was given him, he would push it away and beat it; I presume that the beating was an instinctive sign of anger, like the snapping of the jaws by a young crocodile just out of the egg, and not that he imagined he could hurt the plaything.

The Twentieth Century

By the beginning of the twentieth century, G. Stanley Hall (1846–1924) had incorporated Darwin's views into a psychology—a way of recording and documenting the development of behavior. Hall could thus be considered the first developmental psychologist. In fact, Hall was the first person to do many things. He was the first person to receive a Ph.D. in psychology, and he was the founder of the American Psychological Association. He was also one of the first people to study children in a laboratory, where he investigated the traditional topics of perception, learning, and memory as they applied to children. Hall's interest in child development was extensive, but he didn't stop there. He also published books on adolescence (1904) and even on the aging process (1922).

In the last few decades, interest in adult development has been growing steadily. But adult development is extremely diverse. For example, the behavioral development of men, women, and the elderly can differ greatly from culture to culture. Even the inevitability of death is treated differently in different cultures. The investigative problems posed by this great diversity may have prompted many researchers to concentrate on development during infancy and childhood. But as scientific studies began to be applied rigorously to the development of adolescents and adults, developmental psychology gradually reemerged as a lifespan discipline devoted to the scientific investigation of human development from conception to death.

Compared with what was known in centuries gone by, our current knowledge of development is enormous. In this book, you will learn more about development than was ever known or dreamed of by our ancestors. And you can use this knowledge to be a better parent, teacher, citizen, or researcher—or simply to satisfy your curiosity.

It is also important to note that the field of human development is very broad and that many individuals from related fields have contributed to it (see At Issue).

ISSUES IN DEVELOPMENT

Nature Versus Nurture

As you sit reading this book, you are an excellent example of the interaction of **nature** (the effects of heredity) and **nurture** (the effects of the environment). Your human brain allows you to process and recall vast amounts of information. If you had inherited the brain of a dog or cat, no amount of training would have enabled you to comprehend this chapter.

If this chapter were written in Turkish, you would be unable to understand it (unless through experience, or nurturance, you had come to learn Turkish). It is a combination of your inherited brain and your experience reading the English language, as well as the experience you've gathered about the world, that enables you to understand and make use of the information in this text. All human development can be understood as an *interaction* of nature and nurture (Weisfeld, 1982).

Some behaviors, such as growing physically or learning to walk, seem to be mainly a function of the genetic component. Others, such as driving a car or

NATURE
In developmental research, the hereditary component of an organism's development.

NURTURE
In developmental research, the environmental component of an organism's development.

G. Stanley Hall (1846–1924), who was the first developmental psychologist. He pioneered investigations into many areas of child development.

AT ISSUE

Broadening Horizons

Unlike the fields of mathematics and physics, which seem to be the province of a few specialists, human behavior interests and attracts us all. The study of human behavior is vast in scope, and many researchers who are not psychologists have become involved in it. The study of human development is multidisciplinary and includes contributions made by anthropologists, biologists, physicians, sociologists, and researchers in other social and natural sciences. Psychologists must therefore be careful not to limit themselves to the data developed within their own field. Contributions from other disciplines, as long as they are scientifically gathered, can greatly enhance our knowledge of human development.

TRUE OR FALSE:

1. It is wrong for children to sleep in the same bed with their parents.
2. Adolescence is usually a time of storm and stress.
3. Homosexual behavior among adults is rare.
4. Babies who are held and carried by their mothers too much will become spoiled and fussy.

Cross-cultural research enables developmental researchers to broaden their horizons.

The answer to each of these questions is *false*. In fact, each of the questions was proved false by a researcher from a field other than psychology, and each provides a brief example of such "outside" contributions. For example, statement 1 refers to something many American parents have believed for years—that it is wrong for children to share their parents' bed. But cultural anthropologists have shown that there are a number of cultures that allow children to share their parents' bed, apparently without problems. In Japan, for example, it is customary for children to sleep with their parents, with the youngest child traditionally sleeping closest to the mother, where he or she can be easily nursed. There is no evidence that this practice is harmful to the Japanese child.

Cross-cultural research also helped to show that statement 2 was false. In fact, anthropologist Margaret Mead, who studied the process of "coming of age" in Samoa, demonstrated that adolescence need not be a time of storm and stress (Mead, 1928). Because of cultural factors, adolescents in Western cultures may seem to have more problems in their transition to adulthood, but there is nothing *inherent* in adolescence that makes it more turbulent. Moreover, subsequent research has shown that even in Western cultures, adolescence isn't as stormy as was once thought (Bachman, O'Malley, & Johnston, 1978; Offer, Ostrov, & Howard, 1981).

Statement 3 was proved false by Alfred Kinsey, a zoologist and an expert on sexual behavior in wasps. His pioneering research on the human sexual response helped to dispel many myths and widened our understanding of the development of sexual behavior. Kinsey discovered that many het-

erosexual people had homosexual experiences, and vice versa, and that homosexual experiences were common, with as many as 20 percent of all adults having had a homosexual encounter to the point of orgasm at some time in their lives (Kinsey, Pomeroy, & Martin, 1948; Kinsey, Pomeroy, Martin, & Gebhard, 1953).

Over the years, pediatricians have made substantial contributions to the study of early human development, particularly in babies and young children. Statement 4 was shown to be false by two pediatricians whose research was based on cross-cultural observations (Hunziker & Barr, 1986). In many cultures, infants are carried for extended periods of time by their caregivers. These infants often appear to be less "fussy" than children who do not have this close physical contact. Hunziker and Barr showed that the more an infant was carried and held in close contact, the more its crying and fussiness diminished.

In summary, research on human development is multidisciplinary. Many social and natural sciences other than psychology have made valuable contributions. A significant number of researchers and theorists who study lifespan development come from such diverse fields as anthropology, biology, medicine, and sociology. Without their contributions, our knowledge would be substantially less. Thanks, in part, to the input by researchers in other fields, psychologists have expanded their research to include cross-cultural, pediatric, and demographic studies, as well as other studies once thought to be beyond the scope of psychology.

reading a book, seem to be shaped primarily by the environment. It is important to remember, however, that nature versus nurture isn't a pure dichotomy. Without proper nutrition, a child's growth may be stunted or he may walk much later than he would have otherwise; without a powerful enough brain or the inherited physical capacity, driving a car or even reading might be impossible. It is always the interaction between the two that determines our behavior.

Stability Versus Change

There is much evidence that shortly after birth, babies appear to be different from one another (Eisenberg & Marmarou, 1981). Some cry and fret, some sleep, and some are quietly active. Workers on obstetrics wards are familiar with the great range of personalities noticeable among infants within the first few days of life. Although newborns may behave very differently from one another, their own individual rates of activity and crying are quite stable and consistent during the first days of life (Korner, Hutchinson, Koperski, Kraemer, & Schneider, 1981). **Temperament theories** are based on the belief that these early infant personalities or characteristics may be consistent and stable over even greater lengths of time (Goldsmith, 1983). On the other hand, some of the most interesting changes in development may appear to occur suddenly, sometimes even unexpectedly. In this sense, development can sometimes seem to be an unstable process. In fact, repeated studies of the same individuals have suggested that when considering the great range of human development, *both* components—instability and consistency—are to be found (Costa & McCrae, 1980; Thomas, Chess, & Birch, 1970).

As with the nature-nurture issue, it is important to realize that stability versus change is not a dichotomy. It is not an either-or situation; both are usually involved. In later chapters, we will look at some of these consistencies and changes.

Continuity Versus Discontinuity

Developmental researchers have debated for years whether development can be viewed as a natural, orderly progression or whether it occurs in a series of stages, with abrupt changes occurring from one stage to the next.

Many people automatically assume that human beings follow a fairly **linear** (straight-line) **development**—that is, each new development is built on all the developments that came before. But that isn't the way people develop. Some of the most important phenomena in human development are nonlinear in nature (Roberts, 1986).

Human development may occur rapidly *and* slowly, and it may plateau and even sometimes appear to reverse, all at the same time, depending on which developmental aspect you consider. Some behaviors appear to be acquired in an orderly progression; others may appear in an abrupt shift. In a word, human development is complex. A professor who was once asked if there weren't some aspect of human development that could be counted on to occur at a nice, simple, fixed rate replied, after giving it much thought, "Birthdays!"

Figure 1.2 summarizes the three developmental issues we have discussed so far in this chapter. As you have learned, none of these ideas is simple. No factor can be used to explain any aspect of human development without consideration of the complementary one. Nature is meaningless without nurture; it is impossible to study development without seeing *both* change and stability in the process; and although certain behaviors appear to be acquired in a relatively orderly progression, many others are not. In future chapters, these issues will resurface in our discussions of cognitive, language, moral, and personality development.

CROSS-CULTURAL RESEARCH
Research in which different cultures are evaluated on different behavioral dimensions, such as attachment, emotional development, or intellectual development. Its primary purpose is to isolate and distinguish the effects and influences of culture from those of other variables.

TEMPERAMENT THEORY
Any theory of human development that places an emphasis on the enduring and stable aspects of personality, which are generally considered to be constitutional in nature, that is, due to the biogenetics of the individual.

LINEAR DEVELOPMENT
Development that progresses steadily and continuously (as would a straight line). In this process, each development is dependent on those that came before.

There is evidence to indicate that shortly after birth babies exhibit different temperaments. Some of these temperamental characteristics are quite stable over time.

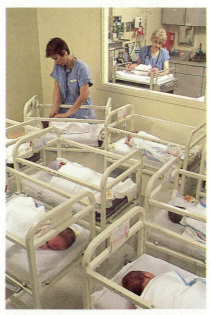

FIGURE 1.2
Concept review of three major developmental issues.

Nature...Nurture	Are certain behavioral characteristics more influenced by heredity or by the environment?
Stability...Change	Are certain behavioral characteristics relatively stable over time, or do changes occur throughout the lifespan?
Continuity...Discontinuity	Can development be characterized as a steady progression, or does it occur in abrupt shifts?

RESEARCH METHODS

All scientific developmental research relies on systematic and objective methods of observing, recording, and describing events. Table 1.1 is an outline of the six dimensions of developmental research. The developmental research discussed in this text (and, for that matter, in all psychological research) will fall on one side or the other of all six dimensions (Reese & Lipsitt, 1970). If you become familiar with these dimensions, you will find it easier to understand the research described in the chapters that follow.

Using Age as a Variable

Developmental researchers are interested in how people change over time, so it's not unusual for them to examine and compare subjects of different ages. There are two basic methods that rely on age as a variable: the **longitudinal approach** and the **cross-sectional approach**. The longitudinal approach involves repeated measurements obtained from the same subject over time, while the cross-sectional approach requires that a number of subjects of different ages be measured, tested, or observed at a given time.

The Cross-Sectional Approach.   Over the years, many cross-sectional studies have been conducted. In 1970, for example, two researchers used the cross-sectional approach to investigate the development of independence in children (Rheingold & Eckerman, 1970). If you had walked into the middle of their experiment, you would have seen an interesting sight. There would be chairs lined up on a large lawn, spaced so that the occupants of the chairs were sitting a fair distance from one another. Sitting in each of these chairs was somebody's mother. And that somebody, namely, one of 54 different toddlers between the ages of 12 and 60 months, was in front of each chair. To the uninitiated, it might have looked like the beginning of an Olympic event for toddlers. Furthermore, hidden observers were watching these youngsters from behind windows at the edge of the lawn. What was actually being measured, however, was how far any given child would travel from his or her mother.

The results of the study revealed a clear relationship between the distance that the child would travel and the child's age. The average distance traveled by 1-year-old children was 6.9 meters. Two-year-old children went 15.1 meters; 3-year-old children went 17.3 meters; and 4-year-old children dared to travel an average of 20.6 meters away. Researchers Rheingold and Eckerman found that for each month of age beyond a year, a child was likely to travel about ⅓ meter farther. By using the cross-sectional approach, these researchers could see how independence developed over time among children of different ages under similar circumstances. As you can see, all these data could be collected in a very short time; if the researchers had wanted to, they could have included other age-groups in their study.

LONGITUDINAL APPROACH

A research study design in which investigators follow an individual through time, taking measurements at periodic intervals.

CROSS-SECTIONAL APPROACH

A research strategy in which investigators examine subjects of different ages simultaneously to study the relationships between age, experience, and behavior.

The cross-sectional approach has some disadvantages. Unfortunately, it won't tell what individual children were like when they were younger or how they developed. It also won't control for *historical variables,* such as an economic depression or a war. Children tested at one time may be very unlike children tested at other times. Any group of people born at approximately the same time is called a **cohort**. People born at about the same time are often exposed to similar cultural and historical experiences. The cross-sectional approach doesn't control for the differences between cohorts. The cross-sectional design will also not help if you have a question such as, Will a very independent 2-year-old child also exhibit great independence at age 6? On the other hand, this is exactly the kind of question that the longitudinal approach addresses.

COHORT

A group of people, all of whom possess a common demographic characteristic; for example, a group of people born at approximately the same time.

Table 1.1 ● Dimensions of Developmental Research

DIMENSIONS OF RESEARCH	DESCRIPTION
Descriptive vs. Explanatory	Descriptive research describes only *what* has occurred, while explanatory research attempts to explain *how* something has occurred, that is, what caused it. Descriptive research is often a good way to begin, as it is generally less subject to error. A caveman describing what has occurred during a thunderstorm might say, "There was a bright flash of light followed by a terrible loud rumble," and he would be accurate. The same caveman attempting to be explanatory might say "The Great God Zog has decided to go bowling." As you can see, the caveman is in trouble already. Descriptions, of course, can be inaccurate. The more objective they are, however, the more accurate they are likely to be; for example, the people standing in a given room can be objectively counted. The more subjective descriptions are, though, the more likely they are to be open to misinterpretation; for example, how many children in a particular school would you describe as happy? In this case, the description is open to personal interpretation and is more likely to be inaccurate. For this reason, developmental researchers often begin with objective descriptions and then, through careful experimental research, begin to examine cause-and-effect relationships in the hope that they may eventually be able to explain how and why the events they have described are occurring.
Naturalistics vs. Manipulative	When conducting naturalistic research, researchers refrain from interacting with the subjects of their observations in order to examine behavior in a natural setting. Careful, detailed records of the observations are kept. Naturalistic research can be conducted in an informal or structured manner, although the more informal the observations, the more chance there is that bias or inaccurate observations and interpretations will result. Parents who simply watch their children are engaged in informal naturalistic observation. In a more structured naturalistic observation, the behaviors observed are clearly defined beforehand, and careful reports are kept. During manipulative research, experimenters purposely expose their subjects to different situations and observe the effects cause by this exposure. This kind of research often can be carefully controlled in a laboratory setting, allowing close and careful observations of each studied behavior.
Historical vs. Ahistorical	If research is fundamentally dependent on past events, it is considered historical research; if not, it is called ahistorical. For example, a study concerned with the effects of a particular therapy for abused children would be historical because a previous history of child abuse would be an important factor, while a study concerned with the effects of brightly colored blocks on an infant's vocalizations would be ahistorical because there would be no particular interest in the infant's experience or history.
Theoretical vs. Serendipitous	Research designed to investigate a particular theory is called theoretical research, while research designed simply to investigate phenomena without regard to theoretical speculation is called serendipitous, or atheoretical.
Basic vs. Applied	Basic research advances knowledge; applied research advances technology. Once the basic knowledge has been gathered, applied research is concerned with assembling it for a particular purpose. The space program is a good example of applied research, as most of the basic knowledge about rockets, aerodynamics, and space had been gathered beforehand. The search for a cancer cure, however, is an example of basic research. No one is certain of the fundamental causes of cancer. so our basic knowledge of biology must be expanded before the next major application of technology can occur. Thus, basic research may seem valueless because it appears to have no immediate application, but it is essential for any science and technology that knowledge be expanded.
Single Subject vs. Group	In single-subject research, the behavior and behavior changes of only one person at a time are of interest, while in group research, the researcher looks at group averages, ignoring whether those averages accurately reflect the behavior patterns of any given individual within the group.

TIME-LAG DESIGN

A research design in which different groups of people are measured on a characteristic or behavior when they are the same age; for example, one group of 2-year-old children are measured in one year, another group of 2-year-old children are measured in a subsequent year, and so on.

SEQUENTIAL DESIGN

A research design that combines elements of different time-dependent research approaches to control for biases that might be introduced when any single approach is used alone.

EXPERIMENT

A test made to demonstrate the validity of some hypothesis or to determine the predictability of a theory. Variables are manipulated during the test. Any changes are contrasted with those of a control that has not been exposed to the variables of interest.

CATHARSIS

In psychoanalytic theory, elimination of a complex by bringing it to consciousness and allowing it to be expressed. Also, any emotional release resulting from a buildup of internal tensions.

The Longitudinal Approach.   Over the years, many important studies have used the longitudinal approach (Schaie & Hertzog, 1982). Among the interesting areas that have been examined by means of longitudinal research is the relationship between intelligence test scores among children and the children's later achievements in adult life. Generally, such longitudinal studies have challenged the old notion that intelligence is an unchanging characteristic (Bayley, 1968). The studies have also challenged the old belief that it isn't good to be too smart. For example, a longitudinal study conducted by Terman examined children whose intelligence scores were in the top 1 percent and then followed these children into adulthood and old age. Terman discovered that bright children tended to become happier, more productive adults than their more average peers (Terman, 1925, 1954). They were also less likely to be institutionalized for emotional problems or to be divorced. (For a more detailed discussion of the Terman study, see Chapter 10.)

There are also some problems associated with longitudinal research. Because social conditions are always changing, we can't be sure that the developmental path followed by people through the middle of this century will be similar to that of people in future generations. Another drawback to longitudinal research is that problems that interested psychologists long ago and that caused them to initiate a longitudinal study may no longer be of interest; thus, by the time the study is completed, the findings may be considered of little value. Also, longitudinal research is often expensive and time consuming. And many subjects simply move away or drop out of the study.

Time-Lag and Sequential Designs.   Through the years, researchers have devised several ways to help eliminate some of the biases introduced when cross-sectional and longitudinal approaches are used. The **time-lag design** has been used to help control for the effects of cultural variation over time. In a time-lag design, different groups of subjects are tested in different years while *age is held constant*. For example, a researcher could study 2-year-old children's ability to perform a certain task during a certain year, could examine a new group of 2-year-old children for the ability to perform the same task in a subsequent year, and so on. This approach may give the researcher information about cultural or historical influences on performance of the task.

Researchers have often combined elements of the cross-sectional, longitudinal, and time-lag designs in a **sequential design**, combining the different methods' strengths and lessening their drawbacks. As you will see in Chapter 14, K. Warner Schaie and his colleagues used a sequential research design to study intellectual functioning through the lifespan. By using such an approach they were able to avoid some of the biases that would have been introduced by the use of just one method.

Figure 1.3 summarizes the cross-sectional, longitudinal, and time-lag approaches by outlining a hypothetical experiment in which all three approaches could be used to help eliminate their individual drawbacks. Over a five-year-period, a researcher could gather information about age differences and cultural variation and could follow one group through time to see the developmental progression.

DESIGNING EXPERIMENTS

When scientists conduct research, it is important that they make sure that their findings will be accurate. One of the best ways to ensure accuracy is to conduct an **experiment**. Perhaps the best way to learn how to conduct an experiment (and how not to conduct one) is to try it yourself. So, for the next few pages, let's work on one together.

First, we need an issue that is testable. If we come up with a question for which no test can be devised, we'll be out of luck. Consider the following questions:

What was the weight of Julius Caesar's liver?
What will the world be like in 20 years?
Is there life on Neptune?

These questions are currently untestable because no one has access to concrete observable information about these subjects, such as a soil sample from Neptune or data brought back by a time traveler. Until we have such information, there is no obvious way to design an experiment that could answer these questions. So, let's examine an issue that *can* be tested: Do violent programs on television cause aggressive behavior in children who view them?

Sigmund Freud (1856–1939) believed that the desire to be violent was instinctive and that viewing violence would satisfy an instinctive urge. In other words, according to Freud, viewing violence would act as a release, or a **catharsis**, reducing the viewer's desire to be violent.

On the other hand, contemporary social psychologist Albert Bandura has developed a social learning theory that leads to predictions contradicting Freud's catharsis hypothesis. Bandura predicts that viewing violence (especially viewing someone being rewarded for being violent, as TV heroes often are) will increase the probability that the viewer will imitate the violence. Clearly, we have a disagreement and one that can be tested.

To conduct a test to decide who is correct, we need some children, some violent TV programs, and some observers to watch the children's behavior. The observers can then record what actually happens when the children are exposed to the shows.

Selecting Subjects

First, we'll select some children. What kinds of children shall we use? Older, younger, boys, girls?

Let's begin with 6-year-old boys and girls. But when we publish our results, will we be able to say anything about 4-, 8-, or 10-year-old children? We probably won't want to say anything definite. If we had adequate time and sufficient research funds, it would be a good idea to use the cross-sectional approach with children of many ages and backgrounds because we always take a risk when we generalize beyond our sample. If we study little boys, for instance, we must be very cautious about generalizing our findings to little girls (and unless we have a sound reason for doing so, we shouldn't attempt it). Researchers should be careful not to go beyond their data unless they specifically state that they are speculating.

Well, I see that we now have a room full of children aged 5 through 10 years. What's next? Shall we show them some violent Saturday morning cartoons? If we do, how could we tell which ones are violent? As a matter of fact, after showing the cartoons, how will we decide whether the children are being aggressive?

Definitions and Reliability

Do we all agree on what "aggression" is? Is a good salesperson aggressive? Are all murderers aggressive? Is it good for a football player to be aggressive? Obvi-

FIGURE 1.3

Hypothetical five-year experiment in which elements of the cross-sectional, longitudinal, and time-lag approaches are combined in a sequential design. In 1991, the researcher used the cross-sectional approach to measure a group of subjects of different ages; the first measurement in a five-year longitudinal study was also made at this time, as well as the first measurement of 2-year-old children for a five-year time-lag study. In 1992, another measurement was made of a different group of 2-year-old children for the time-lag study, and the longitudinal study group from 1991 (who were by then 3 years old) were again measured. In 1993, another group of 2-year-old children were measured, and the 4-year-old children in the longitudinal study were again measured. And so on. Such sequential research designs can help eliminate some of the problems and biases encountered when only one approach is used.

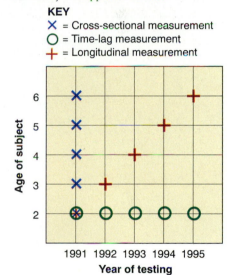

KEY
× = Cross-sectional measurement
O = Time-lag measurement
+ = Longitudinal measurement

INTEROBSERVER RELIABILITY
The degree of agreement or disagreement between two or more observers who make simultaneous observations of a single event.

CONTROL
In a controlled study, experimental or research conditions are arranged deliberately so that observed effects can be traced directly to one or more known variables. The control is similar to the experimental subject but is not exposed to the variable.

ously, aggression has come to mean many different things, and before we can study it (and perhaps conclude that watching TV violence causes it), we must be able to define it. If aggression means something different to everyone who reads our findings, we will have succeeded only in making the issue more confusing.

If a tree falls in the forest and there isn't a creature about to hear it, does it make a noise? Perhaps you've heard this famous question before, but do you know the answer? It depends totally on how you define noise. If you define noise as the production of sound waves, the answer to the question will be yes. If you define noise as the perception of sound waves by a living creature, the answer will be no. The only reason that this question can cause an argument in the first place is that people are often unaware that they are using different definitions of noise.

How would you define aggression to avoid that kind of confusion in our experiment? How about "any act that damages property or physically hurts another person"? But then how would you deal with someone who accidentally stepped on your toe or a sniper who fired at a crowd and missed everyone? Well then, how about "any act committed with the intention of damaging property or hurting another person"? Although intentions aren't easy to observe, let's try this definition, since it fits what most people would call aggression. We must also agree on a definition of violent cartoons (perhaps, "any act that if carried out with live actors would be likely to result in injury"). Once we have defined both terms, we will watch a particular child after the child has viewed a violent cartoon. Your job will be to note whether aggression occurs and how often. Can you be trusted to be accurate in your observations?

Even using our definition, it is possible that you might consider something aggressive that someone else wouldn't. This could be a serious problem. To avoid it, we will use two or more people who will *independently* observe and measure the same child over the same period of time. The observations and measurements can then be compared, and if they are in fairly good agreement, we can conclude that it is possible to observe and record reliably the behavior in question. This technique yields what is known as **interobserver reliability**.

The Control

Now that we have used interobserver reliability to ensure that we agree on definitions of aggression and violent cartoons, what should the next step be? If the children are aggressive after viewing the cartoon, how will we know that it was the violence in the cartoon that was responsible? For that matter, how will we know whether the children wouldn't have been even more aggressive had they not seen the cartoon? If you asked the question "Who won the soccer match?" and the only answer you got was that one team had scored three times, you wouldn't know whether that team had won or lost. You would need the other team's score as a comparison. It's the same with an experiment. As a comparison, or **control**, we must have a second, similar group of children who do not see the violent cartoon. In fact, it is the use of a control that defines a scientific experiment.

Next we must decide whether the second group of children is similar to the first. One of the most common ways to do this is simply to divide the original group of children in half. Then, in all probability, the two groups will be similar. Nonetheless, we must be careful when dividing the original group to do it randomly, so that each child has an equal chance of being placed in either group. For example, we might divide the children into an experimental group and a control group by flipping a coin.

Suppose we have our two groups. What should the next step be? At first it might seem that the experimental group should see the violent cartoon while the control group sees no cartoon. Although that might seem like the correct approach, it is important to remember that the control and experimental groups must be treated exactly the same except for the one variable we wish to measure: in this case, violence. If we show the control group no cartoon, we will fail to control for the effects of simply watching any kind of cartoon. For this reason, the experimental group should see a violent cartoon while the control group watches a nonviolent cartoon of the same length—ideally, the same cartoon with nonviolent rather than violent scenes. In this way, the effect of violence is isolated from all other effects. Anything that happens to the experimental group is *controlled for* if it also happens to the control group. In our case, everything is controlled except viewing violence, which happens to the experimental group.

If the amount of aggression observed in both groups of children is similar before they see the cartoon but different afterward, we have isolated the effect of watching violence and probably nothing else. In this way, researchers are able to separate variables one at a time and observe their effects. A variable is any measurement that may vary, as opposed to a constant, such as the speed of light, which does not vary. Examples of variables include a person's height and weight, the outside temperature or barometric pressure, the miles per gallon obtained by a car, the rainfall in Rangoon, the number of teeth in an audience, and the number of ice cream scoops dropped on the sidewalks of Detroit each day by consequently upset children. To reiterate, in a scientific experiment, both groups share all the variables but one, and both groups are similar to each other at the beginning of the experiment; therefore, if there is a difference between the groups at the end of the experiment, the only variable responsible for the difference is most likely the one variable that they didn't share. Remember, variables shared by both groups are controlled. Or, putting it another way, if it starts to rain on the experimental group, your experiment won't be disrupted as long as it starts to rain on the control group, too. In our experiment,

Research has shown that children who view violence on television are more likely to be violent themselves.

INDEPENDENT VARIABLE
In an experiment, the variable that is manipulated or treated to see what effect differences in it will have on the variables considered to be dependent on it.

DEPENDENT VARIABLE
In an experiment, the variable that may change as a result of changes in the independent variable.

REPLICATION
Repetition of an experiment to enhance the reliability of the results.

EXPANSION
An enlargement, increase, or extension of initial research.

CORRELATION
A relationship between two variables.

the variable that is manipulated—how much and what kind of TV violence we showed—is called the **independent variable**. The variable that may be influenced by the manipulations—the amount of aggression—is called the **dependent variable**.*

Results of Our Experiment

Once we have observed the levels of aggression in the children from both groups, we will analyze the data statistically to determine whether the difference in observed aggression between the control and experimental groups is significantly large. Assuming that the results of our hypothetical experiment are similar to those obtained by researchers who have conducted actual experiments examining the effects of television violence, we will find that the experimental group is significantly more aggressive (Eron, Huesmann, Brice, Fischer, & Mermelstein, 1983; Huesmann, Lagerspetz, & Eron, 1984).

Our conclusion? Viewing TV cartoon violence increases the probability of immediate postviewing aggression in grade school children. Note that our observations fit Bandura's theory. After replicating and expanding on the experiment, we may even suggest that violence in television cartoons should be reduced.

Replication and Expansion

Now that we have completed our experiment, we need to consider two valuable procedures: **replication** and **expansion**. An old rule in research states that if it hasn't happened twice, it hasn't happened. For this reason, it would be a good idea to have other researchers, perhaps at another institution, replicate our study to see whether they obtain the same results. Should their results agree with ours, we will feel more confident about our own findings. Such confirmation is important because there may have been something peculiar about our particular sample of children, or an important event, unknown to us, may have interfered with the treatment or testing (Furchtgott, 1984).

We may also wish to expand on our research. For instance, what would happen if we used live actors instead of cartoons? Would adults become aggressive in the way that children do? How long does this increased aggression last? As you can see, the answer we discovered in our own experiment generated many more questions than we initially faced, perhaps all worth pursuing.

Classifying Our Study

Finally, let's review the kind of research we used in our study:

1. *Explanatory:* We concluded that watching violence was *why* aggression occurred.
2. *Manipulative:* We *altered* the situation so that the children were exposed to the variables that we desired them to see.
3. *Ahistorical:* We were *not* concerned with the children's past *history*.
4. *Theoretical:* We were testing Freud's *theoretical prediction* against Bandura's.
5. *Basic:* We were advancing our *knowledge* rather than attempting to change the technology of the cartoon industry (although that may eventually be the result of our research).
6. *Group:* We worked with *groups* of children rather than concentrating on a single subject.

---

*If you have trouble recalling which variable is which, just think of freedom and independence. The variable that the experimenter is "free" to manipulate is the "independent" variable.

NONEXPERIMENTAL METHODS

The Correlational Method

A **correlation** is defined as the relationship between two variables. For example, there is a strong correlation between height and weight. The taller a person is, the heavier he or she tends to be, and vice versa.

By the late 1800s, army physicians were aware that the best way to stop a malaria outbreak was to move everyone to high, dry ground. Although these physicians were unaware that the disease was carried by mosquitoes, they knew that malaria was well correlated with altitude and moisture. Without knowing the cause, they were still able to predict that the chances of an outbreak were higher in one environment than in the other.

Sometimes psychologists are unable to conduct experiments (or perhaps, like the army doctors, they don't know which experiments to conduct), and they are forced to rely on correlational data. The value of such data is first that they allow predictions to be made and second that they often are the first clue scientists have on the way to making an important discovery. As you can imagine, doctors soon wondered what it was about damp, warm lowlands that related to malaria.

When dealing with a correlation, however, we must be extremely careful not to assume that a cause-and-effect relationship exists simply because the two variables go together. If you were to tell me that ice cream sales in a certain city had increased, I'd be able to predict that the number of drownings had also increased and I'd probably be correct. This does not mean that eating ice cream makes you drown or, conversely, that the possibility of drowning makes you want ice cream! The reason for the correlation between ice cream and drownings is, of course, that in summer both swimming and ice cream sales increase.

Of course, it would be foolish to think that eating ice cream would make you drown or that drowning would make you eat ice cream. But suppose for a moment that you are watching children at play who are being supervised by their parents. You notice that the children of parents who discipline them by yelling at them are more aggressive. Could you conclude that parents who are verbally harsh cause their children to act out and be aggressive? No! All you would have is a correlation that parental yelling coincides with aggressive behavior in children. How do you know that the children weren't aggressive to start with and that their aggression drove their parents to yelling? You don't. To examine cause and effect, you would have to create an experiment by manipulating the variables involved. Until then, you know only that one variable is correlated with the other.

Suppose you walk into a large college classroom, survey more than 100 students, and discover that the only students who became parents before the age of 20 have red hair. Could you conclude that red hair is somehow correlated with extra sex hormones? No. To begin with, you would have "talked beyond your data" because you haven't measured anyone's sex hormones. Actually, before you draw any conclusions, the thing to do is to go to another classroom and *replicate* your observation.

Sometimes things go together (are well correlated) by fluke. Even results from an experiment may be only a coincidence. When you flip a coin, you may get 10 heads in a row, but this doesn't necessarily mean that the coin is weighted.* If there is actually some reason for early parenthood and red hair to be cor-

---

*An unweighted coin has a 50-50 chance of coming up heads. As you know, however, you could get a run of heads four, five, six, or more times in a row by "fluke."

CASE STUDY
An intensive study of a single case, with all available data, test results, and opinions about that individual; usually done in more depth than are group studies.

BABY BIOGRAPHY
A relatively informal naturalistic observation of an infant's routines and behavior.

SURVEY
A method of collecting data through interviews and questionnaires.

related, the correlation should *continue to occur* as you replicate your observation. But if it was only a chance event, it probably won't happen again. Whenever you discover something very unexpected, it's a good idea to replicate your study a few times. Once you've discovered a correlation that replicates, you may wish to begin an in-depth series of experiments (if possible) to try to uncover any cause-and-effect relationships that may explain the correlation.

Case Studies

In a **case study**, a scientist or researcher reports or analyzes the behavior, emotions, beliefs, or life history of a single individual in more depth than is generally done with groups of subjects. Some of the earliest case studies of child behavior were simply informal descriptions of what the child was doing. These were known as **baby biographies**. Even though baby biographies or case studies allow the recording of a personal detailed account of one child over time, biases can easily affect the observations. Sometimes, however, it is impossible for a researcher to gather data by conducting an experiment or observing a correlation. In that case, the researcher may obtain valuable information by viewing a subject carefully and reporting what he or she observes.

Consider the case of a little boy who had deaf parents but was not deaf himself (Moskowitz, 1978). His parents and all the visitors to his home used the American Sign Language for the Deaf to communicate. This was the only way, in terms of language, that the parents and visitors ever interacted with the boy. Unfortunately, the boy had chronic asthma and was housebound. As a result, he never had a chance to interact with anyone who spoke English. But the child's parents wanted him to learn English, so they placed him before a television every day for a number of hours. By the time the child was 3 years old, he was fluent in sign language, but he still couldn't speak any English.

There is no way that such a situation could be investigated by experiment because it would be a violation of ethical principles to isolate children so that the only spoken language they heard came from television. Yet when a case study like that of the little boy is published, it generates interest. Although we always take a chance in generalizing from one child to all children, it appears that for children to acquire language, two-way conversations may be necessary. Reporting of this "accidental" study provided information that otherwise might not have been obtainable; a controlled study would not be acceptable on ethical grounds.

Surveys, Questionnaires, and Statistical Analysis

Although the experimental methods described earlier in this chapter are often preferred by researchers, they are not the only ways of obtaining information about changes through the lifespan. When direct observation is impossible, researchers must sometimes rely on **survey** techniques, such as conducting interviews or administering questionnaires. Among the best-known national surveys are the Gallup and Roper political polls, the Nielsen television survey, and the U.S. Census. In fact, as you will notice throughout this text, a major source of information are the surveys, questionnaires, and analyses of statistics gathered by government institutions. The population pyramid discussed at the beginning of the chapter is one such example. We can gain much information through the use of these data.

Surveys, however, are subject to a number of problems. When people answer questions, they often report what they wish were true or recall things differently from the way they actually happened. For example, married couples asked to report how often they engage in sexual relations per month have a tendency to overestimate. The wording of the questions can influence the results as well. For example, subjects who viewed a traffic accident were more likely to answer yes to the question "Did you see *the* broken headlight?" than they were to the question "Did you see *a* broken headlight?" Also, surveys are often susceptible to sampling error. The classic case is the 1936 political poll in which a random sample was picked from the telephone book and asked, "For whom will you vote in the presidential election, Landon or Roosevelt?" The majority answered that they would vote for Landon, and the pollsters predicted Landon the winner. Unfortunately for the pollsters, in 1936 only richer people had telephones, and Roosevelt won easily.

Throughout this text, you will be given a number of opportunities to see these various methods in action. These methods have given developmental researchers investigative powers undreamed of only a century ago. Bit by bit, we are uncovering nature's secrets. We are learning how nature interacts with the environment. We are gaining a better understanding of human development.

The Ethical and Legal Aspects of Experimenting with Children

Whenever an experiment is conducted with a child as a subject, a very complex ethical and legal question arises, namely, Who gave the right to experiment on children?

CHILDREN IN EXPERIMENTS

In England during the 1700s, Caroline, the Princess of Wales, demanded that before her children be given the new vaccine against smallpox, six charity children from St. James Parish be given the vaccine to make sure of its safety (Lasagna, 1969). Since that time, many children have been the subjects in experiments.

A prominent example of abuse occurred at the Willowbrook School in New York (an institution for the retarded), where children were purposely exposed to hepatitis so that researchers could use them to search for a cure (Mitchell, 1975). The professionals involved made a number of excuses, such as, "A few might suffer but many will benefit," or they emphasized that most of the children in the school seemed to catch hepatitis anyway (yet no one seemed to consider closing the school as a health hazard). The truth of the matter was that these children were forced to suffer for purposes of experimentation. Researchers must be extremely cautious about causing such suffering when conducting experiments.

A child might also, in theory, be injured in a psychological experiment. The child wouldn't be physically endangered as the children at Willowbrook were. But psychologists could, in an experiment, manipulate physical stimuli, social situations, or other variables that might have a direct psychological effect on the child. For example, if a psychologist presents a child with an "impossible puzzle" and, to test frustration, tells

the child that most children can solve it, is the child being psychologically harmed if he breaks down and begins to cry? Even after the child is told the truth about the experiment, might he continue to think less of himself? Could this have a harmful effect on his future life? More than likely, the child won't be permanently harmed by the experience. But the question remains, Should someone gamble with a child's normal development for the sake of an experiment? The use of such deceptions in experiments is common.

It is important to note that thousands of children have served as subjects in important experiments without suffering physical or psychological injury as far as anyone can tell, and eliminating all children as research subjects would be a devastating blow to developmental research.

ETHICS

Sometimes a group of professionals will outline or describe behavior that they consider morally good and appropriate for dealing with the specific issues faced by their profession. Such professional morals are called ethics. Table 1.2 briefly outlines the major ethical principles for research with children. After examining these ethical guidelines, ask yourself whether the experiment on violence and aggression that we conducted in this chapter was unethical.

Among other possible violations, we didn't obtain informed consent. While we were busy defining our terms and considering what we might discover, no one thought to obtain informed consent from the children's parents. Now, aren't you glad that it was only a hypothetical experiment and that you don't have to worry that angry parents who do

not allow their children to see violent cartoons will come knocking on your office door?

THE LAW

You should keep in mind that ethical guidelines are only guidelines. In the United States, the final arbiter of such matters is the court. In actual practice, though, lawsuits are rarely brought against psychologists or educators for experimenting with children. Society appears content that the ethical practices outlined by the profession are adequate, while criminal statutes protect against heinous violations. However, legally there are still two very tricky issues. First, what constitutes psychological damage as outlined in the ethical procedures, and second, can a parent give informed consent for a child by proxy (given that children are probably legally incapable of giving it for themselves)?

When we look to the law for answers, we find that it doesn't say anything about psychological experiments. But after a child was harmed in a medical experiment, the U.S. Supreme Court held, in *Prince v. Massachusetts* (1944), that it wasn't legal for a parent to give the child's informed consent by proxy in such a situation. The Court stated:

Parents may be free to become martyrs themselves. But it does not follow [that] they are free, in identical circumstances, to make martyrs of their children before they have reached the age of full and legal discretion when they can make that choice for themselves.

One legal commentator has further clarified this position in the following way:

It is essential that while humanity and science are served, the individual's rights

APPLICATIONS

Table 1.2 ● Ethical Standards for Research with Children

A CHILD'S LIST OF RGIHTS

1. No matter how young the child, he or she has rights that supersede the rights of the investigator.

2. Any deviation from these ethical principles requires that the investigator seek consultation in order to protect the rights of the research participants.

3. The investigator should inform the child of all features of the research that may affect the child's willingness to participate, and he or she should answer the child's questions in terms appropriate to the child's comprehension.

4. The informed consent of parents or of those who act *in loco parentis* (e.g., teachers, superintendents of institutions) similarly should be obtained, preferably in writing. Informed consent requires that the parents or other responsible adults be told all features of the research that may affect their willingness to allow the child to participate. The responsible adults should be given the opportunity to refuse without penalty.

5. The investigator may use no research operation that may harm the child either physically or psychologically.

6. If concealment or deception is practiced, adequate measures should be taken after the study to ensure the participants' understanding of the reasons for the concealment or deception.

7. The investigator should keep in confidence all information obtained about research participants.

8. The investigator should clarify any misconceptions that may occur during or after the research.

9. When, in the course of research, information comes to the investigator's attention that may seriously affect the child's well-being, the investigator must make all arrangements necessary to assist the child.

10. If, during the research, any previously unforeseen consequences of an undesirable nature should occur, it is incumbent upon the researcher to correct these consequences or redesign the experimental procedures.

11. When experimental treatment is believed to benefit the children, the control group should be offered the same or similar beneficial treatment.

12. Every investigator also has the responsibility to maintain the ethical standards of his or her colleagues.

13. Teachers of courses related to children should present these ethical standards to their students.

14. The research must be scientifically sound and significant.

15. The research should be conducted on animals, human adults, and older children before involving infants.

Source: Adapted, in part, from the Society for Research in Child Development's Ethical Standards for Research with Children and from the standards of the National Commission for the Protection of Human Subjects of Biomedical and Behavioral Research.

---

must be protected with vigor and vigilance. If this means that certain experiments cannot be conducted, it is appropriate that they are not. Medical scientists in the laboratory are privileged to embrace an operative pragmatism during the continuum of inductive and deductive reasoning, intuition, imagination and possibly even serendipity that comprise the scientific method. Occasionally, the means and the end are blurred and may even be indistinguishable. In the clinical experiment with human subjects this facile laboratory stratagem cannot be permitted, for here the end can never justify the means if human rights and dignity are violated. There is a special meaning for the scientist in this cliché, for he above all others exults in his freedom to seek the truth of life and he is first a human, then a scientist. (Ritts, 1968, p. 638)

Psychologists, as human beings first and scientists second, must continue to conduct research with children carefully and conscientiously, placing the children's best interests above any experimental concerns. Failure to do this would be a most serious ethical breach.

SUMMARY

■ All societies are made up of groups of people who are at different stages in their lives—who are different ages. Any study of human behavior must consider the common developmental changes that occur as humans are born, age, and die. Knowledge of the individual changes that take place during a lifespan as well as developmental changes within societies is essential if we are to be prepared for the problems that could be created by these changes.

■ The idea of childhood as a special time did not exist until the Renaissance. By the middle of the 1800s, the first empirical efforts to record and carefully study the behavior of developing organisms were being made. The founder of modern evolutionary biology, Charles Darwin, made a unique contribution: He demonstrated that many important changes can occur over time in a given species.

■ Interest in studying changes during adult development has been growing over the last few decades. Adult development, however, is extremely diverse.

■ An issue that has been of interest to developmental researchers is nature versus nurture, in which the genetic and environmental determinants of a behavior are studied. Stability versus change has also been investigated to determine which aspects of an individual remain relatively stable over a lifetime and which undergo change. Continuity versus discontinuity has been studied to determine whether development can be characterized as a relatively smooth, continuous progression or whether it experiences abrupt shifts.

■ Both longitudinal and cross-sectional research methods use age as a major variable. In cross-sectional studies, subjects of different ages are compared; in longitudinal studies, the same individual is measured repeatedly over time.

■ Time-lag designs incorporate groups of individuals of the same age and measure them in different years. Sequential designs combine elements of different time-dependent research approaches.

■ Researchers conduct experiments to determine the effects of different variables on behavior. When experiments are conducted, terms must be carefully defined to obtain agreement among observers.

■ A control group must be similar to the experimental group; the control group is used for comparison to see whether the variable under study has an effect.

■ It is important to replicate research. We can never be sure that the results obtained from an initial experiment didn't occur by accident or fluke. Successful replication helps to validate the results.

■ Correlational data may be useful because predictions may be derived from them. Correlations are often the first clues a scientist has to an important discovery. Researchers must be careful, however, not to assume cause-and-effect relationships based only on correlations; correlations are often only coincidental.

■ Case studies and baby biographies, although open to bias, often supply valuable information that might otherwise be unobtainable.

■ When experiments are not feasible, surveys or questionnaires often provide valuable data for developmental researchers. They are subject to a number of problems, however.

■ Whenever an experiment is conducted with a child as subject, complex legal and ethical issues arise. It is important that informed consent be given and that no harm occur to the child.

QUESTIONS FOR DISCUSSION

1. Do you believe that parents should have the right to give informed consent for their children by proxy?

2. Ironically, the study conducted at the Willowbrook School, in which children were deliberately exposed to hepatitis, yielded some extremely valuable medical information. The researchers found that hepatitis B, the worst form of hepatitis, is carried by a virus. This discovery actually helped scientists to develop a vaccine that is effective in preventing hepatitis B. In addition, none of the children in the experiment seemed to be permanently injured by the exposure. Does all this information alter your feelings about the ethics of the study?

3. Some developmental psychologists have criticized the emphasis on laboratory research that has occurred during the last few decades (McCall, 1978). They argue that the systematic artificial investigation of single factors has little to do with the behavior of children in their natural interactive environment and that the actual developmental progression has been ignored. What do you think?

4. How important is a person's age to you in social interactions? Would you consider having friends who were substantially older or younger than you? A spouse? Do you always act *your* age?

5. What do you think about violent television programs? What do you think should be the role of researchers who discover information that could have a positive or negative effect on society? Should they do something about it? Should you?

SUGGESTIONS FOR FURTHER READING

1. Aries, P. (1962). *Centuries of childhood: A social history of family life.* (R. Baldick, Trans.). New York: Knopf. (Original work published 1960.)

2. Deese, J. (1972). *Psychology as science and art.* New York: Harcourt Brace Jovanovich.

3. Hannah, G. T., Christian, W. P., & Clark, H. W. (Eds.). (1981). *Client rights.* New York: Free Press.

4. Keuill-Davies, S. (1992). *Yesterday's children: The antiques & history of child-care.* Chicago: Antique Collectibles.

5. Smuts, A. B., & Hagen, J. W. (Eds.). (1985). History and research in child development. *Monographs of the Society for Research in Child Development, 50* (Nos. 4–5, Serial No. 211).

6. Sommerville, J. (1982). *The rise and fall of childhood.* Beverly Hills, CA: Sage.

CHAPTER 2

Theories of Development

A Jigsaw Puzzle

Collecting data is like gathering the pieces of a jigsaw puzzle. By itself, any one piece may be interesting, but it can't reveal the entire picture. To produce the entire picture, you must gather and assemble many pieces. In putting a jigsaw puzzle together, as in gathering data, people usually assemble the pieces in a logical sequence. One person may first work with just the edge pieces, gathering them until the frame is assembled, while another may concentrate on sorting pieces by color or by some other distinguishing characteristic. Someone gathering data or deciding which hypothesis to develop and test works in much the same way. Sometimes an important piece may be found by chance, or sometimes an important piece is overlooked because a researcher has failed to see it for what it is. Both experiences are common to people who conduct research and gather evidence.

While the pieces of a puzzle are being assembled, the picture may suddenly start to emerge. At this point, it may be possible to develop a theory about what the picture is. The person doing the puzzle has seen enough to recognize some sort of symmetry and believes it's now possible to determine what the entire scene will be. Even though only one wall and a part of a door are showing, the puzzle assembler may already know that it is the picture of a house. This person may then feel free to predict the existence of windows and a chimney even before these particular pieces turn up.

*Similarly, when scientists have gathered enough data, they, too, may think that they see an emerging picture. This insightful view of the completed work or section of work is called a **theory**. A theory is a way of organizing data, ideas, and hypotheses to provide a more complete understanding of what the data have been indicating in piecemeal fash-*

THEORY
A system of rules or assumptions used to predict or explain phenomena.

ENVIRONMENTAL THEORY
Theory that attempts to predict or explain behavior based primarily on a person's learning and past experience.

EPIGENETIC THEORY
Theory that emphasizes the interaction between the environment and a person's genetic inheritance.

PRECISION
The accuracy of predictions made from a theory.

ion. Theories can be used to explain or predict phenomena. Of course, theories can be wrong. You may think you see a house as you put the puzzle pieces together, only to find out later that it is a picture of a boat in drydock. But, as Einstein suggested, if your theory is correct, no matter who finds another piece of the puzzle, that piece will always fit perfectly! If, however, someone comes up with a puzzle piece that doesn't fit the picture you had in mind, then you will need to change your guess about the picture. In the same way, if a researcher finds data that don't fit a particular theory, the theory must be changed.

In this chapter, we will examine some of the major theories that have helped researchers to organize and understand human development. Along the way, we'll find some ideas that are mainly of historical interest and others that continue today to be useful in the study of human development.

THEORIES OF HUMAN DEVELOPMENT

There are many different theories of human development. To date, no theory has been found to be the one and only correct theory. Theories often conflict with one another, and there may be arguments among the supporters of the different theories. Sometimes students feel compelled to take sides. The only way to decide among these theories, however, is to conduct further research or experiments. Eventually, the theories will become more accurate and our powers of prediction will become more acute.

Throughout this text, you'll encounter many developmental theories. There are theories that attempt to explain or predict behavior based primarily on a person's learning and past experience, while placing less emphasis on genetics. These are called **environmental theories**. In contrast, there are theories that emphasize the interaction between the environment and a person's genetic heritage. These are called **epigenetic theories**. Both environmental and epigenetic theories can be further divided according to the dimensions of human development on which they focus. Learning or cognitive theories emphasize the individual's developing abilities to learn or think, while other theories emphasize personality or social forces (see Figure 2.1).

These divisions have come about for many reasons. For instance, historically it was common for European theories to be epigenetic, while American theories were more often environmental. This happened because Europeans have traditionally emphasized family ties and lines of inheritance, while Americans believe that all citizens are "created equal." Although there are many modern exceptions, this historical emphasis is still strong and is interesting because it came about for political rather than scientific reasons.

At this point, most of the theories in Figure 2.1 are probably unfamiliar to you. As you continue reading, however, encountering each new theory in the text, you will be able to place it in perspective by referring back to the figure.

	THEORIES	
	ENVIRONMENTAL	EPIGENETIC
EMPHASIS ON LEARNING	*Learning Theory* Watson Skinner	*Ethological Theory* Lorenz Bowlby
EMPHASIS ON COGNITION	*Information-Processing Theory* Gagné Case	*Cognitive Theory* Baldwin Piaget Perry
EMPHASIS ON SOCIAL FORCES OR PERSONALITY DEVELOPMENT	*Social Learning Theory* Bandura	*Psychosocial Theory* Freud Erikson Levinson Vaillant

FIGURE 2.1

A six-way classification of the major developmental theories discussed in this book.

SCOPE VERSUS PRECISION, OR IT'S BETTER TO BE A BIG FISH IN A SMALL POND

As you recall, a theory is a system of rules or assumptions used to predict or explain phenomena. Predictions about human behavior can be derived from psychological theories. To be useful, however, a theory must lead to accurate predictions. If most of the predictions derived from a theory are accurate, the theory is said to have **precision**.

The Astronomer Versus the Meteorologist

On March 7, 1970, a total eclipse of the sun occurred. The shadow of the moon passed over Acapulco, traveled across Mexico, proceeded up the Atlantic coast of the United States, then swept out over the northern Atlantic. More than 50 years ago, astronomers had predicted that an eclipse would occur on this date and that the shadow would pass over exactly these areas. In addition, an exact time for the beginning and end of the eclipse had been predicted.

Twenty-four hours before the eclipse was due, meteorologists (weather scientists) predicted clear skies in Acapulco and rain at Virginia Beach. Accordingly, astronomers with large research budgets went to Acapulco, while some friends and I gambled on the chance of seeing the eclipse through the rain clouds and piled into a van for the ride from Long Island University to Virginia Beach.

The eclipse was spectacular, occurring exactly as it had been predicted many years earlier. Oddly, the weather at Virginia Beach was perfect; the sky was a huge blue hemispheric dome, not a cloud anywhere. And, you guessed it, it rained on the astronomers in Acapulco.

Why did this happen? Is it that astronomers are brilliant, while weather forecasters are simply "not too bright"? Why can't a weather forecaster predict weather 50 years or so in advance? It's interesting that as we drove to Virginia Beach, we gambled that the weather report would be wrong, but none of us considered even for a moment that the eclipse wouldn't occur. Why? Why do astronomers have high precision in predicting eclipses, while meteorologists have relatively low precision in predicting the weather?

The answer lies in the number and accessibility of variables each profession must deal with. In predicting an eclipse, an astronomer must deal with only a few variables and their interactions. Because the number of variables is low, the scope of this "theory of eclipses" is not grand, but limited. Because all the variables involved in predicting an eclipse have been isolated in the past and their interactions are well known, accurate predictions can be made on the basis of astronomical rules applied to astronomers' observations. For this reason, the theory of eclipses has high precision.

But what about the variables that affect the weather? There are air temperatures, ocean temperatures, land temperatures (all of which may vary greatly from one place to another), air pressures, air currents, ocean currents, gases in the atmosphere, solar activity, upper-atmospheric activity, and infrared radiation absorbed and reflected by the seas, cities, and forests. Add to this list all the variables that no one has thought to consider—variables yet to be discovered. Is it any wonder that weather prediction rapidly loses precision when predictions are required more than a few hours in advance? The scope of weather theory is vast (and the headaches of meteorologists many). In weather theory, so many variables are interacting that it's like trying to predict where a dropped gum wrapper will end up after a hurricane has passed.

Unfortunately for developmental researchers, the scope of human behavior is also vast in terms of the variables involved. Human behavior is so complex that when a theory prematurely attempts explanations on a grand scope, precision falls drastically. When precision falls, predictions fail, which of course makes application of the theory pointless. It's only when the scope is limited (few variables involved) that precision becomes markedly strong (predictions become accurate).

Following World War II, a philosophical reorientation occurred throughout most of psychology, including developmental psychology. Increasingly, experiments and investigations were limited to highly specific areas, so that a science of high precision (although of limited scope) might be developed. Grand explanatory theories that attempt to encompass most of human behavior—like those of Freud, whom we will discuss shortly—are now considered an even-

The scope of weather theory is vast. With so many variables involved, predictions lose their accuracy, especially over the long term. The scope of human behavior is also vast in terms of the variables involved, and predictions may become inaccurate when a theory prematurely attempts explanations.

tual goal, but not an appropriate starting point. Creators of modern theories currently hope to develop a high degree of precision *within a limited scope* and then to examine the effects of adding new variables to slowly broaden the scope—essentially adding pieces to the puzzle.

If we continue to conduct experiments, perhaps our understanding of behavior will finally become complete enough so that we can make accurate predictions about human behavior in any given set of circumstances. After all, this kind of experimental approach has served physics well. Physicists have studied the action of fundamental particles and forces, seen how they interact under different conditions, and then made assessments about how these particles and forces can be controlled and manipulated. The development of computers, atomic power, television, and space exploration bear witness to the physicist's success.

Research on human development, however, is more the study of complex systems than of any fundamental particle or force. Children and adults are not uniform in the way that electrons or protons are. They are neither fundamental nor elemental. They are, and will remain, systems interacting in a world that's never quite the same from one day to the next (Manicas & Secord, 1983). As researchers or students of human development, we must always remember that our search for knowledge is somewhat limited by the fact that no two human beings are ever *exactly* the same. Thus, our predictive ability will never be 100 percent, or even close to it. Even so, we can develop a science that is very useful and that will add greatly to our knowledge.

We are now ready to examine some theories that are important to the study of human development.

PSYCHOANALYTIC THEORY

Sigmund Freud: Founder of Psychoanalysis

Sigmund Freud (1856–1939), the founder of **psychoanalytic theory**, derived his system from observation of his many patients. Freud studied human personality development using techniques he developed for probing the hidden and unconscious thoughts or desires of his patients. Because Freud's theory attempted to explain most of human behavior (Freud, 1940/1964), it is often considered a grand explanatory theory.

Freud presented an outline of psychosexual development that focused on the child's level of development and on how that level related to the child's behavior. According to Freud, the child passes through various **psychosexual stages**. The first three stages (**oral**, **anal**, and **phallic**) involve physical satisfaction and are centered around the **erogenous zones**. Freud believed that too much or too little stimulation during any of the stages could cause a child to become fixated at that stage, resulting in immature or incomplete development. Freud argued that many adult personality problems could be traced to such early fixations.

Here are the five psychosexual stages that Freud identified:

Oral Stage (Birth to Approximately 1 Year).   Freud believed that during this time in a child's personality development, the greatest satisfaction is obtained by stimulation of the lips, mouth, tongue, and gums. He noted that sucking and chewing are the chief sources of an infant's pleasure.

Anal Stage (Approximately 1 to 3 Years).   During this time, according to Freud, the child gains the greatest satisfaction by exercising control over the

Sigmund Freud (1856–1939).

LATENCY STAGE
In psychoanalytic theory, the fourth psychosexual stage, occurring between the phallic stage and puberty, during which sexual drives and feelings become lessened or nonexistent.

GENITAL STAGE
In psychoanalytic theory, the final stage of psychosexual development, characterized by the expression of heterosexual desires.

PSYCHOSOCIAL STAGES
Stages of ego development as formulated by Erikson, incorporating both sexual and social aspects.

anus during elimination and retention. Freud believed that the anal stage reaches its peak once toilet training is successful.

Phallic Stage (Approximately 4 to 6 Years). According to Freud, the child's greatest pleasure during the phallic stage comes from stimulating the genitals. It is during this stage, Freud believed, that the identification with the same-sex parent occurs; this identification enables the child to develop into a healthy, mature adult.

Latency Stage (Approximately 6 Years to Puberty). Freud referred to this time as the **latency stage** because he believed that the sexual drive becomes dormant from the age of 6 years until the onset of puberty. According to Freud, children during this psychosexual stage, are free of erotic feelings and instead expend their efforts on acquiring cultural and social skills.

Genital Stage (Puberty to Adulthood). Freud believed that heterosexual desire awakens during the **genital stage**, and provided that no strong, upsetting fixations have occurred, the child is on his or her way to a "normal" life.

Freud's view of personality development had a powerful influence on the history of psychology. A number of his central concepts have been supported by modern research, including the idea that people are often unaware of their unconscious motivations. However, it has proved difficult to test many of Freud's ideas by the scientific method (Hook, 1960). Furthermore, many of Freud's ideas have not been well supported (Erwin, 1980). For instance, modern research indicates that the first six years of a person's life, although important and formative, are not as crucial to the development of adult personality as Freud believed they were.

Whether or not you agree with Freud's theory of human personality development, you should recognize that it is valuable if only because it stimulated so much research. The theory is largely unsupported by scientific data, so its full value will remain uncertain until more ways to test it can be devised.

Erik Erikson: A Modern Psychoanalyst

A number of modern psychoanalysts have had an influence on developmental psychology, and Erik Erikson (1902–1994) is a prime example. As a young student, Erikson worked with Freud, and over the years, he expanded on Freud's ideas. Erikson viewed human development as a progression through eight **psychosocial stages**, roughly equivalent in duration to some of Freud's psychosexual stages (see Table 2.1). Erikson argued that during certain periods in our lives, we are faced with opposing conflicts that must be resolved if healthy development is to occur.

There are three principal ways in which Erikson's theory differed from Freud's. First, Erikson placed a much greater emphasis on social and cultural forces than did Freud. Freud believed that a child's personality was determined mainly by parents and was the result of unconscious processes, whereas Erikson placed the child in the broader social world of parents, friends, family, society, and culture. For this reason, his theory is called psycho*social*. Second, Erikson did not believe that failure at any particular psychosocial stage will have irreversible consequences, such as Freud argued might occur. Erikson argued that setbacks at any stage can eventually be overcome with proper attention, care, and love. And, third, Erikson emphasized the *entire lifespan* of an individual, whereas Freud placed the greatest emphasis on the first six years of life.

Some researchers argue that Erikson's theory is supported by informal observations obtained from many sources and that his theory may have much to contribute as a general outline for healthy socialization and personality development. However, hard scientific proof for Erikson's theory is not easy to come by because of the difficulty of examining Erikson's stages under controlled laboratory conditions or by other scientific methods. Furthermore, it has been argued that Erikson's stages of development have been subjectively determined. George Vaillant and Daniel Levinson, whose work we will be examining in later chapters, have both modified and added to Erikson's work to bring it more into line with their view of normal adult development. Jean Baker Miller, Carol Gilligan, and others have also done research on normal adult development and have formulated a theory of women's psychosocial development as being different from that of men's. We will also be studying their work in later chapters.

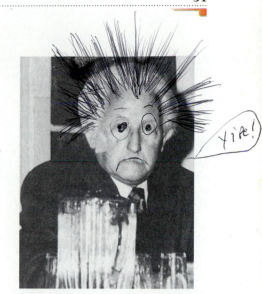

Erik Erikson (1902–1994).

Table 2.1 ● Erikson's Psychosocial Stages (and, for Comparison, Freud's Psychosexual Stages)

PERIOD OF TIME	PSYCHOSOCIAL CONFLICT	DESCRIPTION OF ERIKSON'S STAGES	FREUDIAN STAGES
1. Infancy	Basic trust vs. mistrust	Parents must maintain an adequate environment—supportive, nurturing, and loving—so that the child develops basic trust.	Oral
2. Years 1–3	Autonomy vs. shame or doubt	As the child develops bowel and bladder control, he or she must also develop a healthy attitude toward being independent and somewhat self-sufficient. If the child is made to feel that independent efforts are wrong, then shame and self-doubt develop instead of autonomy.	Anal
3. Years 3–5½	Initiative vs. guilt	The child must discover ways to initiate actions on his or her own. If such initiatives are successful or acceptable, guilt will be avoided.	Phallic
4. Years 5½–12	Industry vs. inferiority	The child must learn to feel competent, especially when competing with peers. Failure results in feelings of inferiority.	Latency
5. Adolescence	Identity vs. role confusion	The child must develop a sense of role identity, especially in terms of selecting a vocation and future career.	Genital
6. Early adulthood	Intimacy vs. isolation	The formation of close friendships and adult sexual relationships is vital to healthy development.	
7. Middle adulthood	Generativity vs. stagnation	Adults develop useful lives by helping and guiding children. Childless adults must fill this need through adoption or other close relationships with children.	
8. Later adulthood	Ego integrity vs. despair	An adult will eventually review his or her life. A life well spent will result in a sense of well-being and integrity.	

BEHAVIORISM

The school of psychology that views learning as the most important aspect of an organism's development. Behaviorists objectively measure behavior and the way in which stimulus-response relationships are formed.

LEARNING

A relatively permanent change in behavior as a result of experience.

CLASSICAL CONDITIONING

An experimental learning procedure in which a stimulus that normally evokes a given reflex is continually associated with a stimulus that does not usually evoke that reflex, with the result that the latter stimulus will eventually evoke the reflex when presented by itself.

CONDITIONED STIMULUS

In classical conditioning, a previously neutral stimulus that, through pairing with an unconditioned stimulus, acquires the ability to produce a similar response.

UNCONDITIONED STIMULUS

A stimulus that normally evokes an unconditioned response, such as the food that originally caused Pavlov's dogs to respond with salivation.

BEHAVIORAL THEORY

John Watson and Black-Box Psychology

Early in this century, an American psychologist, John B. Watson (1878–1958), developed an objective system of psychology he called **behaviorism**. Watson thus took a tremendous philosophical step, rejecting the study of conscious or unconscious thought processes because they were not directly observable. This was a direct response to those, like Freud, who had studied mental processes and their relationship to personality development. Instead, Watson emphasized observable environmental stimuli (e.g., a loud noise, a red stoplight, a candy bar, praise from a friend) and the observable behaviors or responses that occurred in the presence of such stimuli. Behaviorism is sometimes called *black-box psychology* because Watson considered the mind to be like a mysterious black box that could never be examined objectively.

Contrary to psychoanalytic theory, traditional behaviorists believe that **learning** plays the most important role in determining future development. Watson summarized this concept in his 1928 book, *Psychological Care of Infant and Child*:

> Give me a dozen healthy infants, well-formed and my own specified world to bring them up in and I'll guarantee to take any one of them at random and train him to become any type of specialist I might select—doctor, lawyer, artist, merchant, chief, and yes, even into a beggarman and thief regardless of his talents, penchants, tendencies, abilities, vocations, and race of his ancestors. (Watson, 1928, p. 104)

This statement reflected the concept of *tabula rasa* proposed in the eighteenth century by the eminent philosopher John Locke. In this view, the mind of the newborn is like a blank surface on which environment and experience could chisel a unique pattern. Today, our understanding of heredity and genetic mechanisms, as well as our knowledge of how infants actively interact with their environment, lead us to reject the idea that learning is solely responsible for behavior or that the infant is a passive recipient of experience. In fairness to Watson, however, it is important to look at the rest of his famous quote (Horowitz, 1992).

> I am going beyond my facts and I admit it, but so have the advocates of the contrary and they have been doing it for many thousands of years. Please note that when this experiment is made I am to be allowed to specify the way the children are to be brought up and the type of world they have to live in. (Watson, 1928, p. 104)

Ivan Pavlov and Classical Conditioning

In a series of well-known experiments, Russian physiologist Ivan Pavlov (1849–1936) reported an experiment in associative learning. Pavlov was investigating digestion in dogs and was trying to understand why the dogs began to salivate *before* they received food, since salivation is an innate reflex (i.e., unlearned). The salivation reaction seemed to occur when an association was made between the food and another stimulus, such as seeing someone in the laboratory open the cupboard where the dog food was kept. Other researchers had observed this phenomenon, which later came to be known as **classical conditioning**, but had either considered it a nuisance or ignored it. Pavlov, however, became interested in this learning process and began to investigate it systematically. Pavlov chose a stimulus that did not cause salivation in dogs (a

An artist's rendering of Ivan Pavlov (center) and staff.

bell) and began to pair it with the presentation of food. He rang the bell, immediately presented the food, and then observed the salivation. After the bell and the food had been *paired,* or associated, Pavlov was able to elicit salivation without giving food; ringing the bell was enough. The dogs associated food with the bell, and they salivated. The bell had become a stimulus to which the dogs responded in a predictable way, by salivating.

At this point you might be wondering what salivation in dogs has to do with learning in people. But the mechanisms responsible for classical conditioning in dogs apply to human beings as well. A neutral stimulus (known as the **conditioned stimulus**), when paired often enough with another stimulus (the **unconditioned stimulus**) that normally elicits a reflex response, can come to provoke the reflex even when the unconditioned stimulus is not present (see Figure 2.2). Classical conditioning has been demonstrated in children, adults, and even infants (Fitzgerald & Brackbill, 1976). For example, if a child cries (response) when he sees a hypodermic syringe (conditioned stimulus), it is because he has associated pain (unconditioned stimulus) with the syringe; thereafter, the syringe alone can come to elicit the crying response. Furthermore, other kinds of learning play a powerful role in the acquisition of new behaviors for all of us.

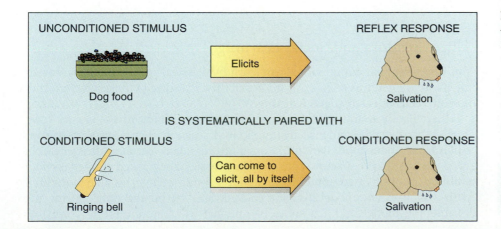

FIGURE 2.2

The classical conditioning paradigm.

FIGURE 2.3

A puzzle box similar to that used by Thorndike in 1898. (SOURCE: Bitterman, 1969, p. 445)

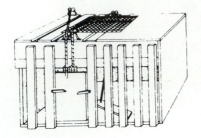

Thorndike, Skinner, and Operant Conditioning

At about the time that Pavlov was studying the behavior of dogs, an American psychologist, E. L. Thorndike (1874–1949), was observing the behavior of cats. Thorndike would deprive a cat of food for some time and then place it inside a puzzle box, a container from which escape is possible if the animal happens to trip a latch that opens the door (see Figure 2.3). Food was placed outside the box in plain view of the cat. Eventually, the cat would accidentally hook a claw onto the wire loop or step on the treadle that pulled the latch, and the door to the box would open. As the cats came to appreciate this way of escaping, each time they were put into the box, they released themselves sooner.

Thorndike's observations of such *trial-and-error* learning led him to consider that the consequences of an act were an important factor in determining the probability that the act would occur:

> Any act which in a given situation produces satisfaction becomes associated with that situation, so that when the situation recurs, the act is more likely than ever before to recur also. Conversely, any act which in a given situation produces discomfort becomes disassociated from that situation, so that when the situation recurs, the act is less likely than before to recur. (Thorndike, 1905, p. 202)

Thorndike's explanation, known as the **law of effect**, is one of the cornerstones of learning. Much of what you've learned in life has been acquired in this way. Because responses are maintained or changed depending on the consequences that *follow a response*, when you respond to something, the response is strengthened if the consequence is pleasant and weakened if the consequence is aversive. For example, if you decide to fry bacon while unclothed and get sprayed with hot grease (aversive consequence), that behavior (cooking while naked) is less likely to occur in the future.

In the 1950s, B. F. Skinner began to systematically study this kind of learning, which he called **operant conditioning**. He explored the concept of **reinforcement**, in which a pleasurable event tends to strengthen the response that preceded it. Skinner argued that behaviors can be made much stronger (reinforced) if they are followed, as Thorndike had originally suggested, by a reinforcing consequence. In this view, a response is initially emitted for unknown reasons. The *probability* that the response will be emitted, again, however, can be predicted by the organism's past experience with the effect of that response on the environment. Responses that had pleasant consequences are more likely to be repeated in similar circumstances, while responses that produced unpleasant consequences are less likely to be repeated. The latter instance is an example of **punishment**.

B. F. Skinner (1904–1990).

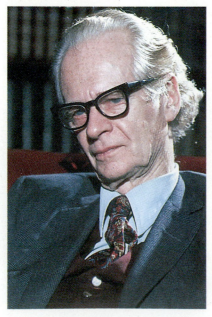

Albert Bandura and Social Learning

You have seen that an individual can learn by classical and operant conditioning. Now we will investigate a third possibility: learning by observing another person's behavior—or **social learning**.

Albert Bandura and several of his colleagues at Stanford University have argued that social learning is a distinct kind of learning that requires new principles to be understood. Bandura, Ross, and Ross demonstrated their thesis in 1963 in an experiment now considered a classic. They asked nursery school children to observe an adult (live) **model** striking a large inflated Bobo doll with a mallet. The model also hit, kicked, and sat on the doll. During the assault, the model said a number of unusual word combinations, probably unlike any sentences the children had heard before. Neither the model nor the observing children were directly reinforced at any time during the session.

Later, after the model had gone, the children were secretly observed as they played in a toy-filled room with the Bobo doll. For comparison, other children who had not seen the model's behavior were also allowed to interact with the doll. The experiment clearly demonstrated that the children who had observed the model were far more likely to be aggressive, in imitation of the model's behavior, than were the other children. Furthermore, many of the children who had observed the model also imitated the model's unusual verbal statements. These results would not have been predicted by other learning theories, inasmuch as the imitation seemed to be occurring without reinforcement.

The question, of course, is why would a child continue to imitate a behavior when the imitation is not reinforced? Although it does seem to happen, no one is quite sure why, which is one reason some researchers view social learning as a distinctly different kind of learning.

In our species, learning by imitating another's behavior is an easy thing to do and in fact is quite commonplace. If you consider that learning by trial and error can be extremely time consuming or even dangerous, you will readily see how valuable it is to learn by imitating the *successful* behavior of another person. If learning were restricted to what we could gain through classical or operant conditioning, our ability to master our world would be severely limited.

The Behaviorist View

As we discussed earlier, John B. Watson argued that any science of behavior must be based on observable events rather than on inferred ones. Watson believed that this would limit the biased and subjective assessments of behavior that he thought were plaguing psychology. His arguments were quite popular in the United States and helped to formulate a particularly American psychology called *behaviorism*.

Behaviorists intended to develop a strong and powerful science based on their acquired knowledge of observable stimuli and responses. They argued that through the scientific manipulation of the environment, a technology of **behavior modification** could be developed. According to behaviorists, as long as you could predict the responses, knowing what went on inside an organism's head was not necessary.

Although this radical approach has produced volumes of valuable research showing how the environment controls and contributes to behavior, it is nonetheless a limited perspective. Humans do think, however unobservably. In other words, the way you internally organize and process information can modify your behavior. People aren't computers; we are not simply the sum of our inputs. Or, as Albert Bandura has stated, to exclude thinking from any theory of learning would be like attributing "Shakespeare's literary masterpieces to his prior instruction in the mechanics of writing" (Bandura, 1978, p. 350).

Although it has its roots in behaviorism, social learning theory concerns the interaction between environment and thought (Bandura, 1978). Social learning theorists, and many other learning theorists, are beginning to incorporate the complexities of internalized thought processes into their research. This synthesis is known as *cognitive behaviorism*.

ETHOLOGICAL THEORY

Although behavioral theory has been emphasized by American psychologists throughout this century, research on inherited behavior has also attracted great

LAW OF EFFECT
Thorndike's principle that responses associated with pleasant consequences tend to be repeated, while those associated with discomforting consequences tend to be eliminated.

OPERANT CONDITIONING
Skinner's term for changes in behavior that occur as a result of consequences that reinforce or punish emitted responses. They are, in turn, shaped by further environmental experiences.

REINFORCEMENT
An event that strengthens the response that preceded it. Operant conditioning is a process by which a response is reinforced.

PUNISHMENT
An aversive stimulus consequence that has the effect of decreasing the strength of an emitted response.

SOCIAL LEARNING
Learning by observing the actions of other people.

MODEL
In social learning theory, anyone who demonstrates a behavior that other people observe.

BEHAVIOR MODIFICATION
A set of procedures for changing human behavior, especially by using behavior therapy and operant conditioning techniques.

Albert Bandura.

ETHOLOGY
The study of human and animal behavior from a biological point of view, characterized by the study of animals in their natural environments.

IMPRINTING
As used by ethologists, a species-specific bonding that occurs within a limited period early in the life of the organism and that is relatively unmodifiable thereafter.

CRITICAL PERIOD
A specific time in an organism's development when certain experiences will have an effect and after which the effect can no longer be obtained through exposure to the experience.

interest, particularly in Europe. People who specialize in this area of research are called ethologists, and their field of study is **ethology**. Ethologists usually conduct naturalistic observations, although they are also interested in learned behavior.

Spalding's Chicks

Ethology traces its experimental roots to nineteenth-century zoology. In an early ethological experiment conducted in 1873, D. A. Spalding discovered that baby chicks tended to follow the first moving object that they saw, usually the mother hen. This tendency seemed to exist either at birth or shortly thereafter. Spalding speculated that the tendency to follow was probably innate, because it helped the chicks to survive by keeping the babies with the mother. Spalding wanted to be sure that the behavior was not learned—that is, acquired through experience—so he covered the chicks' heads with hoods immediately after they were hatched, before they opened their eyes. When the hoods were removed a few hours later, the chicks followed the first object that crossed their field of vision, regardless of what the object was. This result demonstrated that the tendency was not learned, because experience could not have played a role.

Konrad Lorenz and Imprinting and Critical Periods

Research in this new field began to grow significantly after Konrad Lorenz published a paper in 1937 describing the *following response*. As part of his study, Lorenz made certain that he was the first moving object that some newborn goslings saw. From that time on, the ducklings followed "mama" Lorenz everywhere he went, even swimming. It seemed to Lorenz that the first object to move past these ducklings was "stamped into" the animals' brains as the object to be followed. Lorenz called this stamping phenomenon **imprinting**. He also observed that imprinting could occur only during a **critical period** lasting from hatching until about 2 days later. The most effective imprinting occurred approximately 14 hours after hatching. If the chicks were more than 2 days old when they saw their first moving object, imprinting was not

Young ducklings followed "mama" Lorenz wherever he went because they had been allowed to imprint on him.

observed to occur. If the critical period passed without the necessary stimulation, the behavior would *never* be acquired.

Ethologists and other researchers believe that such inherited behavior must serve a survival function. The following response has the obvious function of keeping the chick or duckling close to its mother. Offspring that don't stay close to their mother have less chance of surviving and passing on their genes.

The issue of imprinting is not so clear when we consider human beings. Although infants do generally become attached to parents or caregivers and sometimes show changes in the strengths of their attachments, there appears to be no particular period that is most important in determining their first attachment figure, the way there is with baby ducks or chicks (Reed & Leiderman, 1983). In this sense, imprinting has not been found to occur in human beings. However, modern ethologists, such as John Bowlby, argue that this does not preclude the possibility that infants are still genetically predisposed to form attachments. In their view, even without critical periods, there is an innate drive in humans to form attachments that is as strong as the motivational forces of mating or eating (Bowlby, 1982a). Moreover, other behaviors may be inherited because of the functions they serve.

Sensitive Periods

Although critical periods don't appear to play a major role in human development, there do appear to be times in our lives when certain influences seem to have a greater effect than they would at other times in our lives. As you recall, Freud believed that certain periods in early childhood were sensitive to certain types of stimuli. Ethologists have defined these times as **sensitive periods**; they are those times during an organism's development when a particular influence is most likely to have an effect. Sensitive periods are different from critical periods. If a sensitive period passes without the required stimulation, the behavior still may be acquired, although with difficulty; if a critical period passes, the behavior can never be acquired.

Thus, there could be times in our lives when we are genetically primed to respond to certain influences and other times when those influences will have little or no effect. This is essentially the theory underlying the notion of a sensitive period. As you read other chapters, you may notice that observations of human development often suggest the existence of such sensitive periods. For example, much attention has been given to sexual roles and preferences, but how are they formed? They seem to be shaped early. A study of individuals who desired sex change operations found that most of these people felt that they had been "trapped in the wrong-sexed body" for as long as they could remember (Stoller, 1976). Is this because there is a genetically programmed sensitive period, lasting perhaps a few months, during which a child is extremely influenced by, and easily attracted to, various sexual stimuli? The answers to such questions are not known; it would be exceptionally useful if they were. If scientists knew which sensitive periods existed in our species, then we could be alert to them and could ensure that children and adults would be in a position to profit from them when they occurred.

In Chapter 1, for example, we discussed the effects on children's behavior of viewing violent TV programs. Research has indicated that there may be a sensitive period for children who view such violence. This sensitive period seems to occur around the ages of 8 to 9 years. During this time, the effect of viewing television violence appears to be especially influential in directing a child's behavior (Eron, Huesmann, Brice, Fischer, & Mermelstein, 1983). If they were aware of this sensitive period, parents and educators might be especially cautious about exposing 8- and 9-year-old children to violent television programs.

SENSITIVE PERIOD
A time during which a particular organism is most sensitive to the effect of certain stimuli.

COGNITIVE THEORY

Cognitive theory emphasizes the ability to think. Internal conscious thinking as a vehicle for deciding, choosing, and planning and the way in which that thinking develops are the focus of all cognitive theories.

For a long time, psychology ignored infants' minds. Some psychologists believed that ignoring an infant's mind wasn't a very hard thing to do, because whatever infants thought about, if anything, couldn't be too complex (Pines, 1966). Most early theorists of development were concerned more with physical, biological, or emotional factors or with personality or language development than with what might or might not be going on inside an infant's mind. There was one exception, however—the American psychologist James Mark Baldwin (1861–1934). Even before the turn of the century, Baldwin had outlined a theory describing cognitive development as progressing through stages (Baldwin, 1894). Baldwin was the first person to describe cognitive development in terms of *circular reactions, accommodation,* and *adaptation* (terms we will become familiar with in this and later chapters).

Baldwin's work went largely unnoticed in the United States. He did, however, travel to France, where he worked for a number of years. Some of his writings were translated into French and read by a young man who found them so stimulating that he decided to pursue Baldwin's ideas further. That young man was the Swiss scientist Jean Piaget (1896–1980), whose own work radically altered our study of cognitive development.

Jean Piaget: The Four Stages of Cognitive Development

Next to Sigmund Freud, Jean Piaget is the most frequently referenced researcher in the psychology literature (Endler, Rushton, & Roediger, 1978). In one sense, it's peculiar that this should be so. You see, Piaget was not initially trained as a psychologist; he was a biologist and naturalist. By the time he was 21 years old, he had published over 20 scientific papers on mollusks. Almost all his early research was ethological.

Jean Piaget (1896–1980).

Even before reading Baldwin's work, Piaget had became interested in development as a result of his biological observations. Piaget noticed that when large mollusks were taken from lakes and moved to small ponds, they underwent structural changes because of the reduced wave action in the ponds. Piaget understood this to mean that the mollusks had inherited a structure that was flexible; they would adapt, within limits, to the environment into which they were placed. In other words, the genes in the mollusks carried not only signals for specific biological development, but also signals enabling them to adapt to the environment through exposure to it.

After being exposed to Baldwin's work, Piaget became curious as to whether there were parallels or similarities in our own species. Then, while observing children taking an intelligence test, Piaget noticed that older children seemed to have adapted their thought processes so that they could better deal with the test questions. This observation led him to the conclusion that older children, rather than simply knowing *more* than younger children, actually thought differently about problems. Piaget wondered whether this could be evidence that their brains were flexibly adapting to their environments through experience by altering underlying cognitive structures, much as the mollusks had adapted to the ponds. He asked himself how this interplay between biology and experience might develop, and this question led him to study cognition and thought processing in human beings. Piaget worked in this area for many decades and contributed greatly to our knowledge. Although his training was in biology (which is in many ways closely tied to developmental psychology), he became one of the most widely read and respected psychologists of our time.

In Piaget's view, cognitive development is the combined result of the development of the brain and nervous system and the experiences that help the individual adapt to his or her environment. Piaget believed that because humans are genetically similar and share many of the same environmental experiences, they can be expected to exhibit considerable uniformity in their cognitive development. In fact, he argued, predictable stages of cognitive development will occur during specific periods of a child's life (see Table 2.2).

Piaget believed that all people develop by advancing through the four periods of cognitive development. According to Piaget, cognitive development in all children will follow the outline given in Table 2.2. Intellectually impaired children, however, may develop at a slower rate or may fail to reach the higher stages. If you happen to have a developing child in your home (what other kind is there?), watching the child advance through these cognitive stages can provide endless hours of pleasure.

As you may have already noticed by looking at Table 2.2, infants don't think in the same way that adults do. (In fact, you may have figured this out before you saw Table 2.2.) Adult thinking is based on symbols and logic. We can imagine the future and remember the past in the form of mental images, such as pictures "in the mind's eye," or symbols, such as the words in our language. We can even imagine things that haven't happened or things we wish would happen. Adolescents, of course, also have these abilities, and children as young as 2 years have certain symbolic abilities. Infants, however, don't appear to possess mental images or symbolic skills.

This doesn't mean, however, that the cognitive differences outlined in Table 2.2 occur because adults know more than children do. According to Piaget, it's not a simple matter of children knowing less (a quantitative difference). Piaget argued that children are not simply adults who know less, nor are adults simply knowledgeable children. For instance, older children are capable of thoughts that are, quite literally, beyond the understanding or conceptual abilities of young children. Piaget believed that this is because older children have more extensive cognitive development. On the one hand, they have broader

---

Table 2.2 ● Piaget's Stages of Cognitive Development

Sensorimotor Period (0–2 years)
Characterized by a lack of fully developed *object permanence*, a term used by Piaget to refer to the individual's realization that objects continue to exist even though they are not presently sensed.

Preoperational Period (2–7 years)
Characterized by the beginning of internalized thought processes; it is called preoperational because children haven't yet acquired the logical operations or rules of thought characteristic of later periods of cognitive development; beginning of a sense of self.

Period of Concrete Operations (7–11 years)
Characterized by the beginning of the use of logical operations and rules; the child, however, is limited to the concrete, the world he or she has directly experienced; conservation and reversibility obtained.

Period of Formal Operations (11+ years)
Characterized by the ability to solve hypothetical problems, to make complex deductions, and to test advanced hypotheses; child can analyze the validity of different ways of reasoning (the foundation of science).

ADAPTATION
A term used by Piaget to describe the mechanism through which an organism develops by adjusting to changes; such adjustment occurs through the processes of assimilation and accommodation.

ASSIMILATION
Piaget's term for the act of taking in information and perceptions in a way that is compatible with the person's current understanding of the world.

ACCOMMODATION
Piaget's term for the process in which people adjust or change their understanding to incorporate aspects of an experience not currently represented in their cognitive structures.

EQUILIBRIUM
Term used by Piaget to describe a hypothetical innate drive that forces a person to actively pursue cognitive adaptation. In this view, children have a natural inclination toward cognitive development.

experiences; on the other, they can process the information in more sophisticated ways because of the more advanced biological and adaptive development of their underlying cognitive structures. Because children advance through qualitative changes, it is often necessary to cover old material again at each stage, so that the child can accommodate the information to his or her new understanding of the world (see At Issue).

Now let's see how cognitive structures adapt to the environment.

Assimilation and Accommodation. During cognitive growth, children continue to adapt to their environments. **Adaptation** is a favorite term in biology that describes an organism's ability to change so as to fit in with its surroundings. Borrowing from Baldwin, Piaget argued that children adapt in two ways: through **assimilation** and through **accommodation**.

Piaget defined assimilation as "the integration of external elements into evolving or completed structures" (Piaget, 1970, p. 706). Assimilation, then, is the act of taking in information and perceptions in a way that is compatible with one's current understanding of the world. According to Piaget, we have all developed cognitive structures based on our experience. Anything we perceive that is new can be assimilated and interpreted only by the evolving or completed cognitive structures we already possess.

When we assimilate information or perceptions into our understanding of the world, such additional data may affect underlying cognitive structures and alter them. Such alteration is called *accommodation*.

By bringing new objects into categories they already possess (assimilation) or by creating a new understanding of something (accommodation), children adapt to their environments. Even infants, when first reaching for objects, go through an assimilation and accommodation process as they learn to adjust their reach and grasp in order to touch new objects. For instance, an infant may reach for a new object using the same-sized grasp that successfully obtained an earlier object (assimilation). If he fails, he may adjust his grasp to accommodate the new object's size. His cognitive structure has now further adapted to his environment.

No one knows for certain why children adapt cognitively to their environments. Piaget believed that there is an innate force that drives children to actively pursue cognitive adaptation. In this view, humans desire cognitive **equilibrium**, or balance. For example, when a child feels comfortable with the way she thinks—that is, when she is able to assimilate most of what she finds in her environment into her existing cognitive structures—she feels satisfied and is considered in equilibrium. However, when she becomes aware of the failings of her thought strategies, she experiences disequilibrium. The conflict that arises during disequilibrium, when cognitive structures are unable to comprehend external events, causes the child to become off balance cognitively. This leaves her feeling uncomfortable, and until she acquires a more sophisticated approach for accommodating new information, her equilibrium will not return. In this way, Piaget argued, the struggle to resolve discrepancies between her current understanding of the world and what she observes is the force that eventually propels a child upward through the stages of cognitive development (Block, 1982).

You may have noticed that Piaget listed his last period of cognitive development as beginning at about age 11 years. The question arises, Doesn't further cognitive development occur during adulthood? In fact, there has been considerable debate over this issue. Piaget argued that there is no further cognitive development beyond this stage. Some researchers, however, believe that there may be qualitative advances in cognitive development beyond formal opera-

AT ISSUE

Children's Understanding of Adoption

One of the most difficult tasks faced by adoptive parents is what and when to tell their adopted children about those children's status. Most adoption agencies recommend that a child be told early in life, generally between the ages of 2 and 4 years, that he has been adopted. The typical suggestion is that parents start with the basic adoption facts and then build on them with more and more information until the child comes to deal with and understand what it means to be adopted (Mech, 1973).

The idea of telling the child early and then building on this knowledge is based on the theory that children's knowledge results from a continuous and progressive accumulation of facts. Piaget's theory, however, does not agree with this assertion. In the Piagetian view, children progress through different cognitive stages, and these stages are qualitatively different. Cognitive theorists who have studied Piaget and his work have therefore drawn a different conclusion about how to tell a child that he or she is adopted.

Alan is adopted; he is 5½ years old. He knows he is adopted. Listen, as he discusses adoption with a researcher (Brodzinsky, Singer, & Braff, 1984, p. 873):

Alan: Adoption means you go to try to get a baby, and if you can't, you can't.
Researcher: Where do you get the baby that you adopt?
Alan: From your vagina and your tummy.
Researcher: Whose vagina or tummy?
Alan: The baby's mommy.
Researcher: Is the baby adopted?
Alan: Yes . . . cause the mommy has it now. It came out of her.
Researcher: Are all babies adopted?
Alan: Yep.
Researcher: If a man and a woman want to be parents, what do they have to do?
Alan: Adopt a child.
Researcher: Is there any other way of becoming a parent—a mommy or daddy—besides adopting?
Alan: I don't know.

This example of Alan is typical; very few 5-year-old children who are told that they are adopted understand the difference between adoption and birth or that these can be different paths toward parenthood. They also understand little about the adoption process or the reasons for adoption (Brodzinsky, Singer, & Braff, 1984). Once children enter Piaget's stage of concrete operations, however, their understanding of the different aspects of adoption grow; in adolescence, with formal operations, they reach a sophisticated and abstract appreciation of the adoption process.

The issue is not whether parents should tell children early that they are adopted; adoption experts as well as cognitive theorists generally agree that they should. Rather, it concerns the unrealistic expectations that parents may have concerning the effects of their explanations on a young child. For instance, when the parent of a 4- or 5-year-old girl quite comfortably says, "My child knows she is adopted," we have to wonder if the parent realizes that the child has an extremely limited understanding of adoption. Does the parent realize that when a child reaches concrete operations, it might be good to describe once again, from the start, that she is adopted and what adoption means? Researchers have noted that a false sense of security after telling a young child, and the child's apparent comfort and acceptance of the information, "may well lead to a premature termination of the disclosure process—a factor that presumably could place the child, and parents, at risk for future adjustment problems" (Brodzinsky, Singer, & Braff, 1984, p. 877).

The emphasis, then, is on telling and *retelling* the child about his or her adoption at each successive stage of cognitive development, so that at each stage, the child can understand, to the best of his or her cognitive abilities, what adoption means.

tions (Commons, Richards, & Kuhn, 1982). As you will see in later chapters, theorists such as William Perry have focused on the issue of cognitive development during adulthood.

Criticisms of Piaget.   Without a doubt, Jean Piaget contributed immeasurably to our knowledge of cognitive development in children. His theories have had a wide influence on education and psychology. Throughout the years, however, people have developed some strong arguments against Piaget's view, especially researchers in the United States.

INFORMATION-PROCESSING APPROACH
A cognitive approach to the understanding of intellectual development that relies on the computer as a model. Researchers using this approach are concerned with the storage, processing, and retrieval mechanisms involved in cognition.

PROBABILISTIC EPIGENESIS
Literally, the direction in which growth will probably go. In cognitive development theory, the term is used to describe the stages of cognitive development that typically occur during the development of most individuals, but not necessarily in the development of all individuals.

HUMANISTIC THEORY
A school of psychology that emphasizes the uniqueness of the individual and the search for self-actualization.

SELF-ACTUALIZATION
Maslow's term for an individual's constant striving to realize full potential.

HIERARCHY OF MOTIVES
A theory of motivation developed by Maslow in which more basic needs must first be met before needs of a higher order can come into play.

Throughout the mid-twentieth century, the learning theorist's view was paramount among American psychologists. Proponents of behaviorism, such as John Watson and B. F. Skinner, took a different approach to explain a child's cognitive development. In their view, development does not occur from *within*, as in a living organism, but rather from *without,* by "adding on" to the basic "machine." In other words, cognitive development is the result of learning.

Although Piaget also believed that learning was important, he drew a distinction between development and learning. Piaget believed that the kinds of learning the behaviorists had demonstrated through their conditioning experiments were the equivalent of teaching children "circus tricks" (Piaget, 1952). Behaviorist B. F. Skinner countered by stating that the stages of development that Piaget had observed were nothing more than an illusion based on the kinds of questions that Piaget had asked the children. Skinner argued that children actually developed in a nonstagelike manner according to the principles of cumulative learning—that is, in an orderly and regular *quantitative*, not qualitative, way (Skinner, 1969). In 1970, researcher Robert Gagne outlined cognitive development from the learning theorists' point of view, describing complex cognitive skills as the product of a hierarchy of more elementary skills obtained through prior experience and learning.

Some researchers have postulated that the human mind is similar to a computer and that the computer would be a useful model in the study of cognitive development. This is known as the **information-processing approach**, and we will be touching on the large volume of work generated by this approach as we progress through this book. Unlike the other theories we have been discussing, however, this approach is not cohesive enough to be presented fully in this chapter. In fact, the information-processing approach has been described

> not [as] a single theory, but rather [as] a framework characterizing a large number of research programs. . . Information-processing investigators study the flow of information through the cognitive system. The flow begins with an *input*, usually a stimulus, into the human information-processing system. The flow ends with an *output*, which could be information stored in long-term memory, physical behavior, speech, or a decision. (Miller, 1989, p. 271)

When considering which approach best describes cognitive development, it is important to note that the experiments and observations made by supporters of both Piaget's and the learning theorists' approaches have been extensive and varied. In fact, a number of researchers have come to the conclusion that both views are correct! It may be possible that there are both "stages" and "no stages" in cognitive development. Perhaps cognitive development occurs in a universal stagelike progression, with each stage having a structural organization, *and also* develops in a continuous way, with people showing very different development, depending on their learning, histories, and culture (Fischer & Silvern, 1985). It may be possible to integrate the two approaches.

An Integration

The organism does not stand alone, separate from its environment. Neither does the environment stand alone, separate from the organism. The two must interact. Some of the most ingrained reflexes in human beings show the effects of environmental influences. Even physical appearance, which most people would consider largely determined by genetic inheritance, can be influenced by the environment. For example, human beings who live throughout their lives high in the Andes have great barrel-shaped chests and large lungs to handle the thin air. For these people, the atmosphere at sea level may even pose a threat to health (Gould & Lewontin, 1979). Similarly, cognitive development is shaped simultaneously by our genetics, anatomy, and physiology and also by our behavior, our circumstances, the people around us, and the culture in which we are raised.

What, then, do Piaget's stages actually represent? Piaget and other stage theorists may have demonstrated what is typical under usual environmental and organismic conditions—that is, what is probable. But there always can be variations. When modern theorists talk about stages of cognitive development, they often use the term **probabilistic epigenesis** (Gottlieb, 1983) to reflect the fact that stages describe only the typical or most probable development. In fact, modern cognitive researchers prefer to use the word *level* instead of *stage*, because *stage* has a rigid, inflexible connotation.

Future research may eventually help us understand more fully the cognitive development of human beings and the roles that learning and biology play in this development. Meanwhile, keep in mind that just because Piaget died, his theory isn't necessarily complete. During his lifetime, Piaget was his own greatest revisionist (Block, 1982). He changed old ideas for new and reorganized his thinking many times. As we will see when we study adult cognitive development, contemporary researchers are already revising and extending Piaget's theory.

Abraham Maslow (1908–1970).

HUMANISTIC THEORY

Humanistic theory has often been called the third force in modern psychology, the psychoanalytic and behavioral viewpoints constituting the first two forces. Abraham Maslow (1908–1970) and Carl Rogers (1902–1987) were the leading proponents of the humanistic view.

Humanists regard behavior very differently from psychoanalysts or behaviorists. Humanists don't believe that behavior is governed either by unconscious drives and motives or by external stimuli and rewards in the environment. Instead, they argue that people are free agents, having free will, that they are conscious and creative, and that they are born with an inner motivation to fulfill their potential. Humanists believe that self-initiated learning is the only effective kind of learning. Maslow referred to the inner motivation to fulfill potential as **self-actualization**. The humanists view self-actualization as a lifelong process rather than as a goal that a person eventually reaches.

Abraham Maslow's Hierarchy of Motives

Abraham Maslow postulated that there is a **hierarchy of motives** that determines our behavior. He argued that the higher motivations can come into play only when the basic needs have been satisfied (see Figure 2.4). Before a person can be free to engage in self-actualization—that is, free to continue fulfilling his or her potential—that person has to meet the physiological needs for safety and security, find love and belonging, and have self-esteem and the esteem of others. Accordingly, Maslow placed self-actualization at the top of the hierarchy. Thus, the motivation to realize one's full potential is a fragile thing, easily interfered with by disturbances at the lower levels.

You can see how this hierarchy might explain many of your own motives. Imagine that you arrived in a strange town hungry and broke. According to Maslow, you would be motivated first of all to ensure a supply of food and water to satisfy your physiological needs. Then perhaps you would look for a

FIGURE 2.4

Maslow's hierarchy of motives.

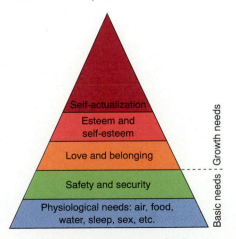

job to obtain money for shelter and security. Only after you had a secure base of operations would you begin to make inroads in the community to develop a sense of belonging, perhaps by forming relationships. Once you felt that you belonged and that you shared love with other people, your sense of self-esteem could develop as your loved ones and friends held you in esteem. At that point, as a fulfilled member of a community, you might begin to develop your full potential.

Today, Maslow's theory, like Freud's, is considered a grand explanatory one. There is little research to support his concepts empirically, but his views have helped stimulate interest in human motivation across the entire lifespan.

Toilet Training in Less than a Day

Throughout the years, most of the theories discussed in this chapter have been applied to everyday situations. Both psychoanalytic and behavior theories have been applied as therapies; Piaget's cognitive theory has had widespread effects on school curriculum; Maslow's theory of the hierarchy of needs has been applied by business organizations to help explain and predict consumer buying patterns; ethological theory has been used to help promote more natural environments for both captive and wild animals and to improve breeding programs necessary to save endangered species. These are just some of the many situations in which these theories have been applied.

Learning theory, in particular, has proved useful for modifying various behaviors, including phobias, and even for promoting certain desirable behaviors. The technology is derived from behaviorism and is known as *behavior modification*.

BEHAVIOR MODIFICATION

A good example of a comprehensive behavior modification program is described in the book *Toilet Training in Less than a Day* by Nathan Azrin and Richard Foxx (1974). Although we can all sympathize with parents for whom toilet training turns out to be a three-year-siege, it does appear that toilet training can be accomplished in under 24 hours by making use of the learning principles described in this chapter. To see how this is possible, let's examine some of the techniques used by Azrin and Foxx. As you'll discover, these techniques take both physical and environmental aspects into consideration.

1. The authors recommend that no attempt be made to train children who are not ready to be trained.

Many parents make the mistake of starting training before their child is cognitively and physically mature enough to be trained. This maturity varies with each child. Some children do not have the muscle development necessary for bladder and bowel control. Others don't have the language development necessary to follow the instructions given. Still others might be unwilling to follow instructions even though they are capable of understanding them. The authors suggest that a simple readiness test be performed to tell whether the child is mature enough to begin training.

2. A learning environment should be created in which the child and parent are together, without distraction, for the whole day. In this way, all their energies can be devoted to learning and strengthening the new behavior.

3. The behavior to be developed is specifically defined; that is, the child will go to the potty-chair when the time arises, lower his or her training pants, urinate or defecate, wipe where appropriate, raise the training pants, remove the plastic pot from

the potty-chair, empty its contents into the toilet, flush the toilet, and return the plastic pot to the potty-chair.

4. The authors give a number of tips for making many of these behaviors easier to accomplish. They suggest, for example, using large, loose-fitting training pants because they are easier to raise and lower.

5. Operant conditioning is achieved as the child's appropriate behaviors are reinforced through lavish praise and the administration of large amounts of juice or soda. Drinking liquid makes urination more likely, giving the child more chances to learn the desired response.

6. The technique of modeling is incorporated in an ingenious way by making use of a doll that wets. At the beginning of the Azrin and Foxx program, before anything else, the child is required to toilet train the doll! In this way, the child observes as the doll models the desired behavior and then sees that the doll is immediately rewarded for its good behavior with praise and juice (administered to the doll in a special baby bottle that refills the doll's reservoir).* This is an effective technique because the child is more likely to imitate the model, even if it is only a doll, if the child sees the model's behavior reinforced (Bandura, 1965).

Behavior modification has been applied to such diverse problems as stopping smoking, ending phobias, and eliminating certain kinds of misbehavior. It has also been used to promote beneficial behaviors, such as that described in this Applications section, and not just in children. It is useful for modifying adult behavior as well.

*Dolls such as these are available in most toy stores.

SUMMARY

- There are many different theories of human development. To date, no theory has been found to be the one and only correct theory. Eventually, theories will become more accurate, and our powers of prediction will become more acute.

- Theories that attempt to explain or predict behavior based primarily on a person's learning and past experience, while placing less emphasis on genetics, are called environmental theories; theories that emphasize the interaction between the environment and a person's genetic heritage are called epigenetic theories.

- For a theory to be useful, it must lead to accurate predictions. If most of the predictions derived from a theory are accurate, the theory is said to have precision.

- Human development is more the study of complex systems than of any fundamental particle or force. Because of this, our predictive ability will never be 100 percent, or even close to it.

- Sigmund Freud, the founder of psychoanalytic theory, derived his system from observations of many patients. He presented an outline of psychosexual development that included five psychosexual stages: the oral, anal, phallic, latency, and genital stages.

- Erik Erikson, a modern psychoanalyst, viewed human development as a progression through eight psychosocial stages, roughly equivalent in duration to some of Freud's psychosexual stages. Erikson's theory differs from Freud's in that Erikson emphasized the important part that society plays in personality development. Erikson also emphasized the entire lifespan, not just the first six years of life.

- Early in this century, an American psychologist, John B. Watson, developed an objective system of psychology called behaviorism. He emphasized observable environmental stimuli and the observable behaviors or responses that occurred in the presence of such stimuli.

- Traditional behaviorists believe that learning plays the most important role in determining future development. This learning takes place through the processes of classical conditioning, operant conditioning, and social learning.

- In classical conditioning, a neutral stimulus (the conditioned stimulus), when paired often enough with another stimulus (the unconditioned stimulus) that normally elicits a reflex response, eventually will provoke the reflex even when the unconditioned stimulus is not present.

- B. F. Skinner studied the kind of learning known as operant conditioning. He argued that behaviors can be made much stronger (reinforced) if they are followed by a reinforcing consequence. Responses that have pleasant consequences are more likely to be repeated in similar circumstances, while responses that produce unpleasant consequences are less likely to be repeated.

- Albert Bandura studied how learning occurs through imitation of other people, known as social learning. In social learning, reinforcement is not necessary for learning to occur.

■ Ethologists study the behavior of animals, including human beings, in their natural environments.

■ Konrad Lorenz, a prominent ethologist, observed the phenomenon called imprinting when he noted that some newborn goslings followed the first object that crossed their field of vision, regardless of what the object was. This phenomenon only occurred during a critical period in the organism's life; thereafter, imprinting could not occur.

■ Cognitive theory emphasizes the ability to think. James Mark Baldwin described cognitive development as progressing through stages. He viewed infants as sensorimotor beings incapable of thought.

■ Cognitive theorist Jean Piaget believed that because humans are genetically similar and share many of the same environmental experiences, they can be expected to exhibit considerable uniformity in their cognitive development. He argued that four predictable stages of cognitive development will occur during specific periods of a child's life: the sensorimotor period, the preoperational period, the period of concrete operations, and the period of formal operations.

■ Piaget argued that children adapt to the environment through assimilation and accommodation.

■ B. F. Skinner and Robert Gagne presented an alternative view of cognitive development: that complex cognitive skills are the product of a hierarchy of more elementary skills obtained through prior experience and learning.

■ Humanistic theory has often been called the third force in modern psychology, the psychoanalytic and behavioral viewpoints constituting the first two forces. Humanists don't believe that behavior is governed either by unconscious drives and motives or by external stimuli and rewards in the environment. Instead, they argue that people are free agents, having free will, that they are conscious and creative, and that they are born with an inner motivation to fulfill their potential.

■ Humanistic theorist Abraham Maslow postulated that there is a hierarchy of motives that determines our behavior. He argued that the higher motivations can come into play only when the more basic needs have been satisfied.

QUESTIONS FOR DISCUSSION

1. According to social learning theory, what special responsibility would the news media have in reporting and covering such events as suicides, snipings, kidnappings, or hijackings?

2. According to Table 2.1, which of Erikson's stages are you in? Are you being successful in resolving the psychosocial conflict for that stage? How important to you is that resolution? For example, how important do you think it is for adults in stage 7 to have a close relationship with their own or other people's children? Do those people who don't have such relationships have unhealthy personalities?

3. How useful would knowledge of Piaget's theory of cognitive development be for parents who are trying to teach their 5-year-old child algebra? (As you will see in Chapter 13, I had trouble with algebra in the ninth grade; it wasn't until I had reached formal operations that I was able to master its abstractions.)

Suggestions for Further Reading

1. Broughton, J. M., & Freeman-Moir, J. D. (1982). *The cognitive developmental psychology of James Mark Baldwin: Current theory and research in genetic epistemology.* Norwood, NJ: Ablex Publishing.

2. Erikson, E. H. (1980). *Identity and the life cycle.* New York: W. W. Norton.

3. Flavell, J. H., Miller, P. H., & Miller, S. A. (1992). *Cognitive development* (3rd ed.). Englewood Cliffs, NJ: Prentice-Hall.

4. Leiser, D. & Gillieron, C. (1990). *Cognitive science and genetic epistemology: A case study of understanding.* New York: Plenum.

5. Miller, P. H. (1989). *Theories of developmental psychology.* (2nd. ed.) New York: W. H. Freeman.

BEGINNINGS
(0–1 Year of Age)

CHAPTER 3
Genetics, Conception, and Prenatal Development

Chapter Preview: How to Build Your Own Human Being
Resources: DNA—The Essence of Life • The Evolution of Life • Chromosomes and Inheritance • Inherited Disorders • Detection of Prenatal Defects • Conception and Prenatal Development • Adverse Influences on Prenatal Development
Applications: Eugenics: Selective Breeding of Human Beings

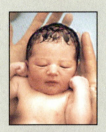

CHAPTER 4
Birth and Competencies of the Newborn and Infant

Chapter Preview: A Doctor Seuss Story
Resources: Labor and Delivery • The Newborn Infant • The Basic Sensory Abilities of the Infant • Other Competencies of the Infant • Infant Physical and Motor Development
Applications: The Value of Infant Walkers

CHAPTER 5
Infant Personality and Social-Emotional Development

Chapter Preview: Check with Mom
Resources: Infant Personality Development • Social Ties • Attachment and Social Development • Social-Emotional Development
Applications: Is Day Care a Good Idea?

CHAPTER 3

Genetics, Conception, and Prenatal Development

CHAPTER PREVIEW
How to Build Your Own Human Being

Thymine, adenine, cytosine, guanine. Often abbreviated as T, A, C, and G, these four simple molecules are abundant in every living creature and are the basis of a larger molecule called DNA. These smaller molecules are typically linked to one another, forming a chain. For example, an A might be joined with a G, and then another G, forming AGG. Or the chain can be longer:

AATTCGCGAATCGCGATCTCGGACCAGCTCGCCACATCGACCCCGAT

Notice how it took nearly an entire line of this book to describe a chain consisting of 47 of these molecules. In fact, these chains can become very long indeed. Instead of an entire line, an entire page or even an entire book may be needed to describe a series!

Dateline: June 3, 2017. *The Massachusetts Institute of Technology, Boston, Massachusetts. Dr. Aaron Steymeyer, director of Biophysical Research and Development at MIT, announced in a press conference this morning that his team of scientists has accomplished a long-awaited breakthrough. The team has successfully manufactured a fertilized human egg.*

Normally, fertilization in humans occurs when a sperm and egg unite after sexual intercourse. But in this case, the MIT team designed and built its own sperm and egg cells using chemicals taken from the laboratory shelf. The manufactured fertilized egg will be implanted into the womb of a female volunteer, where it will develop into a blue-eyed boy. The child-to-be has further been designed to be athletic, 6 feet 1 inch tall, handsome, intelligent, slow to anger, and resistant to disease. The team did not elaborate on other specifics. Of course, the child, when born, will have no real mother or father because he will have been created and designed by the scientists at MIT according to a complex formula.

MOLECULE
A distinct chemical unit or group of atoms that have joined together.

DEOXYRIBONUCLEIC ACID (DNA)
A chemical constituent of cell nuclei, consisting of two long chains of alternating phosphate and deoxyribose units twisted into a double helix and joined by bonds between the complementary bases of adenine, thymine, cytosine, and guanine. It is the substance that enables cells to copy themselves.

GENE
The smallest functional unit for the transmission of a hereditary trait; a section of genetic code.

Dr. Steymeyer explained that the formula's major ingredient was a series of complex chains consisting of the base chemicals thymine, adenine, cytosine, and guanine. Dr. Steymeyer said that if written on paper, the formula would require a few hundred books, each book at least a thousand pages long.

Dateline: April 11, 2031.   Athens, Greece. The International Olympic Committee announced today, "No manufactured human beings specifically designed to excel in an athletic event will be allowed to participate in the Olympic Games."

Dateline: December 3, 2031.   Washington, D.C. Jane Mohr, president of the American Bar Association, gave testimony today before the House subcommittee that is investigating ethical issues involving manufactured humans. The issue brought before the committee concerned the possibility that a manufactured child might one day become a criminal adult. Ms. Mohr said, "Unlike a 'normal' human who would usually be held responsible for his or her actions, a manufactured human who commits a crime should be recalled for repairs by the laboratory that built him or her." Sir Lawrence Arnold, the famed British psychologist and philosopher, is expected to give opposing testimony tomorrow, arguing that environmental influences are responsible for criminal behavior and are therefore not the fault of the laboratory.

Dateline: November 6, 2034.   Harvard University, Boston, Massachusetts. Dr. Sol Crane, the winner of this year's Nobel Prize for social affairs, has voiced his growing concern that the popularity of manufactured fertilized human eggs is steadily increasing "not because the children are certain to be free of genetic disease, or because their sex can be determined beforehand, or even because they are generally intelligent and disease resistant. The major interest seems to center on the fact that the beauty of the child can be guaranteed." Dr. Crane went on to say, "I admit to a growing fear concerning the great emphasis being placed on beauty and the increasing discrimination against the unattractive, which I attribute directly to the ability to make a child look exactly as the future parents desire."

Impossible? Perhaps not.

You would have undoubtedly been confronted with disbelief had you suggested to anyone, in 1956, that men would be driving a car on the moon only 15 years later. In fact, in 1956, many people, including some scientists, believed that travel to the moon was at least a century away. Keep this in mind while you wonder if the news stories presented here could ever occur. Read this chapter—and then decide.

DNA—THE ESSENCE OF LIFE

Presumably, the chemicals mentioned in the Chapter Preview eventually combined to make the first living being. There is evidence that these chemicals occurred quite naturally in the kind of atmosphere that existed on the earth billions of years ago. Experiments that re-create the early earth atmosphere, which use air bubbles trapped in ancient rocks as a guide to the chemicals present at that time, show that such chemicals readily form (Garmon, 1981). For example, among the organic precursors of life that have been discovered in these experiments is the molecule *adenine*.

Adenine and the other simple substances—thymine, cytosine, and guanine—combine to form a chemical molecule known as **deoxyribonucleic acid**, or **DNA**. DNA is a unique molecule. It is sometimes called the essence of life. Every living creature—plant or animal—contains DNA in each cell of its being. Your body is made of cells—brain cells, liver cells, and nerve cells, to name a few. Your body has about 60 trillion (60,000,000,000,000, or 60×10^{12}) cells in all, and each cell contains DNA.

In 1953, the structure of DNA was discovered by James Watson, Francis Crick, and Maurice Wilkins. For this discovery they shared a Nobel Prize.*

The DNA molecule is shaped like a double helix. A phosphate-sugar backbone forms the outside, and the four molecules adenine, thymine, guanine, and cytosine (known as bases) form the inside (Watson & Crick, 1953). This configuration is shown in Figure 3.1. As mentioned in the Chapter Preview, biochemists refer to the four bases by their first letters: A, T, G, and C.

A feature of DNA that makes it truly amazing is that it replicates—that is, makes copies of itself (see Figure 3.2)! This one property, more than any other, distinguishes biology from chemistry.

As you continue to study DNA, you will notice that the horizontal joining of molecules in this incredible substance occurs only in certain ways. An A must join with a T (they are Always Together), and a T with an A. G must join with a C, and a C with a G. However, there are no particular rules for the vertical arrangement of pairs. One strand of DNA may continue for thousands of A-T and G-C base pairs, and the number of different strands that can be made is almost infinite (see Figure 3.3).

DNA is arranged in a code, which is determined by the vertical sequence of the base pairs. The code is divided into sections, and each section orders the building of a sequence of proteins that determines the kind of animal or plant that will be made. Each section of code is called a **gene**. For example, a DNA code consisting of many sections, or genes, exists in each one of your approximately 60 trillion cells. Each one of your cells contains the same code (the same genes), the blueprint for your entire body. Had the DNA code in your body been different, it might have ordered the construction of a box elder beetle, a kangaroo, a great white shark, or an oak tree instead of you! Different DNA codes make different animals or plants or different varieties of the same animal or plant. You look different from a friend of yours mainly because you have a different DNA code in your cells. On the other hand, identical twins share the same or extremely similar codes. Perhaps someday we will fully understand how these codes control and determine the development of living creatures (see At Issue).

A model of DNA.

FIGURE 3.1

The DNA double helix. The external backbone of the structure is formed by phosphate and sugar; the base pairs form the internal core. The completed molecule looks much like a spiral staircase, with the base pairs forming the steps.

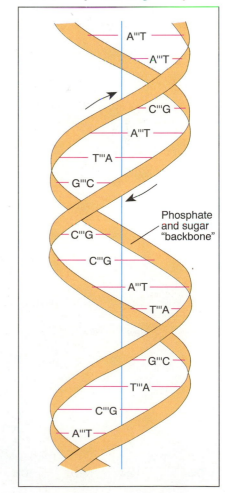

Phosphate and sugar "backbone"

---

*Rosalind Franklin, who also participated in the discovery, would most likely have shared the prize had she not died before the award was given. The Nobel Prize is not awarded posthumously.

HUMAN GENOME
All the genes on all 46 human chromosomes.

FIGURE 3.2

Replication of DNA. As the old DNA, which resides within the nucleus of the cell, begins to unzip owing to the action of certain chemicals called enzymes, free A, T, G, or C molecules floating nearby become attracted to the now unzipped single strands of the original molecule. The new binding of these free-floating molecules with their counterparts on the original strands results in two new and *identical* strands of DNA, both of which are copies of the original.

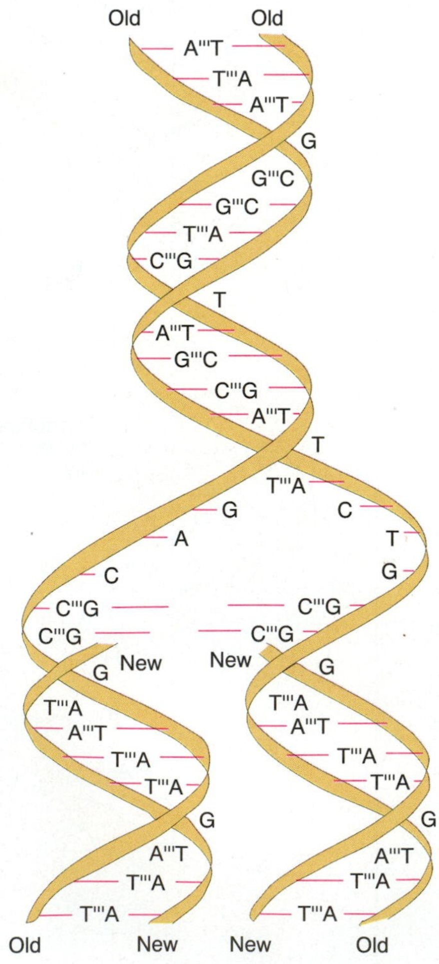

THE EVOLUTION OF LIFE

Around 3.6 billion years ago, forces were at work creating the first single-celled organism—the first life on this planet. It is believed that life began in the clay beds of the oceans with the creation of a stable code that, by chance, ordered up a secure protein "cell" structure that became the first single-celled organism (Dickerson, 1978).

Many things contribute to making a DNA code stable—that is, able to replicate and pass on copies of itself. Some sort of external cell membrane must be ordered by the code. (One possibility is that the first "cell membranes" were a long-lasting type of bubble that could sit quietly attached to nickel-bearing rocks for months at a time while interesting chemical reactions could proceed.) The code must also include orders creating a mechanism for obtaining energy from the environment.

The first stable living cells had, by chance, developed an advantageous trait that enabled them to obtain energy through the process of fermentation. In

FIGURE 3.3

In a DNA sequence of only seven base pairs, 8,192 possible combinations can be made. Four of these possibilities are pictured here. Most DNA strands contain thousands of base pairs, with the result that an almost infinite number of combinations are possible.

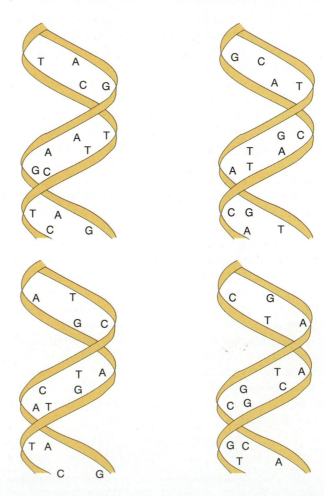

AT ISSUE

Breaking the Code

For centuries, the "holy grail" of biology was to find the essence of life, that is, to discover what it was that made biology different from chemistry. The answer, of course, was DNA, finally uncovered in 1953.

The next great goal in biology is to map the **human genome**, that is, to create a complete guide to the location of every single gene on each of the human chromosomes! This effort is now under way. In the Chapter Preview, you saw a string of 47 bases of A, T, G, and C run together. But the actual code for a human being is estimated to be just a bit longer—about 3 billion bases long, actually. Just imagine trying to pinpoint 3 billion A, T, G, and C bases in their exact order and at their exact locations!

In 1986, when the Human Genome Project was first considered possible, it was estimated that it might take the better part of 50 years to complete. By 1989, however, new breakthroughs in mapping techniques allowed researchers to complete in a single day work that used to take months. Once that fundamental step had been made, James Watson, the co-discoverer of DNA who initially headed the Human Genome Project, asked Congress for more funds, saying, "I have stuck my reputation on getting [an initial general map of all the chromosomes and their genes] done in five years" (Roberts, 1989, p. 424). It is now expected that the complete map, that is, the entire code for a human being, with its complete sequence and exact order, will be ready by the year 2005 at a cost of about $3 billion. And success may come even sooner because the United States is not the only nation in the race for gene technology; Japan and Great Britain are also making a national effort, and many other labs throughout the world are helping as well. Technology continues to make mapping easier as new methods are developed. "It's going at a terrific speed, much faster than anybody anticipated a few years ago." (Service, 1994, p. 1404).

In fact, to avoid overlapping research efforts, Watson suggested that individual countries be responsible for breaking the code of specific chromosomes. The first such breakthrough came in late 1992 when American researchers produced the first complete maps of two human chromosomes, chromosome 21 and the Y chromosome (Vollrath et al., 1992). Although these chromosomes have now been mapped, the genes described on their surfaces remain mostly shrouded in mystery. As an analogy, you might imagine researchers trying to decipher an alien language. Once the chromosomes are mapped, the dictionary of alien words will be complete insomuch as all of the words (genes) will be known, but the definitions of most of the words (what the genes actually do) will remain to be discovered.

Breaking the human code offers tremendous benefits. Once we know the entire code, we will be able to track down the genes that cause diseases like PKU, Huntington's disease, and Alzheimer's disease. But the effort is not without its detractors. Some have argued that if the purpose of the project is to promote good health, the money could be better spent. For example, consider the fact that the greatest threats to humans are environmental rather than genetic. For this reason, the case is put that the $3 billion might be better spent to feed and house people or to fight child abuse and neglect than to discover the causes of the genetic disorders that afflict far fewer individuals (Paul, 1991).

But the effort to map the human genome is being made despite such arguments—in no small part because other nations are also making the effort, and it is feared that failure on the part of the United States to proceed may mean that important discoveries and their salable technological spin-offs may be lost to other nations.

In a less commercial vein, there is the wonder of having the knowledge—to know the chemical formula for a human being. The pure romance of this thought will also draw us forward into the new world that the code will reveal. With such knowledge, we will eventually be able to settle the long-argued issue of nature versus nurture because we will finally discover what, in fact, the genes do control.

What kind of a world will it be for you or your children after the code is broken? We can't know for sure, but you will probably be called on to make decisions you may never have thought about before. What's more, there may be many problems created by breaking the code as well as benefits won. For instance, one thing that breaking the code will show for certain is that we are not all created equal. Take a moment to consider the following situations:

Ellen spent four years completing her PhD in industrial and chemical engineering. Now, wincing as a company doctor draws a few drops of blood for her preemployment physical, she can hardly contain her excitement about the job she's been offered at one of the country's foremost metallurgical research institutes.

Two days later the phone call comes. "You are perfectly healthy," the young doctor says. "But tests have revealed that you harbor a gene that can result in decreased levels of a blood enzyme, glucose-6-phosphate dehydrogenase. Without the enzyme's protection, you have a slightly increased risk of developing a red blood cell disease if you come into contact with certain chemicals in our laboratory."

"I'm sorry," he says. "The job has been offered to someone else."

When Frank married at age 31, he decided to take out a life insurance policy. A swimmer and avid racquetball player with no previous hospitalization, he felt certain that his low premiums would be a worthy investment for his family.

(continued next page)

AT ISSUE

Breaking the Code, continued

Weeks later, after a routine physical exam, he was shocked by the insurance company's response. Sophisticated DNA testing had revealed in Frank's tissues a single missing copy of a so-called RB anti-oncogene and minor variations in two other genes. Computer analysis showed that the molecular misprints more than tripled his risk of getting small-cell lung cancer by age 55. His application was rejected. (Weiss, 1989, p. 40)

As you can see, bit by bit, as scientists break the code, lawmakers will come face to face with a distinctly twenty-first-century problem: *genetic discrimination*. Now is the time to begin thinking about this and other social problems that might be created by our new-found knowledge. If we begin to deal with these issues now instead of waiting until the problems are upon us, the transition into the next century might be considerably smoother. Whatever our future, one thing is certain: Once we break the code, the world will never be the same.

fact, bacteria similar to those first cells are still alive today (e.g., the bacteria responsible for gangrene). Codes favored by the environment—that is, codes that are successful—continue to exist and are passed on to the next generation, while codes that are detrimental eventually die out. This happens because organisms with favorable codes tend to reproduce in greater numbers than do those with less favorable ones, and this **differential reproduction** leads to an increase in the favored codes or traits in the later generations. Supporting this assertion is the fact that far more plant and animal varieties have become extinct than have survived (Fishbein, 1976).

In the mid-nineteenth century, Charles Darwin became the founder of modern evolutionary biology when he realized that natural forces were responsible for the fact that so many creatures were well suited, or adapted, to their individual environments. Also, the creatures that had been ill suited to the environment had generally failed to reproduce or had produced few offspring, leaving few organisms to continue carrying the disadvantageous traits. Darwin called this phenomenon **natural selection**.

Diversification and Mutation

Natural selection is not the only force in the evolution of life. The second major force is **diversification**. For the forces of natural selection to function, there must be a great variety from which nature can select. If all the members of a given species were alike, they would all have an equal chance of succeeding or failing; but they are not all alike. Compare yourself with a close friend. Perhaps you are taller, she is shorter, you have blue eyes, she has brown. There are thousands of other differences between the two of you. Although you are both classified as members of the same species, you are distinctly different creatures. Our species has become diversified; we are not all alike.

But what started diversification in the first place? The answer lies in the biochemical phenomenon of **mutation**. Most people think of mutations in terms of gross body changes that are highly visible. However, mutations are often extremely small changes that result in very minor alterations.

A mutation is likely to alter an organism for the worse. This is because the mutation alters a successful code in a haphazard way. On very rare occasions, however, a mutation may be beneficial. For example, mutations in the first single-celled organism, which used fermentation to acquire energy, may have eventually led to a more advanced single-celled organism, one capable of using photosynthesis to obtain energy. Any code made superior by a lucky mutation would probably be favored during natural selection and passed on to offspring. In this way, mutations initially led to the diversification of species (Stebbins & Ayala, 1985). Eventually, once many members of a particular species are established, they continue to diversify their genetic heritage by mating with one another, thus creating new variations of species members.

Mutations can be induced by ionizing radiation (ultraviolet rays, X rays, or gamma rays), heat, contact with various chemicals, contact with certain viruses, and other processes. It is believed that evolution began when mutations occurred in the offspring of the first single-celled organisms. Table 3.1 is a brief outline of the history of the biological evolution that eventually led to the creation of our own species.

CHROMOSOMES AND INHERITANCE

Throughout millions of years of evolution, genetic material has been passed from one generation to the next. Species have evolved and diversified. A genet-

DIFFERENTIAL REPRODUCTION
A mechanism by which organisms with favorable traits tend to reproduce in greater numbers than those with less favorable traits, resulting in an increase in favored traits in later generations.

NATURAL SELECTION
The process, first suggested by Darwin, through which those individuals of a species best adapted to their environment have a better chance of passing on their genes to the next generation than do those not as well adapted.

DIVERSIFICATION
In evolution, the great range of individual differences in each species, from which natural forces may select.

MUTATION
Any heritable alteration of the genes or chromosomes of an organism.

Table 3.1 ● The Evolution of Life

NUMBER OF YEARS AGO	EVOLUTIONARY ADVANCES
3.6 billion	Primitive one-celled organisms that obtained energy through fermentation
3 billion	Sulfur bacteria that used hydrogen sulfide to conduct photosynthesis. Single-celled organisms able to use water in photosynthesis instead of sulfur; these were the ancestors of the blue-green algae and green plants
2 billion	Oxygen atmosphere
1.6 billion	Bacteria able to use nonsulfur photosynthesis and oxygen in respiration; these bacteria could extract 19 times more energy from food than could the first primitive bacteria.
1.3 billion	Cells with nuclei that concentrated the genetic material, increasing the opportunities for diversification
1 billion	Multicelled organisms; plant and animal kingdoms divide
500 million	Many marine animals, corals, clams, and fishes
300 million	Amphibians, ferns, spiders, insects (over 800 species of cockroach), and first reptiles
150 million	Dinosaurs and reptiles rule the land, sea, and air First birds evolve from small dinosaurs Modern insects (bees, moths, flies)
70 million	Dinosaurs extinct Marsupials and primitive mammals Flowering plants Deciduous trees Giant redwoods 50 percent of North America under water; Rocky Mountains formed
50 million	Modern birds The early horse (only 1 foot high) Ancestors of the cat, dog, elephant, camel, and other mammals Seed-bearing plants and small primates
1.5 million	*Homo erctus* (probable direct ancestor of modern humans)
100,000	*Homo sapiens neanderthalensis* (an extinct variety of human)
100,000	*Homo sapiens sapiens* (modern humans)

NUCLEUS

A central body within a living cell that contains the cell's hereditary material and controls its metabolism, growth, and reproduction.

CHROMOSOME

A thread-shaped body that is contained within the nucleus of a cell and that determines those characteristics that will be passed on to the offspring of an organism. Chromosomes carry the genes; humans have 23 pairs of chromosomes.

GAMETE

Male or female germ cell containing one-half the number of chromosomes found in the other cells of the body.

MEIOSIS

The process of cell division in sexually reproducing organisms that reduces the number of chromosomes in reproductive cells, leading to the production of gametes.

ic heritage now resides within all living creatures. It is formed within the **nucleus** of each cell.

When a certain colored stain is applied to the nucleus of a cell, small bodies within the nucleus absorb the stain and become visible. These small bodies are called **chromosomes**. In fact, the word *chromosome* means "colored body."

In a human body cell, there are 46 chromosomes arranged in 23 pairs. On the chromosomes of each cell lie the genes (made from strands of DNA), which contain the genetic code for your entire body. The number of chromosomes per cell varies from one species of plant or animal to another. It may range from as few as 4 to as many as 254 (Sinnott, Dunn, & Dobzhansky, 1958). For example, toads have 44 chromosomes in their body cells; potatoes have 48. Of the 46 chromosomes in your body cells, you inherited 23 from your father and 23 from your mother.

Human sperm or egg cells, called **gametes**, contain only 23 chromosomes each, rather than 23 pairs. During the creation of these sex cells, a special process known as **meiosis** reduces the usual number of chromosomes to half (Figure 3.4). Thus, when a human sperm and egg unite during fertilization, the next generation will also have 46 chromosomes in each body cell. (Without the process of meiosis, sperm and egg cells would have the same number of chromosomes as body cells, and when they joined during fertilization, the number of chromosomes in each cell of the new generation would be doubled.)

Once chromosomes are made visible by staining, they can be photographed. The individual chromosomes can be cut from the photograph, arranged in

FIGURE 3.4

Unlike the process of mitosis, in which cells replicate, making copies of themselves, the process of meiosis leads to the creation of gametes, which have only one-half the number of chromosomes of a typical body cell.

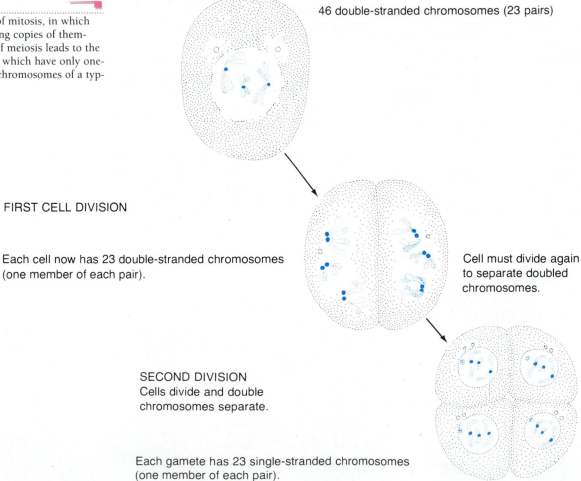

46 double-stranded chromosomes (23 pairs)

FIRST CELL DIVISION

Each cell now has 23 double-stranded chromosomes (one member of each pair).

Cell must divide again to separate doubled chromosomes.

SECOND DIVISION
Cells divide and double chromosomes separate.

Each gamete has 23 single-stranded chromosomes (one member of each pair).

pairs, and placed in rows for easy inspection. Such an arrangement is called a **karyotype** (Figure 3.5). A karyotype can show a number of serious chromosomal abnormalities that are known to be associated with various disorders. The first 22 pairs of chromosomes are called the **autosomes**. The twenty-third pair is labeled separately from the others; these two chromosomes are known as **sex chromosomes**.

Like the autosomes, the sex chromosomes carry many genes. The sex chromosomes are different, however, in that they also carry the genetic codes that determine your sex. Interestingly, these chromosomes are shaped differently, depending on which sex code is being carried. Sex chromosomes carrying the genetic code for a girl are shaped like an X, and those carrying the code for a boy are shaped like a Y. These chromosomes are, in fact, referred to as X and Y chromosomes. As you can see, the twenty-third pair in the karyotype pictured in Figure 3.5 contains both an X and a Y chromosome. In this case, such a child would be male. Males have an XY twenty-third pair, while females have an XX twenty-third pair. Because females are XX, they have no Y chromosomes in their cells. A woman's ovum, or egg, can contain only the X sex chromosome. Therefore, both boys and girls receive one X chromosome from their mother's egg. Because men are XY, their sperm cells created during meiosis may contain either an X or a Y sex chromosome. The child will inherit one or the other, which will then determine the child's sex. If a sperm carrying an X chromosome fertilizes the mother's ovum, a girl will be produced; if a sperm carrying a Y chromosome fertilizes the ovum, the child will be a boy.

There are rare cases, however, of girls who are XY and boys who are XX. They are worth mentioning here to illustrate that the Y chromosome has the effect that it usually does because it is carrying the gene that determines gender. In fact, the actual gene responsible for creating "maleness," discovered in 1990 (Sinclair et al., 1990), sometimes is absent from the father's Y chromosome or present on his X chromosome, causing the aforementioned rare occurrences.

Again, it is only the male who can contribute a Y chromosome, so the gender of the offspring is determined by the father's sperm. Perhaps someone

KARYOTYPE
A photomicrograph of chromosomes in a standard array.

AUTOSOME
Any chromosome that is not a sex chromosome.

SEX CHROMOSOME
In humans, one of the two chromosomes responsible for producing the sex of the child; an X or Y chromosome.

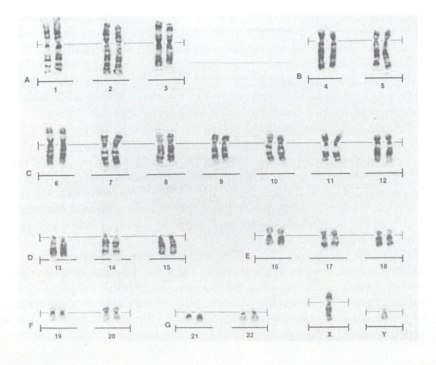

FIGURE 3.5
Humans have 23 pairs of chromosomes. In the karyotype, the pairs are matched. One member of each pair is from the mother, and one is from the father.

ALLELE

Any of a group of possible forms of a gene.

DOMINANT

In genetics, a gene whose characteristics are expressed while suppressing the characteristics controlled by the other corresponding gene for that trait.

RECESSIVE

In genetics, a gene whose characteristics are not expressed when paired with a dominant gene.

CARRIER

In genetics, an organism that carries a particular trait in its genes and, while not expressing that trait itself, is able to pass on the trait to its offspring.

DOUBLE RECESSIVE

A condition in which both allelic pairs for a given trait are recessive and no dominant allelic gene is present to override them. In this case, the recessive trait will be expressed.

HOMOZYGOUS

Describing alleles of a gene pair that are identical.

HETEROZYGOUS

Describing alleles of a gene pair that are different.

PHENOTYPE

The observable characteristics of an organism due to inheritance.

GENOTYPE

The characteristics that an individual has inherited and may transmit to descendants, regardless of whether the individual manifests these characteristics.

Gregor Mendel (1822–1884).

should have told King Henry VIII about that before he had Ann Boleyn executed for, among other things, not having borne him a son! Still, in the sixteenth century, no one knew about the genetic mechanisms of inheritance or the natural laws that they followed.

Mendel's Laws

Gregor Mendel (1822–1884), an Austrian monk, was the first to discover the fundamental laws that govern inheritance. Mendel spent many years carefully crossing garden-variety pea plants with one another and cataloging the results of his experiments. He watched as a number of traits—such as wrinkled or smooth seeds, tall or short stalks, yellow or green seeds—appeared, disappeared, and reappeared from one generation to the next. To understand the mechanisms of inheritance, it's worth examining some of Mendel's observations.

Simple Inheritance

Pea seeds are either yellow or green. Genes that code for seed color are inherited from both parents (even peas have parents). Different genes that can affect the same trait (in this case, seed color) are called **alleles**, or allelic genes. For every allelic gene on one chromosome of a pair, a corresponding allele exists in the same position on the other chromosome of the pair. For example, if the allelic gene for seed color were located at a particular position on a chromosome, another gene for seed color would be found in the same position on the corresponding chromosome of that pair. The letter Y (for yellow) will represent the pea allele responsible for yellow seed color, and the letter g (for green) will represent the allele responsible for green seed color. Notice in Figure 3.6 what occurs when a yellow-seeded plant is crossed with a green-seeded plant. The seed color alleles of all the offspring are Yg.

You might think that all these offspring would have yellowish green seeds. But in fact, the yellow color is controlled by a **dominant** allele, while the green color is controlled by a **recessive** allele. Dominant allelic genes are designated by capital letters, and recessive allelic genes are designated by lowercase letters. When a dominant Y allelic gene inherited from one parent and a recessive g allelic gene inherited from the other parent form a pair in the offspring, the genetic code in the dominant gene is turned on, while the code in the recessive gene stays off. Because of this, seeds that have Yg allelic genes are just as yellow as seeds with YY allelic genes. The difference is that seeds with Yg alleles, even though they are bright yellow, are **carriers** of green color.

Even though yellow is the dominant seed color it is still possible to produce green seeds. Suppose that two plants that have yellow seeds, but that are carriers of green color, are crossed (Figure 3.7). Four kinds of offspring can result: $YY, Yg, gY,$ and gg. When a plant inherits the **double recessive** gg, the seeds will be green. Because no dominant allelic gene is present to override the recessive ones, the recessive alleles are expressed. In fact, when Mendel ran this experiment, he discovered yellow and green seeds in a ratio of 3:1, which is exactly what this example predicts.

When the alleles in a pair are identical, such as with YY or gg, the pair is defined as **homozygous**. If the alleles in a pair are different, as in the case of Yg and gY (yellow seeds that carry the recessive green trait), the pair is defined as **heterozygous**. The observable characteristics of a trait (such as the actual color of the seeds) constitutes the **phenotype**, while the genetic composition of the organism is the **genotype**. Table 3.2 shows the four possible offspring from the crossing of the two pea plants with genotype *Yg*. Notice that the first three off-spring have the same appearance, or phenotype (yellow seeds), but that off-spring 1 has a different genotype from offspring 2 and 3. Offspring 1 is not a carrier of the recessive green trait.

To be perfectly honest, researchers in human development don't really care that much about peas. Not many people do. In fact, Mendel's laws went unno-ticed during his lifetime, and scientists of his day, such as Darwin, never had a chance to examine them. It wasn't until Mendel's laws were "rediscovered" in the early 1900s that his name became prominent.

The reason, of course, for any interest at all in the pea experiments is that these simple mechanisms of inheritance also apply to many other plants and animals, including human beings. In humans, eye color is inherited in this simple manner. Pigmented eyes are dominant (for convenience, let's call all pigmented eyes "brown"), and blue eyes are recessive. Using the capital letter *B* to represent the dominant allelic gene for brown eyes and the small letter *b* to represent the recessive allelic gene for blue eyes, cross two people with het-erozygous brown eyes by filling in the following square:

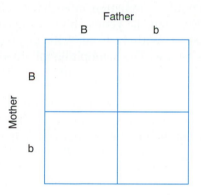

As you can see, it works just like Mendel's peas, with a 3:1 ratio of brown to blue. You should, of course, keep in mind that the 3:1 ratio is derived from an average. On the average, for every three brown-eyed children born from such a cross, one blue-eyed child should be born. But it is possible for such parents to have three or four blue-eyed children in a row, just as it is possible to have six or seven girls or boys in a row.

But not all parents are more likely to have brown-eyed children. Suppose that both parents have blue eyes. Then they must both be homozygous double recessives (*bb*), which means that all their children will have blue eyes. Or if one of the parents is homozygous blue (*bb*) and the other is heterozygous brown (*Bb*), then, on average, half their children will have blue eyes.

Other human characteristics are also inherited in this manner, including hair shape: Kinky is dominant, and straight is recessive. And, more important,

FIGURE 3.6

This diagram is called a Punnett square. It shows the possible interactions, or cross-es, between a green-seeded plant and a yellow-seeded plant. Like a human, the pea plant inherits half of its genetic mate-rial from one parent's gamete and the other half from the other parent's gamete. Remember, these gametes were created during meiosis and contain only one-half of the usual number of chromosomes.

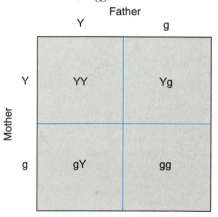

FIGURE 3.7

The recessive trait (green seed color) can be expressed only when no dominant allele is present. Because an allele for seed color is inherited from each parent, the recessive trait can be expressed only as a double recessive (*gg*).

Table 3.2 ● Offspring from the Crossing of Two Pea Plants with Yg Genotype

OFFSPRING	PHENOTYPE (SEED COLOR)	GENOTYPE (SEED COLOR)
1. *YY*	Yellow	Homozygous *YY*
2. *Yg*	Yellow	Heterozygous *Yg*
3. *gY*	Yellow	Heterozygous *gY*
4. *gg*	Green	Homozygous *gg*

Note: The first three offspring have identical phenotypes. However, offspring 1 has a different genotype from that of off-spring 2 and 3. The offspring 2 and 3 have the same phenotype and genotype; there is no difference between *Yg* and *gY*.

CODOMINANCE
Situation in which heterozygous alleles consist of two dominant genes. In such instances, both genes are expressed.

SEX-LINKED DISORDER
A hereditary disorder controlled by a gene carried on the sex-determining chromosome. Color blindness is an example.

blood types follow Mendel's laws. Consider the standard blood-typing system using A, B, AB, and *o*. A and B are dominant; *o* is recessive. Figure 3.8, shows three different blood-type crosses. The first is between a homozygous type A father and a homozygous type B mother. Because alleles A and B are both dominant, both codes in the inherited allelic pair "turn on" and are expressed. This results in the creation of type AB blood in all offspring and is an example of **codominance**, where two dominant genes in one allelic gene pair express themselves simultaneously.

In the second cross, two homozygous type o parents (double recessive) have offspring who are all type o. Because allele *o* is recessive, two parents with type o blood must have a type o child. Notice, though, that in the third cross, a type A father and a type B mother could have children with any of the four blood types, as long as both parents are heterozygous—that is, as long as they are carriers of the recessive *o* allele.

Sex-Linked Inheritance

From 1837 to 1901, Queen Victoria was the ruling monarch of Great Britain. Early in Queen Victoria's life, a mutation must have occurred to one of her genes. This mutation destroyed the gene's ability to make factor VIII, a substance that helps blood clot. Without factor VIII, a person will suffer classic hemophilia, or bleeder's disease. The hemophilia inherited by Queen Victoria's descendants probably began with her, since no case of hemophilia existed in the royal family before her reign.

All the royal descendants of Queen Victoria who suffered from hemophilia were male. This is because hemophilia is a **sex-linked disorder** inherited mostly by males. Neither Queen Victoria herself nor any of her female descendants had hemophilia; instead, they were carriers. Because of the constant hemorrhaging and dark blue bruises that appeared around the joints, these victims were referred to as "blue bloods." After a time, *blue blood* became the term for anyone of royal birth.

Because the defective gene is located on the twenty-third pair of chromosomes, the sex chromosomes, the disease it causes is sex-linked. (All sex-linked disorders involve genes on the sex chromosomes.) Remember that although the sex chromosomes contain the genes that determine your sex, they also contain many thousands of other genes, among them the gene that makes factor VIII.

As a rule, it is men who get sex-linked disorders, while women are only carriers. This has to do with the shape of the Y chromosome. It is similar to an X

FIGURE 3.8

Examples of blood-type crosses between parents with A, B, or o blood type. In human blood, types A and B are dominant (and exhibit codominance in type AB blood) and o is recessive.

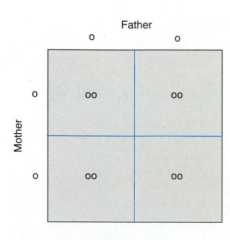

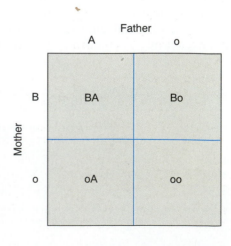

Queen Victoria (center left, foreground), shown here with some of her children, was a carrier of hemophilia. Because hemophilia is a sex-linked disorder, only her sons were at risk for the condition (their father was not hemophilic).

chromosome, but smaller, and it does not contain as many genes. It is as though it is missing a part. And because a part is "missing," so are many of the genes that would normally be on that part. As a result, if a woman inherits a defective hemophilic gene on the X sex chromosome that she receives from her mother, the second X sex chromosome that she inherits from her father will provide a "backup" allelic gene that is not defective. She will be a carrier, not a sufferer, of hemophilia (see Figure 3.9).* In fact, a woman will suffer from hemophilia only if the gene that makes factor VIII is defective on both of her X chromosomes. But this could only happen if her mother were at least a carrier of hemophilia and her father suffered from the disease. Such an occurrence is very rare.

There are a number of other sex-linked characteristics in human beings, including male-pattern baldness, and red-green color blindness. In the United States, approximately 8 percent of men and 0.05 percent of women are red-green color-blind. Because male-pattern baldness and red-green color blindness are sex-linked, grandfathers pass on these characteristics to their grandsons by way of their daughters, who are carriers. In other words, if you are a man and are wondering about your chances of having inherited male-pattern baldness, don't look at your father, but rather, look at your mother's dad. If your X chromosome came from him via your mother (a 50 percent chance) and he has male-pattern baldness, you will have inherited his hair loss pattern. If, however, your X chromosome came down from your maternal grandmother, whether or not you inherit male-pattern baldness will depend on the makeup of that chromosome, and a look at *her* father (your maternal great-grandfather) will give you a 50 percent chance of guessing what it is. It gets complicated, doesn't it?

FIGURE 3.9

Women typically do not suffer from hemophilia because when they inherit an affected X chromosome from their mother (X.), they receive an unaffected X chromosome from their father. Men, however, lack an effective "backup" allele because the Y chromosome does not have the "leg" of the X chromosome in which the allele is carried. Note that a female carrier and a normal male will produce, on the average, one normal girl, one unaffected boy, one carrier girl, and one hemophilic boy.

| | Father | |
	X	Y
X.	X.X (Carrier girl)	X.Y (Hemophilic boy)
X	XX (Normal girl)	XY (Normal boy)

Mother

*Some female carriers, however, do not have reduced levels of factor VIII in the blood; although one working gene is enough to spare them from hemophilia, apparently two working genes are better.

MODIFIER GENES

A gene that acts on other genes and modifies the latter's effects.

PHENYLKETONURIA (PKU)

A genetic disorder marked by an inability to oxidize properly the amino acid phenylalanine. If this disorder is not controlled by proper diet, permanent damage is caused to the developing child's central nervous system.

GENETIC IMPRINTING

The process whereby identical sections of the same chromosome will yield different phenotypic outcomes, depending on whether the chromosome was inherited from the mother or the father.

MONOSOMY

A single unpaired chromosome that is located where there should be a pair of chromosomes.

TRISOMY

A chromosomal abnormality in which a third chromosome occurs on a chromosome pair.

MULTISOMY

A chromosomal abnormality in which more than one additional chromosome is associated with a chromosome pair.

Complex Genetic Interactions

Not all genetic laws follow Mendel's principles or those of sex-linked inheritance. Many complications are possible. For instance, some genes act on other genes. Such **modifier genes** can determine how other genes express themselves. An example of the effects of modifier genes can be found in the disease **phenylketonuria (PKU)**.

PKU is a genetic disorder caused by the inheritance of a double recessive (*pp*) and marked by an inability to oxidize normally the amino acid phenylalanine, which is found in fish, dairy products, and most protein sources. If detected early enough by blood or urine tests, the disease can be controlled by elimination of phenylalanine from the diet. If the disorder is not checked by a suitable diet, however, by-products formed by the incomplete oxidation of the amino acid build up in the infant's body and cause permanent damage to the central nervous system. It is estimated that about 1 percent of the children institutionalized because of mental retardation suffer from PKU.

Even though this disease is caused by a double recessive, children with PKU may exhibit considerably different levels of phenylalanine, and this is where the modifier genes come in. Variations in levels are determined by modifier genes located at positions on the chromosomes different from those of the recessive genes responsible for PKU.

There are probably hundreds, even thousands of complex interactions that can affect the mechanisms of inheritance. Even the "simple" form of inheritance described by Mendel does not take place inviolately. For instance, it is not uncommon for the genes on identical sections of chromosomes to be expressed somewhat differently, depending on whether they are inherited from one's father or one's mother, a phenomenon known as **genetic imprinting** (Sapienza, 1990). Some instances of genetic imprinting are striking. For example, Prader-Willi syndrome, caused by the absence of a portion of chromosome 15, leads to shortness of stature, retardation, and voracious eating. Parents of such children have to lock the refrigerator, hide pet food, and even keep edible garbage out of reach. If the defective chromosome 15 is inherited from the father, Prader-Willi is the result. But if the same defective chromosome 15 is inherited from the mother, the result is Angelman's syndrome, a very different disease, whose sufferers have been described as "happy puppets" because of their constant laughter and jerky movements. The reason for the different outcomes is not entirely clear, since it seems reasonable to assume that identical missing portions of the same chromosome would result in an absence of the same allelic genes. The best current guess is that modifier genes, different in the mother and father, somehow cause subtle biogenetic alterations to these areas, making seemingly identical genetic sections of chromosomes different, depending on whether they are paternal or maternal.

INHERITED DISORDERS

Sometimes during the formation of the sperm or ova, something goes wrong, and these gametes end up missing a chromosome or having an extra one. Such an unfortunate occurrence may result in various disorders, including **monosomies**, **trisomies**, and **multisomies**. Some of these disorders are outlined in Table 3.3. In addition, although chromosomes may appear normal, there can also be various disorders of the genes themselves. Such genetic disorders, unlike chromosomal disorders, are not apparent under a microscope and require special techniques to detect.

Down Syndrome

Of all the disorders listed in Table 3.3, perhaps the best known is a trisomy that occurs on the twenty-first autosome pair, identified by geneticists as trisomy 21. Trisomy 21 always results in **Down syndrome** (Patterson, 1987).* Children with Down syndrome typically have protruding tongues, short necks, and rounded heads. They also often have webbed toes or fingers, unusual dental abnormalities, and a flat-footed clumsy gait. Although children with Down syndrome are usually affectionate and cheerful, most are sufficiently intellectually disabled to need some form of care the rest of their lives. Approximately 10 percent of institutionally retarded persons have Down syndrome.

Although no one knows exactly why Down syndrome occurs, the chances of its occurrence are known to be associated with the mother's age at the time of conception. Offspring who have Down syndrome are more common among older women. For this reason, many doctors suggest routine chromosome testing of the fetus for any pregnant woman 35 years of age or older, so that she has the option to terminate the pregnancy should Down syndrome be discovered (see Figure 3.10).

Out of every 700 babies born in the United States, approximately 1 has Down syndrome (Patterson, 1987). That means that over 250,000 individuals in the United States have Down syndrome, and the population of victims increases by about 5,000 each year. Forty percent of these individuals have congenital heart defects, and heart disease is the principal cause of death. Chil-

DOWN SYNDROME
A chromosomal abnormality that manifests itself in such features as a thick tongue, extra eyelid folds, and heart deformities, as well as deficient intelligence. It is caused by a trisomy of the twenty-first chromosome pair or by a translocation of part of a third chromosome 21 onto another chromosome.

---

*Professionals generally prefer to call this condition Down syndrome rather than the commonly used Down's syndrome, arguing that the possessive form *Down's* is incorrect because Dr. John Langdon Down, who in 1866 was the first to describe the disorder, did not himself suffer from the syndrome. Still, Alzheimer's disease, Wilson's disease, Cushing's syndrome, and so on, are professional terms currently in use, and none of these named researchers ever suffered from the disorder they described. It appears, therefore, to have become a matter of convention as to which form to use. *Down* is currently preferred.

Table 3.3 ● Selected Chromosome Disorders That May Affect Development

TYPE	NAME	DESCRIPTION	EFFECT
Monosomy of sex chromosome 23	Turner's syndrome	Second chromosome of 23rd pair is missing (X–)	Female; short fingers, webbed neck, minimal sexual differentiation, often mildly retarded
Trisomy of sex chromosome 23	Klinefelter's syndrome	Extra X chromosome on XY 23rd pair (XXY)	Male; female body characteristics, minimal sexual differentiation, often mildly retarded
Trisomy of sex chromosome 23	Supermale	Extra Y chromosome on XY 23rd pair (XYY)	Male; tall, acne, sometimes mildly retarded
Trisomy of sex chromosome 23	Superfemale	Extra X chromosome on XX 23rd pair (XXX)	Female; low verbal skills, short-term memory-deficit
Trisomy of autosome 21	Down syndrome	Extra chromosome on autosome pair 21	Retardation; unique appearance; high incidence of heart disease, leukemia, and Alzheimer's disease
Fragility of X sex chromosome	Fragile X syndrome	X chromosome of the 23rd pair breaks easily because of fragile site	Male and female; males show retardation, females are carriers
Multisomes of the sex chromosomes	(Various)	Among known forms are XXYY, XXXY, XXXYYY	Numerous severe physical and developmental impairments
Multisomy mosaics	(Various)	Rare multisomes of the autosomes	(Various)

FIGURE 3.10

Maternal risk of producing a trisomy 21 Down syndrome child (see Chapter 17) among mothers of different ages. (Down syndrome is the most common cause of mental retardation, accounting for 10 percent of all retarded children.) The dark line drawn at the 0.5 percent risk level represents the chance of accidentally producing a miscarriage through use of amniocentesis. As you can see, by the maternal age of 36 years, the mother's risk of producing a Down syndrome child outweighs the risk posed by amniocentesis. In fact, many physicians advocate the use of amniocentesis for all women 35 or older, because many other chromosonal disorders besides Down syndrome can be detected by amniocentesis. (SOURCE: Adapted from Fuchs, 1980)

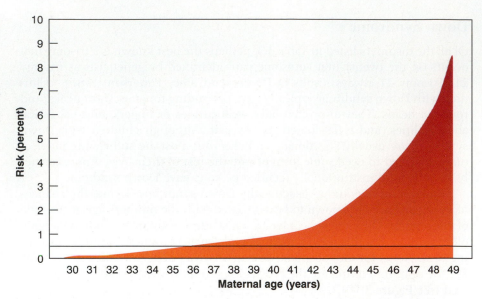

dren with Down syndrome often suffer from congenital intestinal blockages and are 30 times more likely to develop leukemia, probably because of a gene on chromosome 21 that is known to cause leukemia if improperly activated (Siwolop & Mohs, 1985). With modern medical care, fully 80 percent will live to reach their fiftieth birthday (Siwolop & Mohs, 1985). Sadly, people with Down syndrome who survive to middle age invariably acquire Alzheimer's disease, a degenerative brain disorder. For this reason, it is believed that Alzheimer's disease may also, in some way, be associated with damage to chromosome 21 (Patterson, 1987).

Children who have Down syndrome generally have IQs in the range of 30 to 70. Approximately one-half of all children with Down syndrome who are provided with adequate educational facilities can attain reading comprehension at about the second-grade level (Turkington, 1986). They remain intellectually impaired throughout their lives.

Other Chromosomal Abnormalities

Second only to Down syndrome as the leading cause of mental retardation is **fragile X syndrome.** It is believed to affect between 1 in 1,000 and 1 in 1,500 individuals in the general population (Barnes, 1989).

When the X chromosome of people with this syndrome is viewed under a microscope, it shows a distinctive narrowing at a particular location near its tip. The chromosome can easily break at this narrow point. Should the broken piece incorrectly join with other chromosomes during cell division, it can cause translocations of genetic information. Translocations scramble genetic information. Why the X chromosome in these cases is fragile is unknown.

Fragile X syndrome is a sex-linked inherited disorder. Males who receive a fragile X chromosome usually are moderately retarded. Common signs of the syndrome in males include hand flapping, hand biting, poor eye contact, and hyperactivity (Barnes, 1989). Interestingly, unlike the situation with most sex-linked disorders, fully 20 percent of males who inherit the fragile X show no signs or symptoms of the disorder but are able to pass on the disorder to their children! No one yet understands how this unusual mechanism works (Barnes, 1989).

About one-third of female carriers (whose sex chromosome pairs are composed of one normal X and one fragile X chromosome) are mildly retarded. This is similar to the situation in which some female carriers of hemophilia have been shown to have subtle signs of the disease. There are no physical abnormalities associated with fragile X syndrome in females, but these carriers are generally socially withdrawn and shy, and they often have learning disabilities, especially in math (Barnes, 1989; Turner, Brookwell, Daniel, Selikowitz, & Zilibowitz, 1980).

Gene Disorders

Enzymes can now be used to remove individual genes from cultured fetal cells extracted during pregnancy. Before this discovery, scientists were limited to observing gross chromosomal abnormalities—such as an extra or missing chromosome or a fractured or misplaced chromosome—while the condition of the thousands of genes on these chromosomes remained obscure.

Although some gene disorders are directly related to chromosome dysfunctions and are obvious when observed under a microscope (because the larger chromosomes themselves appear to be abnormal), most gene disorders are not so apparent. The defective genes that may cause a disturbance are not visible under the typical microscope and are extremely difficult to isolate and examine. Often the first steps taken to determine if heritable gene disorders are present is to examine the family tree of the parents.

DETECTION OF PRENATAL DEFECTS

Many inherited and noninherited disorders can affect the fetus. Although it is not possible to know for sure if the fetus is healthy, there are ways to discover a number of serious problems prior to birth. When a woman is between the fourteenth and sixteenth weeks of a pregnancy, **amniocentesis** may be performed to examine the chromosomes of the fetus developing within her. The process involves inserting a hollow needle into the woman's abdomen, through which some of the amniotic fluid that surrounds the fetus is drawn out (see Figure 3.11). Body cells shed by the fetus are usually drawn out with the fluid. These cells are then incubated and stained so that the chromosomes can be examined easily. The karyotype obtained will also reveal the sex of the child-to-be. Another method for obtaining this chromosomal information is called **chorionic villi sampling (CVS)**. In this technique, fetal cells are removed through the birth canal without use of a needle at about the tenth week of pregnancy (eighth week since conception). Such techniques are most often used when a chromosomal disorder is suspected.

There are risks involved in the use of these techniques, as both amniocentesis and CVS can cause miscarriage. For CVS, the risk is about 1 to 2 percent; for amniocentesis, the risk is about 0.5 percent. CVS has an advantage of providing results much earlier, when an abortion is easier and safer, but amniocentesis can provide somewhat more information about the fetus. For this reason, doctors often weigh the risks and benefits before recommending either procedure.

Within the next few years, a new technique should remove all the risk from this kind of assessment. The new technique is called *flow cytometry with fluorescent in situ hybridization,* or "flow with FISH" for short. It appears that an extremely small amount of fetal blood normally leaks into the mother's bloodstream, but not enough to cause her body to react (only about 1 fetal blood cell

---

FRAGILE X SYNDROME

A sex-linked inherited chromosomal disorder that produces moderate retardation among males who inherit the fragile X chromosome. After Down syndrome, it is the most common biological cause of retardation.

AMNIOCENTESIS

A medical procedure wherein fetal cells are removed from the amniotic sac by use of a syringe at about the sixteenth week of pregnancy. The technique is used to screen for genetic and chromosomal disorders.

CHORIONIC VILLI SAMPLING

A technique in which a few cells are removed from the chorionic sac that surrounds the fetus via the use of a plastic catheter inserted through the vagina. The cells may then be examined for chromosomal or genetic disorders.

FIGURE 3.11

Amniocentesis may be performed to examine fetal cells for disease or life-shortening disorders. During the procedure, a hollow needle is inserted through the uterus into the amniotic sac surrounding the fetus. Fluid containing the fetal cells is withdrawn through the needle. The cells are then incubated, stained, and examined.

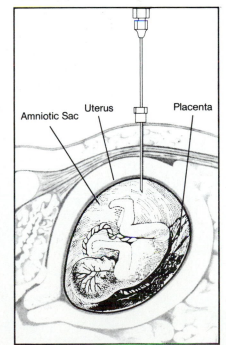

Amniotic Sac   Uterus   Placenta

GENETIC COUNSELING
Services provided to prospective parents that include detailed analysis of genetic inheritance and the possibilities or prospects of the occurrence of genetic disorders in offspring.

for every 20 million maternal blood cells). With the new technique, a blood sample is taken from the mother's arm and processed through a flow cytometer, which uses a laser beam to sort blood cells thousands of times more rapidly than any lab technician with a microscope could hope to do. The fetal blood cells are then given the FISH treatment; that is, they are chemically tagged with a fluorescent dye that highlights the chromosomes when they are exposed to ultraviolet light. The technique is experimental, but it appears to work well (Price et al., 1991) and has already diagnosed one case of trisomy 18, which causes severe mental retardation, from a blood sample taken from a pregnant volunteer. The first full clinical trials of the technique should be ready to begin by 1995.

Genetic Counseling

Parents who are concerned about the possibility of a gene disorder in their offspring may seek help in the form of **genetic counseling**. Genetic counseling provides an opportunity to examine the potential for inherited disorders. As noted earlier, we are just now on the verge of actually examining the fetal genes themselves for possible defects. Such examinations are limited to special cases and are carried out at large research universities. Typically, these methods are unavailable to genetic counselors. Even if they were available, only a few genetic disorders have been isolated by these techniques; the genes controlling most disorders still go unrecognized.

Genetic counselors usually help by investigating the family trees of both potential parents. The counselor looks for incidences of gene disorders. Many gene disorders follow Mendel's laws of inheritance; thus, although no one can say for certain whether a child will be affected, the prospective parents can be told the chances that the disorder will occur.

In some instances, prospective parents can take direct action based on their knowledge. For example, hemophilia is almost exclusively a male disorder; females are carriers of the disease. If medical tests determine that the prospective mother is a carrier of hemophilia, the counselor may then inform the couple that they have a 25 percent chance of producing a hemophilic male child.

Parents who are concerned about the possibility of a genetic disorder in their offspring may seek help in the form of genetic counseling.

The other possibilities, as you will recall, each with a 25 percent probability, are a normal male, a normal female, and a female carrier. Given this knowledge, the mother may choose to have an ultrasound scan of her womb as early as 16 weeks to determine the sex of the fetus (Plattner, Renner, Went, Beaudett, & Viau, 1983). If the fetus is a male, the parents may choose to have an abortion; if a female, they would be assured that hemophilia would not manifest itself. Of course, if parents rely on this method, there is a chance that they will abort a healthy male. Perhaps a less controversial approach would be to rely on a method of preselecting the child's sex, a technique that is currently being developed and refined. Parents in such circumstances might then be free to choose to have only daughters, which would avoid the sex-linked disorders that only sons might suffer.

CONCEPTION AND PRENATAL DEVELOPMENT

Conception

Conception, or fertilization, occurs when a father's sperm cell joins with a mother's egg cell, called an ovum (see Figure 3.12). The ovum is much larger than the sperm. The sperm is microscopic, while the ovum is about half the size of the period at the end of this sentence. Conception typically takes place within one of the **fallopian tubes**, which are part of the female reproductive system. Sometimes, although not often, an ovum is fertilized before it enters the fallopian tube or after it enters the uterus. Prior to fertilization, the egg releases a fluid that attracts the sperm (Ralt et al., 1991). The instant that the sperm penetrates the ovum, a special reaction occurs that immediately makes the ovum impervious to other sperm.

The probability that a woman will become pregnant following intercourse varies from couple to couple, depending on the fertility of the woman and the sperm production of the man. If we assume that both partners are healthy, the one variable that seems the most influential is the woman's age. In France, researchers studied thousands of women who underwent artificial insemina-

CONCEPTION
The moment at which the sperm penetrates the ovum and the ovum becomes impervious to the entry of other sperm.

FALLOPIAN TUBES
The pair of slender ducts leading from the uterus to the region of the ovaries in the female reproductive system.

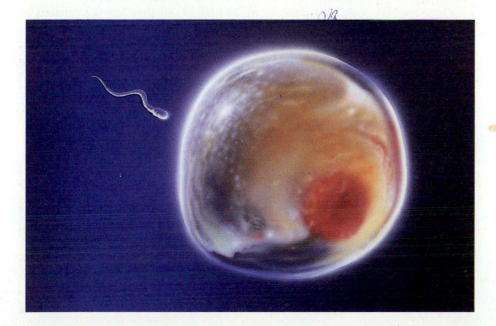

FIGURE 3.12

Conception will occur when the sperm cell penetrates the ovum.

ENDOMETRIOSIS

A pathological condition in which bits of the endometrial lining of the uterus invade the body cavity and periodically bleed during a woman's monthly cycle. The disorder is found more often in women over 30 years of age and may interfere with fertility by producing scar tissue that can damage or block the fallopian tubes.

ZYGOTE

The fertilized ovum that results from the union of a sperm and an egg.

BLASTOCYST

A stage of development during the period of the ovum when the embryo consists of one or several layers of cells around a central cavity, forming a hollow sphere.

TROPHOBLAST

The outer layer of cells by which the fertilized ovum is attached to the uterine wall and through which the embryo receives its nourishment.

PERIOD OF THE OVUM

Time from conception until the zygote is first attached within the uterus, about 2 weeks following conception.

PERIOD OF THE EMBRYO

Time from the attachment of the zygote to the uterine wall until the first formation of solid bone in the embryo, from about 2 to 8 weeks following conception.

EMBRYO

The unborn child from the time of attachment to the uterine wall until the formation of bone (approximately 2–8 weeks from conception).

tion because they wished to become pregnant and their husbands were sterile. This was an ideal way to study the effects of maternal age on the chances of pregnancy, because the amount of sperm given and the timing of its delivery were held constant. The researchers found that the chances of becoming pregnant over a period of 12 menstrual cycles were 73 percent for women age 25 years or younger, 74 percent for women age 26 to 30, 61 percent for women 31 to 35, and 54 percent for women over age 35 (Federation CECOS, Schwartz, & Mayaux, 1982).

The primary reason why older women conceive less frequently is that they often fail to ovulate. This is most likely due to changes in hormone levels associated with aging and the simple fact that the body's metabolism tends to slow down as we get older (Silber, 1980). Other common reasons why older women may have trouble conceiving are scarred or blocked fallopian tubes from past infections and **endometriosis** (which may also affect younger women, but not as often). The chances of conception also decrease with paternal age, but much less significantly.

The chances of conception are also influenced by the woman's ratio of body fat to lean tissue. Loss of fat owing to diet or exercise can lead to infertility; fortunately, fertility is restored once the fat is regained (Frisch, 1988). This particular mechanism probably evolved because of the survival advantages of preventing pregnancy during stressful times.

The Period of the Ovum

The ovum, once fertilized, is called a **zygote**. Assuming that fertilization has occurred in a fallopian tube, it usually takes 3 to 4 days for the zygote to make its way to the uterus. By the time it reaches the uterus, the zygote has become a fluid-filled sphere called a **blastocyst**. The blastocyst may float unattached in the uterus for approximately 48 hours.

An inner cell mass then forms to one side of the interior of the blastocyst (see Figure 3.13). This mass then begins to differentiate into two layers. The outside layer, or *ectoderm*, will later form the skin, teeth, hair, nails, and nervous system of the fetus. The inner layer, or *endoderm*, will eventually develop into most of the body organs. At a later time, a *mesoderm*, or middle layer, will develop, eventually creating the muscles, skeletal system, and circulatory system.

Once the blastocyst enters the uterus (which at this time has the capacity of a thimble), it attaches itself to the uterine wall, and a series of complex connections between the zygote and the mother's body begin to form. The **trophoblast**, which is the external cellular layer of the blastocyst, produces fine spindlelike structures that penetrate the uterine epithelium, or lining, and begins to develop nurturing connections with the mother's body.

The time from conception until the blastocyst is attached within the uterus, or womb, is called the **period of the ovum**; it lasts approximately 2 weeks.

The Period of the Embryo

The **period of the embryo** lasts from the time of the blastocyst's attachment to the uterine wall until the first occurrence of ossification (the formation of solid bone) in the **embryo**. This period usually lasts from the second to the eighth week following conception.

Once implantation has occurred, the trophoblast plays a very important role. It sends signals to the mother's body that "a baby is forming," which in turn triggers a protective "dampening" response from her, preventing her antibodies, which normally fight foreign invaders such as bacteria, from attacking the newly forming embryo (Kajino, McIntyre, Faulk, Cai, & Billington, 1988). It should be pointed out, however, that not all antibodies that reach the embryo are a threat. Certain antibodies from the mother, known as immunoglobulins, are actively carried from the mother to the embryo by special molecules that act somewhat like miniature ferryboats (Simister & Mostov, 1989). Once the immunoglobulins reach the embryo, they help protect it by providing disease resistance—a kind of before-birth inoculation (Beaconsfield, Birdwood, & Beaconsfield, 1980).

During the period of the embryo, cellular division continues at a very rapid rate, and cellular specialization occurs. Although each cell in a body carries the DNA blueprint for that entire body, during cellular specialization, or *differentiation*, different portions of the DNA code in each cell become active, while other portions go dormant, depending on which kind of cell (skin cell, blood cell, etc.) is to be created (Patrusky, 1981). The forces that determine how cells differentiate or specialize are not fully understood. This specialization of cells, however, becomes apparent as skin, hair, sensory organs, a cartilage skeleton, a nervous system, a digestive system, a circulatory system, and other internal organs develop (see Table 3.4).

By the fourth week following conception, a tiny vessel destined to become the heart begins to pulse, even though the embryo is only a little larger than an adult's thumbnail. By 2 months, the embryo is approximately 1 inch long and is beginning to resemble a human being.

As the embryo grows, additional life-supporting auxiliary structures continue to develop. Among these are the **umbilical cord** and **placenta**, which main-

Umbilical cord
The flexible, cordlike structure connecting the fetus at the navel with the placenta. This cord contains the blood vessels that nourish the fetus and remove its wastes.

Placenta
A vascular, membranous organ that develops during pregnancy, lining the uterine wall and partially enveloping the fetus. The placenta is attached to the fetus by the umbilical cord.

Figure 3.13

The period of the ovum.

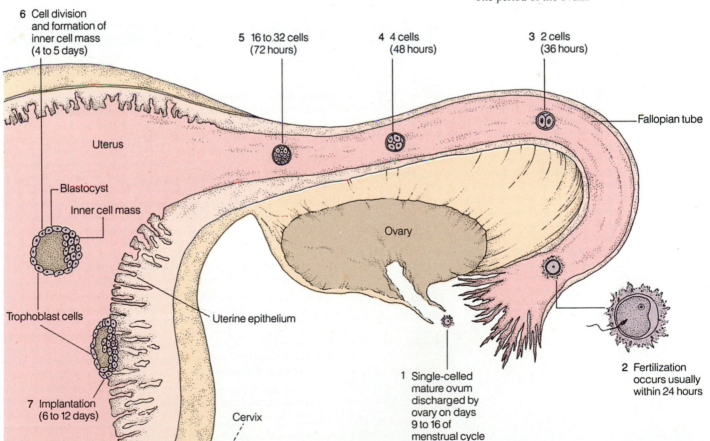

FETUS
The unborn child from the first formation of bone (approximately the eighth week after conception) until the time of birth.

PERIOD OF THE FETUS
Time from the first formation of bone in the embryo until birth, generally from 8 weeks following conception until birth.

tain the connection with the mother's body through which the embryo obtains nutrients and expels wastes. The umbilical cord consists of major blood vessels that pass through the placenta en route to and from the mother's body. The placenta consists of a number of semipermeable membranes that allow only molecules of relatively small size to pass. For this reason, the red blood cells of the mother and those of the unborn infant never mix prior to birth. This separation of blood is essential because the mother's blood type may be different from—and incompatible with—that of the embryo. Moreover, nutrients and wastes can pass through the placental barrier, so a shared bloodstream is unnecessary.

Research has shown that the spontaneous abortion rate is relatively high during the period of the embryo. Approximately 31 percent of all pregnancies end in spontaneous abortion (Wilcox et al., 1988). About two-thirds of the time, the women who undergo spontaneous abortion are unaware that they were ever pregnant, because the spontaneous abortion may seem to be nothing more than an unusually heavy flow during menstruation. It is assumed that the spontaneously aborted embryos are usually abnormal in some way. But there is no assumption that there is something wrong with the women, because 95 percent of women who have spontaneous abortions eventually have normal pregnancies.

The Period of the Fetus

From the time of ossification (approximately 8 weeks after conception) until birth, the developing prenatal organism is called a **fetus**. The **period of the fetus** is marked by continued and rapid growth of the specialized systems that

Table 3.4 ● The Development of the Embryo and Fetus

TIME ELAPSED SINCE CONCEPTION	STAGE
4 weeks	The embryo is approximately ⅕ inch in length. A primitive heart is beating. The head and tail are established. The mouth, liver, and intestines begin to take shape.
8 weeks	The embryo is now about 1 inch in legnth. For the first time it begins to resemble a human being. Facial features, limbs, hands, feet, fingers, and toes become apparent. The nervous system is responsive, and many of the internal organs begin to function.
12 weeks	The fetus is now 3 inches long and weighs almost 1 ounce. The muscles begin to develop and sex organs are formed. Eyelids, fingernails, and toenails are being formed. Spontaneous movements of the trunk can occasionaly be seen.
16 weeks	The fetus is now approximately 5 inches long. Blinking, grasping, and mouth motions can be observed. Hair appears on the head and body.
20 weeks	The fetus now weighs about ½ pound and is approximately 10 inches long. Sweat glands develop and the external skin is no longer transparent.
24 weeks	The fetus is able to inhale and exhale and could make a crying sound. The eyes are completed and taste buds have developed on the tongue. Fetuses born as immature as this have survived.
28 weeks	The fetus is usually capble by this time of living outside the womb, but would be considered immature at birth.
32 weeks	The end of the normal gestation period. The fetus is now prepared to live in the outside world.

emerged during the embryonic phase. Cellular differentiation is quite well advanced by the time ossification begins. As the fetus develops, the muscular and nervous systems grow at great speed. Often, before the twentieth week following conception, the mother is able to feel the fetus move. By the fifth month, reflexes such as swallowing or sucking occur.

By the end of the sixth month, the fetus is a little over 1 foot long and weighs almost 2 pounds. Its skin is thin and there is, as yet, no underlying layer of fat.

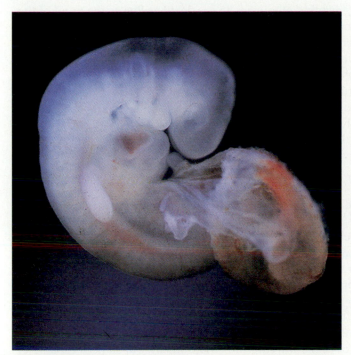

4-week-old embryo.

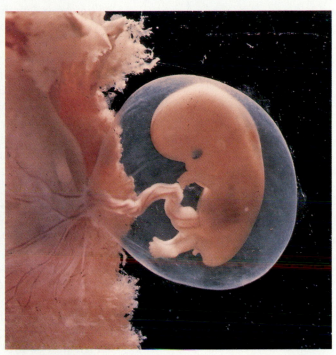

3-month-old fetus.

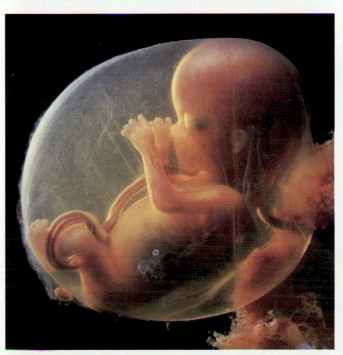

4-month-old fetus.

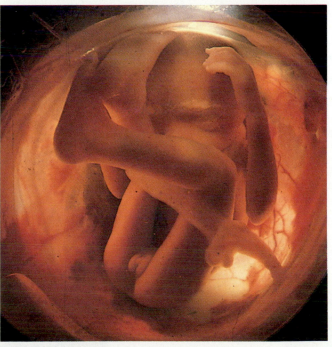

5-month-old fetus.

TERATOGEN
Any substance capable of producing fetal abnormalities, such as alcohol or tobacco.

Fingerprints are visible. The eyelids have developed and are functional. As the fetus grows, it becomes more active.

By the end of the seventh month of pregnancy, a layer of fat is deposited beneath the skin of the fetus. The fetus can also easily respond to stimuli. Should a bright light be surgically passed into the womb, the fetus will close its eyes and perhaps block the light by shading its eyes with its hands. During this time, ultrahigh-frequency sound scans (Figure 3.14) of a pregnant woman's womb may produce a moving image of the fetus hiccuping or even sucking its thumb! The most sensitive of these scanners can resolve objects as small as 1 millimeter in length, enabling physicians to see detail as fine as the pupil of the fetus's eye. A fetus born at this time has a good chance of surviving.

By the end of the eighth month, the fetus is about 18 inches long and weighs about 5 pounds. Development of the brain is especially rapid. Most systems are mature, but the lungs may still need more time in the womb. By the end of the ninth month, the fetus becomes less active, probably because it is feeling confined. The lungs are mature. The fetus's length is about 20 inches and the weight approximately 7.5 pounds. The infant is now ready to be born.

ADVERSE INFLUENCES ON PRENATAL DEVELOPMENT

A number of adverse influences can seriously harm an unborn child. Psychologists are especially interested in these potential dangers because they may seriously affect the child's psychological development or upset the family or social structure on which the child will have to depend. Unfortunately, the reaction of others to a child's handicap can often be the most damaging result of any birth defect or disability. Because many of these dangers to the unborn can be prevented by changing parental behavior or by altering the environment, it is essential that prospective parents be made aware of them. Often, though not always, the greatest burden lies with the mother because she has the greatest control over the intrauterine environment. Substances capable of producing fetal abnormalities are classified as **teratogens.**

FIGURE 3.14

Ultrahigh-frequency sound scans have proved to be a valuable aid. Ultrasound scans can spot fetal cerebral bleeding and its complications and can identify other abnormal difficulaties that may be a sign of developmental problems. Ultrasound scanning, however, may not be completely without risk. Some researchers have argued that ultrasound, in theory at least, may affect fetal cells because of the heat generated by the sound waves. Although no fetal damage directly attributable to ultrasound scans has been documented, the National Institutes of Health has recommended that ultrasound not be used simply for demonstration purposes, to ascertain the sex of the child, or to obtain pictures of the fetus, unless there is a medical reason for doing so.

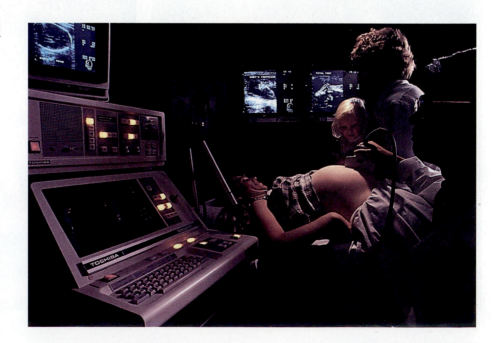

Smoking

By smoking, the mother can create a dangerous environment for her unborn child. When a mother smokes, carbon monoxide levels in her blood (produced by the burning cigarette) increase rapidly. The carrier molecule that normally takes oxygen across the placental barrier to the embryo or fetus will choose carbon monoxide over oxygen whenever possible, and the unborn child will begin to suffocate. This lack of vital oxygen may result in damage to the fetus that is expressed later as a learning or memory deficit (Mactutus & Fechter, 1984).

In addition to the danger from the carbon monoxide, there is the threat of the 3,000 or so other chemicals in the smoke that enter the mother's body. One of the most serious of these is nicotine, an extremely powerful stimulant. Nicotine is a vasoconstrictor: It causes constriction of the capillaries in the mother's body. This, in turn, further deprives the fetus of oxygen by reducing blood flow. Maternal smoking may also affect the ability of the fetus's lungs to grow and mature (Tager, Weiss, Munoz, Rosner, & Speizer, 1983).

But the most damning evidence against cigarette smoking by pregnant women was first brought to light almost 20 years ago by the U.S. Collaborative Perinatal Project. Using data collected from a sample of 50,000 pregnancies at 12 medical centers, the survey discovered that smoking during pregnancy increases the chance of the placenta's separating from the womb too soon and causing a miscarriage. It also discovered that smoking may contribute to the malformation of the heart or other organs in the fetus, again possibly leading to a miscarriage (Himmelberger, Brown, & Cohen, 1978). The project further revealed that cigarette smoking increases the risk of fatal birth defects as well as the possibility of sudden infant death (crib death) following a successful birth (Naeye, Ladis, & Drage, 1976). Furthermore, it was discovered that women who smoked at least 30 cigarettes per day had twice the chance of giving birth to a baby of low birth weight (Niswander & Gordon, 1972). Low birth weight, in turn, has been associated with many negative outcomes, including high infant mortality and low IQ (Broman, Nichols, & Kennedy, 1975). Over the years, many more studies have further supported these earlier findings.

There may also be an increased risk to the fetus if the father smokes. If the father smokes, he may cause the mother to become a passive smoker; that is, she will be living in the smoky environment that he has created. This may be a hazard to the fetus. Research has shown that infants born to nonsmoking mothers who were living in a home with smokers during their pregnancies had significantly high levels of nicotine in their blood, a result of their exposure to tobacco smoke (Greenberg, Haley, Etzel, & Loda, 1984).

Moreover, smoking can affect sperm production. A significantly greater number of abnormal sperm were found among men who smoked than among nonsmokers (Evans, Fletcher, Torrance, & Hargreave, 1981). Abnormally shaped sperm are less likely to reach the ovum and fertilize it. This may help explain why men who smoke generally have higher rates of infertility than those who don't.

All in all, the overwhelming majority of evidence gathered since 1935, when the effects of nicotine on the fetus were first reported (Sontag & Wallace, 1935), indicates that smoking during pregnancy has a high potential to cause harm.

Alcohol

You probably already realize that a pregnant alcoholic may not be doing her unborn child much good. However, there is evidence that even a relatively

When a pregnant woman smokes, she exposes her baby to carbon monoxide nicotine, and thousands of other chemicals. Smoking is associated with low birth weight, which in turn is correlated with high rates of infant mortality.

FETAL ALCOHOL SYNDROME
A disorder suffered by some infants whose mothers ingested alcohol during the prenatal period. It is characterized by facial, limb, or organ defects and reduced physical size and intellectual ability.

FIGURE 3.15

A child with fetal alcohol syndrome. The characteristic facial features include a small head circumference, a low nasal bridge, a short nose, and epicanthic folds of the eyelids. Intellectual deficiency also is common.

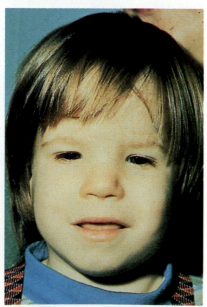

small intake of alcohol can endanger the embryo or fetus (Clarren & Smith, 1978; Streissguth, Barr, & Martin, 1983).

Keep in mind that something that may not be dangerous to the mother may do considerable harm to the unborn child; that is, a safe dosage for a mother may be a huge dose for an embryo or fetus. Think of the embryo or fetus in terms of what it is—the most complex chemical reaction known. With this way of thinking, you might consider it a poor idea to dump unnecessary chemicals on it, alcohol included, while it is developing.

If a mother drinks excessively while pregnant, her child might actually suffer from **fetal alcohol syndrome**, which is associated with facial, limb, or organ defects (Figure 3.15). Furthermore, many of these children are only 80 percent of normal size and are intellectually retarded. In addition, they may exhibit abnormal behavior patterns, such as irritability, short attention span, social withdrawal, poor concentration, impulsiveness, or failure to consider the consequences of their actions (Coles, Smith, Fernhoff, & Falek, 1985; Streissguth et al., 1991). This legacy continues to follow these children into adulthood, often making it impossible for them to have close personal relationships or, in many cases, even hold a job (Streissguth et al., 1991).

Alcohol consumed during pregnancy has also been found to affect the developing brain of the fetus. The brain weight of the affected fetus is generally lower, and specific areas in the brain may be adversely affected (Diaz & Samson, 1980; West, Hodges, & Black, 1981). By the age of 4, children of mothers who drank moderately during pregnancy (on average, three drinks a day) are three times more likely to have subnormal intelligence test scores than are matched peers whose mothers had not consumed alcohol while pregnant (Streissguth, Barr, Sampson, Darby, & Martin, 1989). In fact, 4-year-olds have been found to be progressively more affected in direct relationship to the amount their mothers drank during pregnancy (Barr, Streissguth, Darby, & Sampson, 1990), showing that there probably is no safe limit of alcohol consumption for pregnant woman. Research has indicated that even a small amount taken each day—such as one can of beer, or one glass of wine, or 2 ounces of 86-proof alcohol—could be a hazard (Mills, Graubard, Harley, Rhoads, & Berendes, 1984).

Binge drinking may also be dangerous. A woman may produce a child with fetal alcohol syndrome if she consumes a significant amount of alcohol only once during her pregnancy. Alcohol consumption needn't be continuous or often for damage to occur (Sulik, Johnston, & Webb, 1981). In 1981, the Food and Drug Administration published the surgeon general's advisory to American doctors, which stated that women should totally abstain from all alcohol during pregnancy. No absolutely safe level of alcohol consumption for pregnant women has been identified (Kruse, 1984).

Of course, many mothers who smoke or drink during pregnancy later give birth to normal, healthy children. Most women who drink, even heavily, during pregnancy do not give birth to children with fetal alcohol syndrome (Abel, 1984; Kopp & Kalar, 1989). The reports of the dangers of smoking or drinking are based on averages. You have to play the odds. Similarly, there were soldiers who fought all the way through World War II without ever being injured; that doesn't mean the war was safe. It appears that the more chances you take, the greater the danger. Furthermore, risk factors often have multiplicative effects. For instance, one study has reported that the chance of a growth-retarded infant was doubled if the mother either drank or smoked during pregnancy. However, if she both drank and smoked, the risk quadrupled (became four times as great) (Sokol, Miller, & Reed, 1980).

Other Drugs

Alcohol and nicotine are drugs, of course. But there are many other drugs introduced into the embryonic or fetal environment that may cause damage. There isn't room in this book to consider a detailed analysis of all of them, but it may be beneficial to look at a few. Many drugs are able to cross the placental barrier and have a direct effect on the unborn child. In one study, mothers who were heavy users of marijuana during their pregnancy (four Jamaican marijuana cigars per day) had newborns whose cries were abnormal, indicating some form of neurological dysfunction (Lester & Dreher, 1989). Mothers addicted to heroin or cocaine will give birth to infants similarly addicted. After birth, these infants actually go through withdrawal, which may be life-threatening. Unfortunately, the number of babies born to mothers addicted to cocaine has been steadily growing in the United States. Often these babies are premature, jittery, and extremely fragile (Figure 3.16). These babies are also more likely to have lower birth weight, shorter body length, and smaller head circumference than unexposed infants (Lester et al., 1991).

Many other common drugs, such as tranquilizers, antibiotics, and anticonvulsants, can seriously affect the unborn child. Researchers have concluded that pregnant women should even avoid taking aspirin (which is an anticoagulant, a substance that hinders blood clotting) because of the danger of creating blood disorders in the fetus (Eriksson, Catz, & Yaffe, 1973).

Some antibiotics, especially tetracycline and streptomycin, have also been found to cause damage to the embryo or fetus (Howard & Hill, 1979). Of course, antibiotics (and other drugs, perhaps) may still be useful during a pregnancy because they may stop a disease that is more likely than the antibiotic to have a devastating effect on the fetus. Sometimes drugs are necessary, and good prenatal care requires that all factors be weighed.

It should be pointed out that only a few substances are teratogenic compared with the number of substances to which a woman may be exposed; in this sense, teratogenic substances are relatively rare (Heinonen et al., 1977). It's important to mention this fact, because when you read a chapter like this

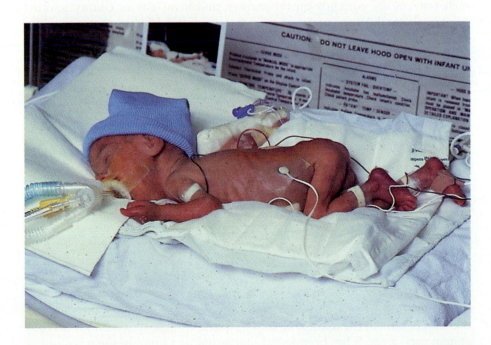

FIGURE 3.16

Babies born to mothers who used cocaine prenatally are often premature, jittery, and extremely fragile. Withdrawal can last up to 1 month after birth.

one, filled with discussions of teratogens, it may appear that everything in the environment might be harmful, when in fact we probably need to be alert to only a limited number of substances.

Environmental Hazards

During the last decade, people have become increasingly aware of the potential dangers from environmental hazards such as radiation or pollution.

Chemical Waste.   Inadequately managed chemical wastes can pervade an environment and make it unhealthy. Scientists believe that such industrial wastes may affect the developing fetus. Of course, pregnant women should not drink contaminated water or live in neighborhoods suspected of being contaminated if they can avoid doing so. Contact with contaminated water may lower a man's sperm count as well.

While it's easy to give such advice, a family with limited resources may find it difficult to move away or otherwise avoid local pollution. In some areas of the world, especially sections of industrialized eastern Europe, pollution is so severe that its harmful legacy may last for years, even after it is cleaned up. Data are only now being gathered for these areas, and the results, when released, are expected to be discouraging.

Heavy Metals.   Heavy metals, such as cadmium, mercury, and lead, have also been found to cause damage to the unborn (Klink, Jungblut, Oberheuser, & Siegers, 1983). In even small amounts, they can be quite harmful to the fetus. This is especially true of lead (Bellinger, Leviton, Waternaux, Needleman, & Rabinowitz, 1987).

Lead is often found as a contaminant of lead water pipes in older houses, and it is also found in newer homes where newly applied lead solder leaches into the copper piping. The problem is so widespread that it is probably a good idea to have your family's water periodically tested for heavy metals. (Many such test kits are currently on the market, and many city or county governments will conduct such tests in your home for the asking or for a minimal fee.) If there is a problem and bottled water is not a reasonable alternative, the water should be run for a few minutes or so before drinking to help eliminate contaminants that may have accumulated in the water that was sitting in the pipe. Lead is also commonly ingested by the use of improperly glazed ceramic or clay dishes, mugs, or cups. This is especially a problem with imported, old, or homemade items, which often contain hundreds of times more lead than is now considered safe.

Lead has also been found in the dust of old houses where lead-based paint was used and in the air from automobile exhausts, although the latter has been reduced significantly since the introduction of unleaded gasoline. In addition, both cadmium and lead are found in cigarette smoke (Klink, Jungblut, Oberheuser, & Siegers, 1983) and can pass directly through the placenta to the fetus (Huel, Everson, & Menger, 1984).

Heat.   Over the last 20 years, hot tubs and spas have become very popular. Hot tubs and Jacuzzi spas are designed for recreational bathing. Their temperatures are generally raised to between 100° F (38° C) and 106° F (41° C). Very hot water surrounding the womb of a pregnant woman may rapidly increase the temperature of the fetus to a point at which damage to its central nervous system may occur. It has been found that as few as 15 minutes in a spa or hot tub at 102° F (39° C) or 10 minutes at 106° F (41° C) is sufficient to cause fetal damage. These studies were made after it was found that some women gave birth to malformed babies after spending from 45 minutes to 1 hour in hot tubs (Harvey, McRorie, & Smith, 1981).

Radiation. Pregnant women in contact with X rays or radioactive materials must also be extremely cautious. As you can well imagine, given the rapid cell division occurring in the zygote, embryo, or fetus, disruption by ionizing radiation can be especially hazardous. Any woman who even suspects that she may be pregnant should inform her doctor before undergoing any tests or therapies that subject her to radiation.

Pathogens

Many disease processes can also threaten the unborn child. Here are the ones that cause the most concern.

Toxoplasmosis. One of the many common infections caused by microscopic parasites is **toxoplasmosis**; it is often found in humans and other mammals. About 35 percent of all adults have contracted toxoplasmosis at one time or another. In adults, the infection usually runs a mild course. However, it has a devastating effect on an unborn child's nervous system, often resulting in retardation, epilepsy, or blindness. Every year in the United States, about 1 in 1,000 infants are born with congenital toxoplasmosis, making it a more common threat to the fetus than German measles, syphilis, or PKU. About half of infected mothers will pass on the parasite to their offspring. At birth, the infant often appears healthy because the devastating effects appear later (from a few months to as long as 9 years after birth).

A test for prenatal toxoplasmosis has been developed (Daffos et al., 1988), but it is expensive and not always readily available. If a woman is found to be infected, however, antibiotics can often control the disease and keep it from reaching the fetus. Should the fetus become infected, treatment in the womb with antibiotics has also been successful. The best treatment, however, is to avoid the parasite in the first place. The best way for a pregnant woman to do that is to avoid contact with animal fecal matter (most often encountered while gardening or changing kitty litter) and never to eat rare or undercooked meat.

Viruses. A virus is typically a segment of nucleic acid (such as DNA) surrounded by a protein coating. When viruses enter the body, they often invade cells, multiply, and rupture the cell they have invaded. From there, they continue to spread unless stopped by the body's defenses. Maternal contact with the **rubella** virus (German measles) can be disastrous for the fetus, especially during the first 3 months of pregnancy. Apparently, the virus interrupts some early development. Although the mother suffers only the mild symptoms of the disease, the fetus may be born intellectually impaired, deaf, or blind. Contact with the virus later in the pregnancy does not usually result in such severe damage.

Cytomegalovirus, a virus that can infect the female genital tract, is extremely common in the United States; 82 percent of American women carry antibodies for the virus, indicating contact at some time in their lives. By the mid-1970s, cytomegalovirus was known to be responsible for approximately 3,700 cases of fetal brain damage per year in the United States (Stagno et al., 1977).

Genital **herpes** is a common venereal disease. For adults, it is more a painful annoyance than a threat to health. For newborns, however, it can be extreme-

TOXOPLASMOSIS
A disease of humans, dogs, cats, and certain other mammals, caused by a parasitic microorganism that affects the nervous system. The disorder is especially damaging to an embryo or fetus.

RUBELLA
A viral infection, commonly known as German measles, that may have a serious effect on an unborn child, especially if contracted by the mother during the first trimester.

CYTOMEGALOVIRUS
A common virus to which a majority of American women have been exposed at some time in their lives. An active infection in a pregnant woman may cause harm to the unborn child.

HERPES
A disease caused by a number of viruses that can attack the skin or mucous membranes. Genital herpes is difficult to treat and can harm an infant born to a mother whose herpes is in an active stage.

CESAREAN SECTION
A surgical incision through the abdominal wall and uterus, performed to extract a fetus.

SLOW VIRUS
A virus that may take years to produce symptoms. Slow viruses have been implicated in some forms of mental retardation.

AIDS (ACQUIRED IMMUNE DEFICIENCY SYNDROME)
A human retrovirus type HIV, which can be transmitted sexually through the exchange of bodily fluids or by shared needle use among infected IV (intravenous) drug abusers. The disease may also be passed by infusion of unscreened blood or blood products. Once the disease process occurs, the immune system fails and death follows. The virus may infect an unborn child by crossing the placental barrier of an infected mother.

ly dangerous. One-third of newborns who contract either the herpes I or herpes II virus die, and another one-fourth suffer brain damage (Sullivan-Bolyai, Hull, Wilson, & Corey, 1983). Most affected infants acquire the disease from their mother at birth, when they pass through her birth canal. Fortunately, most women infected with herpes do not infect their offspring. An obstetrician who is aware that the mother has the infection can often avoid infection of the newborn by performing a **cesarean section**. The herpes virus, however, can invade the mother farther than the birth canal and may cross the placental barrier into the amniotic fluid. In such cases, which are relatively rare, cesarean section will not be effective in avoiding infection of the infant (Silberner, 1985).

The effects of many other viruses on the unborn child, although undoubtedly important, are not as well understood. Sometimes a virus can enter a cell and, rather than multiply, attach its own genetic code to that of the cell's. Such viruses are called **slow viruses** because they may take years to become active or have an effect. A number of disorders that may affect prenatal development or that may lead to mental retardation are now believed to be the result of slow viruses.

Perhaps the most deadly viral infection to which the fetus might be exposed is the one that causes **AIDS**, a lethal immune system disorder. This virus is thought to cross the placenta of infected mothers and infect the fetus. Of women who are infected, the chances of their babies being similarly infected is about 50 percent. Babies who are infected this way are "born dying" and usually succumb during infancy or early childhood.

Rh Factor Incompatibility

Sometimes the disease process may be caused by genetics rather than external pathogens. Consider the case of Rh protein factor incompatibility. Rh stands for rhesus, the species of monkey in which this protein factor was first discovered. Eighty-five percent of the population is Rh positive; that is, the factor exists in their blood. Positive is a dominant trait, while negative is recessive. People who are Rh negative are therefore double recessives.

A problem concerning Rh may occur only if the father is Rh positive and the mother is Rh negative. If their union produces an Rh positive baby, the fetus will possess the Rh factor that the mother does not have. There is generally no difficulty with the first baby, but if its blood mixes with the mother's during birth (which is quite common), the mother's body reacts to the infant's foreign Rh factor by creating antibodies as a defense. If another child is conceived and if it, too, is Rh positive, the mother's body, having been sensitized by the first birth, may recognize her own fetus as foreign and begin to attack it. This is one of the few instances in which the mother's antibodies may attack the fetus. If, through a blood test, physicians are aware of the problem ahead of time, they can use drugs to minimize any damage from Rh incompatibility.

Maternal Diet

Malnourishment, as a single variable, is quite difficult to separate out from generally poor prenatal care, poor sanitation, and lack of adequate shelter (Stechler & Halton, 1982). For example, many studies conducted immediately following World War II strongly indicated that malnourished pregnant women were more likely to give birth to infants who were underweight and at greater than normal risk for developmental disorders. Unfortunately, as is so often the case in naturalistic research, it was impossible to separate the effects of malnourishment from those of the stresses of war. Nonetheless, malnourishment by itself appears to have a deleterious effect on a developing embryo or fetus. Women who were starved during World War II typically gave birth to underweight infants, and of these infants who were girls, they, too, once adults, gave birth to underweight infants, even though they themselves received proper nourishment (Diamond, 1990). In this way, the malnourishment of the grandmother during pregnancy is a legacy passed on even to her grandchildren.

Even when studies control for premature birth, they indicate that malnourished mothers tend to have children who weigh less at birth. Malnourishment doesn't necessarily mean starvation, either. Some maternal diets, while containing sufficient calories, are lacking in important nutrients and vitamins. One study of over 20,000 pregnant women in Boston revealed that diets low in folic acid resulted in underweight babies (Diamond, 1990). For this reason, it is advisable for pregnant women to take vitamin supplements.* Vitamin supplements taken during pregnancy have also been shown to significantly reduce the probability of certain birth defects (Fackelmann, 1991).

Emotional Stress

It is extremely difficult to evaluate the effects of maternal emotional stress on the developing fetus because it is so hard to eliminate this one factor from all the others associated with women under stress, such as malnutrition, poor health, or drug use (Stechler & Halton, 1982). It is known that stress in the mother stimulates the production of adrenaline, which causes capillary constriction and diverts the blood flow from the uterus to other organs of the body. Sufficient stress over enough time might conceivably cause damage by depriving the fetus of needed oxygen.

It is often difficult to tell whether stressed mothers are more likely to have problems with their pregnancies than mothers who are under less stress. In one of the few carefully controlled studies to isolate anxiety as a central factor during pregnancy, it was found that mothers who were most anxious were significantly more likely to give birth to premature infants or infants of low birth weight than were mothers who were less anxious (Lobel, Dunkel-Schetter, & Schimshaw, 1992). Some preliminary studies have also associated job-related stress in pregnant women with low birth weight in their infants (Katz, Jenkins, Haley, & Bowes, 1991). Low birth weight is a major factor in infant mortality.

Birth complications seem to be lessened by the supportive companionship of a close friend or spouse during labor. In fact, one study reported that labor time for mothers who were presumably less anxious because they were supported by a companion was less than half that of women in the control group, who received no such support. The control group's mean length of labor was 19.3 hours; the experimental group's mean length of labor was only 8.7 hours (Sosa, Kennell, Klaus, Robertson, & Urrutia, 1980).

Discussing the dangers faced by an unborn child should not to make you overly concerned about pregnancy, however. After all, most pregnancies go well. The purpose is to alert you to the need for reasonable care. Parents will often spend more time in preparing the baby's new room than they will in dis-

---

*If you are pregnant, be sure that your doctor approves of your choice of vitamin supplements before you take any (some supplements are better than others in terms of content and dosage). Your doctor will probably supply you with vitamins especially formulated for pregnant women.

covering the few precautions they might observe to ensure their future baby's physical health and psychological well-being. By being cautious, you lessen the probability of encountering or creating physical or developmental handicaps that can disrupt the child's life or interfere with the early relationships between child and caregiver.

PARENTAL PLANNING

By planning when to have children and how many to have, couples may lessen the chances of birth defects. The World Health Organization has provided the following advice for parents:

1. Women who bear children should be in their 20s. (Chromosomal abnormalities are least likely to occur in this age range, probably because hormone levels are higher than at other ages.)
2. Men who father children should be between 20 and 55 years of age. (Chromosomal abnormalities are least likely to occur to children fathered by men in this age range.)
3. Pregnancies should be at least 2 years apart (to give the woman's body a chance to recover).
4. Women should limit themselves to five births (to limit wear and tear on the uterus).
5. Women should seek competent prenatal care from the moment they realize they are pregnant.

Eugenics: Selective Breeding of Human Beings

In 1883, Sir Francis Galton, a cousin of Charles Darwin, coined the term *eugenics* and attempted to begin a scientific movement concerned with the selective breeding of human beings. According to this new science, selected human beings would be mated with each other in an attempt to obtain certain traits in their offspring, much the way that animal breeders work with champion stock. The eventual goal of eugenics was to create a better human race.

Galton believed that intelligence was inherited, along with many "civilized" behavior patterns. He believed that the upper class of his day best represented these "inherited" traits, and although his hope was to improve the lot of the common people, the thrust of his argument seemed to be that the English upper class was truly better bred—a concept embraced by the English aristocracy. The idea that learning and experience might play an important role in determining the behavior patterns of the upper, middle, or lower class seemed ridiculous. Nineteenth-century England simply wasn't ready for such democratic notions. In fact, in 1912, when George Bernard Shaw wrote the play *Pygmalion* (later rewritten as the musical *My Fair Lady*), the plot was quite revolutionary because it was about a professor of language *teaching* a street urchin to pass as a lady of great breeding.

From time to time, various groups and sects have incorporated selective breeding into their social doctrine. For example, a nineteenth-century commune in Oneida, New York, begun by John Humphrey Noyes, tried specific breeding with humans, but the commune's efforts were not well documented (Sussman, 1976). Perhaps the most organized and horrifying efforts to carry out a eugenics program were made in Germany during World War II. The leaders of the Nazi Third Reich devised a plan that, in their view, would ensure the continuance and eventual numerical superiority of the Nordic, or German, bloodline. The leaders of the SS (the *Schutzstaffel* elite guard), under Reichsfuhrer Himmler, arranged for babies of "pure stock" to be kidnapped from overrun nations and brought to the German heartland. There the children were placed in luxurious *lebensborn* centers, where they were to be raised according to the ideals of the Nazi high command.

In addition, special houses, or maternity homes, were set aside by the Gestapo so that the SS soldiers, who had already been selected for their light features, height, and robust physique, could impregnate specially selected women who had such physical characteristics as blue eyes, blond hair, and wide hips. These women were to bear the children of the future master race (Hillel & Henry, 1976). All "inferior"

Sir Francis Galton (1822–1911).

humans, especially Jews, retarded children or adults, and individuals with genetic defects, were to be destroyed; and so, along with 6 million Jewish victims, many ill and retarded people were also murdered.

Nazi "scientific" texts concerned with genetics make interesting reading; they are filled with horrifying misconceptions about human inheritance.

NEGATIVE EUGENICS

Negative eugenics is a process of elimination. Thousands of pregnancies are monitored each year, and fetuses found to have serious genetic disorders are often aborted. In this way, parents practice negative eugenics by eliminating defective genes (Miller, 1981). Some people, however, argue that abortion is not a moral or justifiable means to control the spread of genetic disease. The debate over this issue continues.

There are other methods of eliminating unwanted genes besides abortion, such as compulsory sterilization and other restrictions on the right to reproduce. Many argue that because the state has the right to quarantine individuals to prevent the spread of infectious diseases, the state should also have the right to prevent the spread of defective genes.

The following facts are offered without comment:
A. Laws have been suggested that would require people with IQs below 75 to be sterilized.

1. IQ tests measure only limited aspects of a person's ability.
2. Approximately 80 percent of people with IQ scores below 75 are physically normal and have no history of brain or genetic damage (Liebert, Poulos, & Marmor, 1977).
3. IQ scores may change or vary by as much as 40 points or more during

one's lifetime (Skeels, Updegraff, Wellman, & Williams, 1938).

B. A number of years ago, thousands of people in North Carolina were sterilized by law because they were examined and found to be mentally defective by the North Carolina State Eugenics Board (Coburn, 1974).

1. During the 1960s, 63 percent of those sterilized in North Carolina were black, although blacks constituted only 24 percent of North Carolina's population.

2. Black children tend to score from 10 to 15 points lower on IQ tests than do white children (Kennedy, 1969).

3. Many IQ tests have been criticized for asking "white" questions, that is, questions that are easier for white children to answer because of their cultural background (Kagan, 1973).

4. Black children raised in white homes tend to score higher on IQ tests than do black children raised in black homes (Scarr & Weinberg, 1976).

C. A majority of states have had, at one time or another, statutes that allow eugenic measures for controlling the incidence of congenital defects. Many states currently have such laws.

1. Some years back, the Illinois state legislature considered a proposal to disallow marriage licenses to Illinois citizens who are carriers of genetic disorders or diseases that would lead to birth defects.

2. Robert Todd Lincoln, U.S. secretary of war from 1881 to 1885, might never have been born had such a law been in effect during the nineteenth century. His father, a citizen of Illinois, apparently suffered from Marfan's syndrome, a serious and slowly debilitating genetic disease of the body's connective tissue, which causes a weakening of the aorta (and thus heart problems) elongated fingers and toes, and a generally ugly appearance. But then some people are able to endure in spite of their genetic hardships, as did Robert Todd Lincoln's father, Abraham Lincoln, the sixteenth president of the United States (Schwartz, 1978).

POSITIVE EUGENICS

Positive eugenics places the emphasis on creative rather than weeding-out processes. With positive eugenics, selected women would be fertilized with the best sperm.

But who would decide which sperm or egg is "best"? That's the catch. What kind of man or woman represents the best? Mr. Universe, Miss America, a movie star, a Nobel Prize winner? Or if the best seed were to belong to the most socially respectable people, what about "ex-cons" such as Cervantes, Thoreau, Gandhi, and Martin Luther King?

In 1980, in Escondido, California, a millionaire named Robert Graham decided to begin a sperm bank for couples who might need help conceiving a child (Garelik, 1985). His intention also was to practice positive eugenics in a big way. He decided that sperm donated to his bank should be collected only from winners of the Nobel Prize! If the sperm were then given only to women who could prove that their IQ was in the top 1 percent, then the Nobel sperm bank, so the argument went, could be used to improve the lot of humanity

Abraham Lincoln was able to cope despite his genetic handicap.

by creating children of outstanding intelligence.

The first hitch occurred when only two Nobel winners agreed to donate sperm. One of these men remained anonymous. The other was William Shockley, who had received his Nobel Prize for codevelopment of the transistor. Shockley was also well known, however, for his controversial view that whites have a natural intellectual superiority to blacks.

Going on record as refusing to donate, were a number of men who had received Nobel Prizes for their work in genetics and related fields. Some argued that the idea of such a sperm bank smacked of biological elitism. Vance Packard pointed out that J. J. Thompson, a Nobel Prize winner who had discovered the electron, had a mother who couldn't find her way from her home to the railway station, which was about two blocks away! In fact, many illustrious men and women of great intelligence have parents who, on the surface at least, show no particular signs of genius. Although genetics, of course, does play a role in the inheritance of intellectual capacity, environment, it is often argued, may be even more important.

The next problem for Robert Graham's sperm bank occurred when women who applied for his program discovered that the sperm available from Nobel Prize winners was from men well into their 70s. Sperm from men that old are much more likely to contain mutations and genetic defects. None of the women felt comfortable being inseminated by a man in his mid-70s, Nobel Prize winner or no. In response to this, Graham created a new sperm bank with donations from young men of exceptional IQ and achievement.

The first woman to be impregnated through the new bank was Joyce K. She gave birth to a baby girl, Victoria, in 1982. It was only then that the operators of the sperm bank discovered that she and her second hus-

APPLICATIONS

band had lost custody of two children by her first marriage after being accused of abusing them. On the heels of this scandal, she and her husband sold an interview to the *National Enquirer* in which they described expectations for Victoria that were quite extravagant (Garelik, 1985). Interestingly, Graham's response to all this was that although it "may have been a social blunder, it wasn't a genetic one." He added that Ms. K. had "an IQ of 130 or 140" (Garelik, 1985, p. 81).

Many geneticists have expressed concern about possible undue expectations and unrealistic desires placed on a child by parents who may now believe that they have a preordained "Einstein" on their hands. Such pressures could be psychologically or socially detrimental, regardless of the child's capacity for intelligence.

There has been quite a range of reaction to eugenics programs. Roger McIntire, a psychologist, once proposed that anyone who couldn't pass a course in parenting at a community college should be injected with a substance that would prevent reproduction. The antidote, it was argued, should be given only after both parents-to-be passed the course. He received hundreds of letters that, as he noted, ranged from "right on" to "Seig Heil" (Packard, 1977). What do you think?

Summary

■ Among the molecules that formed billions of years ago was DNA, the essence of life. DNA is made of a double strand twisted to form a helix, and it replicates (makes copies of itself).

■ The internal structure of DNA consists of a series of bases made from adenine-thymine and cytosine-guanine pairs. Each section of a code is called a gene.

■ The first life on this planet was a single-celled organism created in the clay beds of the oceans by a combination of chemicals. From this first life, all other life evolved.

■ Genes are located in the nucleus of each cell on small bodies called chromosomes. Each human body cell contains 23 pairs of chromosomes. Because of the process of meiosis, sex cells, called gametes, contain only 23 chromosomes rather than 23 pairs.

■ The first 22 chromosome pairs are called autosomes. The twenty-third pair contain the genetic codes that determine your sex; consequently, the chromosomes in this pair are known as sex chromosomes.

■ Gregor Mendel was the discoverer of the simple laws of inheritance, including the concepts of homozygosity and heterozygosity, dominance and recessiveness, and phenotypes and genotypes. Many human characteristics, such as eye color and blood type, are inherited according to these principles.

■ Some principles of inheritance follow different rules. In the case of sex-linked inheritance, a disorder or trait tends to be carried by women and expressed in men.

■ Other complex genetic interactions include the effect of modifier genes.

■ Through prenatal screening (amniocentesis and chorionic villi sampling) and genetic counseling, prospective parents can help to eliminate possible chromosomal and genetic defects in their children.

■ Fertilization occurs when a sperm penetrates an ovum. This typically takes place in a fallopian tube, which is part of the female reproductive system.

■ During the period of the ovum, which lasts approximately 2 weeks following fertilization, the fertilized ovum, called a zygote, becomes attached to the wall of the uterus.

■ The period of the embryo is marked by the rapid growth and development of the unborn child; it lasts from the time the zygote attaches to the uterus until the formation of solid bone in the embryo, which occurs approximately 8 weeks following conception. From this point until birth, the unborn child is known as a fetus.

■ A number of external influences may cause serious damage to the unborn child. Prospective parents can often avoid these dangers by altering their behavior, so it is important that they be made aware of the possible threats to the embryo or fetus. Among these dangers are behaviors that the mother may engage in, such as smoking, drinking, and the use of drugs.

■ Other hazards that may affect the embryo or fetus include parasites, viruses, emotional stress, and maternal diet.

■ Eugenics refers to the selective breeding of human beings. According to this science, selected humans would be mated with each other in an attempt to obtain certain traits in their offspring, much the way animal breeders work. Positive eugenics places the emphasis on creative rather than weeding-out processes. Negative eugenics is a process of eliminating defective genes, for example, by abortion.

QUESTIONS FOR DISCUSSION

1. Can you conceive of a humane eugenics program that would be just and that would improve the human race? What problems do you immediately encounter?

2. If you could change human genes, how would you alter them? What improvement in our species would you like to see? Are you sure that the behaviors you have chosen are genetic and not learned?

3. In many states, it is difficult for an adopted child to obtain information about his or her biological parents from state agencies because many of these parents wish to remain anonymous. Should *any* information be made available to the adopted child? If so, what information?

4. What are your thoughts about abortion? Do you believe, for example, that severe damage to a fetus caused by rubella should influence a woman's decision concerning abortion?

5. Do you think that pregnant women who knowingly expose themselves to substances known to be harmful to the fetus are guilty of child abuse?

SUGGESTIONS FOR FURTHER READING

1. Cooper, N. G. (Ed.). (1994). *The human genome project: Deciphering the blueprint of heredity.* Mill Valley, CA: University Science Books.

2. Graham, J. (1991). *Your pregnancy companion: A month-by-month guide to all you need to know before, during, and after pregnancy.* New York: Penguin Books.

3. Kevles, D. J. (1985). *In the name of eugenics.* New York: Knopf.

4. Kingdon, J. (1993). *Self-made man: Human evolution from Eden to extinction.* New York: Wiley.

5. Kolata, G. (1990). *The baby doctors: Probing the limits of fetal medicine.* New York: Delacorte.

6. Norwood, C. (1980). *At highest risk: Environmental hazards to young and unborn children.* New York: McGraw-Hill.

7. Nossal, G. J. V. (1985). *Key issues in genetic engineering.* New York: Cambridge University Press.

8. Silber, S. J. (1980). *How to get pregnant.* New York: Scribner.

9. Watson, J. (1968). *The double helix.* New York: Atheneum.

10. Wolpert, L. (1992). *The triumph of the embryo.* New York: Oxford University Press.

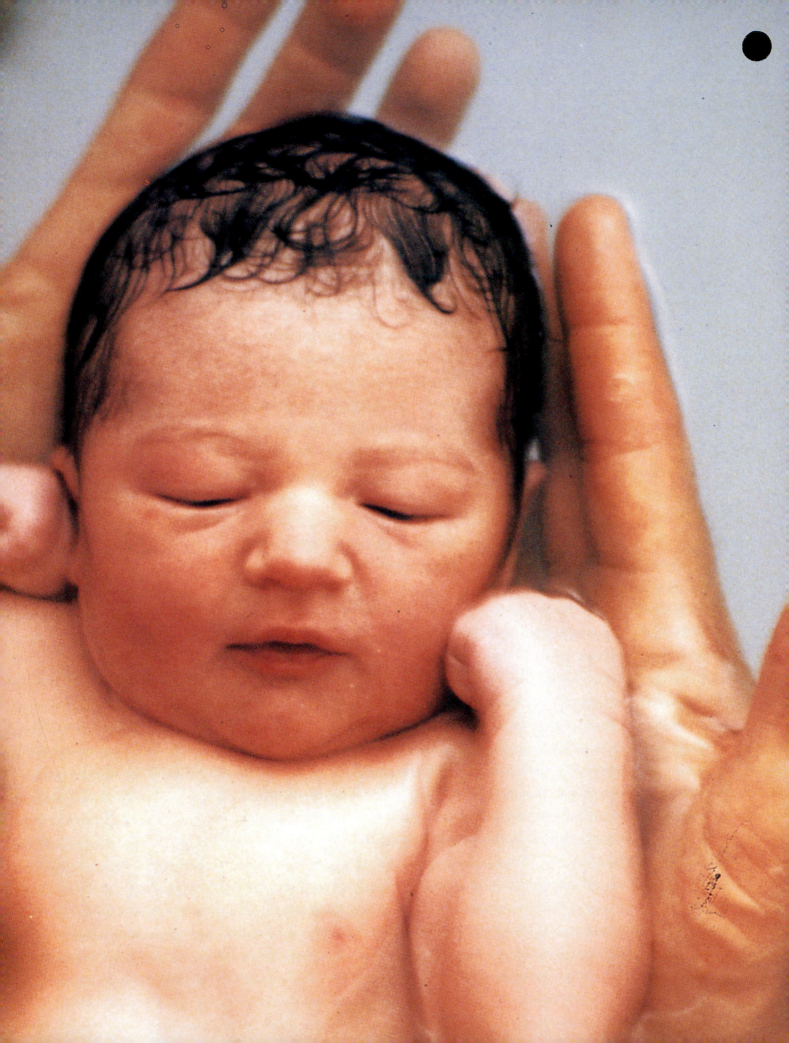

CHAPTER 4

Birth and Competencies of the Newborn and Infant

CHAPTER PREVIEW
A Doctor Seuss Story

Parents enjoy reading to their children, and children especially like to have stories read to them. Among the favorites are the enduring stories of Dr. Seuss. It should come as no surprise, then, to discover that over 150 children observed in a study in North Carolina seemed purposely to attempt, when given the opportunity, to get their mothers to read a Dr. Seuss story to them. But perhaps you'd be surprised to learn that these children were only 2 to 3 days old!

In the experiment, the babies were put in bassinets and small, loose-fitting headsets were placed over their ears. A special nipple was placed in their mouths. If the infants sucked at a selected rate, a tape of their own mother's voice reading a Dr. Seuss story would be played. If the sucking rate deviated from the selected rate, a different woman's voice would continue with the story.

Regardless of whether the selected rate was fast or slow, 85 percent of the infants showed a preference for their own mother's voice over that of a stranger and adjusted their sucking rate to maintain their mother's voice on the earphones. The infants also began new sessions at the correct sucking rate, which demonstrates the presence of a functioning memory (DeCasper & Fifer, 1980).

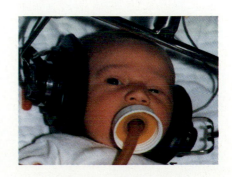

But how could babies know which voice was their mother's? The human ear is developed and functional about 7 months after conception (Birnholz & Benacerraf, 1983), so the fetus probably listens to its mother's voice during the last 2 months of pregnancy, perhaps learning the sound of the voice while still in the womb. Or maybe infants rapidly learn to recognize their own mother's voice the first 1 or 2 days following birth.

BIRTH
The passage of a child from the uterus to outside the mother's body.

LIGHTENING
The rotation of the fetus into a head-downward position prior to birth.

LABOR
The physical efforts of childbirth; parturition.

CERVIX
The opening between the vagina and the uterus in the female animal.

BREECH BIRTH
A vaginal delivery during which the buttocks or feet of the fetus appear first.

Another study was then run to determine when infants learn their mother's voice—before or after birth. This time fathers were used instead of mothers. All the fathers in the experiment were presented with their baby daughters at birth and talked to them as often as possible, sometimes for as long as 10 hours. From after birth to the time of the study, these babies heard no other male voice. The babies, only 2 or 3 days old, once again were equipped with the earphones and the special nipple that allowed them to choose to hear their father or a stranger read Dr. Seuss. The babies showed no preference for one voice over the other (Kolata, 1984). This implies that the infants' reaction in the first study probably was a result of their having had more experience hearing their mother's voice—which of course, implies that they heard it while in the womb. In fact, after listening to their father's voice for a few weeks, the infants preferred it to that of a stranger.

In this chapter, you will see the birth process and learn about some of the infant's amazing abilities. Although scientists used to think that infants were not capable of much, it has become apparent that infants are born with a complex set of capacities and competencies.

LABOR AND DELIVERY

For 9 months, the unborn child has been developing in the womb. Now the fetus is prepared to exit its mother's body. **Birth** in human beings typically occurs 270 days after conception, near the end of a full 9-month period. Shortly before birth (typically a few weeks before first births, but sometimes only a few hours before birth in later pregnancies), the fetus usually rotates into a head-downward position. This movement is referred to as **lightening** because it releases pressure on the mother's abdomen.

For women giving birth for the first time, **labor** usually lasts between 12 and 24 hours, with an average of 14 hours. However, for women who have given birth before, labor usually averages only 6 hours.

The First Stage

Labor is commonly divided into three stages that typically overlap each other. During the first stage, which lasts, on the average, about 13 hours for a woman having her first child, uterine contractions begin. These contractions are usually spaced 10 to 20 minutes apart. Initially the contractions are gentle, but they tend to become more powerful and uncomfortable.

The Second Stage

The second stage of labor usually lasts about 90 minutes. During this stage, the **cervix** opens sufficiently to allow the baby to begin to move down the birth canal. At this point, if the mother has been well prepared, she may use her abdominal muscles to help push the baby along. This second stage of labor often can be shortened considerably by having the mother give birth in a vertical position, for example, by using a chair especially designed for giving birth in an upright position. At the end of the second stage of labor, the baby is born.

Birth.   During birth, the human fetus is forced through the birth canal under extreme pressure and is intermittently deprived of oxygen. During this time, the baby secretes the hormones adrenaline and noradrenaline at levels that are higher than they are likely to be at any other time throughout its life (Lagercrantz & Slotkin, 1986). Adrenaline helps open up the baby's lungs to dry out the bronchi and thus achieve the switch from a liquid to an air environment. Noradrenaline, which is especially prevalent, slows the heartbeat, enabling the fetus to withstand fairly lengthy oxygen deprivation. Babies delivered by *cesarean section*, which we will discuss shortly, are brought out of the mother surgically and do not pass through the birth canal. Interestingly, these infants often have respiratory problems. One reason for such problems might be that the infant has not benefited from the stress of normal birth (Lagercrantz & Slotkin, 1986)!

About 97 percent of babies are born in the head-first position (see Figure 4.1). However, 2.4 percent are born rump first; this is called a **breech birth**.

FIGURE 4.1

Ninety-seven percent of babies are born in the head-first position. The fetus's skull is soft and pliable, which helps the head to pass through the birth canal.

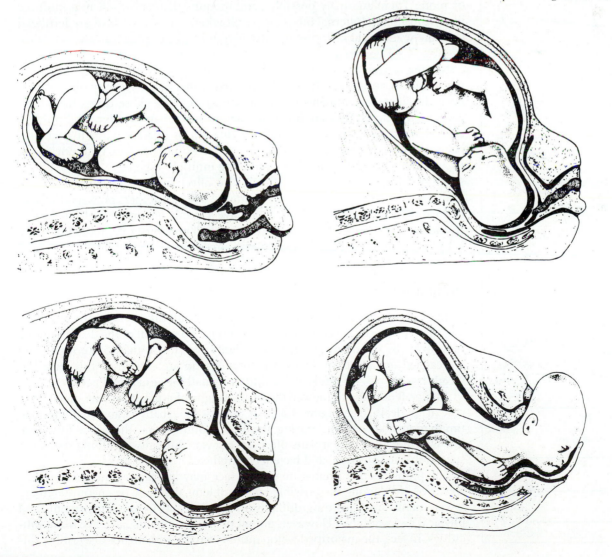

SHOULDER PRESENTATION
During birth, the presentation of the shoulder first, rather than the head.

PREMATURE INFANT
An infant who weighs less than 5.5 pounds at birth and who was carried less than 37 weeks.

FIGURE 4.2

Fraternal offspring result when two or more ova are fertilized separately. Identical offspring result when one zygote splits, or fissions, into two identical zygotes.

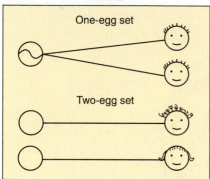

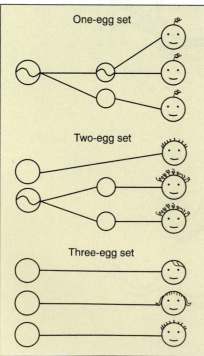

During a breech birth, great care must be taken to avoid damage to the baby's head, which is the largest part of the infant's body and thus has the most difficulty passing through the birth canal. An even more rare occurrence is the **shoulder presentation**. This occurs in only 1 birth out of 200.

If there is a serious problem during birth, or if the woman's obstetrician decides it is necessary for other reasons, the baby may be removed from the uterus by cesarean section. In this procedure, the mother's abdomen is opened surgically and the baby is removed without passing through the vaginal canal. The surgical incision is then closed, as with any other abdominal incision.

The Third Stage

Following the exit of the infant, the third stage of labor occurs, during which the placenta is expelled. The placenta and material expelled during this stage are called the *afterbirth*.

Multiple Births

Sometimes the newborn has company—a twin brother or sister. Sometimes, although less often, the newborn is just one of a crowd—triplets, quadruplets, or more. There are many possible combinations that can result in a multiple birth. In general, fraternal offspring result when two or more ova are fertilized separately; identical offspring result when one zygote splits into two identical zygotes (see Figure 4.2).

No one is quite certain what causes a zygote to split. Researchers are coming closer to an answer, however, and drugs that can trigger twinning have been developed (Kaufman & O'Shea, 1978). Because these drugs have dangerous side effects, they are not available for other than experimental purposes. Certain drugs designed to induce ovulation in infertile women have also been implicated in multiple births. They often stimulate more than one ovum to mature in a single cycle, thus producing multiple zygotes.

Other factors besides fertility drugs also affect the probability of having a multiple birth. Such a birth is more common among mothers between the ages of 35 and 39 and among mothers who have a family history of multiple births. In addition, the more children a woman has had previously, the more likely she is to have a multiple birth in her current pregnancy.

Premature Birth

In the United States, approximately 7 percent of all infants are born weighing less than 5.5 pounds. These infants account for 65 percent of the deaths among newborns. By definition, **premature infants** weigh less than 5.5 pounds and are carried for less than 37 weeks. Infants who are carried to full term but weigh less than 5.5 pounds are said to be "small for gestational age."

As a general rule, the lower the birth weight of a newborn, the greater the risk of its death (see Figure 4.3). An underweight baby is approximately 40 times more likely to die during the first month of life than is a full-term, full-weight baby. These infants often have severe difficulty breathing, are more susceptible to infection, and have feeble reflexes.

The problems that premature infants face may last far beyond the first few weeks of life. Among the possible later problems that may be encountered are lower intelligence, learning difficulties, hearing and vision impairment, and physical awkwardness. However, not all premature infants have eventual difficulties; in fact, the majority develop quite normally and are not discernibly dif-

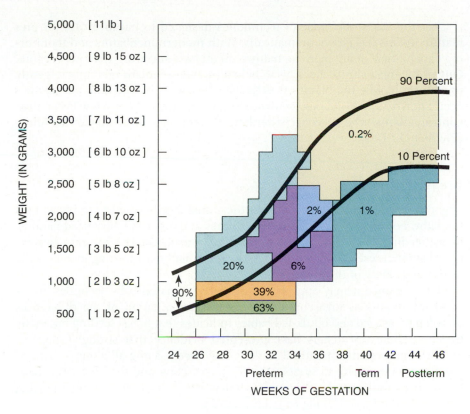

FIGURE 4.3

Neonatal mortality risk by birth weight and gestational age based on 14,413 live births at the University of Colorado Health Sciences Center during 1974–1980. As you can see, infants who were carried full term and who weighed at least 6 pounds (2,725 grams) had the lowest mortality rate (0.2 percent). The mortality rate began to increase dramatically among infants whose birth weight was lower or whose gestation was shorter. Eighty percent of all babies born fell between the 90 percent and 10 percent curves on the graph. (SOURCE: Koops, Morgan, & Battaglia, 1982, p. 972)

ferent from their full-term peers (Cohen & Parmelee, 1983; Roscissano & Yatchmink, 1983).

One of the best ways to prevent premature deliveries is to promote good prenatal care. Expectant mothers who have access to good medical care are less likely to have a premature or underweight baby. Moreover, drugs have been developed to prevent premature deliveries. These drugs prolong pregnancy by relaxing the uterus and postponing labor. According to clinical studies, these medications may help reduce deaths or complications caused by premature birth.

Incubators help provide a carefully controlled and monitored environment for premature infants and those born with life-threatening disorders.

NEONATE
A newborn infant.

Over the years, the range of techniques designed to improve care for premature infants has grown dramatically. With modern incubators and monitoring capabilities, many more premature infants are surviving than ever before. One of the most surprising ways to help a premature infant is simply to gently touch and handle the infant. As little as 45 minutes of touching per day has been shown to help infants in incubators gain weight 47 percent faster than control infants who received stimulation other than touching or handling (Field et al., 1986).

Breast Feeding

One of the first decisions the new mother must face is whether to breast feed her baby. For many years in the United States and other industrialized nations, breast feeding was considered "not modern." During the last 25 years, however, substantial research has supported the idea that breast feeding increases the health and safety of the infant.

At first glance it may appear that properly prepared baby formulas are as good for infants as breast milk, but careful examination of the differences between breast-fed and bottle-fed babies indicates that breast feeding has many benefits. Some researchers have presented evidence that strongly supports what the proponents of natural nursing have been saying all along—that our species did not evolve in symbiosis with Jersey cows and that denying a baby its mother's milk may be denying it vital nutrients as well as antibodies that help to fight disease (Jelliffe & Jelliffe, 1977).

Using complex chemical analysis, the Jelliffes demonstrated, that except for water and lactose, human and cow milk have little in common. Even the attempts at making formulas did not go far enough. For example, human milk had higher levels of the amino acids taurine and cystine than the formulas did. Taurine is absorbed by the infant's brain and plays a crucial role in neural development. Also, mothers who have premature infants generally produce milk with a high protein and fat content, which is valuable to the low-weight infant. It's as though the mother's body adjusts itself to the specific needs of the infant.

Human milk also contains a wide range of resistance factors. White blood cells pass directly from the mother's milk into the infant's intestine, where they confer immunity against many organisms that might cause gastrointestinal infections. These infections are a major cause of infant mortality throughout the world (Short, 1984). Human breast milk also kills intestinal parasites that formulas and cow's milk do not affect (Gillin, Reiner, & Wang, 1983). Breast-fed children are less likely to develop food allergies (Bellanti, 1984), coughs, respiratory difficulties, and diarrhea (Palti, Mansbach, Pridan, Adler, & Palti, 1984) than are bottle-fed ones. Furthermore, breast-fed babies may be less prone to subsequent obesity (Kramer, 1981). In addition to the health and safety advantages it confers, breast feeding may help to establish closer and more affectionate mother-infant ties (Marano, 1979).

In summary, one report concluded that unless the mother's breast milk is suspected of being contaminated by either environmental toxins or disease, it probably is best to breast feed the infant (Coveney, 1985).

Most research shows that breast feeding provides important nutrients and resistance to disease not provided by formulas.

THE NEWBORN INFANT

If you are among the many people who are unfamiliar with **neonates** (newborn infants), if your first reaction to a woman's labor pains is to boil water, or if you've never thought it odd that in old Hollywood movies the delivery room nurse always hands the mother a 40-pound "newborn" possessing a crew cut and a full set of teeth, then you probably would be surprised by the appearance of a real newborn baby.

Real newborn infants (as opposed to the old Hollywood variety) have skin that is soft, dry, and wrinkled. They typically weigh between 6 and 9 pounds and are about 20 inches in length. The newborn's head may seem huge in proportion to the rest of its body, as it is responsible for fully one-fourth of the baby's length. The neonate may appear chinless (which may strike parents as strange because the infant may seem to resemble no other member of the family). In addition, the neonate's forehead is high, its nose is flat, and when it cries, its body turns crimson. Although its eyes may eventually be brown or green or gray, most neonates' eyes are steely blue.

The Apgar and Brazelton Assessments of Neonates

One of the first tasks the health-care team performs when the baby is born is to assess the baby's current physical state. The Apgar Assessment Scale (see Table 4.1) is typically administered to all infants 1 minute after delivery and again after 5 minutes. The scale, devised by Virginia Apgar, measures heart rate, reflex irritability (by facial expression), muscle tone, breathing, and body skin color (Apgar, 1953). Each of the five scales may be rated as 0, 1, or 2; the maximum score is 2 for each of the five scales, for a total of 10 points. A score of 7 or higher is typically obtained by 90 percent of all infants. Generally, an infant with a score of 4 or less is in need of immediate medical assistance. The Apgar score is a fairly good indicator of later neurological or muscular difficulties. A high percentage of infants found to have neuromuscular or developmental problems by 1 year of age had low Apgar scores at birth.

The Brazelton Neonatal Behavioral Assessment Scale (Brazelton, 1973) is also a valuable and popular assessment device. It yields scores on 27 nine-point behavioral scales and 17 reflex scales. The assessment also includes such things as the infant's response to a human voice or face and to being touched or cuddled. The Brazelton scale is more difficult and time consuming to administer than the Apgar is, but it is especially valuable in assessing which infants may need special care and what kind of care they require.

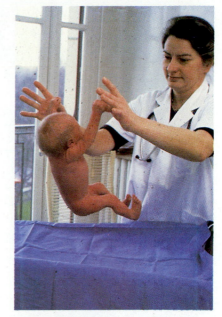

One of the first tasks the health-care team performs when the baby is born is to test its current physical state.

Table 4.1 ◉ Apgar's Scoring Chart for Newborn Infants*			
	SCORE**		
SIGN	0	1	2
Heart rate	Absent	Slow (<100)	>100
Respiratory effort	Absent	Weak cry; hypoventilation	Good, strong cry
Muscle tone	Limp	Some flexion of extremities	Well flexed
Reflex irritability (response of skin stimulation to feet)	No response	Some motion	Cry
Color	Blue; pale	Body pink; extremities blue	Completely pink

*Evaluation 60 seconds after complete birth of infant disregarding the cord and placenta.
**A total score of 10 indicates infant in best possible condition.
Source: Apgar, Holaday, James, Weisbrot, & Berrien, 1958, p. 1988.

REFLEXES
A simple innate response to an eliciting stimulus.

A Competent Individual?

Among most researchers, from the turn of the century until the 1950s, the newborn was considered to be a helpless creature who was handed to the world like a lump of clay ready to be molded and shaped. The newborn was not thought to be competent in any sense of the word. Babies in general were considered to be helpless and *passive*. They cried, they wet, they ate, they slept, they possessed some simple reflexes, and that was about it.

However, during the 1960s and 1970s, there was a sudden surge of research concerning the capabilities of infants. Researchers found, for instance, that throughout infancy, babies initiate social interactions and play an active role in maintaining and developing their parents' responses (Restak, 1982). This sociability begins only moments after the infant is out of the womb. Newborns will look about, and they will turn their heads in response to a voice as though they are searching for its source. Newborns seem especially attracted to faces and show an interest in them. This behavior, in turn, helps to initiate reciprocal interest from the person receiving the infant's gaze (see Figure 4.4). As you read more about newborns, you may be surprised to find how many interesting abilities and competencies they have.

The Neonate's Repertoire of Reflexes

A large number of **reflexes** can be elicited in newborns (see Table 4.2). It can safely be assumed that these reflexes are unlearned and are a result of the child's "nature," because all healthy neonates exhibit them.

Many reflexes apparently evolved because they have a survival value. Coughing, sucking, blinking, crying, and rooting all help the neonate survive. These reflexes are built in; they are needed immediately.

The common assumption about reflexes that don't seem to have any survival value is that they once served a function. When our evolutionary ancestors carried their children, the grasp reflex may have helped babies cling to their mother's hair. A Moro reflex (the extension of the arms on sudden loss of sup-

Human newborns have soft, dry, wrinkled skin. They usually weigh between 6 and 9 pounds and are about 20 inches in length. The neonate's head accounts for one-quarter its entire length. In addition, the neonate's forehead is high and its nose is flat.

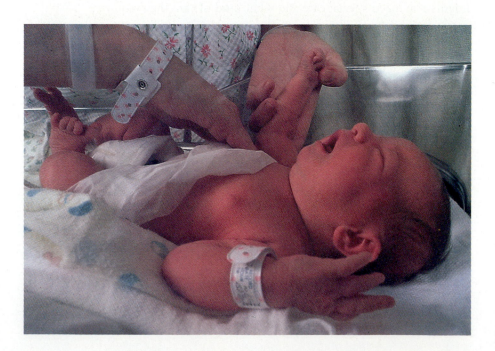

FIGURE 4.4

Newborns seem especially attracted to faces. This facilitates early social interaction between infants and their caregivers.

port) in such a baby may have had the advantage of preventing spinning in a fall, thereby allowing for a more controlled drop and landing. Of course, human mothers don't rely on the ability of their babies to cling to their hair (and quickly learn to keep their hair away from baby's surprisingly powerful grip), and dropping from almost any height would be more than a newborn could handle—spinning or not! It seems likely that many of these reflexes have outlived their usefulness in human beings but continue to exist simply because the environment has never selected against them.

Table 4.2 ● Selected Neonatal Reflexes

REFLEX	ELICITING STIMULUS	RESPONSE	DEVELOPMENTAL DURATION
Babinski	Gentle stroke along sole of foot from heel to toe	Toes fan out, big toe flexes	Disappears by end of first year
Babkin	Pressure applied to both palms while baby is lying on its back	Eyes close and mouth opens; head returns to center position	Disappears in 3–4 months
Blink	Flash of light or puff of air delivered to eyes	Both eyelids close	Permanent
Diving	Sudden splash of cold water in the face	Heart rate decelerates, blood shunts to brain and heart	Becomes progressively weaker with age
Knee jerk	Tap on patellar tendon	Knee kicks	Permanent
Moro	Sudden loss of support	Arms extend, then are brought toward each other; lower extremities are extended	Disappears in about 6 months
Palmar grasp	Rod or finger pressed against infant's palm	Baby grasps object	Disappears in 3–4 months
Rage	Both hands placed on side of alert infant's head and its movement restrained; infant's mouth blocked with cheesecloth or covered for 10 seconds	Baby cries and struggles	Disappears in 2–4 months
Rooting	Object lightly brushed across infant's cheek	Baby turns toward object and attempts to suck	Disappears in 3–4 months
Sucking	Finger or nipple inserted 2 inches into infant's mouth	Rhythmic sucking	Disappears in 3–4 months
Walking	Baby is held upright and soles of feet are placed on hard surface; baby is tipped slightly forward	Infant steps forward as if walking	Disappears in 2–3 months

MYELIN SHEATH
A white fatty covering on neural fibers that serves to channel and increase the transmission speed of impulses along those fibers.

EXPERIENCE-EXPECTANT SYSTEM
A neural model of the central nervous system that pictures the CNS as containing structures that are prepared, or "prewired," to rapidly respond to, or make sense of, experiences that are common to all members of the species. The portion of the CNS that is not experience-dependent.

EXPERIENCE-DEPENDENT SYSTEM
A neural model of the central nervous system that pictures the CNS as containing structures that are flexible and prepared to incorporate information that is unique to each individual member of a species. The portion of the CNS that is not experience-expectant.

The Nervous System of the Neonate

As you might expect, the nervous system of the newborn is less developed than your own. The readouts from an electroencephalogram (EEG), which measures electrical brain activity, may appear to be quite immature in newborns (Berg & Berg, 1979). The newborn's nervous system is still growing. The dendrites (parts of the neuron, or nerve cell, that help to receive and sometimes send nerve messages) are noticeably immature in newborns. Interestingly, newborns have many *more* neurons than adults! As the infant grows and gains experience, neurons not needed are eliminated in a whittling-down process. Some researchers have estimated that neurons in infants are eliminated at a rate of 2 per second (Miller, 1985).

The central structures of the newborn's brain are noticeably immature (Berg & Berg, 1979). In addition, autopsies of newborns have revealed that portions of neurons of the central nervous system, down which neural messages typically travel, are not yet myelinated (Morell & Norton, 1980). That is, there is not yet full development of the **myelin sheath**, a white fatty substance that grows around many of the neural axons in a person's body. Myelin acts as an insulator and aids in nerve conductivity. It also helps provide nutrition for the nerve cells. Without the proper amount of myelin, your body would be incapable of many functions, such as crawling or bowel and bladder control. In fact, the crippling disease multiple sclerosis, which strikes many young adults each year, involves the scarring of the myelin sheath, resulting in weakness and lack of coordination (Bailey, 1975).

To a degree, infants lack strength or coordination because they have an immature nervous system. A great deal of the infant's maturation can be directly tied to a rigid timetable of neural growth (Chugani & Phelps, 1986). For example, it has been observed that human infants, regardless of their culture, begin to smile at about the same age, an occurrence that may be directly related to the amount of myelin that the infant possesses. Some nerve fiber systems develop myelin rapidly, while others take more time. In fact, some parts of the brain aren't fully myelinated until the child reaches puberty.

It is difficult to compare a newborn's nervous system with an adult's. It is harder to study the organization of an entire nervous system than it is to study the structure of individual neurons. The evidence we do have, however, suggests that the organization of the newborn's nervous system is very different from that of an adult's (see At Issue).

THE BASIC SENSORY ABILITIES OF THE INFANT

We know that infants can see, hear, taste, smell, and react to touch. But exactly how developed are these senses at birth? How does learning affect them? What sensory changes take place as the infant develops?

As students soon discover, no overall philosophy encompasses sensory research. From the researcher's viewpoint, the question is which specific sensory area to investigate with whatever techniques are at hand or can be developed. Most of the research is basic, and much of it is serendipitous.

Vision

It was once commonly thought that infants were born blind. It has since been determined that although infants don't see as well as adults, they *can* see. The

AT ISSUE

Are Two Brains Better Than One?

Sensing and perceiving are activities that you and I do without thinking. You see an object and know that it is red and round. You hear a sound and know that it came from behind you. Your friend touches your hand, and you feel the touch. All this is possible because of the way in which your nervous system is organized. The organization of your nervous system also determines how you think and reason; within its organization is held all that you know and believe.

But how much neural organization was already in place at the time of your birth? Was any of it present? Or was there only neural chaos at first, unstructured and unformed, to be shaped only at a later time by your learning and experience? These very questions have interested philosophers for centuries. Much of the work concerning perception that you will read about in this chapter is rooted in philosophical nature-nurture debates. For instance, are we born with the ability to perceive depth, or is it acquired through experience?

Research with humans has shown that in most situations, neither philosophical position is totally correct. In other words, both views are partly right. This conclusion is the result of many years of perceptual research and, more recently, a better understanding of how the central nervous system (CNS) is organized.

There appear to be two separate organizational systems in the newborn's brain (Greenough, Black, & Wallace, 1987). The first organizational system is called the **experience-expectant system**. Through evolution, the experience-expectant system is, to a degree, "prewired," which enables it to make quick sense of aspects of the environment that are common to all members of the species. This does not mean that learning and experience are never involved in this system, only that certain perceptions or actions are very likely to be acquired quickly and with little or perhaps no learning necessary.

Infants actually have more brain neurons (nerve cells) than they will eventually possess as adults (Greenough, Black, & Wallace, 1987). In an experience-expectant system, some neurons will become stronger, while others will remain unstrengthened. The unstrengthened neurons are weeded out of the infant's central nervous system; that is, they die, leaving behind a certain organization of living neurons.

Whether a neuron in this system is strengthened or left to die appears to depend on the infant's exposure to certain stimuli, presumably the common stimuli all healthy babies are likely to encounter (e.g., an edge, a round thing, a figure with a background, the sound of a human voice, or the feel of something smooth). As long as the necessary stimulation is encountered, the experience-expectant neural system will rapidly develop to deal with it.

You may wonder what happens if the necessary stimulation is not received. But remember, we are talking here about stimulation common to all healthy members of a species, not some particular personal experience, so such failures would be quite rare. However, researchers may have answered this question in the laboratory. Through experiments aimed at improving our understanding of blindness and sight, researchers have shown that if animals are denied certain visual experiences during a critical period early in their development, such as the chance to see a vertical edge, they often fail to recover the denied function. In contrast, such deprivation in an adult animal rarely has any long-term effect. It is assumed, then, that exposure to certain phenomena is needed for the experience-expectant system to develop, but that once the system is in place, it is pretty well set.

Interestingly, some computers have even been developed along these same lines. Unlike most computers, these machines have no built-in memory. Instead, the computer strengthens or weakens its circuits based on the experiences it encounters. Computers like these, which learn from experience, are even called neural networks by computer designers because they mimic the hypothesized human experience-expectant system (Allman, 1986).

The second system is called the **experience-dependent system**. In this system, we see the active formation or loss of neural connections throughout the life span in response to experiences. Infants, therefore, will acquire these connections slowly over time as the result of learning and experience and will continue this process throughout life. It is interesting to note that until recently, it was believed that neural connections were pretty well set by adulthood and that any additional changes were the result of the strengthening or weakening of fixed connections. But a growing body of evidence suggests that the creation of completely new neural connections and the disconnection of old neural links are ongoing lifelong processes in response to experience (Reynolds & Weiss, 1992). "Use it or lose it" is a phrase often heard today among brain scientists.

Apparently, the experience-dependent system is needed because the infant's development could not be handled solely by the experience-expectant system. There are too many personal experiences that individuals are likely to encounter in life (e.g., the language they speak, the customs they learn, the books they read). If the brain ever evolved so as to be expectant of every possible experience that a person might encounter (rather than just the ones that all people come across), we would face some rather odd problems. For instance, we might need a 500-pound brain at birth just to hold the neurons required for the monumental lifelong

(Continued next page)

AT ISSUE

Are Two Brains Better Than One? Continued

weeding-out process that such an experience-expectant system would require—lifelong because people are always being exposed to something new. Needless to say, the head needed to hold such a brain would make a cesarean section something of a requirement, would make nodding "yes" a dangerous activity, and would put hats out of the economic reach of most people.

Whether our depiction of what's going on inside the infant's brain is correct remains to be seen. Research will

certainly find it to be more complex than described here. Already there is much agreement that both experience-expectant and experience-dependent systems overlap to a considerable degree, and whether a neural system is experience-expectant or experience-dependent is seen more as a tendency than as a rigid mode of operation. Whatever we discover, it's bound to increase our understanding of infants and all human development.

average 2-week-old neonate has a visual acuity of 20/800 (Fantz, Ordy, & Udelf, 1962)?*

When you have your eyes checked, the examiner can ask you for feedback about what you see. From your answer, the acuity of your vision can be determined. But 2-week-old infants can't give verbal feedback. You can't ask an infant to cover one eye and read the chart! Thus, determining that a newborn's vision is 20/800 is an interesting task. The only responses that can be examined in an infant so young are reflexes or behavior such as sucking or head turning. A reflex is used to determine a neonate's visual acuity. When a series of fine vertical stripes is passed before a neonate's eyes, a reflex can be elicited. The reflex occurs because the eyes reflexively attempt to focus on each stripe that moves through the visual field. If the black vertical lines on the white paper are made finer and finer, the paper will eventually appear gray. Researchers investigating the infant's visual acuity simply continue to use finer gradations of striping until the reflex no longer occurs because the neonate can no longer sense the individual stripes. In this way, visual acuity can be determined.

There's no way of asking newborns if it bothers them that their view of the world is so blurry. We do know, however, that just like you and me, young infants do like to have as clear an image as possible. Infants 1 to 3 months old will learn to operate the focus on a projector to make the picture clearer (Kalnins & Bruner, 1973). The focus is connected directly to a nipple and arranged so that appropriate sucking rates will focus the blurred picture. We also know that infants are sensitive to changes in brightness, that they can detect movement as early as 2 or 3 days after birth (Haith, 1966; Finlay & Ivinskis, 1984), and that they have the capacity to follow a moving object within the first few days of life (Greenman, 1963).

It is generally agreed that visual acuity improves rapidly and comes within adult ranges at about 6 months to 1 year of age. Visual acuity of 20/20 is considered good, but whether an infant ever has 20/20 vision depends a great deal on the genes that determine the eventual shape of the infant's eyes. Remember that there are always individual differences among infants or, for that matter,

*An adult with 20/800 vision would be able to identify from a distance of 20 feet a letter that a person with good vision (20/20) could identify from a distance of 800 feet. Needless to say, if your vision were 20/800, you'd need glasses just to find the front door. Fortunately, by 5 or 6 months, the infant's vision has usually improved to about 20/70.

people in general. Some infants may develop 20/20 vision by 6 months of age, while others never attain that level of acuity. Some children or adults may even have superior vision of 20/15.

Such differences appear to be due to the fact that much of an infant's eventual sensory ability depends directly on inheritance. This is also true for other species. A falcon typically has a visual acuity of 20/1! This means that from a distance of 20 feet away, a falcon could respond to a dot on the wall that you couldn't see until you were within at least 1 foot of the wall. Of course, through evolutionary necessity, superior visual acuity has been naturally selected for in falcons. In evolutionary terms, humans never needed that degree of visual acuity. (When was the last time you had to get your dinner by diving from a great height to snatch a running field mouse?)

As a general rule, infant senses continue to become more refined and sensitive during the first 2 to 6 months of development (Acredolo & Hake, 1982).

Depth Perception. About 35 years ago, Gibson and Walk (1960) constructed a device known as the **visual cliff** (see Figure 4.5). Infant animals, including humans, are placed on the center board between the shallow and the deep sides. Glass covers the surface and prevents any creature from actually falling off the cliff.

Baby animals of many species were tested on the cliff, and the results demonstrated that they possessed innate depth perception. Newborn chicks, whose first visual experience was on the cliff, refused to cross onto the deep side. Kittens, puppies, piglets, and various other infant animals also refused to venture onto the deep end. Baby mountain goats (a species that would have an exceptional reason for possessing a strong cliff-edge avoidance) similarly refused to venture onto the deep side, and if pushed in that direction, collapsed their front legs beneath themselves. Gibson and Walk, along with many other researchers, also demonstrated that human infants were much more easily coaxed onto the shallow side than onto the deep side (although some infants were willing to crawl onto the deep side).

VISUAL CLIFF
An apparatus constructed to study depth perception in humans and other animals. It consists of a center board resting on a glass table. On one side of the board, a checkered surface is visible directly beneath the glass; on the other side, the surface is several feet below the glass, thus giving the impression of a drop-off.

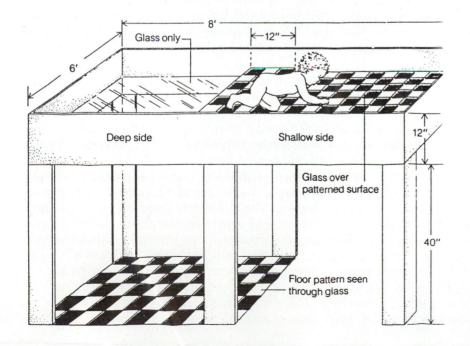

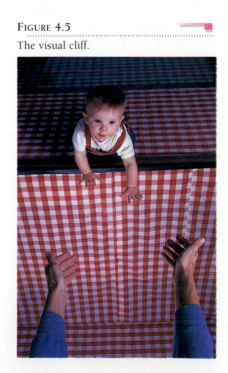

FIGURE 4.5

The visual cliff.

Although infants' visual acuity is limited, it improves rapidly and comes within adult ranges at about 6 months to 1 year of age.

Unfortunately, the results of research with humans were not as clear-cut as with other species. Unlike baby chicks, kittens, or mountain goats, human infants aren't precocious in terms of motor development. Infants are typically unable to crawl (a prerequisite for testing cliff avoidance) until they are about 6 months old. One report suggested that by the time human infants are tested on the visual cliff, they have already *learned* to avoid drop-offs (Campos, Hiatt, Ramsay, Henderson, & Svejda, 1978).

An interesting method called **looming** was developed by researchers who hoped to measure depth perception without requiring the baby to crawl. In this procedure, a large object, such as a bull's-eye target, is rushed directly at a seated infant's face (Bower, Broughton, & Moore, 1970). When this happens, many infants, some as young as 3 to 6 weeks, show what seems to be a defensive reaction by pulling their heads backward as though they were trying to avoid an imminent collision. This reaction appears to indicate an early competence in depth perception (Ball & Dibble, 1980).

Pattern and Form Perception.   Infants can perceive shapes and patterns. In some experiments, even newborn babies were found to discriminate readily between triangles, squares, crosses, and circles (Slater, Morison, & Rose, 1983). Newborns are also able to make even finer visual discriminations and can differentiate between small circles that contain subtly different arrangements of dots (Antell, Caron, & Myers, 1985).

As children become older, their scanning of internal features and objects becomes more complex and detailed. By the age of 3 months, infants show a marked preference for viewing faces (Dannemiller & Stephens, 1988) (see Figure 4.6). Surprisingly, infants even show a preference for the faces of adults and infants whom raters have scored as attractive over the faces of those considered less attractive (Langlois, Ritter, Roggman, & Vaughn, 1991)! This is especially interesting because it had always been assumed that a preference for attractiveness was the result of gradual exposure to cultural forces such as peers, parents, or television. This study, however, points to the possibility of an innate factor in the appreciation of aesthetic beauty or perhaps that there is a preference for some sort of facial symmetry, curvature, or angle that is associated with attractiveness.

By 1 month of age, infants apparently acquire enough information to be able to discriminate between their mother's face and a stranger's (Maurer & Salapatek, 1976). By about 6 or 7 months of age, infants are clearly able to distinguish individuals by their faces (Caron, Caron, & Myers, 1982).

Audition

An infant's sense of hearing is functional prior to birth (Birnholz & Benacerraf, 1983). Many pregnant women have reported that their unborn babies seem to move in response to loud sounds, such as car horns or running bath water. Also, as mentioned in the Chapter Preview, the infant might well be listening to its mother's voice while still in the womb.

As in the case of vision, auditory sensory abilities are tested by examining the infant's responses to different stimuli. For instance, changes in an infant's heart rate will occur when the baby is exposed to sudden alterations of pitch or volume.

Immediately following birth, the newborn's auditory canals often are filled with fluid. Because of this, the newborn's hearing for the first couple of days may be slightly impaired. After the second or third day, however, the neonate's hearing appears to be quite efficient. In fact, audition is initially dominant to vision (which, as you recall, takes about 6 months to reach optimal levels of performance). Supporting this is the evidence that up until about the age of 6 months, infants show greater responsiveness to auditory stimuli than they do to visual stimuli (Lewkowicz, 1988). As a general rule, auditory sensitivity improves continuously from infancy through the preschool period and well into the school years (Trehub, Schneider, Morrongiello, & Thorpe, 1988). Keep in mind, too, that auditory sensitivity can also decrease over the life span. For instance, many older adults do not hear as well as schoolchildren.

Some of the most exciting research in this area includes the findings that newborns are specifically reactive to human voices and to vowel sounds (Clarkson & Berg, 1983). This may indicate a genetic predisposition favoring the sound of the human voice—especially the kinds of sounds later needed for language.

Auditory Perception. Consider the fact that when you hear a sound, you actually sense it twice, once in each ear. Although you *perceive* the sound as occurring only once, you use the difference in the time it takes the two sounds to reach you to localize the source (unless the source is equally distant from

LOOMING
A technique to measure depth perception in infants and animals. A target, usually a bull's-eye, is rushed toward a seated subject's face. Head retraction is taken as a sign that the subject expects collision—an indication of depth perception, as the subject must be assuming that the object is coming nearer.

FIGURE 4.6

These computer-generated faces and patterns were used to test the preference that 3-month-olds have for viewing faces. Unlike earlier studies, this study incorporated the use of computer-generated images instead of photographs of real faces. In the past, when photographs of real faces were used (Fantz, 1961), it was argued that the preference that infants showed for viewing the faces might really be only a preference for contrast or complexity rather than a preference for the human face. To control for these other variables, the computer-generated faces shown in this figure were developed. The infant has a choice of other forms (C and D) that are as complex as the faces (A and B). If high contrast is important, then face A should be preferred to the negative face B. The experiment showed, however, an equal preference for faces A and B over shapes C and D, indicating that it was, in fact, the aspect of "human face" that infants found attractive (SOURCE: Dannemiller & Stephens, 1988, p. 212)

CROSS-MODAL TRANSFER
A recognition of an object as familiar when perceived with a sense other than that previously used when exposed to the object.

both ears). In other words, although your senses send two messages at different times to your brain, you perceive only one sound—but are able to localize it.

There is only one way to find out if this ability is innate; make a sound to one side of a newborn and see if the infant attempts to respond in the direction of the sound. This is what Michael Wertheimer did. He tested a newborn girl in a delivery room by sounding a clicker to the right side and then to the left side of the infant. The baby responded by turning to the right when the clicker sound came from the right, and to the left when the sound came from the left. Wertheimer was surprised to discover that the infant also looked in the direction of the sound, as though she expected to see something! Just seconds after birth, the newborn's visual and auditory senses already were integrated (Wertheimer, 1961). Similar results have been confirmed under more stringent testing conditions (Muir & Field, 1979).

As infants develop, their ability to localize the source of a sound steadily improves (Morrongiello, Fenwick, & Chance, 1990). By 6 months of age, a baby can orient its head toward the source of a sound with no more than a 12-degree error, and by 18 months, the error is reduced to a very small angle of only 4 degrees (Morrongiello, 1988). This is all the more amazing when you consider that as the infant grows, its head size enlarges, making the distance between the ears greater and greater. This means that the infant's brain has to continuously recalibrate the meaning of the time delay between receiving a sound in one ear and receiving it in the other (Clifton, Gwiazda, Bauer, Clarkson, & Held, 1988)! By the age of 7 months, infants sitting in the dark are also able to tell whether an object making noise is within their grasp or too far away to reach (Clifton, Perris, & Bullinger, 1991). Again, this is accomplished by perceiving the angle made between the object making the sound and the ears. Near objects yield wider angles than distant ones, and they are also louder.

Cross-Modal Transfer

Other evidence of sensory integration has been obtained from research on older infants (about 6 months of age), who demonstrated what has been called **cross-modal transfer**. In a typical cross-modal transfer experiment, an infant is allowed to touch and handle, but not to see, a particular object. Then this object and a new object with which the infant has never had contact are presented *visually*. Infants typically will pay the most attention to objects that are new to them. Once they have become familiar with an object, that is, once they have become habituated to it, they will respond less often. Infants as young as 6 months of age often pay less attention to the object they are seeing for the first time but have felt before! This implies that the infant can recognize the object visually from tactile contact with it (Rose, Gottfried, & Bridger, 1981; Ruff, 1980). Another study found evidence that infants of only 4 months of age possess certain forms of cross-modal transfer (Mendelson & Ferland, 1982).

It is believed that cross-modal transfer is based on an experience-expectant rather than an experience-dependent neurological system. This belief is based on the fact that it is very difficult to teach infants *unusual* cross-modal associations (Bahrick, 1988), such as the volume of a sound being inversely proportional to its distance (the closer a sound source gets, the harder it becomes to hear). And yet, infants do clearly show many cross-modal transfers, demonstrating that perceptual associations found in the real world (as opposed to unusual ones found only in a laboratory) are often easily acquired. Also, cross-modal transfer is readily acquired by other species, such as apes (Savage-Rumbaugh, Sevcik, & Hopkins, 1988), implying a fairly broad natural selective process favoring the acquisition of such perceptions. In fact, monkeys that show poor cross-modal transfer are also more likely to show poor cognitive development when they are older (Gunderson, Rose, & Grant-Webster, 1990). With this in mind, researchers are currently investigating cross-modal transfer tests in children as a possible predictor of later cognitive and intellectual development.

Olfaction

The sense of smell is well developed in the newborn (Rovee, Cohen, & Shlapack, 1975). To measure the infant's reaction to odors, an infant polygraph, called a *stabilimeter*, is typically used. The stabilimeter measures the infant's breathing rate and also may measure heart rate, blood pressure, or changes in the electrical potential on the surface of the skin. As cotton swabs dipped in various substances are passed under the infant's nose, any bodily reaction to the presence of an odor will be detected by the stabilimeter. Researchers have discovered that infants are able to sense the odors that adults can sense; odors that adults can't smell, infants can't smell either. In fact, infants have such a well-developed sense of smell that they are capable of some very subtle discriminations (Steiner, 1977; Steiner & Finnegan, 1975; Rovee, 1972).

Infants often express the same likes and dislikes for odors that adults express, but not always. Babies don't seem to dislike some odors that adults generally hate (a full diaper is one example). But by about the age of 3, the odor preferences of children and adults are found to be remarkably alike (Schmidt & Beauchamp, 1988).

Taste

The stabilimeter is also used to measure the infant's sense of taste. We know that infants appear to respond to the four basic tastes to which adults respond (sweet, sour, salty, and bitter), because scientists have found that neonates can discriminate between sugar, lemon juice, salt, and quinine (Cowart, 1981; Harris, Thomas, & Booth, 1990).

Sweet is especially preferred by infants. The presence of sweetness can even have a soothing effect. In one study, for example, newborns from whom blood was drawn for testing were soothed by the administration of a few drops of sweetened water. These newborns cried less in the presence of the sweet water than matched infants who were given either a pacifier or unsweetened water (Smith, Fillion, & Blass, 1990). By the time children are 4 or 5 years old, they often show a preference for salty foods as well as sweet foods. Whether children will eventually develop a desire for extra sugar or salt on their food is very dependent on their early experience. Children who are given extra salt or sugar tend to desire the levels to which they have become accustomed (Sullivan & Birch, 1990). Parents who may wish to teach their children to use less salt or sugar should therefore eliminate early overexposure to salt or sugar. Of course, since just about every snack food in America is loaded with one or the other, keeping preschoolers from eating too much salt or sugar is quite a feat!

Although parents often assume that an infant's appreciation of food is due to a well-developed sense of taste, with the exception of an early attraction to sweet (Pratt, 1954; Engen, Lipsitt, & Peck, 1974), most of the infant's enjoyment of food is due to the sense of smell. It is the same for adults. If you plug your nose and close your eyes, you'll be unable to discriminate between pieces of onion, raw potato, and raw apple!

Infants make pleasant or unpleasant facial expressions in the presence of pleasant or unpleasant odors. These expressions occur even in infants whose higher cortical brain areas have been damaged, indicating that this kind of facial expression does not require higher cortical processing. For this reason, some researchers have referred to such odor-induced expressions as nasofacial reflexes (Steiner, 1973).

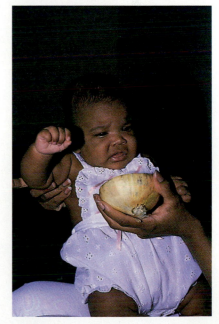

DISTINCTIVE FEATURE
That portion of an object that can be discriminated from other portions.

Touch

Touch really includes many senses. There are different neural receptors for heat, warmth, cold, dull pain, sharp pain, deep pressure, vibration, and light touch, and there are even some receptors that fire only when a touch stimulus starts or stops (Miller, 1983). Most research involving touch in infants involves eliciting reflexes such as those discussed early in this chapter (the Babinski reflex or the palmar grasp reflex, for instance). It has been demonstrated that full-term newborns are sensitive to strong tactile stimulation (Lamper & Eisdorfer, 1971) as well as to mild stimulation (Yang & Douthitt, 1974). Newborns are also sensitive to electric shock (Lipsitt & Levy, 1959) and pain (Sherman & Sherman, 1925). Furthermore, female infants tend to be more sensitive to touch than are males (female adults also are more sensitive to touch than are male adults) (Pick & Pick, 1970).

Even though touch may have great importance, especially in a social sense, "minor senses" such as touch tend to receive little research attention, generally because they are overshadowed by work on vision or hearing. As a result, what you usually discover in reviewing the research on touch are lots of interesting bits of information that no one has really tried to fit into any kind of overall picture. For example, in one study, researchers gave 6-month-olds a vial of warmed colored liquid and let them handle it until they became bored with it. Then a warmed vial of a different-colored liquid was presented. The infants showed little renewed interest. However, when the original vial was presented at a different temperature, the infants acted as though they had received a completely novel stimulus (Bushnell, Shaw, & Strauss, 1985). This shows that for 6-month-olds, anyway, a slight temperature difference can be of overriding interest, even more so than a visual change.

When trying to relate such findings to the broader context of human development, we need to remember that research on the sensory system of the neonate is often basic and serendipitous. Explanations are often not yet available and may require a greater understanding of the human nervous system before they can be found. For the time being, most developmental sensory research is directed at discovering the parameters of sensory abilities among neonates and determining how these abilities change as people age.

OTHER COMPETENCIES OF THE INFANT

To Jean Piaget, the infant's world was quite limited, especially during the early months. Other researchers, however, have found that even the newborn is capable of certain complex cognitive, learning, and memory tasks. In the Chapter Preview, for example, we discussed the fact that not only do infants hear their mother's voice before they are born, but their memory is developed enough so that they recognize that voice again after birth! Soon after birth, infants actively attend and begin the process of encoding information from the environment, placing it into their memory for later retrieval. Experiments have shown that by 3 months of age, infants already can store certain **distinctive features** into their memory.

A distinctive feature is any portion of an object that can be discriminated from another portion. One of the reasons that your cognitive abilities are superior to those of a child is that you are more skilled at attending to the relevant features of an object. Experiments have shown that 3-month-old infants will forget the color of an object before they forget its other features (Fagen, 1984).

The implication is that the object's color has been encoded into the memory *as a distinctive feature*, or how could it have been forgotten separately?

This leads to an interesting question: If memory enables us to keep track of our past, and if even 3-month-old infants are busy encoding information, why can't we remember things that happened to us when we were 1 year old? Researchers have wondered about this for some time. Investigations of the brain, and specifically of those parts of the brain that are most associated with memory, have shown that there are at least two separate memory systems, each making use of its own distinct brain pathways (Mishkin & Appenzeller, 1987). One, called **implicit memory**, stores motor skills or learned actions and procedures, such as those acquired through operant or classical conditioning (see Chapter 2). The other, called **declarative memory**, stores facts and mental images of faces, objects, and events. Implicit memory may develop first, which would explain why as infants we are able to learn or be conditioned but as adults do not have memories of faces or events from that time (Rovee-Collier, Schechter, Shyi, & Shields, 1992). Even the infants in our study who forgot the color of an object "forgot" by failing to show a certain operant response—a function of implicit memory. No doubt, when they are older, these infants will have no recollection of having *seen* the object; such a memory would be a function of declarative memory.

Habituation in newborns and young infants also shows their capacity for learning and can take place only if the infant has a working implicit memory. When a stimulus, such as a sight or sound, is presented repeatedly to the infant, the baby begins to pay less and less attention to it. This suggests that the baby can remember the stimulus and has become bored with it. If another, different stimulus is then presented, the infant often pays attention to it, which shows that the infant has discriminated between the two stimuli. According to psychologist Robert Trotter,

> Habituation is now considered a primary indication of brain and nervous-system functioning and . . . is seen as a good predictor of later intelligence. Habituation, which becomes increasingly acute over the first 10 weeks of life, is commonly assessed as a measure of an infant's maturity and well-being. Infants who have brain damage or have suffered birth traumas, such as lack of oxygen, do not habituate well, and may go on to have developmental and learning problems. (Trotter, 1987, p. 38)

Infants are also capable of being operantly conditioned, as mentioned in Chapter 2. Surprisingly, they can even imitate other people's actions. Among the more interesting experiments in this regard are Andrew Meltzoff's studies of delayed imitation. Meltzoff demonstrated the ability of 14-month-olds to imitate simple behaviors a full week after having seen an adult demonstrate them (Meltzoff, 1988a).

Infants show other amazing capacities. Some researchers believe that the rudiments of language acquisition are present within 72 hours after birth. Evidence for this claim comes from the apparent vocal "dialogues" engaged in by mothers and their newborns. For example, one study analyzed the vocal interactions between mothers and their 3-day-old infants (Rosenthal, 1982). The researchers discovered that the duration and kind of infant vocalization seemed to depend on the presence or absence of the mother's voice. What the mother said and when she said it was in turn affected by the sounds the infant made. Other researchers have documented similar conversations. In fact, this behavior is quite common. Although the newborn has no words to say, this reciprocal pattern of exchange is not too different from one aspect of adult conversation, inasmuch as the mothers and their newborn infants seem to take turns speaking (Bateson, 1975).

IMPLICIT MEMORY
The memory associated with recall of muscular or glandular responses that have been conditioned. Implicit memories are acquired slowly with practice. This type of memory is required to recall the skills necessary for object manipulation and learned physical activity. It is sometimes called skill or motor memory.

DECLARATIVE MEMORY
The memory associated with cognitive skills not directly attributable to muscular or glandular responses. The complete memory may be acquired through a single exposure, but practice is beneficial. This type of memory is required to recall factual information; it is sometimes called fact memory.

HABITUATION
A process whereby an organism ceases to respond to a stimulus that is repeatedly presented.

MATURATION
A genetically programmed biological plan of development that is relatively independent of experience. Maturation is highly correlated with, and dependent on, the growth and development of the nervous system.

As you can see, infants possess a large number of capabilities, many of which help them to organize their world and benefit from their experience. These capacities aren't just sensory and reflexive; the infant has a developing brain with many amazing capacities for learning. You've come a long way, baby!

INFANT PHYSICAL AND MOTOR DEVELOPMENT

The Forces of Maturation

The term used to describe a genetically determined biological plan of development, one relatively independent of experience, is **maturation**. Human growth seems to be mainly a function of maturation; to a large extent, motor development is also. For example, in 1940, researcher Myrtle McGraw decided to examine whether or not early training could facilitate toilet training in babies and young children. She was interested because many experts had suggested that infants even as young as 3 months were ready for toilet training (Scoe, 1933). McGraw took two sets of identical twins, and in an exacting study in which frequency of urination and volume of urination were measured, she systematically gave toilet training to one child from each set of twins, beginning at the age of 1 month. (The control twin in each set received no toilet training at all). Month after month the training continued, and slowly the two boys receiving the training began to have some bladder control. Measurements were taken of success, and by the age of 27 months, toilet training was complete.

However, when the identical twins of the trained boys were tested after just a couple of days of toilet training, they were found to be as successful as their fully "trained" brothers—who had received 26 months of toilet training! This finding led McGraw to state, "Concerning the inception of a training program, the results of this investigation indicate that early toilet training is, to say the least, futile" (McGraw, 1940, p. 588). In other words, until the child is maturationally ready to benefit from the training, no amount of early training will be of any use at all. Physical and motor development during infancy and early childhood are mainly a result of maturation. Experiences often play an important role in maturation, but they tend to be viewed more as accelerators or decelerators of growth or motor development than as the primary cause.

For example, in the early 1930s, Mary Shirley published a series of papers describing the first months of motor development in babies and young children. Her data showed that the average child walked at about 15 months. However, children of today typically walk on their own a few months earlier. For that matter, children in different countries tend to walk for the first time at different ages (Hindley, Filliozat, Klackenberg, Nicolet-Meister, & Sand, 1966), and the rate and steadiness at which their walking develops also differ (Hennessy, Dixon, & Simon, 1984). How might experience account for these different rates and average ages at which children first walk?

Nutrition is a possible explanation. After all, Shirley's data were taken in the 1930s, during the Depression. Or perhaps today's parents are more eager to see their children walk. Such parents might encourage their children to try walking as soon as possible. Parents during the 1930s, on the other hand, often had larger families, and might have been considerably less excited by the first steps of their fourth, fifth, and sixth children. The difference might even be due to the introduction of wall-to-wall carpeting! Perhaps babies who attempted to walk in the 1930s found landing on a hardwood floor punishing enough to deter their efforts for a time. Because of such environmental considerations, motor developments may occur at a slightly faster (accelerated) or slower (decelerated) rate than we might expect—*but only within maturational limits.* Because of the rate of maturational development, it is impossible—regardless of the kind of nutrition, coaxing, or carpeting—to get a 4-month-old to walk on his or her own.

But this doesn't mean that children shouldn't be led into ballet or tennis or any other activity until they are maturationally ready. Although a child may not be maturationally able to engage in certain motor responses, there is no reason why the child shouldn't enjoy attempting to imitate older children or adults. Younger children may have a lot of fun at "ballet" or "tennis," even though they can't actually dance or play well. And by playing at these activities when they are young, they may be highly motivated to continue to develop these skills when they are maturationally ready. It is important for parents to remember, however, that they shouldn't expect their child to perform at a higher level than the child is capable of managing.

Physical Growth

Physical growth and motor development have two things in common. First, they appear to be largely a function of maturation—that is, of nature rather than nurture. Second, they are the most commonly discussed aspects of infant development among parents, simply because they are so readily observable. (Actually, things that seem readily observable often aren't.)

As you can see from Table 4.3, the rate of physical growth is incredibly rapid immediately following conception and decelerates quickly thereafter. You may think that human growth occurs in a fairly linear progression. Well, consider that if your rate of growth during the first 3 months following conception was maintained, by the time you were 20 years old, you'd weigh considerably more than all the planets of the solar system combined, with the sun thrown in for good measure.*

For years, researchers and physicians also assumed that physical growth in infants and young children progressed at a fairly steady rate of roughly 0.5 mil-

---

*Based on a rate of each cell becoming 25 billion cells every 3 months.

Table 4.3 ● The Deceleration of Growth During Prenatal Development

AGE	WEIGHT (IN OUNCES)	PERCENTAGE INCREASE
Conception	0.00000002	
4 weeks	0.0007	3,499,900
8 weeks	0.035	4,900
12 weeks	0.6	1,614
16 weeks	3	400
20 weeks	8	166
24 weeks	22	175
28 weeks	28	27
32 weeks	34	21

FIGURE 4.7

Changes in body form associated with age. (SOURCE: Jackson, 1929, p. 118)

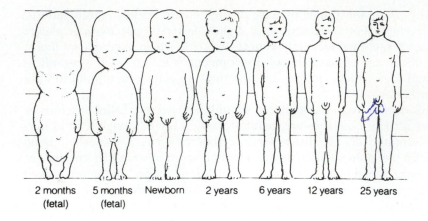

FIGURE 4.8

Selected motor milestones from the Denver Developmental Screening Test. The bottom of the bar represents the age at which 25 percent of the sample could perform the task; the top represents the age at which 90 percent could. (SOURCE: Adapted from Frankenburg & Dodds, 1967, p. 186)

limeter per day. Any "growth spurts" were thought to occur during puberty. However, when researcher Michelle Lampl very carefully measured infants and toddlers on a daily basis, she discovered that there would be long periods of no observable growth (sometimes as long as 2 months), and then suddenly the infant or toddler would grow. During these growth spurts, infants and toddlers typically became excessively sleepy, hungry, or fussy, and then, within just a 24-hour period, grew from 0.1 to almost 0.5 inch (Lampl, Veldhuis, & Johnson, 1992)! At a rate like that, you can't help but wonder if the creaky sound parents occasionally hear in the house at night isn't the kid growing! This kind of development is called **saltatory growth.** Very early results also indicate that grade school children and adolescents may also be growing in a saltatory manner (Lampl, Veldhuis, & Johnson, 1992). Such findings help emphasize that development is rarely a linear process.

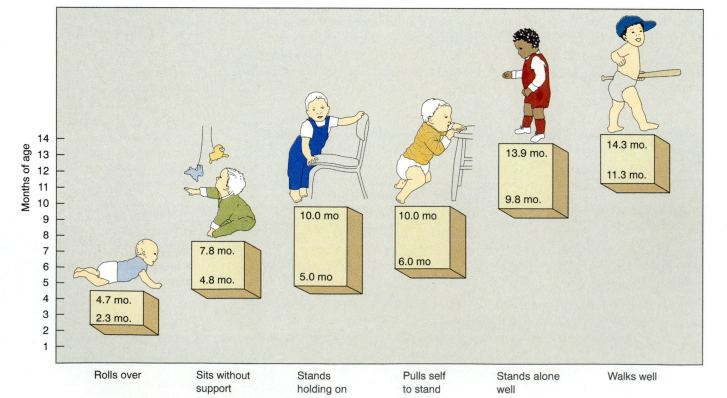

Changes in the relative size of different body parts also take place during growth. The change in the ratio of head to body length is an interesting example of this aspect of growth (see Figure 4.7).

Motor Development

In Figure 4.8, you can see how aspects of a child's motor development also appear to follow a maturational plan. Just as individual babies differ, so, too, do individual rates of motor development. Some infants proceed quickly; others lag behind. Some develop rapidly in one area and simultaneously are slow in another. Like the tortoise and the hare, some infants may race ahead of their peers only to be overtaken later.

Parents often place great importance on the speed of their child's physical and motor development. You can see, however, that they should not be too elated or too concerned if their infant is several months ahead of or several months behind the published norms. A 6-month-old baby may learn to sit by himself and then seem, from the parents' point of view, to develop no further for 4 or 5 months. The frustrated parents may wonder why their baby doesn't stand or crawl—surely a child must learn to crawl before he can walk!—only to have the child suddenly stand up and toddle off somewhere, after 5 months of failing to advance much beyond sitting. Babies are individuals, and they *will* do things their own way, at their own speed.

SALTATORY GROWTH
Literally, growth by leaping. Growth that occurs in "spurts" or sudden leaps.

The Value of Infant Walkers

One of the most important developmental milestones in an infant's life occurs when the infant acquires the ability to move from one place to another. In fact, many of the infant's perceptual advancements appear to coincide with the development of locomotion.

Infants first achieve locomotion by crawling, rolling, scooting, and even, sometimes, walking. For years, researchers have noted that this newly acquired locomotion has a positive effect on other aspects of development, providing the infant with certain experiences that in turn further development (Kermoian & Campos, 1988). For instance, it has been well documented that babies who are able to crawl or walk spend more time near adults, usually their parents. This, in turn, leads to further social contact and interaction (Green, Gustafson, & West, 1980).

Infants who locomote also explore more, and as they go from place to place, typically see and manipulate many objects. Often, when infants first encounter new objects, parents spend extra time naming the object and telling the child about it; detailed discussions may evolve from the baby's exploration. One study noted that

the mothers talked not only about the toys the babies have encountered but also about such minor details as the cracks between the vinyl squares of the floor and its cleanliness, details brought to their attention by the exploratory activities of their infants. (West & Rheingold, 1978, p. 214)

Such findings imply that locomotion may be helpful for the acquisition and development of language.

Locomotion also changes the infant's visual perspective. The interaction of changing visual perspective and locomotion may play an important role in perceptual development by helping to organize the infant's understanding of the surrounding world (Acredolo, 1978). Considering all these effects, locomotion can be viewed as a general reorganizer of the infant's experiences (Gustafson, 1984) and an action that should foster the development of neural experience-expectant systems.

It would also seem reasonable to assume that babies who aren't locomoting relatively early could be missing some of the important experiences obtained by infants who get around. To test this hypothesis, researchers placed infants between the ages of 6 and 10 months in "walkers" and observed the babies' experiences (Gustafson, 1984). Walkers are devices that support infants on wheels such that their feet just touch the ground. By pushing with their feet, babies can propel themselves wherever they wish to go, as long as there are no obstacles or barriers in the way and the surface is relatively flat (see Figure 4.9). Some manufacturers have claimed that the walkers benefit the infant by accelerating development.

Gustafson discovered that nonlocomoting infants who were now getting around in walkers soon encountered the typical experiences of locomoting infants—namely, closer adult contact, greater social interchange, generation of more language by parents, and adjustment to a continually changing visual perspective. By the end of the study, in terms of the experiences they shared, nonlocomoters in walkers were much more like their locomoting peers than like their nonlocomoting peers who had no walkers.

This study might tempt us to say that infants who locomote early have

FIGURE 4.9

Any advantage gained by early locomotion appears to soon be lost, as late locomoters "catch up" to their early locomoting peers. For this and other safety reasons, it is probably not advisable to give infants walkers.

special social, cognitive, and perceptual advantages. And, if babies who would normally walk later are helped by the walkers, then the walkers afford valuable experiences for nonlocomoting infants. Researchers such as Gustafson, however, point out that although it is true that locomotion reorganizes an infant's world, it is not necessarily true that infant walkers are beneficial. Owing to the forces of maturation, healthy infants who are late to start walking quickly catch up to their early walking peers. Similarly, early locomoting infants who may have particular social, cognitive, language, and perceptual experiences as a result of their early locomotion don't seem to hold any long-term

Applications

advantage over peers who are late locomoters.

All healthy children will eventually locomote and gain the experiences that such movement affords. Any early advantage appears to be lost, just as was the case for the toilet-trained twins mentioned in this chapter. It is important to keep such considerations in mind. Parents are so often delighted when their child crawls or talks at an early age and, conversely, dismayed if their child is a little late walking or talking. In general, neither reaction is justified.

As the maturational plan for development unfolds, there is a great range of individual differences. Children who reach certain maturational goals early are typically indistinguishable a few years later from peers who reached those goals at a slower pace.

With this in mind, parents should probably not give their infants a walker. In 1992, both the American Medical Association and the American Academy of Pediatrics argued that infant walkers should be banned. Walkers, they pointed out, are a leading cause of infant injury in the United States. Infants in walkers are simply too likely to fall down stairs or roll up against hot ovens or fireplaces. If, however, parents really wish to purchase a walker for their infant, it is important that it should be a safe walker (one that does not tip over easily or have sharp edges) that they can keep in a safe environment, which means an environment free from stairs or any other hazard. Parents shouldn't think, however, that they are depriving their infant of an important experience if they don't provide a walker.

Summary

- Birth in human beings typically occurs 270 days after conception, near the end of a full 9-month period. Labor is commonly divided into three overlapping stages. During the first stage, uterine contractions begin; at the end of the second stage, the baby is born; during the third stage, the afterbirth is delivered.
- About 97 percent of babies are born in the head-first position. If there is an extremely serious problem during birth, the baby may be removed from the uterus by cesarean section.
- Multiple births result when zygotes split or when there are multiple ovulations. Several factors influence whether or not a woman will have more than one baby, including whether she has taken a fertility drug, is between the ages of 35 and 39 years, and has a family history of multiple births.
- In the United States, about 7 percent of all infants are born weighing less than 5.5 pounds. These infants account for 65 percent of the deaths among newborns. Two of the best ways to prevent underweight babies are to provide proper prenatal care and to use drugs that prevent or stop premature labor.
- Breast feeding confers many advantages to the newborn baby. Breast-fed babies are less likely to develop food allergies, coughs, respiratory difficulties, or diarrhea than are bottle-fed babies.
- Newborn infants typically weigh between 6 and 9 pounds and are about 20 inches in length. One of the first tasks a health team performs when the baby is born is to determine the baby's current physical state. Both the Apgar and Brazelton Assessment Scales are used in this regard.
- Beginning in the 1960s, there was a surge of research concerning the capabilities of infants. Infants were found to possess many interesting competencies.
- A large number of reflexes can be elicited in newborns. These reflexes apparently evolved because they had a survival value.
- The nervous system of the neonate is immature compared to that of an adult. Portions of the infant's central nervous system are not yet myelinated, and the central structures of its brain are noticeably undeveloped.
- It was once commonly thought that infants were born blind. Researchers have since determined that although infants don't see as well as adults, they can see. The average 2-week-old neonate has the visual acuity of 20/800.
- A device known as the visual cliff was constructed to test depth perception in humans and other animals. The results of experiments demonstrated that many newborn animals possess innate depth perception.
- An infant's sense of hearing is functional prior to birth. Auditory sensitivity increases steadily as the child ages.
- Evidence of sensory integration comes from experiments in cross-modal transfer. In such experiments, infants exposed to a stimulus through only one sensory mode will later show familiarity with the stimulus when it is presented to them through other sensory modes.
- The sense of smell is well developed in the newborn. Infants have such an acute sense of smell that they can make very subtle discriminations.
- Infants appear to respond to the same four basic tastes to which adults respond.
- Researchers have demonstrated that full-term newborns are sensitive to strong tactile stimulation as well as to mild stimulation.
- Soon after birth, infants actively attend and begin the process of encoding information from the environment, placing it into their memory for later retrieval. Experiments have shown that by 3 months of age, infants already can store certain distinctive features into their memory.

■ Implicit memory may develop before declarative memory, which would explain why as infants we are able to learn or be conditioned, but as adults we do not remember faces or events from that time.

■ Habituation occurs when a stimulus, such as a sight or sound, is presented repeatedly to an infant and the infant begins to pay less and less attention to it. Habituation is considered a primary indication of brain and nervous system functioning in infants.

■ The term used to describe a genetically determined biological plan of development, one relatively independent of experience, is maturation. Human growth seems to be mainly a function of maturation; to a large extent, motor development is also.

■ Experiences often play an important role in maturation, but they are viewed more as accelerators or decelerators of growth or motor development, rather than the cause.

QUESTIONS FOR DISCUSSION

1. What ethical considerations do you believe should be emphasized in designing research on novel means of human reproduction?

2. Premature infants who would have had no hope of living a decade ago are now surviving, thanks to improved critical care. Many of these infants, however, survive with severe multiple handicaps, often caused by the very equipment that saved their lives, such as a respirator. What role do you think parents, doctors, and society should play in determining whether to treat these infants and when to suspend treatment that is ineffective?

3. Our senses act as filters; there are many things to which we are not sensitive. We can't see X rays, hear dog whistles, or smell carbon dioxide. Why do you think our senses are so selective?

4. National child fitness chains have proliferated in the United States in the past few years. One company even introduced a BabyCise exercise kit for infants with a videocassette of instructions on how to use plastic barbells, a ball, and a little toddler-sized balance beam. What do you think of "workouts" for infants? From what you have learned about maturation, what would you tell a parent who thinks that an early start in exercise will help create a future gymnast like Mary Lou Retton or some other accomplished athlete?

SUGGESTIONS FOR FURTHER READING

1. American Academy of Pediatrics. (1991). *Caring for your baby and young child: Birth to age 5*. New York: Bantam.

2. Dodson, F., & Alexander, A. (1986). *Your child: Birth to age 6*. New York: Simon & Schuster.

3. Haywood, K. M. (1986). *Life span motor development*. Champaign, IL: Human Kinetics.

4. Maurer, D., & Maurer, C. (1988). *The world of the newborn*. New York: Basic Books.

5. Stern, D. N. (1990). *Diary of a baby: What your child sees, feels, and experiences*. New York: Harper-Collins.

6. Stoppard, M. (1990). *The first weeks of life*. New York: Ballantine.

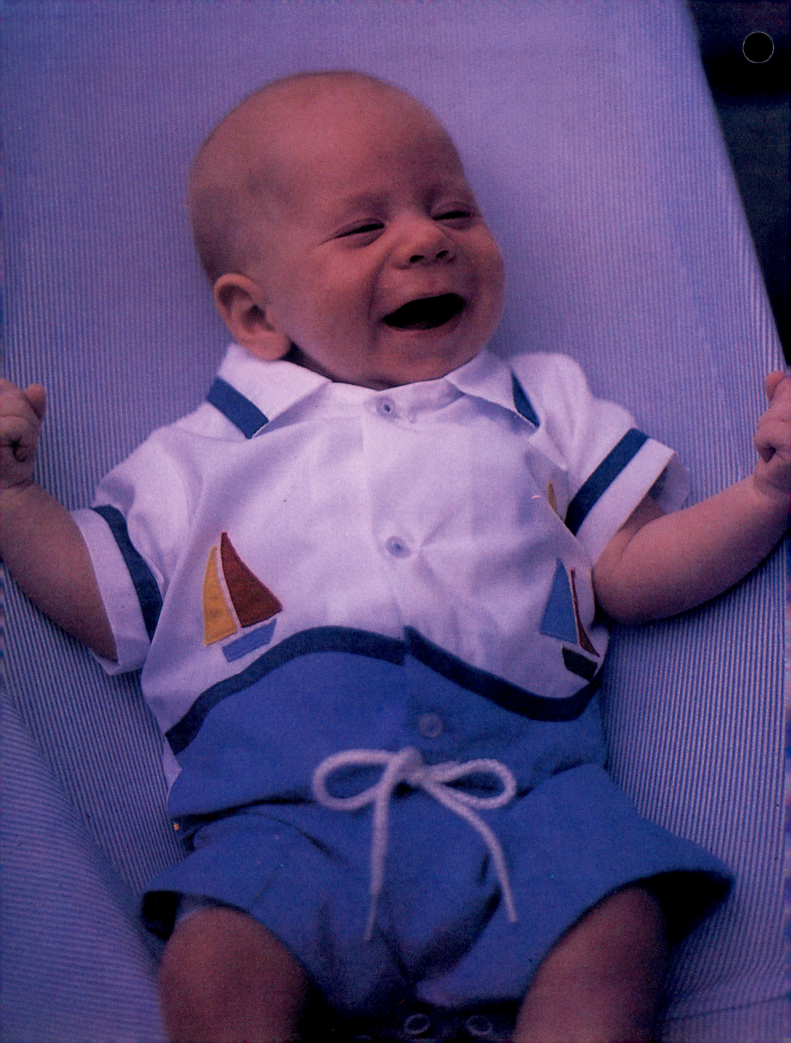

CHAPTER 5

Infant Personality and Social-Emotional Development

CHAPTER PREVIEW
Check with Mom

In a laboratory, researchers place a 1-year-old baby on a visual cliff. This visual cliff, however, is a little different from the one described in Chapter 4. In this case, there's only one drop-off, and it's neither shallow nor deep, but rather somewhere in between. The baby begins to crawl, stops in front of the drop-off, and looks down. It's the kind of drop-off that makes you think, "If I were that baby, would I try it or not?"

Directly across from the baby, on the other side of the visual drop-off, is the baby's mother. She's been instructed to stand still and maintain an expression of fear on her face. The baby looks down at the drop, up at her mother, and then back down at the drop. Once again she looks at her mother, and refuses to crawl any further.

Later, another baby is placed on the cliff. This baby's mother is told to look happy and interested. The baby crawls to the edge of the drop and looks down. He looks at his mother, looks back down again, and crawls across.

*In this experiment, most of the infants who saw fear on their mother's face refused to cross, while those who saw happy, encouraging mothers crossed over the drop (Sorce, Emde, Campos, & Klinnert, 1985). If the drop-off was removed and the visual cliff made flat, the infants crawled about without checking first with their mothers. In the ambiguous situation with the drop-off, however, the babies looked to their mothers for cues about what to do. Looking for cues in this fashion is called **social referencing**, and the emotion that the mother showed was an important communication for her infant. Infants will actively search for emotional cues, not just from their mothers, but from any familiar adult who happens to be present (Klinnert, Emde, Butterfield, & Campos, 1986).*

SOCIAL REFERENCING
The use of emotional signals, or cues, from others as a guide for one's own behavior in ambiguous situations.

In this chapter, we will examine the development of the infant's personality, and we will discuss the social and emotional ties formed between infants and their parents. We'll pay special attention to the relationship between infant and mother, and we'll discuss how theorists believe this important attachment forms. We'll also look at the special relationship that infants have with their fathers. Finally, we'll explore the development of the emotions themselves.

INFANT PERSONALITY DEVELOPMENT

Although the human infant doesn't appear to possess a fully integrated personality in its first few days of life, people have observed that newborns do exhibit considerable differences in temperament. As we discussed in Chapter 1, there is much evidence that babies are different from one another just after birth. Some babies are fussy, some have a high activity level, and some seem to do nothing but sleep. Temperament theories suggest that these early infant personalities, or traits, may be consistent, or stable, over great lengths of time (Goldsmith, 1983).

Although researchers argue over which components of infant personality should be included, any definition of temperament would encompass the ideas that

> temperament consists of relatively consistent, basic dispositions inherent in the person that underlie and modulate the expression of activity, reactivity, emotionality, and sociability. Major elements of temperament are present early in life, and those elements are likely to be strongly influenced by biological factors. As development proceeds, the expression of temperament increasingly becomes more influenced by experience and context. (Goldsmith et al., 1987, p. 524)

The New York Longitudinal Study

In the late 1950s, two physicians, Alexander Thomas and Stella Chess, began what came to be called the New York Longitudinal Study. With their colleagues, they followed 140 children from birth to adolescence. They were initially interested in infant reactivity, but soon came to believe that they were, in fact, empirically documenting differences in temperament. In 1968, they first described their subjects in terms of "easy" or "difficult" temperaments (Thomas, Chess, & Birch, 1968, 1970).

The differences between easy and difficult infants and children are outlined in Table 5.1. These personality dimensions were obtained through interviews with parents, observation of infants and children, and other measures. As you can see, easy infants adapt readily to new situations, are approachable, respond with low or mild intensity, exhibit pleasant moods, and have regular body rhythms.

Not all of the infants studied fell into one or the other category. Some infants fell in between the dimensions of *easy* and *difficult*. Such infants are often referred to as "slow-to-warm-up" babies. Other infants were too inconsistent to categorize, exhibiting "mixtures of traits that did not add up to a general characterization" (Thomas, Chess, & Birch, 1970, p. 105). Among the infants studied, the researchers found that 40 percent were easy, 15 percent slow to warm up, 10 percent difficult, and 35 percent inconsistent.

The categories in Table 5.1 were criticized for a number of reasons. First, fully one-third of the children couldn't be clearly classified. Second, further research showed that a number of the temperament categories tended to overlap each other (Sanson, Prior, & Kyrios, 1990). And finally, it was argued that parents and other raters of temperament sometimes showed bias in their observations.

However, it has since been shown that individuals who are classified according to some of these categories and who are at the extremes of a particular tem-

Table 5.1 ● Stability of Temperaments over Time

TEMPERAMENTAL QUALITY	RATING	2 MONTHS	1 YEAR	10 YEARS
Rhythmicity	Regular	Has been on 4-hour feeding schedule since birth; regular bowel movement	Naps after lunch each day; always drinks bottle before bed	Eats only at mealtimes; sleeps the same amount of time each night
	Irregular	Awakes at a different time each morning; size of feedings varies	Will not fall asleep for an hour or more; moves bowels at a different time each day	Food intake varies; falls asleep at a different time each night
Approach-withdrawal	Positive	Smiles and licks washcloth; has always liked bottle	Approaches strangers readily; sleeps well in new surroundings	Went to camp happily; loved to ski the first time
	Negative	Rejected cereal the first time; cries when strangers appear	Cries when placed on sled; will not sleep in strange beds	Severely homesick at camp during first days; does not like new activities
Adaptability	Adaptive	Was passive during first bath, now enjoys bathing; smiles at nurse	Was afraid of toy animals at first, now plays with them happily	Likes camp, although homesick during first days; learns enthusiastically
	Not adaptive	Still startled by sudden, sharp noises; resists diapering	Continues to reject new foods each time they are offered	Does not adjust well to new school or new teacher; comes home late for dinner even when punished
Intensity of reaction	Mild	Does not cry when diapers are wet; whimpers instead of crying when hungry	Does not fuss much when clothing is pulled on over head	When a mistake is made in a model airplane; corrects it quietly; does not comment when reprimanded
	Intense	Cries when diapers are wet; rejects food vigorously when satisfied	Laughs hard when father plays rough; screams and kicks when temperature is taken	Tears up an entire page of homework if one mistake is made; slams door of room when teased by younger brother
Quality of mood	Positive	Smacks lips when first tasting new food; smiles at parents	Likes bottle; reaches for it and smiles; laughs loudly when playing peekaboo	Enjoys new accomplishments; laughs when reading a funny passage aloud
	Negative	Fusses after nursing. Cries when carriage is rocked.	Cries when given injections; cries when left alone	Cries when unable to solve homework problem; very "weepy" if not getting enough sleep

KEY			
	EASY CHILD	SLOW-TO-WARM-UP CHILD	DIFFICULT CHILD
Rhythmicity	Very regular	Varies	Irregular
Approach-withdrawal	Positive approach	Initial withdrawal	Withdrawal
Adaptability	Very adaptable	Slowly adaptable	Slowly adaptable
Intensity of reaction	Low or mild	Mild	Intense
Quality of mood	Positive	Slightly negative	Negative

Source: Thomas, Chess, & Birch, 1970, pp. 108–109.

perament quality do tend to display such qualities consistently over time (Kagan, Reznick, & Gibbons, 1989; Kagan & Snidman, 1991). For example, a child who doesn't cry much with wet diapers at 2 months of age is also less likely to fuss when a shirt is pulled over the child's head at 2 years of age. Follow-up studies at 5 and 10 years also show a certain stability of these traits. Some studies have found that such stable temperaments may even continue into adulthood (Carey & McDevitt, 1978; Lerner, Palermo, Spiro, & Nesselroade, 1982), although culture and social variables do exert increasing influence on temperament over the life span (Goldsmith et al., 1987).

Goodness of Fit

An interesting question is whether difficult children have more problems adjusting to the world than easy children do. Although it does appear that the kinds of behaviors exhibited by difficult children may be related to more significant behavior problems in childhood (Lee & Bates, 1985), and although there is evidence that difficult children may be at greater risk for psychiatric disorders during adolescence (Maziade et al., 1985), problems faced by a difficult child may be more related to what researchers call *goodness of fit* (Sprunger, Boyce, & Gaines, 1985).

Goodness of fit refers to how suitable a particular child's temperament is to his or her environment. One of the most dramatic examples of the goodness-of-fit concept comes from a study of easy and difficult infants among the Masai, an African tribe of nomadic warriors. In the early 1980s, this tribe, with many other tribes in Africa, suffered the effects of a severe drought and famine. Developmental researchers had already taken initial measurements of which infants were easy and which were difficult. Later, in their follow-up after the calamity, the researchers were shocked to discover that most of the easy infants had died, while almost all of the difficult children had survived (deVries, 1984)! After looking carefully for possible differences that might account for these findings, they observed that the Masai encouraged boldness, outspokenness, and assertiveness in their children and infants—qualities more typical of a difficult temperament. Furthermore, Masai mothers would breast feed their infants on demand, and the researchers discovered that the difficult infants, who by temperament were more fussy and loud, were fed more often. It was a perfect example of the squeaky wheel getting the grease—or, in this case, the milk.

Other studies have shown that children with difficult temperaments are far less likely to develop behavioral difficulties if they are reared in cultural environments that are accepting of these behaviors (Korn & Gannon, 1983; Lerner, 1984). In one study, for example, it was found that difficult infants from upper- and middle-class families, when tested later at age 4, obtained intelligence test scores that were 20 IQ points higher than their matched easy counterparts (Maziade, Cote, Boutin, Bernier, & Thivierge, 1988). The researchers who conducted the study noted that the parents of the difficult children were stimulating them more (talking to, interacting with, and attending to them) in an attempt to deal with their behavior. "Such parents would stimulate the difficult infant more than the extremely easy infant, who is more readily left to himself. Such special stimulation would favor more rapid development" (Maziade, Cote, Boutin, Bernier, & Thivierge, 1988, p. 342). Of course, it is too early to know whether this difference would be sustained over time or provide any lasting advantage. In fact, there is evidence that in the school system, it might be the easy children who have an advantage because they are better able

The Masai people encourage boldness, outspokenness, and assertiveness in their infants and children. Although such qualities are considered "difficult" in Western culture, these same qualities better fit the demands of the harsher environment in which the Masai live.

to attend to tasks and concentrate (Palisin, 1986). As you can see, defining "goodness of fit" is not a simple task.

Environmental Influences

Although there do appear to be biologically determined differences in the individual temperaments of young infants (Matheny, Riese, & Wilson, 1985; Riese, 1987), this doesn't always mean that such traits will continue throughout childhood or, if such traits do continue, that they are the result of a biological constitution. Although studies continue to show that temperaments are stable over time, even in changing environments (Peters-Martin & Wachs, 1984; Rothbart, 1986; Pedlow, Sanson, Prior, & Oberklaid, 1993), this doesn't necessarily mean that the major determinant of this stability is the child's biological constitution. There could be other reasons for such long-term stability.

Consider the following: Researchers have found that mothers who feel that their babies are difficult are less responsive to their infants and less sensitive to changes in their babies' emotional states (Donovan, Leavitt, & Balling, 1978; Klein, 1984). It may be, then, that babies who *initially* have difficult temperaments cause problems or strife between themselves and their parents (Sirignano & Lachman, 1985). Such a situation may in turn lead to a cycle of heavy-handed parental discipline and child rebellion that may, in theory, continue for *environmental* reasons long after any biologically determined temperamental predisposition has ceased to directly influence the child's personality. In other words, whether a baby continues to be easy or difficult throughout childhood may be due to the way the parents initially reacted to the child's temperament.

To address this problem, researchers conducted a study in which they made a special effort to control for the possibility that environmental factors determine temperament. In their study, they examined many different combinations of pairs of siblings, some adopted and some not, some who were identical twins and some who were fraternal twins. The results showed that identical twins were the siblings who were most alike in temperament. But most telling was that biological siblings (who share about 50 percent of their genes with each other) were more similar in temperament than adopted siblings (unrelated biologically) who were living together in the same family. These results "indicate substantial genetic influence on infant temperament" (Braungart, Plomin, DeFries, & Fulker, 1992, p. 45). Further support for the existence of innate components of temperament comes from the observation that identical twins (who share the same genetic makeup) are about twice as likely to share the same fears as are fraternal twins (who are not genetically the same) (Rose & Ditto, 1983). Another study has shown that young Asian infants are less active, irritable, and vocal than their Caucasian counterparts, which also highlights the possibility of a genetic component of temperament (Kagan et al., 1994).

Theories of Personality Development

As we discussed in Chapter 2, both Sigmund Freud and Erik Erikson outlined theories of the development of personality from infancy through adulthood. According to Freud, the focus of personality development in infancy is oral processes. Freud believed that during this *oral stage,* the infant obtains its greatest satisfaction from stimulation of the lips, mouth, tongue, and gums. He noted that sucking and chewing are the chief sources of the infant's pleasure. He also believed that if too little or too much satisfaction was obtained during

ATTACHMENT
An especially close affectional bond formed between living creatures.

this period, a fixation could occur. This fixation might manifest itself in later years in the form of compulsive oral behaviors, such as overeating, excessive smoking, or nail biting. Of course, there are other plausible explanations for these behaviors besides oral fixation; as was stated in Chapter 2, it has been very difficult to test Freud's ideas empirically.

Erik Erikson argued that the first major conflict faced by a child, which occurs during the child's first year, is the establishment of *trust* rather than *mistrust*. During the first year, parents or primary caregivers play the major role in helping the child form a sense of basic trust. The parents should not only feed and care for the child, but also work to build an affectionate and warm relationship. If an infant learns to trust his parents, he is ready to move on to the next psychosocial conflict some time during his second year of life. This idea of Erikson's leads us to a discussion of how this trusting relationship is formed, what effect it has on the infant's future adjustment, and how emotion plays a role in fostering it.

SOCIAL TIES

We humans are social creatures. We live within communities and families; we form social and emotional ties with one another. Such ties are essential for newborns because babies rely on their parents or others for fulfillment of their basic needs. During this time of helplessness, infants come to know their parents socially and form attachments to them.

Early Theories of Attachment

The mechanism of **attachment**, especially between the infant and its mother, has been intensely debated and investigated by developmental theorists (Bretherton, 1985), and the theoretical orientation taken by most researchers over the years has changed (Lamb, 1984). During the first decades of this century, both Sigmund Freud and learning theorists argued that the infant became attached because attachment was associated with the fulfillment of primary biological needs. In other words, infants who were attached to their parents would have their biological needs gratified. However, our theoretical orientation has changed during the past two or three decades. To understand the modern view and to explore why our thoughts about attachment have changed, let's take a look at the work of a well-known researcher, Harry Harlow.

Monkey Love

Both Freud and the learning theorists believed that nursing led to the formation of strong attachments between infant and mother because nursing satisfied the infant's biological needs. However, research with rhesus monkeys, conducted by Harry Harlow and his associates, cast doubt on this speculation (Harlow & Suomi, 1970).

In a series of widely publicized experiments begun about 40 years ago, Harlow and his colleagues separated rhesus monkeys from their mothers at an early age and placed them with artificial surrogate mothers (see Figure 5.1). One surrogate was made of wire; the other was covered with terry cloth and possessed a more rhesus-looking face. Both "mothers" could be equipped with a baby bottle placed through a hole in their chest, which allowed nursing to take place. Regardless of which mother provided food, the baby rhesus spent

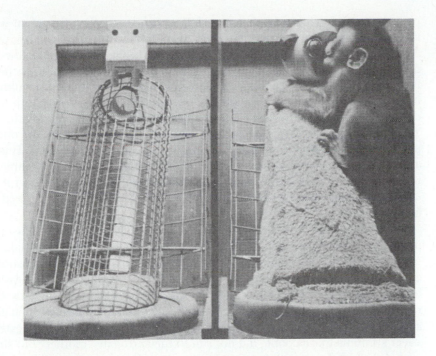

FIGURE 5.1
Baby rhesus monkey with its surrogate cloth mother. The wire mother is also shown.

as much time as possible cuddling and hugging the cloth mother. Even rhesus monkeys fed by only the wire mother formed strong attachments to the cloth mother and spent most of their time hugging it.

Many researchers initially concluded that cloth feels better than wire and that "contact comfort" was more important than nursing in the formation of attachments. But Harlow went further than this in his interpretation. Do you remember those plastic toy insects called "cooties" that you could buy in the store and assemble (see Figure 5.2)? Harlow discovered that baby rhesus monkeys are terrified of cooties. After all, they are about the same size as a baby monkey and they do look scary. Harlow found that when a baby rhesus was

FIGURE 5.2
The dreaded cootie.

INTRAORGANISMIC PERSPECTIVE
The theory, first espoused by Bowlby, that infants possess innate mechanisms that foster and promote the development of attachment. Such mechanisms are believed to have been naturally selected, as they have survival value.

placed in a room with a cootie and a cloth surrogate mother, the infant would run to the surrogate mother and cling to its body. The baby monkey would then become relaxed and calm; apparently, it felt safe. At this point, the baby monkey would often begin to use the "mother" as a safe base of operations from which to explore the environment. Harlow even captured on film one infant who, after a few daring attempts, found the courage to run up to the cootie, pull off one of its antennae, and run back to the surrogate mother.

Harlow arranged a number of variations of this experiment. In one, he placed the cootie between the rhesus and its surrogate cloth mother. This was an interesting experiment because it demonstrated the power of attachment in that the terrified rhesus baby ran *directly toward* the cootie, leaped over it, and landed squarely on the surrogate mother, where it eventually relaxed and became secure.

Interestingly, the baby monkeys did not show such attachment to just a soft piece of terry cloth left lying on the floor. There was something special about "mother" beyond nursing or contact comfort. There may in fact be instinctive components to these attachments. For instance, such attachments are easier to form with objects that appear similar to real mothers. But without early experience, the attachment won't occur. Baby rhesus monkeys raised without either a surrogate or a real mother, when placed in a room with a cloth surrogate and a fear stimulus like a cootie, did not run to the surrogate "mother" but simply curled up and shook with fear or tried to run as far away as possible.

Such early attachments in rhesus monkeys are formed quickly and are long-lasting. Baby rhesus monkeys raised with cloth mothers and then separated from them for 6 months will respond eagerly the instant they are reunited, rushing to the cloth mothers and clinging to them.

Other researchers also have shown that attachment is more than just dependence on someone who fulfills biological needs. For instance, infants may become attached to other infants their own age (Schaffer & Emerson, 1964). Attachment may develop even if an infant is seriously mistreated by the person to whom she is becoming attached (Rosenblum & Harlow, 1963). Infants also respond readily to other people in social situations in which they have never received food or contact comfort (Brackbill, 1958; Rheingold, Gewirtz, & Ross, 1959). Furthermore, infants do not become passive and unresponsive once all their biological needs are met; they continue to be social and to show attachment (Gewirtz, 1961).

The Intraorganismic Perspective

Developmental researchers do not all agree on one view of infant attachment. In recent years, however, the most accepted theoretical orientation has been the **intraorganismic perspective** (Brazelton, Koslowski, & Main, 1974). In this view, attachment is not merely an outward manifestation of a learned, or acquired, behavior pattern. Rather, it is dependent on an internal, or intraorganismic, organization; that is, the infant is biologically organized, or ready, to form attachments to caregivers (Bowlby, 1969; Ainsworth, 1973). Obviously, organisms who are innately predisposed to form attachments to caregivers are more likely to survive than those who are not predisposed to form such attachments. In this sense, parents or other adult caregivers are seen as *intrinsically* attractive to an infant.

Table 5.2 lists many attributes, apparent in infants within a short time after birth, that help the infant and its caregivers to form an attachment relationship. This, in turn, leads to the protection and nurturance of the infant. John Bowlby, one of the most important proponents of the intraorganismic perspec-

Table 5.2 ● Attributes Present at or Shortly After Birth that Facilitate Attachment

INFANT ATTRIBUTE	EFFECT	
Infant cries	Basic needs are met	
Infant is sensitive to touch (Yang & Douthitt, 1974; Lamper & Eisdorfer, 1971)	Promotes close physical contact	
Infant is attracted to faces (Fantz, 1961)	Facilitates mutual interest, involvement	
Infant possesses features innately attractive to adults (Alley, 1981; Lorenz, 1943)	Adults more willing to spend time with infant	**Attachment** (protection, nurturance)
Infant engages in "conversations" with caregiver (Rosenthal, 1982)		
Infant vocalizes more when eye contact is made (Keller & Scholmerich, 1987)	Facilitates social communication	
Infant appears to be specifically reactive to human voices (Hutt, Hutt, Lenard, Bernuth, & Muntjewerff, 1968)		

tive, believed that there is an innate drive in humans to form attachments that is as strong as the motivational forces of mating and eating (Bowlby, 1982a). His paper, "The Nature of a Child's Tie to His Mother" (Bowlby, 1958), is considered by many to mark the beginning of contemporary attachment theory (Joffe & Vaughn, 1982).

Before Bowlby's work, most researchers who studied attachment concentrated on a few specific behaviors, such as how long a child cried after his mother left a room. These behaviors would be counted and sometimes observed for changes over a period of years. Bowlby, however, did not view attachment as a few behaviors that can be counted and measured in the laboratory; rather, he believed that attachment is an *entire way of interacting* with other people, incorporating many different behaviors at different times. Such behaviors initiate and maintain social attachment (Baerends, 1976). Thus, Bowlby argued that researchers must examine a wide range of attachment behaviors in each person they study.

From the intraorganismic perspective, infant smiles are *intrinsically* satisfying to parents, infant cries are intrinsically distressing, and the interaction between parent and child is all that is necessary to foster attachment (see At Issue).

John Bowlby.

The Development of Attachment. Bowlby believed that the attachment system becomes well organized sometime during the second half of an infant's first year of life. By then, the attachment system is already building on earlier behaviors (Bowlby, 1969, 1973, 1982b). For instance, shortly after birth, babies do certain things that might be seen as helping to promote attachment, such as crying, touching, and following their parents with their eyes. A little later, they may display these behaviors as part of an actual attachment by smiling, touching, or especially looking toward a familiar person rather than just anyone (Brooks-Gunn & Lewis, 1981).

AT ISSUE

The Mother-Infant Bond

In 1972, John Kennell and Marshall Klaus thought that there might be a period immediately following birth when a special bond formed between the infant and mother during skin-to-skin contact. Although such a bond might not be as obvious as the kind we see during imprinting, they argued that it would still be one that fostered a special relationship and that a disruption of that bond might leave the infant at a lasting disadvantage (Klaus et al., 1972).

Kennell and Klaus conducted a detailed study to investigate the importance of these first few minutes or hours of contact between a mother and her infant. Twenty-eight healthy mothers with normal full-term infants were divided into two groups. The first group was given more hours of contact (16 hours altogether) with their infants during the first 3 days after birth than was the second group (Kennell et al., 1974). A significant difference was noted between the two groups of mothers when they returned to the hospital 1 month later. During the babies' feeding, the extra-contact mothers cuddled and soothed their babies more and had more eye contact with them.

After 2 years, five mothers randomly selected from each group were reexamined. The extra-contact mothers still showed differences when compared to the less-contact mothers. The conclusion was that the 16 extra hours of contact during the first 3 days of life were still having an effect on the mothers' behavior 2 years after the birth! How the mothers reacted to their infants in turn affected the way the infants responded to their mothers.

These findings, many of which are contained in Klaus and Kennell's *Maternal-Infant Bonding* (1976), led many researchers to conclude that this bond should be encouraged (Klaus & Kennell, 1976; Kennell, Voos, & Klaus, 1979). As a result, many hospitals began changing their procedures. In fact, the hospital procedure of giving the baby to the mother immediately after birth while encouraging her to hold and stroke the infant can be traced, in part, to the bonding research of Kennell and Klaus.

Kennell and Klaus's findings did not go unchallenged, however. The first major criticism of the bonding research was a fairly obvious one, namely, that parents of adopted children feel as close to their kids as any biological parent does—that they do not feel at all distant or "unbonded." This last observation led researchers to conclude that "the initial post delivery bonding, as described by Klaus and Kennell (1976) and others, which is obviously not part of the adoption experience, does not appear to be necessary for the formation of a healthy family relationship" (Singer, Brodzinsky, Ramsay, Steir, & Waters, 1985, p. 1550). These authors argued that whatever the early mother-infant bond was, missing it was something that could easily be overcome.

Intrigued by this observation, researchers Chess and Thomas, well known for their work on temperament, decided to examine the bonding research on their own. After doing so, they argued that Kennell and Klaus's research design had methodological flaws. They concluded that the idea of a unique type of relationship between mother and child due to skin-to-skin contact immediately after birth was unfounded (Chess & Thomas, 1982, 1986b).

Following this, researchers looking at other cultures discovered that motherly affection wasn't any greater in societies that encouraged early mother-infant body contact, that a father's involvement with his child was no greater if he were allowed to attend the child's birth, and that maternal affection or bonding was not greater in societies that encouraged early nursing (Lozoff, 1983).

In the light of these newer findings, Kennell and Klaus agreed that it would be unlikely for the life-sustaining mother-infant relationship to be dependent on any one process such as bonding (although they still believed the bonding effect to be a real one) and that there probably were many other "fail-safe" routes to attachment (Kennell & Klaus, 1984).

The bonding issue continues to flourish, however, because so many hospitals still encourage what they believe to be "bonding" even though research has failed to show a real benefit to be derived from immediate skin-to-skin contact between mother and infant. This attitude may lead to problems if, because of some medical emergency or other valid reason, the infant and mother can't be brought together directly following birth. The mother, if she knows about the supposed importance of bonding, may then feel that she has missed out on something crucial by not being able to "bond" with her baby (Chess & Thomas, 1986b). Still, a number of welcome humanitarian hospital reforms were brought on by this research. These days, parents are encouraged to participate fully in the birth and to become immediately involved with their newborn, which is something that most parents enjoy and appreciate.

By the time these babies are able to crawl, at about 6 months of age, they usually make an *active* attempt to maintain closeness to the person to whom they have become attached. They also begin to demonstrate an awareness of the absence of that person (Bell, 1970). At this time, children may begin to form what are often called **internal working models** of the relationships between themselves and their caregivers (Main, Kaplan, & Cassidy, 1985; Pipp & Harmon, 1987).

The internal working model consists of the child's memories of the attachment relationship—memories on which the child can draw to determine what he or she can expect from caregivers (primarily the mother) in given situations. Such an internal working model also helps the child to develop an appraisal of the relationship. For instance, if the child is rejected or abused when seeking comfort from his or her parents during stressful situations, the child is likely "to develop not only an internal working model of the parent as rejecting but also one of himself or herself as not worthy of help and comfort" (Bretherton, 1985, p. 12). It seems that the *quality* of attachment between child and parent may play a crucial role in a child's development.

The Dynamics of Human Attachment

Mary Ainsworth, who trained with John Bowlby, conducted some of the most interesting, careful studies of human attachment during infancy and childhood. Ainsworth's studies are superior to most others in their scope. They have included a 1-year longitudinal investigation of infant attachments in the home; a 20-minute laboratory test known as the *strange situation*, which demonstrates individual differences in the quality of attachment; and an assessment of the variables that determine the quality of infant attachment.

The strange situation is arranged in the following way. A mother and her young child (approximately 1 year old) enter the experiment room. The mother places her child on a small chair surrounded by toys and then takes a seat on the other side of the room. A short time later, a stranger enters the room, sits quietly for a moment, and then tries to engage the child in play. At this point, the mother abruptly leaves the room. In a short while, the mother returns and plays with the child, and the stranger leaves. Then the mother exits once more, leaving the child completely alone for 3 minutes. Then the stranger returns. A few minutes later, the mother returns and the stranger leaves. All these comings and goings may read like a scene from a Marx Brothers movie, but Table 5.3 will clarify the sequence. Everything that occurs during these 20-minute periods is recorded by an observer sitting behind a one-way mirror.

INTERNAL WORKING MODEL
The memories on which people can draw that help to determine the consequences that may result from actions in a given situation.

Table 5.3 ● The Strange Situation

EPISODE	ACTORS PRESENT IN ROOM	ACTION
1	Child, mother	Mother and child enter room
2	Child, mother, stranger	Stranger enters
3	Child, stranger	Mother exits
4	Child, mother	Mother returns and stranger exits
5	Child, alone	Mother exits
6	Child, stranger	Stranger returns
7	Child, mother	Mother returns and stranger exits

SECURE ATTACHMENT
Most common form of attachment observed by Ainsworth. Securely attached children respond happily to their mother's return, greet her, and stay near her for a while.

ANXIOUS/RESISTANT ATTACHMENT
A form of attachment observed by Ainsworth in which children approach their returning mothers, cry to be picked up, and then struggle to be free. Their behavior is ambivalent; they appear to wish to approach and avoid their mothers simultaneously.

ANXIOUS/AVOIDANT ATTACHMENT
A form of attachment observed by Ainsworth in which children do not approach—but rather actively avoid—their returning mothers.

Securely attached babies tend to show greater competence in early childhood.

As you can see, the organization of the strange situation places the child in a number of circumstances designed to measure the child's sense of security and attachment. It is worth noting that one advantage of the strange situation is that it allows observers to quantify many ways in which an infant can demonstrate attachment, instead of measuring only proximity. This is in agreement with Bowlby's plea that attachment be seen in more global terms. To make this advantage clear, consider that a 1-year-old child who demonstrates avoidance in the strange situation by turning away from his mother may continue to demonstrate avoidant behavior when he is 1½ years old by paying little attention to the mother when she returns. Researchers examining only one kind of behavior (such as turning away) would have missed the continuity that is afforded when the *purpose* of behavior is considered rather than just the behavior itself.

Although earlier studies of separation concentrated on how much infants cried when abandoned or how they reacted to spending time alone, Ainsworth and her associates concentrated on the infant's reaction to the return of the mother. By using a number of observational techniques, they were able to identify three attachment reactions of differing quality.

The first, **secure attachment**, was the most common, accounting for about 65 to 70 percent of children studied. Babies exhibiting this response gave their returning mothers a happy greeting and approached them or stayed near them for a time. The second kind of reaction, **anxious/resistant attachment**, accounted for about 10 to 15 percent of children. Infants who responded in this way approached their mothers, cried to be picked up, and then squirmed or fought to get free, as though they weren't sure what they wanted. The third kind of reaction, **anxious/avoidant attachment** (a rather paradoxical term), accounted for about 20 percent of children; it was demonstrated by infants who didn't approach their returning mothers or who actively avoided them.

It is generally assumed that anxious/avoidant and anxious/resistant attachments are weak attachments, while secure attachments are strong ones (Bretherton, 1985). Supporting this assertion are data showing that babies who are forming secure attachments will get "in tune" with the person to whom they are becoming attached. Their heart rate will become more stable in that person's presence (Izard et al., 1991), and their interactions with that person will become smooth and well timed (Isabella & Belsky, 1991); the same cannot be said for anxious/avoidant and anxious/resistant babies.

If what we are seeing, then, is strength of attachment, it becomes reasonable to wonder whether the way mothers treat anxious/avoidant or anxious/resistant infants is different from the way mothers treat securely attached infants. In fact, mothers of anxious/avoidant infants tend to respond to their infants' cries and demands only when they are in the mood to do so, often ignoring the infants at other times. They also appear to be less sensitive than other mothers to their infants' requests or needs (Smith & Pederson, 1988) and often state that they dislike physical contact with their infants (Ainsworth, Blehar, Waters, & Wall, 1978; Main & Weston, 1982). Infants who are anxious/avoidant may be that way because they expect to be rebuffed rather than comforted in the strange situation. To avoid a rebuff, they may turn away from the person who has been unresponsive in the past.

Anxious/resistant attachment, on the other hand, is not related to rejection but rather to inconsistency by the mother during the infant's first year of life (Ainsworth, Blehar, Waters, & Wall, 1978). Anxious/resistant infants may react the way they do simply because they don't know what to expect because the adult's behavior has been so inconsistent and unreliable in the past. Supporting this idea is the observation that anxious/resistant infants engage in social referencing (just like the ambivalent infants on the visual cliff, as described in the Chapter Preview) more than secure or anxious/avoidant infants (Dickstein, Thompson, Estes, Malkin, & Lamb, 1984).

Mothers who are the most accessible, consistent, and sensitive and who respond most to their babies' cries and signals have securely attached babies (Isabella, Belsky, & von Eye, 1989) and appear to enjoy their babies more than do mothers with less securely attached infants (Pederson et al., 1990). Interestingly, this kind of maternal sensitivity can be promoted just by encouraging the mother to have more physical contact with her baby, which in turn increases the chances that the baby will become securely attached (Anisfeld, Casper, Nozyce, & Cunningham, 1990). Securely attached infants require less proximity and physical contact as they grow older than do anxious/resistant or anxious/avoidant infants (Clarke-Stewart & Hevey, 1981). This might imply that infants who are securely attached have learned to trust and count on the adult who has responded correctly and quickly in the past to their needs or desires.

Until these findings were uncovered, it was commonly believed that infants who were coddled or hugged whenever they cried or showed fear would become dependent. As it turns out, just the opposite happens! Secure babies are more likely to develop independence (Sroufe, 1983).

No one knows why some mothers behave one way toward their infants, while other mothers behave another way. Each mother is an individual and as such has her own personality and beliefs that come into play when she interacts with her child. And of course, each has her own environment filled with various stressors and supports. However, it was also found that mothers of children who showed secure attachment typically recalled from their own childhood that they had felt secure and that attachments to others had been important to them. On the other hand, mothers of anxious or insecurely attached children often recalled feelings of rejection, hurt, or neglect from their childhood (Crowell & Feldman, 1988). It may be, then, that mothers have developed their own internal working models about what attachment between child and mother is, or should be, and this understanding is reflected in their relationships with their own children. Their children, in turn, then use the working models provided by their mothers to form their own ideas of what attachment means and respond accordingly (Crowell & Feldman, 1991).

Highlighting the play of environmental factors in the formation of attachments is cross-cultural research incorporating the strange situation. As it turns out, research conducted in other cultures has produced different results in the strange situation than Ainsworth obtained with her original American samples. For instance, among children who grew up on Israeli kibbutzim (collective farms) and also among Japanese children, there were higher percentages of anxious/resistant attachment in the strange situation. And among a sample of children from northern Germany, anxious/avoidant attachment was the most common form (see Table 5.4).

The results from different cultures may be so varied because the way that children in different cultures initially interpret the strange situation is a product of their experiences (Sagi, Van IJzendoorn, & Koren-Karie, 1991). For example, it has been noted that children on a kibbutz generally are raised communally and not directly by their parents. Thus, the strange situation might really have been "strange" to them because they weren't used to that kind of interaction with their mother. In fact, in this instance, a better choice for the role of parent in the strange situation might have been the child's *metapelet* (care provider on the kibbutz), because attachments don't have to form with the parent but may just as well form with a grandmother, nurse, nonrelative, or, in the case of the metapelet, anyone who fulfills the role of regular caregiver.

Table 5.4 ● The Distribution of Infants Across Cultures by Mode of Attachment Demonstrated During the Strange Situation

	TYPE OF ATTACHMENT		
COUNTRY	SECURE	ANXIOUS/ RESISTANT	ANXIOUS/ AVOIDANT
United States	71%	12%	17%
Japan	68%	32%	0%
Israel	62%	33%	5%
N. Germany	40%	11%	49%

Source: Adapted from Sagi, Van Ijzendoorn, & Koren-Karie, 1991.

Japanese children may have shown more anxious/resistant attachment in the strange situation because they were especially upset at being left alone with a stranger—something that Japanese mothers never do. Differences in German data probably reflect the cultural values of northern Germany that teach parents to keep a certain interpersonal distance from their children.

While these suggestions have received some support, it's probably too early in our research to make the jump from a few samples and results to a description of whole cultures. In fact, when all the studies throughout the world involving the strange situation are examined, one discovers that the variation of results within cultures is 1½ times greater than the variation of results between cultures (Van IJzendoorn & Kroonenberg, 1988). Moreover, many American samples give results very different from Ainsworth's original results, often resembling the Israeli, German, or Japanese findings. American results are probably so different from one study to the next because the American samples were quite diverse, including populations from different socioeconomic strata and ethnic backgrounds.

When examining all these studies, we can say that secure attachment is usually the most common form of attachment exhibited. And we can also say that attachment appears to be strongly influenced by environmental forces. Beyond this, we have to be extremely cautious (Van IJzendoorn & Kroonenberg, 1988).

ATTACHMENT AND SOCIAL DEVELOPMENT

The Flexibility of Human Attachment

Most models of human attachment focus on the importance of a primary caregiver, usually the mother. But recent cross-cultural studies of the Efe, a forest-dwelling tribe in Africa, have raised questions about the assumption that a primary caregiver is necessary for healthy attachment and human development.

Efe babies and toddlers spend about half of their time away from their mothers in the care of many older children and adults. Infants are commonly breast fed by any available woman who is able. Three-year-olds are away from their mothers 70 percent of the time. Contact with fathers stays at about roughly 8 percent during the child's early years.

The infants and toddlers are not left alone, but are usually carried by an older child or adult throughout the day and when set down are typically within earshot of about 10 tribe members. It is not surprising, therefore, that unlike children in other cultures, the Efe children form strong and close emotional attachment to many members of the tribe and have no primary caregiver as such (although some Efe children may, on occasion, show preferences for certain tribe members). The Efe children appear to develop quite well within this arrangement (Tronick, Morelli, & Ivey, 1992).

This mode of child rearing is not really comparable to modern day-care arrangements. Efe infants see the same caregivers each day, while there is often considerable turnover at modern day-care centers. Also, children who must leave their homes each day to go to day care can experience the contrast between the two arrangements. Efe children are all raised the same way and know no other arrangement. The important finding here is not so much a vindication of day care (discussed in greater detail in the Applications section) but rather the realization that infants and toddlers can form very strong emotional attachments to many caregivers at once. That is, infants and toddlers are not limited to one primary caregiver by some innate biological organization; rather, they most often become attached to a primary caregiver because of culture.

Attachment and Social Relationships

Researcher L. Alan Sroufe conducted one of the more detailed investigations of personal competence and peer approval among children in an effort to discover how the kind of attachment that a child shows in infancy affects later social relationships; the study was known as the Minnesota Preschool Project (Sroufe, 1983). Sroufe and his co-workers developed objective measures for observing positive, negative, and inappropriate emotional reactions in preschool children. They designed a rating scale of "social competence" by subtracting the number of inappropriate and negative social-emotional interactions demonstrated by each child from the number of appropriate and positive interactions. Children described by the researchers as securely attached at 15 months tended to have the highest scores and by the age of 3½ years were more likely to be peer leaders in the preschool. They tended to be involved in social relationships and actively engaged in their environments, to be well liked by their peers, and to enjoy sharing good feelings and thoughts with others (Park & Waters, 1989). They also often rewarded their peers for behaving in these ways (Waters, Wippman, & Sroufe, 1979).

Low-ranked children generally were not liked or admired by their peers and were referred to by their teachers as "unpredictable," "a loner," or "a chronic whiner" (Bower, 1985). Other studies have shown the same sort of classifications for school-age children who had not shown secure attachment as infants (Cohn, 1990).

Securely attached infants (at least most of the ones from American studies) also seem to tolerate a moderate amount of separation from their mothers (Jacobson & Wille, 1984), which in turn makes them more comfortable exploring their environments (Joffe, 1980). When faced with something new, such as a toy or game, these infants will persist in examining it. Moreover, they are often encouraged by their mothers in a happy and joyful way to play and explore, which further encourages these children to expand their experiences (Rheingold, Cook, & Kolowitz, 1987). This persistence in exploring and experiencing often provides children with an opportunity to master the new things they have encountered (Frodi, Bridges, & Grolnick, 1985). Not surprisingly, children who exhibit such mastery in infancy tend to show greater competence in early childhood (Messer et al., 1986; Sroufe, 1983), and the persistence and confidence they gain as infants have been shown to have lasting benefits, as reflected in the schoolwork of these same children at age 12 years (Estrada,

Arsenio, Hess, & Holloway, 1987). Securely attached children have also been found to have superior cognitive functioning in adolescence (Jacobsen, Edelstein, & Hofmann, 1994).

Insecurely attached children, once they reach school, show various problems, depending on their gender. Boys who are insecurely attached tend to be more assertive, aggressive, controlling, disrupting, and attention seeking than securely attached boys, while girls tend to be more dependent and compliant than their securely attached peers (Turner, 1991).

Attachment quality can also affect sibling relationships. In families with two children, if both are securely attached, there is less hostility and rivalry than if one or both of the siblings are not securely attached (Teti & Ablard, 1989).

All of these data, however, are correlational (not causal), in that we can state only that high levels of positive behaviors and emotions are correlated with peer approval, acceptance, and early secure attachment, while less desired outcomes are associated with insecure forms of attachment. Again, it may be a third variable that is causing both secure attachment and positive outcomes.

Attachment and Family Stability

Researcher Michael Lamb and his colleagues have pointed out that although there does seem to be some connection between attachment quality and later behavior, the relationship may reflect something more general; according to Lamb, that something probably is family stability. In stable families, attachment is more secure and children tend to be more successful in terms of their social-emotional development. Supporting this assumption is the fact that predictions of future behavior based on findings in the strange situation are more likely to be correct for children who are from stable families, especially those that have stable child-care arrangements. In this view, the results from the strange situation *and* the child's later development simply reflect the more general influence of family and child-care stability, which in turn gives rise to secure attachment and later social acceptance (Lamb, Thompson, Gardner, Charnov, & Estes, 1984).*

The Father's Role

You may have noticed that up until this time, we have hardly mentioned fathers. In fact, fathers have traditionally been shortchanged in the attachment literature. Ainsworth and just about every other researcher prior to 1970 ignored fathers. Happily, however, fathers have attracted attention since then.

One reason for the growing interest in the father's role during his child's infancy is that fathers have been participating increasingly in the feeding, care, and stimulation of their infants (Parke & Tinsley, 1981). This change, which has occurred in most Western industrialized nations, has come about for a number of reasons, the foremost of which is the growing number of working mothers. Also important is the conscious effort on the part of many people to alter or abolish sex stereotypes, which in turn affects the traditional roles of

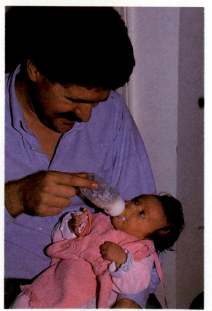

Fathers have been participating increasingly in the feeding, care, and stimulation of their infants, although they are still less likely to be the primary caregiver.

---

*We discussed this logical fallacy in Chapter 1. There, we pointed out that a correlation between increased ice cream sales and increased drownings should not lead us to believe that there is a causal connection between these two variables. Instead, both increases were caused by a third factor—summer. In the same way, the correlation between attachment and later social success may be accounted for by a third factor that is causally related to both—family stability. Whenever you find a strong correlation between two events, it's a good idea to ask yourself whether a third factor could be causing the two you have observed.

"mother" and "father." Even though more than 50 percent of American mothers work, however, these sex role stereotypes are still strong. One study found that, on average, mothers spend 121 hours with their infants for each 26 hours spent by the father (Cowan & Cowan, 1987). As one group of researchers stated, "Mothers more frequently responded to, stimulated, expressed positive affection toward, and took basic care of their infants, while fathers spent more time reading or watching TV" (Belsky, Gilstrap, & Rovine, 1984, p. 702). The same pattern has been found in other Western industrialized nations, such as Israel (Greenbaum & Landau, 1982) and Sweden (Frodi, Lamb, Hwang, & Frodi, 1982). The Swedish study is especially interesting because the difference between mother and father involvement was evident in both traditional and nontraditional families. Fathers are simply less likely to be the primary caregiver, and this holds true across a great range of paternal ages, from teenage fathers to much older ones (Lamb & Elster, 1985).

The attitudes that both parents express before a child's birth concerning how much the father should be involved generally predict how active a role the father will take with his infant (Palkovitz, 1984). Interestingly, when fathers are alone with their infants, they are far more likely to assume the role of primary caregiver and to tend to their infant's needs than they are when the mother is present (Palkovitz, 1980).

Fathers, it should be noted, have been found to spend more time than mothers playing with their infants (Kotelchuck, 1976). This playmate role on the part of fathers also has been observed in other countries (Richards, Dunn, & Antonis, 1977). In one study, 2½-year-old children were given an opportunity to choose either their father or mother in a play situation; more than two-thirds of the children chose to play with their fathers first (Clarke-Stewart, 1977).

John Bowlby once described the distinction between playmate and attachment figure. He noted that while playmates are approached by infants who are in a positive mood, attachment figures are approached by infants who are frightened or under stress (Bowlby, 1982b). In fact, mothers and fathers are *both* attachment figures and playmates for the infant. It's just that generally, the mother is the *primary* attachment figure, while the father is the *preferred* playmate.

This view of father as playmate and mother as caregiver is probably based on culture and tradition and is certainly not the case for every family. Studies from Norway, Sweden, and Australia have shown that the traditional arrangement is not universal and depends on the working arrangements of the parents and other factors, such as the health of the infant and the organization of the family (Gronseth, 1975; Russell, 1980; Radin & Harold-Goldsmith, 1989).

In summary, infants are born into the world with specific behavioral attributes that predispose them to form attachments to their caregivers. These attachments are strong *reciprocal* relationships that help to foster future behavioral competencies. In the next section, we will look at how infant emotions develop and how they contribute to the formation of social relationships.

Research has shown that children especially appreciate the father's role as playmate.

SOCIAL-EMOTIONAL DEVELOPMENT

It has been said that our emotions are what make us most human. We rage, we laugh, we cry, we fear, and we love. To be without emotions is to be unfeeling, perhaps "inhuman." Having feelings is an important part of being human.

Everyone has emotions, even infants. Babies smile and laugh, show fear, and, as you have seen, form loving attachments. Parents often report that the first smile from their baby is a magical moment that seems instantly to create a closer and more meaningful bond. Emotions are so important in forming our social bonds and attachments that researchers often use the term social-emotional development to emphasize the intertwining of the social and emotional dimensions of human behavior.

The Function of Emotion

No one is certain why emotions exist, but many researchers believe that it is because emotions serve important functions. Charles Darwin was the first to espouse this view in his book *The Expression of the Emotions in Man and Animals* (Darwin, 1872/1967). According to this view, emotions perform two valuable services. First, they motivate us. For example, although you might logically decide to get out of the way of a speeding car, you're more likely to do it if you're scared than if you don't particularly feel one way or the other about it; and if you do run, you are more likely to live and pass on the genes for this strong motivational mechanism: the ability to feel afraid. Second, emotions help us to communicate our desires and wishes to others. By looking at others—that is, by engaging in social referencing—we can often sense what others want us to do because we perceive how they feel.

Similarly, emotions motivate infants and also help them to interact. Remember how the infants on the visual cliff in the Chapter Preview relied on their mother's expression for information about whether crossing over the cliff edge was safe. The interpersonal communication provided by facial expressions endows emotion with an important social aspect. In this way, emotion becomes involved in the social process.

The Development of Emotions

The issue of whether infants are born with a full array of emotions or whether they develop emotions over time is central to our understanding of emotional development. This issue, however, remains unresolved. Thirty years ago, most textbooks stated, rather matter-of-factly, that newborns started out by showing only arousal or quiescence. They went on to say that it wasn't until babies were

Young infants show discrete facial expressions.

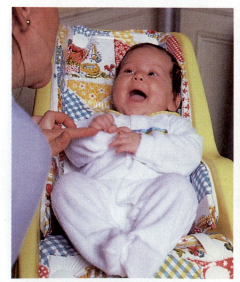
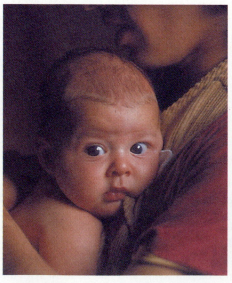

between about 1 and 6 months of age that they displayed weak, less specifically defined emotional states, such as pleasure, wariness, or rage. And it was only older infants, those older than about 6 months of age, who showed distinct emotions, such as joy, fear, or anger. Emotions, therefore, became more differentiated and obvious as infants grew older, and more specific terms were used to denote these emotions as they developed (see Table 5.5). It was also assumed that infants were being socialized, to a great degree, about how to be emotional in certain circumstances. This view of emotional development is still popular today, but it is no longer the only view.

Challenging this long-held assumption is the **discrete emotions theory**. Researchers espousing this view believe that *all* the basic emotions are present in newborns and that as the infants age, they become better able to express these emotions in a way that others can see clearly, which explains the earlier assumptions about the gradual development of emotions (Campos, Barrett, Lamb, Stenberg, & Goldsmith, 1983). Supporting this assertion is a study that shows that infants only 10 weeks old can discriminate their mother's different emotional states. In this study, a mother would face her baby and say, "You make me (happy, sad, angry)," and match her voice to her facial expression. The infant typically acted as though the mother's actions had meaning, and the infant would react.

DISCRETE EMOTIONS THEORY
A view of emotional development that has as its central premise that all basic emotions are present and functional in newborns or very shortly after birth.

Table 5.5 ● The Development of Some Basic Human Emotions*

MONTH	PLEASURE-JOY	WARINESS-FEAR	RAGE-ANGER
0	Endogenous smile	Startle/pain	Distress due to covering the face, physical restraint, or extreme discomfort
1	Turning toward	Obligatory attention	
2			
3	Pleasure		Rage (disappointment)
4	Delight Active laughter	Wariness	
5			
6			
7	Joy		Anger
8			
9		Fear (stranger aversion)	
10			
11			
12	Elation	Anxiety Immediate fear	Angry mood, petulance
18	Positive valuation of self-affection	Shame	Defiance
24			Intentional hurting
36	Pride, love		Guilt

*The age specified is neither the first appearance of the affect in question nor its peak occurrence, it is the age when the literature suggests that the reaction is common.
Source: Adapted from Sroufe, 1979, p. 473.

The happy mothers produced happiness in their infants. Babies exposed to angry exhibitions eventually turned away and stopped looking. Those exposed to sad exhibitions appeared to suck their lips and tried to soothe themselves (Haviland & Lelwica, 1987). The researchers concluded that the mother's demeanor and emotional behavior were triggering the corresponding emotions in her infant. As you can see, this view is quite different from one that supposes that infants have undifferentiated affective states at first and only experience the full range of emotions once they are older.

Central to the discrete emotions theory is the idea that the same basic emotions are common to all people and that they are produced early in infancy or are present at birth, having been brought forth by the maturation of the nervous system. Some evidence for the maturational development of emotion comes from the work of Mel Konner, a Harvard biological anthropologist who has studied the onset of smiling among the !Kung San tribe in the Kalahari Desert in Africa. The !Kung San are one of the last hunter-gatherer tribes in the world. Konner observed more than 60 !Kung infants, and despite the great cultural and environmental differences between the !Kung and industrialized Western cultures, he discovered no differences in the onset and development of smiling (Greenberg, 1977). Konner believes that like motor and physical development, much of emotional development is directly tied to a maturational timetable of neurological growth.

And yet the discrete emotions theory hasn't been fully accepted because no one has found a convincing way to show that young infants acting in what appear to be complex emotional ways actually *feel* the emotions they are displaying. For example, although a baby might smile back at her mother and act in a happy way when her mother acts happily, how can we know if the baby feels happy? Perhaps she is only imitating her mother's facial expression. Some researchers are considering trying to uncover physiological changes that happen during emotions in adults and children and then looking for similar results in young infants. Such findings could indicate that a similar emotional process is going on in both infants and older humans. Until then, however, it remains an open question as to how rich a young infant's emotional experience is compared with older infants and children.

The infant's first faint smile is related to activity in the central nervous system, and this "reflex smile" is replaced by the familiar "social smile" at about 3 or 4 weeks of age.

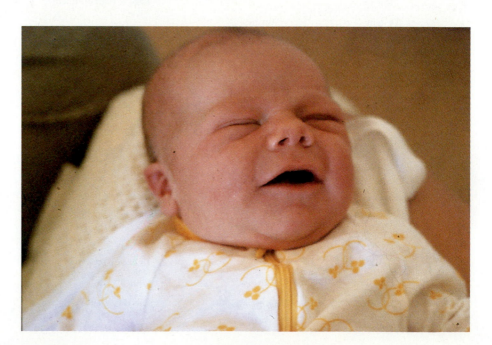

The very existence of biological or maturational components to emotion, however, does not prove that emotions are discrete and present at birth. Other alternatives are possible and are being actively investigated. For example, one researcher, attempting to find emotional correlates with the electrical activity of an infant's brain, noticed that the only emotional activity associated with EEG readings in infants was the initial decision to approach or withdraw from a stimulus (Fox, 1991). Perhaps infants require experience with the environment before these two basic orientations can begin to differentiate into discrete emotional states. If that is the case, human emotions may develop according to the chart shown in Figure 5.3.

At first such findings might appear to be in conflict with the research showing that 10-week-old infants display discrete emotions. But that is not necessarily true. First, as we mentioned, the 10-week-old infants in that study may have just been imitating their mothers without really having yet developed discrete emotions. Second, it is possible that emotions do develop as shown in Figure 5.3, but become discretely differentiated before 10 weeks of age.

Separation Anxiety.   Sometimes emotional development has been used to help assess the overall development of the child. Because of the variability in the onset of emotions, however, this manner of assessment has become less popular. Still, it is not uncommon to hear of certain emotional stages that children are expected to pass through. One such "stage" is referred to as **separation anxiety**. Separation anxiety is the fear expressed by the child when he or she is left alone by the parent or caregiver. Children between 9 and 30 months will often show anxiety at being left, even if the parent is just in another room (sometimes even if the parent is still in view). They will cry and try to regain contact with the parent or caregiver. Separation anxiety is often used to explain the clinging, following behavior of toddlers who may seem driven to be near the adult to whom they have become attached. This anxiety usually reaches its peak at about 18 months of age and declines steadily thereafter. Separation anxiety, however, is often quite variable. Infants who are separated from their primary caregivers on a daily basis often become quite used to the separations and stop reacting to them (Field, 1991a). Some children express separation anxiety far more than others, and some children may express it strongly on one day but not on the next.

Separation anxiety is assumed to have evolved because of the survival value involved in keeping close contact with the caregiver.

Fear of Strangers.   Another emotion that has been of particular interest to developmental researchers is the fear of strangers, which, like separation anxiety, appears to be a universal phenomenon that develops in infants of about the same age worldwide, regardless of their cultural backgrounds.

SEPARATION ANXIETY
The anxiety over the possible loss of anyone to whom a person has become attached.

STRANGER ANXIETY
A fear of unfamiliar individuals that most infants develop when they are about 6 months of age.

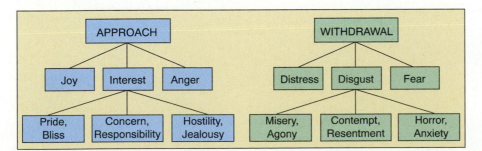

FIGURE 5.3

The possible development of emotions as indicated by Fox's research. Beginning with a mode of responding along a very basic approach-withdrawal continuum, the child eventually develops a refined set of responses, all stemming from the original two of approach and withdrawal. (SOURCE: After Fox, 1991)

Table 5.6 ● Age of Onset of Fear of Strangers in a Group of Children

AGE (IN WEEKS)	PERCENTAGE OF CHILREN AFFECTED AT EACH AGE
21–24	2
25–28	16
29–32	25
33–36	32
37–40	11
41–44	6
45–48	3
49–52	0
53–78	5

Source: Adapted from Schaffer and Emerson, 1964.

Table 5.6 shows the onset of fear of strangers in a group of infants. As you can see, this fear first appears in some babies as early as 6 months of age, but usually begins at about the age of 7½ months.

As with separation anxiety, **stranger anxiety**, as this fear of strangers is called, isn't a clear-cut phenomenon. For many years, for example, it has been known that 9- to 13-month-old infants who have been exposed to only a limited number of adults will often show a strong fear of strangers, while similar infants who have been exposed to many different strangers aren't nearly as likely to be frightened (Collard, 1968). This might mean that infants who react positively to strangers have simply become used to them. Any dog owner can tell you that even the noisiest of dogs will stop barking at strangers if constantly surrounded by them. Perhaps such habituation also occurs in our own species.

Furthermore, fear of strangers is not an extremely reliable phenomenon. Infants who are clearly afraid of strangers on one day will, only a few days later, appear not to be frightened by them at all. At a later time, these same infants may once again manifest fear in the presence of a stranger (Shaffran & Decarie, 1973).

Is Day Care a Good Idea?

Human babies are not precocious. They must be cared for. Infants may need a caregiver for a number of years before they can survive unaided. For this reason, if for no other, it is very much in an infant's best interests to form a strong attachment to a primary caregiver rapidly. As you recall, John Bowlby developed a theory (Bowlby, 1973, 1969) that emphasized the reciprocal nature of such caregiver arrangements. He thought that both infants and their mothers are biologically primed to form special attachments to each other.

If what Bowlby theorized is correct, what happens if we disrupt this very special arrangement between infant and mother and place the infant in a day-care center each day? Is the infant flexible enough to learn to adapt to this situation, or will there be some serious consequences? This issue is an important one, because in the United States, more than 50 percent of mothers of children under 6 are working (see Figure 5.4). In other industrialized nations, a large portion of married women with preschool children are also working, even in countries such as Japan, where mothers have traditionally stayed home with their children. A great number of infants around the world are therefore affected.

For years, developmental researchers studied day care; the general consensus early on was that day care had no effect, one way or the other, on the quality of the infant's attachment to the mother (Belsky & Steinberg, 1978; Farran & Ramey, 1977). Most of these early studies, however, were conducted with infants in high-quality day-care centers, usually at universities. This is not the day-care setting that most infants encounter. Psychologist Jay Belsky examined infants in more typical day-care settings. He concluded that babies who spent more than 20 hours per week with nonmaternal care during the first year of life were more likely to show anxious/avoidant attachment to their mothers than were other babies (Belsky, 1988, 1986). Other researchers have made similar observations and have suggested that infants left in day care might be showing anxious/avoidant attachment because they perceive the mother's daily abandonment as rejection (Barglow, Vaughn, & Molitor, 1987). As you recall, insecure attachment is associated with problems as the infant matures. According to Belsky, "We've identified a window of vulnerability. Now we have to figure out what conditions open it and which shut it" (Wallis & Ludtke, 1987, p. 63).

Some researchers have questioned these findings, however. One of the main criticisms is that Belsky used the strange situation to measure infant attachment. Infants in day care have much more experience with separations and strangers than do those who aren't in day care, and this may affect their performance in the strange situation (Thompson, 1988). Belsky's own research, however, indicates that this is not the case (Belsky & Braungart, 1991). A stronger criticism comes from researcher Michael Lamb, who points out that while it may be true that day-care infants often show more anxious/avoidant attachment, these findings are all based on the strange situation, whose

FIGURE 5.4

The percentage of working mothers of children under 6 years of age was increasing since 1960 until it leveled off in the mid 1980s. It appears that about 45 percent of women with young children will stay at home with their children barring extreme circumstances and that the growing trend for mothers of young children to work outside the home has peaked. Still, because the majority of mothers with young children work outside the home, many preschoolers require some form of nonparental care (SOURCE: Adapted from *Statistical Abstract of the United States*, 1991; Wallis, Hull, Ludtke, & Taylor, 1987)

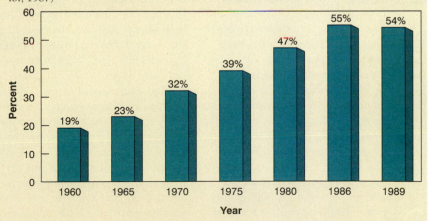

very validity can be questioned (Lamb & Sternberg, 1990). Perhaps, as Lamb and others have argued, other measures should be used to assess the infant's social and emotional well-being, including the long-term effects of day-care quality.

The quality of day care. The greatest difficulty in understanding the issue of day-care quality is that there is such a great range of what we call "day care." Care may be provided in licensed or unlicensed facilities and even in informal family day-care arrangements. For example, one adult on a particular block may take in others' children for profit, in a sense serving as a group baby-sitter. Some states have standards for day care, but most do not. In a number of states, the accepted caregiver-to-infant ratio is 1:10. You can't help but wonder how one caregiver could rescue 10 infants from a fire.

In addition to health and safety standards, many other variables affect the quality of the day-care environment. Unfortunately, longitudinal studies assessing the long-term consequences of different variables in day care are few and far between, and the results we have are highly tentative.

The federal government once developed standards (the Federal Interagency Day Care Requirements, or FIDCR) for day-care centers in terms of child ratios, group size, and teacher training, but they were never implemented. Even so, it has been found that children in day-care facilities meeting those standards were more likely to show secure attachment and to be more competent with peers than children in day-care facilities not meeting the FIDCR standards (Howes, Phillips, & Whitebook, 1992).

These standards were based on earlier findings of what high-quality day care would include. In terms of language, social, and intellectual development, children in day-care

centers were found to do better if they were in small groups (18 or fewer) of children the same age or older (Miller & Greenberg, 1985; Roupp et al., 1979). The most effective teachers, not surprisingly, had the highest education level and the most training in child development. Day-care providers who spoke to the child at an appropriate level and who had conversations with the child often helped to foster language development significantly more than did caregivers who devoted most of their verbal interaction to speaking at an adult level with other staff members (McCartney, 1984). This same kind of involved verbal interaction between caregiver and child was also found to foster successful social development among day-care children (Phillips, McCartney, & Scarr, 1987). Teachers with better training were more likely to become involved with children in this way.

Children who were enrolled in low-quality day care (day-care centers that did not meet the previously mentioned standards) at an early age (1 to 2 years) were found in kindergarten to be more distractible, less considerate, and less able to work at a task than children who had entered low-quality day care at a later age or who had been enrolled in a high-quality day-care facility (Howes, 1990). In contrast, the more time that preschool children spent in high-quality day care, the more likely they were to receive positive ratings in leadership, popularity, attractiveness, and assertiveness once they entered grade school (Field, 1991b). Perhaps most interesting is a Swedish study showing that children enrolled in high-quality day care before the age of 1 performed better in school (when measured at ages 8 and 13) than did their counterparts who had entered day care at a later age (Andersson, 1992). Although some of these results may be related to the fact that families who can afford

high-quality day care may be quite different from families who cannot (Pence & Goelman, 1987), all of these data taken collectively do seem to indicate that the quality of day care is an important factor, probably more so than the age at which the child enters a day-care facility.

Unlicensed or informal care. Little research has been done in the area of home day-care arrangements that are informal or unlicensed, but one study indicated that there probably are no significant differences as long as the caregivers have experience, interact with the children, and provide them with some structure by giving them things to do (Stith & Davis, 1984)—in other words, create a high-quality home-care or unlicensed day-care environment. Of course, the results of this limited study do not mean that unlicensed day-care centers are as good as licensed ones. Unlicensed centers may run the range from excellent to dangerous. (Of course, the same may be true of licensed centers; presumably, however, this is less likely.) Another study did find that children in day-care situations fared better in terms of language, social, emotional, and intellectual development than did those left alone with individual baby-sitters (Miller & Greenberg, 1985).

Choosing a Day-Care Facility. Unfortunately, because of financial constraints and geographical location, parents often accept a day-care facility that does not meet their own personal standards; they simply have little choice to do otherwise (Gravett, Rogers, & Thompson, 1987). Even if this is the case, there are some things parents can do.

First and foremost, parents should get to know the day-care center they are considering. Several studies have found that parents who have chosen a day-care center spend very little time there and interact with the caregivers only occasionally, usually when they are dropping off or picking up their children (Zigler & Turner, 1982; Powell, 1978, 1977). Instead, it's a good idea to spend time getting to know the day-care staff personally. As consumers, parents should feel free to ask questions about the staff's backgrounds, training, and licensing. They should be suspicious of any day-care center that won't let them spend time observing the caregivers at work. Parents should observe how the staff interacts with the children. And they should check that the staff is alert and prepared for medical and safety emergencies. Their questions and pressure may help turn a borderline facility into an acceptable one.

Day-care centers with some structure—that is, those that provide children with things to do—tend to be superior. Parents need to ask what kinds of games, activities, and toys

are available for the children. And parents should certainly look at the staff-to-child ratio. Is the center well enough staffed to meet the individual requirements of the child? Are there regular mealtimes and nap times? Is the place clean? Are children's toilet needs taken care of promptly and hygienically? Are all injuries, bumps, and bruises explained in detail and in writing? These are all concerns that parents might have.

Parents need to be careful consumers and shop around. If there is nothing nearby, they should find out if others in their neighborhood would also like to use a more distant day-care facility. By car pooling, a number of families might be able to benefit from a higher-quality, though more distant, day-care center. Finally, if parents are unhappy with the day-care facilities in their area, they might investigate initiating changes in licensing or practice through local or state government officials.

Day care and child abuse.
Although there have been a few scary headlines of sexual or other forms of child abuse in day-care centers, direct physical abuse is rare. Of much greater concern are questions such as: Are social interactions available (will the child be alone or ignored)? Will the child get a hot, nutritious lunch? Is there adequate fire protection?

Generally speaking, high-quality day care can be very valuable and beneficial because it allows both parents to work, and a family with a higher income may provide a more stress-free and happy environment for its children. There is no question that a child will fare better spending part of the day with a high-quality caregiver than spending the whole day with a depressed or frustrated parent. Parents shouldn't be afraid to use day care; they just need to use a good dose of common sense when choosing a facility.

SUMMARY

■ Although a human infant doesn't appear to possess a fully integrated personality in the first few days of life, scientists have observed that newborns do exhibit considerable differences in temperament. These temperaments may be consistent or stable over great lengths of time.

■ Alexander Thomas and Stella Chess began the New York Longitudinal Study to examine infant reactivity. They have identified a number of temperamental characteristics and have found them to be stable over time.

■ For determining future adjustment, how well a child's temperament is suited to his or her environment may be more important than whether the child is easy or difficult. Researchers refer to this match with the environment as goodness of fit.

■ Although temperament does seem to be determined in part by constitutional factors, the environment can play an important role in shaping and altering it.

■ According to Sigmund Freud, the focus of personality development in infancy is on oral processes. Freud also believed that an infant who obtained too little or too much satisfaction during this time could develop a fixation.

■ Erik Erikson argued that the first major conflict faced by a child, which occurs during the first year of life, is the establishment of trust rather than mistrust.

■ The mechanism of attachment has been intensely debated and investigated by developmental theorists, and the theoretical orientation taken by most researchers over the years has changed.

■ Both Freud and the learning theorists believed that nursing led to the formation of strong attachments between infant and mother because nursing satisfies the infant's biological needs. However, research with rhesus monkeys and surrogate mothers, conducted by Harry Harlow and his colleagues, cast doubt on this speculation.

■ John Bowlby, a proponent of the intraorganismic perspective, believed that the attachment system becomes well organized sometime during the second half of the infant's first year of life. The child may then begin to form internal working models of the relationships between the child and his or her caregivers.

■ Attachment doesn't occur in isolation. To investigate such interactions, Mary Ainsworth devised the strange situation. This experimental design offers many situations in which a child's attachment and exploration behavior can be measured.

■ Ainsworth has identified three kinds of attachment: secure, anxious/resistant, and anxious/avoidant. These attachments appear to be fairly stable over time and may have predictive value in determining the child's social development and behavior throughout life.

■ Michael Lamb and other researchers have pointed out that children's reactions in the strange situation may reflect something more general than quality of attachment—probably family stability.

■ Research concerning the father's role has increased dramatically in recent years. Although fathers are less likely than mothers to be the primary caregiver, they have a special role to play. Fathers are more likely than mothers to be their children's preferred playmate.

■ Emotions are so important in forming our social bonds and attachments that researchers often use the term social-emotional development to emphasize the intertwining of the social and emotional dimensions of human behavior. Emotions motivate infants and also help them to interact.

■ One point that is strongly debated is whether emotions develop gradually or whether they are discrete and fully present at birth.

■ Among the many issues studied concerning infants' emotions are the development of emotions in infants and why they fear strangers.

QUESTIONS FOR DISCUSSION

1. Do you think that "easy" children have an easier life? Do you think that easy children develop effective coping skills? What problems might easy children encounter that difficult children might not? Relate this to the concept of goodness of fit.

2. Do you think that attachment is an adequate way of measuring infant "love"?

3. Would you say that the baby rhesus monkey "loves" its cloth mother? Harlow did.

4. If you were considering leaving your infant in a day-care center, what would be your major concerns? Why? Support your statements.

5. Except for breast feeding, do you think that a mother's ability to function as a caregiver for an infant is biologically different from a father's?

SUGGESTIONS FOR FURTHER READING

1. Brazelton, T. B., & Yogman, M. E. (1986). *Affective development in infancy*. Norwood, NJ: Ablex.

2. Buss, A. H., & Plomin, R. (1984). *Temperament: Early developing personality traits*. Hillsdale, NJ: Erlbaum.

3. Emde, R. N., & Harmon, R. J. (Eds.). (1982). *The development of attachment and affiliative systems*. New York: Plenum.

4. Greenspan, S., & Greenspan, N. T. (1985). *First feelings: Milestones in the emotional development of your baby and child*. New York: Viking.

5. Lusk, D., & McPherson, B. (1992). *Nothing but the best: Making day care work for you & your child*. New York: Teacher's College Press.

6. Reed, G. (1992). *Where are we coming from? Day-care positives & negatives*. New York: Vantage.

7. Shell, E. R. (1992). *A child's place: A year in the life of a day care center*. Boston: Little Brown.

EARLY CHILDHOOD: TODDLERS AND PRESCHOOL CHILDREN
(1–6 Years of Age)

CHAPTER 6

Early Childhood: Physical, Cognitive, and Gender Role Development

CHAPTER PREVIEW
The Dawning of Consciousness

The sense of being conscious, of residing inside of your body, seeing through your eyes, hearing through your ears; the sense of self-awareness; the sense that you exist. When did you first develop it? When did you become aware that you were alive, that you were you, and that on each passing day when you awoke, you would still be you?

You walk into a bathroom and see yourself in a mirror. There you are, it's you all right, as usual. You notice that somehow a smudge of ink has gotten onto your forehead. You wipe it off.

A small smudge of rouge is put on a 5-month-old infant's nose, and she is placed before a mirror. She glances at the reflection in the mirror and at objects in the room; she doesn't seem to realize what the reflection is.

A small smudge of rouge is placed on the nose of a 12-month-old child, and he is placed before a mirror. He reaches out and tries to touch the reflection. He looks behind the mirror. (Is he looking for the baby in the reflection?) He does not seem to realize who the baby with the spot on his nose is (Brooks-Gunn & Lewis, 1975).

A 20-month-old child with a smudge of rouge on her nose is placed before a mirror. She looks at the reflection, reaches her hand to her face, and rubs her nose (Amsterdam, 1972). She is aware; she knows that it is her reflection and that she is seeing herself. Sometime between the ages of 1 and 2 years, children become aware of themselves; they become conscious of being living creatures. The development of self-awareness is one of the major milestones during the early childhood years. It will greatly shape the child's subsequent development.

In this chapter, we will look at some of the physical and motor changes that take place during early childhood, and then we will examine the growing cognitive capabilities of young children. We will see that young children gradually come to use internal representations of the external world and to develop a sense of self-awareness, and that they later use intuition to try to solve problems. We will end our discussion by examining their acquisition of gender roles.

PHYSICAL AND MOTOR DEVELOPMENT

During the early childhood years, the *deceleration* of growth that began just after conception continues. Although the child's height and weight continue to increase, the rate of increase slows down in the latter part of this period. Table 6.1 lists the average gains in height and weight that can be expected in the years from 1 to 6. As you can see, there is a greater increase between the years 1 and 2 than between the years 5 and 6.

Besides physically increasing in size, children show increased motor competence during the early childhood years. Figure 6.1 outlines some of the motor milestones that can be expected to occur in early childhood. During this time, children also continue to hone the motor skills they have already acquired, such as walking. Researcher Kathleen Haywood, an expert in motor development, believes that young children improve their performance of basic skills by increasing their mechanical efficiency. She has stated that children refine their skills gradually by executing each motor behavior in a more mechanically efficient way (Haywood, 1986).

COGNITIVE DEVELOPMENT

Besides the obvious physical and motor maturation that occurs during early childhood, some of the most apparent and interesting development occurs in the way the young child thinks. As we discussed in Chapter 2, Jean Piaget believed that a child's cognitive development is the combined result of the development of the brain and nervous system and the experiences that help the child adapt to his or her environment. As you recall, Piaget outlined two ways in which a child can adapt to his environment—through *assimilation* and through *accommodation*. Table 6.2 outlines the two periods of cognitive development that Piaget believed the infant and young child pass through during their first 6 or 7 years.

Piaget argued that at the beginning, during the sensorimotor period, an infant's "thoughts" are based on his or her physical actions. When an infant recognizes her bottle and reaches for it, she is showing a sensorimotor understanding of her environment because she is able to sense the bottle and reach

Table 6.1 ● Average Height and Weight Increase Between the Ages of 1 and 6 Years		
AGE	WEIGHT INCREASE	HEIGHT INCREASE
1–2 years	5–6 pounds	4–5 inches
2–3 years	3–5 pounds	3–4 inches
3–4 years	3–5 pounds	3–4 inches
4–5 years	3–4 pounds	2–3 inches
5–6 years	3–4 pounds	2–3 inches

Source: Adapted from Dodson & Alexander, 1986, pp. 183, 234, 275.

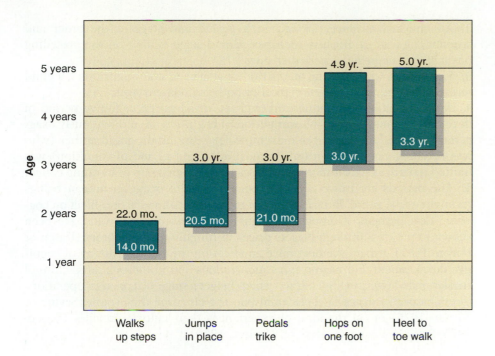

FIGURE 6.1

Some motor milestones that occur during the early childhood years, from the Denver Development Screening Test. The bottom end of the bar represents the age at which 25 percent of the sample could perform the task; the top end represents the age at which 90 percent could perform it. (SOURCE: Adapted from Frankenburg & Dodds, 1967, p. 186)

for it. Piaget used the term **scheme** to describe this basic unit of cognition. A scheme is a sensorimotor reaction by the infant when she responds to something in the environment that her senses have recognized. A scheme is the action equivalent of a concept. With it, the infant can organize her world into categories, such as *things I can touch*, or *things I can eat.*

When the infant becomes aware of a failing in her thought strategies, she experiences disequilibrium. As you recall from Chapter 2, Piaget believed that it was the infant and young child's desire for equilibrium, or balance, that drove her to actively pursue cognitive adaptation.

SCHEME

The comprehensions that an infant, child, or adult has about different aspects of his or her world at any given moment in time. Piaget believed that children develop schematic outlines (or maps) of what the world is like and maintain these outlines in their memories.

Piaget's Periods of Cognitive Development

Before we examine how a child progresses through the periods outlined in Table 6.2, let's discuss a few handy rules:

1. The ages given in Table 6.2 for each period and stage are *only approximate.* A child does not, for example, advance from the sensorimotor to the preoperational period by simply having her second birthday.

Table 6.2 ● Piaget's Periods of Cognitive Development, Years 0–7

Sensorimotor Period (0–2 years)
Stage 1 (0–1 month): reflex activity
Stage 2 (1–4 months): self-investigation
Stage 3 (4–8 months): coordination and reaching out
Stage 4 (8–12 months): goal-directed behavior
Stage 5 (12–18 months): experimentation
Stage 6 (18–24 months): problem solving and mental combinations

Preoperational Period (2–7 years)
Preconceptual stage (2–4 years): emergence of symbolic functions, syncretic and transductive reasoning and animism
Intuitive stage (4–7 years): centers on one aspect at a time, egocentrism

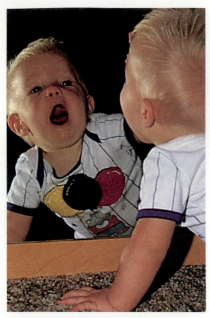

Between the ages of one and two children become consciously aware that they have a self.

2. All children advance through each period and stage in the order and sequence described. Because each period and stage is built on the preceding one, *children never skip a period or stage.*

3. Sometimes, while leaving one period or stage and entering another, a child may exhibit cognitive aspects typical of both periods or stages.

4. An older child or an adult, although at an advanced cognitive period of development, may rely on a lower period of cognition. As a ridiculously exaggerated but perhaps memorable example, my very bright grandmother (who was certainly operating within the most advanced period of cognition) was limited strictly to sensorimotor processes until her first cup of morning coffee!

5. The periods are universal; they are observed to occur in human beings throughout the world. But this does not mean that culture has no effect on cognitive development. Although children in all parts of the world have been shown to progress through Piaget's stages in roughly the same order (Dasen & Heron, 1981), experience does have an effect on the rate and timing of cognitive development. For example, researchers have found through cross-cultural studies that how quickly children enter Piaget's stage of concrete operations (see Chapter 2) depends considerably on the language they speak (Sevinc & Turner, 1976) or on the kind of experiences their culture provides (Dasen, 1975; Price-Williams, Gordon, & Ramirez, 1969).

The Sensorimotor Period (0–2 Years)

The first of Piaget's four periods of cognitive development is the sensorimotor period, which is characterized by a lack of fully developed object permanence. **Object permanence** is the ability to represent an object, whether or not it is actually present. Piaget believed that object permanence is necessary before problem solving or thinking can be carried out internally—that is, carried out by using mental symbols or images.

Look around you. Do you see a redwood tree? Unless you live in a fairly scenic California setting and are sitting next to a window, you probably don't. But can you mentally represent the redwood tree to yourself, even though one isn't actually present? You can do this in a number of ways. You can picture a redwood tree in your "mind's eye" (if you know what the tree looks like). Or you can think of the letter symbols REDWOOD TREE. Or you might actually shape a depiction of a redwood tree with your hands in order to hold on to that

For infants in the sensorimotor period, "out of sight" is often "out of mind."

object mentally, even though it's out of sight. The point is, you can keep any object "permanent," even when it is absent, by using these techniques. Without mental images, symbols, or depictions to represent an object, you would be unable to think of it, because you would have no internal way of representing it. In other words, without object permanence, "out of sight, out of mind."

Piaget argued that during the first two stages of the sensorimotor period, an infant may be unable to think. By the third stage, it becomes apparent that some thought processing does occur, but object permanence is not fully developed until the end of stage 6 (see Table 6.2). Once object permanence is fully developed, the child leaves the sensorimotor period. Indeed, Piaget chose the term *sensorimotor* because all the child's thinking during this period is based on schemes of overt actions in response to what the child senses (*sensori*=stimulus; *motor*=physical action).

The best way to observe the onset of object permanence in infants is to examine each of the six stages of the sensorimotor period in turn.

Stage 1, Reflex Activity (0–1 Month).   This stage involves a systematic and increasingly less awkward use of natural reflexes. In Piaget's words, this is a time of **reflex exercise**. However, accommodation can be observed even during this early stage as the infant learns to distinguish and localize the mother's nipple from the surrounding skin areas.

Stage 2, Self-Investigation (1–4 Months).   During this stage, the infant begins to display a class of behaviors known as **circular reactions**. A circular reaction consists first of

> stumbling upon some experience as a consequence of some act, and second, of trying to recapture the experience by re-enacting the original movements again and again in a kind of rhythmic cycle. The importance of circular reactions lies in the fact that it is the sensorimotor device par excellence for making new adaptations, and of course new adaptations are the heart and soul of intellectual development at any stage. (Flavell, 1963, p. 93)

During this second stage, the circular reactions observed are of a particular type called **primary circular reactions**. Primary circular reactions are simple

OBJECT PERMANENCE
Term used by Piaget to refer to the individual's realization that objects continue to exist even though they are not presently sensed.

REFLEX EXERCISE
Piagetian description of the first stage of the sensorimotor period, during which the infant's reflexes become smoother and more coordinated.

CIRCULAR REACTIONS
A behavior sequence described by Piaget that occurs during the sensorimotor period of development. There are three kinds of circular reactions: primary, secondary, and tertiary.

PRIMARY CIRCULAR REACTIONS
Simple repetitive acts that center on the infant's own body, such as thumb sucking or foot grasping; characteristic of the second stage of the sensorimotor period.

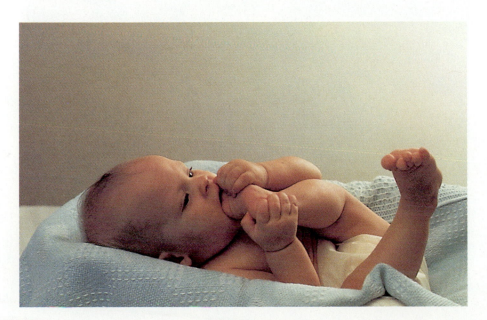

Primary circular reactions are simple repetitive acts that center on the infant's own body, such as thumb sucking, hand clasping, or foot grabbing.

SECONDARY CIRCULAR REACTIONS
Circular reactions characteristic of the third stage of the sensorimotor period, in which the child reaches out to manipulate objects discovered in the environment.

repetitive acts that center on the infant's own body, such as thumb sucking, hand clasping, or foot grabbing. That's why this stage is referred to as a time of self-investigation.

Stage 3, Coordination and Reaching Out (4–8 Months). During this stage **secondary circular reactions** appear. These differ from primary circular reactions in that they no longer center on the infant's own body; instead, the infant "reaches out" to manipulate objects discovered in the environment. Also during this time, a number of coordinations occur that serve to integrate previously isolated behaviors. For example, an infant will shake a rattle in order to hear it or reach for a ball in order to grasp it.

It is also during this stage that object permanence begins to emerge. You can see this by conducting a simple experiment. If you take infants during the first or second stage of the sensorimotor period, show them an object that attracts their attention, and then block their view of the object with a screen, they will act as though the object simply has vanished—"out of sight, out of mind." They won't attempt to look for the "vanished" object, even if it's one of their favorite things (Lingle & Lingle, 1981). But if you do the same thing to infants in the third stage of the sensorimotor period, they will try to regain visual contact with the object that has disappeared from view. This may indicate some object permanence inasmuch as the infants may be searching for the hidden object because they have some internal representation that something was once in view but is now gone. At this stage, however, the object permanence is weak. As John Flavell observed of an infant in the coordination and reaching-out stage,

> His behavior in this situation also testifies to the immaturity of his object concept; if a sufficient fraction of the object shows from behind the screen, he reaches for it; if this fraction is then made to decrease, the reaching hand abruptly drops. More generally, it is characteristic of this stage that the child makes no attempt to retrieve an object manually once it has disappeared from view (e.g., by being covered with a cloth), in spite of the fact that such activity would by this age be well within his physical capabilities. (Flavell, 1970, p. 1010)

During the coordination and reaching out stage infants reach out to manipulate objects in the environment.

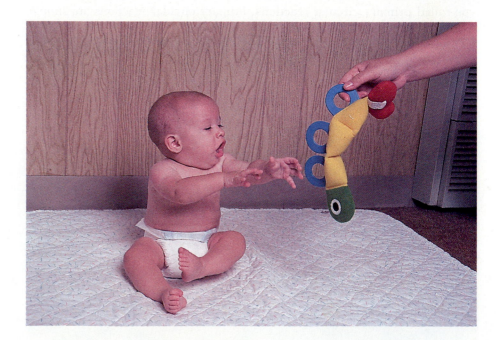

Stage 4, Goal-Directed Behavior (8–12 Months).   During this stage, children integrate and adapt their schemes to attain specific goals. Techniques stumbled on that were successful in obtaining something in one situation may now be generalized to new situations. For the first time, children begin to display purposeful sequential behavior designed to achieve a desired end. Infants accomplish this by integrating previously separate schemes into one overriding scheme (action concept) that controls the sequencing of these once-isolated schemes into a single goal-oriented effort.

For example, an infant may purposely move one object out of the way to reach another or may open something for the purpose of obtaining what's inside. Once, while observing his infant son Laurent, Piaget noted the exact moment when Laurent first exhibited the goal-directed behavior characteristic of stage 4. The infant was 7 months and 13 days old when, for the first time, he moved his father's interposing hand aside to obtain a matchbox. Previously, when Piaget had played this blocking game with Laurent, the infant, although apparently interested in the matchbox, had never made an attempt to move the blocking hand aside (Piaget, 1952).

Object permanence becomes stronger during stage 4. By this time, children begin to search regularly for objects they see disappear. Later in stage 4, as infants continue to develop a system for representing objects that are no longer present, they will even search for an object several minutes after it has been covered or otherwise hidden.

At first glance it may appear that object permanence is fully developed at this stage, but you need only play a simple game with a 10-month-old child who is in stage 4 to discover the serious deficiencies that still exist in the child's object permanence. To play this game, take two cloths of different colors, such as red and blue. Place the infant in front of the cloths and then place something that she wants beneath the red one. She'll probably pull the cloth off the object and then reach for the object because there is purposeful goal-directed behavior during stage 4.

Now, play the game a few more times, each time placing the object under the red cloth. Then play the game once more, only this time, after you've placed the object under the red cloth, clearly remove it, right in front of the infant's eyes, and place it under the blue cloth. You might think that she will look under the blue cloth. But surprisingly, she won't. She'll look where she most often found the object in the past, rather than where she last saw it. Although children in stage 4 have some object permanence, it is not fully developed. (As you can see, 10-month-old babies make a terrific audience for would-be magicians who have not yet perfected their sleight-of-hand technique.)

At first, scientists thought that children at this age simply don't understand the *concept* of an object (including the idea that when an object is moved from one place to another, it can no longer be in that first place). Now, however, researchers think that failure to find the object may have more to do with children's level of memory development. For example, after the child sees the object moved, she must *remember* that it has moved, and she must remember this long enough to enable her to begin her search in the right place. What appears to be happening in this stage 4 game is that during the brief interval between watching the object being moved and searching for the object, the child has *forgotten* what she has seen (Diamond, 1985). Supporting this assertion is the fascinating discovery that adults with certain forms of amnesia fail this particular hide-and-seek game in exactly the same way as do stage 4 infants (Schacter, Moscovitch, Tulving, McLachlan, & Freedman, 1986)!

TERTIARY CIRCULAR REACTIONS
Circular reactions characteristic of the fifth stage of the sensorimotor period, in which the child actively experiments with things to discover how various actions affect an object or outcome.

Stage 5, Experimentation (12–18 Months).   During the fifth stage **tertiary** (third-order) **circular reactions** appear. Unlike secondary circular reactions, in which an infant tries to recapture an external event in a repetitive and mechanical way, in tertiary circular reactions, children begin to experiment actively with things to discover how various actions will affect an object or outcome. Consider, for example, an experimenting toddler sitting in her high chair dawdling over her oatmeal. She drops a handful over the side of the high chair. Then she does it again, this time with more force, and seems to delight in the splat. Then she repeats her actions, only this time she releases the blob gently. She learns that (1) things fall down, not up; (2) the force of the throw determines the radius of the splat; (3) you can make an interesting pattern on the floor with oatmeal; and (4) oatmeal is one of the finer things in life (a discovery not likely to be made by an adult). Whereas stage 4 children can reach goals only by using actions that already exist in their repertoires as a result of accidental discovery, the stage 5 child will *actively* build her schemes through this kind of experimentation.

The beginning of tertiary circular reactions is evidence that the child is developing an appreciation of *cause-and-effect relationships*. Many researchers argue that this comprehension of cause and effect also is reflected in the child's language development (Bates, Camaioni, & Volterra, 1975; Molfese, Molfese, & Carrell, 1982; Sugarman, 1977). Children's attempts to tell adults about events or to give adults commands are believed to be built on their early notions of cause and effect. After all, before the child would make a deliberate attempt to communicate, he would need to "know" that different verbal efforts would result in different effects. Such linguistic efforts are not apparent in children who are between stages 1 and 4.

Stage 5 doesn't begin until children reach about 12 months of age, but you might be wondering about children who are saying words, pointing at objects, and making declarations when they are only 10 months old. So now is a good time to reiterate that the ages we list for these stages are only approximate. Some infants even show evidence of stage 5 acquisition by the age of 8 months (Harding & Golinkoff, 1979).

Such individual differences are probably due, in part, to the child's inheritance or biology. The speed at which the child progresses through the sensorimotor period also depends on the child's environment. If the child has a mother who provides a stimulating environment and who is highly communicative, the child will progress through the sensorimotor period at a slightly faster pace than might be otherwise expected (Chazan, 1981). Interestingly, if children are provided with an enriched environment that helps to accelerate their progress through the sensorimotor period, their verbal requests will begin earlier—but still at the onset of stage 5 (Steckol & Leonard, 1981).

By stage 5, children searching for an object hidden from sight under a cloth will now look for the object where they last saw it rather than where they have found it most often. Even so, object permanence is not complete at this point. If an experimenter picks up an object and closes his hand about it so that it is no longer visible, and then carries it away and appears to deposit it in a hiding place, the observing stage 5 child seems to be able to "see" only part of what has happened. When asked to find the object, the child will search for the object in the experimenter's hand but will not search further by looking in the hiding place. Piaget referred to this behavior as a *failure to infer invisible displacements*; it does not occur if object permanence is fully developed.

Stage 6, Problem Solving and Mental Combinations (18–24 Months).   During this stage, the ability to solve problems by the mental combinations of signs, symbols, or images begins to emerge; the child no longer needs to depend on physical exploration and manipulation of the environment. This ability to think—for that's what it is—can lead to sudden insightful solutions that make little use of the kinds of trial-and-error exploration observed in stage 5. For example, a stage 6 child might set his juice glass down on the floor in order to have both hands free to open a door, and after looking at the door and the juice glass, "realize," through a mental image of the door opening, that the juice glass is in the way. The stage 6 child might then decide to move the glass to a safer place before attempting to open the door. Even so, this child, still in the sensorimotor period, will typically use a certain scheme to aid him in his understanding. The child in this case might be seen to mimic the opening and closing of the door with his hands or his mouth as a way of physically hanging onto the "realization" that he has.

According to Piaget, it is during this stage that children acquire a full understanding that objects continue to exist even after they have disappeared from sight or have been moved by hidden displacement. And that understanding can be quite sophisticated, as researchers have discovered:

> The behavior we describe here [concerned] an 18-month-old infant [who] was asked to gather hidden candies (Cornell & Heth, 1983). The child watched as a treat was placed in each of two cups at differing distances in front of her. We wanted to see which of the two cups she would search first. When released, she did not approach the closer cup, but toddled to a chair at the periphery of the test area and retrieved the full bag of candies from within the tester's purse. (Cornell, Heth, Broda, & Butterfield, 1987, p. 499)

The Preoperational Period (2–7 Years)

The major distinction between the sensorimotor and preoperational periods is the degree of development and use of internal images and symbols. The development of thought, as represented by the establishment of object permanence, marks the dividing line between the sensorimotor and preoperational periods. This internalized thought may be the precursor of a sense of self-awareness. Perhaps, once a child begins thinking to herself by using internal representations of objects (object permanence), she suddenly becomes aware that she has a self. Maybe that's why the child described in the Chapter Preview recognized her own reflection when she looked in a mirror. This may also explain why young infants don't know what the mirror is reflecting. Their object permanence has not developed sufficiently for them to engage in the kinds of internal thinking that may be necessary before a sense of self-awareness can develop.

As the preoperational period sets in, the child demonstrates greater and greater use of symbolic functions. Language development increases dramatically and imaginative play becomes more apparent as children spend much of their time engaging in make-believe. Another difference seen during this period is that children can imitate another person's behavior after some time has passed, implying that they now have a way of symbolically remembering behavior originally observed in a model. All these actions suggest an internal cognitive mediation between incoming stimuli and later responses.

Children's intellectual development during this period is called preoperational because the children haven't acquired the logical operations or rules of thought characteristic of later periods of cognitive development. The first part of the preoperational period is called the preconceptual stage; the second part is called the intuitive stage.

Preconceptual Stage (2–4 Years).   One of the most valuable ways that thinking can be organized is by forming concepts. A **concept** may be defined as a

CONCEPT

An abstract idea based on grouping objects by common properties.

PRECONCEPT

A Piagetian term describing an immature concept held by a child in the preoperational stage.

SYNCRETIC REASONING

A type of reasoning used by preconceptual children, in which objects are classified according to a limited and changing set of criteria.

TRANSDUCTIVE REASONING

A type of reasoning used by preconceptual children, in which inferences are drawn about the relationship between two objects based on a single attribute.

relationship between, or the properties shared by, the objects or ideas in a given group. If you have the concept of "boat" you can recognize something as a boat even though it may look different from all the other boats you've ever seen. A new boat can be included within the concept because it has qualities that are common to the entire class of objects we call "boats": It has a hull; it floats in water; and it's used for transport. Because our concept of boat is highly developed, we are able to tell not only what this new object is (a boat), but also what distinguishes it from other boats. We see the qualities that place it within our conceptual understanding of "boat," but we also see qualities that make it unique. Children, however, as they begin to symbolize their environments and to develop the ability to internalize objects and events, first develop immature concepts, which Piaget called **preconcepts**. For instance, a preconceptual child may have a general idea that winged, flying objects found in trees are "birds" or that wheeled, doored objects found on streets are "cars"— and yet not have sufficient grasp of the conceptual class to isolate and distinguish characteristics unique to any member of that class. For example, it is common for 3-year-old children to refer to every car as "Daddy's car" or to believe that every Santa Claus they encounter on a Christmas shopping trip is the one and only Santa. (Of course, as adults, you and I know that there is only one Santa and the others are just helpers.)

During the preconceptual stage, children's reasoning processes are limited to two kinds of reasoning: syncretic and transductive. **Syncretic reasoning** is the method by which preschoolers tend to sort and classify objects. When disparate things are classified syncretically, they are organized according to a limited and changing set of criteria. A preconceptual 3-year-old child placed before a group of different objects might organize them syncretically in the following manner: "The boats goes with the other boats because they are boats. This glove goes with the boat because they are both green. This block goes with that block because they are both blocks, and the blocks go with the boat because they can fit on the deck."* When the child is asked the question, "Does the glove go with the block?" a common syncretic answer is, "No, the blocks go with the glove 'cause they fit inside."

Syncretic reasoning may occur in part because the child's conceptual understandings are not fully developed. The child isn't necessarily wrong when she says glove and blocks go together, but in this case her reasoning is syncretic because she classified them according to a limited or changing set of criteria ("because the blocks fit inside"). An adult with a fully developed conceptual understanding might easily have placed a glove and a block together and, when asked why, answered, "because they are both manufactured items." Such an advanced classification scheme relies on highly organized and fixed sets of conceptual criteria.

Transductive reasoning involves drawing an inference about the relationship between two objects based on a single attribute. This kind of reasoning doesn't generally lead to correct conclusions, although occasionally it may. An example of transductive reasoning is: If A has four legs and B has four legs, then A must be B and vice versa. If A happens to be a cat and B a dog, a transduction based on legs alone obviously will lead to a faulty conclusion. Transductive reasoning appears to occur because the child's emerging preconcepts are limited to only a few conceptual attributes. In other words: Mommy went to the hospital and had a baby—so when Daddy goes to the hospital, he'll have a baby.

---

*Now that I think about it, things in my garage are sorted in much the same way. Unfortunately, I can't claim to have been 3 years old when I did it.

Transductive reasoning can also lead to animistic thinking. **Animistic thinking** is the belief that inanimate objects are alive. Consider the following conversation between Piaget and a preconceptual child (Piaget, 1960, p. 215):

Piaget: Does the sun move?
Child: Yes, when one walks it follows. When one turns around it turns around too. Doesn't it ever follow you too?
Piaget: Why does it move?
Child: Because when one walks, it goes too.
Piaget: Why does it go?
Child: To hear what we say.
Piaget: Is it alive?
Child: Of course, otherwise it wouldn't follow us, it couldn't shine.

In this case, the child has attributed life to the sun because the sun appears to move, which is a quality of most living objects.

Animism in young children, however, is not as common as Piaget originally thought (Bullock, 1985). In Piaget's initial investigations, he asked children about inanimate entities such as the sun or the wind, which are not as clearly inanimate to children as are things such as rocks or chairs. Had he chosen objects more obviously inanimate, he would have found less animism. For instance, in one study, only 9 percent of 3-year-old children thought that vehicles were alive, even though vehicles move, and only 13 percent of them thought that dead animals were alive, even though pictures of the dead animals looked like those of their living counterparts (Dolgin & Behrend, 1984).

The fact that Piaget found animism to be more prevalent than other researchers did may also be explained by the more recent finding that animism appears to occur in two stages. Whereas 2- and 3-year-old children may show animism outright, 4- and 5-year-old children may infer animism in a less direct fashion (Tunmer, 1985). For example, a 3-year-old child watching a marble roll down an incline may state that the marble is alive. A 5-year-old child watching the same marble may state that it is not alive, but may then say that the marble is moving because *it wants to!* Clearly, the concept of "alive" is difficult for children to grasp and develops over time.

Intuitive Stage (4–7 Years).   The latter portion of the preoperational period is called the intuitive stage because the children's beliefs are generally based on what they sense to be true rather than on what logic or rational thought would dictate.

Piaget once described a problem in which three beads were placed in a narrow, hollow cardboard tube. The tube was held in front of a child so that a blue bead was on the bottom, a yellow bead was in the middle, and a red bead was on top. Even though the child couldn't see through the tube, he knew the order of the beads because he could remember the order in which they had been dropped into the tube. If the tube were turned upside down, the child might still be able to give the correct order of the beads from top to bottom if he could imagine how they might look in the upside-down tube. An intuitive child answers this problem by relying on his ability to imagine the position of the beads rather than by applying any logical operations.

To better understand what is meant by logical operations, suppose that you watch three beads dropped into a tube. Like the child, you know that the blue bead is on the bottom, the yellow bead is in the middle, and the red bead is on top because you can remember the order in which they were placed in the tube. Suppose, now, that the tube is turned vertically 29 ½ times. Which color bead would be on top? You know that it's the blue bead, but how? Did you

ANIMISTIC THINKING
A kind of thinking common in preconceptual children, in which inanimate objects, especially those that move or appear to move, are believed to be alive.

ORGANISMIC-STRUCTURAL APPROACH
An approach to the understanding of cognitive development that takes as its metaphor the growing biological organism. Environmental influences on cognitive development are considered minor, with only extreme environmental forces having any appreciable effect on biological structure or development.

MECHANISTIC-FUNCTIONAL APPROACH
An approach to the understanding of cognitive development that takes the machine as its metaphor. Environmental influences on cognitive development are considered major, since machines don't change from within but must be added to from without.

imagine the column of beads going through 29 ½ turns? Or did you apply a logical rule about full turns and half turns? You probably concluded that any number of whole turns would bring the red bead back to the top position, whereas any number of whole turns plus a half turn would bring the blue bead to the top position. This kind of logical operation is generally beyond the ability of intuitive children. Instead, they rely more on their senses and imagination. Piaget also argued that during this time, the reasoning of intuitive children is further limited because they tend to be egocentric, or conceptually self-centered (Gzesh & Surber, 1985).

Criticisms of Piaget

Without a doubt, Jean Piaget contributed immeasurably to our knowledge of cognitive development in children. His theories have had a wide influence on education and psychology. Nonetheless, a number of researchers have criticized some of Piaget's assumptions.

Ever since Piaget outlined his theory of cognitive development, researchers have been motivated to investigate the way children's thinking develops. Piaget viewed young children as naturally inquisitive beings who adapt to their surroundings by developing cognitive—or mental—structures in a stagelike process. At each stage, Piaget argued, the child is able to handle a more sophisticated logic. Such a view is an example of an **organismic-structural approach**. The root metaphor for this approach is the growing biological organism (Reese & Overton, 1970). In this view, a child will grow mentally according to the biological dictates of the species and will develop into a final adult form following a biologically preordained pattern of development. This, of course, is why Piaget argued that the stages of cognitive development are universal: They are part of our biological heritage and are to be found in all people.

Throughout the years, however, there have been some strong arguments against Piaget's view, especially among researchers in the United States. Throughout the mid-twentieth century, the learning theorist's view was paramount among American psychologists. Proponents of behaviorism, such as John Watson and B. F. Skinner, took a **mechanistic-functional approach** to explain a child's cognitive development. The root metaphor for this approach is the machine (Reese & Overton, 1970). In this view, development occurs not from within, as in a living organism, but rather from without by "adding on" to the basic machine. In other words, cognitive development is the result of learning (the principles of which were briefly discussed in Chapter 2).

The debate, then, boiled down to this: Are there universal discontinuous stages, as Piaget had suggested—stages that are structurally similar and common to all people, regardless of their culture and activity? Or, as learning theorists argued, is development continuous—without stages, with no particular sequence of development—and diversified among people as a function of their previous learning and conditioning? In an effort to answer these questions, researchers have tried to test Piaget's assertions, especially by looking for abilities that Piaget would not have thought possible at certain stages (see At Issue).

It has also been argued that it is not clear exactly how the stages were initially selected (Fischer & Silvern, 1985). For instance, why should the ability to conserve (see Chapter 2) be considered a great cognitive leap marking the start of a stage? Surely, a stage of cognitive development could just as well be based on the dynamic advances that occur during language development (see Chapter 7) or something equally interesting.

AT ISSUE

Reexamining Piaget's Assertions

Since Piaget's death in 1980, a number of experiments have raised questions concerning the validity of Piaget's theory. The most serious challenges questioned Piaget's basic assumptions about the underpinnings of each of the four periods. There are scores of good studies from which to choose, so let's take a moment and quickly survey a few of them.

As you recall, the sensorimotor period is characterized, according to Piaget, by a lack of fully developed object permanence. Piaget argued that it was because of this lack of object permanence that infants younger than about 8 or 9 months generally fail to even look for an object after it has been hidden ("out of sight, out of mind," remember?) (Piaget, 1964). But if strong object permanence could be demonstrated in young infants, Piaget's theory might not be a very helpful place to turn for a satisfactory explanation.

In an ingenious study, Renée Baillargeon (1987) demonstrated object permanence in infants only 3 ½ to 5 ½ months old. In her study, Baillargeon used the habituation method to accustom infants from both the experimental and control groups to the movement of a solid screen that was attached to a table as the screen rotated up and away from the infant, raising up to its full height at 90 degrees and then continuing on over to once again lie flat on the table after a full 180 degrees of rotation (see Figure 6.2). Once the infants from both groups had habituated to the movement of the screen, the infants from the experimental group observed a box being placed in a location that would make it impossible for the screen to rotate more than 112 degrees without hitting the box (see Figure 6.3). In this condition, the infants would first see the box, then watch as the screen was first raised up to 90 degrees (blocking the infants' view of the box—out of

FIGURE 6.2

The apparatus used by Renée Baillargeon to habituate infants in both her experimental and control groups to the action of a moving screen. The infants were allowed to observe a screen raise up in front of them, reach its highest point at an angle of 90 degrees, and then continue on over once again to lie flat on the tabletop, having completed a rotation of 180 degrees. Both groups of infants observed the same stimulation repeatedly until they became "bored" with it. (SOURCE: Baillargeon, 1987, p. 656)

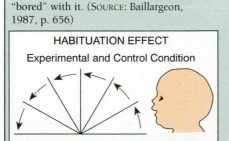

FIGURE 6.3

Infants in the experimental group observed a box placed in a location where it would be struck by the screen should the screen be rotated in the manner in which it had previously been during habituation. Half the experimental group infants were exposed to condition (a), in which the box was secretly lowered though a trap door when the screen had rotated to an angle of 90 degrees. The screen then continued to move the full 180 degrees, a seemingly impossible event to an observer who possessed object permanence, considering the location at which the observer would assume the box to be. The other half of the infants in the experimental group observed the screen strike the out-of-sight box at an angle of 112 degrees, condition (b).

No box was used with the control infants. They either observed a 180-degree rotation (c), as they had seen during the habituation event, or they saw the screen rotate 112 degrees and stop for no apparent reason (d). Of the four conditions, only condition (a) generated prolonged staring from the infants, indicating that these infants were aware that something strange had happened, something that they could not think strange unless they possessed object permanence. (SOURCE: Baillargeon, 1987, p. 656)

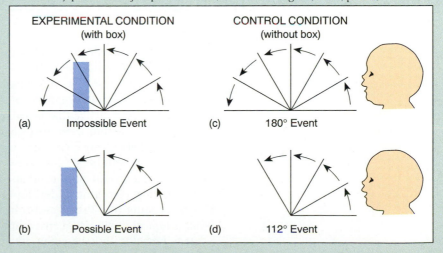

AT ISSUE

Reexamining Piaget's Assertions, continued

sight, out of mind?), then rotated away until it struck the out-of-view box at an angle of 112 degrees (which should come as a surprise if the infant had forgotten that the box was there). The neat trick in this experiment was that for half of the infants in the experimental group, the box was secretly removed via a trap door when the screen was up at the 90-degree angle so that the screen would continue on for its full 180 degrees (just what the infants were used to seeing—what they had been habituated to). In this last situation, however, an adult, who would be expecting the screen to hit the box, would probably ask, "Hey, where'd the box go?" Interestingly, when the infants watched this same situation, they stared at the screen significantly longer when the box seemed to disappear than when the screen struck the box. Infants in the control group were observed to see if they, too, would stare at the 180-degree rotation longer than the 112-degree rotation (which would have indicated that infants in the experimental group had looked longer at the 180-degree rotation probably because they had simply found it to be more interesting than the 112-degree motion), but the results showed that the control group infants did not look longer at the 180-degree rotation.

Now ask yourself, how could the babies in the experimental group have been aware that the 180-degree rotation was something unusual and pay more attention to it—especially after they had been habituated to it—unless, like you or I, they had expected the screen to hit the box, the box that was out of sight but apparently not out of mind. In follow-up studies, Baillargeon and colleague Julie DeVos (1991) further demonstrated object permanence in 3½-month-old infants using similar methods.

Once again, we see the underpinning of the sensorimotor period, namely the idea of a steady and stagelike movement toward object permanence, being called into serious question.

Adding to this impressive body of work, Andrew Meltzoff went on to show that 14-month-olds can imitate actions 24 hours after they have seen them depicted on television (Meltzoff, 1988c). This last finding has implications for parents who wish to control which programs their children view. They might now want to extend that supervision to their infants!

These are just a few of the hundreds of studies that have shown that children's behavior often fails to conform to Piaget's idea of well-defined stages (Carey, 1985; Gelman & Baillargeon, 1983; Keil, 1981).

In addition to the research undermining Piaget's stages of development, some scientists have launched attacks on his work on theoretical grounds. Look again at Table 1.1, p. 11 and review the research dimension "descriptive vs. explanatory." Piaget's cognitive theory has aspects of both. It is descriptive, and it often attempts to be explanatory. As a descriptive endeavor, Piaget's theory is masterful. For over 50 years, Piaget and his colleagues recorded the responses of thousands of children throughout the world to various cognitive tasks. There can be no question that Piaget observed the way children respond to these tasks at different points in their development or that there are many similarities in the way children develop throughout the world.

As a description of a complex matter—the development of thought—Piaget's theory is unequaled. There is no question about the accuracy of what Piaget observed; his findings have been confirmed repeatedly. However, *explanations* of why cognitive development progresses as it does are not as clear.

These attacks on Piaget's theory give strength to the mechanistic-functional approach. Piaget addressed these concerns by creating more substages to explain new findings. Learning theorists saw that numerous substages, when lined up along a graph, began to approach a steady "learning curve" of gradual acquisition of knowledge that learning theorists had envisaged all along. Piaget countered that within each area of investigation, no matter how many areas there are, the stages are clear, showing an abrupt shift from one to the next.

Modern researchers are now attempting to integrate both the organismic-structural and mechanistic-functional approaches into a single coherent view of cognitive development. They have attempted to accomplish this by arguing that Piaget and other stage theorists may have demonstrated what is *typical* under usual environmental and organismic conditions—that is, what is *probable*. But there can always be variations. When modern theorists talk about stages of cognitive development, they often use the term *probabilis-*

tic epigenesis to refer to the fact that stages describe only the typical or most probable development. In fact, researchers currently like to use the word *level* instead of *stage,* because stage has a rigid, inflexible connotation. Table 6.3 outlines the levels of cognitive development from birth to age 5 that best represent a consensus among most researchers (Fischer & Silvern, 1985).

The general consensus concerning cognitive development as it exists today (and there certainly are exceptions) is that there is an interaction between human beings and their environment and that we cannot assume that cognitive development comes mostly from within the organism or mostly from exposure to the environment. Both elements interact in a complex and complete way, resulting in important differences *and* similarities among people, cultures, and the way human cognition develops.

The Development of Memory

Piaget's description of the cognitive development of children didn't say much about the development of memory. Modern cognitive theorists have begun to pay more attention to the development of memory, however, because memory can have an effect on other cognitive processes.

Memory is an important part of human cognition. The power of a computer often is measured by its memory capacity. The more memory a computer can access, the more it can do. Without a memory, a computer wouldn't be able to do much; neither would a human being. The **information-processing view** makes use of such an analogy and incorporates the language used to describe computer memory. In this view, newborns are born with "memory banks," except that theirs are made of developing brain tissue, not silicon chips. And although infants aren't programmed with information simply by being fed prepackaged data, they **encode** much of what their senses record.

Because of their biological organization, infants do have some perceptual understanding of their earliest sensations. As you recall, newborns can track a moving object with their eyes and orient themselves in the direction of a sound (see Chapter 4). In a very limited way, then, newborns can innately engage in **selective attention.** Soon after birth, infants actively attend, thus beginning the process of encoding information from the environment, and placing it in their memories for later retrieval.

MEMORY
The complex mental function of recalling what has been learned or experienced.

INFORMATION-PROCESSING VIEW
A theoretical view that incorporates the computer as an analogy for human processing. Individuals are seen as entities who encode, store, process, and retrieve information.

ENCODE
In memory, to organize a stimulus input into an acceptable form for storage.

SELECTIVE ATTENTION
The process of discriminating one stimulus from multiple stimuli and attending to it.

DISTINCTIVE FEATURE
Gibson's term for that portion of an object that can be discriminated from other portions.

Table 6.3 ● A General Consensus of the Levels of Cognitive Development

COGNITIVE LEVEL	DESCRIPTION	AVERAGE AGE OF CHILD AT FIRST APPEARANCE
1. Sensorimotor actions	Adaptation of single action (child looks at face, grasps a rattle)	2–4 months
2. Sensorimotor relations	Differentiation of a means from an end (child moves object aside to reach for toy)	7–8 months
3. Sensorimotor systems	Organization of schemes into a cognitive system—actions and events no longer treated as unrelated or isolated (child knows that a rattle will make the same noise regardless of which action is used to shake it); actions also unified to make first words	11–13 months
4. Representations	Symbolization of objects, events, and people independent of any particular action by the child (child displays rapid growth of language; pretend play)	18–24 months
5. Simple relations of representation	Coordination of two or more ideas in a single skill (child can take the perspective of another and relate it to his or her own; can perform simplified versions of Piaget's concrete operations tasks)	4–5 years

SCRIPT

In cognitive study, one's knowledge of the appropriate events that should occur in a particular social setting and of how one might carry them out. This includes knowledge of who is expected to do what to whom as well as when, where, and why. A script would include the typical behaviors expected of a person going to a restaurant or movie.

By the time infants are 6 months old, they can encode memories that can last for a very long time. For example, in one experiment, 2 ½-year-old children were retested for a memory of a task they had been trained to do when they were only 6 months old (reaching out in the dark for a rattle they could hear). Children who had had the experience as infants learned faster than control children who had not had such a previous experience (Perris, Myers, & Clifton, 1990).

As children grow older, their memories become more effective. However, not all memory abilities develop at the same rate. Certain components of memory may even be fully developed by the time children are 5 years old. In fact, there are certain memory tasks that a 5-year-old child can do as well as an adult (Kail & Hagen, 1982). For instance, there appears to be little developmental difference between children and adults in the ability to judge recency (Brown, 1973). In one study, subjects were shown two pictures one after the other and were asked to state which picture they had seen first. Five-year-old children performed as well as adults. In fact, by using the habituation method, researchers have shown that even 11-month-old infants are aware of the sequence of two events and can recall, just like adults and children, which of two events came first (Bauer & Mandler, 1992).

Scripts.   Most adults can remember what they did during a whole day, and in what sequence, better than a 5-year-old can. What interests cognitive researchers is *why* an adult can do better. At the moment, researchers aren't sure, but it may have to do, in part, with scripts.

A **script** is a hypothetical cognitive structure that encompasses people's knowledge of the typical events in everyday experience (Abelson, 1981). By using the scripts you have come to know through experience, you can fill in what you may have forgotten with what you think probably happened; you'll just fill in the blank spots, often without being aware that you are doing so, with information based on the common everyday events to which you have become accustomed. It is a valuable ability, because any events you can't recall you just *assume* based on a script—and are right most of the time. Children, on the other hand, with their limited knowledge and experience of the world, may be less successful at developing scripts.

In one study, children were given a detailed story about two boys who had lunch at a McDonald's restaurant. The entire lunch was described in a sequence that was familiar to all children who have been to a McDonald's. Later, when the children were asked to identify which words from a list were also in the story (words such as "wagon," "hamburger," "teddy bear," or "pie"), their memory was extremely accurate (Mistry & Lange, 1985). In this instance, the children were probably helped by their strong and clear script for a visit to a McDonald's. For example, if a child couldn't remember "hamburger," he might assume from his script that a hamburger was probably among the words associated with McDonald's. Children of the same age who were given a less structured story about a picnic in the park were less likely to recall the words on the list, although the same list of items was mentioned.

The children were less likely to recall the words from the picnic story because a script of what happens in the park is less structured than a script of what happens in a McDonald's. Each visit to McDonald's is fairly similar, providing a strong script of what is typical, but one trip to the park might vary quite a bit from another such trip, and so the script is weak because it's not certain what a park visit entails.

Further evidence for the use of scripts in recall comes from the fact that as memories fade, children often replace a missing memory with a "recollection" of what they assume must have happened based on their scripts of day-to-day experience (Myles-Worsley, Cromer, & Dodd, 1986) or based on what they have been repeatedly led to believe has happened (even if not true). Thus, children's memory may sometimes be faultier when they use scripts because they may "fill in" things that never happened to them, but were simply typical of the script (Hudson, 1990).

Scripts also help children remember, or reconstruct, memories they can share. Young children who have similar scripts are more likely to have conversations about these events and share recollections with each other, which in turn facilitates important social interactions and the formation of friendships (Furman & Walden, 1990).

The Development of Memory Strategies.   Successful memory storage and access are important aspects of both computer function and human cognition. We adults possess some knowledge about the problems we are likely to encounter when we put information into our memories or try to retrieve it. For this reason, we often try various strategies to help us remember information.

Children first learn to use specific memory strategies as young as 2 years of age. At that time they engage in simple strategies to remember the existence of a hidden object, such as pointing toward where they last saw it, looking at the hiding place, or talking about it. Such behavior may be evidence of a very early attempt to retain what must be remembered (DeLoache, Cassidy, & Brown, 1985).

As children become older, they attempt more formal memory strategies. One of the most common of these strategies is **rehearsal**, which is repeatedly going over material for the purpose of helping memory. Although rehearsal may seem to be an obvious strategy for aiding memory, it is not commonly observed in children until they reach about 8 years of age (Lovett & Flavell, 1990).In a study in which 5-, 7-, and 10-year-old children were shown seven pictures and asked to remember three specific ones, only 10 percent of the 5-year-old children made some attempt to rehearse at least once, whereas 25 percent of the 7-year-olds and 65 percent of the 10-year-olds regularly rehearsed (Flavell, Beach, & Chinsky, 1966).

Mature strategy efforts appear when children are about 10 years of age (Hasselhorn, 1992). We can thus say that between ages 5 and 10 years, children are beginning to develop **metamemory**; that is, they are becoming aware that their memory works in certain ways and that certain efforts are required to use it effectively (Fabricius & Wellman, 1983). However, children as young as 4 years of age can make effective use of certain memory strategies if carefully instructed about how to incorporate them (Lange & Pierce, 1992).

Metamemory and Culture.   Surprisingly, children throughout the world do not show the same development of metamemory as they grow older, which raises an interesting point. It appears that certain experiences are necessary before the child begins to emerge as a memory strategist.

Advances in memory skills and cognitive development may occur when children are exposed to formal schooling. Evidence for this comes from cross-cultural studies showing that German children are better memory strategists than their same-age American counterparts primarily because memory strategy is given so much emphasis in German schools (Carr, Kurtz, Schneider, Turner, & Borkowski, 1989).

Advances may also be stimulated in any situation in which the advanced skill becomes needed. For example, let's look at the mathematical proficiency of children who have had no formal schooling but who nonetheless require

REHEARSAL
Repetitive review of learned material undertaken to facilitate later recall.

METAMEMORY
Knowledge of how best to use one's memory.

METACOGNITION
All the skills and abilities that encompass one's knowledge and understanding about one's own cognitive and thinking abilities; what one knows about one's own cognition and thinking processes.

GENDER ROLE
The behaviors associated with one sex or the other.

such skills to survive. Geoffrey Saxe (1988) studied Brazilian children between the ages of 10 and 12 who made a living as street vendors. Not too surprisingly, he found them to have mathematical skills far superior to street children who didn't sell for a living. This example further supports the idea that cognitive development cannot be viewed out of its specific environmental context.

Other memory tasks besides the kind of list memorization required by most schools—everyday tasks like recalling the location of objects or remembering incidents—seem to be independent of schooling. In such everyday cases, educated children and uneducated children do equally well (Rogoff & Waddell, 1982).

Metacognition

The information-processing metaphor of the mind as a computer is an interesting model, but it has some obvious limitations. To begin with, the model can't adequately explain why change occurs, that is, why human cognition is a developing rather than a static phenomenon. Perhaps a more important failing of the model is that however you look at it, computers aren't human. They can't think for themselves.

Unlike computers, there is something unique and mysterious about human beings. We are consciously aware, and we deliberately exercise control over many of our own thoughts, thereby demonstrating **metacognition**, the ability to think about thought.

What causes us to have self-awareness is perhaps the greatest philosophical question of all time, and no one so far has an even remotely satisfying scientific answer. All the world's great religions have addressed the issue and refer to a soul or spirit. And until fairly recently, self-awareness was believed to be a uniquely human attribute. But research now suggests that the great apes may share this quality with us (Gallup, 1977).

Data indicating that great apes also pass through a sensorimotor period and develop object permanence may help explain why they share a sense of self-awareness with our species. Perhaps once a creature begins thinking to itself by using internal representations of objects (object permanence), it suddenly becomes aware that it has a self. Maybe that's why children past a certain age—including the young of great apes —can recognize their own reflection when they look in a mirror. This may also explain why young infants don't know what the mirror is reflecting. Their object permanence has not developed sufficiently for them to engage in the kinds of internal thinking that may be necessary before a sense of self-awareness can develop. And once self-awareness develops, thought becomes possible as we begin to mull things over in our minds.

GENDER ROLE ACQUISITION

As young children grow, certain behaviors come to be expected of them, including behaviors associated with the child's gender. The acquisition of these behaviors illustrates the interaction between the child's cognitive development and his or her culture—the culture in essence determining which behaviors are appropriate for each gender. These behaviors constitute what is known as a **gender role.**[*]

Different sexual behaviors are shaped by various social and cultural forces. Culture dictates how long skirts are, whether pants are held by belt or sus-

---

[*]Some researchers prefer the term sex role. In practice, gender role and sex role are synonymous (Maccoby, 1988).

penders, who should or shouldn't wear makeup, and what is considered appropriate behavior for either gender. Each culture expects certain behaviors from its male and female members, and each culture will reinforce and model the "correct" gender role for its children. The process by which an individual incorporates the attitudes, behaviors, and traits deemed appropriate to his or her biological sex is called **sex typing**. The degree of masculinity or femininity that the child eventually displays reflects the amount of sex typing. An extremely masculine male or extremely feminine female is said to be highly sex typed.

With the changing times, our perceptions of which behaviors are appropriate to each gender have changed, too. Just a few decades ago, the use of hair dryers, deodorant, and most jewelry was considered the province of women. However, as cultural attitudes shifted, it became acceptable for men to use these items.

SEX TYPING
The process whereby an individual incorporates the behaviors, traits, and attitudes appropriate to his or her biological sex or the sex assigned at birth.

Early Influences on Sex Typing

The shaping of gender roles may begin as early as birth. In a sense, it can even begin before birth as parents busy themselves preparing color schemes for a nursery or choosing clothing and nursery items for the baby.

From the moment of an infant's birth, parents tend to treat boys and girls differently (Ban & Lewis, 1974; Will, Self, & Datan, 1976). Although there are few behavioral differences between male and female babies, most parents will describe their daughters as cuter, softer, or more delicate than their sons. Fathers tend to emphasize the beauty and delicacy of their newborn daughters and the strength and coordination of their newborn sons (Krieger, 1976).

In one entertaining experiment, the different reactions of mothers and fathers were made apparent. In this study, preschoolers were given stereotypical sex-typed toys to play with, including kitchen play sets, a doll house, an army war game, and cowboy outfits. Both boys and girls were given "girls' toys" to play with on one occasion and "boys' toys" on another. The children were told to play with these toys the way girls would (for girls' toys) or boys would (for boys' toys). What the experimenters were interested in was the reaction of the mother and father when they entered the room and saw which toys their children were playing with. Mothers showed little differential reaction to the toy sets. Fathers, on the other hand, showed far more negative reactions when their children were playing with the "inappropriate" toys. This was especially true if the fathers found their sons playing with "girls' toys" in the way that girls would. Fathers in these cases tended to interfere with the play or show disgust (Langlois & Downs, 1980). Fathers are also more likely to offer sons toys that are stereotypically considered male, such as trucks or footballs (Jacklin & Maccoby, 1983). Mothers are also more supportive of their children's play when it involves "sex-appropriate" toys, but their reactions tend to be more subtle (Caldera, Huston, & O'Brien, 1989). Mothers generally treat boy and girl infants less differently than do fathers. For this reason, fathers, in our culture, may have a greater effect on the early learning of gender roles (Power, 1981).

The shaping of gender roles begins at a very early age.

Gender Role Identification

Researchers are interested in how and when children acquire an understanding of gender roles. Actually, it is more difficult to determine *how* they do it than *when*. "How" requires an explanation, whereas "when" relies mostly on description. Even so, let's begin with a look at "how."

GENDER-ROLE IDENTIFICATION
The degree to which a child adopts the gender role of a particular model.

OEDIPUS COMPLEX
A Freudian term representing the sexual attachment of a boy to his mother. This desire is repressed and disguised in various ways. The child expresses jealousy and hatred of his father because the father can have relations with the mother that the son is denied.

ELECTRA COMPLEX
According to Freud, the female form of the Oedipus complex; the desire of a girl to possess her father sexually.

Determining how children learn gender roles requires a theoretical understanding of **gender role identification**. Psychoanalytic, social learning, and cognitive theories have all addressed this question. Each predicts that a parent's behavior will have a striking effect on the child's developing sexual identity, even though each theory views the development of gender role identification and "appropriate" sex typing differently.

Psychoanalytic Theory

In Freudian, or psychoanalytic, theory, a son's identification with his father results from a drive to avoid retaliation by the father for the son's initially desiring his mother. Once identification with the father is made, the **Oedipus complex**, as Freud called it, is resolved and the boy adopts the father's ways as his own. According to Freud, daughters develop a female identity by resolution of the **Electra complex**, a more roundabout journey. A mirror image of the Oedipus complex was not possible because daughters, too, initially are attached to their mothers through nursing. Freud therefore developed the concept of *penis envy*, in which the girl comes to covet the male anatomy, which would provide her with something she is missing. In this way, the daughter comes to desire the father and identifies with the mother, who possesses the object of the daughter's desire.

The Freudian view of gender role identification has received little empirical support over the years (Jacklin, 1989), and the concept of penis envy has received strong attack (Horney, 1939). Most psychologists find Freud's views historically interesting but scientifically limited, and few currently refer to them or consider them when examining gender role identification. Although some people have developed a more modern psychoanalytic approach to this issue (Chodorow, 1978; Lerman, 1986), their work is viewed as quite subjective (Stoller, 1985). Instead, most researchers currently emphasize social learning theory or cognitive theory.

Each culture expects certain behaviors from its male and female members, and each culture reinforces and models correct gender roles for its children.

Social Learning Theory

Social learning theory is based on the work of Albert Bandura. In this view, children's behaviors are reinforced or punished based on what parents and society deem appropriate for the child's gender. We have already discussed how parents may differentially treat children based on gender. Parents provide different toys for their daughters than for their sons, and they encourage their children to develop sex-typed interests.

Modeling and observational learning are also considered important. Boys learn to observe men, and girls learn to observe women to see how they are expected to behave. Boys observe that men are portrayed more as the initiators of action. On television, for example, about 70 percent of the major characters who initiate action are men. According to social learning theory, parents, television, peers, and society as a whole shape the acquisition of gender roles.

The Cognitive View

Lawrence Kohlberg first proposed a cognitive conceptualization of gender role acquisition way back in 1966 (Kohlberg, 1966). According to this view, a child first comes to realize that he is a male or she is a female, and this cognitive realization then guides the child to change his or her behavior to match what society deems appropriate for the gender of that child. In this view, the time at which children first become aware of their gender and its meaning is an important consideration, because cognitive theory predicts that sex typing will not begin until the child has the concept that he is a boy, or that she is a girl, and an idea of what it means to be one.

Children appear to develop a gender understanding—that is, to comprehend that they are boys or girls—by about the age of 3 (Thompson, 1975). Although a 2-year-old child may tell you that she is a girl, she may have trouble understanding who else is a girl or who is a boy or, for that matter, why she is called a girl. By the age of 3 years, however, children are better able to judge who is a girl and who is a boy. Yet 3-year-old children, whose cognitive processing is necessarily preconceptual, generally fail to understand gender constancy. ✗ — child has this by age 3

Gender constancy is the understanding that your own sex will remain constant: once a boy, always a boy. A girl is demonstrating a grasp of gender constancy when she understands that just because she puts on a jersey and plays football, she does not turn into a boy, but is still a girl.

Once children come to comprehend the anatomical basis of gender distinction, which has been found to be the case in about 40 percent of a population of 3- to 5-year-olds, they will generally acquire gender constancy (Bem, 1989). Most children acquire it by the age of 7 (Emmerich & Goldman, 1972; Wehren & De Lisi, 1983). The progression from rudimentary gender understanding to the completion of gender constancy has been found to be similar in other cultures, although the final age at which gender constancy occurs may vary by a few years (Munroe, Shimmin, & Munroe, 1984).

As noted earlier, Kohlberg's cognitive theory predicts that once children understand which gender they are and that their gender stays constant, they begin to develop "appropriate" gender role behaviors. But in fact, children engage in stereotypical gender role behaviors even before they are cognitively aware of their gender or its constancy. As early as 26 months of age, children are typically aware of the different things that constitute masculine and feminine dress and behavior. They already know that men shave and wear shirts and suits and that women wear blouses, dresses, and makeup. It is quite com-

GENDER CONSTANCY
The realization that one's sex is determined by unchanging criteria and is unaffected by one's activities or behavior; usually develops in children by the age of 6 or 7 years.

GENDER SCHEMA THEORY
The theory developed by Sandra Bem that explains how cognitive advances help the child to organize and integrate the information that he or she has learned about his or her sex.

mon for children as young as 2 or 3 years to show some preference for what are deemed by their culture to be sexually appropriate toys and activities (Jacklin, 1989); yet these children are often unaware that most of the toys they choose for themselves are considered more appropriate for their sex than for the opposite sex. In other words, contrary to Kohlberg's cognitive development view, children demonstrate a certain degree of sex typing before they have a complete understanding of which sex they are or that their sex remains constant.

But if neither the cognitive nor social learning view is correct, how do we explain gender role acquisition in children? This debate has gone on for years. It is now believed by many researchers that the two views may intertwine to create a cognitive-social learning view (Serbin & Sprafkin, 1986).

Gender Schema Theory

In 1981, researcher Sandra Bem suggested the **gender schema theory** to explain the intertwining of the two theories. In her view, as children develop, they reach a point when they are able to integrate cognitively all the different sex-typed behaviors they have acquired through social learning and conditioning. This cognitive integration helps to shape their attitudes and beliefs about gender roles and guides them to their own decisions about what is sex appropriate (Bem, 1981). Bem's view explains how children can show sex-typed behaviors long before they have gender constancy. The theory also explains how, bit by bit, cognitive advances can help the child organize and integrate all the information that he or she has acquired about gender roles up to that point. Supporting this view is research showing that as soon as children acquire even a very rudimentary understanding of gender, sex typing suddenly becomes more prominent as the children rapidly form gender stereotypes and alter their behavior to better fit gender expectations (Martin & Little, 1990). In fact, children as young as 25 months have been observed to incor-

Table 6.4 ● The Development of Gender Identity			
THEORETICAL VIEW	**INITIAL STATE**	**FORCE**	**REACTION**
Psychoanalytic (boys)	Pleasure bond made with mother through nursing	Desires mother, identifies with father	Male gender identity
Psychoanalytic (girls)	Pleasure bond made with mother through nursing	Desires father, identifies with mother	Female gender identity
Social learning (boys and girls)	No differentiation of behavior with respect to gender	Differential reinforcement for and modeling of gender-specific behaviors	Shaping of culturally appropriate gender identity
Cognitive (boys and girls)	No understanding of gender	Advances in cognitive development allow an understanding of gender	Gender identity based on child's comprehension of what culture deems appropriate for his or her gender
Gender schema (boys and girls)	No understanding of gender	Slowly, through reinforcement, modeling, and cognitive development an understanding (schema) of gender-specific behavior is acquired	The child's schema is applied to the self in varying degrees depending on how much the child is reinforced or encouraged to behave in a manner deemed appropriate by the culture for his or her gender.

porate gender schemata in their ability to recall gender stereotypical actions in a model (Bauer, 1993).

Gender schema theory may also apply to the way parents help shape their children's sex typing. For instance, although it is true that parents typically reinforce the use of sex-appropriate toys, parents are more likely to do so for children they know possess gender constancy (Fagot, Leinbach, & O'Boyle, 1992).

Table 6.4 outlines the development of sexual identity according to the four theories we have discussed in this chapter. Research is currently continuing in this area at a fast pace; whether Bem's view is correct remains to be seen. Perhaps a complete understanding of children's sex typing will require an entirely new theoretical view—one not yet considered.

Overcoming Gender Stereotypes

Although it appears that the basic temperamental characteristics of the two sexes are similar, the roles of men and women in society are not. Almost all the nurses and secretaries are women, whereas almost all the engineers, mathematicians, and mechanics are men. Moreover, women earn only about 60 percent as much as men, and large wage differences remain even when comparisons are made within the same occupation.

You might think that things are changing quickly now that so many American mothers are in the workforce. Although a working mother may help to alter the stereotypical sex role socialization of her child, it is not likely. Even after 50 percent of American mothers had entered the workforce, researchers found that the fantasy play of little girls was still focused on a domestic role (Connolly, Doyle, & Ceschin, 1983). There are apparently so many examples of stereotypical sex role behavior in a child's world that a mother's working role is not sufficient to overcome stereotypical sex role socialization. Little girls tended to do what little girls always have done—they played house (Birns & Sternglanz, 1983).

Of course, there's nothing wrong with little girls playing house. A problem occurs, however, when little boys learn that it is not their role to play house and little girls learn that it is their *only* role. Many people have argued that early training in such a domestic role *as the only acceptable female role* is the beginning of second-class citizenship. While this may seem to state the case a little strongly, there may be cause to worry, especially when we examine the changes in the toys themselves. For example:

As in previous decades, girls play with dolls, pots, and toy brooms. Although boys still like blocks and vehicles, some of the traditionally male toys have changed dramatically over time, reflecting technological change. It is hard to find toy horses and bows and arrows today. Cars and trucks are still popular, but space-age toys are quickly gaining in popularity. . . . [I]n the future an additional problem will be that girls will enter high school and college with deficits in computer experience. When boys' toys change as technology progresses and girls' toys do not, it means that we are still preparing men for careers and women for domestic activities and/or low pay, low preparation jobs. (Birns & Sternglanz, 1983, pp. 246–247)

The twenty-first century is about to dawn, and there can be no doubt that computer literacy will be of extreme importance. It may even be that those people unfamiliar with or intimidated by computers will fall behind and create a new lower class of "techno-peasants." Researchers fear that a high percentage of such a class may be women.

Also important is the shaping of attitudes and emotions as they relate

APPLICATIONS

to the sexes. Men and women may be at a certain disadvantage if they are limited to strictly "male" or "female" emotions or attitudes. As researchers have noted,

Nurturance, sensitivity, and compassion are ideal characteristics for physicians (mostly male) as well as for mothers, nurses, teachers, and social workers. However, passivity and dependency are not particularly valuable for mothers, nurses, or anyone else. (Birns & Sternglanz, 1983, p. 248)

Overcoming Stereotypical Sex Typing. It is possible to modify gender-stereotyped behavior to some degree (Katz & Walsh, 1991). In one study, for example, researchers observed children for a period of three years in a special open-school setting that emphasized nontraditional teaching methods. The goal was to respond to each child's individual needs and characteristics. Sex-stereotyped expectations concerning any child's interest, personality, or ability were deliberately avoided. As often as was feasible, both

male and female teachers were together in the classroom and engaged in a wide range of roles and duties. The children were all together; there were no separate classes for preschoolers, kindergartners, first graders, second graders, and so on.

Although the school constituted only a portion of the children's world, and there was no way to insulate the children from sex-stereotyped experiences outside the classroom, the open-school setting provided for much more mixed-sex activity—boys and girls segregated themselves less often—than would a traditional setting. Even among children 7 years of age, when it is most common for boys and girls to associate with their own sex (Freud referred to it as the "latency period"), there was more boy-girl interaction and sharing of ideas, roles, and tasks (Bianchi & Bakeman, 1983).

Similarly, researchers have discovered that children raised in nontraditional families that stress or model atypical gender roles (such as a

mother who is a pilot or a father who does most of the cooking and cleaning in the home) are less likely to adhere to gender stereotypes, although this was more true of girls than of boys (Weisner & Wilson-Mitchell, 1990). These findings add to the evidence that it isn't necessarily the sex of the child that determines playmates and activities; rather, it may be the properties and structure of the environment.

Perhaps by deliberately structuring our environment to help avoid sex-stereotyped representations, we can all help to provide a world in which boys and girls can choose from the greatest possible range of roles and behaviors. This requires the cooperation of parents and, of course, all of society. Perhaps most people don't want to change or get away from the traditional roles; or perhaps they wish to change them only to a limited degree. It will be up to all of us in the future to make these choices and to decide what is best for our children and our society.

SUMMARY

■ During early childhood, the deceleration of growth that began just after conception continues. Besides growing physically, children show increased motor competence during this period.

■ Jean Piaget believed that a child's cognitive development is the combined result of the development of the brain and nervous system and of experiences that help the child adapt to the environment.

■ The first of Piaget's four periods of cognitive development is the sensorimotor period, which is characterized by a lack of fully developed object permanence.

■ During stage 1 of the sensorimotor period, the infant exercises its reflexes.

■ During stage 2 of the sensorimotor period, the infant begins to display primary circular reactions.

■ During stage 3 of the sensorimotor period, the infant begins to perform secondary circular reactions; object permanence also begins to emerge at this stage.

■ During stage 4 of the sensorimotor period, infants first begin to display purposeful sequential behavior designed to achieve a desired end. They also display a more sophisticated appreciation of object permanence.

■ During stage 5 of the sensorimotor period, tertiary circular reactions appear. During this time, there is evidence that the child begins to develop an appreciation of cause-and-effect relationships.

■ During stage 6 of the sensorimotor period, children begin to show an ability to solve problems by the mental combinations of signs, symbols, and images. Object permanence is fully developed.

■ The major distinction between the sensorimotor and preoperational periods is the degree of development and use of internal images and symbols. As they move into the preoperational period, children demonstrate increasing use of symbolic functions.

■ During the preconceptual stage of the preoperational period, children first begin to symbolize their environments and to develop the ability to internalize objects and events. During this stage, children's reasoning processes are limited by syncretic and transductive reasoning.

■ During the intuitive stage of the preoperational period, children's beliefs are generally based on what they sense to be true rather than on what logic or rational thought would dictate. These children tend to be egocentric, or self-centered.

■ Memory is also an important part of cognition. An effective memory encodes, searches for, organizes, and recalls information.

■ Researchers have discovered that an important difference in memory effectiveness between young children and older children and adults may be due to the different ways they organize the information contained in their memories. Older children and adults may use scripts to help them organize the information.

■ Rehearsal is not commonly used as a memory strategy by children less than about 9 or 10 years old.

■ Between the ages of 5 and 10 years, the child begins to develop metamemory, which is an awareness of how memory works and what may be necessary to use it properly.

■ The cultural shaping of gender roles may begin as early as birth. From the moment of birth, parents tend to treat boys and girls differently.

■ Determining how children learn gender roles requires a theoretical understanding of gender role identification.

■ In Freudian, or psychoanalytic theory, a boy's identification with his father results from a drive to avoid retaliation for his initially desiring the mother. Girls identify with their mothers in a more complex way.

■ In the social learning theory of gender role identification, a child's behaviors are reinforced or punished based on what parents and society deem appropriate for that child's gender.

■ In the cognitive theory of gender role identification, children first come to understand that they are either male or female, and this cognitive realization then guides the children to change their behavior to match what society deems appropriate for their gender.

■ Gender schema theory combines elements of both the social learning and cognitive theories to explain gender role identification.

QUESTIONS FOR DISCUSSION

1. If you ask a 1-year-old child, "Where's mommy?" he may actually leave his mother's side to go look for her where he most often finds her (Bower, 1979). What does this tell you about the child's concept of "mother"? Consider stage 4 of the sensorimotor period.

2. Some people have argued that homosexual teachers should not be allowed to teach children because they might adversely affect children's sexual orientation. How well fixed do you think children's sexual orientation is by the time they enter school? Do you believe there is anything wrong with a child's adopting a homosexual orientation? Why or why not?

3. Some of the beliefs about sexual development held by people at the turn of the century were later found to be incredibly inaccurate. Do you think there might be beliefs about sexual development held today that will seem equally foolish 50 years from now? If so, which ones and why?

4. Great apes, including chimpanzees, gorillas, and orangutans, have been shown to progress through the sensorimotor stage of development (Chevalier-Skolnikoff, 1979) and to develop a sense of self-awareness (Gallup, 1977). What does this say about the relationship between cognitive development and the maturation of cognitive structures within the brain and nervous system? What is your feeling about the use of great apes in scientific experiments? Did this knowledge change your feeling?

SUGGESTIONS FOR FURTHER READING

1. Basow, S. (1992). *Gender: Stereotypes & roles* (3rd ed.). Monterey, CA: Brooks/Cole.

2. Brainerd, C. J., & Pressley, M. (Eds.). (1985). *Basic processes in memory development: Progress in cognitive development research*. New York: Springer-Verlag.

3. Dodson, F., & Alexander, A. (1986). *Your child: Birth to age 6.* New York: Fireside.

4. Flavell, J. H. (1985). *Cognitive development* (2nd ed.). Englewood Cliffs, NJ: Prentice Hall.

5. Gross, T. F. (1985). *Cognitive development.* Monterey, CA: Brooks/Cole.

6. Hare-Mustin, R. T., & Marecek, J. (1992). *Making a difference: Psychology & the construction of gender.* New Haven, CT: Yale University Press.

7. Haywood, K. M. (1986). *Life span motor development.* Champaign, IL: Human Kinetics.

8. Liss, M. B. (Ed.). (1983). *Social and cognitive skills: Gender roles and children's play.* New York: Academic Press.

9. Turner, J. S., & Rubinson, L. (1992). *Contemporary human sexuality.* Englewood Cliffs, NJ: Prentice Hall.

CHAPTER 7

Language Development

Categorically Speaking

Do you like to type? I won't blame you if you say no. I don't like to either. In fact, considering the length of this book, I wish I had one of those "speakwriters" that scientists have been working on—the kind you simply talk into and it types what you say! Unfortunately, they're not available yet because computers have a terrible time recognizing the same word when it's spoken by different people.

*Have you ever heard of "voiceprint identification"? It's based on the fact that no two people have exactly the same voice. The way I say "tomato" and the way you say "tomato" sound completely different to a computer. Perhaps the onset of my voice is a little more rapid than yours, or perhaps we differ in our inflections or in which **phones** we use. In general, inexpensive machines programmed to "understand" one person's speech are typically unable to understand anyone else's.*

But why don't people have the same problem that computers do? That's the crucial question. How come babies don't grow up able to understand only their mothers? How is it that they can also understand their fathers, or strangers, or siblings, or anyone else speaking their language? The answer may lie in an inborn mechanism for the perception of spoken words.

In a series of experiments already considered classics, researcher Peter Eimas (1985) examined what it is that infants hear when they listen to spoken language. The infants in the experiments were given a special pacifier to suck, and their rates of sucking were recorded. A word was then spoken by a computer. In this instance, the word bin *was repeatedly said to the infant. When the infant first heard the computer say "bin," the sucking rate increased, indicating that the infant had noticed a*

PHONES

The smallest units of vocalized sound that do not affect meaning but can be discriminated. (Derived from the Greek word *phone*, meaning "voice" or "sound.") Phones are often responsible for regional and foreign accents. For example, someone from Boston might pronounce the word *car* differently than someone from Dallas.

PHONEMES

The smallest units of speech that can affect meaning. For instance, the only difference between *mat* and *bat* is the phoneme sounds *m* and *b*. These two sounds are phonemes because they affect meaning; a mat is certainly not a bat. Phonemes are typically composed of phones. Some languages use more phonemes than others.

PHONEME CONSTANCY

A perceptual ability that develops in infancy in which a phoneme, although spoken or pronounced differently by different individuals, is perceived as a single entity regardless of speaker.

GRAMMAR

A set of rules that determines how sounds may be put together to make words and how words may be put together to make sentences.

change in the environment. After a short time of listening to "bin," the infant became habituated to it. Then suddenly the voice changed from "bin" to "pin," and the infant immediately reacted, showing that the infant had perceived the switch in sound from one letter to the other.

Next, the computer simply said "bin" differently, changing intonation, voice onset, or length of voicing, so that it imitated the way different people might say the word bin. *This time, the baby did not react! It's as though the baby treated different individual voices as not different, while perceiving a change in letter sounds as very different. Eimas argues that this occurs because infants perceive language sounds, called* **phonemes,** *in categories. To an infant, bin is bin,* no matter who is saying it, but *bin is not pin. The baby easily does what most computers find impossible to do. This has led Eimas and others to conclude that babies are genetically "prewired" for language recognition. Eimas refers to this ability as* **phoneme constancy.**

This ability to take the tremendous variety of speech sounds, which are different for each person speaking, and perceive them within category groupings is what makes language perception and production possible. And while it is true that a few extremely elaborate and expensive computers are making some small strides in this same direction, babies have it down pat!

In this chapter, we'll take a closer look at the amazing language capacities of infants, investigate the normal sequence of language acquisition in children, and discuss some of the theories and heated debates concerning language that have been generated by the research of the last few years.

WHAT IS LANGUAGE?

Have you ever seen a dog carry its leash over to its master and drop it at his feet? The meaning is clear, but language isn't necessary. In this way, dogs can communicate, but they don't have language. A language requires more than communication; it requires the use of signs or symbols within a **grammar**—that is, within a structure of rules that determines how the various signs or symbols are to be arranged.

Language also allows the use of signs or symbols within a grammar to create novel constructions. If a myna bird says, "Candy is dandy, but liquor is quicker," you know that the bird is simply imitating someone who has been reading Ogden Nash poems aloud. Myna birds don't use English to express meanings; they only mimic the sounds they have heard. Although the sentence the myna spoke was made with English words and was grammatically correct, the myna is not said to have language. Ogden Nash, on the other hand, as the originator of the statement (a novel construction), has proved his language capability.

THE PRELINGUISTIC PERIOD

Newborn infants don't possess language, of that we are sure. But as infants grow, they gradually develop language in a step-by-step sequence. Interestingly, this sequence of language acquisition is quite similar among children throughout the world.

Newborn Vocalization

Some researchers believe that the rudiments of language acquisition are present within 72 hours after birth. Evidence for this comes from the apparent vocal "dialogues" engaged in by mothers and their newborns. For example, researchers in one study analyzed the vocal interactions between mothers and their 3-day-old infants (Rosenthal, 1982). They discovered that the duration and kind of infant vocalization seemed to depend on the presence or absence of the mother's voice. What the mother said and when she said it were in turn affected by the sounds the infant made. Infants also move their hands and body differently in the presence of their mothers than in the presence of an equally active doll, indicating a social understanding of their interactions (Legerstee, Corter, & Kienapple, 1990). Although the newborn has no words to say, this reciprocal pattern of exchange is not too different from one aspect of adult conversation, inasmuch as the mothers and their newborn infants seem to take turns "speaking" (Bateson, 1975).

The First Language-Like Sounds

The Phonation Stage.   Between birth and 2 months of age, babies are in the **phonation stage** of language acquisition. During this stage, infants often make what are called "comfort sounds." These are "quasi-vowel" sounds ("quasi" because they are not as full or rich as vowel sounds made later). Quasi vowels are made from phones. That is why this period is called the phonation stage.

The Gooing Stage.   "Gooing" might be a better example of a first language-like sound. Between the ages of 2 and 4 months, infants are usually in what is called the **gooing stage.** Young infants typically say "goo," or something similar, by combining the quasi vowels from the phonation stage with harder sounds that they have acquired, sounds that are the precursors of consonants.

The g sound in "goo" is considered a consonant precursor rather than a consonant because when adults attempt to imitate infant gooing sounds, their renditions are quite different; adults' consonants are harder and richer. The reason that an adult's sounds differ from those of a young infant may be that a young infant's developing skull and oral cavity differ from an adult's. Anthropologists comparing the sizes of the skulls and oral cavities of adults and infants have uncovered some evidence that infants before 6 months of age may be physically incapable of making the kinds of sounds necessary for spoken language (Lieberman, Crelin, & Klatt, 1972). For example, the young infant's larynx, or voice box, is very high in the throat. Because of this positioning, newborns are actually able to drink and breathe at the same time! This, in turn, helps them during nursing. As infants grow, the larynx moves lower in the throat, creating the large vocal cavity required for language production. (This lowering of the larynx also makes our species more likely to choke on food, a price we must pay for the ability to speak.)

PHONATION STAGE
A stage of language acquisition that develops between birth and 2 months of age. During this stage, infants often make comfort sounds composed of quasi vowels.

GOOING STAGE
A stage of language acquisition that typically occurs between the ages of 2 and 4 months. During this stage, infants combine the quasi vowels from the phonation stage with harder sounds that are precursors of consonants.

EXPANSION STAGE

A stage of language acquisition that typically occurs between the ages of 4 and 7 months. During this stage, infants produce many new sounds and rapidly expand the number of phonemes they use, giving rise to babbling.

RASPBERRY

In foodstuffs: a rather tasty fruit; a type of berry. In social discourse: an explosive sound caused by the rapid expulsion of air from the mouth. The expelled air vigorously vibrates the lips (especially the lower lip), which have been deliberately placed in a configuration so as to make contact with and surround the protruded tongue. Considered unrequired in most social circumstances.

Infants early in the babbling stage tend to babble just about every phoneme in existence. Babies throughout the world begin to babble at about the same age, and they all produce this expansive and inclusive array of phonemes.

The Expansion Stage.   While the infant's skull and mouth probably need to grow and change shape before the infant is able to make real language sounds, further development of the nervous system also may be needed before an infant is capable of articulation. Interestingly, no one is certain of exactly which neurological or physical prerequisites are necessary for language. However, we do know that infants between the ages of 4 and 7 months typically begin to produce many new sounds, which is why this time is called the **expansion stage**.

The new sounds produced at this time include yells, whispers, growls, squeals, and, every parent's favorite, the **raspberry**. Also during this time, the first fully formed vowels appear. Mature syllables during the expansion stage are rare. As the infant's phonetic repertoire grows, parents become aware that the infant has begun to "babble."

The Conomical Stage.   Between the ages of 7 and 10 months, babbling greatly increases as the infant begins to produce syllables and duplicated sequences such as "dadada" or "mamama." This is known as the **cononical stage**. Interestingly, babies who can hear soon begin to babble cononical syllables, whereas deaf babies, who also babble, do not (Oller & Eilers, 1988). This finding tells us that even very early on, experience with sound has affected the language acquisition of hearing infants. Interestingly, deaf infants who are exposed to sign language also babble, they just do it manually! That is, they babble with their hands, starting out with the basic shapes they have seen adults use and progressing to make various combinations of hand shapes until they say their first signed word at about 1 year of age (Petitto & Marentette, 1991). Apparently, the brain develops language capability in a very similar way regardless of the mode of expression.

When babbling first appears, no differences might be detected between, say, an infant who has been exposed to English and one exposed to Japanese. However, sometime between about 4 and 10 months of age, infants begin to show a preference for the phonemes common to the language they have been hearing and eventually will learn. In one study, the babbling of 6- to 10-month-old infants who came from different language backgrounds was presented to adults from different language communities. The adults were required to judge which infants came from which language background. Although they found it difficult, most judges were able to tell (deBoysson-Bardies, Sagart, & Durand, 1984).

The Contraction Stage.   Following the cononical stage, infants increasingly narrow their use of phonemes, mainly to the ones they will be using in the language they will eventually learn. This is known as the **contraction stage** and generally occurs between 10 and 14 months of age. At this time, infants are also beginning to acquire the pacing and rhythm of their language. In fact, the phonemes an infant chooses to speak in conjunction with the rhythm, pacing, and length of babbled utterances can be so uncannily like the actual language (except that real words are not spoken) that parents swear that their baby has just said a totally intelligible sentence—it's just that they somehow missed what the infant said (and it drives them crazy trying to get their baby to say it again).

It appears that feedback is necessary before phonetic contraction can begin. Infants learn to imitate what they hear. But clearly, they cannot imitate precisely what they hear; otherwise they would be speaking in sentences instead of babbling. We are able to discriminate or recognize individual words only because those words have been associated with particular objects, actions, or circumstances. Until these associations have been made—that is, until these different sounds have meanings—any of us would discern only the phones and phonemes.

Suppose that you were suddenly transported to a foreign land where everyone spoke an unfamiliar language. You wouldn't be aware of distinct words. Everything would sound like gibberish to you. After a short time, though, you might become aware of some aspects of the language. Perhaps you'd become aware of the spacing, when sounds begin and when they end. You might also become aware of the rhythm and tone changes or the differences among the phonetic sounds. Unfortunately, that's not much to go on when you want to communicate. It probably wouldn't be too long before you felt helpless, or even childlike. However, in time you probably could imitate the sounds—that is, you could learn to sound like the native speakers without actually saying a single word of their language. In fact, you've probably heard this done many times. It's how comedians such as Mel Brooks and Robin Williams are able to "speak" many languages. And you can probably tell which language you are hearing by listening to the sound of it, even though you are unfamiliar with any of the words. French simply doesn't sound like Russian, and neither sounds like Swahili.

THE LINGUISTIC PERIOD

Infans is a Latin word meaning "without speech" or "not speaking." The word *infant* is derived from *infans*. It seems logical, then, to consider the first spoken word uttered by a child as the point at which infancy comes to an end.

First Words

To determine when children speak their first word, researchers rely on studies in which two or more observers hear a child use the same first word appropriately at least two times. Only then do they feel comfortable calling it a real "first word." Such studies have shown that first words generally occur between 10 and 17 months, at an average age of 13.6 months (Bloom & Capatides, 1987).

The first words spoken usually relate directly to certain objects or actions (Benedict, 1979). Although generalizing from an adult's experience to a child's is often speculative, you might imagine yourself living in a foreign land, as we discussed earlier. Like a child, you might first acquire words that you could pair directly with some tangible object or obvious action. Children seem to acquire basic nouns and verbs first, such as *mama, wa-wa* (water), or *go;* they learn abstract words later.

The first basic nouns that children use tend to follow the "three bears rule." The three bears rule simply states that a child is most likely to learn a basic noun such as *dog* before learning a subordinate noun such as *collie* or a superordinate noun such as *mammal*. It's called the three bears rule because, as in the story of *Goldilocks and the Three Bears*, the category "mammal" is *too large* and the category "collie" is *too small*, while the category "dog" is *just right* (Gleitman & Wanner, 1984).

Basic words, such as *dog* or *chair*, are perceptually more accessible; to children than are superordinate words. Children don't need abstract cognitive skills to comprehend basic words. And since children are more likely to be aware of what is easiest to perceive, they naturally acquire basic words first, rather than the more abstract superordinate words.

CONONICAL STAGE
A stage of language acquisition that typically occurs between the ages of 7 and 10 months and is typified by an increase in babbling and the production of cononical syllables (made of consonant and vowel sounds of certain intensities). Duplicated sequences such as "dadada" or "mamama" also mark this stage.

CONTRACTION STAGE
A stage of language acquisition that typically occurs between the ages of 10 and 14 months. It is so named because during this time, infants begin to narrow their phoneme production to the phonemes common to the language to which they are exposed. During this stage, infants also acquire the pacing and rhythm of their language.

By 1 year of age, children often show "sign" words to communicate their desires.

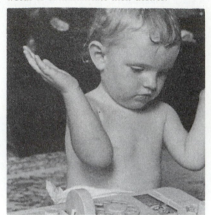

"Beats me!"

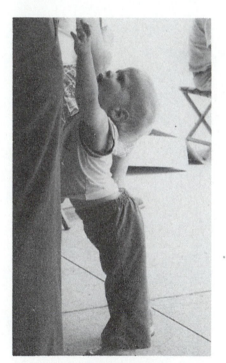

"Pick me up."

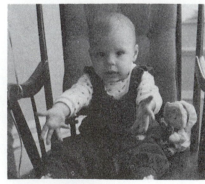

"Get me out of here."

Why they acquire basic words before subordinate words isn't as obvious. It might have to do with the fact that as children acquire language, they continue to organize their experiences into categories in much the same way as when hearing their first verbal sounds. (Recall from the Chapter Preview Peter Eimas's discovery that infants treat all variations of *bin* as identical members of one "bin category.") For example, in one study, 9-month-old infants were habituated to drawings of different kinds of birds (a parakeet, hummingbird, and a hawk). None of these infants knew the word *bird* or were very familiar with birds. After habituation, the infants were shown drawings of two completely different birds (a robin and a toucan) and one familiar bird (the hummingbird, which was used as a control). The infants also saw a horse (see Figure 7.1). When tested, the habituated infants reacted to the new kinds of birds as though they were no different from the birds they had already seen. They treated all new birds as though they were all the same—all members of a "bird" category. They reacted strongly to the horse, however, realizing that it was something very different (Roberts, 1988).

This study indicates that infants appear to form basic categories even before they are able to speak. For this reason, the basic category "dog" might be perceptually accessible, while the subordinates "collie" or "poodle" are not readily sorted out or attended to. This tendency to organize perceptions into categories is probably based on an experience-expectant neural process (see Chapter 4). In other words, it may be the child's nature to do it that way.

Preliminary research has indicated that when children are given a new name for something that they already know by a name, they will treat the new name as a subordinate. For example, in one study, two different-looking toy dogs were shown to 2-year-olds who already knew that both animals were dogs. One dog was then labeled a "fep." Rather than deciding that both animals were now feps or that one should now be called by the proper name Fep, the children appeared to conclude that the one given a new name was a "fep" kind of dog (Taylor & Gelman, 1989). This level of sophistication, shown even by preschoolers, is remarkable when you consider that bilingual preschoolers, like their monolingual counterparts, will readily reject the idea that an object should have two common names unless one is considering a superordinate or subordinate category of that object, but will readily accept that the same object is called by different names in different languages (Au & Glusman, 1990).

Words that are more abstract are acquired after basic nouns and verbs. The first abstract words tend to be adjectives, such as *red, tall,* or *big.* Later, terms that are more abstract are acquired, such as the spatial referents *in, on,* and *between.* Finally, children acquire superordinate classifications and other very abstract words, such as *freedom* or *tangential,* items that philosopher Bertrand Russell called "dictionary words" because we learn their definitions verbally rather than by their relationships to real objects. Use of dictionary words among children younger than 5 years is rare, so you can imagine the shock one father received when his 3-year-old daughter, while looking at the clouds lazily drifting by, sighed and said, "When I'm older, I'll be free." He recovered from his shock when she added, "I mean four" (Whitehurst, 1982, p. 379).

The One-Word Stage

The average 1½-year-old child speaks about four or five words. At first, the child will separate words from sentences by listening for emphases. This is why a giraffe might be referred to by a young child as "raf" or an elephant as "e-fant" (Gleitman & Wanner, 1984). The child speaks these new words that he or she is mastering individually rather than putting them together to form a sentence. Thus, this period of language acquisition is called the **one-word stage**.

Children at the one-word stage may at first only repeat a word that they have heard. But soon it is obvious that they intend to communicate—if only with single words. By the time children have a vocabulary of 100 words or more, there is logic behind their choice of words. They usually choose a word that names or points out something new in a particular situation. Later in the one-word stage, they begin to use a chosen word to ask for things (Greenfield & Smith, as cited in Moskowitz, 1978).

Naming. Children often know what a word means before they are able to say it. In one study, special equipment was used to measure the direction of 13-month-old infants' glances while the infants listened to an adult say the name of an object. Many objects were present, only one of which was being named. The researchers discovered that these infants, although unable to say the word they heard, were commonly looking at the object being named (Thomas, Campos, Shucard, Ramsay, & Shucard, 1981).

In another study, brain waves in 14-month-old infants showed distinct differences when words that the infants had learned were deliberately mismatched with objects that the infants had previously associated with particular names (Molfese, Morse, & Peters, 1990). This finding indicates that during the **naming** process, the brain learns to match objects with names and reacts in a measurable neurological way when a mismatch is perceived. And once naming starts, it is a very important way of acquiring words.

Because naming must first begin with the focusing of attention, it is said that the rudiments of the naming process may be found in infants as young as 1 month, an age when there is already sustained eye contact between infant and parent. By about 4 months of age, infants look at objects simply because parents are looking at them (Bruner, 1983). A little later, the parent can get the child to look just by pointing. It is very difficult to get a dog or even a chimpanzee to do the same thing. Have you ever tried to get a dog to look at something by pointing at it? The dog will look at your finger, not where you are pointing. But young children are different. They usually realize that you are directing their attention. Because of this, by the time children acquire their first words, it's very easy for parents to direct the child's attention to particular objects. As children come to realize that different objects can have names, they begin to pay more attention to those objects (Baldwin & Markman, 1989). This sets the stage for more naming and is a major step in language acquisition.

ONE-WORD STAGE
The universal stage in language development in which children's speech is limited to single words.

NAMING
A development of early childhood in which the child begins pointing out objects and calling them by name. It is considered a special development because it appears to be intrinsically reinforcing and satisfying to humans and seems to occur only in our species.

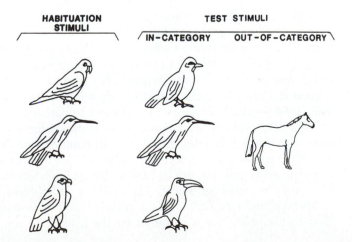

HABITUATION STIMULI   **TEST STIMULI**
                        IN-CATEGORY   OUT-OF-CATEGORY

FIGURE 7.1

The stimuli used in the Roberts experiment. Roberts demonstrated the tendency of 9-month-old infants to perceive different objects within categories. Following habituation to the habituation stimuli, the infants in the experiment showed no significant increase in response to any of the in-category test stimuli but did show a marked response to the out-of-category stimulus (horse).

FAST MAPPING
The ability of children to rapidly narrow down the correct meaning of a word.

Overextension.   It is also interesting that when children first use a word, they may understand it to mean something more than you do. In this way, children often overextend the meanings of words. Researchers have examined hundreds of such overextensions in detail. For example, one child was told that the bright, round object in the night sky was called the moon. The child pointed at the moon and called it "mooi." The next few times she said "mooi," however, occurred when she saw a cake and later when she saw round marks on a window. She appeared to have overextended the meaning of *moon* to include any round shape. In another example, a child was told that the sound he heard the rooster make in the morning was called crowing. He called it "koko." The next time he said "koko" was when he heard a tune played on a violin. Later he used the word to describe any music. He apparently had overextended the meaning of *crowing* to include all musiclike sounds (Moskowitz, 1978).

It really isn't surprising that children often overextend the meaning of words when you think about the task that a child faces when acquiring language. Consider the fact that the average English-speaking high school graduate has a vocabulary of about 40,000 words. If you add in all the names of people and places he or she knows, as well as idiomatic expressions, the number doubles to about 80,000 (Miller & Gildea, 1987). If you figure that this individual has been learning words for about 16 years (since the age of 1), that comes to about 5,000 words a year, or 13 new words each and every day of the young graduate's life! Children with very large vocabularies may acquire words at even twice that rate! No wonder that there is overextension. With a demand to learn at that rate, the only workable strategy would be to grab a word any way you can, get a rough idea of what it means, and go on. The details can wait until later.

Interestingly, when children do nail down a word's definition, they often do it surprisingly quickly. Researchers refer to this ability as **fast mapping**. In a classic study of fast mapping, Susan Carey and Elsa Bartlett (1978) showed 3-year-olds two cafeteria trays, one painted blue, the other olive. The trays were identical in every other way. The children knew what blue was, but most of them called the olive tray either green or brown. The researchers then assigned a nonsense name (*chromium*) for olive. In casual conversation, each child was asked, "Hand me the chromium tray. Not the blue one, the chromium one." Typically, the child would pause, and pointing to the olive tray, ask, "This one?" The experimenter would say, "Yes, that one. Thank you."

One week later, without further guidance, the children were asked to name the colors. Even though they had forgotten the word *chromium*, they *didn't* call the olive tray brown or green. They already knew that the color they were seeing had its own name. Just one exposure had begun the process of reorganizing their color lexicons. Since that experiment was conducted, even children as young as 2 years old have been found able to nail down the correct definitions of words in short order when the words are placed in a context that compels the children to attend to a word's limited meaning (Heibeck & Markman, 1987). And preschoolers were found to fast map new words and acquire a pretty good idea as to their meaning just from watching television (Rice & Woodsmall, 1988)—which, of course, is not news to parents.

Eventually, children do map out most of the definitions of the words they know and bring their usage into line with adults' usage. But how can they do that when it is so easy to become confused? The answer appears to lie in the way that many parents, adults, and older children correct younger children when they mislabel an object. The adult or older child tends to refute the child's label and replace it with the correct one. For instance, if the child says, "The ball is yellow," it is common for the listener to say, "It's not yellow, it's orange" (Au & Lamboise, 1990). This kind of feedback is responsible, in part, for the speed of fast mapping.

First Sentences.   Logically, you might assume that children will speak their first sentence when they say two words—a noun and a verb—together. But "sentences" may already exist in the one-word stage. Although true sentences, do, of course, require a verb and a noun, children in the one-word stage may possess an understanding of **syntax**—the rules that describe how words may be put together to form sentences. (By the way, *grammar* is a broader term than syntax, including both syntax and phonology. **Phonology** is the study of how sounds—phonemes and phones—are put together to make words.) Single words, as spoken in the one-word stage (one word per line), may show evidence of an early attempt at syntactic structure when read vertically. Consider the following conversation between psycholinguist Ronald Scollon and Brenda, a child in the one-word stage (Scollon & Bloom, as cited in Moskowitz, 1978):

Brenda: Ka. Ka. Ka. Ka. (*Car*)
Scollon: What?
Brenda: Go. Go.
Scollon: (*Undecipherable*)
Brenda: Baish. Baish. Baish. Baish. Baish. Baish. Baish. Baish. Baish. (*Bus*)
Scollon: What? Oh, bicycle? Is that what you said?
Brenda: Na. (*Not*)
Scollon: No?
Brenda: Not.
Scollon: No. I got it wrong.

Here Brenda never says more than one word at any given time, which, of course, defines a child in the one-word stage. Still, can we discover an attempt to arrange or structure a "sentence" by reading Brenda's words vertically from top to bottom? Was Brenda saying that hearing the car reminded her that she'd been on the bus the day before and not on the bicycle? What do you think?

As recently as the late 1960s, linguists generally agreed that children in the one-word stage were learning only the names of various objects, actions, or concepts, not syntactic rules. But investigation of the way children order their single-word utterances is turning up evidence that these children already are forming hypotheses about how to put words together to make sentences. In light of these findings, many researchers have begun to use the term *holophrase* to describe these single-word utterances. A **holophrase** is a one-word "sentence" (Molfese, Molfese, & Carrell, 1982).

Figure 7.2 illustrates the extremely rapid acquisition of vocabulary in young children. Most children have mastered over 200 words by the time they begin to speak in true sentences. Children's acquisition of words at this time is truly extraordinary. Very often, they will recall and use words that they have heard only once (sometimes to the horror of the parent, considering what the word could be) (Dickinson, 1984).

The Two-Word Stage

By the time children are between 18 and 20 months of age, they have usually begun to utter two-word statements, called **duos**. During this stage (referred to as the **two-word stage**—what else?), children rapidly learn the value of language for expressing concepts and especially the power of language to aid them in communicating their desires to others. At this time, it is not unusual

SYNTAX
The body of linguistic rules that makes it possible to relate a series of words in a sentence to the underlying meaning of that sentence; that is, the rules governing word order in a language (sentence structure).

PHONOLOGY
The study of how sounds (phonemes and phones) are put together to make words.

HOLOPHRASE
A possible semantic statement made by children in the one-word stage when they utter single words. A holophrase is a single-word "sentence," that is, a one-word utterance that may be interpreted to contain the semantic content of a phrase.

DUO
A two-word utterance made by children during the two-word stage.

TWO-WORD STAGE
The universal stage of language development in which children's expressions are limited to two-word utterances.

FIGURE 7.2

Typical acquisition of vocabulary in children. Chilren's average vocabulary size increases rapidly when they are between the ages of 1½ and 6½ years. The number of children tested in each sample age-group is shown in color. (Data are based on work done by Madorah E. Smith of the University of Hawaii, as presented by Moskowitz, 1978)

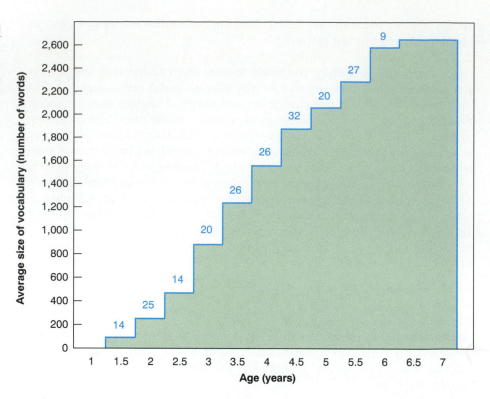

for more than 1,000 new two-word statements to appear monthly (Braine, 1963)! Such two-word utterances enable children to make use of many of the descriptive forms found in language—nominative ("that house"), possessive ("daddy book"), and action ("kitty go"). Throughout the two-word stage, children have a chance to practice these language forms before attempting to expand them. The two-word stage is a universal phenomenon, as shown in Table 7.1.

Telegraphic Speech

Perhaps surprisingly, children do not enter a three-word stage. Unlike the one-word and two-word stages, which appear to be universal among children, there is no specific three-word stage. Instead, following the two-word stage,

Table 7.1 ● The Two-Word Stage: The Same the World Over

FUNCTION OF UTTERANCE	ENGLISH	GERMAN	RUSSIAN	FINNISH	SAMOAN
Locate, name	There book	Buch da (Book there)	Tasya tam (Tasya there)	Toussa Rina (There Rina)	Keith lea (Keith there)
Demand, desire	More milk	Mehr milch (More milk)	Yesche moloko (More milk)	Anna Rina (Give Rina)	Mai pepe (Give doll)
Indicate possession	My shoe	Mein ball (My ball)	Mami chashka (Mama's cup)	Tāti auto (Aunt car)	Lole a'u (Candy my)
Question	Where ball	Wo ball (Where ball)	Gdu papa (Where papa)	Missä pallo (Where ball)	Fea Punafu (Where Punafu)

Source: Liebert, Poulos, & Marmor, 1977, p. 250, as adapted from Slobin, 1970.

children spend the next few years creating many short sentences. Roger Brown at Harvard University has referred to children's sentences during the two-word stage and just after as **telegraphic speech.**

Telegraphic speech is really an apt term. When people send telegrams, at so many cents per word, they want to be brief and to the point; unnecessary words are excluded. Children's telegraphic speech, during the two-word stage and after, is quite similar. A famous example of telegraphic speech can be found in the old Tarzan films. Johnny Weismuller believed that because Tarzan was just getting the hang of English after having lived with the apes for so long, he would speak in a certain way. The speech pattern Weismuller chose in portraying Tarzan was a telegraphic one—that is, rich in important words such as nouns and verbs ("Jane go now," "Boy home soon," "Tarzan help Cheetah"). As you can see, function words are missing; there are no tenses, plurals, conjunctions, articles, prepositions, and so forth. This is typical of telegraphic speech.

To arrange their expressive statements, children in the telegraphic stage often adopt a grammar of rigid word order. In this rigid word order, the subject is usually placed before the verb, just as it is in normal English word order. Children in this stage apparently use a rigid word order because without **grammatical morphemes**—for example, conjunctions, prepositions, and suffixes such as *ing* or the plural *s*—many of the more subtle meanings of a language are difficult to convey. Although children who rely on telegraphic speech make some use of the grammatical morphemes that they hear to comprehend what is said to them (Gerken, Landau, & Remez, 1990), they generally don't use them in their own speech, at least not at first. Because of this, English-speaking children have to rely greatly on word order to make sure that their own meaning is clear, although they may also rely heavily on inflection and emphasis to make their sentences clear (Weist, 1983).

Language and Meaning

Even from this early language use, it is obvious that the development of grammar and semantics (the meaning in the language) are closely allied. English-speaking children are trying to find a way to link the words together to express a meaning, and rigid word order often allows them to communicate a particular meaning effectively. For example, if your 3-year-old child suddenly informs you, "Kitty follow Ann home," you know from the word order that (a) *Kitty* is the subject, (b) *follow* was the action taken, and (c) *Ann* is about to begin imploring you to keep the cat (such is a parent's life). You can tell that young children use rigid word order to express meaning by performing an experiment. Take your 3-year-old child aside and explain to her, using a passive sentence, that "Ann was followed home by the kitty." An interesting thing will happen. A 3-year-old using telegraphic speech and rigid word order will typically ignore such words as *was* or *by* and will only notice that *Ann* came first in the sentence, *follow* came second, and *kitty* came last. The interpretation, as explained by children of this age who hear such passive sentences, would likely be that Ann is now following the cat (Slobin, 1966). Because you and I use function words, we are able to understand that the statement "*Ann was followed* home by the *kitty*" does not mean "Ann follow kitty." Although we sometimes rely on word order to express our meaning, we don't rely on it exclusively.

Some have argued, however, that perhaps children aren't trying to express meaning at all with their word order; perhaps children of this age just have a tendency to string words together in a rigid way. But evidence that children of

TELEGRAPHIC SPEECH
Pattern of speech that develops during and following the two-word stage, in which English-speaking children rely on a grammar of strict word order to convey their meaning and do not use conjunctions, prepositions, or other function words.

GRAMMATICAL MORPHEME
A word or part of a word that helps add meaning to a sentence. Grammatical morphemes are acquired by children generally between the ages of $2\frac{1}{2}$ and 5 years. Conjunctions, prepositions, suffixes, and prefixes are examples of grammatical morphemes. Morphemes are the smallest language units to have meaning and cannot be broken down into smaller meaningful units.

this age use syntactic structure in an attempt to convey meaning, rather than simply showing a tendency to use rigid word order, comes from examining the acquisition of languages in which the use of a rigid word order does not help convey meaning. For example, the Japanese language relies on the use of subjects, objects, and verbs, yet the word order is highly flexible because of the use of small Japanese phonemes called *particles,* which are inserted at different places in the sentence to indicate a word's grammatical role—whether it is a subject, object, or verb. Japanese children in the telegraphic stage, unlike their English-speaking counterparts, show no interest in using a rigid word order; instead, they seem to focus on the position of a particle within a sentence (Hakuta, 1982). It seems, therefore, that a child's early attempts at syntactic use and comprehension are centered on the *semantic* value inherent within the grammatical structure, not on any particular desire to use a rigid word order (Akiyama, 1985). These differences also are observed when considering Western languages. For instance, whereas American children rely on word order to convey and understand meaning, Italian children rely primarily on semantic cues. In one study, American and Italian children were presented with the sentence, "The pencil kicked the cow." The majority of American children chose the pencil as the subject of the sentence (as dictated by word order), whereas most of the Italian children chose the cow (dictated by the fact that pencils don't kick, and therefore a kicking pencil is meaningless) (Bates et al., 1984).

Grammatical Morphemes

Findings indicate that children throughout the world acquire grammatical morphemes in the same general order, although at different rates (deVilliers & deVilliers, 1973). In Table 7.2, you will see 14 grammatical morphemes used in the English language, given in the general order in which children acquire them. This sequence of acquisition is so pervasive that even children who are

Table 7.2 ● Fourteen English Grammatical Morphemes

FORM	MEANING	EXAMPLE
1. Present progressive: *ing*	Ongoing process	He is sit*ing* down.
2. Preposition: *in*	Containment	The mouse is *in* the box.
3. Preposition: *on*	Support	The book is *on* the table.
4. Plural: *s*	Number	The dog*s* ran away.
5. Past irregular: e.g., *went*	Earlier in time relative to time of speaking	The boy *went* home.
6. Possessive: *'s*	Possession	The girl*'s* dog is big.
7. Uncontractible copula *be:* e.g., *are, was*	Number; earlier in time	*Are* they boys or girls? *Was* that a dog?
8. Articles: *the, a*	Definite/indefinite	He has *a* book.
9. Past regular: *ed*	Earlier in time	He jump*ed* the stream.
10. Third person regular: *s*	Number; earlier in time	She run*s* fast.
11. Third person irregular: e.g., *has, does*	Number; earlier in time	*Does* the dog bark?
12. Uncontractible auxiliary *be:* e.g., *is, were*	Number; earlier in time; ongoing process	*Is* he running? *Were* they at home?
13. Contractible copula *be:* e.g., *'s, 're*	Number; earlier in time	That*'s* a spaniel.
14. Contractible auxiliary *be:* e.g., *'s, 're*	Number; earlier in time; ongoing process	They*'re* running very slowly.

Source: Clark & Clark, 1977; based on Brown, 1973.

hard of hearing or who have language disorders acquire these grammatical morphemes in this same order (Khan & James, 1983; Brown, 1984).

Researchers aren't certain why children learn grammatical morphemes in this order, although it may have to do with the complexity of each task. Return for a moment to that foreign land to which you were sent earlier in this chapter. Once you had acquired single words and then two-word phrases and had begun to string them together in a clipped, telegraphic manner, you, too, would slowly begin to acquire grammatical morphemes. But in what order? The answer might be that you would learn the simplest and most obvious ones first. This may be exactly what children do. They learn the easiest and most obvious rule first and then simply begin to apply it.

Other researchers have argued that it's not complexity that determines the order of acquisition, but functionality (MacWhinney, 1978). In other words, the order of acquisition is determined by how much function each grammatical morpheme serves; the ones providing the child with the most value or function are learned first. For example, expressing plurals and locations is more useful in day-to-day conversation than using a copula (you may have even gotten through the whole day without feeling a deep need to use one).

For some time it was assumed that the child's language needed a syntactic structure on which grammatical morphemes could be built. The idea here was that a child needed a certain level of comprehension to grasp the meaning of any of the grammatical morphemes, a comprehension level that included a syntax (i.e., the ability to form a sentence). As you will notice, all 14 of the grammatical morphemes in Table 7.2 have a semantic structure, or meaning; each carries information. However, careful examination has found that the plural may be used correctly by children in the one-word stage, when they may say, for instance, "dogs" when they clearly mean more than one dog (Mervis & Johnson, 1991). Although it might be thought that children who do this don't really understand the rule, but are simply repeating the word *dogs*, there is evidence to the contrary. In 1958, J. Berko asked children to answer the question posed in Figure 7.3. The children correctly answered "wugs," a clear demonstration that they had learned the plural rule, because they obviously had never before heard the word *wugs*. In fact, children often are not aware that they have acquired these rules.

So now we see that even children in the one-word stage are able to grasp some of these rules. To know so much and yet be able to say only one word at a time brings us back to the concept of a holophrase. Although children in the one-word stage may only be able to say single words at a time, their comprehension is clearly much broader than single-word utterances might suggest.

Irregular Words

English, like many other languages, contains a number of words that are exceptions to the rule. Children's early attempts to handle these words give us clues to their acquisition of grammar rules. Parents are sometimes dismayed to hear their young child switch from "Mommy go" to "Mommy goed." At first it sounds as though the child is regressing and is becoming less competent. Actually, the child has advanced and is now using the past regular by adding the suffix *ed*. It's not the child's fault that the past tense of *go* is *went*. *Go* is simply an irregular English word. Frankly, it is hard to argue with the child's logic. Why shouldn't it be *goed* instead of *went*? Children during this time make many similar errors. *One foot*—obviously *two foots; one man—two mans*. Such overregularization—that is, applying the rule in each and every case—demon-

This is a wug.

Now there is another one.
There are two of them.
There are two_____.

strates the rapid acquisition of the general rules of grammar. The exceptions are acquired later.

Children learn the exceptions in the same way they learn regular words. In fact, if adults use a particular irregular word often enough, the child will be far less likely to overregularize it (Marcus et al., 1992). What appears to happen is that the child learns grammar rules and irregular exceptions to those rules separately. For instance, imagine a child who wishes to refer to *feet*. First, she will search her memory for the right word. If she has heard the irregular word *feet* often enough, she will, in fact, use that word, which is why older children almost never overregularize an irregular word. If, on the other hand, she hasn't heard the exception applied correctly often enough, she will come up with the less complex word *foot,* and then apply the plural rule, which yields *foots* (Marcus et al., 1992).

The Development of Syntactic Skills

Beginning with the holophrase, children acquire the rules and knowledge necessary to construct utterances with a growing complexity of syntax. Table 7.3

Table 7.3 ● The Development of Syntactic Skills

AGE (IN YEARS)	MLU	SYNTACTIC SKILLS	EXAMPLES
1½ to 2½	1.5	One-word utterances, called *holophrases,* and two-word utterances, called *duos;* basic semantic relationships, such as:	
		Recurrence	*More ball.*
		Nonexistence	*All gone ball.*
		Attribution	*Big ball.*
		Possession	*My ball.*
		Nominations	*That ball.*
		Agent-action	*Adam hit.*
		Agent-action-object	*Adam hit ball.*
2½ to 3	2.25	Grammatical morphemes added, such as:	
		Present progressive inflection	*I walking.*
		Locative prepositions	*Kitty in basket.*
		Plurals	*Two balls.*
		Possessive	*Adam's ball.*
		Past	*It broke.*
		Verb inflections	*He walks.*
3 to 3½	2.75	Auxiliary verbs	*I am walking.*
			I do like you.
		Negative particles	*I didn't do it.*
			This isn't ice cream.
		Yes-no questions	*Will I go?*
			Do you want it?
		Wh questions	*What do you have?*
			Where is the doggie?
3½ to 4	3.25	Sentence clauses	*You think I can do it.*
			I see what you made.
4 to 5	3.75	Conjunctions of two sentences	*You think I can, but I can't.*
			Mary and I are going.
> 5	> 4	Reversible passives	*The truck was chased by the car.*
		Connectives	*I am going to go although I don't want to.*
		Indirect object-direct object constructions	*The man showed the boy the friend.*
		Pronominalization	*He knew that John was going to win the race.*

Source: Whiteburst, 1982, p. 371.

provides a synopsis of the acquisition of a child's syntactic skills. The second column, MLU (which stands for "mean length of utterance"), is simply the average number of words that a child uses during each utterance at any given time. You may also notice that the example "kitty in basket" (between the ages of 2½ and 3 years) is an instance of telegraphic speech.

Given that children eventually learn the rules of grammar, you might expect that Tarzan would have done so, too. After all, he listened to Jane a lot, and she spoke very well. Edgar Rice Burroughs, the author of the Tarzan books, certainly thought that was how it should be. As his readers know, Tarzan was depicted as an extremely well-spoken man, who eventually became fluent in many languages. And as we pointed out, he listened to Jane and she spoke quite well, which brings us to our next topic: caretaker speech.

Caretaker Speech*

Until about the age of 3 years, children learn to construct their language according to their parents' usage. After this time, peers also become important models. Interestingly, adults who interact with children restructure their language for the children's benefit, often quite unconsciously (Blewitt, 1983). This restructured language is called **caretaker speech**, and it differs in a number of ways from the language generally used by adults to communicate with one another. Caretaker speech is characterized by short, simple sentences. The sentences are usually said in a relatively high-pitched voice, with the highest pitches used for emphasis (Fernald & Mazzie, 1991), and often with exaggerated inflections and intonations (Ratner & Pye, 1984). The vocabulary is simple, and individual words are sometimes simplified by reducing their phonetic complexity. Caretaker speech appears to be a universal phenomenon. It is just as likely to occur, for instance, whether the adult interacting with an infant is speaking English, German, or Mandarin Chinese (Grieser & Kuhl, 1988).

As you can imagine, caretaker speech enables the child to grasp the language more easily. Returning for a moment to the foreign country you visited at the beginning of this chapter, you would no doubt have found it helpful if the local friends you acquired had adjusted their speech for you, so that their sentences were shorter, simpler, and less involved than the speech they used with their native friends. Indeed, you might readily do the same for a friend of yours who is just learning English. Even young children may adjust their speech to the level of the person to whom they are speaking (Dunn & Kendrick, 1982a).

Parents engaging in caretaker speech help their children to acquire language. Parents and older children regularly adjust their speech to a level just slightly above that of the younger child to whom they are speaking. Correcting a child's grammar in slow, easy steps also can help the child to focus on and acquire the next language advances (Goldstein, 1984; Rondal, 1985).

Because caretaker speech is a universal phenomenon, we have few chances of examining what might happen if parents never used caretaker speech and didn't adjust their conversations when they interacted with their child. Without caretaker speech, children might be unable to acquire language. This is not surprising. Do you think that you could learn Turkish by watching old Turkish movies on TV? Perhaps you'd catch a phrase or two, perhaps even a few words, but without caretaker speech or the opportunity to interact in conversations, you might be lost forever among the strange phonemes.

*Also known as "motherese" or "caregiver speech."

CARETAKER SPEECH
A speech pattern used in addressing others who are obviously less competent in their speech than the speaker. Universally applied, caretaker speech is characterized by short, simple sentences, simple vocabulary, a relatively high-pitched voice, and exaggerated inflections. It should not be confused with baby talk, which refers only to the simplification of individual words, such as saying "wa-wa" for water.

Parents often speak to their infants and young children by using short, simple sentences, a higher-pitched voice, and exaggerated inflections. This caretaker speech may facilitate children's language development.

SPOONERISM

An unintentional transposition of sounds in a sentence, as in, "People in glass houses shouldn't stow thrones." Named for the English clergyman William A. Spooner (1844–1930), who was well known for such errors.

PIDGIN

A simplified form of speech typically derived from a mixture of two or more languages. It has as its basis a rudimentary form of grammar and vocabulary and is generally used for communication between people speaking different languages.

The nature-nurture question of why caretaker speech is universal has not been resolved. We do know that the presence of the infant or child is important. Even an experienced parent is unable to produce fully adequate caretaker speech if the child isn't present (Snow, 1972). Furthermore, nonparents who have little experience with infants will engage in caretaker speech that is as rich in quality as the caretaker speech that parents possess (Jacobson, Boersma, Fields, & Olson, 1983). We also know that as the child's world and interests expand, the parents adjust their caretaker speech to keep just slightly ahead of the child's abilities (Molfese, Molfese, & Carrell, 1982). But whether adults change their behavior in these ways owing to a biological propensity or because they are shaped by the child's positive reaction to caretaker speech is unknown (Jacobson, Boersma, Fields, & Olson, 1983).

Nativists, who believe that it is human nature to acquire language, argue that the presence of a child is a sign stimulus that increases the rate of caretaker speech among those present. Learning theorists, on the other hand, argue that when a person is interacting with a child, that person is quickly "persuaded," as a function of shaping, to adjust his or her speech, because the younger child attends more closely to simpler sentences. Learning theorists argue that for the same reason, caretaker inflections may be the result of shaping. For instance, a higher-pitched voice, as a contrasting stimulus, attracts the child's attention and therefore reinforces the caregiver. Theories of language acquisition are ripe with such nature-nurture questions. (See At Issue).

THE FUNCTION OF GRAMMAR

How do children learn to express themselves through language? Can you recall from your own childhood how you learned to express what you wanted to say? In fact, are you even aware of how you currently go about deciding how to express yourself? Suppose that you are working in the hot sun and are becoming thirsty. How do you express a desire for a glass of water? How do you tell your friend on the job that you think it's time to take a break and get a drink? How do you express your meaning in a structured sentence?

You might say, "Let's take a break and get a drink of water," as simply as that. But was that simple? How did you come up with that sentence? Did you just string the words together? Were some words more important than others? Could you have strung them together differently? When you put together that sentence, did you begin by searching your entire vocabulary until you struck upon the contraction *let's*, which you then decided was the best first word? A language computer might perform that way. Then did you go through another search for the next word and finally choose *take?* No, you didn't. People don't sort through their vocabularies before speaking each word, as a machine might. People build the structure or syntax of a sentence to express a meaning, and they do this before they begin to speak.

We can obtain clues about the way people organize syntax to express their meaning by examining **spoonerisms.** Spoonerisms are rather interesting transpositions named after William A. Spooner (1844–1930), an English clergyman well known for accidentally making such rearrangements. No doubt you've occasionally committed a spoonerism yourself. I think of a theater usher who recently baffled my friends and me when he asked, "Would you like me to sew you to your sheets?" Everyone soon realized that he meant to say, "Would you like me to show you to your seats?" What this spoonerism demonstrates, though, is that the usher had to have had the word *seats* in mind (the tenth word in the sentence) before he ever said *show* (the sixth word), or how could

Children and the Origins of Language

One of the longest ongoing debates concerning language development involves whether language is basically a learned phenomenon or whether we, as a species, are biogenetically "prewired" for its acquisition. In fact, research concerning this debate is thousands of years old.

According to the ancient Greek historian Herodotus, in the seventh century B.C. the Egyptian pharaoh Psamtik the First had two newborns raised in silence to see what language they would eventually come to speak. The Egyptians didn't know quite what to make of the "language" that the children eventually spoke, but concluded that it sounded something like Phrygian, although it obviously wasn't.

Other attempts were made throughout history—by Frederick II of Sicily, James IV of Scotland, and Akbar, emperor of India from 1556–1605, to name the most notable. The reports concluded that children not exposed to language either failed to learn any language or spoke a gibberish of some sort. Frederick II was especially disappointed by these results because he had hoped that the children in his experiment, left undisturbed by exposure to common language, would come to speak the pure language that God had intended them to speak—which Frederick assumed to be Latin, although others had argued that it would be Greek.

Akbar, however, noted that all his little victims had turned out mute. He was pleased with this result because he had said all along that exposure to language was a requirement for its acquisition. Fortunately, none of the other emperors of India who followed him were interested in replicating or building on his "research."

Today, of course, we know that children must have contact with a particular language before they can be expected to speak it and that Latin won't spring from the mouth of anyone not exposed to it. But modern researchers still wonder if our childhood isn't a special time during which we apply a natural inborn grammar to the words we hear for the first time and if, in fact, children aren't the ones responsible for the creation of new languages.

But what is an "inborn grammar," and how can children be responsible for the creation of new languages? Let's look at these questions one at a time. First, consider the case of a 13-year-old girl found wandering the streets of a California city in 1970. She was lost, having escaped from an abusive parent who had kept her in total isolation since she was 18 months old. She was unable to speak a single word—because she didn't know any. Like the children experimented on by Akbar, she had not been exposed to any language (Berreby, 1992). After years of rehabilitation, the girl became a functioning adult. Her intelligence scores were adequate so long as the tests given were nonverbal intelligence tests—tests that don't require a verbal answer. In spite of her remarkable

recovery, her language was limited to that of a 2-year-old. As far as complex adult language was concerned, she just never caught on to it. Because it is unethical to conduct the kind of experiment tried by Akbar and various other rulers throughout history, we typically find that case studies like this one form the basis for many of our modern assumptions concerning language formation. Because of this case and others like it, researchers wonder if experience with some sort of grammar during childhood isn't a prerequisite for mature language acquisition.

It might be that a child needs to use a grammar during childhood before speaking a language fully as an adult. Many researchers believe that humans have evolved a language capacity that includes a brain equipped, perhaps at birth, with a form of rudimentary grammar (Chomsky, 1957). Even more controversial is the idea that children naturally impose this inborn grammar early in their development, somehow laying down the neurological groundwork on which the grammar of their own language can be built. The idea, then, is that through corrections and modeling, parents reshape this inborn grammar until the children eventually come to learn the specific grammar of the language that their family is speaking.

There may be a way to tell if children are using an inborn grammar early on in their development. There have been many times and places in history in which peoples of different languages have been thrown together. In Hawaii, for example, there is even the term *four-blood*, which refers to someone whose grandparents are each from a different heritage and culture. For centuries, plantation workers in different parts of the world often found themselves brought together by circumstances. Germans worked with Chinese, French with Vietnamese, and Portuguese with just about everybody. Sometimes, especially on plantations in French Guiana, as many as 12 groups might be working together, each speaking a different language. To get by, people often tried to get a handle on one another's language by picking up a few hundred words and sayings from each other. This approach led to the creation of a "broken" English, French, Japanese, and so forth, known as **pidgin**. For example, to express "They put the body in the ground and covered it with a blanket, and that was all," someone speaking pidgin English was recorded as saying, "Inside dirt and cover and blanket, finish" (Berreby, 1992, p. 47). With a little effort, you might understand what this person was saying, especially if you know the context, but it certainly isn't clear, acceptable English.

But people could usually get by with pidgin while working with others in the fields and then speak their native tongues at home. What makes a confluence of different language

AT ISSUE

Children and the Origins of Language, continued

speakers so interesting, however, is how their children interact. The children typically enrich pidgin by combining many of the words from the languages they use while playing together and then apply a grammatical structure to it. This newly emerging "language," known as a **creole**, may explain how new languages and dialects get started: The children create them!

But is the creole that forms a new language based on an inborn grammar? Some say that it is. Creole "languages" throughout the world appear to be formed by the children of people with different native tongues who come together, usually at the borders of nations speaking different languages. Different creole "languages" also have many points in common. Some argue, however, that most creoles have common antecedents, often Portuguese or African, and that these commonalities among creole "languages" are reflective of common linguistic roots rather than genetic ones. And yet, could it be that creole tongues have much in common because they are reflecting a natural grammar we have all inherited? Researchers like linguist Derek Bickerton believe that even if it isn't so, children's creole is directly based on the deep grammatical structure within us all.

In 1978, Derek Bickerton actually found an uninhabited island 300 miles east of the Philippines for an experiment that might address the question of an inborn grammar. He received a grant to populate the island with six young families, each speaking a language very different from the others. Wells were to be dug and homes built for the experiment, which was to last one year. The idea was to give the six families, including their children, 200 made-up words for different objects and actions, thereby creating a common pidgin that the families could use. Then the children would play together each day and their creole, if they in fact created one, would be examined.

Some felt that the experiment might not be ethical because it required isolating the children for experimental purposes. The legacy of Akbar was still on people's minds five centuries later, and with good reason. Medical facilities and other emergency services were many hours away from the island—which would have virtually marooned the children who were to participate in the experiment. Thus, the National Science Foundation withdrew the grant. Not to be deterred, however, Derek Bickerton is trying again with new funding and a less isolated location on an estate in Europe, where eight families, two each of Greek, Flemish, Basque, and Hungarian speakers, will be living. As to whether his experiment will uncover evidence of an innate grammar, Bickerton probably gave the best answer to that question when he said,

> Whether my hypotheses are supported or not, I don't much care. What I do care about are the things that we shall know for the first time. I want to discover things. And I think we're going to have some fun. (Berreby, 1992, p. 53)

he have gotten them confused? People prepare their syntactic structures before they say them; they don't simply link one word to the next (Motley, 1985).

The question is, how would a child choose a starting place for building a sentence? And it's not an easy question to answer. Language theorists have debated and wondered about this for years. There are those who believe that children use some as-yet-unknown processing system to go from the meaning they wish to express to the syntax they use. Noam Chomsky (1957), a well-known and respected linguist, has proposed the existence of a **language acquisition device**, or LAD, that has evolved in our species to handle the interaction between syntax and semantics. This is akin to the innate grammar addressed by Derek Bickerton when he planned to study the development of creole in children. Others, like Henrietta Lempert (whom we shall discuss in a moment), place greater emphasis on semantic aspects as a driving force behind syntactic structure.

As you recall, earlier we used the active sentence "Kitty follow[ed] Ann home," and then we used the passive voice, "Ann was followed home by the kitty." Both sentences really say the same thing. It makes you wonder why there should even be a passive voice. What's the point of having two ways to say the same thing? I wonder how the passive form got started. I have this fleeting image of a caveman one day announcing to his friends, "This new thing—the passive voice—has been invented by me. With it, we can be amused and our enemies will be confused!" But odds are it didn't happen that way. Instead, the passive voice (as just one of many examples of our grammar) seems to have evolved from our need to express ourselves.

Researcher Henrietta Lempert believes that the way constructions such as the passive voice may have gotten started, and the reason children find them useful to acquire, has to do with the need to express a particular *topic*—not with some rule of grammar. Consider the following incident: A bus hit a dog. If it were your dog and you wanted to talk about what happened to your dog, *your dog* would be the topic of concern. You would start your statement with "My dog." But then where do you go? My dog—what? You can't say, "My dog hit the bus"; that's not what happened. Instead, you are forced to say, "My dog *was hit by the bus*"—the passive voice. Lempert demonstrated in experiments that children of 2 to 5 years could acquire such forms of expression as the passive voice, *especially* if the topic were, like the dog in our example, animate and live (Lempert, 1989). Live and animate things attract children's attention and are likely to become main topics for them. On the other hand, the children had great difficulty understanding the passive voice if the topic was inanimate and stationary (Lempert, 1984, 1989).

The passive voice, then, was easy for the children to learn if their main interest was to express a particular topic. As in our example, they placed the topic first in the sentence, which in turn necessitated use of the passive voice. When it was used simply as a grammatical form without an attractive topic up front in the lead position, children had difficulty understanding the passive voice. Perhaps our grammar works that way. We start with a central topic and then try to build from it. This, in turn, may lead to a series of complicated grammatical forms, all of which have a use, namely, to support the topic. Such an assumption is incredibly difficult to demonstrate, however, and no one knows for sure whether this approach is correct (Bock, 1990).

As you've come to appreciate, language and language acquisition are anything but simple. It may be many years before we fully understand how language develops in humans. But the work has begun, and future results promise to be interesting.

CREOLE
A mixture of language that develops when groups speaking different languages have prolonged contact. Typically, the basic vocabulary of the dominant language is combined with the grammar of a subordinate language, creating an admixture (a mingling within a mixture) of words and grammar that becomes in itself a new subordinate and creolized language.

LANGUAGE ACQUISITION DEVICE (LAD)
As hypothesized by Noam Chomsky, a neural structure inborn in every healthy individual that is preprogrammed with the underlying rules of a universal form of grammar. Once children are exposed to a particular language, they select from the complete set of rules with which they were born only those rules required by the language they will be speaking. Most psychologists and linguists find the idea interesting, but agree that proof of such a device is doubtful because of the difficulties involved in demonstrating its existence.

When children are first learning language live and animate things attract their attention and are likely to become main topics of conversation.

APPLICATIONS

Strike When the Iron Is Hot

Earlier in this chapter, we discussed the importance of naming as a major step in the acquisition of language. But whether a child will learn a new name for something often depends on his or her motivation. For example, let's consider an experiment conducted by Marta Valdez-Menchaca and Grover Whitehurst (1988). In this experiment, English-speaking preschool children were divided into an experimental group and a control group. Then both groups of children were taught the Spanish names of some attractive toys that were out of reach. The children were then told that if they wanted to play with any of the toys, they would have to ask for them by their Spanish names.

When the children were first taught the Spanish names for the toys, however, the two groups were treated differently. Children in the experimental group were taught the Spanish name of a toy only when they expressed an interest in playing with it. Children in the control group were told the Spanish names of the toys just as often, but at random times.

The results were revealing. Children in the experimental group learned the new words at a faster rate and remembered more of them than did children from the control group. The best way to teach children new names for objects, then, is to "strike when the iron is hot"—that is, to engage them in naming when they show an interest in the object to be named.

But does it really matter? Wouldn't children eventually learn the names of things anyway, even if their parents or teachers didn't pay special attention to the times when the children were most interested and moti-

The best way to teach children the new names for objects is to teach them when they show an interest in the object to be named.

vated to learn? No doubt any healthy child would eventually learn the names of things. The main point made by the experiment is not that there is a way to accelerate children's acquisition of names, but rather that children's motivation plays an important role in the acquisition of language.

In fact, the motivational aspect of language acquisition goes beyond just the learning of names for things. To illustrate, consider another experiment conducted by Grover Whitehurst and his colleagues (1988). In this second experiment, it was demonstrated that if parents motivate their children to interact with picture book stories as the stories are being read, the children's overall language development will be substantially boosted. When carrying out this experiment, the researchers gathered 30 middle-class parents and their 2- to 3-year-old children. Half the chil-

dren were placed in an experimental reading program, conducted in their own homes, for 1 month. The other half served as controls.

In the experimental group, one of the parents, most often the mother, was given a one-hour training session in which she was taught a special way to read to her child. Unlike most parents who might simply read a story straight through, she was taught to stop from time to time and ask open-ended questions, often beginning her question with the word *what*. She was also instructed not to ask questions that could simply be answered with a yes or no, or by pointing, or by giving a simple name. For example, "Who's that?" is a poor question because it simply requires the child to give a name. A far better question would be, "There's Eeyore. What's happening to him?" This effective question requires the child to elaborate about the story.

Parents were also asked to expand on the answers that their children gave by providing alternative explanations or by asking progressively more challenging questions.

Parents in the control group read stories to their children in their usual way. Children in both groups were read to just as often—about eight times a week.

At the beginning of the study, children in both groups did not differ in their language ability. This is, of course, what one would expect because the children had been assigned to one group or the other randomly. But after only 1 month with the new reading technique, children in the experimental group were 8½ months ahead of the control group children on a standard measure commonly used to assess verbal expression (the Illinois Test of Psycholinguistic Abilities, which requires children to tell the experimenter as much as possible about various objects) and 6 months ahead on another standard measure commonly used to test vocabulary (the Expressive One Word Picture Vocabulary Test). This all seems to have occurred as the consequence of a change of parental reading style, itself the result of nothing more than a simple one-hour training session!

After 9 months had passed, the children from both groups were test-ed once again. The results showed that the experimental group children still maintained a 6-month advantage over the children from the control group. Further follow-up studies have yet to be conducted, so it is not known if the advantage will continue. However, there are correlational data that show that reading to children is associated with literacy and high teacher ratings of oral language skill as well as with reading comprehension (Wells, 1985). It has also been shown that children who are exposed to interactive reading at age 2½ are among the most advanced in language development at age 4½ (Crain-Thoreson & Dale, 1992).

Thus, something as simple as reading picture books to children, especially in an interactive way that encourages them to think and express themselves, might have important long-term effects. Right now, it's really too early to say. But from Whitehurst's research, we know that the reading experience is likely to help children advance considerably in terms of language and vocabulary skills. Consider, then, a possible snowball effect, in which these children's thought skills also develop faster (because they have more words to use to help them form thoughts) and their interest in reading grows stronger (because reading has been associated with the fun of actively

engaging with their parents). As a result, these children decide to read more often. Reading is a very good way for children to become exposed to new vocabulary and ideas (Miller & Gildea, 1987), which in turn might well expand further the cognitive abilities they will need to perform well in school. Next, because they are more cognitively advanced than their peers, these children succeed in their schoolwork, earning the praise of teachers and parents, which in turn gives them confidence to accept new challenges and progress even further. All this from eight hours per week of interactive reading with their parents when they were little!

Of course, I'm not saying that this is what would happen or that it would be as simple as I've made it sound. Many more experiments and more data are needed before we can fully know the long-term value of such an experience. But it does seem possible, even probable, given the value of reading in our society, that it could all happen in just the way I've described. The point is that such interaction with children might be a great help and requires little effort, so it's worth a try.

SUMMARY

- A language requires the use of signs and symbols within a grammar. A language also allows novel constructions to be created by manipulation of the various signs and symbols within the grammatical structure.
- There is evidence for the existence of vocal "dialogues" between mothers and their newborns within 72 hours following birth.
- Language acquisition may begin when the infant acquires the first language-like sounds. An infant's gooing sounds seem vowel-like, although the sounds differ considerably from the vowel-like sounds produced by adults, probably because of the differences between infant and adult skulls and oral cavities.
- Infants progress through a number of stages during their acquisition of language. These are the phonation stage (0 to 2 months), the gooing stage (2 to 4 months), the expansion stage (4 to 7 months), the cononical stage (7 to 10 months), and the contraction stage (10 to 14 months). Babbling begins with the onset of phonetic expansion. During the contraction stage, infants often imitate the tones and inflections of the language to which they have been exposed.
- Infants perceive language sounds in categories. To an infant, a phoneme is a phoneme, no matter who is saying it, even when there is a change in intonation, voice onset, or length of voicing. The ability to perceive that the phoneme remains the same even with these changes is known as phoneme constancy.
- By 1 year of age, children often have begun to speak their first words. This developmental period is known as the one-word stage. The first words that children acquire usually are concrete nouns, and these tend to follow the "three bears rule."
- Naming is a very important way of acquiring words. By the time the child has acquired his or her first words, it's easy for a parent to direct the child's attention to particular objects. As the child comes to realize that different objects have different names, this sets the stage for a major step in language acquisition.
- Careful examination of the way children in the one-word stage order their single words indicates that children are already forming hypotheses about how sentences are constructed. For this reason, many researchers refer to single-word utterances as holophrases. A holophrase is a one-word "sentence."
- After the one-word stage, children enter the two-word stage. Both the one-word and two-word stages appear to be universal among children. During the two-word stage, the child may utter over 1,000 new statements every month.
- Interestingly, children don't enter a three-word stage, but instead begin to use telegraphic speech; that is, they form sentences without using function words. They learn grammatical morphemes later, in a specific sequence that is probably dependent on the difficulty of mastering each rule.
- Both adults and children engage in caretaker speech, which appears to be a universal way of addressing other people whose language competence is less than one's own. Such speech helps children to understand what is being said and to learn how to use more advanced forms of the language.
- Children may be the ones responsible for the formation of new languages. Creole is an example of the possible influence that children may have on language formation.
- Spoonerisms give a clue to the way people organize their syntax to express their meaning. People prepare their syntactic structures before they say them;

they don't simply link one word to the next. Many researchers believe that the first focus of a sentence is the topic at hand and that certain aspects of grammar derive from the need to emphasize a topic.

■ Reading picture books with children in an interactive way has been found to increase children's vocabulary and descriptive verbal skills and may promote later school achievement.

QUESTIONS FOR DISCUSSION

1. If you had no language, how do you think this would affect your thought processes?

2. Would an Italian baby learn Italian in the same way as an American college student taking an Italian language class? What differences would there be? After five years, who would know more Italian?

3. Do you think that you could restructure the language class so that the college student in question 2 would be sure to win the "race"? How would you make the class different?

4. Eskimo children have a better recall of what kind of snow was on the ground the day before than do children from warmer climates. Eskimo languages also include many more words for different kinds of snow than languages used in warmer places. What do these two statements tell us about language and memory? If the Eskimos had no language, do you think that they would still remember the kind of snow that fell the day before better than someone from a southern climate, simply because the Eskimos have learned to pay more attention to things that are meaningful in their culture?

5. We know that it is beneficial to engage young children in an interactive dialogue while reading to them. Do you think that it might also help young children to develop their thought skills if parents spent time engaging them in an interactive dialogue about the television programs that they watched together? Do you think that it could help older children?

SUGGESTIONS FOR FURTHER READING

1. Baron, N. S. (1992). *Growing up with language: How children learn to talk.* Reading, MA: Addison-Wesley.

2. Bickerton, D. (1990). *Language and species.* Chicago, IL: University of Chicago Press.

3. Hulit, L. M., & Howard, M. R. (1992). *Born to talk: An introduction to speech & language development.* New York: Macmillan.

4. Miller, P. J. (1982). *Amy, Wendy, and Beth: Learning language in South Baltimore.* Austin, TX: University of Texas Press.

5. Terrace, H. S. (1979). *Nim.* New York: Knopf.

6. Wang, W. S-Y. (Ed.). (1990). *The emergence of language: Development and evolution.* New York: W. H. Freeman.

CHAPTER 8

Early Childhood: Personality and Social-Emotional Development

CHAPTER PREVIEW
"Lead Me Not into Temptation"

Have you ever tried to diet? Quit smoking? Save money? Watch TV only after you've studied? Good luck! It isn't easy to resist immediate gratification in exchange for a long-term advantage. Some people can do it. We like to say that they have willpower.

Two researchers once gathered together a group of kindergartners to investigate willpower in young children. The children were asked to make some drawings. When they were finished, they were offered candy for having done such a good job. But before they took the candy, they were told that if they wanted to give up candy today and wait until tomorrow, they could have twice as much. Before the children decided which they would prefer, they were asked what they thought a "dumb kid" and a "smart kid" would do in the same situation. Most of the children said that a dumb kid would take the candy today, whereas a smart kid would wait until tomorrow and get twice as much. Yet even after making this statement, most of the children took the candy rather than wait (Nisan & Koriat, 1977).

It is unlikely that these children thought of themselves as "dumb kids." They knew the intelligent thing to do; it's just that for some reason, they couldn't bring themselves to do it. Is there any one of us who hasn't done the same thing at one time or another?

In this chapter, we will examine personality development during early childhood, including the development of self-regulation and competence. We'll also discuss the important effects that parents, siblings, and peers can have on young children and the development of friendships and other relationships during play. In addition, we'll take time to examine the important topics of working mothers and child abuse.

PERSONALITY DEVELOPMENT IN EARLY CHILDHOOD

Erik Erikson believed that after a base of trust has been laid down during infancy, the child must then develop autonomy. Failure to do so, he argued, will lead to unhealthy ego and personality development. It is during this time that children come to regulate their own behavior. They see themselves as separate from their parents; they begin to develop a sense of autonomy. This is the time of the second psychosocial conflict (autonomy versus shame or doubt), which Erikson asserted develops between the ages of 1 and 3 years.

According to Erikson, children start to develop autonomy when they learn how to master tasks or do things for themselves. Each success teaches them that they are important and can control their lives. Erikson believed that children who are not encouraged to develop this self-confidence may come to doubt themselves or to be ashamed of their inability.

Between the ages of 3 and 5 years, children who have a sense of basic trust and who see themselves as autonomous or competent may feel free to initiate their own activities. At this point, the third psychosocial conflict emerges (initiative versus guilt). Erikson argued that during this time, children should be encouraged to initiate activities on their own. Sometimes, of course, the activities that a child initiates may run counter to parental or social rules of conduct. Erikson argued that the best way to deal with this problem is to forbid the inappropriate behavior, but to do so in a manner that won't unduly upset the child. When, for example, a 5-year-old child decides it would be fun to play with delicate stereo equipment, a parent should forbid the activity firmly but also gently, so as not to make the child feel guilty for having initiated the behavior in the first place. In this way, according to Erikson, children can develop confidence in their own planning without fear that an initiated activity will meet with a severe reaction.

Children begin to develop autonomy when they learn how to master tasks or do things by themselves.

Self-Regulation

Parents usually discover that regulation of their children's behavior becomes necessary during the child's second year. This is when the child begins to display sufficient autonomy to interfere occasionally with parental desires. For this reason, parents will wish to instill in the child an understanding of what is acceptable. This, of course, is an important step in the child's development. As researcher Claire Kopp has stated,

> During the second year of life, children increasingly demonstrate signs of selfhood and autonomy. This growing sense of identity, coupled with the ability to recall the dictates of caregivers, leads to a new dimension in behavior. Children begin to appraise the requirements of social and nonsocial situations and to monitor their own behavior accordingly. Slowly and precariously they move toward self-regulation, an achievement that Flavell (1977) describes as being "one of the really central and significant cognitive-developmental hallmarks of the early childhood period." (Kopp, 1982, p. 199)

This does not mean that it is the parents' job to inhibit autonomy when children begin to express themselves. On the contrary, encouraging autonomy is often beneficial. However, the child must *not* be allowed to express inappropriate behavior at inappropriate times. The parents' job is to teach the child which behaviors, under which circumstances, should be inhibited or expressed. In this way, *unlimited* autonomy is kept in check. The encouragement of such self-regulation in the child is one of the parents' most important tasks (Maccoby & Martin, 1983).

To examine how parents teach young children what is allowed, researchers in one study looked at disciplinary interactions in the homes of 90 2-year-old children. The interchange between parent and child was recorded whenever the child engaged in an inappropriate behavior, such as temper tantrums, physical or verbal aggression, actions that might damage household objects, or other behaviors that were not allowed (Minton, Kagan, & Levine, 1971). The parent's initial reaction was typically mild. If the child did not comply, pressure to behave escalated and became more active and forceful.

Although the initial motivation to behave may be brought on through external pressure, such as parental commands, even children as young as 2 years will begin, after exposure to such external pressure, to develop their own self-regulation based on their understanding of what their parents allow (Lytton, 1980; Dunn & Munn, 1985). The acquisition and consolidation of self-regulation are considered by many researchers to represent a major developmental milestone (Vaughn, Kopp, & Krakow, 1984).

When children begin to regulate their own behavior, they come to appear to rely on internalized value and reward systems. They can behave appropriately without being forced by external pressures, they can ignore immediate gratification in favor of long-term goals, and they may adhere to personal standards of moral behavior in the face of opposition.

Babyproofing.   Any home should be "babyproofed" to the extent that all potential poisons (including medicines and vitamins) and other dangerous objects should be kept well out of reach of children. It's probably not advisable, however, to babypoof the home further by taking away every object that might possibly be damaged by a young child. Most preschoolers eventually comply (although it may take some parental insistence) with requests to leave appealing objects alone. Apparently, the presence of the objects can help children to acquire their own impulse control as they learn to leave the objects alone (Power & Chapieski, 1986). Furthermore, completely babyproofing a home may make it somewhat sterile, limiting the opportunities for the exploration of new and interesting things. This, in turn, may hinder the development of nonverbal competence. In fact, children from heavily babyproofed homes tend to score slightly lower on the nonverbal items in IQ tests (Power & Chapieski, 1986).

The Development of Competence

In 1965, Burton L. White and his colleagues at Harvard University began a longitudinal study of approximately 400 preschoolers to investigate the development of competence in young children. This study became known as the Harvard Preschool Project. White identified several characteristics of the competent child. The most competent children in his sample displayed superior social skills and cognitive abilities. He found that the mothers of the most competent children usually had three things in common (White, 1975, p. 264):

1. **Designing the living area.** They protected the child from the dangers of the home . . . usually ahead of time. They then provided maximum access to the living quarters. They particularly made the kitchen safe and useful. They made kitchen cabinets, and safe utensils, etc. available for play.
2. **Consulting.** They were available to the child several hours each day to assist, enthuse and soothe when necessary. . . . They would usually respond promptly even if only to delay action. . . . They would provide what was needed *with* some language, on target and at or slightly above his level of comprehension. . . .

PERMISSIVE-DEMANDING DIMENSION
One of two major dimensions used by Baumrind to describe parenting; denotes the degree of parental permissiveness.

ACCEPTING-REJECTING DIMENSION
One of two major dimensions used by Baumrind to describe parenting; denotes the degree of affection within the parent-child relationship.

3. Authority. Though loving and encouraging and free with praise, these mothers were firm. *No matter how young the infant, they set clear limits. . . .* They did not overintellectualize or expect the baby to do more than he was capable of, like control strong impulses indefinitely, etc.

THE FAMILY

In much early research on child development, the focus was on the parents' (usually the mother's) effect on the child's development. That focus has changed, however. Researchers now recognize that any child within a family is bound to have a reciprocal effect on the family and on its attempts to socialize the child (Brunk & Henggeler, 1984; Maccoby & Martin, 1983; Bell, 1979). Families are complex; they consist of numerous two-way relationships and interactions. For this reason, researchers who study the family are faced with the formidable task of studying its many interactions. How is the child affected by parent-child relationships? How is the husband and wife's relationship affected by the relationships between their children? How does parental behavior affect a child's ability to form peer friendships? The number of possible interactions is extensive; and adding to the complexity, family relationships often differ among families and across cultures (Maccoby & Martin, 1983). (See At Issue)

Parenting

Over the years, developmental researchers have examined many different kinds of parenting techniques. Building on the earlier work of Earl Schaefer (1959), Diana Baumrind (1980, 1971, 1967) has become one of the most prominent researchers in parenting styles. Baumrind has examined the interaction of two of the most important dimensions of parenting. One dimension indicates the degree of parental permissiveness. This is the **permissive-demanding dimension**. The second dimension indicates the degree of affection. This is the **accepting-rejecting dimension**. These two parenting dimen-

Part of the socialization process includes parental efforts to help children acquire self-regulation.

AT ISSUE

Born to Be Wild: An Evolutionary Theory of Social-Emotional Development

Every once in a while, a theory comes along with a broad enough sweep to take your breath away. Such a theory has been proposed by Jay Belsky and his colleagues (Belsky, Steinberg, & Draper, 1991). Essentially, their theory suggests how the process of natural selection may influence social-emotional development. The researchers readily admit that their theory is unproved; but like any good theory, it explains a great deal and contains many features that are testable.

The argument they make is a bit shocking at first, but in many ways it does make sense. Belsky and his colleagues claim that human beings, as products of natural selection (see Chapter 3), are genetically "programmed" to a certain degree to raise and socialize offspring in a way that will provide the best chance for the continuation of their own genetic line. Of course, people aren't like insects or lower animals. Culture, religion, learning, and tradition all play a role in the procreative process. If there were an unrelenting drive to reproduce, we wouldn't be able to explain the use of birth control or, for that matter, people who opt to have no children. What is argued in their theory is that there is an inherited tendency to socialize children in a way that fosters their reproductive fitness, that is, in a way that best ensures that the offspring will survive to maintain their gene line.

Addressing this point, Belsky, Steinberg, and Draper argue that there are two somewhat distinct paths along which reproductive fitness may travel. First, parents may make a long-term investment in their children, caring for and nurturing each child for a lengthy time and in so doing expend many resources to protect their genetic "investment." Or second, parents may expend their resources to reproduce often, giving up the time they might otherwise have spent giving special care to a few offspring to mate many times and have many children. The researchers compare these approaches by thinking in terms of quantity (low resource investment in many children) versus quality (high resource investment in fewer children).

Consider what would determine which path was the most advantageous in terms of fostering one's genetic line. In times of upheaval—for instance, during forced migrations, when families are broken apart and resources uncertain—the quantity approach is more likely to result in the passing on of one's genes because these tend to be times of high infant mortality. Anyone who puts off having children to wait for better times or who has few children may well end up not producing at all or losing the few children that he or she does have. In other words, during such times, there is genetic safety in numbers. In stable times, however, when families can stay together and resources are more certain, the quality approach, in which

fewer offspring are protected and nurtured for long periods of time, produces better results because resources (food, shelter, parental attention) can be concentrated to benefit the few and almost guarantee their survival.

The major feature of the quality approach is the stable, caring family. Therefore, in very stable times with ample resources, a family with even a dozen children would still be seen as following a quality approach if sufficient time was invested in each child. On the average, however, the quality approach will result in fewer births (but a greater likelihood of survival for each individual birth) than will the quantity approach. It should also be noted that the quantity approach will outproduce (in terms of live births) the quality approach. For instance, a man with many mates who expressed the quantity approach could in one lifetime father scores of children—something beyond the reach of a man and woman who had bonded together for life.

Belsky and his colleagues argue that during the first five to seven years of a child's life, the child comes to understand how generally trustworthy his or her parents are, how available certain resources (food and shelter) tend to be, and how much he or she can count on relationships to endure. If the family is in upheaval—if the family suffers from violence, divorce, a missing parent, or fewer resources owing to poverty—a series of genetically programmed triggers will ensue within the family that will direct the child toward the "quantity" line of reproduction! For genetic reasons, then, as well as environmental ones, parents in such circumstances will become harsh, rejecting, insensitive, and inconsistent toward their children. In fact, it is interesting that when times get tough, parents often turn on their children. Wouldn't you think it would be the other way around—that tough times would foster extra kindness from parents?

You might think that it is because parents under stress become frustrated that they act in this manner. While this may be true, Belsky argues that parents have been naturally selected to react to frustration by turning on their children. Furthermore, when parents reject their children, the children are accelerated toward early puberty.

No one is sure why parents who reject their children cause puberty to occur earlier in those children, but it does appear to occur. Some have argued that what really happens is that accepting parents cause a genetic delay in puberty, a delay naturally selected for as a way to lessen incestuous pregnancies brought on by fathers who become too close to early-maturing daughters (Maccoby, 1991). But Belsky believes that early puberty occurs because the parents' behavior of rejection, triggered by hard times, helps bring on early

AT ISSUE

Born to Be Wild: An Evolutionary Theory of Social-Emotional Development, continued

puberty for the child as a preparation for early pregnancy, so that the child may begin down the "quantity" reproductive track. For example, daughters who are treated harshly at home are more likely to become depressed, which in turn causes them to internalize their problems, which lowers metabolism, which in turn stores fat, which in turn brings on an early menarche (the first reproductive cycle and period). In this sense, then, harsh parenting and the resulting depression in children, aspects of family life usually considered pathological or dysfunctional, are in fact highly adaptive!* Furthermore, Belsky argues that children who come from broken or "dysfunctional" homes, or who are raised in poverty, or whose families are in upheaval will not only strive for early pregnancy by being sexually promiscuous, but will not invest in long-term relationships, nor will they be very interested in being close, loving parents!

Meanwhile, children raised in stable, loving families with sufficient resources will find their genetic "quality" program triggered and will be more amenable to socializing processes that lead to trusting relationships, delayed sexual activity, long-term relationships, and greater parental investment (see Figure 8.1).

*Researcher Robert Hinde makes the comparison that fear of the dark used to be classified as an "irrational fear of childhood." After John Bowlby's work demonstrated that such fears were probably the product of natural selection because of the survival value of children staying close to the parent during the night, children's fear of the dark was no longer seen as irrational, but as adaptive (Hinde, 1991).

No one knows how much of this theory is correct, but it explains a great deal. For example, why are kids who live in poverty more likely to be aggressive, sexually promiscuous individuals who fail at long-term relationships and make poor or abandoning parents? Of course, there may be other reasons, but this theory yields a potentially viable explanation—and one that is testable to a considerable degree. For instance, exactly how do parenting techniques and behaviors influence the onset of puberty? We know that harsh treatment of animals brings on early puberty and that early puberty is also associated with poverty and upheaval in humans. But to be definitive, Belsky proposes a study of identical twins reared apart to see if different parenting directly affects the timing of puberty.

If it does turn out that this theory is correct or that major portions of it are, it would mean that we might be able to solve many serious social problems by finding ways to keep troubled families together while teaching them ways to interact that foster closeness and caring. If a national effort along those lines was feasible, it would, in one generation, transfer millions of children over from the quantity line to the quality line of social development simply because they had experienced a stable and loving environment during the first five to seven years of their lives. While such ideas may seem naive, the theory must be given a full examination if there is even the remotest possibility that such changes could be implemented.

sions have been observed in all human societies (Rohner & Rohner, 1981). As you might imagine, Baumrind's work has generated a great deal of research over the years.

The field created by the interaction of these two dimensions can be seen in Figure 8.2. For example, if a mother scored –60 on the accepting-rejecting dimension and –80 on the permissive-demanding dimension, her form of parenting would fall within the rejecting-demanding field and would be labeled authoritarian-dictatorial. We can study various points within four fields—accepting-permissive, accepting-demanding, rejecting-permissive, and rejecting-demanding—by examining the interaction of these dimensions.

No one knows for certain what makes parents select a particular mode of interaction. A parent's own upbringing may have a bearing on his or her choices. Experiences with other parents and parental models from television or other media probably also play a role. There is even evidence that the choice of any of these dimensions, except for demanding, is influenced to a degree by the parent's genetics (Plomin, McClearn, Pedersen, Nesselroade, & Bergeman, 1988). Research also shows that once a particular mode of parenting is estab-

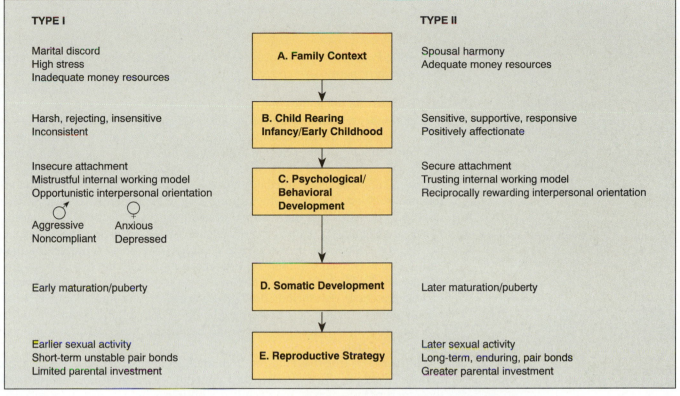

FIGURE 8.1

Two pathways of reproductive development; quantitative (type 1) and qualitative (type 2). (SOURCE: After Belsky, Steinberg, & Draper, 1991)

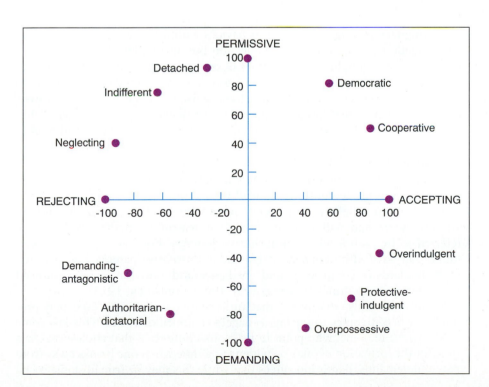

FIGURE 8.2

Modes of parenting. The interaction of two important dimensions of parenting, permissiveness and affection, describes many different environments in which children may be reared. (SOURCE: After Schaefer, 1959)

AUTHORITATIVE PARENTS
Parents who set strict standards, but who are also warm and willing to explain their reasoning to their children.

lished, it tends to remain in place; that is, the parent is generally consistent in the mode of parenting (McNally, Eisenberg, & Harris, 1991).

Accepting-Permissive.   Parents who are loving and accepting and at the same time are fairly permissive create what is referred to as a democratic environment. Each child is treated as an individual and held in esteem. Although democratic parents do not allow complete freedom and do enforce rules of conduct, their children are relatively free to try new things and are encouraged to develop independently. Children raised in this kind of environment tend to be independent, outgoing, active, and assertive (Baldwin, 1949). They are also friendly and tolerant and have a high sense of self-worth (Kagan & Moss, 1962).

Diana Baumrind has defined accepting-permissive parents as those who are tolerant, who take an accepting attitude toward their children's desires, who rarely use punishment, and who try to avoid using restrictions and controls when possible. These parents rarely demand mature behavior, such as engaging in proper manners or carrying out family assignments; they allow their children to make many of their own decisions and rarely have strict rules governing the children's time (such as when to go to bed or how much television may be watched) (Baumrind, 1967). Of course, no one functioning as a parent, by the very nature of the role, could ever be completely permissive, nor is it necessarily a good idea that one should be. All parenting requires some control over children.

Although it is true that children from loving, permissive families (those that might be considered cooperative or democratic in Figure 8.2) often do well, too much permissiveness may result in children who are immature and who have poor impulse control (Baumrind, 1967). It should also be pointed out that permissiveness is an inappropriate response if the child is engaging in excessive aggression. Researchers have observed that there is a positive correlation between permissiveness toward aggression and children's aggressive behavior toward parents and other family members (Yarrow, Campbell, & Burton, 1968).

Accepting-Demanding.   Parenting behaviors within the accepting-demanding field include not only warmth and affection but also a high degree of control. Children of such parents can sometimes be overprotected or taught to be dependent on adults. If these children become too dependent, they may be unable to stand up for themselves and may develop a sense of insecurity (Becker, 1964). Creativity can also be restricted in the accepting-demanding environment. Children of overprotective parents are generally dominated excessively and tend to be submissive, dependent, polite, and obedient, whereas children of overindulgent parents are more disobedient, rebellious, and aggressive.

While parents, in the very act of parenting, must exert some control, excessive or inappropriate control may lead to overprotection. Judicious and fair control is often beneficial, however. Parents who set strict standards but who are also warm and willing to explain their reasoning to their children are referred to by Baumrind as **authoritative parents.** For instance, it has been found that boys with high self-esteem had authoritative parents who required high standards of competence and obedience and who consistently enforced these standards and rules (Coopersmith, 1967; Comstock, 1973).

Baumrind has also discovered that authoritative parenting is especially productive when it comes to raising teenagers (Baumrind, 1991). This has come as a surprise to some, who point to Erikson's contention that adolescence is a time for the formation of one's own identity, a time when one breaks away from parental demands. Baumrind agrees that while this may be true in stable social environments, in today's often unstable world of working mothers, high divorce rates, and accessible illicit drugs, adolescents do best when parents are both demanding and sensitive to their teenager's growing need for independence. Baumrind has shown in her research that adolescents from authoritative (accepting-demanding) families are less likely to abuse drugs than are those from democratic (accepting-permissive) families and are also likely to become competent, mature, and optimistic. Other researchers confirm that authoritative parenting fosters academic achievement in adolescents. Adolescents who describe their parents as being democratic and warm, but at the same time firm, are more likely than other adolescents to develop positive attitudes toward their achievements and therefore do better in school (Steinberg, Elmen, & Mounts, 1989). As Baumrind points out,

> Authoritative parents are not bossy. They make it their business to know their children, how they're doing in school and who their friends are. Their control reflects a high level of commitment to the child, and they are not afraid to confront the child. (Bower, 1989a, p. 117)

Rejecting-Permissive.   Rejecting parents who do not control their children's behavior are creating an environment that fosters rebellion, anger, and disharmony. Children in these settings tend to be disobedient, aggressive, and delinquent (Sears, Maccoby, & Levin, 1957; Becker, 1964). The high rate of aggression in this group may be because hostile parents so often model aggression themselves.

Rejecting-Demanding.   Parents who are demanding but at the same time hostile, or rejecting, are referred to by Baumrind as **authoritarian parents**. These parents put forward a strict set of rules and require unquestioned obedience. Physical punishment is commonly used by the parent to enforce the rules, and reasoned discussion with the child is rare. Children reared by rejecting, demanding parents tend to be socially withdrawn and sullen. Their friendships are marked by quarreling and shyness (Becker, 1964). Because of the high degree of control maintained by authoritarian parents, these children are unable to express their hostility outwardly and may have a tendency to turn their aggression inward. This group exhibits a high degree of self-punishment and suicide compared with the other groups.

It is important to note that the four modes of parenting discussed here are not guaranteed to create the kinds of outcomes we have described. This is perhaps a good place to point out that these findings not only are general but also are often limited to middle-class populations in Western industrialized nations. For instance, parenting within the accepting-demanding dimension is perceived by Korean children as far more loving and acceptable than parenting that falls within the accepting-permissive dimension (Rohner & Pettengill, 1985). This is probably because despite Western influence, the Korean family stresses obedience to its authority and deference to its elders. The child is viewed as a fractional part of the more significant whole—the family. A Korean child treated with too much permissiveness is, unlike his or her Western counterpart, quite likely to feel rejected.

The Discipline of Children.   Three distinct kinds of disciplinary practices used by parents have been described (Hoffman, 1970). These are power assertion, love withdrawal, and induction.

Power assertion refers to the use of physical punishment, the removal of privileges, or the threat of these actions, and is commonly associated with the

AUTHORITARIAN PARENTS
Parents who put forward a strict set of rules and require unquestioned obedience to them. They are both demanding and hostile. Authoritarian parents often use physical punishment to enforce their rules, and reasoned discussion with the child is rare.

POWER ASSERTION
A disciplinary technique in which caregivers use physical punishment, removal of privileges, or the threat of these actions.

LOVE WITHDRAWAL
A disciplinary technique in which care-givers express disapproval by ignoring, isolating, or expressing lack of love for the child.

INDUCTION
A disciplinary technique in which care-givers try to show the child the reasoning behind the discipline.

authoritarian parent. With this practice, some parents hope to control their children by exploiting the child's weakness and lack of power. The use of physical punishment may, however, create serious problems for the child and family because of the potential for abuse.

Love withdrawal is a nonphysical attempt to discipline the child. Parents using such methods ignore or isolate their children or express lack of love for them. Parents usually resort to this technique because they are frustrated and because it does often create a high level of compliance (Chapman & Zahn-Waxler, 1981). The child becomes very willing to "behave," apparently because of the great anxiety he or she feels at the threat of loss of love. Some researchers have argued that this technique may be more harmful than physical punishment because it holds within it the constant threat of abandonment (Meyer & Dusek, 1979).

Induction is a disciplinary technique by which the parent either attempts to give the child an understanding of the reasoning behind the discipline or appeals to the child's pride or desire to be grown up. Induction is more commonly associated with the authoritative parent. For example, parents using this technique may warn a child not to tease an animal by describing how the child may be bitten or injured. Through induction, parents attempt to build children's comprehension of the perspective of others and to help children realize how their actions may affect the people around them. Parents who use induction often augment it with praise for appropriate behavior. Parents use induction more often when they want long-term compliance from their children rather than the immediate cessation of some action (Kuczynski, 1984). By the time children are about 4 or 5, parents usually begin to favor induction over distraction as a way of preventing children from engaging in some action, simply because older children are beginning to understand the parent's reasoning. Interestingly, at about the same time, children will switch from noncompliance or direct defiance to the more sophisticated strategy of negotiation, also attempting to use reason (Kuczynski, Kochanska, Radke-Yarrow, & Girnius-Brown, 1987).

Exactly why a parent might choose one technique over another in any given situation is not clear. Some researchers believe that it has to do with the parent's perception of why the child is behaving as she is or of which technique will provide the best results. For instance, data indicate that parents who score low (more rejecting) on the accepting-rejecting dimension are more likely to use power-assertive disciplinary techniques, whereas parents who score high on this dimension (more loving) are more likely to use praise and induction (Becker, 1964).

Parents are more likely to use power-assertive discipline with boys than with girls (Kuczynski, 1984), probably because parents often expect boys to be harder to control. Because parents who use physical punishment are more likely to have aggressive children (Martin, 1975), it would be expected that parents who score low on the accepting-rejecting dimension would raise children who are more aggressive. According to the data, this is exactly what happens (Becker, 1964). In fact, harsh parenting techniques tend to be passed down from generation to generation. This finding suggests that modeling such parenting techniques teaches children how to act once they themselves become parents (Simons, Whitbeck, Conger, & Chyi-In, 1991). Research examining such perceptions and beliefs, however, is still in its earliest stages; too little is currently known for us to draw firm conclusions.

How To Parent.   There is probably no one best way to treat children. Nonetheless, the following guidelines won't lead you too far astray, and for the most part they probably will be helpful:

1. Try not to be excessively demanding. Parents who control their children too much are often more concerned with meeting their own needs than with meeting those of their children. Although the children of such parents may grow up to be self-controlled, they may fail to develop confidence and self-assurance.

2. Try not to be extremely permissive. Be sure to reinforce responsible behavior while discouraging disruptive or immature acts. Without this feedback from you, your child may not learn to be adequately self-controlled.

3. Try to maintain a warm, accepting home where independent actions and thinking are encouraged, where rules are firm but fair, and where children know they are loved.

4. Be consistent. Don't change rules suddenly without a reason.

Child Abuse and Neglect

An issue that continually comes up during discussions of parental styles and discipline techniques is that of child abuse. Abuse is often begun during a simple attempt to discipline a child. The parent or caregiver, however, goes too far and harms the child. Child abuse has been with us for all recorded history—and no doubt long before that. In the United States, child abuse can be traced back to the first settlers to come ashore (Pleck, 1987). But it wasn't until the early 1960s, when researchers first coined the term *battered child syndrome* (Kempe, Silverman, Steele, Droegemueller, & Silver, 1962), that the nation's interest in the problem was aroused.

There is no one accepted definition of **child abuse** (Emery, 1989). Although the term *child abuse* implies the physical assault or sexual abuse of a child by a parent or caregiver (Starr, 1979), defining the term can be quite tricky. Consider the following case. In 1974, a woman who had recently immigrated to England slashed the faces of her two young sons with a razor blade and then rubbed charcoal into the lacerations. When the woman was found out, she was arrested and charged with child abuse. Later, however, it was discovered that she was a member of the Yoruba tribe of Nigeria, a group that traditionally practices scarification as part of a rite of manhood. All the Yoruba boys get scarred, and the scars are then stained with charcoal. The Yorubas think it quite proper and manly (Korbin, 1977). The woman was found guilty, but con-

CHILD ABUSE
Behavior by parents, caregivers, or other people responsible for children's welfare that, through malice or negligence, results in psychological or physical injury to a child.

Parents are more likely to use power-assertion discipline with boys than with girls, probably because parents often expect boys to be harder to control.

CHILD NEGLECT
Failure by parents, caregivers, or other people responsible for children's welfare to provide reasonable and prudent standards of care for children in their charge, which thereby threatens the child's well-being.

PSYCHOLOGICAL MALTREATMENT
Mistreatment of children in a psychological way, as distinguished from physical abuse or neglect; includes verbal abuse, failure to provide warmth or love, and belittlement or berating.

sidering her culture, was given a suspended sentence. If you think that the court was too lenient, consider what anthropologist Jill Korbin has pointed out: Some cultures, including the Yoruba, find the Western practice of forcing an infant to sleep alone, away from its parents in a separate room, very cruel! As you can see, cultural factors must also be considered when defining abuse.

Occasionally, acts of omission are also incorporated in a definition of child abuse. These include failure by parents or other caregivers to provide the child with adequate food, shelter, safety, or health care. Such acts of omission are sometimes classified as **child neglect** and are more common than acts of child abuse (Wolock & Horowitz, 1984). For example, consider that in the United States, fully 40 percent of all children have not been immunized against certain common diseases, and a majority of the 5 million handicapped children in America are not receiving the help they need. Over half a million children have no home at all.

More recently, **psychological maltreatment**, such as constantly berating or humiliating a child or continuously showing resentment or coldness toward the child, has come under consideration (Garrison, 1987). Psychological maltreatment may actually be the most prevalent form of child abuse and potentially the most destructive, because in the long run, it tends to destroy the child's self-image and distort his or her relationships with other people (Hart & Brassard, 1987). Psychological maltreatment is so difficult to define, however, that it is not likely to be controllable through state intervention (Melton & Davidson, 1987). Any major effort toward prevention of psychological maltreatment will probably have to focus on public education to make people aware of the problem and teach them how to lessen it.

If we include child neglect and psychological maltreatment in our definition, then child abuse is believed to be very common indeed, although specific numbers are unknown. If we limit ourselves to the consideration of violence alone, the prevalence of child abuse is easier to calculate. In 1991, almost 2.7 million cases were reported in the United States alone (U.S. Bureau of the Census, 1993). Child abuse and neglect are so prevalent that the federal government has classified the situation as a national emergency.

Child abuse is seven times more likely to occur in families earning less than $15,000 per year (U.S. Advisory Board on Child Abuse and Neglect, 1990), but there is also considerable child abuse among parents who are at middle or high socioeconomic levels. Child abuse is also more common in families where parents are under stress or are unemployed (Elder, Nguyen, & Caspi, 1985) or where parents were themselves abused as children (Knutson, 1978; Newberger & Bourne, 1978; Parke & Collmer, 1975; Oliver & Taylor, 1971). Generally, however, there are no characteristics especially associated with abusive parents that are not also seen in nonabusers (Spinetta & Rigler, 1972).

Abuse of children is rarely systematic. Abusers often are surprised at their actions and usually are remorseful. This reaction may in turn lead to a sense of guilt and worthlessness that raises the chances of another outburst of anger.

Psychological Effects of Abuse. The psychological effects of child abuse depend on the type of abuse and its severity. Among the most common findings are that abused children often come to see themselves as "bad" and often assume that their behavior legitimately merited such abuse (Dean, Malik, Richards, & Stringer, 1986). Younger abused children studied in the *strange situation* (see Chapter 5) often show such unusual patterns of behavior that they can't be assessed according to the commonly used type A (anxious/avoidant), type B (secure), and type C (anxious/resistant) classifications. More than 80 percent of these children show such similar odd behaviors that they are classified as a distinct group, type D (disorganized/ disoriented) (Carlson, Cicchetti, Barnett, & Braunwald, 1989).

Another unfortunate outcome of child abuse is that the more children are exposed to adult anger, the more sensitized and upset they become by it (Cummings, Iannotti, & Zahn-Waxler, 1985). As an interesting example of this, consider one study in which abused and nonabused children, both from socioeconomically disadvantaged backgrounds, responded to the distress of a child the same age. The nonabused children showed concern, sadness, and empathy; not one of the abused children, however, showed such a reaction. Instead, the abused children reacted to their peer's distress by engaging in disturbed behavior, such as physical attacks or displays of anger or fear (Main & George, 1985).

Researchers in another study found that by the time abused children enter kindergarten, they are almost three times as likely to be aggressive and violent than nonabused children (Dodge, Bates, & Pettit, 1990). This ratio was found to hold true regardless of whether the abused children came from poor or well-to-do families or whether they came from two- or one-parent homes. The abused children continually expressed anger and incited conflict, often attributing hostile intentions to others and considering aggression as the only solution to problems. They were also more emotionally withdrawn and socially isolated than their peers.

The emotional outbursts, anger, and fear shown by abused children often fuels the cycle of abuse because abused children are more difficult to control and are more often noncompliant with their parents' requests. The parents are more likely to become angry, furthering the likelihood of abuse (Trickett & Kuczynski, 1986; Oldershaw, Walters, & Hall, 1986).

Preventing Child Abuse.   Among the treatment efforts currently being pursued to prevent child abuse are individual therapy, child foster care, and self-help groups such as **Parents Anonymous**. Parents Anonymous groups have been created by abusive parents who want to talk about their difficulties with others who share their problems (Lystad, 1975). Parent aides, crisis nurseries, and short-term residential treatment for entire families can also play an important role.

A **crisis nursery** is a place where a parent can bring infants and young children and leave them for a short time, until the parent is better able to deal with his or her stress and the danger of abuse is lessened. Mandatory counseling for parents is usually a condition for leaving children in a crisis nursery. Unfortunately, there are very few crisis nurseries available for those who need them.

Parents Anonymous, in conjunction with casework, generally has been the most effective at reducing abuse or neglect, but programs rarely have a success rate higher than 40 to 50 percent (Berkeley Planning Associates, 1977).

If you know anyone who is abusing or neglecting a child, don't hesitate to notify the police or child protection authorities in your community. In almost every case, the end result will be constructive, and both parents and children will receive help. The staff of professional agencies that deal with child abuse are usually tactful and compassionate and are concerned that every member of the family be helped. You might also make an effort to support or develop a crisis nursery for your community.

Also, if you know of an abused child and are in a position to provide emotional support for that child, you might be able to help break the cycle of violence. It has been shown that abuse becomes less likely to occur in the next generation if an abused child receives emotional support from a nonabusive adult (Egeland, Jacobvitz, & Sroufe, 1988).

PARENTS ANONYMOUS
An organization to help parents who abuse their children make constructive changes in their responses; uses the same intensive contact and principles as Alcoholics Anonymous.

CRISIS NURSERY
A place where parents may leave infants and young children for a short time, until the parents are better able to deal with their stress and the danger of abuse is thus lessened.

Additionally, be prepared to support local and state efforts to raise funds for abuse prevention. Many states are now attempting to do this "painlessly" by establishing trust funds drawn from add-on fees to marriage or birth certificates. Check and see if your state has such a system, and if not, consider writing to your state representatives suggesting the implementation of one.

Parental Roles: On Being Mothers and Fathers

All parents have desires and hopes for their children. The way parents achieve these ends can differ greatly from family to family. Researchers do not agree on which of the many child-rearing practices is best. It is known, however, that parents provide role models for their children and that children rely on their parents to teach them about the world.

Mothers and fathers who have assumed the traditional gender roles behave differently toward their children (McHale & Huston, 1984). From the time the child is born, mothers are more likely to assume caregiving responsibilities, even if the fathers are home and are free to help. Fathers, on the other hand, are more likely to engage the infant in active and stimulating play (Parke & O'Leary, 1976; Yogman, Dixon, Tronick, & Brazelton, 1976). As the child grows older, the mother's role of primary caregiver and the father's role of playmate generally continue (Lamb, 1978). Because mothers and fathers behave in this distinctive way, they come to represent different types of experiences for their babies (Lamb, 1979). Both parents, however, transmit and enforce the rules and expectations of society.

It is sometimes difficult for parents to adjust to their changing roles in a modern society. When values and traditions in a culture begin to undergo rapid change, it becomes difficult to decide which attitudes and beliefs children should be taught. As one researcher has stated,

> Today's children are the first generation to be raised amid doubt about role prescriptions that have long gone unchallenged. This makes their socialization especially difficult. Traditionally, socialization was a process of raising the young to fill major roles in a society when the present incumbents vacated them. Yet today we do not know what type of society our children will inherit, nor the roles for which they should be prepared. (Lamb, 1979, p. 941)

Working Mothers.   For many years, our society favored a working father and a homemaker mother. Mothers who worked outside the home were considered neglectful of their children (if they didn't "have to" work) or unfortunate (if they did).

Now all of that has changed. The statistics tell the story: Beginning in 1986, the labor force included for the first time a majority of mothers whose children were not yet grown. This was double the percentage found in 1970. Nearly half of these working mothers were married women who had a child at home under 1 year of age. By 1992, there were 8.5 million mothers of preschool children in the U.S. labor force (U.S. Bureau of the Census, 1993).

The large increase in working mothers is most likely due to financial need. There was a time when a single wage earner could sustain an entire family; but things are different today. Many families are finding it easier to make ends meet if both husband and wife hold full-time jobs. Moreover, in 1984, 1 out of 4 mothers were single; by 1993, the statistic was 1 out of 3. The financial burden faced by these women typically requires them to work outside the home.

Fathers are more likely than mothers to engage in active and stimulating play with their children.

The Effect on Children.   In all honesty, it will probably take another generation before we can know how the increase in working mothers will affect children. However, in one of the most comprehensive, long-term studies of its kind, the National Longitudinal Survey of Youth, results indicated that maternal employment during an infant's first year of life was detrimental in terms of cognitive and behavioral dimensions, regardless of the infant's gender or socioeconomic status (Baydar & Brooks-Gunn, 1991).

Results for children older than 1 year of age generally support a different outcome. Typically, data show that there are no adverse outcomes if the mother of a toddler or older child is employed. As measured by achievement on IQ, reading, arithmetic, spelling, and linguistic tests during an eight-year longitudinal study, young children of working mothers were not ordinarily adversely affected by their mother's absence (Cherry & Eaton, 1977). More recent studies have come to a similar conclusion (Gottfried & Gottfried, 1988), especially for girls (Baydar & Brooks-Gunn, 1991).

In fact, many children of working mothers have been found to be superior to the children of nonworking mothers in terms of cognitive and social development. Furthermore, although data have shown that working mothers spend about 2 hours per day less alone with their children than do nonworking mothers (Easterbrooks & Goldberg, 1985), these mothers can compensate for their absence by interacting frequently with their children when they are at home (Moorehouse, 1991). The total amount of time that the entire family (mother, father, and child) spends together is unaffected by maternal employment (Easterbrooks & Goldberg, 1985).

It is also worth noting that the stability of infant attachments to mothers and fathers appears generally to be unaffected by maternal employment (Hoffman, 1989). And if an employed mother is happy with her job and is able to provide for her child's daily needs so that she need not worry about her child's security, she may perform as a parent as well as or better than an unemployed mother. Unemployed mothers, in contrast, often find their homemaking job overly stressful because of money problems. Unemployed mothers are also more likely to be depressed if they want to work but are unable to (Hock & DeMeis, 1990).

Day-care centers often differ greatly one from another. Parents considering placing their children in a day-care center should investigate it thoroughly beforehand.

Finally, and perhaps most importantly, employed mothers tend to encourage their children to be more independent and self-sufficient from an early age (Hock, 1978). It appears that self-sufficiency may be a valuable attribute for children to acquire. Children who are encouraged to participate in household tasks and to organize and plan their daily activities often discover (as long as they are not forced to attempt tasks beyond their capabilities) that they can be successful. Such early independence training has been shown to increase achievement motivation and competence (Woods, 1972).

Researchers have wondered it these differences between children of employed and unemployed mothers might not stem from the fact that employed mothers are better educated. In a study done by Birnbaum (1975), educated full-time mothers were compared with professionally employed mothers. The full-time mothers had lower self-esteem, felt less competent and less attractive, and expressed more feelings of loneliness than did their professional counterparts. Data have shown that a mother's morale is positively correlated with her effectiveness as a parent (Hoffman, 1979). However, if working fathers support nonworking mothers by providing intellectual and stimulating company and by sharing many of the child-care duties, mother-infant relations become more affectionate, competent, and sensitive (Pederson, Anderson, & Cain, 1977). One study that examined employed mothers' feelings about being separated from their firstborn infants found that mothers who chose to work were better able to cope than those who had to work but didn't want to (DeMeis, Hock, & McBride, 1986). Still, there are many exceptions. Quite a few women do find it stressful to combine the dual roles of primary caregiver and employee. Such stress may offset any advantages gained from their employment (Hoffman, 1989).

Gender Effects.   Employed mothers provide an incentive to children to set higher occupational and educational goals for themselves (Stein, 1973). This is especially true for daughters. Daughters of working mothers perceive the woman's role as more satisfying and women as more competent than do daughters of nonworking mothers (Broverman, Vogel, Broverman, Clarkson, & Rosenkrantz, 1972). Daughters, therefore, may admire their working mothers and see them as an important role model. Sons, on the other hand, are often more resentful when their mothers work. These differences appear to be especially pronounced among preschool children (Bronfenbrenner, Alvarez, & Henderson, 1984). Of course, as was said earlier, these are only general findings and cannot be applied in every instance.

In general, most of the effects that we have examined concerning working mothers are not due to employment of the mother per se, but rather to the circumstances, attitudes, and expectations that both parents experience as they relate to the mother working outside the home (Scarr, Phillips, & McCartney, 1989).

The Development of Sibling Relationships

Although parents are usually the primary agents of socialization for the young child, in most families the child also has a relationship with one or more siblings. Siblings can have a powerful effect on one another. Research indicates that siblings spend a great deal of time together, that they interact on many different levels, and that they are often deeply emotionally involved with one another (Abramovitch, Pepler, & Corter, 1982). Because siblings are of the same generation, have a common genetic heritage, and share many of the same experiences, they often have a significant effect on one another throughout their lives (Cicirelli, 1982).

Cross-cultural research has shown that even though the sibling relationship in non-Western cultures is different from that in industrialized Western nations, it is still an important one. In non-Western cultures, siblings are more commonly involved in cooperative child rearing and in day-to-day activities necessary for survival, such as defense and food gathering.

In many ways, the interactions among siblings can be much like interactions among peers. In both we see a high frequency of interaction, an uninhibited emotional quality, mutual interest in one another, and evidence of imitation and attachment (Dunn, 1983). These similarities are especially evident among siblings who are close in age (Berndt & Bulleit, 1985). When siblings are more than a few years apart, the older siblings tend to influence younger siblings in a way that is more parentlike than peerlike, often acting as teachers and role models for their younger brothers and sisters (Brody, Stoneman, MacKinnon, & MacKinnon, 1985; Dunn, 1983). Although siblings may show antagonism and rivalry, most sibling interaction is friendly and playful (Abramovitch, Corter, Pepler, & Stanhope, 1986).

Fully 80 percent of the children in the United States and Britain have siblings (Dunn, 1983). Siblings often are different from one another in terms of intellectual development and personality (Scarr & Grajek, 1982; Rowe & Plomin, 1981). Researchers have been interested in what determines differences between siblings living in the same family, and a number of important factors have been noted. First, there are genetic differences. Any two siblings will share about 50 percent of the same genes, but the other 50 percent will be unique to each sibling, allowing for considerable differences in temperament and other aspects of behavior strongly influenced by genes. Another important factor is the differential treatment of siblings by their mother. Differential treatment is the rule rather than the exception; mothers simply don't treat each of their children in exactly the same way. This is not to say that one child will be treated well and another poorly, but rather that children are individuals and end up being treated as such. This differential treatment no doubt accounts for some of the differences observed between siblings raised in the same family (Stocker, Dunn, & Plomin, 1989). Some of the differences observed between siblings may also be due to the fact that siblings may create very different family environments for one another as a result of their behaviors toward one another (Daniels, Dunn, Furstenberg, & Plomin, 1985; Stocker, Dunn, & Plomin, 1989). In this sense, because siblings directly affect the family unit, they may have a greater effect than do peers, especially during a child's first 5 years.

Strong sibling relationships have been shown to persist across life spans and throughout the world. And because of shared genetic, experiential, and cultural heritage, the sibling bond can be a very powerful one indeed.

THE DEVELOPMENT OF PEER RELATIONSHIPS

Although parents and siblings seem to have the greatest effect on young children's social development, peers begin to have an increasing influence as the child grows older. Strictly speaking, **peers** are equals. Nonetheless, children often have playmates who are three or four years older or younger than they are. Many researchers therefore consider children who are interacting at about the same behavioral level to be peers, regardless of age. Even so, explorations of peer relationships usually concentrate on children of approximately the same age, because these children are most likely to be interacting with one another (Roopnarine, 1981).

PEERS
Equals; developmentally, people who interact at about the same behavioral level, regardless of age.

The Second Year: Emotional and Cognitive Changes

Between the ages of 1 and 2 years, children's social skills and peer interactions remain at a rudimentary level (Hartup, 1983). However, the complexity and amount of peer interaction is greater than during infancy (Eckerman, Whatley, & Kutz, 1975). Some researchers have argued that the development of peer relationships during the first year or two may pass through three distinct stages (Mueller & Lucas, 1975; Mueller & Vandell, 1977). In the first stage, the *object-centered stage*, children occasionally interact with one another, but most of their attention is focused on objects or toys. During the second stage, the *simple interactive stage*, which begins at about 1½ years of age, infants respond primarily to one another and prefer social play to solitary play (see Figure 8.3). By the age of 2 years, children enter the *complementary interactive stage*. During this final stage, many complex social interchanges occur. Imitation becomes more likely, and positive social interactions often are accompanied by appropriate emotional responses, such as smiling or laughter (Mueller & Brenner, 1977).

Emotional reactions of children to one another appear to become more important during the second year. Although 1-year-old babies laugh and smile at one another, most of their interactions appear to be absent of any discernible emotional tone (Rubenstein & Howes, 1976). By the age of 2 years, however, emotions become a more important part of social interaction (Mueller & Rich, 1976; Ross & Goldman, 1976). By this time, children take careful note of one another's emotional expressions and dispositions before acting or responding socially. Adults do this as a matter of course, and it is an important part of any social interaction. Further evidence of the social influence of peers comes from the fact that, by the age of 18 months, children are more likely to leave their mother's side and explore a room in the presence of a peer than they are when no peer is present (Gunnar, Senior, & Hartup, 1984).

Cognitive changes during the second year also play an important role in social interaction. Six-month-old infants rarely show distress when a peer takes a toy away; such an interaction between children 20 months of age or older, on the other hand, is likely to start a fight. In the Chapter Preview for Chapter 6, we noted that a 20-month-old child probably knows her own reflection and recognizes her own face, whereas younger children and infants typically do not (Amsterdam, 1972). This occurs, researchers argue, because at about 20 months of age, children become aware of themselves; they develop a

Figure 8.3

By the age of 1½ years, chilren engage more often in social play than in solitary play. (Source: Eckerman, Whatley, & Kutz, 1975, p. 47)

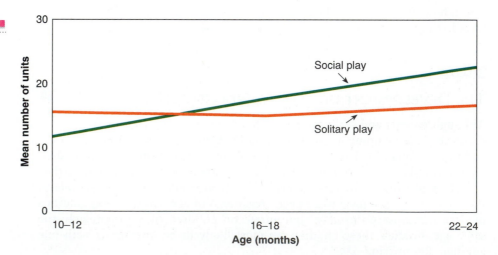

sense of self. In one study, researchers found that as children develop this self-awareness and are able to see themselves as distinct from other people, they begin to claim toys and other items as "mine" (Levine, 1983). Once they've defined "mine," they are more likely to become possessive.

This does not necessarily mean that children become selfish at 20 months of age. Children of this age often share, especially if they become familiar with one another, or if other children have shared with them (Levitt, Weber, Clark, & McDonnell, 1985). What has happened, however, is a basic developmental step toward becoming a social being, a step that shouldn't necessarily be equated with "selfishness." Before any mature or complex social interaction can take place, a child must have a clear understanding of "you" and "I." As children develop this awareness, their behavior with peers will follow a different pattern:

> Specifically, they would attempt to define their territory by claiming toys as *mine*, and they would comment on the other child or his possessions. These children would also show a different pattern of interaction that reflected their increased self-awareness and social awareness. They would be wary initially of a new peer in an unfamiliar setting. However, they would then try to define their boundaries by claiming toys. Once this issue appeared to be clarified, they might then express increased social interest in the other child. (Levine, 1983, p. 544)

Longitudinal studies have shown that throughout the second year of life, a child's social behavior becomes more consistent and predictable (Bronson, 1985). This increased stability of social behavior may indicate that by the age of 2 years, children are beginning to regulate their own behavior internally in a consistent way. Consistency of behavior in different situations marks the beginning of what psychologists call **personality**. By 2 years of age, a social person is emerging; the child has a unique personality.

The Preschool Years

Most interactions among children between the ages of 2 and 6 years have been studied in day-care centers or in nursery schools. During the preschool years, both friendly and, less commonly, antagonistic social interactions emerge.

PERSONALITY
The organization of relatively enduring characteristics unique to an individual, as revealed by the individual's interaction with his or her environment.

By the time children reach the age of 2 years, fights over toys are more likely to occur because the children have developed self-awareness, which enables them to conceive of things as "mine."

FRIENDSHIP
Close emotional tie formed with another person through mutual preference for interaction, skill at complementary and reciprocal peer play, and shared positive affect.

Friendships.   Major changes occur in children's social relationships between the age of 2 years and the time the children enter school. By the age of 3 or 4 years, most children overcome their reluctance to join other children fully in play. They begin to interact with one another (Hinde, Stevenson-Hinde, & Tamplin, 1985) and to form **friendships**.

Although it's hard to imagine 8- or 9-month-old babies having friends, infants of this age have been observed, in nurseries and day-care centers, to have definite preferences for certain peers (Lee, 1973). These preferences, however, are not complex enough to be considered friendships in the general sense of the term.

Friendship has been defined as "mutual preference for interaction, skill at complementary and reciprocal peer play, and shared positive affect" (Howes, 1983, p. 1041). As you can see, friendship involves more than just friendly interaction. Children who form friendships do many things together; most important, they form emotional ties with one another.

By the age of about 6 years, most children have a sufficient understanding of the distinction between themselves and other people to know that other people may not feel or react the same way they themselves do (Selman, Schorin, Stone, & Phelps, 1983). Because of this, children at this age are better able to predict one another's characteristics (Ladd & Emerson, 1984). Preschool children, on the other hand, typically adopt another child as a "best friend" in a rather one-sided way, without the same mutual understanding or sharing of knowledge and feelings that older children have. These findings show that as children grow older, a shared knowledge about one anothers' unique characteristics helps to form and cement a friendship. And as children grow older, they spend more and more time with other children, especially with close friends (Howes, 1983). In fact, by the age of 7 years, the average child will have as much social contact with friends and peers as with adults (Wright, 1967).

When children first meet, they are more likely to become friends if they are able to exchange information successfully, to establish a common-ground activ-

Children who form friendships do many things together; most important, they form emotional ties with one another.

ity, and to manage conflicts (Gottman, 1983) (see Table 8.1). After this initial relationship has been established, other processes become more important. Among these are the exploration of similarities and differences, self-disclosure, and amity (peaceful relations) (Gottman, 1983) (see Table 8.2). As children become older, they improve their acquaintanceship abilities. They become more successful at exchanging information, establishing common-ground activities, resolving conflicts, and exploring differences. They also share intimate details of their lives. This last characteristic is especially true among girls (Furman, 1987). These characteristics, along with the emotional exchanges, become the most important aspects of the friendship (Diaz & Berndt, 1982; Furman & Bierman, 1983; Newcomb & Brady, 1982).

Play. One of the most obvious occurrences during the preschool years is the development of **play**. Although children often may play alone, as they grow older play becomes more of a social phenomenon (Cooper, 1977; Hartup.

PLAY
Pleasurable activity engaged in for its own sake, with means emphasized rather than ends. Play usually is not engaged in as a serious activity and is flexible in that it varies in form or context.

Table 8.1 ● How Children Establish an Initial Relationship

CATEGORY	EXAMPLE
Information exchange	
Success	A: What's this?
	B: This is my room right here. This is my farm here. Look how very, very large.
Failure	A: How come we can't get this off?
	B: You know, I'm gonna get the rolling pin so we can roll this.
Common-ground activity	
Success: A joint activity is successfully initiated	A: And you make those for after we get in together, okay?
	B: 'Kay.
	A: Have to make those.
	B: Pretend like those little roll cookies, I mean.
	A: And make, um, make a, um, pancake too.
	B: Oh rats, this is a little pancake.
	A: Yeah, let's play house.
	B: Okay, play house.
Failure: initiation is ignored, or disagreed with, activity does not develop	A: Let's play house.
	B: Nope, nope, nope, nope, nope, nope.
	A: Because you're coloring that brick wall?
	B: Yep.
Conflict	A: This is stretchy.
	B: No, it's not.
	A: Uh huh.
	B: Yes.
	A: Uh huh.
	B: It's dirty.
	A: Uh uh.
	B: Uh huh.
	A: Uh uh.
	B: Uh huh.
	A: Uh uh.
	B: Uh huh.
	A: Uh uh. It's not dirty.

Source: Adapted from Gottman, 1983, pp. 27, 53–54.

Table 8.2 ● The Development of Friendship

CATEGORY	EXAMPLE
Similarity: Children note that they are the same	A: Mine's almost finished. B: Mine's too.
Contrast: Children note that they are not the same	A: I'm gonna be 5 at, in my birthday. B: Well, I'm 5 now.
Self-disclosure: Any personal statement about one's feelings that is intimate; excludes low-intimacy statements (e.g., "I love chocolate"), even if they are strongly stated	A: She didn't say anything about the dress. She said leave me alone. B: Why'd she say that? A: She doesn't love me.
Amity: Validation or approval of the other person; affirmation of the relationship; sympathy; offers of affection; wit and hilarity; or shared deviance	A: (kisses B) B: Oh gosh. A: What? B: You just kissed me on the cheek. Thank you. A: I'll kiss you on the forehead. B: I'll kiss you.

Source: Adapted from Gottman, 1983, pp. 54–55.

1983). Playing can be simple and unstructured, as in a game of hide-and-seek, or it can be more complex and structured, as in a school basketball game.

Curiously, *play* has never been defined precisely (Rubin, Fein, & Vandenberg, 1983). Part of the problem is that the word *play* is used to describe such diverse behaviors as adolescents assembling model ships and dogs frolicking in a yard (Vandenberg, 1978). Most people do seem to know what is meant by play (Smith & Vollstedt, 1985). Still, researchers, in an effort to define play, have attempted to isolate different aspects of the behavior. In fact, it has been suggested that there are five descriptors of play and that the greater the number of descriptors that can be applied in any given situation, the more likely people are to call those circumstances play (Rubin, Fein, & Vandenberg, 1983; Smith & Vollstedt, 1985). Here are the five descriptors of play:

1. **Intrinsic motivation.** The behavior is motivated from within; that is, it is done for its own sake and not to satisfy social demands or bodily functions.
2. **Positive affect.** The behavior appears to be pleasurable or fun to do.
3. **Nonlaterality.** The behavior is not lateral; that is, it does not follow a serious pattern or sequence, but rather has more of a pretend quality about it.
4. **Means/ends.** The means are emphasized rather than the ends; that is, there is more interest in the behavior itself than in any outcomes it may produce.
5. **Flexibility.** The behavior is not rigid: it shows flexibility in form and context and across situations.

If we use all five descriptors, we might say that a child who is manipulating toy animals in a flexible way with no apparent goal in mind, who is pretending, who is enjoying herself, and who is doing the activity for its own sake is playing. Such an activity fits all five criteria, and almost any observer would call it playing. A major league baseball player at bat, however, may fit only one or two of these criteria. For this reason, fewer people would call this activity play, although some would.

However play is defined, playing and playful interactions with peers seem to have an important role in the social and cognitive development of children.

Why Children Play.   No one is certain why children play. Social scientists generally believe that play has evolved because it has a function (Vandenberg, 1978). It may be that playing with objects, playing make-believe, or playing together at various games helps children to become skilled at manipulating objects (Cheyne & Rubin, 1983), and to learn adult roles or, once they are grown, to cooperate while dealing with serious and complex tasks.

Some ethologists have argued that there is an **exploration-play-application sequence** found in humans and in the more advanced animals (Wilson, 1975; Vandenberg, 1978). When children are confronted with an extremely novel toy, they tend to explore it before playing with it (Belsky & Most, 1981; Vandenberg, 1984). It's as though they want to be sure that it is safe before they play (Weisler & McCall, 1976). This same kind of exploration-before-play sequence has been observed in chimpanzees (Loizos, 1967; Mason, 1965).

During play, the skills necessary for serious application are acquired. For example, it has been found that chimpanzees need to spend time playing with sticks before they can use sticks for purposeful applications such as food gathering (Birch, 1945; Schiller, 1957). Researchers have found similar play-before-application sequences while investigating human children (Sylva, Bruner, & Genova, 1976; Vandenberg, 1978). Perhaps, then, play has evolved as a means of helping children practice motor and cognitive skills they may later apply.

Types of Play.   In what has since become a classic study of play, Mildred Parten observed 42 nursery-school children between 2 and 4½ years of age while they played (Parten, 1932). Parten observed six distinct kinds of behavior in the play situation. These included unoccupied behavior, **solitary play**, **onlooker play** (watching others but not participating in play activity), **parallel play** (playing alongside other children but not directly interacting with them), **associated play** (playing and sharing with other children), and **cooperative play** (playing structured games with other children according to rules). After 60 one-minute observations of children's play, Parten noticed that older children spent more time in social play (associated and cooperative), whereas younger children were more likely to engage in parallel or solitary play (see Figure 8.4).

EXPLORATION-PLAY-APPLICATION SEQUENCE
An ethological term describing the function of play as a bridge between the cautious exploration of the unfamiliar and its eventual application for useful purposes.

SOLITARY PLAY
According to Parten's classification, the type of play children engage in when they play by themselves.

ONLOOKER PLAY
According to Parten's classification, the type of play in which the child watches other children play but does not participate.

PARALLEL PLAY
According to Parten's classification, the type of play children engage in when they play alongside other children but do not participate directly with the other children.

ASSOCIATED PLAY
According to Parten's classification, the type of play in which children play and share with others.

COOPERATIVE PLAY
According to Parten's classification, the type of play in which children play structured games with other children according to rules.

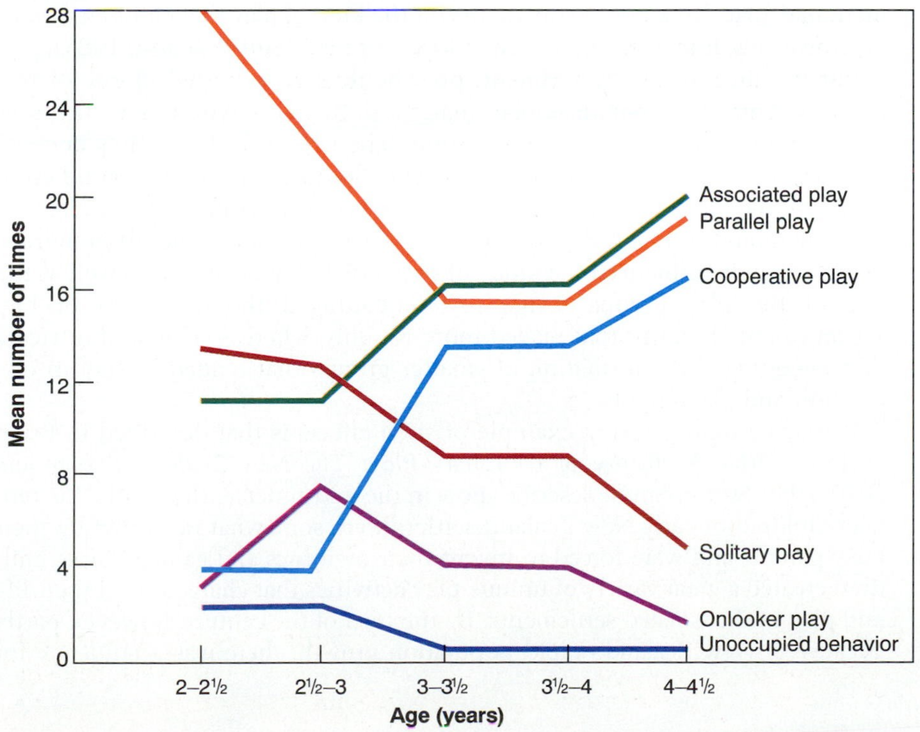

FIGURE 8.4

Developmental changes in play according to Parten's 1932 study. As children become older, the social kinds of play increase while the solitary forms of play decrease. (SOURCE: Parten, 1932)

REALITY PLAY
Play devoid of fantasy or in which fantasy is an insignificant part; essentially, play in which an object or situation is treated as what it actually is.

FANTASY PLAY
Play in which an object, person, or situation becomes a target for fantasy and is not treated as what it actually is.

SOCIAL FANTASY PLAY
Play in which one pretends to be someone else or adopts a role other than one's own; common to children age 5 years or older.

Children who prefer solitary play are not necessarily maladjusted or withdrawn. Most researchers believe that solitary play has an important function and is not usually a sign of maladjustment (Rubin, Maioni, & Hornung, 1976). About 50 percent of all solitary play involves educational activities, and an additional 25 percent focuses on large-muscle activity such as dancing, spinning, hopping, or running (Moore, Evertson, & Brophy, 1974).

Fantasy Play.   Certain cognitive abilities must be present before a child is able to pretend (see Chapter 6). Object permanence—the ability to imagine an object even though it is not presently sensed—is a basic requirement. This ability generally develops by the age of 2 years; any form of social pretend play with others is quite rare in children younger than 2 years of age (Howes, 1985).

Although object permanence appears to be a prerequisite for pretending, pretend play doesn't appear all at once but emerges gradually (Pederson, Rook-Green, & Elder, 1981). Among 2-year-old children, **reality play** (play in which an object or situation is treated as what it actually is) is the most common form of play. By the age of 3 years, **fantasy play** becomes more likely, and children begin to make believe that objects or people can be things other than what they are (Field, De Stefano, & Koewler, 1982). Also by about the age of 3 years, fantasy play and social play merge to yield **social fantasy play**, where children who are playing together come to agree on fantasy themes for their play (Howes, Unger, & Seidner, 1989). It has been shown that children who engage the most in social fantasy play are also more likely to be popular with their peers and to receive high teacher ratings of social skill than are those who do not (Connolly & Doyle, 1984). These findings may indicate that social fantasy play is meaningful for the development of important social skills (Doyle, Doehring, Tessier, de Lorimier, & Shapiro, 1992).

The Environmental Structuring of Play.   The trend from nonsocial play to a more social play appears to be universal, but the kinds of play that children engage in can be quite different from culture to culture. A particular environment may place all kinds of constraints on the kind of play that children engage in; conversely, it may promote certain forms of play (Sutton-Smith, 1985).

For instance, in one experiment, preschoolers were placed in one of two environments that contained play materials. In one environment, the toys were aimed at large-muscle coordination. The toys were large, they encouraged action, and the environment provided a lot of room. In the second environment, the play materials were aimed at fine-muscle coordination. The toys were small and intricate (Vandenberg, 1981). In this study, the play environments strongly influenced the kinds of social play that occurred, as well as the size of the play groups. Large toys encouraged the formation of big, action-oriented groups that played more roughly, whereas small and intricate toys encouraged the formation of smaller groups that tended to stay in one location and play quietly.

Perhaps a more striking example of such effects is that described in Brian Sutton-Smith's *A History of Children's Play: The New Zealand Playground 1840–1950.* Sutton-Smith describes how in the mid-nineteenth century, the pioneer children of early New Zealand settlers were somewhat neglected by their busy parents and were forced to invent their own toys and games. These children created a great variety of unique play activities that characterized their life and play in the isolated settlements. By the turn of the century, however, partly because of New Zealand's rapid population growth, there was a tendency for adults to make educational reforms and to organize children's play. Regulations were passed; teachers were even graded according to their ability to organize children's games. Rugby became a national game, and children were pressured to participate in order to develop skills such as leadership and discipline.

In his epilogue, Sutton-Smith describes the current ongoing processes by which every part of the children's lives and their play have become organized for them, in school and at home, through television and by the use of commercial toys. The great variety of play that once existed is now absent, he notes, and all children engage in the same general list of expected activities (Sutton-Smith, 1981). No doubt, much the same is true in the United States and in other industrialized nations.

Overcoming Childhood Fears: "Things that Go Bump in the Night"

When Brian was 5 years old, he stayed with his grandmother while his parents went out for the evening. While at his grandmother's, he watched an old "Dracula" movie. That was when the nightmares started. He had them for a week, and his parents began to get concerned, but then they stopped. Unfortunately, they started up with a vengeance again after Brian contracted chicken pox and ran a very high fever. While he was running the fever he began to hallucinate and to scream that Dracula was there in front of him. The nightmares got worse—they began occurring several times a night, and his parents eventually began letting Brian sleep with them. Everyone reacted with tension as evening approached; would Brian's nightmares continue? Soon, Brian's daytime behavior also changed. He began to act fearful and withdrawn, and insisted on staying near his mother (Kellerman, 1981).

One of the common emotional developments in young children's lives is the development of fear. In most cases, the fear is transitory and doesn't interfere with the child's development. But in some cases, like Brian's, the fear becomes debilitating. It can even come to hold an entire family hostage. A fear that is excessive, unrealistic, maladaptive, and persistent, and that can be neither reasoned with nor explained away is known as a *phobia* (Marks, 1969).

Most of the fears that develop in young children are transient, develop between the ages of 2 and 5 years, and include the fear of animals, imaginary creatures, the dark, and being alone (Murphy, 1985). Because these fears are often short-lived or mild or involve things that can be easily avoided by the young child (such as a roller coaster), they often do not require any special treatment. In certain cases, however, it may become necessary to intervene:

To avoid needless suffering in young children, a child-care worker confronted with a fearful child should ask the following questions: Has the fear been persistent? Is it painful to the child? Is it adversely affecting the child's usual behaviors or relationships? Is it preventing the child from participating in activities that are conducive to health or happiness? (Murphy, 1985, p. 180)

Fortunately, several techniques have proved successful in helping children overcome their fears. Among these are desensitization procedures, modeling of fearless behaviors, rewarding fearless behaviors, and cognitive control or competence training. Most programs that have been developed to help eliminate fears in young children have used a combination of these techniques because the approaches seem to be more effective when used in concert (Murphy, 1985).

Desensitization. When desensitization is used, the child is gradually exposed to the feared stimulus, while he attempts to remain relaxed. In the

Count Dracula.

case of fear of the dark, for example, the child might be trained to gradually dim the light in his room through the use of a rheostat, or he might be trained to gradually spend longer and longer periods of time in the dark, all the time trying to remain calm. In one experiment that used several methods for eliminating a fear of the dark in thirty-two 4- and 5-year-old children, the researchers found that only the group that had received *some* exposure to the fear stimulus (the dark) were able to show significant changes in dark tolerance (Sheslow, Bondy, & Nelson, 1982).

In Brian's case, desensitization was accomplished with help from Jonathan Kellerman, a child psychologist. Kellerman had Brian draw pictures of Dracula and talked about Dracula with Brian. At the end of his therapy, Brian was even allowed to purchase a cape, mask, and some fangs! (Kellerman stopped short of buying Brian a ticket to Transylvania.)

Modeling Fearless Behavior. Modeling fearless behavior has also been shown to be effective in reducing or eliminating fears in children. To help children overcome an unrealistically intense fear of dogs, Albert Bandura and his colleagues at Stanford University organized a treatment based on social learning theory. In this treatment, young children who showed an extreme fear of dogs when actually confronted with one were allowed to watch a fearless child of their own age initiate play with a dog. At each stage of the treatment, the fearless model came closer to the dog than before, until finally the model played inside a closed playpen with the dog (Bandura & Menlove, 1968).

By watching a fearless child approach a dog in slow, successive stages without any adverse consequences, fearful children could be coaxed into following the model's lead. Of the children who observed the model play with the dog, 67 percent were able to stay alone with the dog in the playpen. As a control, Bandura used fearful children who had not seen the model play with the dog. Only an extremely small percentage of these children were willing to join the dog in the playpen.

Children can become fearful or their fears can be exacerbated if they observe someone react with fear to a stimulus. In Brian's case, his parents became very anxious as nighttime approached (fearing Brian's nightmares). Brian saw his parents' anxiety and reacted with more anxiety himself (Kellerman, 1981). As another example, I know of a case of a woman who has a Santa Claus phobia as a result of a fearful encounter with a boisterous (and somewhat inebriated) Santa while she was still a child. Two of her three daughters also grew up to fear Santa Claus, to the extent that during the Christmas shopping season, they avoid shopping centers and other places where a Santa might be. The third daughter, now an adult, admits to once having a little bit of the "Santa feeling," but was too attracted by gifts and shopping to pass him up and was thereby counterconditioned. Children take emotional cues from their parents, and if the cue is one of fear, then the child is more likely to be fearful as well (Kellerman, 1981).

Rewarding Fearless Behaviors. Many programs that have been developed to control or eliminate children's fears have included some element of rewarding children when they exhibit fearless behavior. For example, when the child shows control of his fear, he may receive money or other reinforcers, such as praise. Brian was given money (5 cents) for each "good night" he had.* Eventually, the rewards can be eliminated as the child conquers the fear.

Cognitive Control or Competence Training. Besides desensitization, one of the most effective ways of helping children is to teach them that they can learn to control their fear in their own mind. Such training often includes teaching the child things to say or do when he is fearful. Brian was taught to tell Dracula, "I'm mad at you, you rotten bum!" and was told "You can be the boss over Dracula. You can be in charge" (Kellerman, 1981, p. 67). Research has shown that using some form of cognitive or competence training in combination with other techniques, such as desensitization, is an effective way of eliminating fears in young children (Kanfer, Karoly, & Newman, 1975; Giebenhain & O'Dell, 1984). According to researcher Donna Murphy,

The cognitive aspect of fear intervention is enticing in that it has—theoretically, at least—the potential to increase the likelihood of maintenance of effects and feelings of self-control. (Murphy, 1985, p. 186)

Children almost always have specific fears, but it's not always obvious to the adults what those fears are. For example, Kellerman reported a case in which a 4-year-old boy began to wake up screaming in the middle of the night. The child was never able to remember the episodes when he woke up the next morning. Such a phenomenon is known as a *night terror*. Night terrors typically occur when the child is deeply asleep.

This child's mother began to listen carefully to what the child was saying when he woke up screaming. She heard him clearly yell, "No wolf house! No wolf house!" (Kellerman, 1981, p. 71). After she had deciphered his statements, the meaning became clear to her. She and her husband were thinking of moving to a new home, and one of the homes they were considering was owned by a couple with the last name of Wolf. Obviously, she and her husband had spoken of going to see the "Wolf house" without realizing that their son would misinterpret this to mean that they were going to visit a home populated with wolves (Kellerman, 1981). This example illuminates something that is important for parents and caregivers to remember: Young children function on a different cognitive and experiential level, and they often believe in the literal meaning of what they hear. By keeping in mind the cognitive and emotional capabilities of young children, we can often uncover and eliminate their fears.

*Frankly, I'm not sure I'd be willing to face Dracula alone in a dark room for a crummy 5 cents!

SUMMARY

- Erik Erikson believed that after a base of trust has been laid down during infancy, the child must then develop autonomy. This is the time of the second psychosocial conflict (autonomy versus shame or doubt). After children develop autonomy, they begin to initiate activities. At this point, the third psychosocial conflict emerges (initiative versus guilt).
- Regulation of the child's behavior by parents usually begins during the second year of life. This in turn allows children to be able to begin to regulate themselves.
- There are many things that parents can do to encourage competence in their children; among them are designing the living area, consulting with the child, and showing loving authority.
- The number of possible interactions within families is extensive. Furthermore, family relationships often differ among families and across cultures.
- Belsky's evolutionary theory of socialization incorporates the idea that harsh environments trigger a series of behaviors in parents and their children that foster goals that encourage early puberty, early pregnancy, short-term commitments, and weak parenting in children as a way of increasing the quantity of offspring in difficult times. In this view, many behaviors thought dysfunctional are, in fact, highly adaptive.
- Baumrind has examined four modes of parenting: accepting-permissive, accepting-demanding, rejecting-permissive, and rejecting-demanding. Each mode is likely to produce different kinds of behavior in children.
- Three distinct kinds of disciplinary practices used by parents have been described. They are power assertion, love withdrawal, and induction.
- Occasionally, parents' attempts to discipline their children result in a situation that gets out of control. This loss of control may lead to child abuse. Child abuse is more common among persons from lower socioeconomic levels and is also more common in families where parents are under stress or unemployed or were themselves abused as children.
- Researchers do not agree on which of the many child-rearing practices is best. In recent years, there have been changes in the traditional roles of parents. One of these changes has been that more and more mothers of young children work.
- Although parents usually are considered to be the primary agents of socialization for the young child, in most families the child has a relationship with one or more siblings. Strong sibling relationships have been shown to exist across the life span and throughout the world. Because of shared genetic, experiential, and cultural heritage, the sibling bond can be very powerful.
- Peers begin to have an increasing effect as children grow older. Peers are generally defined as children who are interacting on the same behavioral level, regardless of age.
- Between the ages of 1 and 2 years, children's social skills and peer interactions remain at a rudimentary level. However, the complexity and amount of peer interaction is greater than during infancy. By the age of 2 years, emotions become an important part of social interaction with peers.
- Cognitive changes during the second year also play a role in social interaction. As children develop a sense of self-awareness, they begin to claim toys and other items as "mine."
- Most interactions among children between the ages of 2 and 6 years have been studied in day-care centers or in nursery schools. During the preschool

years, both friendly and, less commonly, antagonistic social interactions emerge.

■ When children first meet, they are more likely to become friends if they are able to exchange information successfully, to establish a common-ground activity, and to manage conflicts.

■ One of the most obvious occurrences during the preschool years is the development of play. Although children often play alone, as they grow older play becomes more of a social phenomenon.

■ There are five descriptors of play: (1) the behavior is motivated from within, (2) the behavior appears to be pleasurable to perform, (3) the behavior does not follow a serious pattern or sequence, (4) the means rather than the ends are justified, and (5) the behavior is not rigid.

■ Some researchers believe that play develops according to an exploration-play-application sequence.

■ The trend from nonsocial play to a more social play with increasing age appears to be universal, but the kinds of play that children engage in can be quite different from culture to culture.

QUESTIONS FOR DISCUSSION

1. Some researchers have argued that inconsistent discipline techniques can be worse than harsh discipline or no discipline at all. What kinds of difficulties might arise when parents are inconsistent in applying discipline?

2. Of the people sampled in a large nationwide poll, 28 percent said that neither of their parents had ever used physical force against them. How do you think these parents maintained discipline?

3. Do you have a strong emotional relationship with a brother or sister? What do you remember from your early childhood about this relationship? Was there sibling rivalry?

4. Do you remember having close friends during early childhood? What factors attracted you to them? Was the relationship reciprocal?

5. Many states have laws that require children under a certain age to be in a special child safety seat when they are riding in the family automobile. Are parents who fail to protect their children in this way guilty of child neglect?

SUGGESTIONS FOR FURTHER READING

1. Bell, R. Q., & Harper, L. V. (1977). *The effect of children on parents.* Hillsdale, NJ: Erlbaum.

2. Boer, F., & Dunn, J. F. (Eds.). (1992). *Sibling relationships: Developmental & clinical issues.* Hillsdale, NJ: Erlbaum.

3. Borman, K. M., Quarm, D., & Gideonse, S. (Eds.). (1984). *Women in the workplace: Effects on families.* Norwood, NJ: Ablex.

4. Dunn, J. (1990). *Separate lives: Why siblings are so different.* New York: Basic Books.

5. Kellerman, J. (1981). *Helping the fearful child: A parent's guide.* New York: Warner Books.

6. Lamb, M. E. (1981). *The role of the father in child development* (2nd ed.). New York: Wiley.

7. Rubin, Z. (1980). *Children's friendship.* Cambridge, MA: Harvard University Press.

8. Walker, M. (1992). *Surviving secrets: The experience of abuse for the child, the adult, and the helper.* New York: Taylor & Francis.

9. Wiehe, V. R. (1992). *Working with child abuse and neglect.* Itasca, IL: Peacock.

MIDDLE CHILDHOOD
(6–12 Years of Age)

CHAPTER 9

Middle Childhood: Physical, Cognitive, and Moral Development

CHAPTER PREVIEW
The Moral of the Story

Piaget once conducted an experiment in which two groups of children (one group approximately 5 years old and the other group approximately 10 years old) were told two stories. In one story, a boy attends a dinner party and accidentally breaks 15 cups. In the second story, a boy breaks a cup while trying to steal jam from a cupboard. Piaget then asked the two groups of children which child had been naughtier.

The younger children responded that the one who broke 15 cups had been naughtier. Piaget believed that this response was the result of the younger children's simple "fixed-law" morality. From the younger children's point of view, the fixed law that "thou shalt break no cups" had been violated 15 times. The 10-year-old children, on the other hand, said that the child who had broken one cup while attempting to steal jam had been naughtier. They based their judgment on a more adultlike social-oriented morality, in which justice plays a key role. In this morality, laws are not rigidly fixed, and qualities such as intentions (to harm or to steal) and a sense of fairness (accidents can happen to anyone) prevail. Other researchers have also found that younger children tend to measure immoral actions by harm done, whereas older children are more concerned with intent (Ferguson & Rule, 1982; Surber, 1982). As children advance in their cognitive development, they begin to use a more sophisticated moral reasoning.

During middle childhood, many physical and cognitive changes take place. In this chapter, we will look at some of these changes, and we will also examine the relationship between children's cognitive development and their moral development, just as Piaget did in his experiment. We will see that during middle childhood, children come to employ more sophisticated cognitive strategies for solving problems and begin to show more complex moral and prosocial behaviors.

PHYSICAL GROWTH AND MOTOR DEVELOPMENT

Middle childhood is a time of continued physical growth and motor development. Until school-age children reach puberty, their rate of growth is relatively steady. Both sexes show an average weight gain of about 7 pounds and gain about 2 to 3 inches in height each year. There is a wide variation among individuals, however, owing to both genetic and environmental variables. On the average, girls and boys perform physically at about the same level, at least until the beginning of puberty (Hall & Lee, 1984).

Although most basic motor skills have been learned by middle childhood, there is an increase in the ability to perform these skills:

> With experience, instruction, and imitation of others, children become more efficient in their performance of the basic skills. This improvement happens gradually, with the child continually refining the skills to more closely approximate a form consistent with mechanical principles of movement. Increases in body size and strength account for many of the improvements achieved during childhood. . . . [T]he development of the basic skills generally follows a trend toward increased mechanical efficiency. (Haywood, 1986, pp. 95–96)

Health During Middle Childhood

In Western societies, children in middle childhood are usually the healthiest group in the population. This is because they aren't exposed to deficiencies in nutrition such as those faced by children in developing countries. Furthermore, they have passed the dangerous first few years when birth complications and early childhood diseases take their toll, and they haven't yet reached adolescence, when their bodies undergo rapid change, or adulthood, when major diseases become more prevalent (Shonkoff, 1984). For this reason, the major health risks faced during middle childhood are due to accidents, with motor vehicle accidents accounting for about 50 percent of all deaths.

Middle childhood, however, *is* the time when many behaviors relating to lifestyle are formed, including "physical fitness, coping with stress, tobacco and alcohol abuse, and dietary habits" (Shonkoff, 1984, p. 24). For this reason, middle childhood is the best time to focus on health programs designed to modify unhealthy behavior patterns that otherwise might be carried into adulthood. The prevention of smoking is an example:

> The problem of cigarettes is particularly compelling. Of all the major risk factors for serious illness, disability, and premature death in the United States, the U.S. Public Health Service . . . noted that smoking may be the most important preventable one. (Shonkoff, 1984, p. 47)

Obviously, the best time to stop people from smoking is *before* they become addicted. By adolescence it is often too late; during middle childhood, because few children smoke, health programs that emphasize prevention can have a major effect. These programs usually focus on social forces, because these children haven't developed enough cognitively to be very concerned about hypothetical future health problems, perhaps because they haven't yet reached the period of formal operations, when such sophisticated reasoning comes into play.

AT ISSUE

Children in Sports

Twenty million children between the ages of 6 and 16 participate in non-school sponsored sports programs each year in the United States. At least another five million children participate annually in a variety of school-sponsored sports programs (Brown, 1988). In the past, both the National Education Association and the American Medical Association have opposed organized sports activities for children under the age of 14 because of the dangers of physical injury or psychological stress (Seefeldt, 1982). In spite of these cautions, organized sports for children under 14 years of age are growing, and the controversy over whether it is a good idea to let children engage in organized sport, has grown along with it.

In an effort to address these concerns, a number of researchers have gathered empirical data that might shed light on this issue. Let's look at some of their findings. As you'll soon see, the issue is a complex one with no easy answers.

PHYSICAL INJURY

The number of physical injuries among children who participate in organized sports is increasing (Micheli, 1988). This is probably due to the fact that more children are involved in organized sports than ever before. The most common injuries are fractures, sprains, and twisted ligaments. In football, wrestling, and gymnastics, head and neck injuries also are common. Death in children owing to an injury during an organized sport activity is extremely rare, however (Dyment, 1988). Interestingly, football injuries to little children (for instance in Pop Warner football) have not turned out to be as common, or as severe as originally feared, most probably because young children aren't heavy enough to do much damage to one another when they collide (Micheli, 1988).

Another kind of physical injury, however, often gets overlooked; the overuse injury. Overuse injuries occur when many little traumas add up to cause swelling, inflammation, or pain. This usually happens because of too much exercise or stimulation to the muscles or tendons. The results can have long term consequences that can be debilitating and require considerable therapy. Interestingly, "safe sports" (safe in that they rarely lead to sudden or acute injury) such as swimming or tennis, often are associated with overuse injury. Overuse injury in organized sport can almost always be traced to poor coaching or athletic training. Trainers or coaches who know what they are doing are careful not to "overtrain" children (Micheli, 1988). Unfortunately, many schools do not provide a well trained coach to train children.

SOCIAL ASPECTS

Competitive youth sport is a social experience, and the cast of characters is enormous. Involved are peers in the form of both teammates and opponents and a myriad of adults, including coaches, parents, officials, spectators, record and score keepers, and sometimes judges. And yet, we have been reasonably remiss in sport psychology in that we are just beginning to study the impact that these people have on the young athlete's sport experience (Scanlan & Lewthwaite, 1988, p. 41)

What do children learn from sport in its social context? The psychological experience of organized sport on children may be far more profound than the threat of injury, and yet, as Scanlan and Lewthwaite point out, we know precious little about it. For instance, does sport participation unstill the valued moral fiber in our children that we like to think it does? In fact, what are the goals of organized sport for children, and are they met?

When organized sport was first proposed in the United States its purpose was "developing strong men so our nation would be better prepared in the event of war. This may have been a useful purpose in the past, but today few accept preparation for war as an objective of children's sport programs" (Martens, 1988, p. 297). Today, the goals of organized sport for children focus on helping to build physical skills and develop an active lifestyle for good health, to enjoy sport for the fun of it, to develop interpersonal skills, and to come to know oneself better. Sports can also help children to develop self-worth and self-confidence. But, do children's sports achieve these ends? Researcher Rainer Martens believes that these goals are often *not* achieved, because they become overshadowed by the desire to "win." Martens argues that trainers, teachers, parents, and coaches must come to think of "athletes first, winning second" and keep this in mind at all times when dealing with children (Martens, 1988). Too often, undue pressure is placed on children to win, to do well for Dad, Mom, or for the coach, rather than to discover and enjoy what sport has to offer (Scanlan & Lewthwaite, 1988).

If sport is considered in terms of what it can provide children, if proper safety measures are observed, and if training is competent, organized sports for children may provide valuable benefits. If, on the other hand, there is nothing but pressure to be better than the next player, to win because "no one likes a loser," to blindly train and compete, the harm caused by organized sport to the development of a child may be considerable. In the end, it comes down to the adults. Are the children first? Is winning second? Let's hope so.

CONCRETE OPERATIONS
A set of logical operations listed by Piaget as indicative of the third period of cognitive development, occurring roughly between the ages of 6 and 11. Such operations are logical, but still tied to the physical world and physical actions.

CONSERVATION
The principle that quantities such as mass, weight, and volume remain constant regardless of changes in the appearance of these quantities and that such changes in appearance can be undone, thereby regaining the original state by reversing any operations that had been performed. The concept of conservation encompasses the concepts of identity, decentration, and reversibility.

COGNITIVE DEVELOPMENT

According to Jean Piaget, at about the time children enter school, they develop the ability to rely on logical rules, or operations, to form their conclusions. Preoperational children, Piaget argued (see Chapter 6), do not rely on logic to form their conclusions. Children in the period of **concrete operations**, though, are able to use such logical rules to deal with problems. How children acquire a logical understanding of the world is not clear, but they seem to do it rather abruptly.

This change is commonly viewed as a qualitative change because preoperational children, who can't comprehend the logic of concrete operations, will, as soon as they advance to concrete operations, suddenly see the logic of these operations as self-evident and unmistakable (Miller, 1986). This finding supports the idea that these children have moved into a qualitatively new and more advanced stage—that of concrete operations. Such children however, are limited to the concrete, to the world they have directly experienced. They are not yet able to comprehend the hypothetical—to compare what is with what may be.

Conservation

Piaget stated that the onset of the child's understanding of **conservation** marks the end of the preoperational period and the beginning of concrete operations. The major difference between the preoperational and concrete periods is that children are beginning to use logical operations and rules rather than intuition. This change is viewed as a shift from reliance on perception to a reliance on logic, and as you will soon appreciate, it is a giant leap.

During the period of concrete operations, children's thought processes become more competent, flexible, and powerful as they come to understand and apply identity, decentration, and reversibility.

A child who is not yet able to conserve may believe that the taller glass holds more liquid, even though it has been demonstrated that they contain the same amount.

Identity refers to the fact that the amount of a material does not change unless something is added to it or taken away from it, even though its form or distribution may change. For example, both a preoperational and a concrete operational child presented with two identical glasses of water will realize that they are equally full. But suppose that we pour the water from one of the glasses into a dish while both children watch. The preoperational child most likely will say, when comparing the dish of water with the remaining glass, that there is now less water in the dish because it is at a lower level than the water in the glass (see Figure 9.1). The concrete operational child, however, will know that the amount of water is the same as before. He will understand that no water has been added or taken away. Another way of saying this is that he is able to break away from centering his attention on only one aspect of the problem (e.g., how tall the column of water looks) and *decenter* his attention so he can now conserve quantity (one aspect), even though the shape has altered (another aspect). **Decentration** enables the child to conserve. In this way, the identity of the water as comprising a particular amount is maintained.

Another way to solve the problem posed in Figure 9.1 is to imagine that the water from the dish is being poured back into the glass. This action would bring us right back where we began, and it is one way of proving that the dish holds the same amount of water as the glass. Here we are using the concept of **reversibility**; we are able to imagine reversing what we have just done. The ability to reverse operations in your mind is another key aspect of the concrete operational period. Preoperational children have a terrible time with this seemingly simple way of thinking. For example, consider the following 4-year-old preoperational child who is having difficulty with the "rule of reversal" (Phillips, 1969, p. 61). He is asked, "Do you have a brother?" He says, "Yes." Then he is asked, "What's his name?" He replies, "Jim." But when asked, "Does Jim have a brother?" he says, "No."

The Horizontal Decalage

Figure 9.2 outlines the many different kinds of conservations that children acquire during the period of concrete operations. The ages given are only approximate and vary, depending on the method employed to test the particular conservation (Baer & Wright, 1974). Piaget used the term **horizontal decalage** to refer to the fact that some conservations are mastered before others. It's fascinating to observe children dealing with conservation tasks before the horizontal decalage is complete. For instance, a child who has grasped conservation of substance may realize that a ball of clay rolled into the shape of a

IDENTITY
The concept that two objects will remain identical in some elemental way even though one of the objects may have its appearance altered in some dramatic way. In Piagetian theory, children achieve a deep understanding of identity during the period of concrete operations.

DECENTRATION
In Piagetian theory, the cognitive ability to break out of the frame of thought that causes one to focus on only one aspect of a changing situation.

REVERSIBILITY
The concept that actions that affect objects, if reversed in sequence, will return the objects to their original state. In Piagetian theory, the ability to understand reversibility is obtained during concrete operations.

HORIZONTAL DECALAGE
Term used by Piaget to describe the onset and order of different conservation abilities.

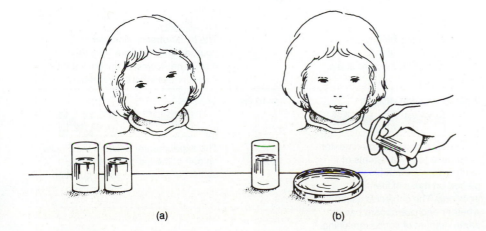

(a)   (b)

FIGURE 9.1

Testing a child for the ability to conserve: (a) The child agrees that glasses A and B contain the same amount of water. (b) Water from one of the glasses is poured into a dish. The child doesn't realize that the dish and the remaining glass contain the same amount of water—that is, the child is unable to conserve one aspect (amount) when another aspect (height of water column) changes. This inability is typical of children in the preoperational stage.

hot dog still has the same *amount* of clay as when it was a ball. But since conservation of weight is farther along the horizontal decalage, the same child may fail a conservation of weight test. For example, if the child is shown two clay balls and watches as they are weighed on a balance scale, the child sees that they weigh the same. But then suppose that one of the clay balls is rolled out into a hot dog shape. If the child is asked whether the rolled-out clay still weighs the same as the ball, the child may not know the answer. Although this child can conserve substance, he is unable, as of yet, to conserve weight, and although the child knows that the *amount* of clay has remained the same despite the change in shape, he does not realize that the two pieces of clay still *weigh* the same!

Seriation

Besides conservation, children in the period of concrete operations are able to engage in three other important logical operations. The first of these is under-

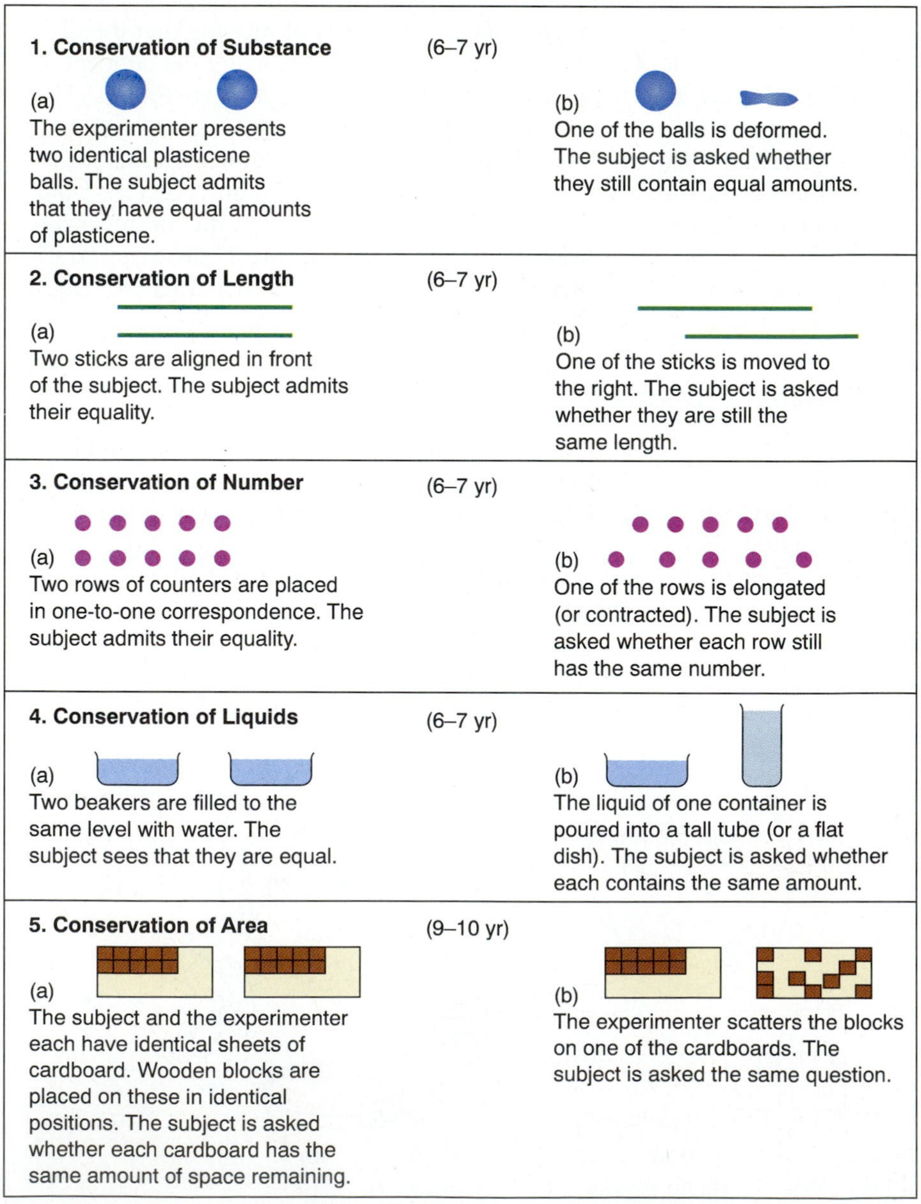

FIGURE 9.2

Examples of the many kinds of conservation tasks investigated by Piaget. The ages at which the conservations generally are first obtained are shown in parentheses. (SOURCE: Lefrancois, 1983, p. 327)

1. Conservation of Substance   (6–7 yr)

(a) The experimenter presents two identical plasticene balls. The subject admits that they have equal amounts of plasticene.

(b) One of the balls is deformed. The subject is asked whether they still contain equal amounts.

2. Conservation of Length   (6–7 yr)

(a) Two sticks are aligned in front of the subject. The subject admits their equality.

(b) One of the sticks is moved to the right. The subject is asked whether they are still the same length.

3. Conservation of Number   (6–7 yr)

(a) Two rows of counters are placed in one-to-one correspondence. The subject admits their equality.

(b) One of the rows is elongated (or contracted). The subject is asked whether each row still has the same number.

4. Conservation of Liquids   (6–7 yr)

(a) Two beakers are filled to the same level with water. The subject sees that they are equal.

(b) The liquid of one container is poured into a tall tube (or a flat dish). The subject is asked whether each contains the same amount.

5. Conservation of Area   (9–10 yr)

(a) The subject and the experimenter each have identical sheets of cardboard. Wooden blocks are placed on these in identical positions. The subject is asked whether each cardboard has the same amount of space remaining.

(b) The experimenter scatters the blocks on one of the cardboards. The subject is asked the same question.

standing serial position. In Figure 9.3, you will see the falling-stick cards. Children in the period of concrete operations are able to place these cards in correct sequence—quite an advance over preoperational children, who can't order objects according to a particular dimension, such as height, length, or size.

Classification

The second additional acquisition is the ability to deal with classes of objects. Unlike a younger, preoperational child, the average 8-year-old child would be able to answer the following class inclusion question: In a bunch of flowers with two yellow daisies and six red roses, are there more roses or flowers? This new-found ability to sort subclasses from the original class and to understand that they are not two equal items but that, instead, one is part of the other is an important cognitive advance. When combined with an understanding of serial order, the ability to classify according to groups and subgroups can enable the child to attain the third important acquisition: the concept of number.

Numeration

Although preoperational children can count and relate numbers to certain objects before they reach school age, their understanding of numbers is quite limited (Halford & Boyle, 1985). Before they enter the period of concrete operations, children generally have a poor grasp of the ordinal relationships among numbers (Michie, 1985). Once they obtain an understanding of serial order and classification, however, children begin to comprehend the sequence of numbers as well as classes and subclasses of numbers. For example, during the period of concrete operations, a child will come to understand that a group of six is made from three subgroups of two. As you can see, this kind of understanding forms the foundation on which concepts such as multiplication and division can be built.

The Social-Cognitive Theory of Lev Vygotsky

The Russian researcher Lev Vygotsky, a critic of Piaget's, has been receiving much attention lately. It is somewhat odd, because he died of tuberculosis at the age of 37 in 1934.

Following his death, Vygotsky's work remained little known outside the former Soviet Union because it had been banned by Stalin. During this time, many of Vygotsky's colleagues secretly continued to pursue the work that he had begun. However, even after Stalin's death, Vygotsky's work remained unknown to most Western scholars because English translations of his writings were rare. All these circumstances help to explain why he remained relatively obscure for more than half a century.

Happily, the collapse of the Soviet Union has opened up a greater dialogue with Russian researchers, who are still elaborating on Vygotsky's work and who are both willing and able to discuss their efforts openly. In addition, English translations of Vygotsky's work are becoming more common.

In Chapters 1 and 2, we briefly discussed the social learning theory of Albert Bandura. As you recall, Bandura argued that much of children's behavior is shaped by social exposure—that is, that children learn how to act by watching people model different behaviors. In Chapter 6 and again in this chapter, we have looked at Jean Piaget's cognitive theory, in which he argued that the child's mind develops through interaction with the environment. Vygotsky's

FIGURE 9.3

The falling-stick cards represent a temporal, or time, order when placed in the correct sequence. Preoperational children seem unable to comprehend this kind of ordering.

ZONE OF PROXIMAL DEVELOPMENT
In Vygotsky's cognitive theory, any or all activities that a child is almost able to perform or is able to perform with a little help.

theory encompasses both these domains, emphasizing the social and the cognitive aspects of development. Both these motifs run throughout his work and can be found in the themes that underlie his intricate and encompassing theory. These themes are the influence of culture, especially the predominant role of language, and what Vygotsky called the zone of proximal development.

Culture, Language, and Thought.   In Vygotsky's view, each person is born with a set of elemental cognitive functions, such as the ability to attend, perceive, and remember. These abilities are innate (unlearned). Each person's culture then transforms these elemental abilities into higher cognitive functions, largely through social interaction, especially through the teaching and use of language.

Vygotsky argued that it is language that makes thought possible. He further argued that language eventually comes to govern behavior. He supported his argument by describing three types of speech—external, egocentric, and internal—that make up the stages of language-thought development.

In the first stage of "language-thought," called external speech, thinking comes from a source external to the child. Typically, the source will be an adult's speech directing the child in some way. For example, a child might be scribbling and his mother might ask, "What are you drawing?" The child might reply, "A doggie." His mother might then ask, "Where's the tail?" and so on, directing the child's thoughts (Smolucha, 1988, p. 3).

In the next stage, called egocentric speech, the mother's speech is no longer required. The child now speaks out loud as a way of thinking. For example, while drawing, he might now be heard to say aloud, "This is a doggie. Here's his tail."

Vygotsky conducted a number of experiments to test his assumption that this shift from external to egocentric language was related to thinking. According to Piaget, the way children talked to themselves out loud (egocentric speech) was not social and was not related to problem solving but was simply an expression of the child's egocentric thought. Vygotsky was familiar with Piaget's view on this issue, and it stimulated him to test it. In experiments, Vygotsky discovered that children's egocentric speech increased in direct proportion to the amount of thought required of them to solve a problem (Vygotsky, 1934/1962). This finding, since replicated by American researchers (Berk, 1986; Kohlberg, Yaeger, & Hjertholm, 1968), demonstrated that egocentric speech is directly tied to the thought process, not what Piaget had supposed it to be.

By about the age of 6 or 7, children rely on what Vygotsky called internal speech and have fully internalized their thought processes. For example, a child might think to himself, "What should I draw? I know, I'll draw a picture of my dog" (Smolucha, 1988, p. 3).

Another important aspect of cognitive development, according to Vygotsky, is the **zone of proximal development**. According to this view, at each level or stage, individuals are prepared to be responsive to a particular environment and the people in it. A collaboration then occurs between one's cognitive structures and the environment. In this way, different experiences and cultures can shape a child's naturally developing cognitive processes, which then create a particular way of thinking about one's world. As an analogy, think of the developing child as a building under construction. Adults provide children with a *scaffolding* that helps direct and nurture their cognitive development. Thus, adults provide children with the kinds of special support needed for accomplishing what would normally be beyond a child's ability. In other words, adults guide children to discover gradually what adults already know (Radziszewska & Rogoff, 1991). Adults provide similar kinds of scaffolding for one another when they help each other develop different cognitive skills and ways of thinking.

Let's look at a cultural example of scaffolding, although families and individuals also shape cognitive development. One study found that illiterate adults in the African nation of Liberia had a very difficult time when they tried to organize, categorize, and sort pictures of geometric shapes, such as differently colored triangles and squares. According to Piaget, this sort of task should be quite simple for someone who has achieved concrete operations, but these adults were confused by it and couldn't decide where to begin. When these same adults were given bowls containing many different kinds and colors of rice, an important food in their country, they quickly organized them into sensible and reasonable categories (Irwin & McLaughlin, 1970).

In a follow-up to that study, American undergraduates given the same pictures of differently colored geometric shapes had no trouble sorting or categorizing them into meaningful groups. When given the many bowls of rice, however, the undergraduates showed the same bewilderment and hesitation that the illiterate adults in Liberia had shown when faced with the geometric shapes (Irwin, Schafer, & Feiden, 1974). These findings support Vygotsky's view that the scaffolding of each culture appears to have shaped its members' thinking and thought processes along different lines, depending on what is important to each culture.

As you might imagine, the concept of a zone of proximal development and the idea of scaffolding are having an impact on American education. While Piaget saw the drive toward cognitive development as stemming mainly from within the child, Vygotsky emphasized the spoken interaction between the child and his or her teacher, parent, or culture as the force that drives the child forward toward higher levels of thinking that might not be achieved independently. If you recall Piaget's quote—"Every time we teach a child something, we prevent him from discovering it on his own"—you'll see immediately how diametrically opposed Piaget's ideas are to Vygotsky's.

Vygotsky's ideas are stimulating research in the areas of language and teaching cognitive skills. His views will no doubt continue to stimulate research for many years to come. One can only wonder what might have been if Vygotsky had worked in a free society and had, like Piaget, lived well into his 80s.

Information Processing

The information-processing approach is yet another way of looking at cognitive development. Even its supporters readily admit that it is not yet a theory, but only a useful approach to the study of the field (Kuhn, 1984). At its center is the idea that the human intellect may function like a computer. Both the human and the computer are seen as information-processing systems.

One reason that developmental researchers became interested in using the computer as a model for the human intellect was Piaget's emphasis on the growth of logic as the centerpiece of his theory. Although Piaget discussed the acquisition of logic and its development, he never dealt with the way in which it might be operating or combining to produce the performance of a given individual (Siegler & Richards, 1982). Researchers thought that by closely examining the way in which computers "think," they might find important parallels in human development. After all, like humans, computers have memories and can solve problems.

ARTIFICIAL INTELLIGENCE
A computer simulation of human cognitive ability and performance.

MORALS
The attitudes and beliefs that people hold that help them to determine what is right and what is wrong.

As far back as 1958 (the Dark Ages, by modern computer standards), Allen Newell and his colleagues developed a special problem-solving logic for their computer (Newell, Shaw, & Simon, 1958). They fed in a sequence of elementary logic problems and compared the results with solutions given by human subjects. The computer and the human subjects performed equally well. The computer even made many of the same errors that the humans did! To the shock of just about everyone, the fit between computer and human was remarkably good (Case, 1985).

Since that time, progress in **artificial intelligence** has continued at a rapid pace. Nobel laureate Herbert Simon, who was one of Allen Newell's colleagues during those early years, now believes that it is perfectly reasonable to assume that someday computers will be able to think like people (Holden, 1986)! Although no one has ever asserted that computers and children are the same, the computer provides a model of cognitive development that stimulates research. Prior to the advent of the computer, areas of current interest, such as attention and memory, had been given little consideration by either Piaget or learning theorists.

THE DEVELOPMENT OF MORAL THOUGHT AND BEHAVIOR

The attitudes and beliefs held by children and adults that help them to determine what is right and what is wrong are called **morals**. The development of moral thought may be influenced by a child's level of cognitive development. Piaget argued that moral judgments are dependent on cognitive development. This position is supported by the finding that problem solving and the ability to take the role of others are positively correlated with cognitive development (Kurdek, 1978). Children must have both of these abilities before they can make sophisticated moral decisions.

Piaget's Approach to Moral Development

In 1932, Piaget published *The Moral Judgment of the Child*. Until that time, morality generally had been an issue debated by philosophers, who were concerned mainly with adult behavior. Rarely had the moral development of children been discussed; when it had been, it was considered a process of socialization in which adults taught children what was right or wrong so that children slowly acquired adults' moral standards (Durkheim, 1925). Piaget, however, broke with the idea that moral development was due solely to socialization and argued instead that a child's cognitive development was most responsible for developmental changes in moral thinking (Piaget, 1932). In his book, Piaget supplied the following foundation on which modern moral theory is based:

1. No subject's reaction to any moral situation or dilemma can be fully understood without considering the subject's current scheme (this statement is in keeping with Piaget's cognitive theory). This idea broke away from the behaviorists' view that the external force of socialization was most important.
2. The process of socialization is not discounted as a factor in moral development. The child's *first* experiences with social rules typically are commands handed down by authorities who deserve respect, usually parents. The child behaves as though these social rules are fixed in nature, as are the laws of

physics. At this point, the child does not yet know that social rules are agreed-on instruments designed to structure cooperation. Later, as children play together and come to arrangements and agreements, they begin to understand that rules are based on social contracts that encourage mutual cooperation and respect. This new understanding changes the child's schemes qualitatively.

3. These two moralities—fixed law and social contract—involve different principles and dynamics, each organized in a unique way. Although Piaget referred to the two moralities as stages of morality, he did not argue that they were clear-cut and distinct stages, as are the stages in his theory of cognitive development. Rather, the two moralities are extremes on a developmental scale; children develop by progressing from one extreme to the other through all the gradations in between (Carroll & Rest, 1982).

The example given in the Chapter Preview shows how Piaget's work helped to highlight the influence of cognitive development on moral thought and understanding. Although many refinements have been added to Piaget's speculations, research generally has supported his view.

Kohlberg's Moral Stage Theory

If moral judgments and thinking are tied to cognitive development, as Piaget believed, then perhaps moral reasoning does progress through a series of developmental stages as the child develops. The question of developmental changes in moral reasoning has attracted the attention and interest of researchers.

Building on Piaget's work (Piaget, 1932), Lawrence Kohlberg postulated three levels of moral development: the **preconventional**, the **conventional**, and the **postconventional**. Within each level are two stages. According to Kohlberg's theory, moral development begins with preconventional thinking, in which children obey to avoid punishment, and ends with the development of a sense of universal justice.

To determine which stage of moral development a person is in, Kohlberg devised a test. Subjects are presented with a moral dilemma, and the reasoning they use as they resolve it determines how advanced their moral development is. Table 9.1 gives an example of one of these moral dilemmas. For each stage, actual answers have been provided that demonstrate the kinds of reasoning involved. The headings above each set of answers describe, in general terms, the quality of moral reasoning that defines each stage.

Before his death, Kohlberg revised his methods for scoring these interviews. This revision has proved to be a powerful improvement over his older technique. With these new methods, Kohlberg and others have examined the data collected over the years from the use of the moral interview. This extensive new review of the data strongly supports Kohlberg's position that moral thinking progresses sequentially through a series of stages (Carroll & Rest, 1982; Colby, Kohlberg, Gibbs, & Lieberman, 1983; Fischer, 1983; Saltzstein, 1983; Snarey, Reimer, & Kohlberg, 1985; Walker, de Vries, & Bichard, 1984). As with Piaget's cognitive theory of development, individuals assessed by Kohlberg sometimes were between stages, leaving one stage and entering the next. Advances in moral thinking, though, always proceeded sequentially, never skipping a stage and never backing up. The data supported this hypothesis for all stages of moral development except stage 6. It was not possible from the data to make a clear distinction between stages 5 and 6 (Colby, Kohlberg, Gibbs, & Lieberman, 1983). For this reason, stage 6 has been dropped from current assessment procedures. This doesn't necessarily mean that stage 6

PRECONVENTIONAL LEVEL
According to Kohlberg, a level of moral development in which good or bad is determined by the physical or hedonistic consequences of obeying or disobeying the rules.

CONVENTIONAL LEVEL
According to Kohlberg, the level of moral development in which the individual strives to maintain the expectations of family, group, or nation, regardless of the consequences.

POSTCONVENTIONAL LEVEL
According to Kohlberg, the level of moral development characterized by self-chosen ethical principles that are comprehensive, universal, and consistent.

Lawrence Kohlberg (1927–1987).

doesn't exist, but rather that the data failed to support stage 6 as distinguishable from stage 5. Perhaps a more sensitive interview instrument could make the distinction.

It is interesting to note that children in the more advanced stages of development don't necessarily behave better. It's not a matter of "good" or "bad" behavior. Each stage in Kohlberg's theory is value-free. What determines a child's position in the stages is not whether the child chooses "right" or "wrong" according to some value system, but the moral *reasoning* the child uses in making the choice.

Table 9.1 ● Presentation of a Moral Dilemma with Answers Graded According to Kohlberg's Six Stages of Moral Development

In Europe a woman was near death from cancer. One drug might save her, a form of radium that a druggist in the same town had recently discovered. The druggist was charging $2,000, 10 times what the drug cost him to make. The sick woman's husband, Heinz, went to everyone he knew to borrow the money, but he could only get together about half of what it cost. He told the druggist that his wife was dying and asked him to sell it cheaper or let him pay later. But the druggist said "No." The husband got desperate and broke into the man's store to steal the drug for his wife. Should the husband have done that? Why?

Preconventional

Punishment and obedience orientation (physical consequences determine what is good or bad).

Stage 1	*Pro* He should steal the drug. It isn't really bad to take it. It isn't like he didn't ask to pay for it first. The drug he'd take is only worth $200; he's not really taking a $2,000 drug.	*Con* He shouldn't steal the drug. It's a big crime. He didn't get permission; he used force and broke and entered. He did a lot of damage, stealing a very expensive drug and breaking up the store, too.

Instrumental relativist orientation (what satisfies one's own needs is good).

Stage 2	*Pro* It's all right to steal the drug because she needs it and he wants her to live. It isn't that he wants to steal, but it's the way he has to use to get the drug to save her.	*Con* He shouldn't steal it. The druggist isn't wrong or bad, he just wants to make a profit. That's what you're in business for, to make money.

Conventional

Interpersonal concordance or "good boy—nice girl" orientation (what pleases, or helps others is good).

Stage 3	*Pro* He should steal the drug. He was only doing something that was natural for a good husband to do. You can't blame him for doing something out of love for his wife; you'd blame him if he didn't love his wife enough to save her.	*Con* He shouldn't steal, If his wife dies, he can't be blamed. It isn't because he's heartless or that he doesn't love her enough to do everything that he legally can. The druggist is the selfish or heartless one.

"Law and order" orientation (maintain the social order, doing one's duty is good).

Stage 4	*Pro* You should steal it. If you did nothing you'd be letting your wife die; it's your responsibility if she dies. You have to take it with the idea of paying the druggist.	*Con* It is a natural thing for Heinz to want to save his wife, but it's still always wrong to steal. He still knows he's stealing and taking a valuable drug from the man who made it.

Postconventional

Social contract—legalistic orientation (values agreed upon by society, including individual rights and rules for consensus, determine what is right).

Stage 5	*Pro* The law wasn't set up for these circumstances. Taking the drug in this situation isn't really right, but it's justified to do it.	*Con* You can't completely blame someone for stealing, but extreme circumstances don't really justify taking the law into your own hands. You can't have everyone stealing whenever they get desperate. The end may be good, but the ends don't justify the means.

Universal ethical principle orientation (what is right is a matter of conscience in accord with universal principles).

Stage 6	*Pro* This is a situation which forces him to choose between stealing and letting his wife die. In a situation where the choice must be made, it is morally right to steal. He has to act in terms of the principle of preserving and respecting life.	*Con* Heinz is faced with the decision of whether to consider the other people who need the drug just as badly as his wife. Heinz ought to act not according to his particular feelings toward his wife, but considering the value of all the lives involved.

Source: Description of Kohlberg's stages from Shaver & Strong, 1976. Dilemma and pro and con answers from Rest, 1968.

According to Kohlberg's theory, each stage builds on the previous stage. More advanced stages of moral development encompass earlier stages and reorganize them in a way that provides the child with new criteria and perspectives for making moral judgments (Hoffman, 1979). Kohlberg assumed that all children begin at the first stage and progress through each stage without skipping any of them. As with Piaget's cognitive theory, in which there is no assurance that the period of formal operations will be reached, Kohlberg maintained that many children may never reach the final stage. In fact, most people do not appear to develop beyond stage 4 (Shaver & Strong, 1976).

Kohlberg argued that children advance to a higher stage of moral development when they are exposed to moral reasoning slightly more advanced than their own. According to Kohlberg's theory, this places the child in a cognitive conflict that is resolved by acceptance of the more advanced moral reasoning. Experiments with children have indicated that exposing them to moral reasoning that is one or two levels above their own is a strong inducement for them to advance to the next higher stage (Walker & Taylor, 1991a). Often, parents are the ones who provide the child with exposure to a more advanced level of moral reasoning (Walker & Taylor, 1991b).

Because moral development appears to be tied to cognitive development, it is reasonable to expect that certain cognitive abilities must exist before advances in moral development can occur. Studies have indicated that the period of concrete operations is a prerequisite to stage 3 moral reasoning, and the period of formal operations (see Chapter 12) is a prerequisite to stage 5 moral reasoning (Kohlberg & Gilligan, 1971). Such cognitive development, however, does not ensure that these moral stages will be reached.

Criticisms of Kohlberg's Theory

Although Kohlberg's theory presents a well-organized depiction of how moral development may occur, it has been criticized.

Moral Development and Moral Behavior.   Perhaps the most serious problem with Kohlberg's theory of moral development is that it correlates poorly with moral behavior. What people say they will do and what they actually will do are often two very different things (Kurtines & Greif, 1974). With this in mind, some researchers have argued that the approach that Kohlberg took when examining moral development may have been a poor one. It is argued that Kohlberg would have learned more about moral life by studying the behaviors that arise from actual experiences rather than examining the verbal responses given to hypothetical moral dilemmas (Vitz, 1990).

Furthermore, whether a person will choose to behave in a moral way often depends more on the immediate situational forces than on the person's level of moral reasoning. For instance, people are more likely to act in a moral way if the moral imperative requires that they *not do* something (e.g., steal money for food) rather than if it requires that they *do* something (e.g., give food to the hungry) (Kahn, 1992). Of course, the fact that moral behavior often is situationally dependent doesn't necessarily mean that moral reasoning doesn't progress through stages, as Kohlberg suggested, but it does indicate that fostering high levels of moral reasoning might not help create moral behaviors.

Some researchers have also argued that Kohlberg's theory is culturally biased in favor of Western ideas of what is morally "advanced" (Huebner & Garrod, 1991). Other people have concluded that Kohlberg's theory is an accurate description of moral development through childhood and adolescence but that it is not a valid way to measure moral development among adults (Gibbs,

PROSOCIAL BEHAVIOR
Behavior that benefits other people and society.

ANTISOCIAL BEHAVIOR
Behavior that shows little or no concern for other people and little sense of right and wrong.

COOPERATION
Working together toward a common end or purpose.

1979). Still others have criticized Kohlberg for ignoring the powerful effect that emotions often have on determining our moral judgments (Shweder, 1981).

Women and Moral Development.   Kohlberg's original sample, on which most subsequent analyses and reanalyses have been made, consisted solely of white lower- and middle-class males. This has led to one of the most interesting criticisms of Kohlberg's work by one of his colleagues, Carol Gilligan, who has argued that women typically approach moral problems differently than men (Gilligan, 1982).

Gilligan states that women, more often than men, will focus on the interpersonal aspects of morality and on minimizing suffering. These assertions have come from interviews made by Gilligan with many women who were facing interpersonal crises. In this view, the moral development of women can better be understood as a morality of mercy and caring, which leads women, more often than men, to consider the concrete issues of who is being hurt, what has happened each step of the way, and how help can be forthcoming. Kohlberg, Gilligan argues, presented his moral dilemmas with a male bias, stating them as an exercise in logic, a cold balancing act devoid of a morality of caring for others (Vitz, 1990). If gender differences do play an important role, then Kohlberg's work could hardly be considered a model of "human" moral development.

Conclusions.   If we wish to be extremely conservative and not speculate beyond the data that have been gathered, we may conclude that "it now seems that Kohlberg's first five stages can be accepted as a legitimate description of the development of moral judgment in . . . white lower- and middle-class males" (Fischer, 1983, p. 98) and that "for a limited range of situations an individual can gradually develop the ability to apply a single type of reasoning" (Fischer, 1983, p. 104). Of course, because Kohlberg was creating a theory, it is proper to speculate, to try to form a greater whole from the component parts that the data present, and from this organization to extract a greater meaning. Whether the sequential development of moral reasoning that Kohlberg discovered will eventually be considered an important part of a child's development remains to be seen. For the moment, it certainly is intriguing.

PROSOCIAL BEHAVIOR

Prosocial behavior is the opposite of **antisocial behavior**. Prosocial behaviors benefit others and society. During our lives, we are often encouraged to be prosocial. We are asked to cooperate, to help, and to share. How children come to acquire prosocial behaviors and how these behaviors are maintained have become areas of increasing interest to developmental researchers.

Cooperation

When two or more people work together for their mutual benefit, they are cooperating. **Cooperation** is a prosocial behavior, because societies would not be possible without cooperative efforts. Researchers showed little interest in cooperation until Azrin and Lindsley demonstrated in their classic study that direct reinforcement could increase cooperation among children (Azrin & Lindsley, 1956).

Children often are spontaneously cooperative. In our society, however, and in others, individual competition often is reinforced. This is especially true for boys. In fact, by the time they reach high school, boys show strong positive correlations between competitiveness and a sense of self-worth and almost no correlation between cooperativeness and a sense of self-worth (Ahlgren, 1983). Sometimes, the desire for competition can be so intense that it interferes with the need for cooperation. Such irrational competition can spoil the success that cooperation might bring.

M. C. Madsen and his associates conducted an experiment that clearly depicts this problem. They discovered that in certain cases, cooperation *declines* as children grow older and that competition may become the most common mode of responding, even when it cannot possibly lead to success. In his experiment, Madsen had children of the same age sit across from each other at opposite ends of a small table (see Figure 9.4). Narrow gutters ran down the length of the table on both sides. The table surface was arched so that a marble placed anywhere on the table would roll immediately into the nearest gutter. Embedded in the tabletop in front of each child was a cup. To start the game, a marble was placed into a free-sliding marble holder in the center of the table. The marble holder prevented the marble from running into a gutter. Each child had a string attached to one end of the marble holder. For a child to score, he need only pull his string and cause the marble holder to pass over his cup. The marble would then drop into the cup, and he would have succeeded. However, if both children pulled their strings simultaneously, the marble holder would come apart, and the marble would roll into the gutter.

When Madsen had children play the game, he discovered that cooperation was common among 4- and 5-year-old children. During the first 10 trials, the children usually would negotiate and arrange that each received about half of the marbles. However, when Madsen tested schoolchildren in the second through fifth grades, he found their desire to compete so strong that a majority of them failed to obtain a single marble (Madsen, 1971). In a later study, some of the children were so competitive that they argued that it was impossible to get a marble! One child pointed out that success might be possible "if I could play alone" (Kagan & Madsen, 1971, p. 38). Other studies have also supported the fact that older children tend to be more competitive (Herndon & Carpenter, 1982).

Older children appear to be much more competitive because of their experience and learning. Cross-cultural research supports this supposition. When Madsen examined children from different backgrounds, he obtained different results. His data indicate that a strong competitive outlook is more likely to develop among older children in urban surroundings. For instance, it was observed that city-dwelling Israeli children were more competitive than Israeli children raised on a kibbutz (Madsen, 1971; Shapira & Madsen, 1974).

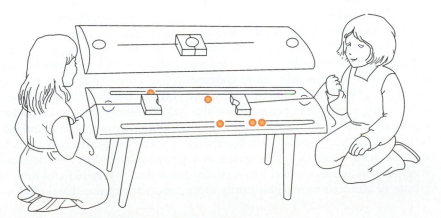

FIGURE 9.4

Marble-pulling apparatus used by Madsen and his colleagues to measure the extent of cooperation and competition among chilren. (Adapted from Madsen, 1971)

A strong competitive outlook is more likely to emerge in urban surroundings. Israeli children raised on a kibbutz were less competitive than those raised in an urban setting.

American children were generally most competitive, regardless of their race, sex, or background, perhaps because competition is so emphasized in American society (Madsen & Shapira, 1970; Nelson & Madsen, 1969). And more recently it has been shown that children reared in family environments in which competition is emphasized tend to be more competitive (Monsaas & Engelhard, 1990).

It was suggested by some, however, that urban children and older children might simply be more familiar with these kinds of games and know that such games usually require competitive strategies. To address this criticism, in 1981, Madsen took his game to Papua, New Guinea, where he used it to test two different groups of children. One group of children belonged to an intact rural tribe, whereas the other group lived in a more heterogeneous urban setting. Neither group was particularly familiar with similar games of any kind. The results were in keeping with Madsen's earlier studies: The children from the rural tribe demonstrated more cooperation, whereas those from the urban setting were more competitive (Madsen & Lancy, 1981).

Teaching Cooperation.   A number of things can be done to teach children the value of cooperation. Spencer Kagan has suggested that creating a "we" rather than an "I" atmosphere can make it easier for children to conceive of themselves working *with* rather than *against* other children (Kagan & Madsen, 1971). Mexican American children, more than Anglo-American children, perceive their parents as expressing this kind of "we" attitude in the home (Knight, Kagan, & Buriel, 1982). This may help explain why Mexican American children are generally more cooperative, whereas Anglo-American children tend to be more competitive (Knight, Kagan, & Buriel, 1981, 1982).

Modeling cooperative behavior can also help children choose cooperation as a primary method for dealing with problems when competition wouldn't be beneficial (Liebert, Sprafkin, & Poulos, 1975). The long-term effectiveness of such modeled cooperation, however, may be age related. For instance, in one study in which cooperation was modeled for 6- and 8-year-old children, both groups of children were significantly more cooperative immediately following the modeling than the control group was. Seven weeks later, however, only the 8-year-old children maintained significantly greater cooperation, whereas the effect of the observed modeling on the 6-year-old children had apparently worn off (Sagotsky, Wood-Schneider, & Konop, 1981). For the modeling of cooperation to be effective, then, it should be modeled often, especially for younger children.

Still another way of teaching children to be more cooperative is to guide them through cooperative ventures so they can see for themselves the value of working together. Through firsthand experience, as children come to appreciate how their prosocial actions can help others and how others can come to depend on their behavior, they begin to develop a greater sense of social responsibility. In turn, this growing sense of social responsibility tends to foster further prosocial behavior (O'Connor & Cuevas, 1982).

You should keep in mind, however, that there are times when competition is the most beneficial strategy. Competition becomes a problem only when it is inappropriate or when it interferes with cooperative efforts that are essential for the society. The race among many nations to obtain nuclear weapons and other means of mass destruction perhaps provides the most striking example in which further competition is an inappropriate strategy and cooperation is essential, in this case for the well-being of millions of people.

Helping

Cooperating with someone is not the same as helping that person. When people help, they provide services, skills, or information necessary to others. The most extensive studies of helping in children have been conducted by psychologist Ervin Staub.

Staub tried to determine what made one child help another. Staub hypothesized that there are two factors that are important in helping. First, an individual must possess the skills or knowledge needed to help effectively; second, the individual must have **empathy** with the person in need of help (Staub, 1978). If this hypothesis is correct, it should be possible to foster helping in children by teaching them the necessary skills and by training them to empathize.

It is generally true that grade school children, especially those in higher grades, are more likely to offer help to someone in need than younger children are (Ladd, Lange, & Stremmel, 1983; Peterson, 1983), especially if the help involves sharing or generosity (Barnett, King, & Howard, 1979). Research indicates, as Staub has suggested, that when older children give help, it is because they know they have better helping skills and also because they have developed greater empathy; both factors are important (Radke-Yarrow, Zahn-Waxler, & Chapman, 1983). Let's take a moment to examine the influence of each.

Knowing How to Help. Offering help to another is not an uncommon behavior among children. Even very young children willingly provide assistance. In studies conducted in a laboratory that simulated a home environment, children between 18 and 30 months of age were observed while parents and other adults performed some common household chores. The researchers noted that the children promptly and spontaneously helped the adults during most of the tasks (Rheingold, 1982). Interestingly, the offer of cooperation and helping from toddlers has been observed to increase greatly at about the time that children first become aware that there is a distinction between themselves

EMPATHY
An insightful awareness and ability to share the emotions, thoughts, and behavior of another person.

and others (Brownell & Carriger, 1990). You may recall our discussion of the dawning of conscious awareness in the Chapter Preview for Chapter 6. It seems reasonable that once children understand that there is a difference between themselves and others, they might grasp the idea that others could possibly need something at a particular moment that they themselves didn't need—such as help.

Evidence gathered during the research indicated that the children showed more than just simple imitation—that is, they weren't just imitating the adults without really knowing that they were "helping." This is evidenced by the fact that they often added appropriate behaviors that the adults had not modeled. Furthermore, they said things that indicated that they knew what the goals of the tasks were and how they were helping. For instance, the older children made such statements as, "I'm going to pick up these books" and "I'm all through with my little broom" (Rheingold, 1982, p. 119). Even the youngest children made appropriate statements while they worked, such as "Sandy sweep," "fold clothes," and "all clean" (Rheingold, 1982, p. 119). This willingness among preschoolers to help is also found in their pretend play, during which they often take on the imaginary role of someone about to render help or aid (Bar-Tal, Raviv, & Goldberg, 1982).

As we noted before, grade school children are more likely to help than preschoolers. But this doesn't seem to be because grade school children are more *willing* to help; younger children are also willing. Rather, older children have greater knowledge and skills that facilitate their deciding when and how to help. Initial knowledge and skills about the requirements of helping (such as knowing your own attributes, the attributes of the one to be helped, the demands of the task, and the intervention techniques required) can be used to determine the difficulty of a task and the appropriateness of different helping strategies (Barnett, Darcie, Holland, & Kobasigawa, 1982). In other words, older children are more likely than younger children to be familiar with the circumstances in which others need help and with the methods for providing that help (Ladd, Lange, & Stremmel, 1983). Children are more likely to help when they know how and when to help (Pearl, 1985). The same is true of adults. In fact, the best way to teach helping behavior to children, especially young children between ages 2 and 7 years, is to have them role-play or act out the kinds of helping that they might be able to offer another (Staub, 1971). In this way, they come to learn how best to help and which situations require them to help.

Hoffman's Stages of Empathy Development. As you may recall, Staub suggested that it takes more than skills and knowledge to motivate a child to help; a child's empathy—that is, aroused feelings over someone else's distress—can also be a motivating factor. Telling children about the value of empathy and explaining how it would benefit another person (a technique known as induction) is likely to initiate helping behavior in children, but generally only among those who are 7 years of age or older (Howard & Barnett, 1981).

Because induction is more successful with older children, it has been argued that empathy does not come into being suddenly but develops over a number of years. In fact, researcher Martin Hoffman has observed four stages of empathy development (Hoffman, 1979). As you can see from Table 9.2, Hoffman's four stages roughly correspond to Piaget's stages of cognitive development (see Chapter 2).

The first stage of empathy, according to Hoffman, occurs during early infancy. Babies appear to be aware if someone in their immediate vicinity is in distress (Yarrow & Waxler, 1977). However, the infant has no awareness of which particular person it may be (Sagi & Hoffman, 1976). In the second stage, or person-permanence stage, the older infant will know that someone is in distress and be able to locate that individual. Still, the infant or young child does not seem to understand that the person in distress has inner feelings or thoughts that may be different from his or her own. In the third, or role-taking, stage, the child demonstrates an increasing ability to respond to others' inner states. The fourth stage emerges in late childhood and is achieved when a child's understanding of another's emotional responses is synthesized with a "mental representation of the other person's general life experiences" (Hoffman, 1977, p. 300).

Hoffman argues that comprehensive empathy, during which the child becomes aware of the stress within the larger life experience, begins in late childhood or early adolescence. Some naturalistic data, however, do not support this assertion. For instance, in one study, it was noted that a 4-year-old boy, when told about the death of his friend's mother, said sadly, "You know, when Bonnie grows up people will ask her who was her mother and she will have to say `I don't know.' You know, it makes tears come to my eyes" (Radke-Yarrow, Zahn-Waxler, & Chapman, 1983, p. 493). This statement

Table 9.2 ● Hoffman's Hierarchy of Empathy Development

	DESCRIPTION	EXAMPLE	PIAGET'S STAGES OF COGNITIVE DEVELOPMENT
DISTRESS REACTION	Child responds to another's distress. Shows no indication of knowing which particular person is in distress.	11-month-old sees another child fall and begin to cry, looks as if she, too, is going to cry, then hides her head in her mother's lap and sucks her thumb.	Sensorimotor period (0–2): Reflex reactions.
PERSON PERMANENCE	Child knows someone is in distress and knows who that person is, but is unaware that the other person may have needs different from his own and therefore may respond inappropriately.	2-year-old sees another child fall and begin to cry, brings his own mother to comfort the other child, even though that child's mother is also present.	Preoperational period (2–7): Object permanence obtained; egocentrism common.
ROLE TAKING	Child responds appropriately to another's distress because he is able to imagine himself in the other's position.	7-year-old child comforts his friend who is sad because he lost his lunch money, and shares a sandwich with him.	Concrete operations (7–11): Egocentrism ends; conservations obtained.
COMPREHENSIVE EMPATHY	Child becomes aware of distress within the larger life experience. Empathy develops for chronic as well as acute situation.	12-year-old collects money for a charity to help alleviate the distress of those less fortunate than she.	Formal operations (11+): Able to deal with the hypothetical.

Source: After Hoffman, 1979.

appears to be a fairly comprehensive empathetic response. Even children as young as 2 have been observed to show empathy for others (usually their mothers) and to show some sensitivity to even unfamiliar persons (Zahn-Waxler, Radke-Yarrow, Wagner, & Chapman, 1992). Because of such findings, some researchers have argued,

> More systematic data are needed on children's empathy in real-life situations before we have a good understanding of how far empathic distress arousal extends for children at various developmental levels, how empathy is molded and moderated by cognitions, how empathy enters into prosocial behavior in later childhood and adolescence. (Radke-Yarrow, Zahn-Waxler, & Chapman, 1983, p. 493)

There are some major differences between the theories of Hoffman and Piaget. To begin with, Hoffman's stages of empathy development, unlike Piaget's stages of cognitive development, are not qualitatively different from one another. Empathy, as a quality, may occur at any age. According to Hoffman, advancing cognitive development only modifies the expression of empathy—it doesn't create it (Radke-Yarrow, Zahn-Waxler, & Chapman, 1983). Second, Hoffman argues that the more primitive forms of empathetic arousal are not replaced in the course of development. They can occur throughout life. For instance, the emotional distress reaction felt by the 11-month-old child seeing another child fall, as depicted in Table 9.2, may also be felt by a 30-year-old adult, although the adult no doubt will continue from that initial point to a more complex empathetic reaction. Nothing similar to this is found in Piaget's stages of cognitive development. For instance, no normal and healthy 30-year-old would still show instances of a lack of object permanence, as is common in the sensorimotor stage.

A final, and perhaps major, difference between the theories of Hoffman and Piaget concerns the amount of research supporting each theory. Piaget's theory has been with us for many years, and the descriptive research supporting it is voluminous. In contrast, Hoffman's theory of empathy development is still relatively new, and many exceptions and modifications may be forthcoming.

Empathy and Prosocial Behavior. Hoffman's description of the development of empathy in childhood may help explain why induction works best with children older than 7 years. Hoffman's hierarchy tells us that 5-year-old children, for instance, who are in the second, or person-permanence, stage, although able to understand that another person is in distress, may not fully realize why that person is in distress. For this reason, to discuss with them how helping can better the distressed person's life (induction) may not be as effective as it would be with an older, third- or fourth-stage child, who has role-taking ability, the ability to take another person's perspective. With younger children, it may be best to act out helping and to teach them when helping is appropriate.

It seems reasonable that induction would work only on those children who were capable of role taking, because induction calls attention to the plight of others. To examine this issue experimentally, researchers divided 18 middle-class 7-year-old boys and girls into two groups, depending on their ability to role-take. High role takers (those found to be most able to understand the feelings of others) were placed in one group, while those lower in role taking were placed in the other. Each child was then videotaped while teaching kindergartners how to make caterpillars with paper, glue, scissors, and crayons. Researchers observed and recorded 16 categories of prosocial behavior. High role takers were found to show greater empathy with the kindergartners struggling to make their caterpillars and were more likely to offer help than were the low role takers (Hudson, Forman, & Brion-Meisels, 1982). These results indicate that children who are high role takers, independent of age, are more likely to be sensitive to another's distress and therefore are more likely to help. As you recall, such role taking is closely tied to a child's cognitive development.

Interestingly, children who are role takers are more likely to help another child in distress when there is an adult present to evaluate their behavior than when no adult is present. This appears to occur because role takers, who are able to understand the stress of another child, also can take the role of the adult who is watching and realize that the adult will be pleased if the child tries to help (Froming, Allen, & Jensen, 1985).

There is some evidence that the children who express the most empathy are the most likely to offer help or cooperation (Buckley, Siegel, & Ness, 1979; Marcus, Telleen, & Roke, 1979), whereas those expressing the least empathy are most likely to be delinquent (Ellis, 1982). Surprisingly, though, most researchers have found that a child's level of empathy is often a poor predictor of prosocial behavior (Radke-Yarrow, Zahn-Waxler, & Chapman, 1983; Chapman, Zahn-Waxler, Cooperman, & Iannotti, 1987). No one is quite certain, however, why a child's level of empathy doesn't always correlate well with prosocial behavior. Part of the problem may be that different studies have sometimes used different definitions of "empathy" (Eisenberg-Berg & Lennon, 1980). Some definitions rely heavily on cognitive changes, others on affective changes. Only in the last decade have serious attempts been made to create a uniform definition. Another reason for the occasional failure of levels of empathy to predict prosocial behaviors may be that other variables often affect children's willingness to help. Although helping increases with the intensity of a child's empathy, children who find the observed distress too severe may focus on their own "empathetic distress" rather than on the plight of the victim (Barnett, Howard, Melton, & Dino, 1982; Hoffman, 1979). Furthermore, children often behave differently in different situations. For example, children respond "more empathetically to others of the same race or sex and . . . to others perceived as similar in abstract terms (e.g., similar 'personality traits')" (Hoffman, 1979, p. 963). If these additional factors are not taken into account, predictions of prosocial behavior based on a child's measured level of empathy are not likely to be accurate.

Meta-Emotion. **Meta-emotion** refers to one's knowledge about one's own emotions. Researchers have begun to examine how a child's understanding of his or her own emotions may influence the development of empathy. Although researchers have just scratched the surface of this area, some interesting speculations and findings have been forthcoming.

Part of having empathy for others is the ability to put oneself in the other person's shoes, that is, to know and understand other people's experiences. This is, of course, what Hoffman meant by role taking. Perhaps to have empathy for another person requires that you yourself, at some time, need the empathy of others. With this in mind, it has been argued that childhood illnesses may be one of the more interesting forces behind role taking as it concerns the development of empathy. Oddly, illnesses may have a beneficial effect on behavior and development because they provide a child with experiences that require the help and empathy of other people, which may in turn teach the child to understand what it is like to be in need and to understand how others must feel when they are in a similar situation (Parmelee, 1986).

Children also acquire greater meta-emotion when they come to understand that previous emotional experiences may affect the way that they or someone

META-EMOTION
One's knowledge about one's own emotions.

ALTRUISM
Behavior that benefits someone other than the actor, with little or no apparent benefit for the actor.

else assesses a current situation. In one study, children of different ages and college students were told stories that included a description of an earlier emotional experience. One story was as follows:

> This is a story about a boy named Pat. One day Pat picked up his gerbil, and the gerbil bit him, and it hurt. The next day in school, Pat's teacher said, "Pat, it's your turn to feed the gerbil." (Gnepp & Gould, 1985, p. 1455)

The subjects were then asked how Pat would feel after having heard the request. Kindergartners generally thought that Pat would be happy, considering only the immediate circumstances. Second graders were somewhat more likely to realize that the previous emotional experience would make Pat feel frightened. Fifth graders were more likely still to realize that the earlier experience would affect the boy, and college students understood immediately (let's hope so!) (Gnepp & Gould, 1985).

Another important concept incorporated within meta-emotion is the ability to generate strategies that can help to change emotions. In general, 5-year-old children attempt to help other children feel better after something sad has happened by providing material goods. As one young child said, "I would give her some toys" (McCoy & Masters, 1985, p. 1221). Older children, however, are more sophisticated. By the age of 10 years, children often attempt to mediate cognitive processing of emotions with verbal interventions, such as, "Tell him it's not worth thinking about" (McCoy & Masters, 1985, p. 1221).

Future discoveries concerning the development of meta-emotion will no doubt help researchers to better understand prosocial behavior and the development of empathy.

Sharing and Altruism

"Most children in middle childhood will verbally, if not behaviorally, support the principle that one should aid the needy" (Bryan, 1970, p. 61). Both sharing and **altruism** are prosocial behaviors. How these behaviors develop and how they can be encouraged have become the focus of a large amount of research.

Children share whenever they give some of what they have to another person. However, sharing may or may not be altruistic. Altruism takes into consideration the motive behind the act. An altruistic act is one that is not motivated by self-interest. Sometimes children share altruistically; at other times, they share for reasons of self-interest (e.g., to avoid punitive action or to obtain a future good). When children are governed by self-interest, adults often find it necessary to structure the contingencies in the children's environment in a way that will ensure sharing or fairness. Consider the mother whose two children constantly argued about who would get the "larger half" of the apple or the "larger half" of the doughnut. Her solution was to alter the external contingencies to make the children share equally. She instructed the first child to divide the food in two and then gave the second child first choice as to which piece she wanted. From that day on, food was always divided right down the middle—unless the children were alone, in which case the older child got all the apple if the younger child did not threaten to tell. As you can see, this is not altruism. Still, many children will share when no adult is around to make them do so, and they also will share even when there is no chance that their actions will be reciprocated.

Intrinsic Motivation. Psychologists and others are interested in altruistic behavior, especially among older children and adults, because most often it

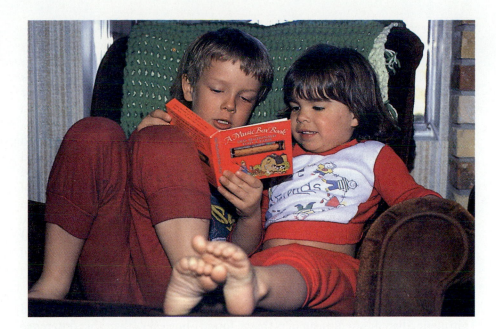

Children often share with each other without being pressured to do so.

appears to be controlled by internalized systems of self-reward and morality (Peterson, 1982). These internalized systems may in turn have developed after long exposure to altruistic individuals, especially parents (Clary & Miller, 1986). In many cases, intrinsic motivation has been found to be superior to extrinsic motivation in creating and maintaining prosocial behavior.

In one experiment, researchers attempted to teach fifth graders not to litter and to help clean up after others. The children were divided into two groups. The first group was told each day for eight days that they should be neat and tidy, and the reason this behavior would be good for them was explained. The second group was told, for the same number of days, that they were neat and tidy people. Littering and cleanliness were measured on the tenth and fourteenth days. The differences were considerable. The children in the first group, who were motivated extrinsically, were far less likely to help clean up than were the children in the second group, who had begun to think of themselves as neat and tidy and who wanted to maintain this positive attitude (intrinsic motivation) (Miller, Brickman, & Bolen, 1975).

Both role playing and empathy are important in developing intrinsically motivated sharing and altruism in children, just as they are in promoting helpful behavior. In one study, researchers found that 6-year-old children who had been trained through role playing were more likely than other children to share with a needy child, even though they were not given extrinsic rewards for doing so (Iannotti, 1978).

The degree of a child's intrinsic motivation is also related to age and experience. As older children develop more competence and a greater sense of responsibility, they come to understand better the needs of others and the benefit that their giving may bring. These greater feelings of competence and responsibility may be one of the reasons that sharing and altruism increase during late childhood and early adolescence (Peterson, 1983). By the age of 9 years, nearly all children are willing to share (Green & Schneider, 1974).

The Effects of Modeling and Culture.   Modeling can affect sharing. Children who view a generous model usually will share more than children who do not view a model (Lipscomb, Larrieu, McAllister, & Bregman, 1982), and children who view a stingy model will share least of all (Ascione & Sanok, 1982). Understanding sharing or other prosocial behaviors is a complex task. Many factors besides role playing, empathy, and modeling can be influential (Hampson, 1981). For example, sharing can be increased by asking children to think happy thoughts (Isen, Horn, & Rosenhan, 1973; Moore, Underwood, & Rosenhan, 1973), by asking them to share (Bryan, 1975), or by providing them with more than they think they deserve (Olejnik, 1976).

Sharing also can be influenced strongly by culture. In one study conducted in Israel, two groups of children were asked to share with other children based on how much work the other children had done. One group comprised 10-year-old city children raised in Jerusalem; the other group consisted of 10-year-old children who had been raised on an Israeli kibbutz (a collective in which sharing is strongly emphasized). The city children shared based on how much work other children produced. The kibbutz children, however, shared even with those children who produced little, as long as the other child tried hard (Nisan, 1984).

Gender Differences.   It is a common belief that girls are more sharing and altruistic than boys. Researchers have found, however, that the difference between boys and girls is extremely slight (in favor of girls being more altruistic and sharing) or nonexistent (with no difference between the sexes) (Shigetomi, Hartmann, & Gelfand, 1981; Zarbatany, Hartmann, Gelfand, & Vinciguerra, 1985). In any case, no research has ever supported the popular belief that girls are overwhelmingly more sharing and altruistic than boys.

Some have wondered if there once was a real sex difference many years ago; perhaps girls today are simply becoming more like boys. However, the first study of gender and altruism was conducted well over half a century ago (Hartshorne, May, & Maller, 1929), and those researchers discovered, as have modern researchers, that although girls were only slightly more likely to help or to share than boys were, girls had a far greater reputation for altruism than boys did. The researchers concluded that "a sex prejudice may be at work" (Hartshorne, May, & Maller, 1929, p. 156). It appears that more than 65 years later, the same prejudice is still at work!

Altruism and Natural Selection.   At first glance, it may appear that altruistic acts should run contrary to our "natural grain" because it would seem reasonable that natural selection would choose against any creature with a propensity to give without receiving. Depending on species and circumstances, however, selfishness may not necessarily aid in procreation. The animal kingdom is filled with examples of selfless altruistic behavior, behavior that often helps a species pass on its genes to the next generation. Birds risk their lives and sometimes die to attract attention away from the nest. Among baboons, zebras, moose, and wild dogs, often there are "stubborn, doomed guardians, prepared to be done in first in order to buy time for the herd to escape" (Thomas, 1982, p. 58).

Human beings, too, evolved in societies and groups, and it is reasonable to assume that altruism in our species may be easy to learn for genetic reasons (Rushton & Sorrentino, 1981). In this sense, then, altruism may be acquired easily by our species because of our inheritance. It should be emphasized that even if altruism exists to a degree because nature has selected in favor of it, the effects of our society's teachings, our own experiences, and the individual differences among members of our own species also appear to play extremely important roles in determining the presence of altruism. These biological and social learning views are not incompatible; both probably explain the existence of altruism (Rushton & Sorrentino, 1981; Sharabany & Bar-Tal, 1982).

Why Children Stop Believing in Santa Claus

Or, "Daddy, Based on Your Midnight ETA for Santa, I Don't See How Only Eight Reindeer Can Handle the Fuel-to-Load Ratio"

Let's take a moment to examine Piaget's theory as it might be applied to an interesting problem—namely, why children stop believing in Santa Claus. Because all children progress through stages of cognitive development in a specific order, and because each stage is said to define the child's cognitive abilities, studying each stage of their child's cognitive development might help parents to understand changes in the child's thinking, such as why the child stops believing in Santa Claus.

Once again, it is helpful to remember that Piaget's descriptive data are generally undisputed, although there are a few exceptions. The explanatory nature of his theory is what is typically debated. Thus, we are probably on fairly safe ground when we describe a child as being in, say, the stage of concrete operations, if by that we mean that the child will most likely approach certain problems in a certain way and will most likely perceive the world with certain limitations. Why the child thinks as he or she does is another matter, and there we may agree or disagree with Piaget's assessment. The point is that the "stages," whether they exist or not, can still function surprisingly well as descriptive terms. They can, of course, also function as explanatory terms, but with advised caution, considering that there are many unresolved issues concerning the data that Piaget's work has generated.

But let's get back to our important issue. Do you remember when you stopped believing in Santa?* I do. I recall that there was this one day shortly before Christmas when something seemed all wrong to me about the whole idea of Santa Claus. I sud-

Santa Claus and a "true believer."

denly began to wonder how Santa could possibly get all the toys that I wanted, along with the toys that I knew my friends wanted, not to mention the toys that all of the rest of the kids in the world wanted, into one sleigh. Conservation had struck with a vengeance. My mother recalled when it happened because I wandered about for days worried about this knotty problem that Santa faced and how it was likely to influence my Christmas.

Have you ever wondered what kind of thinking is required to believe in Santa Claus? Look again at Figure 9.2, and you will see why children in the period of concrete

operations—children capable of conserving—would come to doubt Santa's existence.

Can you see how a child who conserves amount will realize that for every child in the world to receive at least one gift, the number of toys must be at least equal to the number of children? Any child who has seen that seven or eight packages can just barely fit into the trunk of the car will be as perplexed as I was. How can Santa put all those presents in one sack (or even two or three)?

Furthermore, a child engaging in concrete operations, who can understand the temporal sequence of events, will begin to wonder how

*Assuming you ever believed in Santa.

Santa can visit every house in the world on one night. As you can see, even if the mean kid on your block hadn't told you that there was no Santa Claus, you'd probably have deduced it sooner or later on your own. I had just turned 6 when I found out. I suppose that was pretty old to finally get the picture. It probably took that long because the older kids on my street were kind and didn't say anything, and all my friends were just as gullible as I was.

I was proud after I found out, though. I felt as if I had accomplished some kind of mental breakthrough into the secret world of adults. Unfortunately, I had a touch of horizontal decalage. By the following March, I knew full well that there was no Santa, and was still proud of knowing that fact, but was happily waiting for the Easter Bunny to arrive. Maybe parents shouldn't lie to their kids in the first place. I still feel bad about the Easter Bunny, which had seemed quite a reasonable concept at the time. I wasn't ready for the truth about that, but my parents broke it to me rather than have me get much older and embarrass them. I suppose I had to grow up. There was no way to hold onto my old concepts once I had advanced cognitively, or was there?

It is possible that a cognitively advanced child might continue to believe in Santa Claus (and still be normal). It would be possible to maintain the Santa myth if you solved the child's cognitive dilemma. Parents sometimes try to accomplish this with statements such as, "Santa can do all these things because he has many helpers," or "Santa uses magic." Interestingly, if peers and other adults support the myth and supply such answers, the child may continue to believe. There are many cultures in which superstitions or myths, certainly as wild as the Santa Claus one, are firmly believed by even the adult members. This distinction is important. The fact that we develop more complex cognitive reasoning doesn't necessarily mean that we develop the ability to distinguish truth from fiction. To answer the question, Why do children stop believing in Santa Claus?, we must admit that it is not because children develop cognitively; it is because members of the society confess to the myth when a conserving child begins to chip away at it. If peers, parents, and other adults supported the myth and provided answers *satisfactory for the child's cognitive level,* Santa could be expected to survive the onslaught of concrete and even formal operations. (The Easter Bunny, too!)

SUMMARY

■ Middle childhood is a time of continued physical growth and motor development. Until school-age children reach puberty, their rate of growth is relatively steady, and their motor skills show an increased mechanical efficiency.

■ Children in middle childhood usually are the healthiest group in the population. Middle childhood is the time when many behaviors related to lifestyle are formed, and health programs designed to prevent future problems can help to modify unhealthy behaviors.

■ At about the time children enter school, they develop the ability to rely on logical operations to form their conclusions. This was called the period of concrete operations by Jean Piaget.

■ During the period of concrete operations, children's thought processes become more competent, flexible, and powerful as the children come to understand and apply decentering, reversibility, and conservation.

■ Piaget used the term *horizontal decalage* to refer to the fact that some conservations are mastered before others.

■ During concrete operations, children begin to understand serial position, begin to deal with classes and subclasses of objects, and acquire a sophisticated knowledge of the ordinal relationships among numbers.

■ Russian researcher Lev Vygotsky described how environmental influences might mold and shape cognitive structures. Adults provide children with a scaffolding that helps to direct and nurture the child's cognitive development.

■ The information-processing approach is yet another way of looking at cognitive development. At its center is the idea that the human intellect may function like a computer.

■ The attitudes and beliefs held by children and adults that help them to determine what is right and wrong are called morals. The development of moral thought may be influenced by a child's level of cognitive development.

■ Piaget believed that a child's cognitive development was most responsible for developmental changes in moral thinking. He believed that moral thinking evolved from fixed-law morality to social contract morality.

■ Building on Piaget's work, Lawrence Kohlberg postulated that there are three levels of moral development: the preconventional, the conventional, and the postconventional. Within each level are two stages.

■ Each stage in Kohlberg's theory is value-free. What determines a child's position in the stages is not whether the child chooses "right" or "wrong" according to some value system, but the moral reasoning used in making the choice. According to Kohlberg, each stage builds on the previous stage.

■ Although Kohlberg's theory presents a well-organized depiction of how moral development may occur, it has been criticized. Perhaps the most serious problem with Kohlberg's theory is that the expressed moral beliefs it measures correlate poorly with moral behavior.

■ Prosocial behaviors are moral behaviors that benefit others and society. During our lives, we are often encouraged to be prosocial.

■ There is some evidence that the children who express the most empathy are the most likely to offer help or cooperation, but surprisingly, researchers occasionally have found a child's level of empathy to be a poor predictor of prosocial behavior. Part of the problem may be that different studies have used different definitions of empathy and that other variables also may affect children's willingness to help.

■ Cooperation is a prosocial behavior. Children often cooperate spontaneously. In our society, however, and in others, individual competition is so often reinforced that children's efforts to surpass other people sometimes interfere with the need for cooperation.

■ Staub believes that to help, a person must possess the necessary skills or knowledge and also must empathize with the person in need.

■ Both sharing and altruism are prosocial behaviors. Sharing may or may not be altruistic. Altruistic acts are not motivated by self-interest. Altruistic behavior is usually among children who are intrinsically motivated, who have more empathy, or who observe altruistic models.

QUESTIONS FOR DISCUSSION

1. Do you think that children should participate in competitive sports during their middle childhood years? If not, why?

2. Researchers at the Johns Hopkins University studied 131 college students who were 12 and 13 years old and found that the children were maintaining a grade point average of 3.59 (A students). There have been no reports of 8-year-old children attending regular college classes. Do you think this is because 8-year-old children haven't reached the level of formal operations, or because they haven't lived long enough to gain the information-processing capabilities needed for college classes, or both? Might there be (as yet undiscovered) teaching techniques that could prepare an 8-year-old child for college?

3. How might a child's cognitive development be affected if she was raised in a one-parent family? (Consider scaffolding.)

4. In what ways might Kohlberg's theory of moral development be biased in favor of Western ideas of what is or isn't morally advanced?

Suggestions for Further Reading

1. Eisenberg, N. (1992). *The caring child.* Cambridge, MA: Harvard University Press.

2. Eisenberg, N., & Mussen, P. (Eds.). (1989). *The roots of prosocial behavior in children.* New York: Cambridge University Press.

3. Flavell, J. H., Miller, P. H., & Miller, S. A. (1993). *Cognitive Development* (3rd ed.). Englewood Cliffs, NJ: Prentice Hall.

4. Howe, M. L., & Pasnak, R. (Eds.). (1992). *Emerging themes in cognitive development.* New York: Springer-Verlag.

5. Keil, F. (1992). *Concepts, kinds & cognitive development.* Cambridge, MA: MIT Press.

6. Perkins, D. (1992). *Teaching children how to think: New strategies for parents and teachers.* New York: Free Press.

7. Sutherland, P. (1992). *Cognitive development today: Piaget and his critics.* New York: Taylor & Francis.

8. Tappan, M. B., & Packer, M. J. (Eds.). (1991). *Narrative and storytelling: Implications for understanding moral development.* San Francisco: Jossey-Bass.

CHAPTER 10

Intelligence and Creativity

CHAPTER PREVIEW
Smart Is as Smart Does

In the summer of 1942, psychologist Seymour Sarason was working at the Southbury Training School for the Mentally Retarded, a school in Connecticut. Among Sarason's many jobs was giving various intelligence examinations to the handicapped students. One of the tests he commonly used was the Porteus Mazes Test. This test demanded no spoken response; rather, it simply required those taking it to trace their way through a series of printed mazes with a pencil. Perhaps you have come across similar puzzles; some are very easy, while others can be quite complicated. Many of the handicapped students at the school, however, weren't able to do even the simplest puzzle. This came as a great surprise to Sarason.

The reason that he was surprised was because a number of the students who failed his mazes had previously broken out of the institution and had successfully negotiated the woods of the Connecticut country-side in an effort to return to their homes! Sarason has said, "That was when I realized that what these kids could plan on their own was in no way reflected by how they did on tests" (McKean, 1985, p. 25). Although testing can be a powerful and helpful tool, the relationship between a test score and what is commonly thought of as intelligence is a complicated one.

In this chapter, we will examine the development of intelligence, the ways in which it is measured, and the problems faced by researchers interested in studying developmental changes in intelligence. We will also see how researchers attempt to deal with what Sarason and others have discovered—that the concept of intelligence isn't always as clear or obvious as one might imagine.

INTELLIGENCE
A general term for a person's abilities in a wide range of tasks, including vocabulary, numbers, problem solving, and concepts. It may also include the ability to profit from experience, to learn new information, and to adjust to new situations.

EUGENICS
The science of improving the genetic characteristics of humans through breeding; term coined by Sir Francis Galton.

PHRENOLOGY
A system for identifying types of people by examining their physical features, especially the configuration of the skull.

WHY PSYCHOLOGISTS STUDY INTELLIGENCE

People within every group or society are aware that some of their members have superior abilities to analyze problems, to find solutions, to comprehend ideas, and to accumulate information. Such people are valued because they can help the society to reach its goals. They are considered intelligent.

We revere those people whose insights, gifts, and knowledge have enabled them to make brilliant deductions or to see things as no one has seen them before. We know their names—Galileo, Einstein, Newton, Michelangelo, Darwin, and Beethoven, to name a few. But why do some people have these abilities and not others? Are their gifts present at birth, or are they acquired through experience and learning? Can **intelligence** be taught? Can intellectual potential be found and cultivated? Can we prevent it from being lost or wasted? Does intelligence change over time, or does it remain stable? Is there a general kind of intelligence, applicable in all situations, or are there many kinds of intelligence? Psychologists are interested in all these questions. In fact, intelligence is such an intriguing subject that nearly everyone takes an interest in it.

DEFINING INTELLIGENCE

What is intelligence? Is it the ability to do well in school or to figure things out? Is it having the skills to find happiness or knowing when to come in out of the rain? Think about the following people and ask yourself if they are intelligent:

• The physician who smokes three packs of cigarettes per day
• The Nobel Prize winner whose marriage and personal life are in ruins
• The corporate executive who has worked to reach the top and has earned a heart attack for the effort
• The brilliant and successful composer who handled his money so poorly that he was always running from his creditors and sometimes paid for a night's lodging with the rights to a great work (Incidentally, his name was Mozart.)

Examine any of these paradoxes, or consider the lives of your friends or even your own life, and it will be clear to you that intelligence is not an easy thing to define.

The first scientific interest in defining and measuring intelligence can be traced to the nineteenth-century inheritance theories of Sir Francis Galton (1822–1911). Galton was interested in the success that English dog breeders had had in creating so many varieties of dogs. He wondered if it wouldn't be possible to also breed humans for desirable characteristics, intelligence being one of them. Galton founded a **eugenics** movement that advocated mating the best men and women for the purpose of producing superior offspring.

The movement never went very far, mostly because people preferred to marry for love rather than genes. Still, Galton's studies of supposedly superior and inferior qualities of people marked the start of the entire psychological testing movement, and people began to think about differences in mental abilities in a way they never had before. By 1900, the public had come to accept the idea that science could measure psychological differences to identify superior and inferior abilities. Clouding serious scientific research, however, were numerous nonsensical but popular theories, which were often the product of charlatans or pseudoscientists who purported to be able to measure "inherited traits." One such theory was **phrenology**. Phrenology is the study of personal-

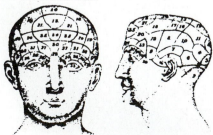

Phrenologists attempted to measure personality by examining the contours or bumps on the human head.

ity based on the contours and bumps of the head. It works about as well as trying to figure out how much money someone has by feeling the outside of his safe. Another idea was the notion that criminal tendencies were mostly inherited and were directly related to such physical features as a low forehead or "shifty" eyes. We now know that this idea is foolish. Among thousands of counterexamples is the fact that Australia was settled two centuries ago mostly by criminals banished from England. Many of today's Australians can trace their genetic roots back to these criminals, and yet Australia has a low crime rate. The list of foolish beliefs about inherited characteristics is long. Nevertheless, as the twentieth century dawned it was a common public belief that most human characteristics, including intelligence, were the result of heredity; the influence of learning or experience was discounted.

More recently, however, the contributions of experience and environment have been widely investigated, and the more modern view is that a characteristic such as intelligence develops out of an interaction between inherited capacity and environmental influence.

MEASURING INTELLIGENCE—IQ TESTS

In 1905, Alfred Binet (1857–1911) and Theodore Simon (1873–1961) developed the precursor to the modern intelligence test. Its purpose was to determine which Parisian schoolchildren would benefit from regular classes and which should receive special education.

Binet established which tasks or questions could be solved easily by children in each of the school grades and which were difficult. Carrying his research further, he developed a concept of **mental age (MA)**. For example, a 5-year-old child who performed as well on the test as an average 6-year-old child would be said to have a mental age of 6. A 10-year-old child who performed only as well as an average 5-year-old child would be said to have a mental age of 5. Binet used the term **chronological age (CA)** to represent the actual age of the child.

A few years later, the German psychologist L. William Stern developed a formula to avoid fractions when comparing MA and CA. It yielded a score he called the **intelligence quotient**, or **IQ**. Stern's formula, IQ=MA/CA × 100, gave a rough index of how bright or dull any child was in comparison with his or her school peers. In the case of the 5-year-old child (CA = 60 months) with an MA of 72 months, the IQ is 120, more than sufficient for schoolwork. But the 10-year-old child (CA = 120 months) with an MA of only 60 months has an IQ of 50, which would be defined as developmentally retarded—not sufficient for schoolwork.

In 1916, Lewis Terman (1877–1956) and his colleagues at Stanford University in California revised the original Binet-Simon intelligence scale and incorporated Stern's idea of the IQ. Their revision, known as the Stanford-Binet, became the first of the modern IQ tests. Using the Stanford-Binet test, most IQ scores in a normal population fall between 85 and 115, although some are higher or lower. Figure 10.1 depicts the distribution of scores.

Test Validity

Although we now have IQ tests, intelligence itself has never been adequately defined, and there is some question about the **validity** of these tests. A test is said to be valid if it measures what it claims to measure. Do IQ tests measure

---

MENTAL AGE (MA)
A concept developed by Alfred Binet that was subsequently incorporated into the formula IQ=mental age/chronological age × 100. The mental age of a person is derived by comparing his or her score with the average scores of others within specific age-groups.

CHRONOLOGICAL AGE (CA)
A concept developed by Alfred Binet that was subsequently incorporated into the formula IQ=mental age/chronological age × 100. The chronological age of a person is his or her actual age.

INTELLIGENCE QUOTIENT (IQ)
A quotient derived from the formula MA/CA × 100, where MA is mental age and CA is chronological age. The intelligence quotient was devised by German psychologist L. William Stern and introduced in the United States by Lewis Terman.

VALIDITY
The capacity of an instrument to measure what it purports to measure.

Alfred Binet (1857–1911).

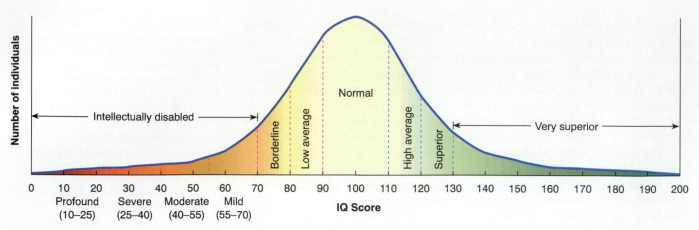

FIGURE 10.1

The standard distribution of IQ scores within the general population. The most common IQ score is 100. Approximately two-thirds of all scores fall within the IQ range of 84 to 116.

intelligence, as most people use the term? Generally, IQ tests measure common skills and abilities, many of which are acquired in school. Consider the areas covered in a widely used intelligence test, the revised Wechsler Adult Intelligence Scale (WAIS-R), shown in Figure 10.2 on pages 268–269* Does the ability to answer the sample questions correctly coincide with most people's understanding of intelligence?

Many people think that intelligence also includes such attributes as creativity, persistent curiosity, and striving for success. IQ test scores aren't always good indicators of a person's abilities in these areas. For instance, two researchers worked with a number of bright mathematicians whose IQ test scores were very similar, who were all about the same age, and who all had a Ph.D. from a prestigious university. They found that these subjects had remarkable differences in creative output, as measured by other mathematicians (Helson & Crutchfield, 1970). IQ test scores, then, are not generally a valid measure of creativity.

Still, IQ tests have been found to predict other behaviors. They are generally able to predict success in school with a fairly high degree of certainty—not surprisingly, perhaps, since this is what they were originally designed to do. IQ tests are also sometimes valid for clinical assessments of people who have mental disorders or neurological and perceptual deficiencies.

Whether an IQ test will be a valid predictor often depends on the particular situation and the population being considered. Although people have attempted to use IQ tests to predict the likelihood of success on the job (Cronbach, 1970), the tests are fairly inaccurate at making such predictions (McClelland, 1973). If the job in question requires the academic skills most often learned in school, however, the IQ test will be a better predictor of success. This again shows the relationship between IQ scores and the ability to do well in school. In one study (Ghiselli, 1966), IQ test scores moderately predicted job success among stockbrokers (a more academic job) but poorly predicted job success among police officers (a less academically oriented job). As you can see, IQ tests may be useful predictors of success in some situations, but they don't necessarily measure the great number of abilities that might be included under the term *intelligence*.

---

*There is also a child's version of this test (WISC-3), which asks similar but easier questions.

Factor Analysis

Some IQ tests are given individually, one on one, such as the Stanford-Binet or the WAIS-R, while others are given to groups. Some IQ tests are designed to be taken exclusively by infants, or by children, or by adults. All the IQ tests ask different questions, and, although they are all called intelligence tests and they all yield an IQ score, they may measure different abilities. Furthermore, some tests measure the same ability more than once and thereby give that one ability more weight in the final score. The weight, or emphasis, given to any one ability is known as a **factor load**.

To understand factor load better, let's look at an example from athletics. Think of an Olympic decathlon athlete who must compete in the following 10 events:

- pole vault (requires running start)
- 100-meter dash
- javelin (requires running start)
- 110-meter high hurdles
- 400-meter run
- high jump (requires running start)
- 1,500-meter run
- discus
- running long jump
- shot put

As you can see, one ability is measured more than once; that is, it has a heavy factor load. This ability is running. The idea of trying to balance tests—including IQ tests—for factors, so that each ability is tested only once, was advocated by L. L. Thurstone in 1938. To accomplish this, Thurstone relied on a technique known as **factor analysis**. Of course, who's to say that a test equally weighted for all factors is the best indicator of what we call intelligence? Perhaps intelligence is measured better by tests that have more weight for some factors than for others. Factor analysis is still valuable, however, because if the factors can be isolated, the value of each factor and the weight it should be given can be determined more accurately.

Although the factor analysis approach has been challenged, there is no doubt that some IQ tests are loaded in favor of particular factors. For instance, I do fairly well on the Stanford-Binet test; this test is heavily loaded in favor of verbal skills, and I enjoy talking and writing. But when I take the WAIS-R, my IQ is 15 points lower; the Wechsler includes many tasks that require eye-hand coordination, and it turns out that I am a clod with blocks. Yet both tests give me an IQ score. People often assume that an IQ is an absolute value regardless of the test; as you can see, they are mistaken.

Thurstone was a mathematician who worked in Thomas Edison's laboratory, solving the straightforward arithmetic that Edison seemed unable to comprehend. Edison's inability in this area led Thurstone to conclude that rather than a single quality called general intelligence, there must be many, perhaps unrelated kinds of intelligence. One of Thurstone's hopes was that it would eventually be possible to distinguish social from nonsocial intelligence, academic from nonacademic intelligence, and mechanical from abstract intelligence.

Since Thurstone's day, many people have attempted to isolate different kinds of intelligence. One of the most exhaustive efforts was made by J. P. Guilford. He developed a model of intelligence based on factor analysis of the human intellect. In his most recent version of the model, Guilford proposed that there are as many as 150 different factors, or kinds, of intelligence (Guilford, 1982).

FACTOR LOAD
The weight, or emphasis, given to any factor or ability.

FACTOR ANALYSIS
A statistical procedure aimed at discovering the constituent traits within a complex system such as personality or intelligence. The method enables the investigator to compute the minimum number of factors required to account for intercorrelations in test scores.

FIGURE 10.2

Subtests of the Weschler Adult Intelligence Scale (WAIS-R, 1981).

VERBAL SCALE

1. INFORMATION: Twenty-nine questions covering a wide range of general knowledge that people have presumably had an opportunity to gain simply by being exposed to the culture.

   EXAMPLE: How many zeros are there in 1 billion?

2. DIGIT SPAN: Fourteen groups of from two to nine digits presented orally, one group at a time. After hearing a group, subjects must repeat it from memory. Some require repitition forward, others backward.

3. VOCABULARY: Thirty-five vocabulary words of increasing difficulty presented visually and orally. Subjects must define each word.

   EXAMPLE: "What does parsimony mean?"

4. ARITHMETIC: Fourteen problems similar to those encountered in elementary school. The problems must be solved without paper or pencil.

   EXAMPLE: "How much would three cigars cost if each cigar was $1.80 and the store was offering a 10 percent discount on all puchases?"

5. COMPREHENSION: Sixteen questions that ask subjects to indicate the correct thing to do under varied circumstances, what certain proverbs mean, or why certain practices are followed.

   EXAMPLE: "What is meant by 'too many cooks spoil the broth'?"

6. SIMILARITIES: Fourteen items requiring that subjects explain the similarity between two things.

   EXAMPLE: "In what ways are red and hot alike?" (ANS.: Both can be sensed; both are stimuli.)

PERFORMANCE SCALE

7. PICTURE COMPLETION: Twenty pictures. In each picture something is missing. Subjects must identify the missing part.

   EXAMPLE:

8. PICTURE ARRANGEMENT: Ten sets of cards. Each set contains cartoon characters performing an action. If the set of cards is placed in the proper sequence, it will depict a sensible story. Subjects must place cards from each set in the proper order.

   EXAMPLE: "Place the cards in the proper sequence so that they depict a sensible story." (ANS.: Corect order should be 3, 1, 4, 2.)

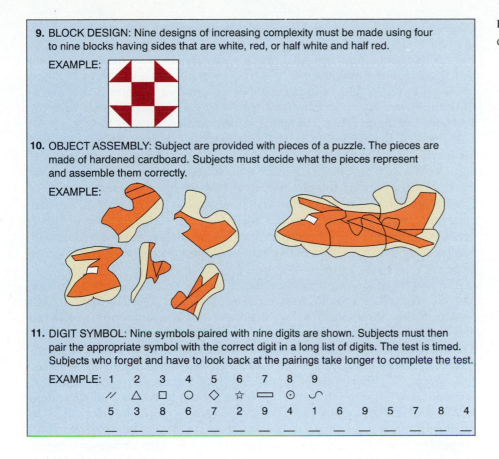

FIGURE 10.2

Continued

9. BLOCK DESIGN: Nine designs of increasing complexity must be made using four to nine blocks having sides that are white, red, or half white and half red.

EXAMPLE:

10. OBJECT ASSEMBLY: Subject are provided with pieces of a puzzle. The pieces are made of hardened cardboard. Subjects must decide what the pieces represent and assemble them correctly.

EXAMPLE:

11. DIGIT SYMBOL: Nine symbols paired with nine digits are shown. Subjects must then pair the appropriate symbol with the correct digit in a long list of digits. The test is timed. Subjects who forget and have to look back at the pairings take longer to complete the test.

EXAMPLE:

Other researchers agree with Guilford that there are different kinds of intelligence, but disagree as to the number. Psychologist Howard Gardner, for example, has proposed that there are seven different kinds of intelligence (Gardner, 1983). Gardner's categories are quite broad in their definition of intelligence, including such aspects as social grace and athletic skill.

The view that there are different kinds of intelligence lies in direct contradiction to an idea proposed early in this century by Charles Spearman (1863–1945). Spearman argued that there was only one kind of general intelligence (*g*) and that g represented the amount of mental energy that a person could bring to bear on any given mental task (Spearman, 1927). A number of modern researchers also hold this view. Of course, because no one has been able to define intelligence adequately, no one is sure how many kinds of intelligence there may be—a state of affairs that plainly illustrates the difficulty of measuring intelligence (Weinberg, 1989).

Currently, this issue is unresolved. Two camps remain. There are the *lumpers,* who believe that all intelligence stems from one general ability, and the *splitters,* who argue in favor of many separate kinds of relatively independent intelligence (Mayr, 1982). There are even some who take a middle ground, arguing in favor of a hierarchical organization of specific skills stemming from only one or two factors (Horn, 1986).

THE TRIARCHIC THEORY OF INTELLIGENCE

After having studied the issues of intelligence and intelligence testing for many years, psychologist Robert J. Sternberg has reached a conclusion: Intelligence tests are simply too narrow. According to Sternberg, "Most psychologists and

COMPONENTIAL INTELLIGENCE
From Sternberg's triarchic theory of intelligence, that aspect of intelligence encompassing the cognitive problem-solving and information-processing skills measured by most IQ tests.

CONTEXTUAL INTELLIGENCE
From Sternberg's triarchic theory of intelligence, that aspect of intelligence encompassing the ability of the individual to adapt to his or her environment or culture.

EXPERIENTIAL INTELLIGENCE
From Sternberg's triarchic theory of intelligence, that aspect of intelligence encompassing the ability to take a newly learned skill and make it routine.

others who have studied intelligence have attempted to 'look inside the head' in order to understand the nature of intelligence" (Sternberg, 1985, p. 1111). By this he means that most intelligence tests rely solely on problem-solving skills and cognitive abilities, which is true. In fact, if the tests commonly used by Piaget to test children's cognitive development (see Chapter 2) are assembled and given as an "intelligence" test, they correlate quite well with the Wechsler Intelligence Test (Humphreys, Rich, & Davey, 1985).

In his book *Beyond IQ* (1984), Sternberg proposes an information-processing approach (see Chapter 9) to the study of intelligence, one that would encourage a step-by-step analysis of cognitive processes and be *applicable in any sociocultural context*. Toward this aim, Sternberg has developed a triarchic theory of intelligence that would account for what he argues are the two missing legs necessary to support the concept we call intelligence. This triarchic view of intelligence is far broader than the perspective that psychologists have traditionally accepted, and it may be more in line with what most people believe intelligence to be.

The first leg of the theory, of course, includes the cognitive problem-solving and information-processing skills measured by most IQ tests. This is what Sternberg calls **componential intelligence**—what the layperson might call "book smart" or "school smart."

The second leg concerns the ability of individuals to adapt to their environment or culture. This is known as **contextual intelligence**. For years, people have referred to this as "street smart," knowing the ins and outs, the angles, knowing how to get by in a given situation. Learning how to survive and do well in your cultural and social environment is important and, after all, is an intelligent thing to do. In fact, when Sternberg teaches his psychology graduate students, he likes to include contextual training, such as how to compete for a top job, or how to obtain the biggest financial grants, or how to publish in the journals that have the biggest circulation (and why it's smart to do so). Some of Sternberg's colleagues have argued that by discussing the "inside" ways to get ahead, he is covering the seedier side of office politics and that it is inappropriate. Sternberg argues that such inside contextual knowledge is important, that contextual intelligence can be learned, and that it's about time we recognize this fact.

The third leg is **experiential intelligence**. Sternberg argues that an important part of intelligence is the ability to take a newly learned skill and make it routine. We have phrases to describe this kind of intelligence, such as "learning from your mistakes" and "capitalizing on your experiences." People with this intelligence quickly develop expertise by making their newly acquired skills routine. By so doing, the mental tasks that once required thought become almost effortless or automatic.

Sternberg has developed a test to measure these three components (the Sternberg Multidimensional Abilities Test). Perhaps this new test will be better able to predict performance and to help individuals discover their weaknesses and identify ways to correct them than standard IQ tests can (Weinberg, 1989).

For Sternberg, as for most modern psychologists, intelligence is understood to be a series of skills—not something that you're born with, something that you either have or do not have. These skills, admittedly influenced by heredity, can be nurtured and developed as well. For this reason, correcting weaknesses in intelligence may well become an important part of applied psychology. Sternberg's book *Intelligence Applied* (1986) even provides a training program, based on the author's theory, to help individuals strengthen any or all of the three forms of intelligence he identifies.

Robert Sternberg.

HOW MUCH OF INTELLIGENCE IS INHERITED?

Your brain, your nervous system—indeed, your entire body—is made according to instructions received from the genes you inherited from your parents. It would seem reasonable that superior genes would endow a child with superior intellectual capacity. And in fact, researchers have discovered that parents with high IQs tend to have children with high IQs, while parents with low IQs tend to have children with low IQs.

This finding might appear to prove that intelligence is inherited. But does it really? Rich parents tend to have rich children, and parents who like tostadas and enchiladas tend to have children who like tostadas and enchiladas; it doesn't necessarily follow that these characteristics are carried by genes. Environment also can play an important role. Perhaps being raised by intelligent parents in a stimulating or intellectual home tends to increase a child's IQ.

Nature and Nurture

Genetics determines brain structure and differences within that structure, and obviously, brain structure is related to intellectual functioning. In fact, in one study, the brain sizes of young adults who had IQs above 130 were compared with the brain sizes of matched subjects (in terms of body size, gender, etc.) who had IQs that were slightly below the average of 100. An extremely sensitive imaging technique called **magnetic resonance imagining**, or **MRI**, was used to compare the brains of the two groups. Brain size and IQ were found to correlate +.35 (Willerman, Schultz, Rutledge & Bigler, 1991). What this means is that if we compared two women who were about the same physical size and age, we would expect the one with the higher IQ to have the larger brain. Psychologist Lee Willerman, who conducted this study, points out that those with higher IQs appeared to have more myelin in their brains, especially in areas of the brain associated with higher mental processes, which seems to account for the larger size of their brains. Young adults with lower IQs had brains that more closely resembled the less myelinated brains of older adults. Other studies have lent further support to this finding (Andreasen et al., 1993).

Psychologists often debate the importance of genetics in determining IQ. What you should remember is that intelligence is not just something children are born with—that they either have or don't have—but is rather an attribute greatly determined by the interactions between genetic inheritance, culture, and experience. This is true even in the case of something such as brain size, which at first glance may seem to depend solely on genetics. It may be, for instance, that the young adults with higher IQs in Willerman's study came from more stimulating homes where they were also provided with better nutrition. Either of these environmental factors may possibly lead to a greater production of myelin. If this were the case, larger brains to a great degree could be the result of environmental forces.

This example also helps us to understand that if some aspect of intelligence is inherited, it doesn't necessarily mean that that aspect, whatever it might be, is right there at birth and is rigidly fixed in the child and unchangeable from that point on. Because intelligence is determined by more than one gene, and because it is also a complex response to the environment, it doesn't follow Mendel's simple laws for the inheritance of traits (see Chapter 3). Richard Weinberg expressed this point when he said, "There is a myth that if a behavior or characteristic is genetic, it cannot be changed. Genes do not fix behav-

MAGNETIC RESONANCE IMAGING (MRI)
A technique that makes internal body structures clearly visible. It uses radio waves to excite atoms in the body, and the excitations, monitored by a huge magnet, are interpreted by a computer to produce a composite picture.

TWIN DESIGN

A research design used for sorting the influence of nurture from nature. A characteristic or behavior is compared between identical twins; then the same characteristic or behavior is compared between fraternal twins.

ADOPTION DESIGN

A research design used for sorting the influence of nurture from nature. Genetically related individuals who are reared apart or genetically unrelated individuals who are reared together are studied.

ior. Rather, they establish a range of possible reactions to the range of possible experiences that environments can provide" (Weinberg, 1989, p. 101).

Methods of Behavioral Genetics

There are two basic ways to study the inheritance of human intelligence. The first is the **twin design**, in which a characteristic or behavior is compared between identical twins and then between fraternal twins. The second method is the **adoption design**. Researchers who use this design study genetically related individuals who are reared apart or genetically unrelated individuals who are reared together. As you can see, these designs allow the effects of nature and nurture to be separately examined. It is not uncommon for both designs to be incorporated into a single study.

As an example of this kind of behavioral genetic research, consider the fact that relatives share many of the same genes, while unrelated people do not (which no doubt has some bearing on why relatives are related to each other and unrelated people aren't). Keeping this in mind, look at Table 10.1, and you'll see categories of related and unrelated people, with a correlation coefficient next to each. These correlations represent the relationship between the IQ scores of pairs of individuals within each category (the scores of two first cousins, of a parent and child, etc.).

Let's look at parents and their children to see how these correlations are derived. Each parent and his or her child are given an IQ test. Then a computation is made that allows these test scores to be compared with each other; each parent's score is compared with his or her own child's score. The more alike these compared scores are, the closer to +1.00 the correlation coefficient will be. A high positive correlation means that the test scores of the parents and their children are similar. We can predict from a positive correlation that if a parent's IQ is high, his or her child's is likely to be high, or that if a parent's IQ is low, his or her child's is likely to be low also. A correlation of zero, or near zero, indicates no relationship between the two scores. If that were the case, the parent's score would tell us nothing about the child's score. A correlation approaching −1.00 indicates an inverse relationship; that is, if one score is high, the other is likely to be low, and vice versa. As you can see, the actual correlation between parents and their children is +.40, a moderate positive correlation.

Table 10.1 ● Correlations of Intelligence Test Scores*	
CORRELATIONS BETWEEN INDIVIDUALS	**MEDIAN VALUE**
Genetically Related Persons	
Identical twins reared together	.86
Identical twins reared apart	.72
Parent—child	.40
Fraternal twins reared together	.60
Siblings reared together	.47
Siblings reared apart	.24
Half-siblings	.31
Cousins	.15
Unrelated Persons	
Nonbiological sibling pairs (adopted/adopted pairings)	.34
Adopting parent-offspring	.19

*Based on a study of 111 studies which reported on familial resemblances in intelligence.
Source: Adapted from Bouchard & McGue, 1981, p. 1056.

One of the areas of greatest interest in Table 10.1 is the "twins reared apart" category. It is rare for identical twins to be reared apart, but when they are, it provides an ideal chance to study the IQs of two people sharing the same genes but having different upbringing and experiences. As you can see from the table, identical twins reared apart have an even higher correlation than do siblings reared together (Segal, 1985). In the Minnesota Study of Twins Reared Apart, one of the most extensive studies of its kind, Thomas Bouchard and his colleagues at the University of Minnesota found the correlation for IQs among identical twins reared apart to range from +.69 to +.78 (strong positive correlations), depending on the IQ test used (Bouchard, Lykken, McGue, Segal, & Tellegen, 1990). In this survey, the researchers were careful to use only identical twins who were separated at infancy and who were raised in different environments. Identical twins reared apart were also found to show many other similarities, including shared aspects of personality and social attitudes. This has led Thomas Bouchard to say:

> For almost every behavioral trait so far investigated, from reaction time to religiosity, an important fraction of the variation among people turns out to be associated with genetic variation. This fact need no longer be subject to debate; rather, it is time instead to consider its implications. (Bouchard, Lykken, McGue, Segal, & Tellegen, 1990, p. 227)

At first glance, this result would seem to indicate that inheritance plays a greater role in the determination of IQ than the environment does. However, the "twins reared apart" category is not without problems. As you might imagine, it isn't easy to find twins who have been reared apart. In earlier studies, from which much of this table was developed, "reared apart" often turned out to mean that they were living next door to each other, or that they went to the same school, or that one was with the father and the other with the mother; and because married couples tend to have similar IQs, the "reared apart" environments may have been quite alike in terms of intellectual stimulation. Therefore, the "twins reared apart" category might be contaminated (in a research sense). If so, IQ similarities between identical twins reared apart could no longer be sorted in terms of heredity or experience, and researchers began to question these earlier data.

In an effort to overcome such problems, many rigorously sampled twins reared apart were studied for the Minnesota Study of Twins Reared Apart. These newer data tripled the current number of subjects in the "twins reared apart" category. Even so, some researchers are still concerned that there may have been some contamination of the "reared apart" category even in these new studies (Dudley, 1991). But Thomas Bouchard and his colleagues point out that they were very careful with their selections and that even if there were some contamination, there is no doubt that twins reared apart are far more alike along many dimensions than are siblings reared together and that this could not possibly be explained by shared environments (Bouchard, Lykken, McGue, Segal, & Tellegen, 1991).

Identical twins raised together have the highest correlations between their IQ scores.

The Texas Adoption Project

In one of the most detailed efforts to differentiate the effects of the environment and heredity, researcher Joseph Horn examined 300 adoptive families who had acquired their children at birth (Horn, 1983). He compared the IQs of these children with the IQs of both the adoptive mother and the biological mother. In all, 469 adopted children were tested. The results showed that the children's IQs were more strongly correlated with their biological mothers'

(+.28), even though the children had never met these women, than with the IQs of the adoptive mothers who had raised them, (+.15).

At first glance, it might appear that heredity is the most important factor in intelligence, but that is not the finding of the study. To begin with, the difference between correlations of +.15 and +.28 is very small, almost insignificant (Walker & Emory, 1985). Given these small correlations, the statistical analysis shows us that the biological mothers' IQs accounted for (or, in statistical terms, explained) only about 8 percent of the scores obtained by the adopted children. The IQ scores of the adoptive mothers explained only about 2 percent of their adopted children's IQ scores.* In other words, fully 90 percent of the variables that accounted for the children's IQ scores were unaccounted for, even after the contributions of both adoptive and biological mothers had been considered.

The unaccounted variables could include, among other things, the contributions of the fathers, both biological and adoptive. Assuming that the fathers contributed as much to the children's intelligence as the mothers, however, would still leave a large percentage of the variables unaccounted for. These variables may very well have to do with the children's environment—the environment beyond that supplied by exposure to the adoptive parents. These variables might include television, school, friends, and a host of other possible factors. Joseph Horn, who conducted the Texas Adoption Project, states unequivocally that he believes that IQ can be strongly affected by environmental factors (Horn, 1985).

The Texas Adoption Project also produced a surprise when the same children were retested after a 10-year interval. The researchers running the project discovered that

> the popular view of genetic effects as fixed at birth and environmental effects as changing has got matters almost backward, at least for the trait of intelligence in this population during these developmental years. . . . Especially provocative is the finding that genes seem to continue actively contributing to intellectual variation at least into early adulthood, whereas the effect of shared family environment appears to be largely inertial after early childhood. (Loehlin, Horn, & Willerman, 1989, pp. 1000–1001)

In other words, the influence that genetics was having on intelligence increased as these children aged, while the effects of environment decreased. Other studies support these data and yield estimates showing that by age 3, while the shared family environment accounts for about 70 percent of IQ correlations among twins, its influence decreases dramatically to 30 to 40 percent in middle childhood and drops to about 20 percent by age 15 (Wilson, 1983).

At first it may be difficult to see how genes could have a greater effect on the expression of intelligence the older a child gets. But remember what the authors of this research said about needing to break away from the idea that genetic effects are fixed at birth, expressing themselves only then and there. Perhaps an example from another field will help to clarify this apparent paradox. Consider the effectiveness of the heart at pumping blood when a person is resting. Among a population of 20-year-olds, environmental factors (exer-

---

*By squaring the correlation coefficient, you can derive what statisticians refer to as the explained variance. For example, Table 10.1 shows that siblings reared together have an average correlation of +.47 when their IQ scores are compared, and. +.47 × +.47 = +.2209, or, when rounded off, +.22, which equals 22 percent. This means that whichever variables are responsible for one sibling's IQ score, 22 percent of those same variables are responsible for the other sibling's test score. In other words, 22 percent of the variance has been "explained" (although we still may not know which variables, environmental or genetic, they are sharing). As you can see by using this formula, correlations such as +.28 or +.15 are really quite weak.

AT ISSUE

Birth Order and Intelligence

In 1986, Galton observed something intriguing about the order in which children were born. He noticed that an exceedingly large number of prominent British scientists were firstborn children. Since Galton's time, a number of studies have indicated that firstborn children have a distinct advantage in certain areas of development over other children (Koch, 1955). Firstborn children are more articulate and tend to score higher on intelligence tests than children born later. Firstborns also tend to be more reflective, whereas later children are more impulsive. When dealing with important choices, reflective children tend to examine a number of opinions and delay decisions so that they can minimize their errors. Impulsive children, on the other hand, are eager to rush to a solution when dealing with problems (Kagan, 1966).

Firstborn children also appear to have a greater need to achieve (Sampson, 1962), to be more active (Eaton, Chipperfield, & Singbeil, 1989), and to perform better academically (Altus, 1967). Firstborn children are more likely to attend college (Bayer, 1966) and have higher educational aspirations (Falbo, 1981). Interestingly, 21 of the first 23 astronauts to travel into space were firstborn children.

The meaning of these birth-order data is not clear. The answer may have something to do with the size of the family into which children are born. Perhaps firstborn children enjoy a more stimulating environment than do later children because they have the undivided attention of both parents.

Supporting this interpretation is the fact that firstborn children develop language rapidly, whereas twins develop language at a slower rate, and triplets more slowly still (Davis, 1937). Research has shown that twins tend to be short-changed by their parents because parents don't like to repeat themselves. In other words, a twin is likely to be spoken to less often because parents treat the twins as a unit rather than doubling their verbal interactions (Lytton, Conway, & Suave, 1977). Because IQ scores reflect verbal skills to a considerable degree, it would not be surprising if firstborn children tended to have higher IQ scores than twins—and they do. Furthermore, while firstborn children tend to have higher IQ scores than second children, second children also tend to have higher scores than third, third than fourth, and so on (Zajonc & Markus, 1975); in other words, children from families with many siblings tend to have poor verbal skills (Blake, 1989).

Zajonc and Markus have developed a model of intellectual climate designed to help predict the differences among the average intelligence scores in children from large and small families (see Table 10.2). In their model, the parents are each assigned a value of 30, and the children are assigned a value equal to their chronological age. These values are added and then divided by the number of family members. For example, a firstborn child would enter an intellectual climate equal to [30 (father) + 30 (mother) + 0 (baby)] ÷ 3 = 20. A child born to a single parent would be born into a intellectual climate of

Table 10.2 ● Zajonc-Markus Model of Intellectual Climate As Applied to a Large Family Over an 18-Year Period with Chidlren Spaced 2 Years Apart

YEAR OF BIRTH OF CHILD	NUMBER OF CHILDREN	VALUE OF INTELLECTUAL CLIMATE: FORMAL	RESULT
1975	1	$\dfrac{\text{mother (30) + father (30) + baby (0)}}{\text{number in family (3)}} =$	20.0
1977	2	$\dfrac{\text{mother (30) + father (30) + 2 yr old (2) + baby (0)}}{\text{number in family (4)}}$	15.5
1979	3	66 ÷ 5	13.2
1981	4	72 ÷ 6	12.0
1983	5	80 ÷ 7	11.4
1985	6	90 ÷ 8	11.3
1987	7	102 ÷ 9	11.3
1989	8	116 ÷ 10	11.6
1991	9	132 ÷ 11	12.0
1993	10	150 ÷ 12	12.5

AT ISSUE

Birth Order and Intelligence, continued

$(30 + 0) \div 2 = 15$. A second child with a 6-year-old brother would be born into a family with an intellectual climate of $(30 + 30 + 6 + 0) \div 4 = 16.5$. And so on. With this formula, Zajonc and Markus found close agreement between their values of intellectual climate and the average IQ scores among children in different-sized families.

For instance, the model predicts that the birth of a baby will reduce the average intellectual climate in the home. Researchers have since found that the birth of a baby does, in fact, appear to result in a slight decrease in the IQs of older siblings (McCall, 1984). This model has also been used to explain the decline in SAT (Scholastic Aptitude Test) scores among high school students prior to 1980 and the rise in scores following that time (Zajonc, 1986). Just prior to 1980, when test scores were low, a high percentage of later-born students were taking the test. That trend is now reversing, as many of the baby boomers' firstborn children are now in high school and taking the test. The model predicts that SAT test scores should continue to rise until the year 2000, level off, and then start to decline once again. Findings such as these help to validate the model (Berbaum & Moreland, 1985; Berbaum, Moreland, & Zajonc, 1986).

Changes in the average number of siblings per family are also expected to make a difference in the years ahead (Blake, 1989). For instance, in the 1930s, less than half of all children were reared in families with three or fewer siblings, and one-quarter were reared in families with seven or more. Today, for the first time in U.S. history, three-fourths of children are being reared in families with three or fewer siblings, and only 5 percent are being reared in families with seven or more.

The Zajonc and Markus formula for intellectual climate shown in Table 10.2 was developed for a family of up to 10 children spaced two years apart and shows the lessening of intellectual stimulation for children reared in larger families. Of special interest is the model's prediction that in such a large family, with children spaced two years apart, the intellectual climate actually *increases* for the eighth, ninth, and tenth children. This is because, by the time these last children arrive, older siblings are in their late teens and provide a more stimulating intellectual environment.

It's not easy to find a great number of eighth, ninth, and tenth children. However, one large study conducted in Israel, which included almost 200,000 subjects, closely fit the predictions made by the Zajonc-Markus model (Davis, Cahan, & Bashi, 1977). The Israeli researchers found that firstborn children scored highest on cognitive and intellectual mea-

sures, whereas second, third, and subsequent children showed progressively lower scores. However, this trend reversed after the seventh child.* Eighth children were found to have higher scores than seventh, ninth higher than eighth, and tenth higher still!

Extra attention may be helpful. On the other hand, there may not be great cause for concern, because the difference between firstborn and later children on IQ tests is generally only 3 or 4 points, which, in practical terms, is not significant. In addition, the fact that firstborn children tend to be more successful may be related to many other factors besides extra parental attention or stimulation. Larger families, for example, often are of lower socioeconomic status, and a later child, who is simply more likely to come from a poorer family, is more likely to be at an economic disadvantage than is an earlier child, who is more likely to come from a financially better-off family. For this reason, later children typically are found to have fewer opportunities made available to them. You may find more firstborn children among scientists or astronauts simply because, as firstborns, they were given opportunities that those born later were denied. Finally, it should be noted that not all scientists agree that there is a real or significant birth-order effect (Grotevant, Scarr, & Weinberg, 1975). Some studies have reported finding no such effect (Galbraith, 1982; McCall & Johnson, 1972). Nonetheless, studies that include large samples of subjects generally support the theory that birth order is related to achievement motivation and IQ test scores (Belmont & Marolla, 1973; Berbaum, Markus, & Zajonc, 1982; Berbaum & Moreland, 1985).

As you can see, the birth-order effect is at best a very subtle and small one, although it is interesting. Unfortunately, in just about any bookstore, you can find books claiming all sorts of fantastic things about birth order—books that tell you that first children act this way, middle children act that way, and last-born children act still another way. Many of these books—to boost sales, no doubt—treat birth order as though it were destiny itself, making ridiculous and extravagant claims about its effects. The birth-order effects described in this text are subtle, and as far as we know, that's all there is (Ernst & Angst, 1983). Books claiming to tell how any individual child will develop based solely on birth order are nonsense and should be treated as such.

*So much for Sinbad, the sailor, whose luck was said to stem from being the seventh son of a seventh son!

cise, diet, etc.) may play a greater role in heart efficiency than do genetic factors. It is simply rare for a 20-year-old to have a bad heart. By the time these same people are 80 years old, however, genetic factors will probably account more for their heart efficiencies than environmental factors. If you want to live a long time, exercise and diet are important, but nothing beats a great set of genes.

Similarly, genetic influences, for reasons yet unknown, play a greater role in intellectual variation among children as they grow older. And this leads us back to the ultimate question: Are genes more important than environment, or is it the other way around? The answer for now is that no one really knows, but the general consensus of over 1,000 psychologists is that both genes and environment play a major role (Snyderman & Rothman, 1987). If you pressed me for a current assessment as it stands today, I would say that on average, environment and inheritance each account for about 50 percent of the differences observed in intelligence as measured by traditional tests. This still leaves great room for the effects of environment. Even with our limited understanding of intelligence, we can often boost IQ 20 to 25 points with environmental intervention (Weinberg, 1989). And with advanced technology coming our way, we may be able to engage in genetic intervention sometime in the next century. Imagine finding the genes responsible for some of the variance of IQ and medically adjusting them in a living person to raise intelligence. Although it may sound like science fiction, there is a good chance that you will live to see it happen. In fact, a few years ago, the National Institute on Child Health and Human Development awarded psychologist Robert Plomin $600,000 to head a project to search for more than 100 genetic "markers" in the blood of over 600 schoolchildren in an effort to find alleles (see Chapter 2) associated with intelligence and giftedness. Plomin says that he expects the most interesting results to come from the blood of "the really smart kids [because] the only way to get high scores is if you've got everything going for you, including the positive alleles" (Holden, 1991, p. 1352).

CULTURE-FAIR TESTING

Any intelligence test that makes use of language is likely to be culturally biased. Consequently, people have attempted to produce language-free, **culture-fair tests** that would be equally difficult for members of any culture. The first such tests generally relied on pictures and nonverbal instructions, but these still tended to favor some cultures. Children in some cultures were simply more familiar with pictures or the requirements of certain tasks (Vernon, 1965). Still, some tests are self-explanatory and do not require pictures of familiar objects. One of the most widely used culture-fair tests is the Raven Progressive Matrices Test. In Figure 10.3, you will see a sample question from the Raven test. Even without instructions, you can understand what is required. But in this test, too, people from cultures in which fill-in or matching exercises are more common may have an advantage over people from other cultures. To date, no one test has been developed that is completely culture fair.

Over the years, researchers have tried to eliminate some cultural bias from tests that are given to large and diverse populations. Still, the concept of intelligence—and intelligence tests—remains fairly mysterious. For instance, researcher James Flynn examined IQ scores obtained from 14 nations around the world, all the way from the Netherlands to New Zealand, and discovered that there had been a significant jump in IQ scores from the last generation to

CULTURE-FAIR TEST
A test that is supposed to be free of cultural biases, usually constructed so that language differences and other cultural effects are minimized.

FIGURE 10.3

Sample item from the Raven Progressive Matrices Test.

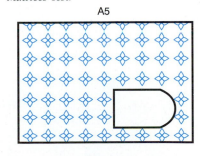

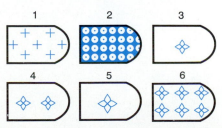

NATURAL SELECTION
The process, first suggested by Charles Darwin, through which those individuals of a species best adapted to their environment have a better chance of passing on their genes to the next generation than do those not as well adapted.

the current one, an increase ranging from 5 to 25 points (Flynn, 1987). No one knows why there should be such an increase. It can't be genetic, because the forces of **natural selection** couldn't have caused such a change in only 30 years. The real surprise was that the greatest gains occurred on the Raven test, which is purported to measure intellectual aptitude free of cultural bias. Clearly, culture-fair tests aren't culture fair. One researcher trying to solve this dilemma has argued that so-called culture-fair tests become easier if your culture has provided you with training, as many modern schools do, emphasizing intelligent guessing (which modern students exposed to multiple-choice testing often raise to an art form) and speed of thought (Brand, 1987).

THE EFFECTS OF ENVIRONMENTAL STIMULATION

One way to assess environmental influences on intellectual development is to alter the environment on purpose and then to observe the effect on IQ scores. Ethically, of course, it's proper to create only a stimulating environment in the hopes of raising IQ scores.

Project Head Start was designed in the 1960s to help disadvantaged preschool children do better in school as they grew older. At first, research results from the Westinghouse Learning Corporation and researchers at Ohio State University indicated that Head Start was making little difference in the long-term intellectual development of its children. However, researchers David P. Weikart and Lawrence J. Schweinhart released an interim report in 1980 on an 18-year study of the progress of 123 children at Perry Elementary School in Ypsilanti, Michigan, which indicated that good-quality preschool education does benefit the disadvantaged. The Ypsilanti Project offered 12½ hours of education per week at ages 3 and 4 years, plus 90-minute weekly home visits. Children in the enrichment program scored higher on reading, math, and language achievement tests than did those in the control group. They also showed fewer antisocial and delinquent tendencies (Williams & King, 1980a).

An executive report released in 1986 noted that although it was not known whether all Head Start programs in the United States were producing beneficial results, such results could be achieved if the programs were adequately funded and the teachers well trained and competent (Schweinhart & Weikart, 1986). Among the benefits are

> improved intellectual performance during early childhood; better scholastic placement and improved scholastic achievement during the elementary school years; and, during adolescence, a lower rate of delinquency and higher rates of both graduation from high school and employment at age 19. (Schweinhart & Weikart, 1985, p. 547)

A 20-year follow-up study of children from two American cities who were enrolled in Head Start, preschool, or no school during the school year 1969–70 showed that although the value gained from Head Start had diminished over the years, some benefit was still observed. The benefit gained, however, was somewhat comparable to the long-term value of preschools in general. The long-term benefits were obvious when those who had participated in preschool programs were compared with those who had had no school during that year, and this was especially true of members from the lowest socioeconomic group (Lee, Brooks-Gunn, Schnur, & Liaw, 1990).

There have been other programs like the Ypsilanti Project that have been effective (Gray & Ruttle, 1980; van Doorninck, Caldwell, Wright, & Frankenburg, 1981). A notable example of institutional enrichment can be found in

Israel, where children of European Jewish heritage have an average IQ of 105, while those of a Middle Eastern Jewish heritage have an average IQ of only 85. Yet when raised on a **kibbutz**, children from both groups have an average IQ of 115.

Early intervention projects have not been uniformly successful. Depending on the program, how it is implemented, and the population that receives the intervention, early intervention may produce many different outcomes. Programs with a high academic content are generally the most successful in producing increases in IQ and achievement (Miller & Dyer, 1975; Stallings, 1975). Special programs aren't always required to give an intellectual boost, however. For example, good-quality day care has been found to improve the intellectual development of socioeconomically disadvantaged children (Burchinal, Lee, & Ramey, 1989).

In summary, there is no clear-cut way to predict whether early intervention will be effective. Many programs claim success, but their work is often hard to assess because the criteria they use to define success and to define which children are needy often differ (Scarr & McCartney, 1988). The general consensus appears to be that early intervention can have lasting and valuable effects (Lazar & Darlington, 1982; Casto & Mastropieri, 1986), but there is no guarantee for any given program with any given group of children (Ramey, 1982; Woodhead, 1988).

KIBBUTZ

An Israeli farm or collective where children are often reared in groups and receive nurturance and guidance from many different adults and older children.

INTELLECTUAL CHANGES OVER TIME

Problems arise when IQ tests are used to measure intellectual changes during a life span. In the 1930s, Nancy Bayley developed a test called the Bayley Mental and Motor Scale to evaluate infants' intellectual and motor skills. Interestingly, subjects who were measured by the Bayley test when they were 9 months of age often had very different IQs when they were retested at 5 years of age with the Stanford-Binet IQ Test. In fact, the correlation between the two IQ scores was zero (Anderson, 1939), indicating that the infants' IQ scores at 9 months of age on the one test were totally unrelated to their IQ scores at 5 years on the other test. Table 10.3 shows the correlations obtained between the children's scores at various ages and the scores at 5 years.

The correlation between 9 months and 5 years was virtually zero because tests given at different ages often measure different abilities. Tests for very young children and infants generally emphasize motor skills, whereas tests for older children tend to emphasize verbal and cognitive skills. Yet both are said to measure intelligence.

A number of other tests were then designed to assess infants' intellectual development. They included the Griffiths Test of the Abilities of Babies (Griffiths, 1954), the Cattell Test of the Measurement of Intelligence of Infants and Young Children (Cattell, 1966), and the Bayley Scales of Infant Development (Bayley, 1969). As with the Bayley Mental and Motor Scale, these tests all failed significantly to predict what the IQs would be once the children reached school age (McGowan, Johnson, & Maxwell, 1981). Although such tests have some limited utility for describing the infant's current state, they simply cannot predict intellectual changes over a long time.

As Figure 10.4 shows, IQ scores don't tend to become consistent over time or reliable until children are about 10 years old. This means that IQ scores obtained from children younger than 10 years may not be reliable; they may change considerably as the children grow up.

Table 10.3 ● Correlation Between IQ Scores of 91 Children at Various Ages (Bayley Mental and Motor Scale) and Their Scores at 5 Years (*Stanford-Binet)

AGE	TOTAL CORRELATION COEFFICIENT
3 months and 5 years	.008
6 months and 5 years	−.065
9 months and 5 years	−.001
12 months and 5 years	.055
18 months and 5 years	.231
24 months and 5 years	.450

Source: Adapted from Anderson, 1939, p. 204.

Correlations between children's IQ scores at various ages and their IQ scores at maturity, according to several studies. (SOURCE: Bloom, 1964)

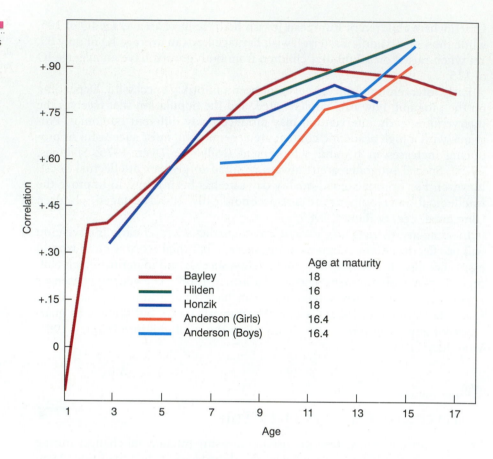

Psychologists have wondered if it might not be possible to develop an infant IQ test that would have scores well correlated with later intellectual performance. But unless there were some common denominator that could be measured in infancy that was also related to IQ in childhood, it would not be possible. And for a long time, it was believed that no such denominator was likely to be found. Slowly, however, this view has begun to change (DiLalla et al., 1990).

In one study, for example, 4-month-old infants were given both repetitive and new sounds to listen to. An intelligence score was developed based on how easily they recognized a new stimulus (measured by a change in heart rate) and how quickly they came to recognize a repeated stimulus as familiar. The children were followed until they were 5 years old and were then given the Stanford-Binet IQ Test. The correlation was an impressive +.60 (O'Connor, Cohen, & Parmelee, 1984). It was assumed that in this instance, a basic memory skill had been tapped.

Similar results have been obtained with the use of a visual habituation test developed by Joseph Fagan (see Figure 10.5) (Rose, Feldman, & Wallace, 1988). This test appears to be most useful with infants who are deemed at risk for retardation due to premature birth or other reasons. This test was used on 128 infants between 3 and 7 months of age, who were then retested with the Stanford-Binet at age 3 years. Fagan discovered that he was able to correctly predict 101 of the 104 children whose IQs would be within the normal range by age 3 and also predict fully half of the infants whose scores would be in the retarded range by that age (Bower, 1988). The test may also be able to predict certain memory and language abilities that are relatively independent of IQ (Thompson, Fagan, & Fulker, 1991).

FIGURE 10.5
The baby in this photograph is looking at pictures of two faces. One of those faces he has seen before; the other is new. The researcher is measuring how long the baby looks at each of the faces. Babies who spend less time looking at the familiar face tend to have higher scores on intelligence tests when they reach school age.

Overall, infant habituation tests are able to predict childhood IQ with some success, correlating with childhood IQ roughly at about +.36 by age 8 or 9 (McCall & Carriger, 1993).

Terman's Study

In 1921, psychologist Lewis Terman received a grant from New York City to conduct an extended longitudinal study of children with IQs above 140. Terman selected his 1,528 subjects from grade schools in California. Their average IQ was 150, and 80 of them possessed IQs of 170 or higher (Terman, 1925). Follow-up studies were conducted in 1922, 1927–28, 1939–40, 1951–52, 1960, 1972, 1977, and 1982. Terman strongly believed that intelligence, or giftedness, was an inherited quality. In fact, during his life, he often turned a blind eye toward any evidence that there was also a strong environmental component to IQ (Cravens, 1992). Even so, his data do tell us a lot about men who have high IQs.

Because few women were encouraged during the 1920s to seek professions, most of the follow-up studies of professional accomplishments concentrated on the approximately 800 men in the original selection. This is not to say that the Terman women didn't choose professions; many of them did, but there were few professional women in the average general population with whom to compare them. By 1950, at an average age of 40 years, the men had written and published 67 books, over 1,400 articles, and 200 plays and short stories; they had obtained over 150 patents; 78 of them had received a Ph.D., 48 an M.D., and 85 an LL.B; 74 were university professors, and 47 were listed in *American Men of Science*. As Terman noted, "The number who became research scientists, engineers, physicians, lawyers, or college teachers, or who were highly successful in business and other fields, is in each case many times the number a random group would have provided" (1954, p. 41).

Among the Terman women there were also some surprises. According to Pauline Sears, who reviewed the data, the Terman women

were way ahead of several trends that have only lately become true for the nation as a whole. They were quicker to join the work force. They took longer to marry and have children, and more were childless. A high proportion were in managerial positions; I

Lewis Terman.

suspect that because they were bright, they got ahead faster. Their brightness made another intriguing difference: the divorced women among them were happier than most, at least on our measure of satisfaction with their work pattern. Almost all divorced women worked full time, and their work was satisfying to them. The same was true of the women who remained single. All of them worked, and they were much happier with their work than most women are. Their satisfaction wasn't from income, either, but from the work itself. (Sears quoted in Goleman, 1980, p. 44)

Pauline Sears's late husband, Robert Sears, was in charge of overseeing the Terman study. Robert Sears was formerly head of the psychology department at Harvard and dean of Stanford University. He was also one of the 1,528 children in Terman's original study (Goleman, 1980).

The Terman "kids" are now in their late 70s and early 80s, and compared with the average person of that age, they are healthier, happier, and richer and have had a far lower incidence of suicide, alcoholism, and divorce. These studies also dispel the myth that genius is next to insanity, since few of the Terman subjects have suffered from serious behavioral disorders compared with the average populace.

A possible reason for high correlations between high IQ scores, and happiness, wealth, and low incidence of alcoholism or divorce may be that the subjects in Terman's study stayed in school (probably because they were good at it, which is what a high IQ would indicate). If you stay in school long enough and do well, you're likely to obtain an advanced degree. And generally, if you have an advanced degree, you'll earn more money. People who are richer tend to be happier (perhaps that doesn't surprise you). If you are better educated, wealthier, and happier, you probably can afford better medical care, are more aware of how to take good care of yourself, and are under less stress. Finally, happier people get divorced less often.

With these results in mind, one researcher studied 26 of Terman's subjects who had IQs of 180 or higher and compared them with 26 randomly selected subjects from the rest of Terman's sample, curious to see if this group did even better than the typical Terman subject. But the differences turned out to be negligible (Feldman, 1984). This finding helps to emphasize that extra IQ points needn't make an important difference, at least at the upper end of the scale. What did seem to make a difference for Terman's "kids" is that they all were at the upper end of the IQ spectrum.

CREATIVITY

Individual differences in intellectual capacity are not the only characteristics that have attracted interest in recent years. Psychologists are also concerned about the development of **creativity**. One researcher pointed out:

Some of the controversy about the concept of creativity surrounds the question of the extent to which it is a personality trait, a specific cognitive ability, or a type of problem-solving strategy that might be learned (Michael, 1977). If it is the latter, there is less need to search for those who know the process than to teach the process to everyone. (Fox, 1981, p. 1108)

Defining creativity is difficult, but we all seem to have some idea of what it means. Look at the picture in Figure 10.6 and decide what it is. A fairly common but rather uncreative answer is that it looks like a broken window. But what if someone told you that it was a boat arriving too late to save a drowning witch? That's a more creative response.

FIGURE 10.6

What do you see?

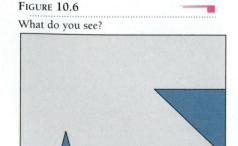

One way of defining creativity is to apply the four criteria of *novelty, appropriateness, transcendence of constraints,* and *coalescence of meaning* (Jackson & Messick, 1968). Novel, of course, means new. Something creative should be new. However, spelling *cat* Q-R-S would be new but it wouldn't be appropriate. Jackson and Messick therefore included appropriateness as a necessary dimension. Something transcends constraints when it goes beyond the traditional. A creative idea may transcend constraints by lending a new perspective to something with which we are all familiar. Finally, the most creative ideas have meanings that coalesce over time. In other words, the depth and value of an extremely creative idea often are not apparent at first, but become more obvious as time passes. When Thomas Edison first developed the motion picture projector, many people wondered why the great genius was wasting his time on something of so little value. It was only after some time that the full significance of the invention became apparent.

High creative ability is poorly predicted by IQ tests. Individuals with very similar IQs often differ considerably in their creativity (Torrance & Wu, 1981). This failure of IQ tests to predict creativity was investigated by Guilford and his colleagues in 1957. They believed that IQ tests typically measure a kind of intelligence different from that required for creativity. Two of the factors Guilford mentioned in his model of the intellect were **convergent production** and **divergent production**. Guilford argued that most IQ tests rely heavily on convergent production, in which people search their knowledge for all that they can find to help them converge on one correct answer. In divergent production, they use their knowledge to develop as many solutions as possible to a given problem. Figure 10.7 illustrates the difference between these two thought processes. Creativity, Guilford believes, relies more on divergent production (Guilford, 1983). If Guilford's view is accurate, then the ability to see many solutions to one problem is very different from the ability to develop one correct answer from a store of information.

The skills needed for both convergent and divergent production appear to be acquired, at least in part, through experience. In one study, 3- and 4-year-old children were given convergent games to play: blocks that had to be inserted into particular forms cut from a board. These children spent two-thirds of their time placing the pieces into the forms on the board. Another group of children, the divergent group, played with blocks only. Using the different block pieces, they engaged in a wide variety of activities. A third group, a control group, did not partake in either the convergent or the divergent games. After the play period, the divergent group performed better than did the other two groups on new divergent tasks, whereas the convergent group performed better than the other two on new convergent tasks (Pepler & Ross, 1981).

CREATIVITY
The ability to originate something new and appropriate by transcending common thought constraints.

CONVERGENT PRODUCTION
In Guilford's model of intelligence, a type of thinking in which an individual searches through his or her knowledge and uses all that can be found to converge on one correct answer.

DIVERGENT PRODUCTION
In Guilford's model of intelligence, a type of thinking in which a person searches for multiple ideas or solutions to a problem. It is characteristic of the creative thought process.

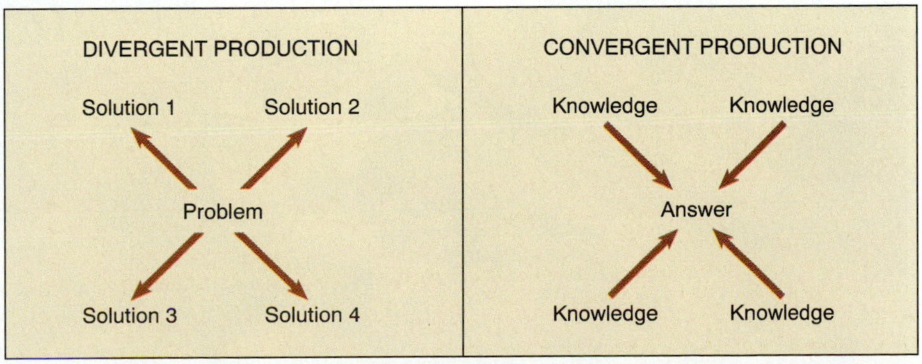

FIGURE 10.7
Divergent and convergent production.

IDEATIONAL FLUENCY
A term used by Michael Wallach to describe an individual's ability to produce many ideas. Ideational fluency is sometimes used as a measure of creativity.

Some tests have been designed to predict creativity by measuring divergent production. One such test, described by Michael Wallach (1970), employs the concept of ideational fluency. **Ideational fluency** is the ability to develop a large number of ideas appropriate to a particular task. To measure ideational fluency, researchers might ask someone to name as many uses as possible for a common object such as a cork or a shoe or to point out all the similarities between a train and a tractor. People with high ideational fluency produce many answers. Divergent production tests such as this one are much more accurate in their predictions of creativity than are IQ tests. In a study of almost 500 college students (Wallach & Wing, 1969), researchers found that ideational fluency correlated well with creative attainments such as receiving prizes in science contests, publishing original writing, or exhibiting artwork. Like IQ test scores, ideational fluency scores among older children appear to be fairly stable over time (Kogan & Pankove, 1972).

SOME FINAL THOUGHTS ON INTELLIGENCE

Biology is not democratic. Some of us are tall, some of us are short, and some of us are no doubt better biologically organized to develop skills considered indicators of intelligence. Inheritance is important. Yet, as the Ypsilanti Project showed, intelligence (or whatever it is that our "intelligence" tests measure) can be dramatically affected by the environment. Intelligence might best be considered a complex interaction between genetic heritage and experience. The Terman subjects probably did well in school, and therefore did well on IQ tests, which ask academic types of questions, because they inherited excellent brains and nervous systems and also because they were stimulated at home and school to learn and to develop their cognitive and intellectual skills.

IQ, CULTURE, AND ETHNIC DIVERSITY

A serious controversy concerning the heritable aspects of intelligence developed immediately after researcher Arthur Jensen published an article in the

Part of being creative includes the ability to transcend constraints, that is, to make something different, something unique.

1969 *Harvard Educational Review.* Jensen suggested that the reason whites scored higher than blacks on IQ tests by an average of 15 to 18 points was probably related more to genetic variables than to the effects of experience. In other words, Jensen was saying that whites were naturally intellectually superior to blacks. The ensuing debates on radio, on television, and in the press were stormy, usually generating more heat than light. In 1994, a book written by researchers Charles Murray and Richard Herrnstein, *The Bell Curve,* was published. In it, the authors reiterated the differences in IQ scores among different ethnic groups in the United States, including African, European, and Asian Americans. It, too, generated much controversy.

Cultural and Educational Bias

No one disputes that whites generally score higher than blacks on IQ tests. But this does not necessarily mean that Jensen, Murray, and Herrnstein were right. There are other interpretations. The kinds of observations that Jensen made were not new. In 1912, the U.S. Public Health Service gave the then-new IQ tests to immigrants arriving in New York. It was discovered that 87 percent of Russians, 83 percent of Jews, 80 percent of Hungarians, and 79 percent of Italians were feebleminded. It didn't matter to the supervisor of the testing, Henry Goddard, that many of the immigrants couldn't speak English. He was convinced that the tests were adequately translated to suit the immigrants. Unfortunately, a considerable knowledge of American culture was also necessary to score well; thus, 79 percent of the Italians tested were not feebleminded, but rather were ignorant of the answers to culturally biased questions.

When the United States entered World War I, the army administered the same IQ tests to all inductees. It was at this time that blacks were first tested in large numbers. Their average mental age was only 10.41, just behind recently immigrated Poles (10.74), Italians (11.01), and Russians (11.34). Of all those who were tested, including the recently naturalized immigrants, blacks were the poorest financially and were the least educated. In other words, educational bias may have influenced test scores. Because of inferior schooling, black children may have been less likely than white children to be exposed to the kinds of strategies and knowledge required by IQ tests. This interpretation, however, was not considered at the time. Instead, the army findings were commonly used to support unfounded racist beliefs that blacks were intellectually inferior.

A similar kind of educational bias may explain the fact that Japanese children tend to outscore white American children on IQ tests by about 7 points (Mohs, 1982). Although a few researchers believe that this, too, may be due to genetic differences, most point to the possible effects of the superior Japanese school system. The effect of schooling cannot be too strongly stated. IQ and schooling go hand in hand: Schooling boosts IQ (Cahan & Cohen, 1989), and IQ predicts school performance mostly because IQ tests are typically filled with the kinds of questions children encounter in school. Supporting this assertion is the interesting finding that the IQs of schoolchildren tend to make a small, but measurable decline just following summer vacation (Ceci, 1991) and typically lose up to 6 IQ points for each year of missed school. Considering that year after year, Japanese schoolchildren spend many more days in school than their American counterparts, the differences in IQ should not be surprising.

In an effort to shed some light on this issue, psychologist Sandra Scarr gathered data on the IQ scores of black children adopted and raised by white families. Scarr discovered that the younger the black children were at the time of adoption, the closer their scores were to the white IQ averages (Scarr & Weinberg, 1976). Similarly, the IQs of poor children increased when they were adopted by affluent families (Schiff, Duyme, Dumaret, & Tomkiewicz, 1982).

These results strongly suggest that background, experience, and culture can influence a person's knowledge and thought processes as measured by any particular intelligence test. Different cultures teach not only different things but also different ways to think about things. And different cultures require their children to meet different educational standards. As Jerome Kagan once said in reference to two of the best-known IQ tests, "If the Wechsler and Binet scales were translated into Spanish, Swahili, and Chinese and given to every ten-year-old child in Latin America, East Africa, and China, the majority would obtain IQ scores in the mentally retarded range" (1973, p. 89). Of course, these children wouldn't be mentally retarded in the commonly understood sense of the term, but they would be at a disadvantage in taking the tests until they learned to adapt to our culture. In this case, a low IQ score would represent cultural ignorance or lack of education, not lack of intelligence. Any of us would be at the same disadvantage if we took a test developed in another culture.

The Kaufman Assessment Battery for Children

The Kaufman Assessment Battery for Children (K-ABC) was developed by Alan and Nadeen Kaufman in the early 1980s, in part to eliminate black-white differences. While field-testing the K-ABC, the Kaufmans discovered that the test cuts the IQ differences between blacks and whites by 50 percent (to about 7 points) and eliminates the difference between white and Hispanic children. The Kaufmans argue that this is because the test reduces cultural and educational bias.

Initially, there were worries that the design of the K-ABC might result in its scores concealing important differences that should be exposed. In other words, it might appear to be fairer but in fact might be hiding serious educational deficits displayed by minorities who had been victims of discrimination, poverty, and poorer schools. The K-ABC, however, has been found to correlate well with achievement tests (Childers, Durham, Bolen, & Taylor, 1985; Valencia, 1985), which implies that the K-ABC distinguishes those individuals who have acquired knowledge from those who haven't, while at the same time avoiding a racial bias.

The K-ABC is just now coming into wider use. Eventually, we will be able to judge whether it has actually overcome some of the cultural bias that other tests include.

The Proper Use of Intelligence Tests

Ever since Alfred Binet first began to use intelligence tests to differentiate between normal and dull students in the Paris school system, there has been controversy over whether IQ tests are a valid measure of intelligence:

Intelligence tests have been under attack practically since their inception (Cronbach, 1975; Haney, 1981). Critics have claimed, among other things, that intelligence and aptitude tests measure nothing but test-taking skills, have little predictive power, are biased against certain racial and economic groups, are used to stigmatize low scorers, and are tools developed and fostered by those in power in order to maintain the status quo. . . . Though perhaps not as apparent as 10 (or 60) years ago, such criticisms remain prevalent (e.g., Gould, 1981; Lewontin, Rose, & Kamin, 1984; Owen, 1985). (Snyderman & Rothman, 1987, p. 137)

The following case study illustrates the problem. Some time ago, when Gregory Ochoa was a high school student in California, he and his classmates, most of whom also had Spanish surnames, were given an IQ test. The result of the testing was that Gregory was placed in a special class. Gregory didn't fully realize what this would mean. All he knew was that his special class didn't do regular schoolwork. Any class member interested in intellectual pursuits, such as going to the school library, was told that such activities were out of bounds.

Gregory soon dropped out of school. He was sent to reform school, where he received some remedial reading. After finishing reform school, he joined the navy. There Gregory earned high school credits, which eventually enabled him to attend college as a student on probation. In college, he received high grades and graduated with honors—while *still* on probation! He believes that this occurred because the college never stopped thinking of him as "retarded." By the time he was 40, Doctor Gregory Ochoa was an assistant professor at the University of Washington in Seattle, where he taught classes in social case work.

Ochoa's problems in school had started when he was given his first IQ test and was placed in a special class for no other reason than that his IQ test score was low. No one considered that cultural differences might have played a role in his low score. He was lucky to have received remedial training; other children with low IQ scores were not so lucky.

This ongoing problem finally reached the courts in the 1970s. Larry P., like Gregory Ochoa, was a student in California who had been placed in a special class as a result of his low score on an IQ test. In the court case *Larry P. v. Wilson Riles,* it was argued that IQ tests should no longer be used to assign students to such "special" classes. The prosecutor maintained that a disproportionate number of blacks such as Larry P. had been wrongly assigned to special classes for the mentally retarded because of nothing more than their IQ scores. In these classes, they were taught little. Furthermore, assignment to such classes stigmatized them. A federal appeals court agreed, and IQ tests were no longer allowed to be used for this purpose.

The case of Larry P. was somewhat offset by the ruling of a federal district judge in 1980 in *PASE v. Hannon.* In that case, a federal district court judge in Illinois ruled that IQ tests could still be used to place minority students in special education classes *as long as other factors* were considered when placing the students. That ruling applies to only federal law, however. The states are still free to ban IQ testing based on their own laws or constitutions, and California is one of those states where IQ tests cannot be administered to students for identifying or placing them in special education (Landers, 1986).

This, of course, has left the schools with a problem—to find alternative assessment devices that are valid and can indicate the need for special help. These include assessments of the pupil's past personal history, adaptive behavior, classroom performance, and past academic achievement and use of instruments designed to point out specific deficits in specific skill areas. Unfortunately, these assessment devices have been shown to be even less valid indicators of future academic achievement than IQ tests, and psychologists and educators are therefore left with the requirement of identifying pupils in need of special help but with few valid ways of doing so.

In a survey of over 1,000 professionals with expertise in intelligence testing, most were found to favor the continued use of intelligence tests at their present level (Snyderman & Rothman, 1987). But the question remains: Can the tests be used without being misused? In the words of Gregory Ochoa,

I think first of all, one would have to ask why you want to know what this person's intellectual capacity is. Are you using it in order to make sure that every horizon available to him is reached, or are you using it to diminish his opportunities or to prove to him, or to oneself, that Blacks, or Chicanos, or other minorities are inherently inferior to others. I think that is the critical issue—what is it being used for? ("The IQ Myth," 1975)

Summary

- The first scientific interest in intelligence and intelligence testing can be traced to the inheritance theories of Sir Francis Galton.
- In the modern view, intelligence is an interaction between inherited capacity and environmental influences.
- In 1905, Alfred Binet and Theodore Simon developed the precursor to the modern intelligence test. Its purpose was to determine which Parisian school-children should receive special education.
- Binet developed the concept of mental age (MA). By comparing mental age with chronological age (CA), Binet was able to make comparisons among children. The German psychologist L. William Stern developed the formula $IQ = MA/CA \times 100$, which yielded a rough index of how bright or dull any child was compared with school peers.
- Although we have IQ tests, intelligence itself has never been defined adequately, and there is controversy over whether these tests measure intelligence as most people use the term.
- A test is said to be valid if it measures what it claims to measure. IQ tests have been found to be valid for predicting school performance and as tools in clinical assessment.
- The amount of weight, or emphasis, given to any one ability measured on a test is called a factor load. Some IQ tests measure particular factors more than others do. For this reason, the same individual may score differently on different IQ tests.
- To balance a test for factors so that each ability is tested only once, L. L. Thurstone advocated use of a technique called factor analysis.
- According to Thurstone and other factor analysts, there is no general ability called intelligence; rather, there are many different kinds of intelligence. The debate over this issue continues today.
- Psychologist Robert J. Sternberg has developed a triarchic theory of intelligence that includes componential intelligence, contextual intelligence, and experiential intelligence.
- Psychologists have studied the heritability of human intelligence and other characteristics by examining people who are related to one another. Based on current data, many psychologists agree that heredity does play a role in determining individual differences and intelligence. How important it is in comparison with environmental experiences has yet to be determined.
- Attempts have been made to devise a culture-fair test, one that contains no cultural bias. However, even on tests that do not use language, an advantage will go to people from cultures incorporating any types of skills or activities required by the test.
- The Ypsilanti Project and home-based early intervention projects have generally been successful in raising the intellectual levels of the children who participated.
- Intellectual changes are difficult to measure over time. Tests measure different skills in subjects of different ages; as a result, reliability is not always high.
- Lewis Terman conducted a study that has surveyed gifted children for over 70 years and is still in progress. The Terman kids are now in their 70s and 80s, and compared with the average person of that age, they are healthier, happier, and richer, and they have a far lower incidence of suicide, alcoholism, and divorce.
- Jackson and Messick have judged creativity by four criteria—novelty, appropriateness, transcendence of constraints, and coalescence of meaning. High creativity is poorly predicted by IQ tests.

■ Some tests have been designed to predict creativity by measuring divergent production. One such test, described by Michael Wallach, employs the concept of ideational fluency, or an individual's ability to produce many ideas.

■ According to researcher Arthur Jensen, the fact that whites generally score higher than blacks on IQ tests was mainly the result of genetic variables. Other people argue that cultural bias on the tests accounts for the discrepancy.

■ In one study, Scarr and Weinberg gathered data on the IQ scores of black children adopted by white families. They discovered that the younger the black children were at the time of adoption, the closer their IQs were to white IQ averages.

QUESTIONS FOR DISCUSSION

1. How would you define *gifted?* How would you discover whether your definition was valid?

2. Think of intelligent people whom you know well. What unintelligent things do they do? All of them are bound to do some unintelligent things, so why did you consider them to be intelligent people? Were you emphasizing some factors at the expense of others?

3. Did you ever consider that your class might be filled with people of tremendous potential? There might be a world-class archer, a great poet, a magnificent violinist, and a great president. However, the archer never happened to try the bow, the poet never tried writing, the violinist ignored music, and the president never ran for office. Instead, they worked at other things and weren't very good. They all think of themselves as failures, although they would have been successful if they had only tried these other things.

What argument is being made by these statments? How would the concept of a general intelligence refute this argument?

SUGGESTIONS FOR FURTHER READING

1. Anastasi, A. (1988). *Psychological testing* (6th ed.). New York: Macmillan.

2. Chapman, P. D. (1988). *Schools as sorters: Lewis M. Terman, applied psychology, and the intelligence testing movement. 1890–1930.* New York: New York University Press.

3. Fancher, R. E. (1985). *The intelligence men: Makers of the I.Q. controversy.* New York: Norton.

4. Lazar, I., & Darlington, R. (1982). *Lasting effects of early education: A report from the Consortium for Longitudinal Studies.* Monographs of the Society for Research in Child Development, 47(2-3, Serial No. 195).

5. Lewontin, R. C., Rose, S., & Kamin, L. J. (1984). *Not in our genes.* New York: Pantheon Books.

6. Minton, H. L. (1988). *Lewis M. Terman: Pioneer in psychological testing.* New York: New York University Press.

7. Sternberg, R. J. (1986). *Intelligence applied: Understanding and increasing your intellectual skills.* New York: Harcourt Brace Jovanovich.

8. Terman, L. M., & Oden, M. H. (1959). *The gifted group at midlife.* Palo Alto, CA: Stanford University Press.

CHAPTER 11

Middle Childhood: Personality and Social-Emotional Development

Learning to Be Helpless

*During middle childhood, many attitudes are formed and many behaviors are learned. Some of these attitudes and behaviors persist to become part of the child's later personality and adult lifestyle. Some of these behaviors are desirable; others are not. One undesirable learned behavior that might persist is known as **learned helplessness**.*

It's possible to teach an animal to become helpless. Dogs trained to avoid a shock by jumping from one side of a box to another will soon give up jumping when the shock is applied to both sides of the box. And no wonder—there is no escape once both sides are electrified. The more interesting outcome is that the dogs rarely try again to avoid the shock. When the electric current on the far side of the box is turned off, affording the dogs an escape if they would only try, the dogs will simply stay where they are, suffering the shock when it comes. They never discover that the other side is now safe. They have given up (Seligman & Maier, 1967).

Animals will also generalize learned helplessness to new situations. When placed in water-filled mazes, rats who had previously learned to be helpless will stop swimming and will drown if not rescued. Rats who have not learned to be helpless will complete the swim to safety (Altenor, Kay, & Richter, 1977).

Children can also learn to be helpless. Researcher Carol Dweck and her colleagues have examined the learning of helplessness among school-age children (Dweck, 1975; Diener & Dweck, 1980; Dweck, 1986). They identified schoolchildren who had learned to be helpless and who subsequently generalized their helplessness to new situations. They found that those schoolchildren who attributed their failure at a task to a lack of competence were much more likely to respond in a helpless fash-

LEARNED HELPLESSNESS
Giving up even though success is possible because of previous experience with situations in which success was impossible.

ion on subsequent tasks than were children who attributed their failure to a simple lack of sufficient effort (Dweck & Reppucci, 1973).

As a result of their research, Carol Dweck and her colleagues designed a program to help alleviate this learned helplessness (Dweck, 1975). Dweck found that the best way to change helpless behavior in children was to help children relearn to attribute their failure at a task to nothing more than their own lack of sufficient effort. Accomplishing this, however, required more than simply giving the children problems in which they would be successful. In fact, it was important to include tasks at which the children would fail and then to teach them new attitudes:

> An instructional program for children who have difficulty dealing with failure would do well not to skirt the issue by trying to ensure success or by glossing over failure. Instead, it should include procedures for dealing with this problem directly. This is not to suggest that failure should be included in great amounts or that failure per se is desirable, but rather, that errors should be capitalized upon as vehicles for teaching the child how to handle them. (Dweck, 1975, p. 684)

In this chapter, we'll examine the school-age child's personality and social-emotional development. Along the way, we'll study important behaviors and attitudes such as learned helplessness, which may be learned in childhood and continue into adulthood. We'll study the effects that families and peers have on the developing child. We will also have a chance to see how schools and television influence children.

PERSONALITY DEVELOPMENT IN MIDDLE CHILDHOOD

During middle childhood, children's personalities become increasingly complex and more like that of their future adult selves. According to Erik Erikson, during this time the psychosocial conflict to be resolved is *industry versus inferiority*. During this period of development, Erikson argued, children should be encouraged to produce things and complete the activities they have initiated. Through such efforts, they attain a sense of industry. Erikson believed that failure to be successfully industrious will lead to feelings of inferiority. The conflict between industry and inferiority becomes especially strong among schoolchildren, who are often in competition with their peers. As we saw in the Chapter Preview, children who fail can even learn to be helpless, which can lead to a negative self-concept and peer rejection.

Self-Concept Tasks of Middle Childhood

Children face a number of tasks as they enter middle childhood. Researchers Hazel Markus and Paula Nurius have described four areas in which children must refine and improve their self-concept: (1) developing a relatively stable and comprehensive understanding of the self; (2) refining their understanding of how the social world works; (3) developing standards and expectations for their own behavior; and (4) developing strategies for controlling or managing their behavior (Markus & Nurius, 1984).

Self-Understanding. The school-age child has come a long way from the rudimentary self-concept acquired between the ages of 2 and 3 years. This

> self-understanding now also includes some awareness of more achieved characteristics, such as values, norms, enduring goals, ideals, future plans, and strategies. . . . A key feature of this period is an increasing sensitivity to the needs and expectations of others and to the knowledge of the self that comes from them. (Markus & Nurius, 1984, p. 151)

Children change their view of themselves during middle childhood. As children grow older, their self-concept goes from the concrete to the more abstract (Livesly & Bromley, 1979; Rosenberg, 1979). "While young children are quite likely to confuse the terms *body*, *self*, *mind*, and *brain*, the 8-year-old child begins to appreciate that a mind is separate from the body and has control over behavior" (Markus & Nurius, 1984, p. 155). For example, children begin to understand that they can fool themselves, or that they can talk themselves into doing or saying one thing while they are thinking another thing (Selman, 1980).

In middle childhood, many children's feelings of self-esteem are related to their success or failure in school (Epps & Smith, 1984; Markus & Nurius, 1984). As we saw in the Chapter Preview, children who learn to be helpless can carry this legacy of helplessness into their future lives, to the detriment of their self-esteem. Children who learn to attribute their success or failure to the amount of effort they expended on a task, however, are more likely to succeed in the future (Dweck, 1975) and may therefore be less likely to have negative self-esteem.

Social Roles. School-age children begin to acquire a better understanding of the complexities of other people's social roles, including the fact that people can have many different social roles. For example, they can understand that the same person can be both a father and a son or that someone can be both nice and mean (Fischer, Hand, Watson, Van Parys, & Tucker, 1986).

As children enter the period of concrete operations (see Chapter 9), they begin to appreciate that other people's viewpoints may be different from their own. A child who engages in **social role taking** during this period can appreciate that any two individuals who experience an event may interpret it differently. In other words, the child now knows that "knowledge" does not lie in the event itself, but rather is symbolic and resides within the observer's own perceptions.

Standards and Strategies for Self-Control. School-age children begin to integrate the standards of their society into their own personal system. As they do this, they come to acquire control over themselves and begin to use increasingly sophisticated strategies to achieve this self-control. The kinds of strategies used by children appear to follow an age-related progression that is tied to the child's cognitive development (Mischel & Mischel, 1979).

For example, you may recall from the Chapter 8 Preview that preschoolers who are given the choice of waiting for a big reward later or taking a little reward now are very unlikely to wait (Mischel & Ebbesen, 1970). Preschoolers in this kind of situation make waiting more difficult by using a poor delaying strategy. They focus their attention on the smaller reward that they could have right now. As a result, they often give in to their immediate desire (Yates & Mischel, 1979). By the third grade, however, children have become aware of some effective delay strategies. For example, some children advocate not looking at the little reward. Some children make waiting easier by reminding themselves over and over again that if they wait they will receive the big reward, but if they don't wait they will receive only the small one.

SOCIAL ROLE TAKING
The act of taking or understanding the perspective of another.

Although school-aged children show an increasingly sophisticated use of self-control strategies, sometimes (as is the case with adults) the strategies just don't work.

By the time children reach sixth grade, their strategies may be fairly sophisticated. For instance, in one experiment some of the older children used the effective delay strategy of thinking of the reward (marshmallows) as round or white (neutral attributes) instead of as sweet or fluffy (positive attributes), as the younger children often did (Mischel, 1979).

SOCIAL-EMOTIONAL DEVELOPMENT IN MIDDLE CHILDHOOD

During middle childhood, many institutions have an influence on a child's socialization. Among them are the family, peers, school, and even television. Whereas preschoolers rely mostly on their parents for information about the world, school-age children have much wider and varied social interactions, partly because of increased autonomy, and partly because of increased competencies. Figure 11.1 outlines the amount of time spent by school-age children at various tasks. As you can see, the most common activities of children in this age-group are sleeping, going to school, and watching television.

During this formative time, however, there are some situations that can have a negative effect on the child's development. Divorce is one such situation.

Divorce and One-Parent Families

Divorce rates in the United States have increased dramatically in the past 30 years. According to current assessments, 40 to 50 percent of marriages among young people will end in divorce. Of the children born in the 1980s, almost 50

FIGURE 11.1

Amount of time that school-age children spend per week at various tasks. (SOURCE: Adapted from Collins, 1984, p. 18)

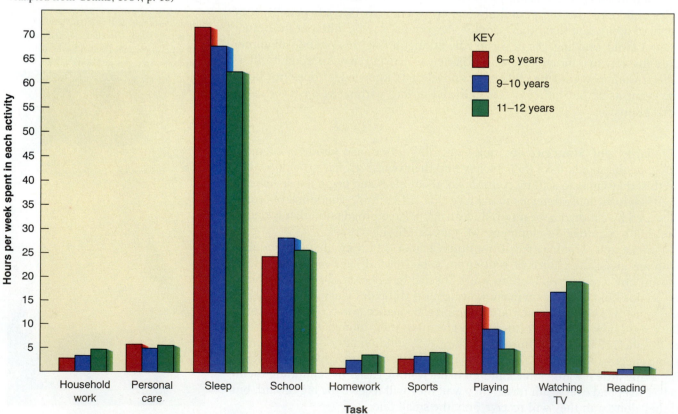

percent spent an average of 5 years in one-parent households (Hetherington, Stanley-Hagan, & Anderson, 1989).

The number of single-parent families has increased more than 400 percent since 1970. As of 1990, 50 percent of all children under 18 years of age were spending some time in a single-parent household as the result of divorce or separation.

Because 80 percent of men and 75 percent of women eventually remarry, 25 percent of all children will spend some time as a member of a step family before they are 18 years of age (Hetherington, 1989; Bureau of the Census, 1993). Thus, the period of transition and disequilibrium for children following a divorce can continue for a considerable time, since they must become accustomed to stepparents and to new environments. Sadly, of the 75 to 80 percent of divorced parents who do remarry, more than half will get a second divorce (Hetherington, 1989). Divorce rates are accelerating too quickly for longitudinal data on these changes to be available yet, and very little is known about the effects of a second divorce on children.

Joint Custody.   It used to be common practice following a divorce to award sole custody of the children to the mother. It was believed to be in the best interest of the children and occurred in about 90 percent of all cases. Although little was said about it, fathers often suffered severely from this practice (Meredith, 1985).

Now most states provide for an arrangement known as **joint custody**. Unlike sole custody, joint custody ensures that both parents have access to their children. It also provides the parents with an opportunity to share in the responsibility of raising the children. With joint custody, both parents can take part in important decisions, such as schooling and medical care. In fact, it has been found that fathers with joint custody are more likely to maintain a high degree of involvement with their children and are more likely to provide economic support (Grief, 1980; Meredith, 1985). Parents who choose joint custody generally work out agreements that better cover their children's needs than when sole custody is awarded (Phear et al., 1983).

Sometimes, however, joint custody isn't the best solution, especially when parents won't cooperate with each other (Atwell, Moore, Nielsen, & Levite, 1984). In a study of over 100 children of divorcing parents in which custody was being bitterly contested, access to both parents was often found to increase the child's emotional distress (Johnston, Kline, & Tschann, 1989).

Children's Initial Reaction to Divorce.   The largest data source concerning the effects of divorce on children comes from the Virginia Longitudinal Study, conducted by E. Mavis Hetherington. Hetherington discovered that at first, most children respond with anger, fear, and shock. It is also common for children to feel guilty about or in some way responsible for the divorce and to become withdrawn and depressed (Hetherington, 1979; Kalter & Plunkett, 1984). Still, most children can adapt to a divorce within a couple of years; if the crisis is aggravated by additional stresses or conflicts, however, serious developmental disruptions may result.

Whether children fare well may depend on their past experience, their age, and the support they receive from their parents (Hetherington, 1989). Parental support often is lacking, however, because parents become so wrapped up in their own problems during a divorce that their ability to function as parents diminishes (Wallerstein & Kelly, 1975, 1976, 1981; Wallerstein, 1985).

Temperament can also play an important role in the child's ability to adjust to a divorce. Temperamentally, children labeled as "difficult" (see Chapter 5)

JOINT CUSTODY
An arrangement in which more than one person shares legal custody of a child.

have been found to be more vulnerable to the stress of a divorce than "easy" children (Hetherington, 1989). This may be because difficult children are more likely to elicit anger and hostility from parents who are already under considerable stress because of the divorce.

The Stress of Divorce.   There are many stresses associated with the divorce of one's parents (Hetherington et al., 1992). The child's bedtime and eating schedules may be disrupted. The parents' emotional state and the lessening of adult contact are likely to place stress on the child. Also, the level of income in the household usually decreases, which accounts for a significant portion of the stress that children encounter following a divorce (Guidubaldi & Perry, 1985). In fact, about 45 percent of mothers who have custody of their children following a divorce report an annual income of less than $10,000 per year (Hernandez, 1988), which is well below the poverty level. Ex-husbands who fail to pay child support are often partly to blame for this state of affairs (Haskins, Schwartz, Akin, & Dobelstein, 1985).

A lower income often forces the parent to move, which in turn may cause the child to lose close friends and neighbors. In addition, the child may have to change schools or move to a neighborhood that has a higher rate of crime and delinquency (Tessman, 1978). Furthermore, if the mother is forced to take a job, the child may now feel abandoned by both parents. This is especially true for preschool children (Hetherington et al., 1982). As you can see, divorce is not a single event but a complex series of transitions requiring considerable adjustment.

Gender Differences.   Generally, girls are better able to cope with the effects of divorce than boys (Guidubaldi & Perry, 1985; Hetherington, 1989). Following a divorce, boys usually have more behavior disorders and problems relating to others. The reason may be that in 90 percent of divorces that do not involve joint custody, the mother still receives custody (Hetherington, Stanley-Hagan, & Anderson, 1989). The children "lose" their fathers, and boys are usually more attached to their fathers than girls are. The extra difficulties associated with boys may also stem in part from the fact that mothers who have custody of their sons may expect greater discipline problems from them because the fathers are absent, and they may try to forestall such problems by being stricter with them than they are with their daughters. In general, mothers tend to view their sons more negatively after a divorce than they do their daughters (Santrock & Tracy, 1978).

Girls, however, often have a more difficult time than boys adjusting to a remarriage (Hetherington, 1989; Vuchinich, Hetherington, Vuchinich, & Clingempeel, 1991). No one is sure why this is. Hetherington has argued that it might be because

> daughters in one-parent families have played more responsible, powerful roles than girls in nondivorced families and have had more positive relationships with their divorced mothers than have sons. They may see both their independence and their relationship with the mother as threatened by a new stepfather, and therefore resent the mother for remarrying. (Hetherington, 1989, p. 7)

The effect is apparently quite a strong one, because as Hetherington notes about the girls in her study whose mothers had remarried, "No matter how hard stepfathers tried, their stepdaughters rejected them" (Hetherington, 1989, p. 7). Sons, however, are more likely to view the stepfather as a source of support, a companion, and a role model (Vuchinich, Hetherington, Vuchinich, & Clingempeel, 1991).

Long-Term Effects of Divorce on Children.   In a 10-year study of over 130 children of divorce, researcher Judith Wallerstein found that the effects of a divorce can last a long time (Wallerstein, 1984a, 1984b, 1985). Even after 10 years, the young men and women she interviewed typically perceived the divorce as the most stressful event in their lives. Many felt that they had missed something important by not growing up in a family with both parents. Many were angry because of their parents' extramarital affairs and were determined to avoid such experiences in their own future marriages. (Unfortunately, research indicates that children from divorced families are themselves more likely to become divorced.)

Although many researchers have noted that boys typically react more severely at the beginning of the divorce, Wallerstein found that after 10 years, it was the girls who seemed to face the most difficulties. Many were afraid to make a commitment and feared betrayal and rejection by men. They were more likely to become involved in sexual relationships of shorter duration, occasionally with older men. Another interesting finding was that children of divorced parents had formed closer relationships with their siblings 10 years following the divorce.

Children and One-parent Families.   Considering how stressful divorce is for children, you might wonder if parents should make every effort to stay together, rather than get a divorce. Years ago it was a common belief that parents should do anything to "stay together for the kids." But research has consistently shown that children are better off in single-parent families than in stressful families in which parents are in continual conflict with each other (Hetherington, Cox, & Cox, 1978). Divorce in certain instances may also be helpful in putting distance between a disturbed parent and a child (Wallerstein, 1985). Also, it's been found that children, especially boys, often become more aggressive and uncontrollable many months, sometimes even years, before a separation or divorce as compared with children whose parents have no desire to separate (Block, Block, & Gjerde, 1986; Cherlin et al., 1991). These findings indicate that predivorce marital stress may be having a significant influence on children's development.

Although many children fare well in single-parent families, the chances of problems increase. Whether children in single-parent families have adjustment problems may depend greatly on the community support services available to the parent, such as day care or financial aid.

Single parents often find it particularly helpful to be relieved of the burdens of parenting 24 hours a day or to receive added financial support to make ends meet. Any warm, structured, and predictable environment, whether a day-care center, school, or extended family, can be of great help to children suffering the turmoil of divorcing parents (Hetherington, Stanley-Hagan, & Anderson, 1989). One study even found that when medical and social services, including day care, were provided for single parents, beneficial effects were evident even a decade after the support had ended (Seitz, Rosenbaum, & Apfel, 1985); the single mothers receiving the help had children with better school attendance and were themselves more likely to be self-supporting, to attain a higher education, and to maintain a smaller family when compared with mothers in a control group who did not receive support. Furthermore, the mothers and children in the study's control group (who had not received the services) required far more financial assistance when the children reached early adolescence than did the mothers who had received help. This shows that failing to provide early help for single parents may be more costly in the long run.

PEER GROUP
A group that develops its own set of values and goals and establishes durable social relationships. Generally, each member has a specified role or status.

Peer Relationships

For the school-age child, peer relationships both in and out of school become extremely important. Being accepted by one's peers and belonging to **peer groups** are major concerns (Zarbatany, Hartmann, & Rankin, 1990).

Between the ages of 7 and 9 years, children generally form close friendships with peers of the same sex and age (Roopnarine & Johnson, 1984). After the eighth grade, however, it is not uncommon for adolescents to have friends of the opposite sex as well (Buhrmester & Furman, 1987).

The older children become, the more likely they are to share with friends (Berndt, Hawkins, & Hoyle, 1986) and the more they come to value friends according to their personal attributes. For instance, one study found that whereas 5½-year-old children might be more interested in making friends with another child who had a new game or toy, 9-year-old children were more interested in making friends with another child because "he's real nice" (Boggiano, Klinger, & Main, 1986). Throughout the school years, children also rely on their peers as important sources of information and may use peers as standards by which to measure themselves. By the age of 7 or 8 years, children tend to look to their peers as models of behavior and for social reinforcement as often as they look to their own families. Research also has shown that by the fourth grade, children have come to rely on friends as an important source of social and moral support (Berndt & Perry, 1986).

Peer Acceptance.   The kinds of behaviors accepted or rejected by a band of children can vary greatly from one group to the next. Some peer groups reinforce aggression, whereas others promote cooperation. Peer groups may be as diverse as a gang of 13- or 14-year-old adolescents that reinforces killing and a local Boy Scout troop that reinforces social and achievement-oriented skills. Nonetheless, we can make several general statements about peer acceptance or rejection.

Among grade school children, peers who are rejected tend to behave in ways that are more aggressive and *inappropriate* than do peers who are accepted (Dodge, Coie, Pettit, & Price, 1990). Inappropriateness is an important con-

For the school-aged child, peer relationships both in and out of school become extremely important.

sideration when appraising the effect of aggression because research has shown that no more than half of aggressive children are rejected by their peers. What we find, then, is that rejected children are generally those whose aggression violates the norms set by the group; it's not just that they are aggressive (Coie, Dodge, Terry, & Wright, 1991). In fact, among older children (9-year-olds), aggression in reaction to provocation, as well as some bullying, were positively correlated with higher peer status (Coie, Dodge, Terry, & Wright, 1991). The behavior of hyperactive children is also often seen as inappropriate and as proper grounds for rejection by the group (Pope, Bierman, & Mumma, 1991).

One of the most important moments determining later acceptance or rejection is the first interaction. Children who are best able to fit in and to engage in conversation with a new group *when they first meet* show skills that predict later popularity among their peers (Black & Hazen, 1990; Putallaz, 1983). Furthermore, children who have the social skills to evoke humor and laughter among their peers have been found to be more academically and socially competent and to be viewed by their peers as fun to be with and as having good ideas for things to do (Masten, 1986). Also, children who have the most positive parent-child relationships tend to form the most positive friendships (Youngblade & Belsky, 1992), and children who acquire many friends are more likely to do well in school (Ladd, 1990).

Interestingly, once a child has been accepted by a group, that child is not likely to be rejected, even if he is as aggressive as peers whom the group initially rejected (Coie & Kupersmidt, 1983). A bias exists in that once a child has been accepted by his peers, aggressive and inappropriate behavior may be overlooked; but once a child has been rejected by his peers, even relatively mild behavior may be considered undesirable by those who were rejecting (Hymel, 1986). These findings underscore the importance of possessing the social skills necessary to be accepted *initially* by a peer group.

Occasionally, peers are neglected instead of being actively rejected. Neglected children tend not to display aggressive or task-inappropriate behaviors any more than do accepted peers. Neglected children, however, often are shy and rarely approach their peers in a social way (Dodge, Coie, & Brakke, 1982).

If children who are rejected or neglected by their peers don't find ways to be accepted, they can sometimes turn to a close sibling for support (although that can't fully make up for peer rejection) (East & Rook, 1992) (see At Issue). Children who lack close sibling relationships and who fail to find peer acceptance, or who fail to learn the appropriate behaviors demanded by peers, face a loneliness in childhood that often continues into adulthood (Cassidy & Asher, 1992; Hojat, 1982; Parkhurst & Asher, 1992). Grade school teachers know that social isolation is a genuine risk of early childhood (Hymel, Rubin, Rowden, & LeMare, 1990) and that part of their job is to nip such rejection in the bud by forcing, if necessary, peer-group acceptance and tolerance. Such initial forced acceptance often develops into real acceptance as the children come to accommodate one another.

Factors Affecting Peer Acceptance.   Children generally prefer to be with members of their own race and sex (Schofield & Francis, 1982). Such preferences are found throughout grade school, from kindergarten (Finkelstein & Haskins, 1983) to the sixth grade (Sagar, Schofield, & Snyder, 1983). Learned prejudice may account for racial preferences among children to a small degree, but the main factors appear to be related to social class and levels of academic achievement. Research indicates that there is more interracial acceptance among children if they meet at the same academic and social level (Schofield & Whitley, 1983).

AT ISSUE

Sibling Rivalry: Fact or Fiction?

When a second-born infant joins a family, especially a family in which the firstborn is under the age of 4, there is likely to be some conflict. Over the years, terms such as *dethronement*, *displacement*, and *regression* have been used when describing the firstborn's reaction to the new situation. These terms are still used to describe a firstborn's typical reaction, although *imitation* is now considered a better descriptor than *regression*; both refer to a strategy of acting like the baby to maintain or regain parental attention (Stewart, Mobley, Van Tuyl, & Salvador, 1987).

Although it was traditionally thought that conflict was the inevitable outcome of a sibling relationship, research has shown that rivalry and conflict are not necessarily the norm. In fact, the most common mode of sibling interaction is often that of cooperation and helping (Abramovitch, Pepler, & Corter, 1982).

Judy Dunn and her colleagues at Cambridge University closely examined sibling relationships among preschool children and came to several interesting conclusions. First, they found that the mother's behavior following the birth of a new baby was a factor in determining the presence or absence of rivalry and conflict. They also noted that it was helpful to include the older sibling in baby-care activities and to refer to the baby as a person instead of simply as "the baby":

> In families where the mothers discussed caring for the baby as a matter of joint responsibility and talked about the baby as a person from the early days, the siblings were particularly friendly over the next year. Most encouraging of all, our findings show that in families where the first child was interested and affectionate toward the baby, the relationship continued to be rewarding, loving, and supportive for both children—not just the first year, but over the next three years. (Dunn & Kendrick, 1982b, pp. 220–221)

The second important finding made by Dunn and her colleagues was that the sibling relationship could not be characterized as being of any one type, that such relationships showed incredible variability and complexity. Furthermore, even though siblings may seem to get along well with one another, they can still have episodes of conflict, perhaps because they are together so much of the time.

A third finding of Dunn's study was that even when the older sibling was "naughty" after the birth of the new baby, the naughty behavior was commonly directed against the mother and usually occurred when the mother was interacting with the new baby. For example, one child deliberately began to sprinkle his milk all over the sofa while his mother was interacting with his baby sister, and another child, observing a similar interaction between mother and baby, ran outside, laughing, and let down a full line of clean clothes

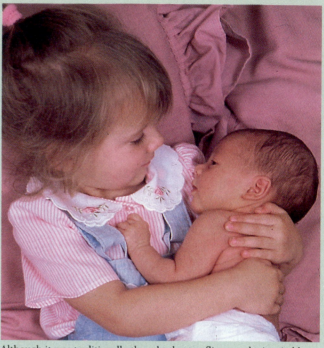

Although it was traditionally thought that conflict was the inevitable result when a new baby joined a family that had at least one child already, research has shown that the *most* common mode of sibling interaction is cooperation and helping.

that had been drying onto some muddy grass (Dunn & Kendrick, 1982b).

Dunn and her colleagues also found that the gender of the siblings had a bearing on whether or not there would be conflict, with opposite-gender siblings having a stormier relationship than same-gender ones. They also found that the temperament of the firstborn child may play a role in fostering conflict (Dunn, 1984). Parents have no control over gender and little control over temperament and so can modify a stormy sibling relationship only to a certain extent.

As a general rule, however, sibling relationships become less intense as children grow older. Older children report that their sibling relationships are on a more equal footing than they were previously, with a lessening of both aggression and nurturance between themselves and their siblings (Buhrmester & Furman, 1990).

In conclusion, sibling rivalry occurs, but contrary to common belief, it is not the typical way siblings interact. Sibling rivalry is not a natural or necessary aspect of every sibling relationship, and the rivalry that does exist generally diminishes with age.

Children who are physically attractive are also more likely to be accepted (Vaughn & Langlois, 1983). Children as young as 3 to 6 years of age show a strong preference for attractive rather than unattractive children (Dion, 1973). This inclination is especially marked among girls (Langlois & Styczynski, 1979; Vaughn & Langlois, 1983).

The physically attractive also tend to be more resistant to peer pressure (Adams, 1977). This may be because attractive children expect to be accepted as leaders, whereas unattractive children may capitulate and be followers in order to gain acceptance. Among boys, those who mature early and have a masculine build are more likely to be imitated and accepted by their peers.

A child's name may also affect peer acceptance. Through associative learning (see Chapter 2), names such as Rose or Bertha, which were popular at the turn of the century, have become unpopular. The names Scott and Jennifer, on the other hand, have become more popular.

Although name, race, sex, and physical attractiveness initially may be most important in peer acceptance of a child (Furman & Bierman, 1983), as peer relationships grow and develop, a child's character often emerges as the most important attribute in determining continued acceptance (Reaves & Roberts, 1983). For character to play an important role, however, children must first become known by their peers, and this may not be possible if they already have been rejected because of peer-group determination that their overt aspects are undesirable. Such initial rejections may have an unfortunate influence on a child's personality, and the child may become depressed or aggressive or may change in some way as to make future peer acceptance even less likely.

Peer-Group Organization. Among 6- or 7-year-old children, peer groups tend to be informal and unstructured, but as children grow older, their peer groupings sometimes become more organized and formal. The different skills, powers, and abilities of group members become important distinctions. Status ordering based on characteristics such as appearance, pubertal development, athletic skill, academic achievement, or leadership ability is common (Savin-Williams, 1979).

Members of the peer group, in an effort to be admired and accepted, will attempt as best they can to conform to the standards and values of the group. Generally, conformity to peer-group standards increases with age, but a great deal depends on the tasks or behaviors demanding conformity. Older children who are certain of the position they take on an issue are less likely to be influenced by peers than are younger children. In ambiguous situations, however, when children are uncertain of their position, conformity with peers is more likely with increasing age (Hoving, Hamm, & Galvin, 1969).

Adult Versus Peer Influence. The desire to interact with peers grows throughout childhood. By the age of 10 or 11 years, peer friendships are extremely important. If a child's peers exhibit values and behaviors that conflict with those espoused by the child's family, challenges to parental authority and serious family arguments may occur (Elkind, 1971). Generally, however, there is remarkable agreement between a child's peers and family members in terms of accepted values and behaviors (Douvan & Adelson, 1966; Hartup, 1970). This is probably because children are socialized first by their families, and they later choose playmates and friends who hold values similar to those they have been taught.

In some situations, peers are more likely to have a greater influence than adults. For instance, peers usually have a greater influence over a child's choice of friends and in situations involving challenges to authority, personal or group identity, interpersonal behavior, language fads, and clothing choices (Brittain,

Peer groups include individuals who share similar beliefs and attitudes.

1963). Peers are also more influential in shaping sexual attitudes and behaviors (Vandiver, 1972). Although adults, especially parents, are more likely to influence the child's future aspirations, academic choices, and political views, children's behaviors are usually the result of both peer and parental influence (Siman, 1977).

Parents who are warm and supportive are likely to have the greatest influence on their children. Parents who are too permissive or too punitive are usually less accessible to their children and as a result have less influence. When children rely on their peers excessively or acquire antisocial behaviors supported by the peer group, the reason is often disillusionment with adult wisdom, justice, or status. Children who are disillusioned with their fathers are especially susceptible to becoming highly peer oriented (Bixenstine, DeCorte, & Bixenstine, 1976).

Given the strong influence that peers can have on a child's development, parents often wonder if they should try to exert more control over their child's choice of friends and associates. Although much of a child's early socialization is the result of family influences, in practically every culture, peers have been found to affect strongly the development of many behaviors, ranging from aggression to cooperation and sharing (Whiting & Whiting, 1975). Parents, of course, want their children to behave in certain ways, and if parents find that their children's peers are promoting behaviors that conflict with parental values and desires, it is understandable that they may wish to control peer relationships. This is especially true when peers are modeling aggression and antisocial behaviors. There is evidence that among all the social agents in a child's life, peers are the most effective models of aggression (Cohen, 1971).

Parents face two problems when trying to control peer influence. First, as children grow older and spend less time at home, parents may find that they have less influence and that any attempts to control the child only drive the child toward a greater peer orientation. In fact, by adolescence, the average child will spend more than twice as much time with peers as with parents (Condry, Siman, & Bronfenbrenner, 1968). The second problem faced by parents who wish to control the influence of peers is that of overcontrol. Overcontrolling children by limiting their social contacts may inadvertently keep them from developing adequate social skills or the confidence to interact in groups.

The Influence of Schools

A school serves the purpose of systematically passing on the wisdom (or prejudices) of the culture to its young. There is probably no such thing as the average school or the average student. Because of this, it is impossible to discuss the effect of the school on the child (Sarason & Klaber, 1985). Unquestionably, however, many attitudes, feelings, and beliefs are created, maintained, and altered by schools. Schools are a significant force, not just because they teach reading, writing, and arithmetic, but because they expose the child to new ideas, important new adult models, and greater contact with peers.

Each society also depends on its schools to produce its most important resource: the next generation of educated citizens. A decade ago, however, the National Commission on Excellence in Education reported that the United States had become a "nation at risk." Supporting its claim, the commission noted that 23 million Americans were functionally illiterate, including 13 percent of all 17-year-olds and 40 percent of minority youth, that average high school test scores had been dropping steadily over the previous 26 years, that half of gifted students failed to match their abilities in school, and that almost 40 percent of high school seniors could not draw inferences from written material, while 80 percent could not write a persuasive essay and 67 percent could not solve math problems requiring more than a few steps (Gardner, 1983).

Following that report, a growing awareness developed that something had to be done to improve American education. The government and its citizens became more interested in the effect of schooling on the development of children and demanded to know why some schools turned out well-educated, motivated children, while other schools were failing in this important task.

All investigations in this area agree that huge differences exist among schools, and not just in the United States (Rutter, 1983). In studies conducted in Great Britain, for example, the great range in schools was obvious. In one school, 50 percent of the pupils went on to college; in another, fewer than 9 percent did. Delinquency rates varied from 1 percent to 19 percent, and absenteeism ranged from 6 percent to 26 percent (Power, Alderson, Phillipson, Schoenberg, & Morris, 1967; Reynolds, Jones, & St Leger, 1976; Rutter, Maughan, Mortimore, Ouston, & Smith, 1979). The range among American schools was even greater.

At first it might seem that these differences are due to the neighborhoods the schools serve rather than the schools themselves. But researchers have studied many pairs of schools that differ greatly in their delinquency, attendance, and college acceptance rates but that serve similar student populations in terms of intellectual characteristics and socioeconomic status (Finlayson & Loughran, 1976; Reynolds & Murgatroyd, 1977). Furthermore, a number of schools consistently turn out students who attain high levels of scholastic achievement despite the fact that these students come from inner-city neighborhoods generally associated with low achievement (Weber, 1971). All these findings indicate that different schools may provide their students with very different educations, regardless of the neighborhood. Moreover, schools that show superior student achievement—whether the students come from poor neighborhoods or affluent ones—tend to maintain their high standards of excellence year after year. Schools with poor performance records, regardless of neighborhood, also tend to be consistent (Rutter, 1983).

Successful Schools. Successful schools generally have an academic emphasis. Academic goals are clearly stated, there's a certain degree of structure, and there are high achievement expectations (Linney & Seidman, 1989). Effective schools are also characterized by regularly assigned and graded homework (Bales, 1986) and by a high proportion of time devoted to active teaching instead of to miscellaneous activities such as calling the roll, handing out papers, setting up equipment, and disciplining students. Effective schools also have a system of checks to make certain that teachers are following the intended practices of the school. This is especially important for inexperienced teachers, who tend to be the most inefficient in classroom management (Rutter, Maughan, Mortimore, Ouston, & Smith, 1979).

Although the age of the school and the size of the classrooms were once thought to affect student achievement, such factors don't seem to make much difference (Rutter, Maughan, Mortimore, Ouston, & Smith, 1979). This, of course, assumes that reasonable minimal standards are met, that facilities are not completely dilapidated, and that the school has funds for rudimentary equipment.

Another very important factor in school success may be the presence of just a handful of excellent and dedicated teachers. In one study (Pedersen, Faucher, & Eaton, 1978), researchers found that the children in a particular elementary school who had achieved the highest grades and who later demonstrated superior status as adults all had one thing in common—the same first-grade teacher! This in and of itself seems amazing. The simple academic material that the teacher presented obviously would have little effect on the children once they had become adults. However, it has been shown that when children first enter school, their attitude toward learning and their desire to achieve undergo a major revision. As they come to know their school and teacher, they begin to realize what is expected of them (Alexander & Entwisle, 1988). Thus, the first teacher or two have a unique responsibility to help students set their sights on goals and to instill confidence in the student, both for the current year and for the future. Here, the teacher may make a lasting contribution.

Think of the few teachers you've had in your life whom you greatly admired and respected. They taught you more than just academic material. They taught you to do your best, to have confidence in yourself, to set high standards, and then to attain them. Or, perhaps most important, they made you want to stay in school and continue to learn. Furthermore, most of the research indicates that it is what the teacher does in the classroom—how and what he or she teaches—rather than personality that makes the difference (Linney & Seidman, 1989). Perhaps such teachers, more than anything else, help make a school successful.

School and Social Class.   Children from low socioeconomic classes have severe disadvantages in school. Before such children ever enter school, they often have become victims of poverty and are suffering from poor health or inadequate family care, which has a direct adverse effect on their academic performance, which in turn makes it more likely that they will drop out of school (Cairns, Cairns, & Neckerman, 1989). Many economically disadvantaged children do not receive sufficient food, sleep, or stimulation (see Figure 11.2). The extent of this problem was highlighted by the discovery that one way to improve the grades of impoverished children by as much as 2 to 6 percent is simply to provide them with a nutritious breakfast once they arrive at school (Meyers, Sampson, Weitzman, Rogers, & Kayne, 1989).

Another problem associated with poverty is that while some disadvantaged families are supportive of high academic achievement and good grades (Greenberg & Davidson, 1972), many belittle their children's efforts toward scholastic success and encourage early employment as a more responsible choice. In

Just a handful of dedicated teachers may make the difference between successful and unsuccessful schools.

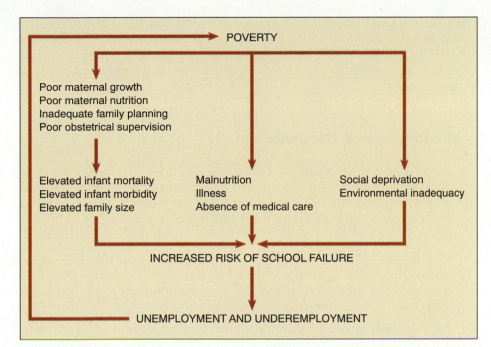

FIGURE 11.2

Children from low socioeconomic classes face a vicious cycle of poverty that can have a devastating effect on their school performance. (SOURCE: Birsch & Gussow, 1970, p. 268)

addition, many schools in lower-class neighborhoods are so pressed for funds that school activities and school-supported programs must be cut back or eliminated. Such schools also have problems attracting the best teachers because of the crowded conditions and the high incidence of violence. In almost every lower-class neighborhood, schools spend more to repair the damage done by vandals than to buy textbooks. Teachers in these schools often expend a disproportionate amount of time on custodial and disciplinary tasks at the expense of teaching. Given these factors, it is not surprising to find substantial differences in academic achievement among children of different socioeconomic backgrounds. Greater national attention is required to solve this problem. Although it will be expensive, the costs of doing nothing are much greater. Ignorance is always more costly than education.

Role of the Parents.   Most researchers believe that although the teacher is an extremely important influence on the child's educational development, parents are even more important. Parents set and model academic standards for their children. They are a source of encouragement or discouragement. In fact, one study has found evidence that parental appraisal of a child's ability has an even greater effect on the child's self-appraisal than does feedback from actual schoolwork (Phillips, 1987). Parents also enforce, or fail to enforce, school attendance, completion of homework, and respect for the educational system. Furthermore, when parents take an active interest in their children's daily activities at school and keep abreast of their children's academic performance, their children are apt to receive better grades and have fewer conduct problems (Crouter, MacDermid, McHale, & Perry-Jenkins, 1990).

When intelligent, caring parents are combined with a good school, the combination is likely to produce results. As a demonstration of this, consider an interesting study conducted in Paris in which children from disadvantaged backgrounds were placed for adoption and raised in well-to-do families. The children's school performance over many years was found to be significantly superior to similar children who were not adopted and who were raised in the poorer neighborhood and went to poorer schools (Duyme, 1988). This study also helps to deemphasize the idea that genetic differences may be the prime factor in the failure of disadvantaged students, because different environments were all that accounted for the differences in the children's academic development.

The Influence of Television

> To put the matter most boldly: Children, at least those in the United States, are growing up in an environment in which babies and toddlers must not only process the shapes, contours, and objects of their own rooms or decode and imitate the sounds and gestures of the adults or siblings around them; they must also relate to a small box on which figures leap, dance, laugh, scream, destroy each other, and urge purchases of food and toys. (Singer, 1983, p. 815)
>
> By the time American children are 18 years old, they have spent more time watching television than in any other activity than sleep. Moreover, their experiences with television begin long before exposure to school or, in many cases, any socialization agent other than the family. (Huston, Wright, Rice, Kerkman, & St. Peters, 1990, p. 409)

No one really knows what children learn from television and how it affects them. The effect must be considerable, however, because by the time most children are 18 years old, they have logged 3 hours watching television for every 2 hours spent in school! American children between the ages of 5 and 13 years have been found to spend more time watching television than they spend participating in any other waking activity (Huston & Wright, 1982; Liebert & Sprafkin, 1988). And even children as young as 3 or 4 spend about 2 to 4 hours a day watching television (Huston, Wright, Rice, Kerkman, & St. Peters, 1990). Parents also report having lost some control over their children's viewing habits, and this is confirmed by research showing that most children view television 6½ hours a week more than their parents want them to (Sarlo, Jason, & Lonak, 1988). Television is so wide-ranging in its content that it probably has both detrimental and beneficial effects on children (Liebert & Sprafkin, 1988; Singer & Singer, 1983a).

Television has changed the way we live and has influenced family life. Just having a television set in the house affects family interaction patterns. Although families spend time together watching television, they spend less time than they used to directly engaging in activities with one another. Some have joked that you can always spot a television-oriented family because none of the conversations among family members ever lasts longer than the average commercial.

As never before, children can isolate themselves for hours in front of the tube. True, before TV was invented, children could have done the same thing with books. But whereas books excluded preschoolers and infants, television doesn't. To the dismay of some people, television is far more popular than books ever were.

Television actually competes for the role of socializing agent with parents, school, and peers. Children spend a huge amount of their time in front of the TV. For instance, approximately 25 percent of all sixth to tenth graders surveyed were found to be viewing at least 5½ hours of television on any given school day (Lyle & Hoffman, 1972). Moreover, as many as 25 percent of sixth graders sampled were still watching television at 11:30 P.M. These children are probably being socialized by television at the expense of family or school. In fact, one-third of parents surveyed more than three decades ago stated that one of television's major uses is as a baby-sitter (Steiner, 1963). Twenty years following this survey, parents still stated that one of television's major advantages is that it keeps the kids occupied—it is a baby-sitter (Singer & Singer, 1983a).

Children's Television.   The idea behind "Sesame Street" was to give preschool children the basic knowledge and cognitive skills they would need in elementary school. Unfortunately, "Sesame Street" has not had as great an effect as originally hoped, although children can benefit from watching it, especially in regard to vocabulary development (Rice, Huston, Truglio, & Wright, 1990).

"Mr. Rogers' Neighborhood," another PBS children's program, and "Here's Humphrey," a similar television program in Australia, seem to be beneficial in other ways. These programs were shown to increase interpersonal prosocial behaviors in preschoolers, although the effect was short-lived (Friedrich & Stein, 1973; Stein & Friedrich, 1972; Singer & Singer, 1976; Tower, Singer, Singer, & Biggs, 1979).

Most important, however, is the finding that such children's programs are most effective in teaching preschoolers if parents or teachers interact with children as they watch the programs (Friedrich, Stein, & Sussman, 1975; Singer & Singer, 1974). If an adult calls a child's attention to the significant features of a program and discusses some of the content, the child is much more likely to benefit. This finding fits well with Gibson's theory of distinctive features (see Chapter 4), inasmuch as it may well be necessary for an adult to help a less experienced child discriminate the important points in a program. Perhaps such active participation—discussing as often as possible the various aspects of the program and helping the child interpret and understand the important information (Rubinstein, 1983)—is the best way for parents to handle their children's exposure to television. Unfortunately, research shows that parents don't usually watch television with their children and that there isn't very much parental control or supervision over what the children watch (St. Peters, Fitch, Huston, Wright, & Eakins, 1991).

If we combine the findings of all the research conducted over the past 40 years, we can summarize the effects of television on children by placing the data into two categories: influences that are well documented and influences we suspect to be occurring.

Documented Influences.   Heavy viewing of violent programs has been associated consistently with aggression in both children and adults (Liebert & Sprafkin, 1988; Pearl, Bouthilet, & Lazar, 1982; Rubinstein, In general, heavy television viewing is associated with poor school achievement (Rubinstein, 1983), poorer reading comprehension (Singer & Singer, 1983a), and poorer language useage (Singer & Singer, 1983b). Interestingly, for children of lower socioeconomic status, heavy TV viewing has been associated with *higher* reading comprehension and *higher* scholastic achievement. Television viewing, therefore, appears to have a leveling effect, often raising the abilities of disadvantaged children while lowering the abilities of children with higher socioeconomic status (Gerbner, Gross, Morgan, & Signorielli, 1980; Morgan & Gross, 1982). Heavy television viewing also appears to inhibit the development of imagination.

Children who are heavy viewers of television do not need to engage in as much self-generated imaginative thinking because the television provides its own fantasies. Instead of making up stories and imaginative encounters, children who are heavy watchers often reenact by rote the stories they have seen. It thus appears that imagination is somewhat dampened by heavy television viewing (Singer, 1982).

Although heavy television viewing may have a negative effect on children, television can also be educational.

Television also influences children's concepts of sex roles. Children who watch more television tend to view the male and female roles in a more stereotypical fashion (Williams, 1986), although the more recent trend toward showing female TV characters in traditional male roles (lawyers, police officers, private detectives) has increased girls' interest in these professions as acceptable careers for females (Wroblewski & Huston, 1987).

Television also shapes what is called "world knowledge": By being exposed to television, children form attitudes and beliefs about their world. This is a good thing only insofar as TV reflects reality. To the extent that it doesn't, this exposure can cause problems. For example, children who are heavy viewers of television, especially of graphic action shows, such as police dramas, tend to view the world as a mean and scary place and as more dangerous than it really is (Rubinstein, 1983). Television instills a certain paranoia in these children and may tend to make them more fearful and less trusting of others.

Many controlled experiments have been conducted over the years that support the findings we have discussed. And then there is the interesting case of the small Canadian town that in 1973 still had no television. This town was not particularly isolated, but it was in a geographical "blind spot" where microwave transmissions and cable simply couldn't reach. In all other aspects, it was a normal North American community. For the sake of anonymity, let's call the town Notel. In 1973, it was finally possible to bring television to Notel. This provided an opportunity for researchers to enter the town, make observations, take naturalistic data, and compare their findings with data collected from the same people after two years of television viewing. The scientists found that television generally affected the viewers in a negative way.

One negative effect had to do with displacement: When you're watching television, you can't be doing something else. The number of hours people spent participating in outdoor activities, community events, and sporting games decreased. And after two years of watching television, children were found, relative to their age-mates, to have poorer reading skills and to score lower on tests of creative thinking. Aggressive behavior increased, and sex stereotyping became more extreme, as girls and boys became more strongly sex typed (Williams, 1986).

Suspected Influences. Young children don't watch television in the same way that older children or adults do. They simply are unable to attend to an entire plot line or story with full comprehension (Anderson, Lorch, Field, Collins, & Nathan, 1986). This has led researchers to suspect that TV producers who argue that violence is all right as long as justice and morality triumph in the end are overlooking the fact that younger children may see the violence but miss the just or moral conclusion. It is also suspected that exposing children to greater amounts of television violence may lead them to behave apathetically when they observe real violence (Rubinstein, 1983). Television may also be sending subtle messages about health practices. On the good side, it must be said that very little smoking occurs on programs today. TV characters, however, are far more likely to consume alcohol than to gulp down soft drinks. Furthermore, very few TV characters buckle up their seat belts while driving, and many of them exceed speed limits and drive recklessly. It is suspected that modeling these behaviors may influence children (Rubinstein, 1983).

In fairness, television may also be providing a great deal of good information and exposure for children. For the first time, children, no matter how rural or distant from major centers their homes are, are growing up with exposure to events on the entire planet. Television may thus broaden the horizons and stimulate the curiosity of millions of children who would not otherwise have known what the world might hold for them.

Studies have also shown that children can acquire good nutritional habits from television programs designed to teach such habits (Campbell, 1982) and that children can learn to help others or to give to charities from watching such behavior modeled on TV. They can also learn to cooperate, to share, and to be imaginative under certain conditions, all from being exposed to particular TV shows (Pearl, Bouthilet, & Lazar, 1982). Appropriate television programming can enhance friendliness and generosity. It can help children learn to delay gratification as well as to overcome fears of strange and unusual situations (Rubinstein, 1983). So, TV certainly has its "good side."

In fact, it's still not that easy to say exactly which is television's good or bad side. In a very intensive review of the effects of television on children (Anderson, 1989), a number of surprises were uncovered showing that we still have much to learn. For instance, although school-age children might spend many hours in front of the television, careful observation shows that they only spend about two-thirds of that time actually watching. The rest of the time is devoted to other activities. During these times, children often monitor the television, waiting for something that might catch their interest, which in itself might be a cognitively enriching activity in that it requires a certain amount of attention and information processing.

Television also doesn't seem to interfere that much with homework. It seems that children who do their homework get it done in spite of the presence of a television set in the house, while those who don't do their homework tend not to do it anyway, even if the television is turned off.

Perhaps the best way to put television to good use is to cast your consumer vote by watching programs you deem appropriate and by purchasing the products associated with those programs. Sending letters to the networks describing the kinds of programming you prefer can also be helpful. Also important is selecting the programs that you and your family watch with some care. Of course, you can't keep children away from every show you don't want them to see, and perhaps you don't need to as long as you take the time to discuss in detail what the children have seen and what it means in terms of the real world. Let them know what is pretend and what isn't, what is really acceptable and what isn't. Let them benefit from your experience.

"All That Glitters . . ."

The average American 19-year-old has spent more total time just watching TV commercials than a full-time employee spends on the job during an entire year! Commercial TV is very much part of our environment.

Adults tend to assume, falsely or not, that they are in control of their behavior and that TV commercials don't have much effect on them. Because of this belief, most of the concern about commercial television has focused on children's television, or "kidvid," as it is known in the advertising industry. The majority of kidvid ads are for toys, cereals, and candy and other food snacks. On a typical Saturday morning, for instance, 40 percent of commercials advertise sugar-laden breakfast foods. One ad executive was quoted in *Advertising Age* as stating, "If you truly want big sales you will use the child as your assistant salesman. He sells, he nags, until he breaks down the sales resistance of his mother or father" (Packard, 1977, p. 134).

Congress, spurred by powerful lobbying organizations such as Action for Children's Television, has been investigating how commercial television attempts to alter children's emotions or attitudes toward a particular product. The process by which advertisers get children to want their products relies heavily on the principles of associative learning (see Chapter 2). For example, associations are made between a product and a favored cartoon character: Fred Flintstone says, about a sugared breakfast food, "CoCo Pebbles are CoCo-moko good." Associations are also made between a child's use of a product and a resulting gleeful hysteria (called "super-joy" in the ad trade) exhibited by the actors portraying parents. And toys may be

associated with exciting music and interesting animations that often are hard for a child to replicate in the home (Greer, Potts, Wright, & Huston, 1982). Another advertising technique, begun in the 1980s and disturbing to many parents, is to create children's programs that are, in essence, advertisements. This is done by making available for sale toy versions of the cartoon characters and the objects used on the program. These are but a few examples. Keep in mind that advertisers spend about $500 million per year systematically working to shape the attitudes of preschoolers. Judging by the sale of sugared snacks and foods, as well as the volume of the toy market, such campaigns are successful.

Furthermore, children, especially those younger than 5 years, can be terribly misled by TV advertisements. They simply do not process what they see in the same way as you or I might. For example, children younger than 5 years often fail to make the distinction between what may appear to be real and what is actually real. In other words, they don't know that what you see is not always what you get (Flavell, 1986).

THE APPEARANCE-REALITY DISTINCTION

For many years, John Flavell and his colleagues at Stanford University experimented with children's understanding of what is real and what is not. Often, Flavell gave the child a brief lesson in appearance-reality distinction by introducing the child to a Charlie Brown puppet inside of a ghost costume. Flavell would explain that although Charlie Brown "looks like a ghost to your eyes right now," the puppet is "really and truly Charlie Brown," which means that "some-

Advertisers spend hundreds of millions of dollars every year in an effort to get children to want certain products.

times things look like one thing to your eyes when they are really and truly something else" (Flavell, 1986, pp. 39, 42). After this lesson, the child would be shown an object that looked like a rock; however, when it was picked up and felt, it was obviously a sponge! Or the child would first be shown a red car, then shown the red car again through a blue filter, which made the car appear black. After these experiences, most 6-year-old children would realize that the rock was really a sponge and that the red car was still red even though it had been covered by a blue filter. Children 3 or 4 years old, on the other hand, would typically argue that the sponge is a rock when it's not being felt and that the car seen through the filter is really and truly black. Even in simpler tests, 3- and 4-year-old children often showed a surprising inability to realize that looks can be deceiving.

These younger children also rely very strongly on appearances to decide about the goodness of something they've seen. In one experiment, children were presented with two versions of a story. One group was given the "kind" version, in which a woman picks up a cat gently and pets it, then adds that she wishes people, too, would visit her. Then she feeds the cat some cream. In the "cruel" version, the woman grabs the cat by the neck, shouts at it, and adds that she's glad that people are smart enough to stay away from her home. Then she threatens to starve the cat and throws it down the basement stairs. At the end of the story, the researcher tells the children that at this point the woman has noticed that there are children hiding under her table who do not belong in her home. The question then is, "What will happen next?" Will the children be asked to stay and have milk and cookies, or will the woman grab them and throw them into a closet (Hoffner & Cantor, 1985)? As a further manipulation, the

FIGURE 11.3

Illustration of the manipulation of protagonist's appearance and behavior. (SOURCE: Hoffner & Cantor, 1985, p. 1067)

children are shown two versions of the woman in the kind story and two versions of the woman in the cruel story. In one version the woman is middle-aged and plump; in the other, she is old and witchlike (see Figure 11.3). The researchers referred to the two portrayals as "attractive" and "unattractive."

Children aged 3 to 5 years generally agreed that the attractive woman would ask them to stay and have milk and cookies, while the unattractive woman would throw them into a closet, *regardless* of how the woman had treated the cat. Children aged 6 to 10 years, on the other hand, disregarded the woman's looks and considered only her behavior (Hoffner & Cantor, 1985). Once again, we have evidence that children under 5 years rely strongly on appearance to determine what is good or desirable.

The failure of young children to make appearance-reality distinctions,

as well as their reliance on liking whatever looks attractive, makes the job of advertisers that much easier. It is easy to sucker young children into believing, through super-joy or glitz, that their parents will love them more or that they will be much happier if they have a certain toy or breakfast food.

To lessen the indoctrination of young children, it has been argued that commercials should be banned from all children's television. Such legislation has been before Congress on and off for the last two decades, but has yet to be enacted. In the end, it is the public who must decide what will or will not be allowed on television. Perhaps knowing how susceptible children are to the manipulation of advertisers—how younger children are unable to tell the difference between glitter and gold—will help us to decide.

Summary

- During middle childhood, children's personalities become increasingly complex and more like that of their future adult selves. According to Erik Erikson, the psychosocial conflict to be resolved at this time is industry versus inferiority.
- During middle childhood, children face a number of tasks. They must develop a relatively stable self-concept, refine their understanding of how the social world works, develop standards for their behavior, and develop strategies for self-control.
- During middle childhood, many social institutions have an influence on a child's socialization.
- Many children initially respond to a divorce with anger, fear, and shock. It is also common for children to feel guilty about the divorce.
- Generally, girls are initially better able to cope with the effects of divorce than are boys. Wallerstein found that after 10 years, however, it was typically the girls who seemed to face the most difficulties.
- Children may fare well in single-parent families, but the chances of problems increase.
- For the school-age child, peer relationships both in and out of school become extremely important. Being accepted by one's peers and belonging to peer groups are major concerns.
- Children who fail to find peer acceptance or who fail to learn the appropriate behaviors demanded by peers face a loneliness in childhood that often continues into adulthood.
- Although a child's overt aspects may be the most important for peer acceptance, as peer relationships grow and develop, a child's character often emerges as the most important attribute in determining continued acceptance.
- Parents who are warm and supportive are likely to have the greatest influence on their children. Disillusionment with adult wisdom, justice, or status may lead children to rely on their peers excessively or acquire antisocial behaviors supported by the peer group.
- Schools serve the purpose of systematically passing on the wisdom (or prejudices) of the culture to its young. In addition to teaching reading, writing, and arithmetic, schools also expose the child to new ideas, important new adult models, and great contact with peers.
- Different schools may provide their students with different educations despite the neighborhood from which the students come. Schools that show superior student achievement tend to maintain their high standards of excellence year after year, while schools with poor performance records also tend to be consistent.
- No one is certain, but the existence of just a handful of excellent and dedicated teachers may be an important factor in making a successful school.
- Children from low socioeconomic classes may face severe disadvantages in school.
- Television has been shown to have a great influence on the development of school-age children. Television competes with parents, school, and peers for the role of socializing agent.
- Heavy viewing of violent television programs has been consistently associated with increased aggression in both children and adults. In general, heavy viewing also is associated with poor school achievement, although children

from lower socioeconomic levels may achieve some beneficial effects from heavy television viewing and may perform at a higher level than expected.

■ Television also influences children's concepts of gender roles. Children who watch more television tend to view the male and female roles in a more stereotypical fashion.

■ Television also has its good side. It can broaden horizons, teach good nutritional habits, and model prosocial behaviors.

■ Children, especially those younger than 6 years, can be terribly misled by TV advertisements. They fail to make the distinction between what may appear to be real and what is actually real.

QUESTIONS FOR DISCUSSION

1. How might single parents compensate for their children's lack of a second parental role model?

2. What factors do you believe have contributed to the rising divorce rate in the United States? Do you think the trend will continue?

3. Were you ever placed in conflict between the desires of your parents and those of your friends? Who had the most influence? Why?

4. The efforts of commercial television to get children to like broccoli or other such vegetables haven't been too successful. What does this indicate about the limits of the power of advertising?

5. Can you recall one or two teachers who had an important influence on your life? What qualities made those teachers special?

SUGGESTIONS FOR FURTHER READING

1. Boer, F., & Dunn, J. F. (Eds.). (1992). *Sibling relationships: Developmental & clinical issues*. Hillsdale, NJ: Erlbaum.

2. Comstock, G., & Paik, H. (1991). *Television and the American child*. San Diego, CA: Academic Press.

3. Dunn, J. (1990). *Separate lives: Why siblings are so different*. New York: Basic Books.

4. Leder, J. M. (1991). *Brothers and sisters: How they shape our lives*. New York: St. Martin's Press.

5. Liebert, R. M., Sprafkin, J. N., & Davidson, E. (1982). *The early window: Effects of television on children and youth*. Elmsford, NY: Pergamon Press.

CHAPTER 12

Adolescent Physical and Cognitive Development

Algebra and Formal Operations

When I was in the ninth grade, my cognitive development must have been coming along a little slowly. At the age of 13, before I was well enough along toward formal operations to deal with abstractions, I had the misfortune of running into algebra. I can remember the previous year, seeing the older kids in the hallway with math books that had covers showing letters being multiplied by numbers. I remember wondering how that was possible. I asked my father if it was hard, and he asked me, "How many numbers are there?" I said that there must be a zillion. And he said, "Well, how hard can letters be, there are only 26 of them." A solid picture of a small group of finite letters seemed simple enough to deal with, and so I entered algebra class with confidence.

The instructor began by placing an x on the board. I remember thinking that it seemed to me he had passed up a lot of the alphabet and didn't have very far to go, but that was all right. I raised my hand and asked him what x was. I wanted something concrete. He said, "x is an unknown." In my notebook I wrote, "x = ?" I liked that. I decided that whenever he used an x, I would use a question mark because it would make everything easier. After a while, he wrote a y on the board. I raised my hand and asked what y was. He replied that it, too, was an unknown. So I wrote in my notebook, "y = ?" It didn't take an Einstein to figure out that if x = ? and y = ?, then x must equal y, because they were both question marks. So I raised my hand and volunteered, "Then x = y!" The instructor said, "Well, that can happen sometimes, but it usually doesn't." I don't remember much more about that instructor, but I do remember my friend John, who sat next to me in class. He and I spent the rest of that year talking about less confusing things.

The second time I took algebra I think I had the same instructor; at least he looked familiar. This time when he said that x was an unknown and y was an unknown, it seemed very clear to me that this meant that they could be anything—equal to each other or not equal to each other. By that time, abstract thinking didn't seem so foreign to me. I didn't know it then, but I was slowly entering what Piaget called the period of formal operations and was beginning to be able to handle abstract concepts.

In this chapter, we'll examine the physical and cognitive changes that mark the period of adolescence. We will also see how these changes can affect feelings, attitudes, and behavior.

PHYSICAL GROWTH

Behind each maturational change lies the development of essential cells within the brain and body. Most aspects of a child, including emotions, skills, and aptitudes, are related directly or indirectly to body structure. Feelings about body image underlie many social interactions. This is especially true during adolescence, when many obvious physical changes occur (Chumlea, 1982).

Psychologists are aware of how physical growth and development affect a person's emotions and behavior. In fact, if most people had a better understanding of the physical changes that take place during adolescence, they would better understand an adolescent's feelings and behavior. For instance, most people know that girls mature earlier than boys do, but few people give much thought to the fact that adolescents of the same age may be either pre-pubescent or physically mature (see Figure 12.1). Yet the timing of physical development can profoundly affect adolescents and their interactions with peers and the school environment.

The Timing of Maturity

Maturing before your friends do can be lonely. Often there is a sense of being separated from peers by some barrier, some obvious alteration that has made an important difference. Also, adults may unconsciously expect greater maturity from a physically advanced adolescent, whose appearance begins to be more adultlike than childlike. However, emotional maturity develops more slowly than physical maturity, and many adolescents, especially those who are physically mature at an early age, may have difficulty living up to the new demands made of them. This, in turn, can lead to disappointment, doubt, and insecurity.

Among boys, however, early maturation can have its advantages. An appearance of being more "mature," thanks to the development of a visible sexual characteristic, such as a beard, can enhance a boy's status in his peer group. Early physical maturation can also enhance athletic ability, which often leads to increased status among peers, members of the opposite sex, and adults. However, the desire among boys to be physically mature and to excel in sports can sometimes lead to dangerous behavior. Among high school students, for instance, it has been found that 1 out of every 15 males have taken anabolic steroids (Buckley et al., 1988). The boys obtained these drugs, mostly illegally, from coaches, gym employees, bodybuilders, doctors, veterinarians, and

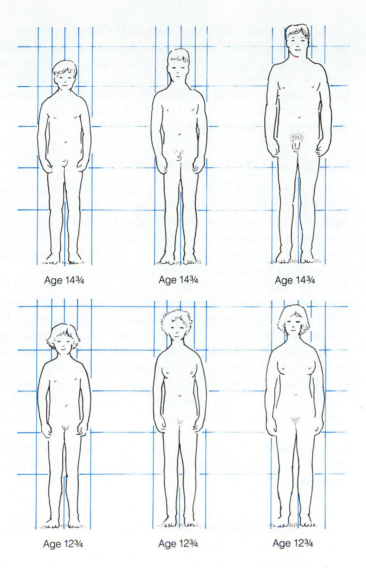

Age 14¾   Age 14¾   Age 14¾

Age 12¾   Age 12¾   Age 12¾

FIGURE 12.1

Differing degrees of pubertal development at the same chronological age. Upper row: three boys all age 14¾ years. Lower row: three girls all age 12¾ years. (SOURCE: Adapted from Tanner, 1969)

pharmacists. These hormones increase muscle mass but at the same time place the body under considerable stress. Serious heart disease and behavioral changes are associated with their continued use. Many of these boys began steroid use before the age of 15.

In general, girls find early maturity more stressful than boys do (Nottelmann & Welsh, 1986; Petersen, 1979). Although a girl may find herself suddenly attractive to older males, she often lacks the emotional maturity to deal with the situations that may result. It is also true that girls who mature early are given higher social status by their peers; the increased status, however, is markedly less than that enjoyed by boys who mature early. This may be because of the greater emphasis given by boys to athletic ability. But as girls participate more and more in athletic events formerly restricted to boys, girls maturing earlier will find their social status enhanced by athletics, just as boys do.

Late maturity among boys can be very stressful. Besides being teased and verbally ridiculed by more physically mature age-mates, boys who mature late often fear that they may never develop further or grow taller. These factors can lead to a negative self-image that can continue even after physical maturity has been reached (Siegel, 1982).

PUBERTY
The stage of maturation in which the individual becomes physiologically capable of sexual reproduction.

GROWTH SPURT
The time during puberty in which an adolescent's growth undergoes a marked acceleration.

Girls who mature late share many of the same problems. They may fear that they will remain flat-chested or that boys won't like them. And if boys don't like them, they may be left out of activities considered important by their peers. Such physically immature girls tend to be less socially mature. Nonetheless, in terms of current standards of physical attractiveness, girls who mature late may have an advantage, becoming generally taller and slimmer as adults than those who mature early.

Puberty and the Growth Spurt

At the beginning of adolescence, a number of physical changes occur. These changes are controlled by genetics and hormones. One change is the development of sexual maturity, which occurs during a period called **puberty**. It has been found that the hormone melatonin, which is secreted by the pineal gland, is responsible for the onset of puberty. As puberty nears, melatonin concentrations show a marked decrease (Waldhauser et al., 1984).

At the onset of puberty, the testes or ovaries enlarge. During puberty, the reproductive system matures, and sexual characteristics such as facial hair or breast enlargement emerge. At this time, the adolescent's growth undergoes a marked acceleration. Height and weight increase dramatically, and body proportion changes. This occurrence is known as the **growth spurt.** The growth spurt lasts for 2 to 3 years and begins in girls about 2 years earlier than it does in boys (see Figure 12.2). As you can see, the rate of growth in centimeters per year declines from birth through age 10 years in girls and through age 12 years in boys. This trend reverses during the growth spurt, when the rate of growth accelerates. During the growth spurt, the legs grow more rapidly than other parts of the body, which often gives the adolescent a disproportional appearance. It sometimes takes a while to become accustomed to a body of new proportions. Perhaps this is one of the reasons adolescents occasionally appear clumsy. Other physical changes that may occur include the development of acne, caused by the activity of sebaceous glands beneath the skin, and the vocal changes that sometimes embarrass maturing boys when their voices suddenly drop an octave in midspeech.

Because girls begin their growth spurt a year or two sooner than do boys, there is an awkward time when they are taller than boys their own age.

The Secular Trend.   In past years, the onset of puberty and the completion of growth typically occurred at a later age than they do now (Tanner, 1968). Evidence that children are now maturing earlier comes from data indicating that the average age of **menarche** (onset of menstruation) is getting lower. The range of nonpathological onset of menstruation is between 9 and 16 years of age (Bullough, 1981). Today, the average age of menarche is 12.3 to 12.6 years, a year or two below some previously reported averages (Bullough, 1981). This decrease in the age of menarche, together with the corresponding tendency of children to mature and grow taller at an earlier age, is known as the **secular trend.** It is believed that the secular trend is the result of improvements in diet, sanitation, and medical care. There is evidence, however, that the secular trend has reached its biological limit. For the first time, the most recent generation to reach adulthood has been found to average the same height and onset of puberty as the generation just before it.

Exercise and Menarche.   More and more evidence has been gathered that strenuous exercise can delay menarche. Researcher Michelle Warren has discovered that young ballet dancers usually have their first menstrual period about 3 years later, on the average, than age-matched controls. Among the dancers, menarche didn't occur until they were an average of 15.4 years old (Warren, 1980).

   At first, some researchers believed that the reason for the delay in menarche was that young ballet dancers were generally lighter and had less body fat than other girls. This might mean that menarche might be triggered when a child reached a certain proportion of height and weight. However, when the ballet dancers were measured after menarche, they were found to be heavier and to have more body fat than the younger nondancers who had also reached menarche. Furthermore, the dancers generally experienced their first menstrual period when they were not exercising because of vacation or injury. Exactly why vigorous exercise should postpone menarche is unknown, but it is suspected

MENARCHE
The first occurrence of menstruation.

SECULAR TREND
The tendency during the last century for children to mature and grow taller at a younger age.

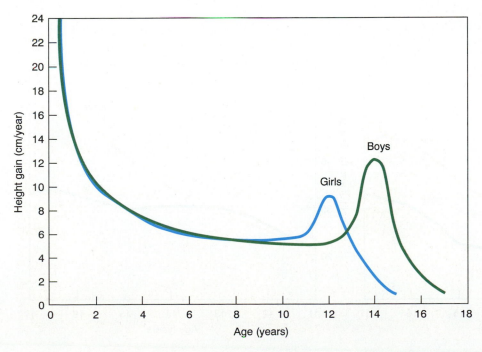

FIGURE 12.2

Typical growth curves for boys and girls. As you can see, height gain declines from a rate of about 24 centimeters (9½ inches) per year just after birth until the years of puberty, when the curve again accelerates. This growth spurt occurs earlier for girls. (SOURCE: Tanner, Whitehouse, & Takaishi, 1966)

Young ballet dancers and gymnasts often show delay of menarche and sexual characteristics.

that it may be the body's way of postponing childbearing during times of stress. It has also been found that strenuous exercise not only can delay menarche, but can also lead to a disruption of the menstrual cycle (Bullen et al., 1985). Again, this may be the body's way of postponing childbearing until the mother is better able to handle a pregnancy.

Muscle Development and Strength in Adolescence

Data indicate that boys are only slightly stronger than girls before the age of 12 years (Malina, 1978). During puberty, however, as muscle growth increases, there is a corresponding increase in strength. From measurements of changes in power during this period, it has been found that girls increase their strength by about 45 percent (Faust, 1977), whereas boys increase theirs by about 65 percent. Following puberty, boys continue to gain in strength (see Figure 12.3).

Males also have an advantage over females in their ability to sustain effort. Their larger hearts and lungs help to supply needed oxygen to the muscles. In addition, during puberty, boys develop greater amounts of oxygen-carrying hemoglobin through the action of testosterone. In practical terms, these differences are slight, however, and many women are able to increase their muscular endurance substantially by engaging in the kinds of bodybuilding exercises that once were considered solely the province of men. Following puberty, the average male can bench press (raise a weight above his chest while lying on his back) about 1.7 times as much weight, relative to his own body weight, as the average female can. However, the average female athlete, after about 6 months of weight training, can bench press 150 pounds, considerably more than the average untrained male (Douglas & Miller, 1977).

Following puberty, boys secrete about 30 to 200 micrograms of testosterone each day, compared with about 5 to 20 micrograms a day in girls. Because testosterone is necessary for the extensive muscle growth that occurs with exercise, girls do not develop much muscle tissue in response to strenuous exercise. After 6 months of weight training, a girl's flexed biceps are not likely to have increased by more than ¼ inch. And yet her arm strength will have grown considerably (Douglas & Miller, 1977). No one fully understands the relationships between muscle mass and strength. Although girls do not have

FIGURE 12.3

Strength of arm pull and arm thrust in children from ages 11 to 17 years. Mixed longitudinal data, 65 to 93 boys and 66 to 96 girls in each group (SOURCE: Tanner, 1962; data from Jones, 1949)

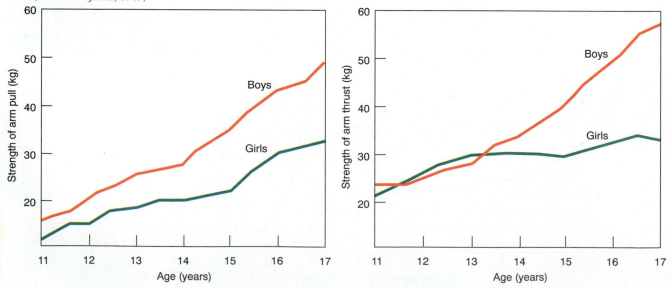

the muscle mass possessed by most boys, they can approach a boy's strength. Still, between the ages of 12 and 17 years, boys tend to become progressively stronger than girls (Malina, 1979).

Nutrition and Its Effects

A considerable amount of energy is required to maintain the rapid growth rate characteristic of adolescence. This energy can be measured in terms of kilocalories. A kilocalorie, more commonly called a calorie, is a measurement of food energy. Adolescents consume a lot of calories and a lot of food. Adults are sometimes surprised at how much food an adolescent can put away without becoming overweight.

Of course, good nutrition is essential for proper development. Malnourished adolescents may suffer from delayed puberty and poor physical growth. Although hunger and starvation in the United States are minimal compared with other nations, many American adolescents are not adequately nourished. Adolescents are more prone than adults to consume inordinate amounts of carbohydrates or junk food and to engage in fad diets. When I was about 15, I had a good friend who wanted to lose about 12 pounds so that he could improve in gymnastics. A normal diet didn't seem interesting enough to him, so he began a kind of Zen macrobiotic transcendental diet (or something like that). At any rate, it seemed to me that for the next three weeks, he ate only brown rice and cherries. I suppose he was lucky that he was healthy to start with, and I must admit he did get thin. He also got mean and sick (he's better now).

Many young women are able to increase their muscle strength substantially through weight-training exercises, once thought to be solely the province of men.

Self-Imposed Malnourishment.   A growing number of children in the United States are underweight and underdeveloped because of self-imposed malnourishment caused by an obsessive fear of "becoming fat" (see At Issue). Such deliberate undereating is believed to be responsible for approximately 7 percent of the stunted growth and delayed puberty found in underdeveloped children. These children, who habitually skip meals, often eat as little as one-third of what they need.

We have to wonder why these children are so afraid that they'll become overweight. Sometimes, children have parents who are preoccupied with slenderness and who often express concern about the child's figure and caution him or her about "becoming fat" (Pugliese, Lifshitz, Grad, Fort, & Marks-Katz, 1983). Because children especially need to fill their nutritional requirements, any dieting for the control or avoidance of childhood obesity should be handled only under a doctor's care. Children who undereat for considerable lengths of time may never be able to make up their lost growth.

Obesity.   Obesity results when the number of calories stored is greater than the number used or passed by the body. It has been determined that the prevalence of obesity (where a person is 20 percent above appropriate weight) has increased by 39 percent among 12- to 17-year-old adolescents during the past two decades (Kolata, 1986).

One hypothesis as to why there are more obese teenagers now than before links television watching to obesity. It seems that children who watch large amounts of television are more likely to be overweight, perhaps because they tend to consume more of the kinds of foods they see in commercials and also because they tend to be less active than children who don't watch as much television (Dietz & Gortmaker, 1985; Palumbo & Dietz, 1985). Fast foods generally have more of their calories in fat than in protein or carbohydrates.

The Pursuit of Thinness

During adolescence, children become more preoccupied with their body image. This may lead to some strange eating habits. The following case study illustrates what can happen to teens who become so concerned about their weight that they resort to bizarre weight control regimens:

> The first vomiting period perpetuated itself into a five-year-long habit in which I had daily planned and unplanned binges and self-induced vomiting sessions up to four times daily. I frequently vomited each of the day's three meals as well as my afternoon "snack" of three or four hamburgers, four to five enormous bowls of ice cream, dozens of cookies, bags of various potato chips, packs of Swiss cheese, two large helpings of french fries, at least two milkshakes, and to top it off, an apple or banana followed by two or more pints of cold milk to help me vomit more easily.
>
> During the night, I sneaked back into the kitchen in the dark so I would not risk awakening any family member by turning on the light. . . . Every night I wished that I could, like everyone else, eat one apple as a midnight snack and then stop. . . . Then I tiptoed to the bathroom to empty myself. Sometimes the food did not come up as quickly as I wanted; so, in panic, I rammed my fingers wildly down my throat, occasionally making it bleed from cutting it with my fingernails. Sometimes I would spend two hours in the bathroom trying to vomit, yet there were other nights when the food came up in less than three minutes. (Muuss, 1986, p. 261)

This case study illustrates a growing problem in the United States. Approximately 1 to 2 percent of the U. S. population either starve themselves or binge on food and then use laxatives or induce vomiting in an effort to remain slender.

Those people who starve themselves are said to be suffering from *anorexia nervosa*, which is characterized by "progressive and/or significant weight loss, alternate binge eating and dieting with avoidance of any 'fattening' foods, amenorrhea [absence of menstruation], hyperactivity and compulsive exercising patterns, and preoccupation with food and nutrition" (Lucas, 1977, p. 139). In severe cases of anorexia, death from starvation or other health problems associated with it (such as heart disorders) may occur. It has been estimated that as many as 20 percent of the people who have the disease eventually die from it (Brumberg, 1985). Anorexics are often extremely emaciated and dangerously underweight, even though they may still report that they feel "fat" and need to lose just a little more weight. Different sources estimate that there are between 150,000 and 500,000 anorexics in the United States.

Regular purging without weight loss is called *bulimia* and is approximately four times as common as anorexia. Bulimics may suffer from dental and digestive problems brought on by the incessant vomiting they induce following their binges, all

In our culture, there is great pressure on women to be slender and attractive.

in an effort to keep from gaining weight. They are also often anxious and depressed over their bizarre and secretive habit. Bulimics, like anorexics, tend to be adolescent females. They may be less likely to receive help for their problem because outwardly, at least, they may appear perfectly normal.

It's hard for some people to understand why anyone would want to follow every meal of the day with the disgusting experience of vomiting or how anyone who looked like she just stepped out of a concentration camp could insist that she needs to lose weight. Psychologists and physicians have searched for physical causes to explain these disorders. There is evidence of hypothalamic dysfunction in anorexics, although it has not been determined whether this dysfunction is a cause or merely an effect of the disease (Casper, 1984; Gold, Pottash, Sweeney, Martin, & Davies, 1980). Thyroid disease may account for a small minority of cases. There is also evidence that the physical mechanism that signals satiation in bulimics may be faulty, thus allowing them to con-

AT ISSUE

The Pursuit of Thinness, continued

tinue to eat large quantities of food without feeling "full" (Geracioti & Liddle, 1988). Moreover, there is evidence that hormones may play a role, because levels of the hormone vasopressin are found to be higher in bulimic than in nonbulimic women (Demitrack et al., 1992).

Another hint about the cause of these disorders is that males rarely have them. Adolescent females account for 90 to 95 percent of all cases of anorexia and bulimia, which has also led researchers to look for possible social or environmental causes. In our culture, there is great pressure on women to be slender and attractive. Adolescent females, especially those who have low self-esteem or who come from families in conflict (Grant & Fodor, 1986; Johnson & Flach, 1985), often try to emulate their vision of the slender models depicted on television and in magazines. This may be a way for them to show their control and to increase their sense of self-worth. One study demonstrated that adolescent girls in

competitive environments that emphasize weight and appearance face more pressure to have the "thin" ideal body (Brooks-Gunn, Burrow, & Warren, 1988). And girls who attend schools in which social acceptance into a clique or group is highly valued tend to be less satisfied with their body weight than are girls who attend less cliquish schools (Richards, Boxer, Petersen, & Albrecht, 1990).

Some researchers have argued that it is essential that society decrease the pressure it places on adolescents to have a certain body physique in order to be loved and admired. Many bulimics and anorexics may indeed be casualties of the pursuit of thinness. On the other hand, the American emphasis on being slender may help some people to maintain suitable weight and avoid obesity. Perhaps if the emphasis were more on the weight appropriate for good health than on what would look best in chic clothes, it would help remove some of the pressure to be inordinately thin.

Research has shown that fat calories are far more likely to be stored than are calories from other sources. For this reason, 400 calories of french fries are actually more fattening than 400 calories of plain baked potato (Miller, Lindeman, Wallace & Niederpruem, 1990).

It has also been shown that obesity is mostly determined by inheritance (Grilo & Pogue-Geile, 1991). Children inherit different numbers of fat cells, and the number they inherit determines, in part, how well their bodies will store fat. Children from families in which parents or other family members are overweight may be able to store excess food more efficiently than other children do and may therefore be considered genetically obese. For example, among the Pima Indians in Arizona, a farming tribe for the last 2,000 years, the vast majority are extremely obese. Their obesity begins in childhood. By the time they are 35, about half of the population have diabetes. It appears that through natural selection, the Pima body is prepared for a famine. However, in the food-rich United States, body preparation for a famine may no longer be an advantage.

During adolescence, obesity can present severe problems because of the adolescent's preoccupation with self-image. Overweight adolescents may be socially isolated. Often, the social isolation is self-imposed out of fear of ridicule. Adolescents who are teased because of their obesity often take comfort by eating more, which perpetuates the cycle.

COGNITIVE DEVELOPMENT IN ADOLESCENCE

In most individuals, the ability to reason and to think probably becomes fully developed during adolescence. Erik Erikson (1968) described adolescence as a time of identity crisis when the questions "Who am I?" and "What is my role in life?" become dominant themes. Without the cognitive changes that occur, it would not be possible for adolescents to consider such complex philosophical questions.

Consider the cognitive changes that occur during adolescence. First, the adolescent becomes capable of dealing with the logic of combinations, which requires the simultaneous manipulation of many factors, either singly or in conjunction. Second, the adolescent becomes able to use abstract concepts to make thought more flexible. And third, the adolescent becomes able to deal with the hypothetical as well as the real (Piaget & Inhelder, 1969). According to Piaget, this last step is the most advanced form of cognition, and it defines formal operations.

The Logic of Combinations

In 1958, Inhelder and Piaget presented a chemistry problem to a number of children and adolescents of different ages. The subjects were shown four containers (A, B, C, and D), each of which contained a different colorless liquid. They were then shown a separate container and were told that it contained a catalyst, or activating agent. It was explained that the catalyst in combination with one or more of the other liquids would produce a yellow mixture. The subjects were then asked to discover which combination or combinations would produce the colored liquid. How would you solve this problem? Many of the subjects began by examining what happened when the catalyst was mixed independently with each of the colorless liquids. This first attempt did not produce a yellow liquid. This was a simple enough place to start, but where would you go from there?

Figure 12.4 shows the correct strategy. As you can see, there are only four possible combinations of the catalyst (1) with only one of the unknown liquids (A, B, C, or D): 1 with A, 1 with B, 1 with C, and 1 with D. Then you need only progress through the other possible combinations of three (1 with A and B, 1 with A and C, etc.), four, and five substances to test every possibility. The combinations that will produce the yellow liquid are circled in the figure.

Children who have not begun to enter the period of formal operations use less sophisticated reasoning and attack the problem with a hit-or-miss strategy. This ineffective approach leads them to repeat combinations they have tried

As adolescents begin to acquire formal operations thinking, they come to understand the logic of combinations and are able, for the first time, to think scientifically.

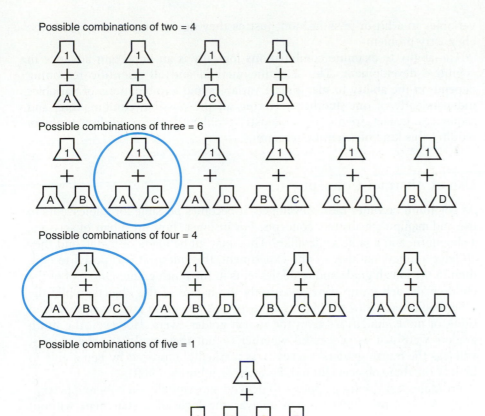

Possible combinations of two = 4

Possible combinations of three = 6

Possible combinations of four = 4

Possible combinations of five = 1

Key
1 = potassium iodide
A = diluted sulfuric acid
B = water
C = oxygenated water
D = thiosulfate

FIGURE 12.4

A chemistry problem requiring a logical analysis of combinations.

before or to overlook some of the possible combinations. As young adolescents begin to develop formal operations, they become capable of examining combinations systematically, in a scientific way.

This ability to examine combinations logically was also demonstrated by Inhelder and Piaget in their famous pendulum problem. A pendulum can be created by suspending a weight from a string and allowing the weight to swing free. In the pendulum problem, the subject is asked to determine which of four factors affects the rate at which the weight will swing. The four possibilities are the force of the initial push that you give the weight, the amount of weight suspended from the string, how far out you pull the weight before you let it go, and the length of the string. The subjects are allowed to experiment with the pendulum to determine which of these variables affects the rate of the swinging (how many complete swings per unit of time the pendulum makes).

Adolescents who are able to examine logically the possible combinations discover that only the length of the string affects the rate at which the pendulum swings. Once the length of the pendulum string is set, each completed swing (once back and forth) takes the same amount of time regardless of how fast or slow the pendulum swings (because a faster swinging pendulum has farther to travel). This is why pendulums make good timepieces; even as they slow down, their rate stays constant. Children who have not yet attained formal operational thinking attempt to manipulate the different variables in a hit-or-miss fashion, just as they do when presented with the chemistry problem.

The ability to examine combinations logically is an important advance in cognitive development. The scientific method and all scientific reasoning depend on the ability to manipulate variables and combinations of variables independently of one another, covering all the possible combinations and sequences. In fact, solving the chemistry problem or the pendulum problem requires this kind of scientific reasoning.

Use of Abstract Concepts

As cognition becomes more developed, it becomes possible for adolescents to use and manipulate abstract concepts. For instance, how are a pair of scissors, a shoehorn, and a table knife alike? They may all be made of metal, and they all have a functional use. In one experiment, this question was posed to children in the fourth grade and to adolescents in the ninth grade. One-half of the children in each group were given only the names of the objects, while the other half actually saw the objects. As expected, the ninth graders were able to think of more similarities than the fourth graders were. However, the ninth graders were just as successful whether or not they could see the objects, whereas the fourth graders' success was markedly improved by being able to look at the three objects (Elkind, Barocas, & Johnsen, 1969).

Preadolescent thinking appears to depend substantially on concrete perceptions. Adolescents, however, can analyze the logic of a statement without becoming tied to its concrete properties. In a series of experiments, adolescents and preadolescents were asked to judge whether certain statements were true, false, or impossible to know (Osherson & Markman, 1974–75). The subjects were told that the experimenter had hidden a poker chip in his hand and that "either this chip is green or it is not green." Most of the preadolescents thought that it was impossible to judge because they could not see the hidden chip. The adolescents, however, were able to deal with the concept of green abstractly. They realized that something must either be a particular color or not be that color. The adolescents realized that the statement had to be true. For that matter, everything in the universe is either green or not green. Preadolescents have trouble comprehending such an abstraction. This is one of the reasons why educators usually wait until children reach adolescence before they seriously present them with abstractions such as algebra, as described in the Chapter Preview.

Using and Understanding the Hypothetical

By the time adolescents have reached the age of 15 years, they are often capable of the most advanced cognitive thinking (Niemark, 1982). As cognitive processes mature, the adolescent comes to respond to the world and its institutions with a more encompassing view (see Figure 12.5). In part, this is because of the adolescent's ability to develop abstract hypothetical ideas. The adolescent's concepts of morality become more philosophical. Religious and political views often undergo considerable analysis and change during this time. Adolescents who have treated religion in concrete terms may begin to ask questions about the nature of morality or religion, and their beliefs may become more mature and personal (Kuhlen & Arnold, 1944). During the transition into the formal operations period, the adolescent begins to view political institutions as governed by general principles. Older adolescents often are capable of considering the hypothetical potential outcomes of decisions made

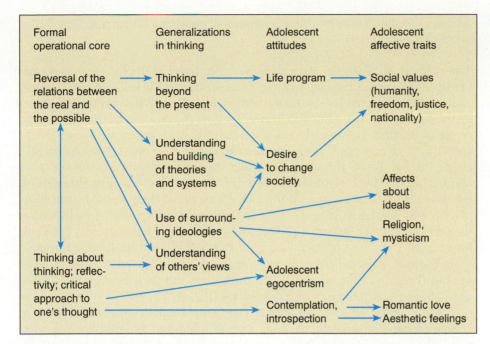

FIGURE 12.5

Model relating formal operations to the characteristic of adolescence. (Adolescent egocentrism is discussed in the Applications section.) (SOURCE: Blasi & Hoeffel, 1974, p. 345)

by governments. The development of political ideology is closely tied to the cognitive development that occurs during adolescence. In one study, adolescents who demonstrated advanced moral and cognitive development were found generally to be the most politically active (Haan, Smith, & Block, 1968).

It's not uncommon, however, for individuals to fail to reach the period of formal operations during adolescence or even during adulthood (Blasi & Hoeffel, 1974). In fact, cross-cultural studies generally find that among rural and non-Western societies, the majority of adolescents fail to complete the development of formal operations (Ashton, 1975; Glick, 1975). In the United States, a comprehensive longitudinal study of adults and adolescents found that only 30 percent of adults attained formal operations (Kuhn, Langer, Kohlberg, & Haan, 1977).

In one of the most detailed studies of formal operations, a researcher examined children in the sixth, eighth, tenth, and twelfth grades, whose ages were between 11 and 18 years. Each child was given a total of 10 different tasks, each of which had been used by Inhelder and Piaget to demonstrate formal operational thinking. Among these 10 tasks was the pendulum problem described earlier. Interestingly, only about 2 percent of the subjects who were able to perform at the formal operational level on one task were able to do so on all tasks. Almost all the subjects showed inconsistency in their ability as they moved from one task to the next (Martorano, 1977). Subjects who used advanced formal operational thinking to solve one problem often were found to use rudimentary forms of concrete operational thinking in solving another problem.

Such results demonstrate the complexity of measuring advanced cognitive processes. In fact, some psychologists have argued that if advanced human cognition were closely tied to maturational changes, as Piaget suggested, then evidence for these developmental changes should be more apparent from cross-cultural research. The fact that adolescents in Western cultures are better able to solve problems designed to measure formal operational thinking has been thought by some scientists to indicate a cultural bias in the testing. There is evidence to support the argument that specific experience can improve an adolescent's ability to solve formal operational problems (Danner & Day, 1977; Siegler & Liebert, 1975).

The Effect of Specific Experiences. Gottfried Wilhelm von Leibnitz (1646–1716) was a famous German philosopher and a brilliant mathematician. Leibnitz is credited by many with independently developing calculus. People in Leibnitz's day liked to gamble, just as they do today. Dice were particularly popular. Fortunately (or unfortunately, whichever way you see it), gambling houses weren't always successful, because no one knew how to calculate the odds of throwing particular numbers on dice. Leibnitz was approached by "businessmen" who wanted his help in calculating the odds of any given throw. For instance, if three dice were used, what would be the odds of rolling a 3—that is, three 1s? Again, using three dice, how much harder would it be to roll a 3 than a 4? And so on. Leibnitz worked on this problem for over 20 years, and he finally decided that it could not be solved! Interestingly, though, many college students, some with no college math at all, can figure out the odds of throwing a 3 with three dice, and they can figure out how much harder it would be than throwing a 4 (Bower, 1979).*

While it might seem amazing that a great mathematician couldn't solve a simple probability problem, we must keep in mind that Leibnitz undoubtedly would have been capable of the mathematics involved if he had ever thought of *probability!* But Leibnitz had never been exposed to probability theory, and no one else in his day had either. Leibnitz spent most of his time trying to understand how dice might bounce when they struck a surface! The idea of *odds* never crossed his mind. When adolescents are asked to solve formal operational tasks such as the pendulum problem, they may rely on previous exposure to the general concepts of the scientific method. Perhaps children in non-Western cultures who haven't had such experiences are unable to solve the pendulum problem, and are unable to understand it when it is explained to them, because they have not had enough exposure to the general principles involved. After all, until Galileo solved the pendulum problem, no one had. This is an information-processing view of advanced cognitive thinking.

---

*The odds of rolling a 3 (1, 1, 1) with three dice are $\frac{1}{6} \times \frac{1}{6} \times \frac{1}{6}$, or $\frac{1}{216}$ (1 chance in 216 throws). The odds of rolling a 4 with three dice are three times more likely, because there are three ways to do it (1, 1, 2 or 1, 2, 1 or 2, 1, 1, or 1 chance in every 72 throws.

Adolescent Egocentrism: Understanding Adolescents Even Though They May Not Understand You

By the time children enter adolescence, they have been found to demonstrate a kind of egocentrism. Adolescents aren't egocentric in the same way preschoolers are—that is, only able to understand the world from their own perspective. Adolescents are certainly aware that others may have perspectives different from their own and that the sun doesn't shine to light their path. (Preschoolers often say that the sun shines "so I can see.") An adolescent is far removed from that kind of egocentrism. However, as children enter adolescence, the limits of their judgment and logic make them susceptible to another kind of egocentrism: They may become deeply involved with themselves.

Initially, as adolescents become able to deal with abstractions, they also become capable of thinking in greater detail about the thoughts of others. They form hypotheses about what others may be thinking (Elkind, 1967). As Elkind has said, "It is this capacity to take account of other people's thoughts . . . which is the crux of adolescent egocentrism" (Elkind, 1967, p. 1029). The adolescent believes, "If I'm thinking about me, they must be thinking about me" (Looft, 1971). Adolescents may also discover conflicting thoughts and behaviors in themselves because, for the first time, they are able to compare the different ways they may behave in school, with their friends, with their family, and in their romantic relationships (Harter & Monsour, 1992). This may not only leave adolescents unsure of what others think of them, but make them unsure even of what they think of themselves!

I can recall first being concerned in this way about what other people were thinking when I was 12 years old and was playing with my friend Vinny, who was 11, and his 10-year-old brother, Junior. I had toy hand grenades loaded with caps that would go off when the grenades hit the ground. Vinny and Junior had a metal replica of a 50-caliber machine gun that seemed to weigh a ton. With this arsenal, we decided to go across to a vacant city lot and destroy "the enemy" (I think it was the Nazis at the time).

As we were winning the war, I noticed a young couple walking down the street past where we were playing. Even so, my friends continued the attack, and perhaps a few months earlier I would have, too. But now, for the first time, I felt embarrassed. I hid my grenades and walked about nonchalantly, inspecting the bits of weedy botany growing about the lot until the couple had passed.

After they had gone, I started to assault the one lump of remaining high ground (only to discover that I was too late—the Nazis had gotten Vinny and Junior because I hadn't been there to back them up; I live with the guilt to this day). Now that I look back at it, I doubt that the young couple really would have given much thought to whether I was too old to play "army," but at the time I was sure I was the most important thing on their minds.

Because of this egocentrism, adolescents often place an inordinate emphasis on acne blemishes, physical features, and size. They may think that their parents, friends, teachers, and siblings are as concerned about them as they are themselves. A further consequence of this egocentrism is that an adolescent often feel like he is "on stage," playing to an "imaginary audience" (Adams & Jones,

Adolescents who are egocentric believe that others are often thinking about them.

1981; Elkind & Bowen, 1979; Gray & Hudson, 1984). "Moreover, because he believes he is of importance to so many people, he comes to regard himself, and particularly his feelings, as something special and unique" (Elkind, 1967, p. 1031). This sense of being unique becomes obvious when adolescents make statements to parents or other adults such as, "You can't possibly know how I feel" or "You just can't understand how much I love him" (Elkind, 1978).

All of us are concerned about ourselves to some degree, and many of us wonder from time to time what others may think of us. However, most of us are aware that others have their own lives and concerns and that we are not on stage everywhere we go. Most of us are no longer as egocentric as we may have been during adolescence (Enright, Lapsley, & Shukla, 1979). This lessening of egocentrism, or decentering, as it is called, appears to occur when formal operations finally become established (Elkind, 1967). Through social interactions and objective analysis of our own thoughts, we come to realize that although we may be important to some, we are not the center of everyone's attention.

There may also be ways to help adolescents from becoming excessively egocentric. For example, it might be helpful for adolescents to discuss their feelings in detail with many different peers and adults. In this way, they may be better able to evaluate their own position and to understand positions different from their own. Perhaps the best way for adolescents to overcome their egocentric thoughts and feelings is to develop a genuine, intimate relationship with another person. This, more than anything, may foster mature interpersonal relations (Elkind, 1967; Looft, 1971; Piaget, 1967).

SUMMARY

- Almost every aspect of a child, including emotions, skills, and aptitudes, is related directly or indirectly to body structure. Psychologists are aware of how physical growth and development affect a person's emotions and behavior.

- Adolescents of the same age may be prepubescent or physically mature. Level of development can profoundly affect adolescents and their interactions with peers and the school environment.

- At the onset of puberty, the testes or ovaries enlarge. During puberty, the reproductive system matures, and sexual characteristics develop. At this time, the adolescent's growth undergoes a marked acceleration. Boys usually reach their full height between the ages of 18 and 20 years, whereas girls reach this plateau between the ages of 16 and 17 years.

- The decrease in the age of menarche, along with the corresponding tendency of children to mature and grow taller at an earlier age, is known as the secular trend. It is believed that the secular trend is the result of improvements in diet, sanitation, and medical care. Increasing evidence indicates that strenuous exercise can delay menarche and disrupt the normal menstrual cycle.

- During puberty, as muscle growth increases, there is a corresponding increase in strength. Measurements of changes in strength during this period show that girls increase their strength by about 45 percent, whereas boys increase theirs by about 65 percent.

- During adolescence, children become more preoccupied with their body image. This, in turn, may lead to self-imposed starvation (anorexia nervosa) or a cycle of binging and purging (bulimia).

- During adolescence, obesity can present severe problems because adolescents often are preoccupied with self-image. Overweight adolescents may be socially isolated. Often, the social isolation is self-imposed out of fear of ridicule.

- A number of cognitive changes occur in adolescence. First, the adolescent becomes capable of dealing with the logic of combinations, which requires the simultaneous manipulation of many factors either singly or in conjunction. Second, the adolescent becomes able to use abstract concepts to make thought more flexible. Third, the adolescent becomes able to deal with the hypothetical as well as the real.

- As cognitive processes mature, the adolescent comes to respond to the world and its institutions with a more encompassing view. The adolescent's concepts of morality become more sophisticated, and religious and political views often undergo change.

- By the time children enter adolescence, they are well beyond the egocentrism of preschoolers, yet they still demonstrate a kind of egocentrism.

QUESTIONS FOR DISCUSSION

1. Because cognitive development appears to be completed by the time adolescents are about 15, should 16- and 17-year-olds be given the vote?

2. Do you think that other factors besides changes in cognitive development may contribute to adolescent egocentrism? For example, how might the emphasis in TV commercials on appearance affect an adolescent's concern with self?

3. Can you recall specific instances from your adolescence when your thinking underwent a change? How might this change have related to your cognitive development?

SUGGESTIONS FOR FURTHER READING

1. Elkind, D. (1981). *Children and adolescents: Interpretive essays on Jean Piaget* (3rd ed.). New York: Oxford University Press.

2. Graydanus, D. E. (1991). *Caring for your adolescent: Ages 12 to 21.* New York: Bantam.

3. Kaplan, L. J. (1984). *Adolescence: The farewell to childhood.* New York: Simon & Schuster.

4. Klausmeier, H. J., & Allen, P. S. (1978). *Cognitive development of children and youth: A longitudinal study.* New York: Academic Press.

5. Santrock, J. W. (1990). *Adolescence* (4th ed.). Dubuque, IA: Brown.

6. Stein, P., & Unell, B. (1986). *Anorexia nervosa: Finding the lifeline.* Minneapolis: CompCare.

CHAPTER 13

Adolescent Social and Personality Development

CHAPTER PREVIEW

Rites de Passage

In some cultures, there is no social period of adolescence. There are only childhood and adulthood. In such cultures, when a child enters puberty, it is a sign that he or she has become an adult. In many groups and tribes throughout the world, the social change from childhood to adulthood happens in a single day. For instance, a boy might be summoned by his elders, along with other children his age, and taken to a place where a ceremony is conducted that marks his passage into adulthood. Such a ceremony is called a rite de passage, *or rite of passage. The ceremony is often stressful. A tribe in the South Pacific requires that boys leap from a 100-foot-high platform built in a tree, with nothing to protect them but some 90-foot-long vines tied to their feet. Many of the boys said that it was scary, but that it was exhilarating, too. Western observers of this practice went on to invent bungee jumping!*

Among the Mandan, a now-extinct American Plains Indian tribe, boys had their pectoral muscles pierced with sharp sticks and then were suspended by ropes attached to the sticks (as depicted in the film A Man Called Horse*). The boys who could last the longest were thought of as the most manly. Among the Australian aborigines, a boy is held by his sponsor while circumcision is performed with a sharp stone tool. In each case, the ceremony represents a transition to adult status.*

In the Jewish religion, when a boy turns 13, he goes through a bar mitzvah ceremony to mark his passage into adulthood. Traditionally, the bar mitzvah was a true rite de passage, *but not as it's practiced today. In a real* rite de passage, *the child's social environment would change radically. He would leave his village as a child, treated as such by his parents and other adults; but when he returned, he would have the full status of an adult and would be treated as an adult. In our culture, after a boy is bar mitzvahed, he goes right back to school, and nobody expects that he will immediately vote, drive a car, or be married.*

For our children, the transition to adulthood is slow, marked by many separate changes over the period of adolescence. A 12-year-old girl may be allowed to wear nylons and makeup, a 16-year-old may be allowed to drive, an 18-year-old may marry or vote, and in many states individuals must be 21 years old to drink alcohol legally. For this reason, adolescents often regard smoking, drinking, driving, and sexual activities as indications of adult status.

In this chapter, we'll examine the social world of adolescence in our society and see how personality can be shaped during the transition from childhood to adulthood.

THE EMERGENCE OF ADOLESCENCE

In 1904, G. Stanley Hall published the first scientific study of adolescence. His ideas were published in a two-volume work titled, curiously enough, *Adolescence,* and they had a tremendous influence on subsequent thought concerning the subject. Hall saw adolescence as a period of storm and stress. He believed the adolescent period to be full of many changes in direction and swings in mood—a time of turbulence and turmoil.

Most people would agree that adolescence is a time of conflict and stress. Think of all the changes that an adolescent must face. Adolescence is a time when self-concept and attitudes may alter considerably (McKinney & Moore, 1982; Harter & Monsour, 1992). Adolescents must deal for the first time with sexual relationships, the choice of a career, political decisions, economic alternatives, and a host of other "adult" tasks. As Erik Erikson pointed out, there is an important struggle to establish an identity during adolescence. With so many major conflicts and decisions to face, it's no wonder that the journey from puberty to adulthood is turbulent—quite unlike the more gentle and serene adult years. This is why the adolescent . . . wait a minute! The "more gentle and serene adult years? Is that right? Let's start again. Adolescence is a time of unusual turbulence and conflict (so far, so good) unlike—when? Now that we think about it, life at any age can become turbulent and filled with conflict. Unfortunately, life's problems don't end when one turns 20.

Actually, an 8-year nationwide study conducted at the University of Michigan concluded that adolescence is fairly benign. The study, which followed 2,000 adolescent males as they went from tenth grade to the age of 20 years, revealed that self-concept, outlook on life, and a number of other attitudes were well formed by the time adolescents entered tenth grade. Moreover, when the subjects were retested at age 20, their attitudes were found not to have undergone the dramatic changes that might be expected following a turbulent adolescence (Bachman, O'Malley, & Johnston, 1978). Others have confirmed these findings (Offer, Ostrov, & Howard, 1981; Savin-Williams & Demo, 1984). According to one group of researchers,

> The most dramatic . . . findings are those that permit us to characterize the model American teenager as feeling confident, happy, and self-satisfied—a portrait of the American

adolescent that contrasts sharply with that drawn by many theorists of adolescent development, who contend that adolescence is pervaded with turmoil, dramatic mood swings, and rebellion. (Offer, Ostrov, & Howard, 1981, pp. 83–84)

One common assumption has been that the activation of hormones during adolescence causes upset and stress. But the surge in hormones during the adolescent period doesn't in itself appear to cause undue stress (Buchanan, Eccles, & Becker, 1992), although it is difficult to separate cultural forces from hormonal ones that might, for example, encourage adolescent boys to be aggressive.

Without a doubt, there are stresses associated with being an adolescent. It's just that we might be hard pressed to say for sure that these stresses are more severe than those encountered during other periods of life. Even so, although adolescence may not generally be a time of unusual turbulence, some adolescents may have a particularly difficult time coping with the changes that occur. There is a great range and diversity of adjustment patterns during adolescence (Boxer, Gershenson, & Offer, 1984). There may also be specific stresses associated with adolescence that are qualitatively different from the stresses of adulthood.

A Changing Philosophy

As adolescents develop cognitive skills, they are confronted for the first time with the overwhelming complexities and abstract qualities of the world. Suddenly, nothing is simple. Religious values, political values, social concepts, and questions about personal identity seem to encompass endless hypothetical possibilities from which the adolescent is expected by parents and society to draw conclusions and adopt a life philosophy. During our adult years, we have time to organize and make sense of this confusion. We adopt a philosophy. We take political, social, and moral positions and incorporate them into our identity. In this sense, adulthood would have a stability that is not immediately available to the adolescent.

Our culture demands that adolescents handle a number of developmental tasks. As we have discussed, sexual relationships must be faced. Social maturity in dealings with both sexes is expected. The adolescent's own masculine or feminine role must be realized and adjusted to his or her satisfaction. And the adolescent must come to terms with his or her physical development. Our culture also expects adolescents to achieve emotional independence from parents and other adults. Decisions about whether to marry or have children become more pressing. Adolescents are expected to develop a philosophy and moral ideology as well as to achieve socially responsible behavior.

Choosing a Career

Pursuing a career choice is an essential part of adolescent development. Researchers Inhelder and Piaget have stated, "The adolescent becomes an adult when he undertakes a real job" (Inhelder & Piaget, 1958, p. 346). Piaget argued that once adolescents have entered formal operations, their newly acquired ability to use the hypothetical allows them to create ideal representations. Piaget believed that the existence of such ideals, without the tempering of reality, rapidly leads adolescents to become intolerant of their nonidealistic world and to press for reform and change in a characteristically idealistic and adolescent way. Piaget has said,

An adolescent's first job has a way of bringing the "real world" into sharp focus.

True adaptation to society comes automatically when the adolescent reformer attempts to put his ideas to work. Just as experience reconciles formal thought with the reality of things, so does effective and enduring work, undertaken in concrete and well-defined situations, cure dreams. (Piaget, 1967, pp. 68–69)

Of course, youthful idealism often may be a valid response to the ills of society, and most people don't like to give up their dreams. Perhaps, taken slightly out of context, as it is here, Piaget's quote seems a little harsh. What he was emphasizing, however, is the way reality can modify and shape idealistic conceptions. Some people refer to such modification as "maturity." Piaget argued that attaining and accepting a vocation is one of the best ways to modify idealized conceptions and to mature.

As careers and vocations become less available during times of inflation, lowered productivity, or rising unemployment, adolescents may be especially hard hit. Difficult economic times may leave many adolescents confused about their role in society. For this reason, government job programs as well as community interventions that provide summer and vacation jobs not only provide economic relief but also, in the view of many developmental researchers, help to stimulate needed adolescent ego development (Vondracek & Lerner, 1982).

This might lead one to wonder if adolescents who take part-time jobs during the school year are at an even greater advantage than those who work only during the summer. Interestingly, just the opposite is true. Adolescents who held part-time jobs during the school year were found to have poorer grades, greater psychological and physical stress, more drug and alcohol use, and greater delinquency. They did not show any benefits from their added work experience, such as increased self-reliance or self-esteem (Steinberg & Dornbusch, 1991). While summer jobs and vocational training may stimulate adolescent ego development, for most adolescents, school is a full-time job. Taking on what amounts to a second job during the school year is not advisable.

A Crisis of Identity

According to Erik Erikson, the adolescent is faced with the task of developing an acceptable, functional, and stable self-concept. Those adolescents who succeed, Erikson argued, will establish a sense of identity, and those who fail will suffer **role confusion.** Erikson said that the sense of identity is experienced as a sense of self as distinct from others. The most obvious concomitants of a sense of identity are "a feeling of being at home in one's body, a sense of 'knowing where one is going,' and an inner assuredness of anticipated recognition from those who count" (Erikson, 1968, p. 165). In other words, adolescents need to maintain a meaningful connection with the past, establish relatively stable goals for the future, and keep up adequate interpersonal relationships in the present to feel that they have an identity. As Erikson said, "The adolescent needs to integrate a conscious sense of individual uniqueness" with an "unconscious striving for a continuity of experience" (Erikson, 1968, p. 165).

Many other psychologists have found the concept of identity a valuable tool for understanding adolescent psychosocial development. Research and case studies have indicated that the resolution of the identity crisis depends greatly on the adolescent's society, family, and peer groups. Ideally, adolescents achieve their new identity by abandoning some of the values and aspirations set for them by their parents and society while at the same time accepting others. A number of investigations have found that a mature adolescent identity is more likely to be achieved when there is a mutual redefinition of the parent-child relationship (Grotevant & Cooper, 1985), that is, when both parents and children share their own perspectives in a mutually supportive way (Powers, Hauser, Schwartz, Noam, & Jacobson, 1983). Occasionally, the adolescent fails in this task, which results in the formation of a premature identity. This identity may develop when an adolescent hasn't actively questioned alternatives and has made a commitment to a particular identity too early. This **foreclosure** often occurs when adolescents accept the beliefs or expectations of parents or others before having a chance to explore on their own.

Other adolescents may experience **identity diffusion** and find themselves committed to few goals or values and apathetic about searching for their own identity. And some individuals may even adopt a **negative identity,** one that is opposite to what they were expected to adopt. An adolescent who is still in the process of searching for an identity is said to be in **moratorium.**

The following case study illustrates how family, peers, future goals, and other forces can create role confusion.

ROLE CONFUSION

A consequence of the failure to establish a sense of identity during Erikson's fifth psychosocial stage. Without a sense of identity, the individual will be confused about his or her role in society and will find it difficult to form a life philosophy or create a stable base on which to build a career or have a family.

FORECLOSURE

The failure of an adolescent to explore and discover a self-identity; the unquestioning acceptance and adoption of the identity demanded by parents or other important adults.

IDENTITY DIFFUSION

A problem faced by adolescents who find themselves committed to few goals or values and who are apathetic about searching for their own identity.

NEGATIVE IDENTITY

A development among some adolescents in which the identity adopted is the opposite of what parents and society desired or expected.

MORATORIUM

The time during which an adolescent is searching for an identity.

LINDA C.—A CASE OF ROLE CONFUSION.

Linda C. was successful in high school. She was well liked by other people and maintained a B average. She was the second child in a fairly strict Italian Catholic family. Her brother Thomas was 1 year older than she was.

Her two closest girlfriends in school were sexually active and had steady boyfriends. Linda felt a great deal of peer pressure to find a boy to "go with," so she developed a relationship with a boy in her class, a relationship that was sexual but excluded intercourse because she believed that it was wrong outside of marriage.

Linda's father was an alcoholic. Often, she was embarrassed by her father's drinking. For example, she was very upset when her boyfriend arrived one day to see her father drunkenly falling down the stairs. She thought that her father's behavior reflected on her.

Linda was determined to go to college and make a better life for herself than the one her family provided. Her father, however, believed that girls shouldn't go to college, and he spent his savings to finance his son's education at a private university. Linda's brother had been a poor student in high school, and eventually he failed at college, having spent the family's savings. Linda, still determined, decided when she was 19 years old to attend night school.

She had been much influenced by reading about Madame Curie in high school, and she decided to become a physicist. She took physics and math classes. She was the only woman in many of her classes; the other students were mostly employees of an aerospace company who were taking classes to help advance their careers. Linda was attractive and had several admirers who accompanied her for coffee during class breaks.

Unexpectedly, her high school boyfriend, with whom she had been going steady for four years, left to take up with her best friend. Linda's father's alcoholism became more severe, and Linda spent more time at school to escape from her family. She fell in love with a 54-year-old draftsman in her class who talked kindly to her and made her feel wanted. She began a sexual relationship with him. Later she discovered that he was married and had three children (all older than she). She ended the relationship. Her grades suffered; she failed her courses.

During this time, Linda continued to live at home. She quit night school, but found that her days and nights were still turned around. She slept until 3 P.M. and walked her German shepherd until dawn. She gained weight and became less attractive; men stopped approaching her. She thought it was just as well. She continued to stay at home. Her parents tolerated her, hoping that eventually she would marry. She took some boring night jobs and couldn't seem to adjust her sleep schedule. She didn't like going out on her own. She had no close friends. To placate her parents, she began to do volunteer work for the church, where, for the first time, she felt she had found her identity. She gained more weight, worked longer hours for the church, and lived at home. She gave up paying jobs, with her parents' permission, so that she could devote even more time to the church. She did not want to become a nun, because her parents wanted grandchildren. The more her father drank, the more he referred to her lack of a husband. She remained at home until she was 28, at which time she took her own life.

Statistically, one wouldn't consider Linda's adolescence and later life normal. Most adolescents and young adults don't commit suicide. However, an alarming number do.

Just consider the problems that Linda had with her "identity." She had one boyfriend and few girlfriends. It was the fashion to go steady and pay total attention to your partner instead of to friends of the same sex. Part of her identity, then, was that she was this boy's girlfriend. (Many women find that their identity after marriage is that of, say, Mrs. John Jones—no first name or last name of their own.) Eventually, Linda's "girlfriend" identity was rejected by her boyfriend.

Then there was Linda's identity as a sexual woman. She found herself torn between the desires of church and family and those of peer group and boyfriend. "Everything but intercourse" was her solution. Then her boyfriend left her for her best friend, who was more sexually willing. That must have intensified the conflict she experienced between competing values.

Was Linda physically attractive or not? At different times she held the identity of sexually attractive or nonattractive. She never achieved emotional independence from her parents. She failed to develop a career identity or goal for work. She tried to develop an ideology within the church, but she did this mostly to placate her parents. Linda had failed most of the developmental tasks that an adolescent faces. At 28, emotionally she was still an adolescent.

Adolescent Suicide

Suicide is one of the leading causes of death among adolescents. Since 1965, the rate of suicide among adolescents and young adults ages 15 to 24 years has more than doubled in the United States (see Figure 13.1) (U.S. Bureau of the Census, 1993). Every year in the United States, approximately 2,000 adolescents between the ages of 15 and 19 take their own lives and about 250,000 adolescents attempt suicide. Because many attempts go unreported, there is reason to believe that this figure is conservative. Moreover, the increase in suicide rate among teenagers is an international phenomenon; from the 1950s to the 1980s, suicide rates in most European countries also increased (Sainsbury, Jenkins, & Levey, 1980; McClure, 1986).

Among teenagers who commit suicide, the ratio of boys to girls is about 4:1 or 5:1 (Holden, 1986). This is because males tend to use means that are immediately lethal, such as shooting or hanging, while females tend to favor means that are less violent and take more time, such as poison or gas. Girls are therefore more likely to be rescued and so are more likely to make an unsuccessful suicide attempt—at a ratio that has been estimated at anywhere from 2:1 to 8:1 (Holden, 1986).

Interestingly, the majority of adolescent suicides occur among those who are currently using alcohol or other drugs (Fowler, Rich, & Young, 1986; Rich, Sherman, & Fowler, 1990). It is difficult, however, to determine whether the drugs contribute directly to the suicide or whether they, like the act of suicide itself, are simply related to depression and poor impulse control.

Depression and poor impulse control are both considered common precursors to suicide and may be considerably influenced by genetics and brain chemistry (Gross-Isseroff, Dillon, Israeli, & Biegon, 1990). It is possible, then, that there may be an inherited predisposition toward suicide and that someday, medical testing will be able to determine individuals who are at risk.

Warning Signs.   A number of signs may warn of a potential suicide. The first sign is an adolescent's failure to achieve in school, a sign that should be heed-

Many adolescents who commit suicide first give an indication that suicide is on their mind.

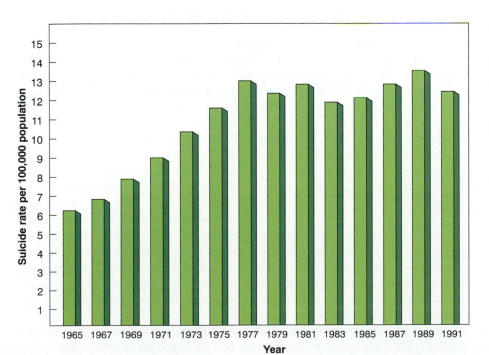

FIGURE 13.1

Rates of suicides per 100,000 population among adolescents and young adults ages 15 to 24 years, 1965 to 1991. There was a sharp increase throughout the 1960s and early 1970s that leveled out in the late 1970s and 1980s. (SOURCE: U.S. Bureau of the Census)

ed, especially in students who have better-than-average ability. Of those adolescents who have committed suicide because of perceived school failure, only 11 percent were actually in serious academic difficulty (Jacobs, 1971). The second sign is an adolescent's withdrawal from social relationships. Suicidal adolescents often feel unwanted by their families or parents (Rosenkrantz, 1978). Rejection by teachers and peers can also contribute to social withdrawal. Another indication may be the termination or failure of a sexual relationship. Many adolescents fearful of venturing into sexual relationships become overly attached to the one boyfriend or girlfriend with whom they feel comfortable. And one study found that adolescents who were less able to cope with the stresses of life and who had difficulty dealing with their angry and sad feelings were more likely to attempt suicide (Khan, 1988).

The most powerful and consistent warning signs, however, are expressions of hopelessness—that life isn't worth living and that suicide is a way out. For this reason, any attempts at suicide, however mild, must be taken seriously. Any jokes about suicide, however lightly made, should alert people to a possible risk. Almost every adolescent who commits suicide first gives an indication at one time or another that suicide is on his or her mind. In fact, concerned parents can probably best identify a teenager at risk by simply asking the adolescent about feelings of hopelessness or thoughts of suicide (Swedo et al, 1991). (See At Issue.)

THE PEER GROUP

Adolescent peer groups may be of different sizes and may be devoted to different interests. Adolescents often belong to more than one peer group at a time. Such peer groups may consist of a few close friends of the same sex or a larger group of both sexes who hang out together. Peer groups provide an important social structure for most adolescents and can serve many other functions (Brown, Eicher, & Petrie, 1986). They can be sources of ready companionship and adventure and providers of standards against which to compare oneself. As a result, a peer group can be a powerful influence.

To become or to stay a member of a desired peer group, adolescents need to appear desirable. They also need certain social skills. Adolescents who lack social skills or who are deemed socially undesirable by their peers may find themselves living a lonely or isolated existence, and eventually they may be adversely affected by the experience. To avoid rejection, adolescents may go to extremes to please their peer group. They may radically change their dress, appearance, or behavior, or they may adopt the group's jargon. Adolescents who attempt to adjust to a group that has views or values opposed to those held by their families may experience considerable conflict and stress (P. R. Newman, 1982).

A peer group may function as a reference for adolescents (Petersen & Taylor, 1980). Adolescents often resolve differences between themselves and their peer group by changing their behavior to match the group's norms. The group can influence susceptible teenagers either to perform or to avoid misconduct (Brown, Clasen, & Eicher, 1986). It has been shown, however, that peers are less likely to encourage misconduct than they are other types of behavior (Brown, Lohr, & McClenahan, 1986).

There are some important exceptions to conformity with the group's norms, however. For instance, how adolescents first evaluate themselves may have a great bearing on which peer group or peer-group behaviors they find most

Peers can have an enormous influence on adolescent behavior, particularly in such areas as dress, general appearance, and adoption of special slang or jargon.

AT ISSUE

Is Suicide Contagious?

In a 12-month period beginning in February 1983, seven teenagers in the town of Plano, Texas, committed suicide. In February 1984, five boys, all from neighboring New York counties, killed themselves. In one 5-day period in 1986 in Omaha, Nebraska, three teenagers from the same suburban high school took their own lives. In March 1987, four teenage boys and girls killed themselves with carbon monoxide by allowing their car to run in an airtight garage in Bergenfield, New Jersey. The day after the bodies were discovered in Bergenfield, two teenage girls were found dead under similar circumstances in Illinois (Wilentz, Gorman, & Hull, 1987). Such clusters of suicides have been documented in several other places in the United States as well (Leo, 1986).

Researchers believe that imitation may play an important role in suicide clusters (Fox, Manitowabi, & Ward, 1984; Gould & Shaffer, 1986). The simple knowledge that a suicide has occurred may make some teenagers more likely to commit suicide. In fact, it has been known for years that suicides reach a peak just after a nationally publicized suicide, especially if the person who died was famous. Publicizing suicides could therefore be dangerous, an idea that is counter to the traditional wisdom that thoughts of suicide should be brought into the open, discussed, and dealt with. Perhaps this wisdom does hold when professionals are present to deal with the feelings generated by talk of suicide. But what about the disturbed adolescent, alone in his or her room, who hears about another teen who just committed suicide? Could it put an idea in this young person's head that must now be dealt with alone?

Imitative suicide may be more common than we know. One researcher who carefully studied automobile fatalities discovered that such deaths increased by an average of 9.12 percent following well-publicized suicides (Phillips, 1977). This is especially important because it implies that some deaths listed as accidents may really have been suicides.

Researchers studying the relationship between nationally televised news or feature stories about suicide and the fluctuations in suicide rates among American teenagers, both before and after the publicity, found a significant correlation between suicide rates for teenagers and news stories about suicide (Phillips & Carstensen, 1986). They noted that suicides increased as much after general-information suicide

features as after stories about specific suicides. They concluded:

> The findings of this study strongly suggest that televised news stories about suicide trigger a significant rise in teenage suicides; that the more publicity the news story receives, the greater is the increase in teenage suicides; and that news stories providing general information about suicide are just as dangerous as specific stories. In view of these findings, educators, policy makers, and journalists may wish to consider ways of reducing public exposure to stories, both general and specific, about suicide. (Phillips & Carstensen, 1986, p. 689)

Preventing Imitative Suicides. The major U.S. television networks attempted to overcome the problem of imitative suicides by producing educational programs that depicted fictional suicides. Some of these programs focused on the teenager who committed suicide, others on the family left behind. They were produced, once again, with the idea that bringing more information about suicides into the open might help prevent them. In many cases, the networks worked with suicide prevention centers, provided hot-line numbers for teenagers to call if they felt troubled after viewing the program, and offered educational materials and teachers' guides for use in classrooms across the country.

The results of studies analyzing these fictional accounts of suicide have been mixed. One study (Gould & Shaffer, 1986) concluded that even these fictional stories could increase teenage suicide rates. A subsequent study that replicated and expanded Gould and Shaffer's analysis concluded that there was no such increase (Phillips & Paight, 1987).

More research needs to be conducted to determine whether any stories or programs about suicide among teenagers can help to inhibit rather than to provoke the act. Obviously, some elements in such broadcasts can provide help for troubled teens and their parents. Researchers need to determine what these elements are and how to apply them carefully to decrease the rate of suicide among teenagers (Davidson, Rosenberg, Mercy, Franklin, & Simmons, 1989).

important and desirable (Eisert & Kahle, 1982). One study discovered that college students (mean age 18.95 years) who evaluated themselves as having high self-esteem chose groups to join and to emulate that were composed of students of high socioeconomic status (Filsinger & Anderson, 1982). This is not just a one-way street, however; the groups with whom adolescents choose to compare themselves can in turn directly affect an adolescent's self-evaluation. No doubt, the students who associated and became friends with high-status peers found their own self-esteem enhanced.

Adolescent Versus Parental Values

In a study of over 18,000 adolescents between the ages of 12 and 17 years, researchers asked questions about the degree to which adolescents valued their mothers', fathers', and friends' opinions (Curtis, 1975). Among adolescents at every age, the advice of parents was more valued than was the advice of friends. Among 12-year-old adolescents, parental opinions far outweighed advice offered by friends. By the age of 17 years, however, although teenagers still valued parental opinions more, they placed friends' opinions a close second.

Another study found that the more that adolescents are removed from adult supervision after school, the more susceptible they are to peer pressure to engage in antisocial activities (Steinberg, 1986). This is especially true among those who were rejected by their peers during childhood or who are failing academically (Dishion, Patterson, Stoolmiller, & Skinner, 1991).

Although it can be exasperating to be an adolescent and contend with your parents, or to be a parent and contend with your adolescent, researchers have found that both parents and adolescents typically share the same views on sex, war, drugs, religion, law enforcement, and politics (Lerner & Weinstock, 1972; Weinstock & Lerner, 1972).

The influence of the adolescent peer group seems to be a worldwide phenomenon (B. M. Newman, 1982). In almost every culture, adolescents congregate for companionship and adventure. The way the society views the adolescent peer group, however, quite often differs from one culture to the next. For instance, in American society, adolescent peers may more often seem to ignore or deviate from the values of the culture, whereas in other countries, such as Switzerland or Iran, adolescent peer groups are viewed as actively supporting and maintaining allegiance to the society's norms.

Drug Use and Abuse

The use of drugs by adolescents has decreased dramatically in all categories from what it was 15 years ago, with one exception, the use of tobacco, which has remained steady (see Table 13.1). Educational efforts and peer pressure have apparently made a considerable difference. As one researcher has noted,

> Ten years ago, students would brag about how drunk or stoned they got. It's no longer "in" to talk that way. Ten years ago kids who went to what would be called a "sober" party would have been really considered nerdy. They would be ashamed of it. Now that's one of the "in" things to do. Popular kids go to "sober" parties. . . . There are still the addicts, of course, but they're not the "in" kids anymore. (Peck, as cited by Freiberg, 1991, p. 28)

However, despite the improved outlook, drug use among adolescents remains a serious problem, and drugs remain readily accessible, even in elementary schools.

Table 13.1 ● Drug Use Among High School Seniors (1991)

CATEGORY	1991	PEAK YEAR
Used illicit drugs at least once	62.2%	70.5% in 1986
Used illicit drug in previous month	15.1%	40% in 1979
Used alcohol during past month	54.0%	72.1% in 1978
Used marijuana in previous month	13.8%	37.1% in 1978
Used cocaine within the last year	3.5%	19.7% in 1986
Used crack within the last year	1.5%	3.2% in 1986
Used amphetamines during the previous month	3.2%	15.8% in 1981
Used PCP within last year	1.4%	7.0% in 1979
Used cigarettes daily		Rate remaining steady since 1980
Used cigarettes during the past month	28.3%	Rate remaining steady since 1980

Source: Adapted from Johnston, Bachman, & O'Malley, 1992.

For some adolescents, drug use provides an element of excitement and daring. Some find peer acceptance by using drugs or by demonstrating a comprehensive knowledge of street drugs and their effects. For others, selling drugs is a quick way to be admired and to make money. However, peer pressure to use drugs is only one of 17 major correlates associated with adolescent drug use (see Table 13.2). Moreover, each of the 17 factors appears to correlate somewhat separately and independently with drug use. That is, each factor carries its own impact, and each time a factor is added to the mix, the chances of drug use increases (Hawkins, Catalano, & Miller, 1992). By isolating the factors associated with drug use, hopefully we will be able to address each factor in an effort to lower the incidence of drug abuse. It should also be noted that adolescents who use drugs because of one particular factor may be more likely to curtail use than would those taking drugs for a different reason. For example, adolescents who use drugs because their friends are using them are more likely to give up drugs in adulthood than are adolescents who take drugs for physiological reasons (Kandel & Raveis, 1989).

How involved someone is with drugs and how long that individual has been taking them also play an important role. For instance, longitudinal studies indicate that those who briefly experimented with drugs (primarily marijuana) during their adolescence were fairly well adjusted as adults, while those who used drugs frequently as adolescents showed signs of maladjustment later on, including alienation from others, poor impulse control, and emotional distress (Shedler & Block, 1990).

The Most Commonly Used Drugs

The drugs most commonly used by adolescents are alcohol, tobacco, and marijuana (see Table 13.1). Alcohol use and abuse can be a serious problem among adolescents—or any group, for that matter. In a national survey of over 17,000 high school seniors conducted by the University of Michigan, nearly 3 out of every 5 students admitted to drinking alcohol within the previous month, and 1 out of every 3 acknowledged consuming five or more alcoholic drinks in a row within the prior two weeks (Johnston, Bachman, & O'Malley, 1992).

During the 1980s the use of cocaine by adolescents became a serious problem.

Table 13.2 ● Factors Associated with the Incidence of Adolescent Drug Use

FACTORS ASSOCIATED WITH DRUG USE	HOW FACTOR WOULD INCREASE THE PROBABILITY OF ADOLESCENT DRUG USE
Laws and norms	Drug is legal; use is socially acceptable
Availability	Drug is readily available
Extreme economic deprivation	Living in poor or overcrowded conditions
Neighborhood disorganization	Neighborhood has poor surveillance, mobile residents, and high rates of adult crime
Physiological factors	Individual is genetically prone to addiction; shows sensation-seeking behavior and has low impulse control
Family drug use	Family members model drug use
Poor or inconsistent parenting	Lack of maternal involvement; inconsistent discipline; low parental aspirations for children
Family conflict	Adolescent comes from a broken home; family members often fight
Low bonding to family	Adolescent is not close to parents; finds parents cold and untrustworthy
Early and persistent behavior problems	Adolescent has shown tendency to be aggressive and antisocial from as early as age 5
Academic failure	Adolescent is truant, placed in a special class, drops out of school, or has failing grades
Little commitment to school	Adolescent is not interested in education; does not expect to attend college
Peer rejection in grade school	Child was aggressive, shy, or withdrawn and had few or no friends
Association with drug-using peers	Adolescent has many friends who use drugs
Alienation and rebelliousness	Adolescent rejects dominant values of society; has low religiosity; is often delinquent
Personal attitude	Adolescent believes using drugs is okay
Early onset of drug use	Adolescent tried drugs for the first time before the age of 15

Source: Adapted from Hawkins, Catalano, & Miller, 1992.

Peer use of alcohol is the most powerful predictor of adolescent alcohol use, at least in the United States. The general rule is, if your friends drink, you are likely to drink. In other countries, patterns of alcohol use often differ. For instance, one study in Israel found that the most powerful predictor of adolescent alcohol use was parental use (Adler & Kandel, 1982).

Although most adolescents keep their drinking under control, the number of adolescent alcoholics is alarming. Four percent of high school seniors state that they are daily users of alcohol (Johnston, Bachman, & O'Malley, 1992). These data are also from the University of Michigan survey, and like the other data compiled from that survey, they did not include the 30 percent of adolescents who have dropped out of high school. It is suspected that alcohol and other drug use among dropouts is at higher rates than found among adolescents who remain in school. Alcohol use among adolescents can also be a fatal choice. Alcohol is believed to be responsible for between 30 and 50 percent of all vehicular deaths among teenagers.

About one-fifth of high school seniors reported being daily cigarette smokers (see Table 13.1). Cigarette smoking by adolescents is the only area of drug use that has not declined since the University of Michigan began tracking high school drug use in the late 1970s. For many researchers, this is the saddest part of the story because tobacco use is among the most deadly of addictions. Smoking is known to be a major cause of heart disease, cancer, stroke, and emphysema—four of the leading causes of death in the United States. Perhaps the most shocking statistic of all is that in the twentieth century, smoking has killed more people than war.

Parents and siblings have a considerable influence on a teenager's smoking habits. If a parent or older sibling smokes, the chances that the teenager will smoke are 1 in 5. If neither the parents nor older siblings smoke, the odds become less than 1 in 20. In general, adolescents who have friends who smoke are more likely to smoke. The single most reliable predictor of continued smoking by teenagers has been their own statement that they believed that they would still be smoking in 5 years.

Some adolescents who fear the health effects of smoking have taken to chewing tobacco. Chewing tobacco, however, poses hazards in the form of oral cancer and dental damage. Publicizing these dangers more widely might make greater numbers of adolescents aware that chewing tobacco is not a safe alternative to smoking.

After alcohol and tobacco, marijuana was found to be the most widely used illicit drug among high school seniors. Other abused drugs include amphetamines, cocaine, and hallucinogens such as LSD or PCP (see Table 13.1).

SEX AND THE ADOLESCENT

"Sex is exciting."

"It's a way to show your love."

"It's a way to prove yourself."

"Everyone else is doing it."

"It's okay for boys but not for girls."

"Sex is wrong."

Adolescents must learn to deal with physical maturity and their own sexual desires.

Many of these attitudes and beliefs are held by teenagers. In our culture, "children" of 13 years of age often are physically capable of having children of their own but are not capable emotionally or economically of maintaining and supporting a family.

Every society has standards that define acceptable and unacceptable sexual behaviors among its members. Traditionally, the majority of American adults have not condoned premarital sex among adolescents. At the turn of the century, 75 percent of all women under the age of 20 were virgins. Since then, however, American attitudes toward adolescent sexuality and dating have become more permissive (Rubinson & de Rubertis, 1991). Following the "sexual revolution" of the 1960s, only 45 percent of all women under the age of 20 were virgins. During the same time, the number of virgin males under the age of 20 dropped from approximately 50 percent to 15 percent (Sorensen, 1973; Reiss, 1976).

Nevertheless, it would be an error to assume that the majority of teenagers are capriciously engaging in sexual relations with many partners. Table 13.3 describes the sexual behaviors engaged in by a group of college-aged males and females. As you can see, intercourse was engaged in by a majority only when they considered themselves to be in love with one person.

SEXUALLY TRANSMITTED DISEASE (STD)
A disease that is primarily transmitted through sexual intercourse.

Teenagers often think of sexual partners as future marriage partners. Furthermore, it is common for a teenage boy and girl to latch onto each other instantly. As a result, some adolescents live as pseudomarried couples and eventually may marry without ever getting to know other potential partners—all because they've learned to feel safe with their "first love" and because "sex" and "marriage" are so often paired. Unfortunately, early marriages have a poor track record compared with marriages of more experienced or mature couples.

Sexually Transmitted Diseases

One of the more unfortunate results of an increase in sexual activity among adolescents is the resultant increase in **sexually transmitted diseases (STDs)**. Diseases primarily transmitted through sexual contact include chlamydia, gonorrhea, syphilis, venereal warts, genital herpes, and AIDS. Some of these diseases, such as chlamydia, gonorrhea, and syphilis, are treatable with drugs—although if left untreated, they can cause extensive damage to the reproductive system and even death, in the case of syphilis. Venereal warts, herpes, and AIDS, because they are caused by viruses, are more difficult to treat. AIDS, of course, is invariably fatal, although adolescents rarely die from it because the period from the time of infection to the full-blown symptoms of the disease can be many years. However, since so many individuals are first diagnosed with AIDS in their 20s, it is assumed that many were infected in their teens. Unfortunately, although use of condoms is up among sexually active teens, it remains low (21 to 37 percent) among those teens at highest risk (IV drug users, homosexuals, and those with many partners per year).

Preventing the Spread of AIDS.   Education seems to be the best hope for preventing the spread of AIDS. This is especially true for those teens at highest risk. In one study, researchers provided intensive education for 450 runaways and gay male youths in five New York City shelters (Rotheram-Borus, Koopman, Haignere, & Davies, 1991). When first admitted to the program, 21 percent of the teens were engaging in high-risk behavior, defined as having 10 or more sexual encounters with three or more partners during the past three months while at the same time being inconsistent concerning condom use. After six months of education conducted in 15 sessions, none of the original 21 percent fit the high-risk profile. In her testimony before congress, Rotheram-Borus recommended setting up "HIV [the AIDS virus] prevention programs in shelters, foster care, group homes and other social agencies." (Youngstrom, 1991, p. 39).

Table 13.2 ● Percentage of College-Aged Males and Females Reporting Specific Sexual Behaviors

SEXUAL BEHAVIOR	GENDER	DATING WITH NO PARTICULAR AFFECTION	DATING WITH AFFECTION BUT NOT LOVE	DATING AND BEING IN LOVE	DATING ONE PERSON ONLY AND BEING IN LOVE	ENGAGED
Light petting	M	25	50	81	92	94
	F	8	26	59	88	98
Heavy petting	M	18	33	68	81	88
	F	6	19	42	82	93
Intercourse	M	15	18	49	63	74
	F	4	11	32	68	81
Oral sex	M	10	32	59	78	82
	F	2	11	24	59	66

Source: Adapted from Roche, 1986, p. 110.

APPLICATIONS

Preventing Teenage Pregnancy

Before the baby came, her bedroom was a dimly lighted chapel dedicated to the idols of rock 'n' roll. Now the posters . . . have been swept away and the walls painted white. Angela Helton's room has become a nursery for 6-week-old Corey Allen. Angie, who just turned 15, finds it hard to think of herself as a mother. "I'm still just as young as I was," she insists. "I haven't grown up any faster." Indeed, sitting in her parents' Louisville living room, she is the prototypical adolescent, lobbying her mother for permission to attend a rock concert, asking if she can have a pet dog and complaining she is not allowed to do anything. The weight of her new responsibilities is just beginning to sink in. "Last night I couldn't get my homework done," she laments with a toss of her blond curls. "I kept feeding him and feeding him. Whenever you lay him down, he wants to get picked up." In retrospect she admits: "Babies are a big step. I should have thought more about it."

The rhythm of her typing is like a fox trot, steady and deliberate. It is a hot summer day in San Francisco, and Michelle, a chubby black 14-year-old, is practicing her office skills with great fervor, beads of sweat trickling down her brow. She is worried about the future. "I have to get my money together," she frets. "I have to think ahead." Indeed she must. In three weeks this tenth-grader with her hair in braids is going to have a baby. "I have to stop doing all the childish things I've done before," she gravely resolves. "I used to think, 10 years from now I'll be 24. Now I think, I'll be 24, and my child will be 10." (Wallis, Booth, Ludtke, & Taylor, 1985, pp. 78–79)

If the present trend continues, almost 40 percent of today's 14-year-old girls will have been pregnant at least once before the age of 20. One of the unfortunate consequences of teenage pregnancy arises from the higher risk of medical complications faced by pregnant teenagers and their babies.

Research has indicated that about 40 percent of today's 14-year-olds will have been pregnant at least once before the age of 20.

Teenage mothers, who are often under more stress than mothers better able to cope with pregnancy, are also more likely to become child abusers. Pregnancy is also the most common reason that adolescent girls leave school, which means that teen mothers tend to have far less promising educational or economic futures than do their counterparts who delay parenting (Subramanian, 1990). Although the rate of pregnancies among teenagers has increased in many other countries, the United States leads by a large margin (see Figure 13.2). The tragedy is that few of these teenagers are in a position to provide a stable family environment or to care for their infants. In our society, they are children with children. The major factor affecting the difference in pregnancy rate among

teenagers in the United States and other countries appears to be the level of contraceptive use. The Alan Guttmacher Institute, which conducted a comparative study of pregnancy rates among teenagers in six nations throughout the world, concluded, "It is likely that the United States has the lowest level of contraceptive practice among teen-agers of all six countries" (Adler, Katz, & Jackson, 1985, p. 90).

While it is true that condom use has increased somewhat, the number of adolescents who don't use condoms or any contraception remains at an alarming level. In general, the rate of teen pregnancy has not declined since 1985 because more teens are sexually active now and begin sexual activity at an earlier age than they did in 1985.

It is also difficult to assess the rate of condom use among adolescents. The largest study concerning this matter, the National Survey of Adolescent Males, has found in a 10-year follow-up that the rate of condom use among adolescents ages 17 to 19 had increased from 21 percent in 1979 to 58 percent in 1988 (Landers, 1990). But again, in 1979, 67 percent of males 17 to 19 reported being sexually active, but by 1988, 75 percent were sexually active. The use of condoms or other contraceptives also appears to be far less frequent among teens ages 13 to 16 (Youngstrom, 1991).

There are a number of reasons why teenagers don't use birth control methods more often. Some teenagers have religious or moral objections to the use of contraceptives. Some are fearful that birth control methods may be unsafe, or they believe that the risk of AIDS in their case is mini-

FIGURE 13.2

Pregnancy rate per 1,000 teenage females in selected countries. (SOURCE: The Alan Guttmacher Institute, 1985)

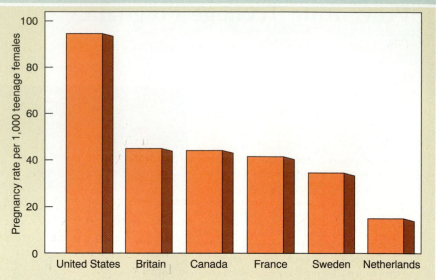

mal (because, for instance, their partner "looks healthy"). Furthermore, many teenagers know amazingly little about sexual reproduction. Still others simply believe that sex should be unplanned, or spontaneous. In fact, teenagers who feel guilty about the sex may have a need to convince themselves that they just "got carried away." But that can be hard to do if they've just spent a minute or so in technical preparation.

Interestingly, in some cultures, "technical" prenuptial arrangements are considered part of the romance. However, our associative learning has been such that many forms of contraception appear to us to be unromantic. After all, many of us were raised to believe that sex was an embrace, a kiss, and a camera pan to the breakers of the surf (with, of course, full orchestration). At times, expectation and reality can seem far apart.

Careful investigation has found that there are four major risk factors that indicate which teenage girls are most likely to become pregnant. The girls most at risk are those who begin sexual activity at an early age, who are depressed, whose mothers are depressed, or whose mothers have left home within the past 15 months (Horwitz, Klerman, Kuo, & Jekel, 1991). Hopefully, girls who fit this profile will receive extra counseling concerning bearing and raising children at an early age.

Abortion. Whether to have an abortion is, among other things, a moral decision that an individual must make for herself (or, when the father is a party to the decision, himself). Many teenagers prefer to keep their children whether they are able to care for them or not. Astonishingly, among those young women who choose abortion, the New York Planned Parenthood Society has found that many return for a second, third, fourth, or even fifth abortion.

One possible solution to this problem is to develop programs to educate teenagers. Some schools have on-campus health clinics that are authorized to dispense contraceptives to students who have parental permission. Unfortunately, not enough sex education programs are available in high schools, and many of the available programs don't discuss the kinds of issues we have been addressing here; instead, they tend to be courses in "plumbing" (a relentless pursuit of the fallopian tubes).

In 1987, the National Academy of Sciences Panel on Early Childbearing recommended programs to help reduce teenage pregnancy. They recommended that these programs increase the options available to teenagers, such as improving school performance, providing employment opportunities, and providing role models. The panel also recommended that sex education programs be explicit and include information on contraception. The panel also recommended changes in the media—that programs glorifying sex be discouraged and that advertisements for contraceptives be available.

There is also a need for effective counseling and support programs for pregnant teenagers. One of the first such programs was developed by Janet Hardy and Theodore King at the Johns Hopkins Medical Institution in Baltimore. In this program, medical and psychological services are offered to pregnant teenagers. Classes are conducted from the first prenatal visit through labor and delivery, and, most important, they continue for three years after delivery. The relationship between the staff and teenage mothers is close and supportive ("One Solution," 1979).

Among teenage mothers enrolled in the Johns Hopkins program, 85 percent returned to school and only 5 percent became pregnant again within one year of delivery. The mothers in the program also had statistically fewer premature deliveries, medical complications, or unhealthy babies. Among teen mothers who weren't in the program, only 10 percent returned to school, and 47 percent became pregnant again within one year of delivery ("One Solution," 1979). As you can see from these data, the Johns Hopkins program was successful. This program is now used as a model for developing a nationwide program for preventing pregnancy among teenagers.

SUMMARY

- Teenagers may seem to be a distinct and special group with special problems and needs, but their status may be more a function of culture and economics than of age.

- During adolescence, individuals must deal for the first time with sexual relationships, the choice of a future career, political decisions, economic alternatives, and a host of other "adult" tasks.

- As adolescents develop cognitive skills, they are confronted for the first time with the overwhelming complexities and abstract qualities of the world. Sexual relationships must be faced. Social maturity in dealings with both sexes is expected. The adolescent's own masculine or feminine role must be realized and adjusted to his or her satisfaction. The adolescent must come to terms with his or her physical development. Our culture expects adolescents to achieve emotional independence from parents and other adults. Decisions about whether to marry or whether to have children become more pressing. Pursuing a career choice is also an essential part of adolescent development.

- According to Erik Erikson, the adolescent is faced with the task of developing an acceptable, functional, and stable self-concept. Those adolescents who succeed, Erikson argued, will establish a sense of identity, and those who fail will suffer role confusion.

- Suicide is one of the leading causes of death among adolescents. Since 1965, the rate of suicide among adolescents and young adults ages 15 to 24 years has more than doubled. Every year in the United States, approximately 2,000 adolescents between the ages of 15 and 19 take their own lives and about 250,000 adolescents attempt suicide. Females are more likely to attempt suicide than males are, but males are more likely to actually kill themselves.

- Adolescent peer groups may be of different sizes and may be devoted to different interests. Peer groups provide an important social structure for most adolescents. Such groups can be sources of ready companionship and adventure and can provide standards for adolescents.

- Some adolescents gain peer acceptance by using drugs or by demonstrating a comprehensive knowledge of street drugs and their effects. The drugs most commonly used by adolescents are tobacco, alcohol, and marijuana. In the last 15 years, drug use among high school students has declined, except for the use of tobacco, which has remained constant.

- American attitudes toward adolescent sexuality and dating have become more permissive. Nevertheless, it would be an error to assume that the majority of teenagers are capriciously engaging in sexual relations with many partners.

- One of the more unfortunate results of an increase in sexual activity among adolescents is the resultant increase in sexually transmitted diseases.

- Researchers have estimated that if the present trend continues, about 40 percent of today's 14-year-old girls will have been pregnant at least once before the age of 20. Programs to help prevent teenage pregnancy have been developed.

QUESTIONS FOR DISCUSSION

1. What are the implications for families and society if more and more unwed teenagers wish to keep their babies?

2. Was your adolescence benign? If not, was it more stormy than other times in your life have been?

3. What circumstances have influenced your identity development?

4. How can parents help their teenagers deal with the conflicts of adolescence?

SUGGESTIONS FOR FURTHER READING

1. Adelson, J. (1985). *Inventing adolescence: The political psychology of every-day schooling.* New Brunswick, NJ: Transaction Books.

2. Gilligan, C. (1990). *Making connections: The relational worlds of adolescent girls at Emma Willard School.* Cambridge, MA: Harvard University Press.

3. Graydanus, D. E. (1991). *Caring for your adolescent: Ages 12 to 21.* New York: Bantam.

4. Group for the Advancement of Psychiatry, Committee on Adolescence. (1986). *Crises of adolescence: Teenage pregnancy, impact on adolescent development.* New York: Brunner/Mazel.

5. Hauser, S. T., Powers, S. I., & Noam, G. G. (1991). *Adolescents and their families: Paths of ego development.* New York: Free Press.

6. McAnarney, E. R. (1983). *Premature adolescent pregnancy and parenthood.* Orlando, FL: Grune & Stratton.

7. Offer, D., Ostrov, E., & Howard, K. I. (1981). *The adolescent: A psychological self-portrait.* New York: Basic Books.

8. Offer, D., Ostrov, E., Howard, K. I., & Atkinson, R. (1988). *The teenage world: Adolescents' self-image in ten countries.* New York: Plenum.

9. Simmons, R. G. (1987). *Moving into adolescence.* Hawthorne, NY: Aldine de Gruyter.

10. Youniss, J., & Smollar, J. (1985). *Adolescent relations with mothers, fathers, and friends.* Chicago: University of Chicago Press.

UNIT SIX

EARLY ADULTHOOD
(18–40 Years of Age)

CHAPTER 14
Early Adulthood: Physical, Cognitive, and Personality Development

Chapter Preview: Reaching for the Stars
Resources: The Study of Adult Development • Physical Development and Health Concerns in Early Adulthood • Cognitive Development in Early Adulthood • Moral Development in Early Adulthood • Personality Development in Early Adulthood
Applications: Thinking about Changing Your Life?

CHAPTER 15
Early Adulthood: Loving and Working

Chapter Preview: Homework
Resources: Liking and Loving • Social Participation and Intimacy • The Traditional Family • Divorce • Homosexual Relationships • Unmarried Heterosexual Cohabitation • Singlehood • Working
Applications: Finding Your One and Only

CHAPTER 14

Early Adulthood: Physical, Cognitive, and Personality Development

Reaching for the Stars

> This game is all confidence. And, you know, sometimes it's scary. When I'm at my best, I can do just about anything I want, and no one can stop me. I feel like I'm in total control of everything. (Callahan, 1985, p. 53)

These words were spoken by Larry Bird when he was 28 years old. By the time he had turned 30, Bird had won three Most Valuable Player (MVP) awards in the National Basketball Association. But the words might just as well have been said by Martina Navratilova, who at age 33 had won her ninth Wimbledon Singles Tennis Championship, or by Wayne Gretzky, when at age 28 he won his ninth MVP award in the National Hockey League, or by Greta Waitz, who at age 33 had won her eighth New York City marathon. We've come to expect and envy this kind of confidence in our sports champions, who dazzle us with their speed, agility, and lightning-fast reflexes. And we pay them good money to keep doing it!

Almost always, sports stars fall into the age range of 18 to 40 years, as do other world-class contenders:

> The young challenger abandoned his aggressive assaults and settled into a defensive stance . . . the grind began to tell on the slight champion. Kasparov seemed to be physically finished. It was then that the president . . . halted the match, contending that everyone was exhausted. Kasparov erupted in anger, charging that he had been robbed. (Schmemann, 1986, p. 42)

A boxing match? No. It was the next to decisive game in The World Chess Championship, a match that ran from July 23 until October 5, 1986, when Gary Kasparov, at age 23, finally defeated Anatoly Karpov, 35, to retain his world title.

Early adulthood is the time when most people are at their peak physically and intellectually. It is also a time to try out new roles and identities, and young adults often are in the forefront of social movements. In the 1940s, the White Rose at the University of Munich was preeminent among resistance groups raising their voice against Hitler's "atheistic war machine" (Dumbach & Newborn, 1986). In the 1960s, students protested the Vietnam War. And although we reflect on him as having been an elder statesman of the U.S. Civil Rights Movement, Dr. Martin Luther King, Jr., was only 34 years old when he stood on the steps of the Lincoln Memorial and shared his dream that someday people of all races would sing together, "Free at last! Free at last! Thank God Almighty, we are free at last!"

In this chapter, we will first look at some general issues relevant to the study of adult development. Then we will examine physical, cognitive, and personality development during early adulthood, which we define roughly as the period between 18 and 40 years of age.

THE STUDY OF ADULT DEVELOPMENT

Had early developmental psychologists heeded the "life cycle" lessons of Confucius or the Talmud or Shakespeare, they might have lengthened the scope of their inquiry to include adulthood. Instead they focused on infancy, childhood, and adolescence, creating the state of knowledge reflected in the following table of contents, taken from a very fine human development textbook (Nash, 1978):

Unit 4: Growth and Maturation

Conception

Prenativity

The Femaleness of Man

The Perinativity

Infancy

Preschool Period

Preadolescence

Adolescence

Death

After charting our course through adolescence, researchers either ignored adults completely or perpetuated the myth that after 18 years it's all downhill, then we die. And, perhaps when you're 17 years old, it does seem that way. But then comes the shock of discovering that you're 19, then 20, then 21. (By the way, the shock keeps right on happening every year, and there appears to be no way to stop it.) Following this discovery, the whole idea of adulthood becomes very interesting, because it's happening to you, of all people!

You would think that developmental researchers, themselves adults, would have become interested in adulthood sooner, especially since the age range of 18 years until death usually has more years in it to study than the period between birth and 18 years. A key reason why researchers ignored adulthood for so long is that age-related changes in behavior, cognition, physical development, and such are much more difficult to identify and trace in adulthood than in childhood. In childhood, these changes often are due to forces of biological maturation and are universal. In adulthood, however, social and cultural factors often play a much greater role than biological factors, and we can't count on the changes to be universal. In fact, the timing of the changes varies so much from one person to another that chronological age becomes an increasingly poor guide as we grow older, and it is far more difficult to generalize about a group of, say, 50-year-old adults than about a group of 6-year-old children. Bernice Neugarten explains the situation this way:

> The stereotype has it that as people age they become more and more like one another. In truth, they become less and less alike. If you look at people's lives, they're like the spreading of a fan. The longer people live, the greater the differences between them. (Neugarten & Hall, 1980, p. 78)

As we proceed to examine adult development, we will look at general trends in physical, cognitive, and social functioning. But we must remember that among a group of adults of the same age, the variability in functioning will be enormous.

Child development played a key role in the investigation of adulthood, as diligent and committed researchers followed into adulthood many of the subjects from prestigious early projects (Eichorn, Clausen, Haan, Honzik, & Mussen, 1981). Another key factor was the publication of Erik Erikson's highly influential essay "The Eight Ages of Man" in 1950. In this essay, Erikson described a stage theory of personality development that, unlike Freud's or Piaget's theories, included adulthood as well as childhood and adolescence. The key issues we deal with in adulthood, Erikson said, are intimacy versus isolation, generativity versus stagnation, and ego integrity versus despair. Over the next few chapters, we will look at each of these conflicts in detail.

Also during the 1950s, some key longitudinal studies of adult development were initiated. These included the Seattle Longitudinal Study, the AT&T Longitudinal Studies of Managers, the Baltimore Longitudinal Study of Aging, and the Duke Longitudinal Study (Schaie, 1983). More recently, George Vaillant, Daniel Levinson, and many other researchers have made important contributions to our understanding of adult development.

Despite the progress, however, the study of adult development today is still what Levinson once called "Dozens of Fragments in Search of an Animating Source and a Unifying Plot" (Levinson, 1986, p. 8). By this Levinson meant that the fragments of research cover personality, cognitive, and moral development, career choice, marriage, the family, biological development, and so on, but that studies of one fragment usually have no evident connection with studies of others. Furthermore, no larger, empirically tested "scheme of things" exists in which to place the research findings (Levinson, 1986).

For these reasons, the research you'll read about in this and subsequent chapters is not nearly as neat and tidy, or as conclusive, as the research you've read about so far. As we turn now to early adulthood, we'll examine the physical, cognitive, and personality changes that generally take place some time during the age span of 18 to 40 years.

PHYSICAL DEVELOPMENT AND HEALTH CONCERNS IN EARLY ADULTHOOD

As is the case with the champions in the Chapter Preview, most Olympic and professional athletes are between 18 and 40 years old. However, it is not only

NEARSIGHTEDNESS
The inability to see distant objects clearly.

PUPIL
The dark circular opening in the center of the eye that helps to regulate the amount of light entering the eye.

PRESBYCUSIS
The progressive, age-related decrease in the ability to hear high-frequency tones.

athletic superstars who accomplish amazing feats during these years. College students carry full course loads, work, play sports, and socialize with friends. Young executives work 70 hours per week to establish their careers. Mothers care for babies, run a home, and pursue careers or graduate school. Young construction workers do hard physical labor 8 hours per day, then play softball. Trust me, by middle age you're likely to look back at your early adult years and wonder how you ever did it!

Early adulthood is marked by such outstanding vitality because during that time, so many of our body's organ systems work so well together. The nervous system coordinates movement of muscles that have the potential to be stronger than ever. The heart pumps blood effectively from the lungs to these working muscles, and the lungs move air in and out and exchange vital gases with peak efficiency. The kidneys remove waste materials from the blood, the endocrine glands synchronize metabolic processes, and the blood's buffer systems maintain the body's chemical environment with tremendous ease and efficiency (Shock, 1962).

Continued Growth

You may have heard that humans are physically grown by age 18, and for many years, our data on physical development appeared to support this idea. By making careful measurements, however, we now know that this isn't true and that growth continues for many years after adolescence. In fact, the long bones of the skeleton grow until we're about 25 years old, and the vertebral column until we are about 30. This may add as much as an inch to our height (Tanner, 1978). Men tend to grow in stature more than women do, while women's skulls tend to grow more than men's do. However, men who wear hats will probably notice the skull size changes, because as they age, they have to buy larger hats. Some bones in the skull actually continue to grow throughout our lives (Garn, 1980).

Myelinization and differentiation of the central nervous system continue until about age 25 years. Our muscles strengthen to peak efficiency between 25 and 30 years. Women reach the peak of their reproductive capacity during their 20s, while the uterus is still growing and the lining is most amenable to implantation (Timiras, 1972). We even get new teeth—so-called wisdom teeth—which usually erupt in our early 20s, although their roots may not fully develop until we are about 25 (Lowrey, 1978).

All this may sound too rosy, however. Age 18 to 40 years is a long time, and 40-year-old adults do look different from 18-year-old ones. Some unwelcomed changes do occur during these years, and a look at a group of, say, 35-year-old adults will convince you that not all of them are in peak physical condition. What will probably strike you is the enormous variation in how those 35-year-old adults look and act. Some watch their diets, consume only moderate amounts of alcohol, and exercise regularly. Others eat anything they want and exercise by pushing buttons on the remote control of the television. By age 35 years, it is usually clear who is in which group.

Research showing age-related physical changes is typically based on measurements drawn from many different subjects and averaged. We must be careful in applying data based on averages, however, because how someone ages depends on many factors, and average curves give only a rough approximation of the pattern followed by specific individuals (Shock, 1985).

Because our society places so much value on looking young, the changes that often distress us most are those that physically harm us least. For example, we discover that "smile lines" around our eyes and mouth remain, even

Physical prowess peaks in early adulthood because different organ systems work together so efficiently.

when we've stopped smiling. Gray hairs appear, and men start experimenting with interesting hairstyles or new drugs such as minoxydil to conceal thinning hair. Both women and men commonly color the gray in their hair. (Apparently, no one "dyes" hair anymore.)

Vision and Hearing

Visual acuity usually is sharpest in young adults around 20 years of age. **Nearsightedness**, the inability to see distant objects clearly, may begin in childhood or adolescence and usually doesn't change much during early adulthood. As the years progress, however, depth perception and the ability to adapt to darkness decrease slightly. It may take a bit longer, for example, for your eyes to adjust when you go from a lighted lobby into a dark movie theater. This happens because as we age, the **pupils** of the eyes gradually get smaller, and the muscles that cause the pupils to dilate and constrict gradually weaken (Fozard, Wolf, Bell, McFarland, & Podosky, 1977).

Hearing usually peaks at about age 13 years. It then begins to decline, especially for higher-frequency tones, a condition known as **presbycusis**. The decrements are so gradual, however, that 90 percent of Americans in their mid-30s can still hear a whisper (National Center for Health Statistics, 1980). As is the case with visual deficits, more men than women suffer hearing impairments (U.S. Bureau of the Census, 1986). One reason for this is that noise pollution is a major cause of hearing loss, and men traditionally work in noisier occupations. Prolonged exposure to noise levels above 75 decibels may cause irreversible damage, as may a sudden, single exposure to an extremely high-pitched loud noise. The damage occurs because the noise destroys the tiny hairlike sound receptors in the inner ear. Work environment noise levels can legally reach 90 decibels. If workers don't wear noise protectors, their hearing can be damaged in only a few years. (See Figure 14.1 for decibel levels of common activities.)

Factors Affecting Health Status

For most people, early adulthood is a time of exceedingly good health. Illnesses are usually acute and are readily shaken off with minimal disruption to normal routine. Fewer than 1 percent of young adults are incapacitated by chronic illnesses (Scanlon, 1981).

Despite this generally positive picture, many people do begin to develop certain silent diseases that will be problematic later on. These diseases include the beginnings of atherosclerosis, emphysema in heavy smokers, cirrhosis of the liver in heavy drinkers, kidney disease, and arthritis (Scanlon, 1981). The leading causes of death prior to age 35 years are accidents, suicide, AIDS, and homicide, followed by cancer and heart disease (National Center for Health Statistics, 1991). After 35 years, however, cancer and heart disease emerge as leading causes of death, followed by accidents, suicide, and liver disease (U.S. Department of Health and Human Services, 1985).

We inherit predispositions to certain diseases or to good health from our parents. In addition, several other factors affect the status of our health, and these tend to become apparent during early adulthood.

One such factor is gender. Throughout adulthood, the death rate for women is lower than that for men, partly because women are more sensitive to early warning signs of illness and more willing to ask for help. During adulthood, women pay three visits to a doctor for every two paid by men. Many women's visits are for routine gynecological procedures, such as Pap smears to check for

FIGURE 14.1

Loudness is measured in decibels (db). A 10-db sound is 10 times louder than one of 0 db (which is the faintest sound that can be heard); a 20-db sound is 100 times louder than one of 0 db and 10 times louder than one of 10 db. The average loud conversation (60 db) is 1 million times louder than the faintest sound that can be heard.

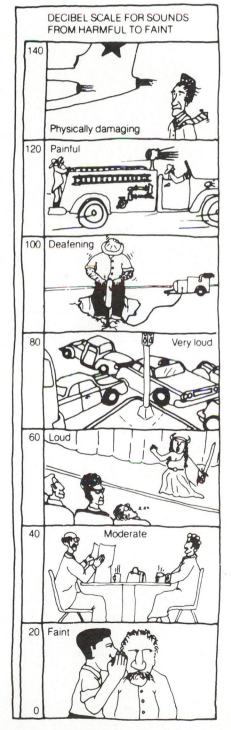

DECIBEL SCALE FOR SOUNDS FROM HARMFUL TO FAINT

140 — Physically damaging
120 — Painful
100 — Deafening
80 — Very loud
60 — Loud
40 — Moderate
20 — Faint
0

AMENORRHEA
The absence of the menstrual period from any cause other than pregnancy or menopause.

DYSMENORRHEA
Painful menstruation.

cervical cancer or checkups during pregnancy. Some visits are for reproductive problems such as infertility, or for **amenorrhea, dysmenorrhea**, or heavy menstrual periods.

In addition, it is thought that female hormones may play a beneficial role in preventing heart disease. On the whole, women have healthier lifestyles than men in that they generally don't smoke or drink as much. However, the increase in women's smoking is now being reflected in health statistics. Between 1970 and 1990, deaths from lung cancer doubled among the general population, but they tripled among women (U.S. Bureau of the Census, 1993).

Better health is consistently correlated with better education (Fuchs, 1974), which often goes hand in hand with higher socioeconomic status. It is likely that more money enables people to buy better food and health care and that better-educated people pay more attention to lifestyle factors such as nutrition, exercise, smoking, and alcohol consumption.

Lifestyle behaviors heavily influence a person's health status. Exercise strengthens muscles—including heart muscle—lowers blood pressure, increases lung capacity, and even alleviates anxiety and depression (Lee, Franks, Thomas, & Paffenberger, 1981; McCann & Holmes, 1984). Smoking increases a person's risk of many different types of cancer, as well as heart disease and emphysema, and we now know about the dangers of passive smoking. Passive smoking has been estimated to increase the heart disease death rate of those who have never smoked by 20 to 70 percent (Wells, 1994). Passive smoking is also a significant risk factor for obstructive respiratory disease (Dayal, Khuder, Sharrar, & Trieff, 1994). And children of heavy smokers have a higher incidence of respiratory problems than do children whose parents don't smoke (Chen, Li, & Yu, 1986; Guneser, Atici, Alparslan, & Cinaz, 1994).

Alcohol is a major factor in car fatalities, suicides, drownings, and family violence. Moreover, fraternities that require pledges to chug-a-lug a fifth are endangering their pledges' lives, because consuming such large quantities of alcohol so quickly can paralyze breathing mechanisms and result in death. High cholesterol levels, which can be influenced by diet, increase our risk of heart disease, and being obese (more than 20 percent over desirable body

Aerobic exercises provide both physical and psychological benefits.

weight) increases our risk of diabetes, heart disease, and hypertension (high blood pressure). In addition, our society places so much value on being slim that being overweight can seriously damage a person's self-esteem.

Interestingly, developmental psychologists weren't always concerned with how behavior might be related to health. While it is true that some of the early psychologists, such as William James and G. Stanley Hall, dealt with health-related issues from time to time, health was generally considered a matter for physicians. In 1964, however, a presidential commission took note of the fact that the leading causes of death were no longer the terrible diseases of the past, such as plague, diphtheria, typhoid, or cholera. These scourges are now prevented or controlled by inoculation, sanitation, or antibiotics. Instead, the report noted that every year, hundreds of thousands of Americans and millions around the world were dying prematurely as a result of their own detrimental *behavior* (Fisher, 1986; Taylor, 1990). These behavior-related disorders, for the most part, are the ones we have been discussing. But if many of these disorders are influenced by behavior, then it stands to reason that by modifying our behavior, we can actually lessen the chances of developing these disorders. With this in mind, refer to Table 14.1, which lists ten major threats to life that are related to behavior and some of the things you can do to add healthy years to your life.

COGNITIVE DEVELOPMENT IN EARLY ADULTHOOD

Had we written this book in the 1920s, we would be reporting to you that you are past your intellectual prime—unless, that is, you entered college at a very early age. Almost three-quarters of a century ago, the findings of a group of army psychologists were that the average intelligence of white draftees was roughly equivalent to that of an average 13-year-old child, while that of black draftees was equivalent to that of an average 10½-year-old child (Yerkes, 1921). A 1933 study was considered optimistic because the researchers found that intelligence did not peak until 18 to 21 years of age. After 21 years, the researchers said, intelligence declined steadily, so that by the time a person reached 55 years, that person was functioning at the intellectual level of a 14-year-old adolescent (Jones & Conrad, 1933).

Many researchers thought that these findings ran counter to common sense. Well into adulthood themselves, they knew that they were smarter than they had been in their teens. One of the first studies to support this theory was conducted in 1949–50, when William Owens located and retested 127 men who had taken the Army Alpha IQ Test in 1919 as a college entrance exam. Owens's findings were dramatic: Overall, the men showed a significant increase in their total IQ scores and on many individual subtests, and on no single subtest did they show a significant decrease (Owens, Ortmeyer, & Helmstadter, 1953). At about the same time, other researchers looked at the adult IQ scores of Terman's child geniuses (see Chapter 10). They found that on most subtests, the scores of these subjects had increased between ages 20 and 50 years (Bayley & Oden, 1955).

It is interesting to consider how researchers could come to such contradictory conclusions. One key factor in these and subsequent studies is that those using cross-sectional designs (see Chapter 1) tend to show IQ decreasing with age, while those using longitudinal designs tend to show it increasing. Many people think that the decrements shown by the former studies are caused by cohort, or generational, differences. Different cohorts are exposed to different

PRACTICE EFFECT
The improvement in performance that comes about from doing a task more than once.

SELECTIVE ATTRITION
The tendency of people who do not perform well in a given situation (e.g., college, a job, a research project) to leave that situation.

educational opportunities and other historical circumstances that are likely to affect their performance on IQ tests. How can you fairly compare, for example, 50-year-old adults who grew up during the depression with 30-year-old adults who grew up in the age of television? If the 30-year-old adults score higher on an IQ test, is that because they are brighter or because they have been reared in a different environment?

Longitudinal designs eliminate the problem of cohort differences, but they may bias the results to support the hypothesis that IQ increases with age. One reason for this is the **practice effect**. Taking a test several times often improves performance on the test, and that is what longitudinal tests do: test and retest subjects. Then there is the problem of **selective attrition**, in which subjects who believe they don't do well on the tests drop out, leaving a biased sample

---

Table 14.1 ● Selected Threats to Your Life (Presented in Order of Actual Danger) Against Which You Can Take Defensive Action

1. Heart Disease
Cholesterol is a major factor in promoting heart disease. See your doctor now and discover your blood serum cholesterol level and HDL levels. (You may need to have them checked a number of times to obtain a valid average level.) The blood should be drawn from the arm and not the finger for more accurate results. The ratio of total cholesterol to HDL should be 5 or less. Avoid fatty foods and keep fat intake to 30 percent of daily calories or less. Don't smoke. Know your blood pressure. Exercise regularly. Control your weight. Have the entire family learn cardiopulmonary resuscitation (CPR). Be alert for health problems following a strep infection because of the danger of rheumatic fever (especially in children). After age 40 get an EKG stress test every 3–5 years.

2. Cancer
Don't smoke, and try to avoid second-hand smoke; smoking is a known cause of lung cancer and leukemia. Know the levels of radioactive radon gas in your home (see July 1987 *Consumer Reports*, pp. 440–447); this hazard is believed responsible for up to 20,000 cancer deaths per year. Know your family history and take special care to watch for kinds of cancers that run in your family (especially cancers of the colon or breast). Avoid getting a sunburn. Avoid the sun in general; wear sunblock and a hat. See your doctor for complete and regular checkups, and learn how to check yourself. (Learn how to do a self-examination of your skin from a dermatologist; for women, learn how to do a self-examination of your breasts from your family physician or gynecologist.) For women, obtain a mammogram if over age 40, and have a Pap smear on a regular basis. Avoid excessive alcohol consumption. Avoid mouthwash containing alcohol (people who use mouthwash regularly have the same rate of oral cancer as heavy drinkers). See your doctor promptly about anything unusual that doesn't go away.

3. Stroke
(Review all the behaviors listed for heart disease.) Avoid excessive alcohol consumption.

4. Diabetes
Have your doctor do an annual check of your blood for sugar (glucose). Know your family history. Avoid obesity. Get checked immediately following symptoms such as light-headedness, unexplained fatigue, persistent thirst, or frequent urination.

5. Motor vehicle accidents
Wear a seat belt with shoulder harness (use proper protective seats for infants). Avoid alcohol consumption before driving. Obey speed limits. Be very vigilant at intersections and while making left turns. Don't be an impatient driver eager to get a jump on the next guy; follow the rule "When in doubt, wait it out"—an extra minute at an intersection might be worth years of life. Drive a large car with air bags. Don't ride a motorcycle.

6. AIDS
Avoid sharing needles if taking drugs. Avoid intimate sexual contact with an infected partner. Assume that everyone is infected and use a condom to reduce chances of infection; practice abstinence for complete protection. If possible, prepare for transfusions in advance of surgery by "stockpiling" your own blood; although blood-borne AIDS is now rare, this may protect you from other diseases as well.

7. Suicide
Immediately seek professional help for depression or suicidal thoughts. Know your family history. Avoid keeping a gun in the house.

8. Liver disease and cirrhosis
Avoid unprotected sex (because of the hepatitis B virus). Don't drink to excess (98 percent of all cirrhosis is alcohol related). Keep all drug use to the absolute minimum, including the taking of common painkillers.

9. Homicide
Don't keep a gun in your home. If possible, avoid dangerous neighborhoods or jobs. Don't be confrontational.

10. Emphysema
Don't smoke. Get regular checkups. Get early and regular help for asthma.

of bright people. As you can see, this would lead to a finding that IQ increases with age, which may or may not be true.

In an effort to overcome these problems, K. Warner Schaie and his colleagues in the Seattle Longitudinal Study developed what is known as a **cohort sequential design**. In 1956, they began administering the Primary Mental Abilities (PMA) Test (see Figure 14.2) to subjects in each 7-year age interval from 20 to 70 years, and they retested as many of those subjects as possible every 7 years from 1956 to 1991.

Schaie and his colleagues measured changes in cognition based on six abilities they termed "latent ability constructs." These constructs were measured using the PMA and other measurements, which were added at later retestings. They found that using multiple measures increased the validity of their results. Table 14.2 shows the variables that they used to measure the constructs. Also, at each testing, they added new subjects at each age interval (see Figure 14.3).

Schaie and his colleagues believe that the cohort sequential design allows them to identify changes in intelligence that are due to aging rather than to cohort differences, the practice effect, or selective attrition. (Another example of such a longitudinal, cross-sectional, time-lag design can be found in Figure 1.3, on p. 13.) The most recent report of their 21-year study was published in 1994 (Schaie, 1994). When cohort differences are taken into account, it is apparent that

> for the longitudinal data, a pattern of linear age-related decline for young adulthood appears plausible only for perceptual speed. . . .Numeric ability shows an early plateau with linear decline, beginning in the 60s. The other four abilities, however, reach an asymptote by age 53 and show only modest decline thereafter. (Schaie, 1994, p. 307)

COHORT SEQUENTIAL DESIGN
A research design in which both longitudinal and cross-sectional data are gathered and compared. It allows researchers to separate changes due to aging from those due to cohort differences, the practice effect, or selective attrition.

FIGURE 14.2

Subtests of the Primary Mental Abilities (PMA) Test battery. (SOURCE: *SRA Primary Mental Abilities*, Ages 11–17, Form A.M.)

1. **VERBAL MEANING (V):** 50 multiple-choice items that test the subject's ability to understand ideas expressed in words. Time limit: 4 minutes.

   Example: Select the alternative that is most similar to the first word:

   BIG   A. ILL   B. LARGE   C. DOWN   D. SOUR

2. **SPACE (S):** 20 items that measure the subject's ability to imagine how an object would look if it were rotated or to visualize objects in two or three dimensions. Time limit: 5 minutes.

   Example: Mark every figure, except the mirror image, that is the same as the first figure:

3. **REASONING (R):** 30 items that measure the subject's ability to foresee and plan the solution of logical problems. Time limit: 6 minutes.

   Example: The following letters form a series based on a rule. Mark the letter that should come next in the series:

   a b x c d x e f x g h x   h i j k x y

4. **NUMBER (N):** 60 items that measure the subject's ability to work with figures and to handle simple quantitive problems rapidly and accurately. Time limit: 6 minutes.

   Example: Determine whether the solution to the following problem is right(R) or wrong (W):

   17
   84   R   W
   29
   140

5. **WORD FLUENCY (W):** A measure of the speed and ease with which the subject can recall words. The subject is required to write as many words beginning with the letter "s" as possible. Time limit 5 minutes.

Table 14.2 ● Variables Used by Schaie and Colleagues to Measure Latent Ability Contructs

Construct	Measurements (Variables)
Inductive reasoning	PMA Reasoning Letter series Word series Number series
Spatial orientation	PMA Space Object rotation Alphanumeric rotation Cube comparison
Verbal ability	PMA Verbal Meaning ETS Vocabulary Advanced vocabulary Word fluency
Numerical ability	PMA Number Addition Subtraction and multiplication Number comparison
Perceptual speed	PMA Verbal Meaning Identical pictures Number comparison Finding A's Word fluency
Verbal memory	Word fluency Immediate recall Delayed recall

Source: Adapted from Schaie, 1994.

As you can see from Figure 14.4, during early adulthood, many of these cognitive abilities are either increasing or remaining relatively steady. In fact, Schaie and his colleagues maintain that any decline prior to age 60 years "does not appear to be of sufficient magnitude to be practically important" (Schaie & Hertzog, 1983, p. 540).

Figure 14.3

Design of the Seattle Longitudinal Study. The number of subjects in each sample is indicated within the circle. As you can see, attrition would have substantially influenced the results had not Schaie and his colleagues added subjects during each retesting. (Source: After Schaie, 1994)

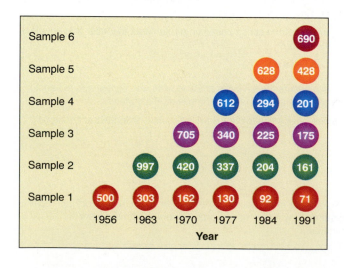

Fluid and Crystallized Intelligence

Other researchers have used different constructs to measure cognitive abilities throughout the life span. Psychologist Robert J. Sternberg believes that intelligence tests are too narrow, and he is currently designing a test that he hopes will measure three types of intelligence: componential, contextual, and experiential (see Chapter 10). In formulating his ideas, Sternberg built on the work of John Horn, Raymond B. Cattell, and Gary Donaldson, who have looked at the data from the Seattle Longitudinal Study in a different way (Horn & Cattell, 1966, 1967; Horn and Donaldson, 1980; Horn, 1982).

These psychologists believe that there are essentially two types of intelligence, fluid and crystallized (Schulz & Ewen, 1993). **Fluid intelligence**, they say, reflects our innate ability to learn and understand things. It depends primarily on heredity and on how well our nervous system works, and not so much on education or environment. Tests of short-term memory, abstract thinking, reasoning, speed of thinking, creativity, and problem solving are thought to measure fluid intelligence.

The other type of intelligence is **crystallized intelligence**, which consists of stored information that we can readily call on and use. Formal education, traveling, reading, and being around intelligent, stimulating people are all ways of increasing our crystallized intelligence, which is measured by tests of vocabulary, information, social judgment, numerical ability, and the ability to understand and use mechanical principles and tools.

Horn and Donaldson found that fluid intelligence peaks between ages 20 and 30 years and declines thereafter. This is the time, they say, when we have to make so many difficult decisions about careers and intimate relationships, decisions that tax our fluid intelligence to the utmost. We keep accumulating information about our world throughout our lives, however, so crystallized intelligence naturally keeps increasing as we age (see Figure 14.5).

FLUID INTELLIGENCE
The innate ability to learn and understand information and to solve problems.

CRYSTALLIZED INTELLIGENCE
Stored information about oneself and the world.

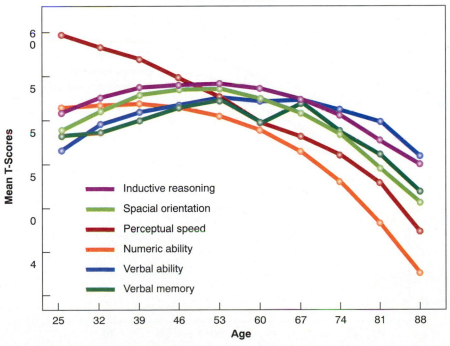

FIGURE 14.4

Longitudinal estimates of mean factor scores for the latent ability constructs. (SOURCE: Schaie, 1994, p. 308)

Note. From 7-year within-subject data.

FIGURE 14.5

Smoothed curves summarizing several studies indicating aging changes for fluid and crystallized intelligence abilities. (SOURCE: Horn & Donaldson, 1980, pp. 469, 471)

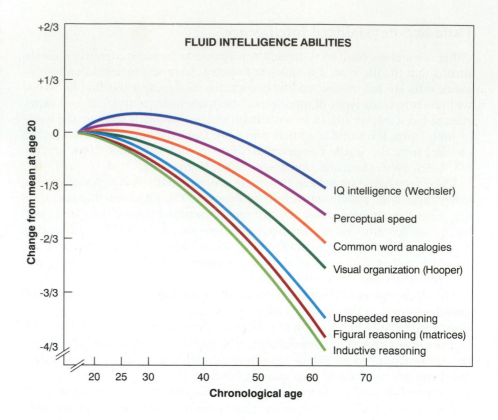

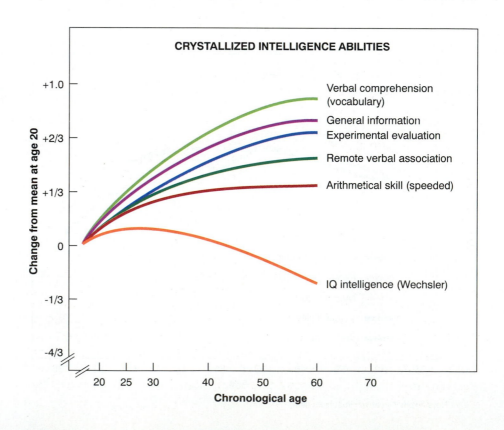

The Structure of Thinking in Adulthood

While the psychologists discussed above have taken a quantitative approach by trying to measure how much adults know, other psychologists have followed Piaget's qualitative approach by looking at how adults think. They have tried to answer a difficult question: Is there a stage of cognitive development beyond Piaget's formal operational stage?

You may recall that in Chapter 8 we said that many adults never even attain formal operations. Even college students have been found to use formal operational thought easily in their majors but not in unrelated subjects (DeLisi and Staudt, 1980). Be that as it may, many researchers and theorists believe that there may be something beyond formal operations and have attempted to describe what is sometimes called **post–formal operational thought**.

One of the earliest attempts to examine how adults think was a study conducted by William Perry and his colleagues in the 1960s. The team interviewed 67 Harvard students during each of the students' four years in college. Although the variability in development we have noted was certainly evident among these students, there was a general progression in how they thought about knowledge and about their place in the world.

Initially, many students believed that there was a single right answer to every question and that professors either should teach the right answers or give them assignments to force them to figure out the right answers themselves. Up to this point, their formal operational skills served them well, but a different kind of thinking was needed for what was to come.

As the students were exposed to more and more competing and contradictory opinions about life, they began to see that knowledge and values are relative and that each person has to work out these issues for him- or herself; no "authority" is going to give us *the answer* or tell us what the *right* thing is to do. At first the students were overwhelmed by the diversity of ideas and tended to conclude that since everyone has a right to his or her own opinion, one opinion must be as good as any other. Eventually, however, most students came to see that some opinions are more reasonable and more easily defended than others. They eventually realized that even though they could understand many different options and conflicting opinions, they had to make choices and commitments that, at least at the time, were "right" for their own lives (Perry, 1970).

Dialectical Thinking.   Many of the themes sounded by Perry have been elaborated by other psychologists. Klaus Riegel (1973, 1975), for example, examined the issue of how we handle competing and contradictory opinions and proposed that a primary characteristic of adult cognition is what he calls **dialectical thinking**. By this he means that adults readily recognize, accept, and even enjoy conflict and contradiction in values and possible courses of action because sorting out these conflicts forces them to grow intellectually.

Dialectical thinking occurs even among concrete operational children as they try to understand concepts like "big," "small," "old," and "young." But adult dialectical thinking often deals with contradictory ideas about morality, religion, ethics, and the like, and adults don't necessarily feel compelled to resolve the contradictions. Take, for example, the difficult dilemma of whether a comatose person should be removed from a respirator. Adults engaging in dialectical thinking can list the many reasons for and against such an action and can come to a conclusion about what action they think they would pursue. Whatever their decision, however, they still are likely to acknowledge that a good argument against that decision could be made.

POST–FORMAL OPERATIONAL THOUGHT
A type of thinking that may develop in late adolescence or adulthood. No widely accepted definition yet exists; in general, characteristics include an ability to understand relativity, contradiction, and subjectivity and to integrate these into decision making.

DIALECTICAL THINKING
Thinking characterized by an understanding of the advantages and disadvantages of any idea or course of action.

Concrete and Abstract Thinking.   Deirdre Kramer has identified a key paradox in adult thinking that she believes distinguishes it from the formal operational thinking characteristic of adolescence. She sees adult thinking as being simultaneously more concrete and more abstract (Kramer, 1983).

Teenagers so much enjoy their newly acquired formal operational skills that they often construct abstract and sometimes grandiose plans, despite parents' advice to be practical. As they enter adulthood and are forced to make commitments to jobs and other people, their thinking usually becomes more practical and concrete. However, it simultaneously gets more abstract and detached, because they can step back and view their own thought processes and realize just how subjective their "pragmatic" decisions really are.

Kramer (1983) has reviewed the literature on adult cognition and has concluded that mature adult thinking is characterized by (1) the realization of the relativistic, nonabsolute nature of knowledge; (2) an acceptance of contradiction; and (3) an integration of contradiction into an overriding whole to which the person can commit him- or herself. Whether this kind of thinking represents a fifth stage of development that is qualitatively different from Piaget's formal operational stage, or whether it is merely an elaboration of that stage, is still an open issue.

Systematic and Metasystematic Reasoning.   It is difficult to imagine how the issue of whether there are operations beyond formal operations might be resolved. It would probably depend on how we define cognitive operations. Piaget argued that any cognitive advance beyond formal operations was not *qualitatively* significant but rather was "mere window dressing." But as you have seen, some researchers believe that there may be qualitative advances in cognitive development beyond formal operations. It has been argued by some that for such advances to be truly *qualitatively* different, higher levels of reasoning beyond formal operations would have to be demonstrated (Commons, Richards, & Kuhn, 1982). These researchers refer to such post–formal operational reasoning as systematic and metasystematic reasoning.

Systematic reasoning, they argue, relies on the ability to build operations on operations, such as would be required to build entire abstract representational systems from the hypothetical constructs generated by formal operational thinking.

Metasystematic reasoning would be the next step beyond systematic reasoning. According to these researchers, an example of metasystematic reasoning can be found in Einstein's general theory of relativity. Such an ability allows entire systems to be built on each other. However, whether such reasoning is "qualitatively" different from what Piaget considered to be formal operations is still debatable. For this to be demonstrated, further research would have to show that the cognitive advance required for systematic and metasystematic reasoning depends on, and is separate from, the cognitive advance to formal operations. It may be that future research will show that such post–formal operational abilities exist.

MORAL DEVELOPMENT IN EARLY ADULTHOOD

In Chapter 9, we presented Lawrence Kohlberg's theory of preconventional, conventional, and postconventional moral development. Kohlberg and his colleagues followed their original 84 white, lower- and middle-class male subjects into adulthood and found that postconventional reasoning did not emerge until their subjects were at least 18 years old. Moreover, no more than 10 percent of the sample ever demonstrated this high level of moral reasoning, and those who did reached only stage 5 (Colby, Kohlberg, Biggs, & Liberman, 1983) (see Figure 14.6).

Postconventional morality doesn't appear earlier because formal operational thinking appears to be necessary for postconventional moral reasoning. As we learned earlier, this kind of thinking often doesn't emerge until young adulthood, if then. Moreover, postconventional morality demands that we be exposed to many different values and opinions, and most of us get this exposure only after we leave high school and our parents' homes. In one study, no one without postsecondary education attained even stage 4 moral reasoning (Walker, 1986).

Stage 6 Individuals

Kohlberg constructed his definition of stage 6 from a small, elite sample consisting of people such as Martin Luther King, Jr., and Ghandi. Unfortunately, no one in any longitudinal research has attained stage 6. And although Kohlberg believed that stage 6 was "an ideal endpoint" for his theory (Kohlberg, Levine, & Hewer, 1983) he admitted, near the end of his life, that he had been unable to demonstrate a clear distinction between stages 5 and 6 (Colby, Kohlberg, Gibbs, & Lieberman, 1983).

Women's Moral Development

Kohlberg's theory of moral development was called into question by Carol Gilligan, one of Kohlberg's graduate students. When she presented the standard moral dilemmas to women, she discovered to her dismay that the women were far less likely than men to reach postconventional reasoning. Refusing to conclude that women's moral judgment is inferior to men's, she designed a research project to look at how women resolve a very difficult real-life dilem-

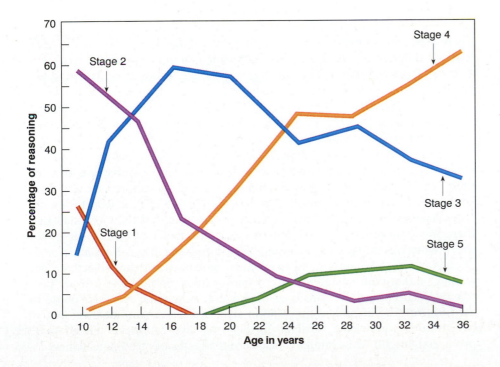

FIGURE 14.6

Follow-up of Kohlberg's study; mean percentage of moral reasoning at each stage for each age-group. (SOURCE: Colby, Kohlberg, Gibbs, & Lieberman, 1983, p. 46)

ma, the decision about whether or not to terminate a pregnancy. Her subjects were 29 women, ages 15 to 33 years, of diverse ethnic backgrounds and social classes, referred by abortion and pregnancy counselors. From this and other research, Gilligan concluded that women tend to conceptualize moral problems in terms of *care and responsibility in relationships*, while men tend to think more in terms of *justice* (Gilligan, 1982).

Gilligan found that her subjects initially focused on caring for themselves to ensure survival. Then they began to criticize themselves as selfish for considering their own needs first and to consider more their responsibility for others, especially the dependent and unequal. This second stage, which Gilligan called traditional maternal morality, was characterized by much self-sacrifice. Eventually, the women were able to fuse an awareness of their own needs with their wish to care for others and to see as moral those actions that showed care and responsibility both for themselves and for other people.

Gilligan's work has not gone unchallenged. For example, Lawrence Walker has repeatedly reported that he has been unable to find gender-related differences in moral orientation or stage of development in his own research or in that of other people (1986). His research, however, yielded inconsistent findings about gender and moral orientation. No differences were found among younger boys and girls. However, contrary to Gilligan's theory, adolescent boys showed more of a responsibility orientation than did adolescent girls; consistent with Gilligan's theory, women showed a stronger responsibility orientation than did men. One of the most intriguing findings is that people at higher stages of moral development tended to include both orientations in their reasoning, that is, both an orientation toward caring for others with whom they have a relationship and an orientation toward universal justice and what is generally fair (Walker, de Vries, & Trevethan, 1987).

Women's Cognitive Development

Carol Gilligan examined how women solve a difficult real-life dilemma to determine their level of moral development.

Mary Field Belenky, Blythe Clinchy, Nancy Goldberger, and Jill Tarule (1986) have challenged existing theories about the structure of thinking in adulthood and now maintain that women's ways of knowing are different from men's. These researchers interviewed 135 women, including students or recent graduates of different types of colleges and women in family agencies that offer training about parenting. The subjects came from a variety of ethnic backgrounds, and their socioeconomic status ranged from being recipients of welfare to being members of the upper middle class. The researchers maintain that this diverse population "provided us with an unusual opportunity to see the common ground that women share, regardless of background" (1986, p. 5).

Belenky and her group identified five *epistemological perspectives* from which women know and view the world. The first perspective was held by their youngest and most deprived subjects, who had no appreciation of their ability to learn or even to reason. The women who viewed the world from the second perspective knew that they could learn facts, but they assumed that there was only one right answer to any question and that other people, not they themselves, knew right answers. In the third category, self-reliance was a distinguishing characteristic, as the women came to trust their subjective, "gut feeling," rather than relying on external authorities. From the fourth perspective, women engaged in conscious, deliberate, systematic analysis. Those in the fifth category integrated this kind of analytical knowing with their subjective, intuitive knowledge. Women in these last two categories tended to be privileged, bright, white students or recent graduates of prestigious colleges.

Belenky and her colleagues did not interview a comparable group of men, so male and female "ways of knowing" cannot be compared and contrasted according to their scheme. However, they do report that their women did not fit Perry's scheme well. Be that as it may, their second-perspective women do resemble those students Perry interviewed who looked for a single right answer from their professors. And their fourth and fifth perspectives are quite compatible with the progression Perry saw as his Harvard students moved through their college years.

PERSONALITY DEVELOPMENT IN EARLY ADULTHOOD

As we have seen, both our bodies and our minds are still undergoing dynamic changes right through early adulthood. But what about our personalities? Not surprisingly, researchers are finding that adult personalities change, too. Norma Haan, Roger Millsap, and Elizabeth Hartka reported a longitudinal study in which they assessed changes and stability on key personality variables over a 50-year period. One of their conclusions is especially relevant to early adulthood:

> Great shifts in personality organization are ordinarily thought to occur during adolescence, but these findings suggest that more marked shifts occur, not during adolescence, but at its end when most people make the profound role shifts entailed by entry into full-time work and marriage. (Haan, Millsap, & Hartka, 1986, p. 225)

In an effort to examine the personalities of young adults and to discover how stable these personalities might be over time, a group of researchers studied 79 identical twins and 48 same-sexed fraternal twins. These twins were tested over a 10-year period during which various dimensions of their personalities were measured. It was discovered that the stability of their personalities was largely due to genetic factors and that what changes did occur were largely due to environment (McGue, Bacon, & Lykken, 1993). This interesting discovery highlights once again the diversity of adult development and how such development is tied to culture and social conditions, as opposed to the development of children, which is often more tied to biological or maturational factors.

What, then, are the demands and developmental tasks of early adulthood? What happens to our personalities as the environment shapes us during these years? We'll look first at the theory set forth by Erikson in his classic essay "The Eight Ages of Man." Then we'll look at more recent theorists who have added to or otherwise modified Erikson's ideas.

Intimacy Versus Isolation

According to Erikson, our chief developmental task in early adulthood is to form an intimate relationship with another person. If the young adult is secure in his identity, he should be "eager and willing to fuse his identity with that of others" (Erikson, 1950, p. 263). This may occur in the context of intimate friendships, which require personal compromises and sacrifices, as well as in the special relationships of spouses or lovers.

Erikson believed that much of a person's sexual activity prior to this stage serves mainly to help define and clarify the individual's identity. Now, however, what Erikson called "the utopia of genitality" becomes possible. The word *genitality* is a bit misleading here because of its sexual connotations; Erikson used the term in a broad sense. His "utopia" does include "mutuality of

YOUTH
A stage of development that some people go through following adolescence and prior to assuming full responsibilities of adulthood.

orgasms with a loved partner of the other sex," but he also insisted that the two partners be able to share and regulate the cycles of work, procreation, and recreation "so as to secure to the offspring, too, all the stages of a satisfactory development" (Erikson, 1950, p. 266).

As you may have noticed, this is an extremely traditional view. In effect, it excludes single people, homosexuals, and people without children from the realm of healthy development. In an interview near his eightieth birthday, Erikson was asked what he thought about people deciding not to have children. His reply was that people who do so defy a "procreative urge" and that they need to acknowledge the sense of loss that often accompanies this decision. He went on to say, however, that this urge can be satisfied by caring for other people's children, making creative contributions to the world, and doing things for the community, what the Hindus call "the maintenance of the world" (Hall, 1983).

Erikson said that if people do not form intimate relationships at this stage, they run the risk of becoming isolated and self-absorbed. They can become so convinced of the righteousness of their own position and so mistrustful of people who disagree that they develop prejudices and may even seek to destroy people who seem to threaten their position.

Youth: A Special Time of Life

In 1960, Erikson was appointed professor at Harvard. Kenneth Keniston, a young faculty member, was asked to assist Erikson in preparing a course on the life cycle. Recalling those years, Keniston stated that Erikson's theories, especially his ideas about the identity crisis, caught on quickly among undergraduates, but Erikson worried about this because he feared that students would use them to justify evading responsibility. "Having an identity crisis," he said, "is neither a boast nor an excuse for late papers" (Keniston, 1983, p. 29).

Keniston was impressed by Erikson's theories, but the more he taught, the more college students he found who did not fit Erikson's scheme. He decided that perhaps there was another, optional stage of development that some people experience after adolescence and before becoming full-fledged adults; he called this stage "**youth**" (Keniston, 1968, 1970).

The people Keniston called "youth" were men and women of college and graduate school age who were unable to settle down as their parents had, who didn't consider themselves adults, and who often strongly challenged the existing social order. Many were at least partly dependent on their parents financially, and they often postponed marriage because it implied settling down. Keniston knew that there have always been tiny minorities of people—often the very creative or very disturbed—who fit into this category. In the 1960s, however, many young people did so.

But such people aren't just in an extended adolescence. They usually have already lived through the identity upheavals of adolescence and have a fairly stable sense of who they are. In their view of what must be done in the world, they are "less impelled by juvenile grandiosity than by a rather accurate analysis of the perils and injustices of the world in which they live" (Keniston, 1970, p. 634). They begin to experience a real tension between themselves and society, and they struggle with the question of how they can simultaneously maintain their personal integrity and be an effective member of society.

This tension between self and society leads youths to value change and transformation and often to panic when they feel "stuck in a rut." Sometimes, they believe that it is they themselves who need to change, and they'll use whatever means available: monasticism, psychoanalysis, religious conversion,

"Youths," whatever their ages, often lead all kinds of social movements.

drugs, hard work, cults, encounter groups, and so on. At other times, they try to change the world, as did the young radicals protesting the Vietnam War or the college students who demanded an end to apartheid in South Africa.

Another way that youths differ from adolescents is that the identities and roles that they assume lie somewhere between the ephemeral enthusiasms of adolescents and the established commitments of adults. The roles may last for months or years, and the youths are deeply committed to them. Almost always, however, the youths know that the roles are temporary and that aging will change their status. For some youths, the roles do provide the foundation for later professional commitments; for others, the roles are merely experiments that allow them to grow, then to move on in other directions.

It may seem to you that this is a stage that mainly upper-middle-class college students go through. No doubt affluence and education provide the freedom and intellectual stimulation that help promote the transformations of youth. But many well-to-do college students go directly from adolescence to adulthood, while many poorer young people have a youth stage. Abraham Lincoln is a good example. A friend of his thought there was "suthin' peculiar-some about Abe" because he "picked out such a question as 'Who has the most right to complain, the Indian or the Negro?' and would talk about it, up and down in the cornfields" (Sandburg, 1954, p. 14). At the age of 19, Lincoln set off with a friend on a 1,000-mile trip down the Mississippi River to New Orleans. Later, he judged horse races and cockfights while working as a store-keeper, rail splitter, mill hand, farmhand, and postmaster, before finally settling into politics and law, and finally marrying at age 33.

It is hard to say when youth ends. Development proceeds unevenly. If we analyze someone's life at any given time, we'll find a mixture of adolescent, youthful, and adult features. In general, however, economic independence and the ability to make autonomous decisions about a career, values, and relationships often mark the end of youth. The age at which these occur, however, varies enormously from one person to another.

Career Consolidation

While Keniston was developing his ideas about youth, George Vaillant was gathering and analyzing data for the Grant Study, a major longitudinal study of adult development. In 1937, William T. Grant, philanthropist and owner of the W. T. Grant variety stores, provided Harvard with a substantial sum of money to make a systematic inquiry into healthy students who function well (Heath, 1945). The Grant Study staff recruited 268 Harvard undergraduates who had good grades, were especially self-reliant, and were superior to their peers in both emotional and physical health. Ninety-five of these men were followed into their 50s.

Vaillant, an admirer of Erikson's work, found that the Grant Study data provided objective support for Erikson's contention that an individual must pass sequentially through the stages of development. The men who failed to master one stage generally weren't able to master later stages. However, the age at which the men mastered the stages varied considerably. The data further suggested, Vaillant decided, that Erikson's theory needed to be modified somewhat (Vaillant, 1977).

Vaillant inserted a new stage, career consolidation, between Erikson's stages of intimacy versus isolation and generativity versus stagnation. He found that between 20 and 30 years of age, most of the men in his study married and established strong friendships. Once the men had established these relationships, usually while they were 25 to 35 years old, they focused almost exclusively on their careers. They were not good at self-reflection, and much like conscientious elementary school children, "they were good at tasks, careful to follow the rules, anxious for promotion, and willing to accept all aspects of the system" (Vaillant, 1977, p. 216). They sacrificed play for work, deceived themselves about the adequacy of their marriages and careers, and became "colorless, hardworking, bland young men in 'gray flannel suits'" (Vaillant, 1977, p. 217). In Chapter 16, we'll see what happened to these "bland young men" in middle age.

We can also learn other things from Vaillant's work, not the least of which is a lesson about the value of longitudinal research. The lesson is well illustrated by one man who, in 1941, when there was a growing movement in favor of the United States entering the war against Germany, told the researchers, "I feel extremely disheartened. The war in Europe is none of our business." In 1966 and 1967, this same man fully supported U.S. involvement in Vietnam and condemned his sons for protesting the war. When asked then about his beliefs just prior to the U.S. entry into World War II, he could only recall his active, patriotic participation! Vaillant concluded that "Maturation makes liars of us all." (1977, p. 197)

Now let's turn to another research project aimed at helping us understand adult development.

The Seasons of a Man's Life

Daniel Levinson and his colleagues at Yale were initially interested in what they called the midlife transition in men, which we'll look at in Chapter 16. They recruited 40 men, ages 35 to 45 years, 10 in each of four occupations: hourly workers, business executives, academic biologists, and novelists. In lengthy, in-depth interviews, the researchers asked the men about their occupations, relationships, hopes, dreams, and frustrations, both in their current lives and during their late adolescence and early adulthood (Levinson, Darrow, Klein, Levinson, & McKee, 1978).

The key concept to emerge from Levinson's research is that of the **life struc-ture**, the underlying pattern of a person's life at a given time. Levinson argues that the life structure evolves through a series of stable, structure-building periods alternating with transitional, structure-changing periods. The stable periods generally last 5 to 7 years—10 at the most (see Figure 14.7).

Early adulthood in Levinson's scheme encompasses ages 17 to 45 years. First came a transitional time (ages 17 to 22 years), during which the young men moved out of their parents' homes and began to take steps toward emotional and financial independence. At ages 22 to 28, the men's lives generally were stable. During this time, the men developed a dream of the kind of life they wanted, especially in terms of relationships and careers. Although some men used these years to try various jobs and relationships, most got married, had children, and invested in a career. Many were aided by a **mentor**, an older man who offered guidance and support and helped them in their career develop-ment. Around age 30 years, the men went through another transition, during which they reexamined their earlier commitments and often found them want-ing. Marital problems and job changes were common. From about 33 to 40, Levinson's men strove to establish themselves in society and made stronger commitments to work and home life. They often set goals for themselves, with age 40 being the target date for the goals' accomplishment.

Toward the end of this stable period, from about age 36 to 40 years, came what Levinson calls BOOM (Becoming One's Own Man). His subjects began to feel constrained by authorities and wished for more independence. They broke off relationships with their mentors, and now felt compelled to become senior members of their professions themselves.

Levinson notes that the 28-year era of early adulthood is the time "of great-est energy and abundance and of greatest contradiction and stress . . . we are most buffeted by our passions and ambitions from within and by the demands

LIFE STRUCTURE
The underlying pattern of a person's life at a given time.

MENTOR
A more experienced person in a work set-ting who provides guidance, support, and advice about career development to a less experienced person.

FIGURE 14.7

Developmental periods in the eras of early and middle adulthood. (SOURCE: Levinson, 1986, pp. 3–13)

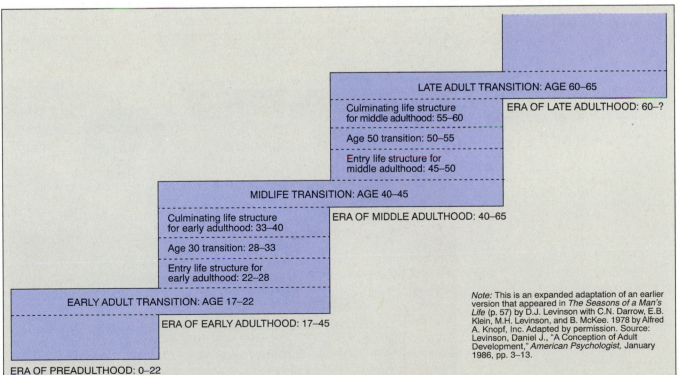

LATE ADULT TRANSITION: AGE 60–65

Culminating life structure for middle adulthood: 55–60

ERA OF LATE ADULTHOOD: 60–?

Age 50 transition: 50–55

Entry life structure for middle adulthood: 45–50

MIDLIFE TRANSITION: AGE 40–45

Culminating life structure for early adulthood: 33–40

ERA OF MIDDLE ADULTHOOD: 40–65

Age 30 transition: 28–33

Entry life structure for early adulthood: 22–28

EARLY ADULT TRANSITION: AGE 17–22

ERA OF EARLY ADULTHOOD: 17–45

ERA OF PREADULTHOOD: 0–22

Note: This is an expanded adaptation of an earlier version that appeared in *The Seasons of a Man's Life* (p. 57) by D.J. Levinson with C.N. Darrow, E.B. Klein, M.H. Levinson, and B. McKee. 1978 by Alfred A. Knopf, Inc. Adapted by permission. Source: Levinson, Daniel J., "A Conception of Adult Development," *American Psychologist,* January 1986, pp. 3–13.

SELF-IN-RELATION THEORY
A theory in which the goal of personality development is a deepening capacity for competence in relationships, in contrast to theories that emphasize autonomy, self-reliance, and separation from other people.

of family, community, and society from without" (Levinson, 1986, p. 5). It can be a "season" of much satisfaction in terms of love, sexuality, family life, occupational achievement, and creativity. But it can also inflict crushing stresses as men simultaneously undertake the demands of marriage, parenting, and building a career before they have the maturity to choose wisely. Ironically, it is making and living with these choices that help men mature.

Self-in-Relation Theory of Development

You may have noticed that Levinson, Vaillant, and Kohlberg's subjects were all men. Erikson called his life cycle stages the eight ages of man. But what about the other 51 percent of the population? (See At Issue.)

Psychologists have repeatedly constructed models of normal development based on observations of male subjects, and repeatedly women have not fit these models. You can imagine what some people thought was the "obvious" conclusion: There must be something wrong with women! Not until the late 1960s did writers begin to challenge this conclusion and develop theories of normal female development. To date, there are relatively few broad-based studies of women, and many people believe that women's lives, especially in adulthood, defy classification and categorization even more than men's do. Much of the research on women has focused on the effects of traumatic experiences, such as rape. Although this is now changing, most of the writings on normal female development are still in the theoretical, hypothesis-generating stage, similar to where the writings on men were in the 1950s.

Twenty years ago, Jean Baker Miller published *Toward a New Psychology of Women*, a landmark book that, among other things, set forth the proposition that "women's sense of self becomes very much organized around being able to make and then to maintain affiliation and relationships" (Miller, 1976, p. 83). Miller's book and the writings of Nancy Chodorow (1974, 1978) formed the basis for what has come to be called the **self-in-relation theory** of development (Surrey, 1985). According to this theory, the basic goal of a woman's development is the "deepening capacity for relationships and relational competence" (Surrey, 1985, p. 2), and development consists of "a process of growth

New theories of female development stress the importance of developing and maintaining close relationships throughout a person's life.

AT ISSUE

Women's Achievement Motivation

When Lawrence Terman first examined his group of gifted children in 1921, he found that the girls were more talented artistically and that the seven most talented writers were girls. But when these children grew up, the eminent artists and writers were all men. Furthermore, almost half the men in the study were professionals in high-level occupations, whereas only 11 percent of the women were professionals, and most of these were teachers (Terman & Oden, 1947, 1959). The finding that gifted girls usually fail to grow into achieving women appears with alarming frequency in the literature on achievement. In the next chapter, we'll look at some of the very real external barriers that hamper women's achievement in the workplace. But for now, we'll examine a highly controversial concept known as "fear of success."

In 1968, Matina Horner asked college women to complete a story that began with the sentence, "After her first term of medical school, Ann finds herself at the top of her medical school class." Sixty-five percent of the women responded with negative stories, including violent ones such as, "Her fellow classmates are so disgusted with her behavior that they jump on her body and beat her" (Horner, 1968). When men were asked to complete the same story about a male student, only 10 percent responded with negative statements. Horner concluded that women's achievement strivings often become thwarted because they fear success and that this fear "exists because for most women, the anticipation of success in competitive achievement activity, especially against men, produces anticipation of certain negative consequences, for example, threat of social rejection and loss of femininity" (Horner, 1968, p. 125).

As you might expect, Horner's report generated considerable attention and controversy. Many people criticized the use of fantasy as a technique to assess motivation, and they developed objective instruments aimed at measuring fear of success. Moreover, different researchers defined "fear of success" differently, so for a time it became a "now-you-see-it-now-you-don't" phenomenon. A review of 64 studies found that an incredible range of anywhere from 6 to 93 percent of the female subjects and 7 to 95 percent of the male subjects could be classified as fearers of success (Paludi, 1979, reported in Paludi & Fankell-Hauser, 1986).

Michele Paludi and Jean Fankell-Hauser (1986) used the technique of biographical interviewing, which Levinson and his colleagues used in studying their male subjects (1978). This technique, they believe, allowed them to elicit information not readily obtainable from either Horner's fantasy-based measure or the newer objective measures. Their subjects were 80 predominantly white, middle-class women ranging in age from the late teens to the 80s.

When these women were asked whether they had ever been in a situation in which they were about to succeed and

Women are more likely to score high in achievement motivation and low in fear of success if their parents reinforced their achievement strivings and if their mothers enjoyed a career of their own.

had feared the success, 91 percent replied "no." However, 96 percent did report that they sometimes wondered whether their achievements were worth the cost to themselves and their families. Interestingly, this concern seemed to be determined by specific situations. The women reported consciously summing up specific situations and deciding whether to engage in behaviors such as playing dumb, hiding their achievements, and letting men win at games or to indulge their achievement wishes.

Paludi and Fankell-Hauser also found age differences in women's achievement strivings. Compared to the older women, the younger women tended to be more concerned with maintaining relationships and less concerned with competitive achievement. Women aged 50 to 80 years reported that their achievement motivation increased when their children began moving out of the house and no longer needed so much of their time. Moreover, these older women said that they felt that their successes were accepted by both male and female peers and relatives. Other writers have suggested that it is mature women who become innovators and pioneers (Kaufman and Richardson, 1982), and this study lends support to this hypothesis. Finally, high achievement motivation and low fear of success were most characteristic of women whose parents reinforced and encouraged their efforts and who were raised in dual-career families.

In sum, fear of success is clearly a complex construct, and the very existence of such a fear is still open to question. What is clear, however, is that women's achievement motivation and their willingness to act on that motivation probably do vary a great deal, depending on family background, relationships, and developmental stage of life.

within relationships, where both or all people involved are encouraged and challenged to maintain connection and to foster, adapt, and change with the growth of the other" (Surrey, 1985, p. 8).

Think, for a minute, about how this theory contrasts with Erikson's. His initial stage of trust versus mistrust does emphasize the importance of relationships, but the developmental tasks of his next four stages are aimed at increasing autonomy, self-reliance, and separation from other people. He believed that intimacy is possible only after a person is secure in his identity. Self-in-relation theory maintains that intimate relationships are important throughout life, and that the development of a woman's identity is closely tied to those relationships, whether they are with parents, siblings, other relatives, friends, lovers, spouses, or whomever.

As this chapter has illustrated, early adulthood is a time of dynamic development for our bodies, our minds, and our personalities. In the next chapter, we will look more closely at loving and working, two issues that we have touched on in this chapter and that are clearly among the major preoccupations of early adulthood.

Thinking About Changing Your Life?

A friend of mine in college had trouble "finding himself," despite searching through fraternity parties, football games, and Mardi Gras. One semester, his grades consisted of three D's and an F. His father responded by sending a booklet on job opportunities in Alaska, a poster proclaiming "Uncle Sam Wants You!" and an announcement that he was cutting off tuition support until he felt he could get his money's worth. Disliking his father's options, my friend joined the Peace Corps, spent two years in Somalia, and returned settled enough to earn himself a doctorate in economics and continue working in Third World countries.

So what can we say about dramatic alternative lifestyles? Are they really viable ways of changing your life for the better? Many people think both the Peace Corps and the military may be.

"The thing about the Peace Corps is that it doesn't end after two years, it lasts a lifetime" (Landrum, 1986, p. 87). The words of this volunteer were echoed by former senator Paul Tsongas, who called his years in the Peace Corps "the formative experience of my life" (Landrum, 1986, p. 88). In a 1965 study, most of the early volunteers acknowledged changing career directions during their Peace Corps years; most were back in school, and many planned careers in international work. By 1980, 15 percent of the then nearly 100,000 veterans worked for the government either at home or abroad, and many others held prestigious jobs with various international agencies (Landrum, 1986).

That the military also can serve as a positive turning point in a person's life has been demonstrated by data from the longitudinal Berkeley Guidance Study (Elder, 1986). Born in 1928 and 1929, the men in this study were children during the depression, and early in their lives knew deprivation and uncertainty. By the time these men reached early adolescence, the United States was mobilizing for World War II, and military personnel provided models of courage and mastery. Seventy percent of the men served at least two years in the armed forces. Some entered during the closing months of World War II, and many others served in the Korean War. Only one died in the service, a prisoner of war in Vietnam.

The men who entered the armed forces before age 21 are of special interest because they appeared to be the least likely to succeed. Their parents were the hardest hit by the depression, most of them had below-average grades in school, and most scored toward the bottom on measures of goal orientation, self-adequacy, assertiveness, and social competence as adolescents. However, the military provided these men with new options and experiences that drastically changed their lives.

First, people from deprived backgrounds who also are poor achievers through adolescence tend to complete their education, marry, have children, and get jobs at an early age. As a result of the demands of the military, most of these men delayed these events until later in their lives, and in so doing, gave themselves much-needed time to grow up. Only one-third completed high school

It may not be everyone's idea of fun, but the military certainly provides a unique perspective on life.

before entering the military, but all earned diplomas in the service or shortly after leaving it. Thanks to the GI Bill, most went on to junior colleges or vocational schools.

Following the military, the men had something of a youth stage in that they made many changes in jobs, employers, aspirations, and lines of work. By midlife, however, they were quite stable professionally, and their occupational achievements equaled those of the nonveterans who had come from much more promising and supportive backgrounds. Their personal lives also tended to be good. Seventy-four percent had formed stable marriages, compared to only 46 percent of the nonveterans. Finally, in terms of psychological functioning, these men showed much greater social competence and assertiveness than their performance during adolescence would have led one to expect.

In a 1982 interview, 94 percent of these men reported that the military had been a positive influence in that it was "a maturing experience," "developed character," or provided "greater educational opportunity" (Elder, 1986, p. 244). Like the Peace Corps veterans quoted earlier, these men clearly saw the time they spent living a dramatically different lifestyle as a positive experience that drastically altered the course of their lives.

SUMMARY

- The timing of developmental changes varies so much from one adult to another that chronological age becomes an increasingly poor guideline as we study adults.
- The outstanding vitality of early adulthood comes about because so many of our organ systems work so well together during those years.
- Leading causes of death prior to age 35 are accidents, AIDS, homicide, suicide, cancer, and heart disease, in that order. After age 35 years, cancer and heart disease emerge as the leading causes.
- Gender, socioeconomic status, education, exercise, smoking, alcohol consumption, and diet all play important roles in determining the status of our health.
- In studying cognitive development, those researchers who use cross-sectional research designs generally conclude that IQ decreases with age, while those who use longitudinal designs generally conclude that IQ increases with age.
- Fluid intelligence reflects our innate ability to learn and understand, while crystallized intelligence consists of stored information that we can readily call on and use.
- Mature adult thinking is characterized by the realization of the relativistic, nonabsolute nature of knowledge, an acceptance of contradiction, and an integration of contradiction into an overriding whole to which the person can commit him- or herself.
- Postconventional moral reasoning did not emerge among any of Kohlberg's original subjects until age 18 years, and no more than 10 percent of them ever demonstrated this stage of reasoning.
- According to Erikson's stage theory, the primary developmental task of early adulthood is to establish intimate relationships with other people.
- The youth that Keniston described is an optional stage of life between adolescence and adulthood, through which some but not all people pass.
- Vaillant inserted a new stage called career consolidation between Erikson's stages of intimacy versus isolation and generativity versus stagnation.
- The life structure described by Levinson is the underlying pattern of a person's life at a given time.
- By and large, the writings on normal female development are still in the theoretical stage and may be thought of under the general heading of self-in-relation theory.
- According to Gilligan, women tend to conceptualize moral problems in terms of care and responsibility in relationships, while men tend to think more in terms of justice.

QUESTIONS FOR DISCUSSION

1. Consider the characteristics of the subjects who participated in the studies done by Vaillant, Levinson, Gilligan, and Belenky and her colleagues. How applicable do you think the findings of these studies are to other populations?

2. Which of the theories of personality development best describes you? Your best friend? Explain your answer.

3. Why do you think many young adults ignore what is known about the dangers of smoking and alcohol abuse? Might their level of cognitive development have something to do with it?

SUGGESTIONS FOR FURTHER READING

1. Gilligan, C. (1982). *In a different voice.* Cambridge, MA: Harvard University Press.

2. Keniston, K. (1970). Youth: A new stage of life. *The American Scholar,* Autumn, 39(4), 631–654.

3. Schaie, K. W. (1995). *Intellectual development in adulthood: The Seattle Longitudinal Study.* New York: Cambridge University Press.

4. Schulz, R., & Ewen, R. B. (1993). *Adult development and aging* (2nd ed.). New York: Macmillan.

5. Sheehy, G. (1977). *Passages: Predictable crises of adult life.* New York: Bantam.

CHAPTER 15

Early Adulthood: Loving and Working

Homework

Gregory, age 31, is an actuarial analyst for a large insurance company. The company headquarters is in New York, and every day for the last nine years, he boarded the Long Island Railroad, took the 50-minute ride from his home into Manhattan, and battled the congestion and crowds to get to his small office on the nineteenth floor of an 80-story building. There he worked with the information and the figures provided him, consulted his colleagues, and produced reports for the company. But he dreamed about living elsewhere. He always wanted a small home in the mountains in some rural upstate location far from the city, where his children could grow up surrounded by the forests and the hills.

Now, after nine years, Gregory has his wish. He, his wife, and his children are living in a small rustic home in the Adirondack Mountains in a New York town of 1,300 people. His children attend the local school, and Gregory no longer has to commute to his office in Manhattan. What's most amazing is that Gregory never quit his job. He's still doing the same work for the same corporation, only he doesn't have to be in a company office to do it.

Gregory wakes up each morning and goes to work by simply walking across his living room to a small office in his home. There, he turns on his computer, takes the telephone off the hook, and connects it to the computer modem, which puts him in direct contact with the main office in New York City. All the information he needs for that day—all the information he would have received in his office—is immediately sent to his home. Any books or literature he needs are delivered by mail or are available by computer access. Consultations with colleagues are accomplished by conference calls or electronic mail. He sits at his computer, prepares his reports, makes his suggestions, and does all the work he would normally do in his little office in downtown Manhattan. Three times a year Gregory travels to New York City for major conferences, which he enjoys.

In the United States, the number of home-working professionals like Gregory is growing rapidly. The latest government figures indicate that there are nearly 20 million workers in the United States who conduct all or some of their work at home by computer (U. S. Bureau of the Census, 1993). This situation may sound ideal, but if you talk with Gregory, you will discover that this new circumstance in his life has also brought about some unexpected changes in his work and in his close relationships.

To begin with, Gregory reports touches of cabin fever. He doesn't leave the house as much as he used to. Because he doesn't need to get up at a certain hour, some days he sleeps late. There have been days when he never bothered to get dressed. He says that he seems to be disorganized, although he gets his work done.

He also reports that he misses socializing with his colleagues at work. Although he has made friends with neighbors and local residents, these relationships can't replace the camaraderie that he shared with others who are doing the same work. He feels a little lonely. Nonetheless, when asked whether he'd like to go back to the way he lived before, with the long commute, he says, "No way!"

Does he like the way things are now? He says that it is different from what his wife and he thought it would be. For example, Gregory is finding it difficult to separate work and family life. His wife and children have the same difficulty. Because he is always at home, he is accessible to them. His roles as husband and father become intermixed with his role as employee. It's very difficult for him to say, "I'm going to my office now; don't bother me no matter what," because when he's home he finds himself involved with his family.

Other things disrupt his work and influence his motivation. To begin with, no one is expecting him to "arrive" at work at a certain time. He has deadlines he must meet, but he can meet them in any way he wishes. He often gives himself a day off to be with the children, but the next day he has to do twice as much work. This practice is extremely common among people who work at home with fixed deadlines. Rather than work a steady 8 hours every day, they tend to take extra days off followed by 13- or 14-hour marathons of work. Their work often expands to fill weekends and holidays, times they would have normally been forced to take off. It's hard for Gregory to relax when he's not working, because he knows his work is building up. When he worked at the office in New York, he could leave his work behind him when he left for the day. Now it's somehow always there in the back of his mind. He knows he should organize his work more carefully, but he doesn't seem able to. He's never been one for making his own schedules and adhering to them. It was different before, when the structure was imposed from the outside.

Workers like Gregory are obviously going to face new kinds of stresses and dilemmas while working at home. And once the information superhighway comes on-line, millions more can be expected to join the ranks of the "homeworkers." Psychologists have only recently begun to examine how to help these workers organize their time better, separate family from work psychologically, and socialize with people who do not necessarily share their work interest but must now take the place of co-workers. No one really knows how these sweeping changes will affect the work and relationships of young adults as they enter the workforce and begin their families. But ready or not, the changes are on the way!

In this chapter, we will look first at the varieties of intimate relationships that people form during early adulthood, and at what happens when these relationships go awry. Then we will turn to another great preoccupation of this stage in our lives—the need to form a professional identity and to establish ourselves in the world of work.

LIKING AND LOVING

> I have sought love, first, because it brings ecstasy—ecstasy so great that I would often have sacrificed all the rest of life for a few hours of this joy. I have sought it, next, because it relieves loneliness—that terrible loneliness in which one shivering consciousness looks over the rim of the world into the cold unfathomable lifeless abyss. I have sought it, finally, because in the union of love I have seen, in a mystic miniature, the prefiguring vision of the heaven that saints and poets have imagined. (Russell, 1951, pp. 3–4)

These eloquent words of philosopher and mathematician Bertrand Russell make clear why the search for love is so central to human experience. Those of us who profess to study human experience naturally want to know more about this thing called love. Unfortunately, our funding sources have not always been sympathetic. When two psychologists requested an $84,000 federal grant to study love, Senator William Proxmire called the request the "biggest boondoggle of the year" and told the National Science Foundation to "get out of the love-racket" (Reston, 1975, p. 39). But *New York Times* columnist James Reston came to the defense of the psychologists:

> If the sociologists and psychologists can get even a suggestion of the answer to our patterns of romantic love, marriage, dissolution, divorce and the children left behind, it could be the best investment of federal money since Mr. Jefferson made the Louisiana Purchase. (Reston, 1975, p. 39)

As soon as we attempt to dissect and analyze love, however, we run into problems. The first is that we cannot always agree on what we mean by the word *love*. It is used to refer to everything from the heart-pounding excitement of a first sexual encounter to the gentle affection between two elderly sisters or

PASSIONATE LOVE
An intense emotional reaction to another person characterized by feelings of romance and excitement.

COMPASSIONATE LOVE
A feeling of closeness to and companionship with another person that grows stronger over time.

brothers. In an attempt to clarify matters, researchers have outlined the following behaviors of love (Kelley, 1983, p. 274):

1. Verbal expression of affection
2. Self-disclosure: revealing intimate facts
3. Nonmaterial evidence of love: giving emotional and moral support, showing interest in the other's activities and respect for his or her opinions
4. Feelings not expressed verbally: feeling happier, more secure, more relaxed when the other is around
5. Material evidence of love: giving gifts, performing physical chores
6. Physical expressions of love: hugging and kissing
7. Willingness to tolerate less pleasant aspects of the other: tolerating demands in order to maintain the relationship

Although by no means as eloquent as Russell's description, these behaviors are far easier to measure and are therefore more suitable for research.

Passionate and Compassionate Love

Love is often classified as either passionate or compassionate. **Passionate love** is an intense emotional reaction to another person characterized by feelings of romance and excitement. If you fall passionately in love with someone, you constantly think about and yearn to be with that person, and you probably idealize him or her. Not all cultures have a concept of love at first sight, or romantic love. In contemporary Western culture, however, we not only believe in this type of love, but expect to be swept away by it (Berscheid, 1983). In fact, the first step to falling in love is to live in a culture that expects this to happen. Second, you must meet an appropriate person, which in this context means someone to whom you are sexually attracted. Third, you must experience an intense emotional arousal, which you interpret as love (Berscheid & Walster, 1978).

The process of interpreting an emotion as love can be somewhat tricky. Have you ever found yourself head over heels in love, only to wonder a week later how you could possibly have felt so strongly about that particular person? One reason we periodically "go out of our heads" with love may be that we misattribute general feelings of arousal (Adler & Carey, 1980). In fact, research has found that sexual attraction increases when people are feeling hate (James, 1910; Suttie, 1935), anger (Barclay & Haber, 1965), and even pain (Ellis, 1936). This kind of mislabeling is probably responsible for many whirlwind courtships. Blinded by passion, people enter into mariage hastily, only to wonder later how they could ever have done such a thing!

Some people think that another reason we periodically go crazy over someone has to do with our brain chemistry. They note that passionate love and its demise are similar to an amphetamine high followed by withdrawal symptoms. Phenylethylamine is a substance in the brain whose chemical structure is similar to amphetamines. Researchers studied subjects with a history of roller-coaster love affairs and found that these subjects often craved chocolate after a breakup. Yes, chocolate is high in phenylethylamine (Liebowitz & Klein, as cited in Adler & Carey, 1980)!

In most lasting relationships, passionate love evolves into **compassionate love**. This type of love involves the willingness to make sacrifices for each other, and it becomes deeper and more powerful as the years progress and the partners share more experiences with each other.

You might wonder if passionate love can occur during a compassionate relationship. Conventional wisdom has it that passionate love rarely lasts for more than 6 months to 2½ years (Walster & Walster, 1978). However, at least one

Movie producers have always catered to our penchant for passionate love, and have perpetuated the notion that this is what "true love" really is.

longitudinal study found that for some couples, both types of love did remain powerful throughout the years (Traupmann & Hatfield, 1981). At this stage of our knowledge, however, we really don't know how to ensure that such an ideal combination will last over time.

SOCIAL PARTICIPATION AND INTIMACY

Social involvement is an important part of the lives of young adults. A lot of their time is spent thinking about and taking part in social interactions with friends, family, and romantic partners (Reis, Lin, Bennett, & Nezlek, 1993). Researchers have found that the most satisfying source of happiness and well-being for young adults is the social bonds they form (Argyle, 1987). In fact, young adults with the most social support have been found to enjoy the best physical health (Cohen, 1988). Young adults who are without social bonds or who have few social contacts often experience problems ranging from mild loneliness to extreme depression or suicide (Reis, 1990). In later years, when people think back on their early adult life, it is usually family, friends, or lovers that they recall most fondly. As a result, developmental psychologists and other researchers are interested in understanding the development of social participation and intimate relationships.

In one study, the social patterns of college students and young adults (ages 18 to 31) were examined from detailed records kept by the subjects. There were three interesting findings. First, from age 18 to 31 there was an important shift during which young adults changed from spending most of their time with same-sexed partners to spending most of their time with opposite-sexed partners. Part of this was due to marriage, but as a rule it was found that "the preference for same-sexed partners [so common in adolescence] ends in adulthood" (Reis, Lin, Bennett, & Nezlek, 1993, p. 641) (see Table 15.1). Also, by the time adults had reached their 30s, they showed a marked preference for a smaller number of good friends and had generally reduced the size of their social circle.

It was also found that intimacy increased from ages 18 to 31 in all social categories. You may recall that Erik Erikson spoke of early adulthood as a time of forming and nurturing an intimate relationship with another. These research findings showed, however, that intimacy in young adulthood was more diffuse than just a single heterosexual bond and occurred in all social relationships. Friendships, family relationships, and romantic involvements all tended to become richer and more intimate as individuals reached their 30s. Women appeared to reach this deeper level of intimacy sooner than men, often in their early to mid-20s (Reis, Lin, Bennett, & Nezlek, 1993).

Why intimacy in social relations increases at this time is not known, but it might have to do with maturation. Some studies have shown growing levels of

Table 15.1 ● Time (in Minutes) per Day Spent Socializing

Group	All Interaction College*	Adult	Same Sex College	Adult	Opposite Sex College	Adult	Mixed Sex College	Adult	Group College	Adult
Men	329.0	263.5	143.6	86.2	53.5	89.3	32.2	53.0	100.8	34.8
Women	390.7	332.6	131.2	86.6	118.8	145.4	41.4	58.8	91.7	41.7

*Measurements were made when subjects were in their first year of college and then again during early adulthood, a span of 9 to 11 years.
Source: Adapted from Reis, Lin, Bennett, and Nezlek, 1993, p. 638.

intimacy throughout adolescence. This growing intimacy in adulthood, then, may be an extension of that development (Reis, Lin, Bennett, & Nezlek, 1993).

Another possibility is that certain cognitive developments might be required before deeper social intimacy can emerge (Reis & Shaver, 1988). Some researchers disagree with Piaget and assert that cognitive development continues into adulthood. These researchers propose that the ability to relate several aspects of two or more abstractions to one another might not develop until age 19 or 20 and that the ability to form general principles from this systematic manipulation of these various aspects might not emerge until age 25 (Fischer, Hand, & Russell, 1984). If an individual's understanding of personal relationships qualifies as "an abstraction," then the depth of our understanding of another person may be limited by our cognitive development. If this is true and cognitive development continues into adulthood as Fischer suggests, our growing ability to understand another person might lead to greater intimacy than was possible at an earlier time, when our cognitive abilities were not as fully developed.

It could also be that lack of intimacy during the early college years reflects the fact that the first few years of college can be a pretty transitional time, a time when new friendships and romantic involvements are often formed and re-formed. This in itself may appear to make freshmen and sophomores less intimate in social situations. However, data show a steady increase in intimacy in social relationships during early adulthood, and this could not be explained only by the transitional nature of the first few years of college.

The last finding of the study was that the trends toward greater intimacy in young adulthood were very consistent over time, adding to our belief that we are observing a real developmental change and not just the effects of a historical variable or some other transient phenomenon (Reis, Lin, Bennett, & Nezlek, 1993).

We will now look at traditional and nontraditional relationships in adulthood and at what happens when intimate relationships go awry.

THE TRADITIONAL FAMILY

Most young adults hope and dream that their lives will include an intimate relationship and love. These desires generally focus on the idea of marrying and having a traditional family. If we look at the most recent census data, however, it becomes clear that these hopes and dreams have a greater chance of being shattered than ever before.

Between 1980 and 1992, almost 15 million *new* households were formed in the United States. However, 69 percent of these new households consisted of people living alone or with unrelated people or of women heading households without a man present (U.S. Bureau of the Census, 1993). When *all* households were considered, almost 66 percent were made up of only one or two persons, up from about 41 percent in 1960 (U.S. Bureau of the Census, 1984, 1993). These statistics mean, of course, that two-parent families with children have finally become a minority. The average size of the U.S. household has declined from 5.79 in 1790, to 4.76 in 1900, to 2.62 in 1992 (U.S. Bureau of the Census, 1984, 1993).

These changes have attracted researchers' attention, and studies have now been launched to examine the family as a unit, especially its life cycle, to understand better the stresses and strains that a family is likely to face over the years.

Parents of preschool children may become so preoccupied with the children's growth and nurture that they have trouble finding time for each other.

The Family Life-Cycle

Many researchers have come to believe that family life moves through a series of stages, each with unique developmental tasks to which the family members must attend (Duvall, 1977; Aldous, 1978; Nock, 1982). Drawing on the work of earlier researchers, David Olson, Hamilton McCubbin, and their associates (1983) divided the family life cycle into seven stages:

I. Young married couples without children
II. Families with preschool children
III. Families with school-age children
IV. Families with adolescents in the home
V. Launching families
VI. Empty-nest families
VII. Families in retirement

They then conducted a cross-sectional survey of 1,140 couples and 412 adolescents located in 31 states. Each stage was represented by at least 100 couples or families chosen because they were "normal," "typical," "nonclinical," and "ordinary" intact units. Although there was enormous variability in the length of time a given family might spend in a particular stage, the early adulthood years typically encompassed stages I through III. Key stresses in each of these stages are shown in Figure 15.1.

Stage I: Young Married Couples Without Children.   The average age of stage I husbands was 27.6 years; that of wives was 25 years. These couples were not yet faced with the demands of young children, but were formulating and negotiating individual and couples' goals and mutually acceptable lifestyles. Financial burdens and work-related difficulties were their key problems. Their relationships were characterized by considerable cohesion and adaptability, and they reported high marital and family satisfaction. Only 10 percent said they had ever considered separation or divorce.

Stage II: Families with Preschool Children.   The average age of stage II husbands was 30.5 years; that of wives was 29 years; that of the oldest child was

FIGURE 15.1

Profile of family stresses and strains in early adulthood. The top four stressors for families in each stage are listed. (SOURCE: Adapted from Olson et al., 1983, pp. 125–126)

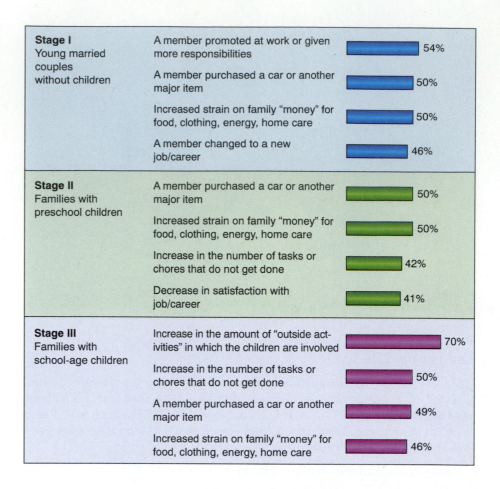

3 years. Children spent most of their time at home, and the families were essentially child-centered. Parents were preoccupied with the children's growth and nurture and were primary sources of information and control. Family cohesion and overall quality of life were high for stage II families, but adaptability and marital and family satisfaction dropped off slightly. Twenty-one percent of the couples now reported having considered separation or divorce.

Stage III: Families with School-Age Children.   The average ages of stage III husbands and wives were 35 and 33, respectively, and the couples had been married for an average of 11 years. They generally had two children, and the average age of the oldest was 9 years. One reason the family income did not increase from stage I to stage III may be that many mothers with small children either were unable to work outside the home or chose not to.

Given that there were now more people to support on the same amount of money as in earlier stages, you might suspect that financial problems would be paramount for these families. However, parents reported that the most stressful life events came from activities related to the children's education and socialization—that is activities outside the home. Cohesion continued to be high, and these families actually reported slightly higher levels of marital satisfaction than did stage II families. However, family satisfaction continued to drop, especially for the women. This meant that the spouses continued to be happy with their relationship but they were not so pleased with the family interactions as a whole.

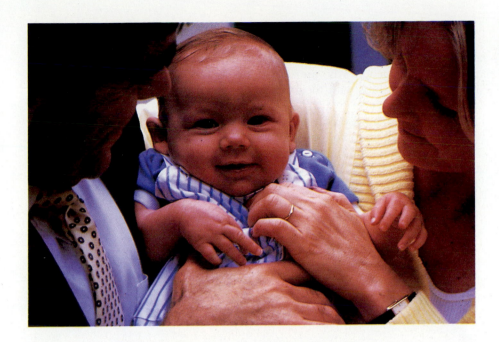

Parenting can be happy and rewarding, but it also is difficult and demanding. The decision to have children should be made carefully, with sound, educated judgment.

Family life cycle theorists have been criticized for not taking into account divorces, remarriages, childless couples, or intergenerational relations. For example, a person may be in stage I in his nuclear family but stage VII in his family of origin. Moreover, Olson and McCubbin's study is cross-sectional in design. Although it does let us examine differences among families at various stages, "it is impossible to assess with certainty which are developmental differences and which are due to the varying ages, maturity level, or historical contexts of the people studied" (Olson et al., 1983, p. 36). Despite these difficulties, the family life cycle is a useful concept for helping traditional families understand what may be happening within their family unit at any given time. In Chapters 17 and 19, we'll look at the stages that families go through in middle and late adulthood.

Parenthood

You probably noticed that in the two stages that include children, family satisfaction dropped off a bit. Moreover, as of 1995, it cost about $182,000 to raise a child to 18 years of age, more than the price of the average house! In fact, while data indicate that spousal support is a very helpful and constructive influence on parenting, economic strain on a family has been found to be one of the most destructive (Simons, Lorenz, Conger, & Wu, 1992). There is no doubt that children are expensive and that they can disrupt a couple's life together, but most couples still want to have children.

Many couples have very good reasons for wanting children. They may feel a sense of responsiblility toward the next generation, or they may feel that children can provide a lifetime of love and joy. Unfortunately, some couples decide to have children for very poor reasons. They may want a chance to raise children according to a particular philosophy, or they may want to have someone who will love them or whom they can dominate. Some people have children because other people, especially their own parents, want them to. Some people have children simply because they assume that's what adults do. And yet others have children unintentionally and decide to "make do" with their situation.

Needless to say, wanting children for "good" reasons can make a tremendous difference in the quality of life for both the children and the parents. Having children is a decision that should be made carefully, with sound, educated judgment. For people who are stable, mature, and sensitive enough to form healthy relationships with their children, parenting can be a very happy and rewarding experience.

Some couples, however, decide not to have children. They might believe, for example, that children will interfere with their relationship with each other or will distract them from their other interests. Some feel that they themselves are not stable enough financially or otherwise to be responsible for raising a child. The decision not to have children is probably easier for people in their 20s to make, because these people still have plenty of time to change their minds. The decision is more complex during the 30s, however, because, at least for women, the biological clock starts ticking more loudly.

We noted earlier that the hopes and dreams of marrying and raising children in an intact traditional family don't always come true. In Chapter 11, we looked at how children react to divorce. Let's look now at general divorce trends and at the effects of divorce on the adults involved.

DIVORCE

The divorce rate in the United States more than doubled between 1950 and 1981. As of 1995, it had decreased only slightly from its high in 1981. It is especially sobering to realize that almost *half* of all new marriages in the United States will end in divorce. Ours is not the only country grappling with this problem; many other Western industrialized nations have similar rates. Most divorces occur in early adulthood, usually within the first 7 years of a marriage (Reiss, 1980).

Although these high numbers understandably generate concern, we should be aware that the divorce rate has been generally rising since the mid-nineteenth century (see Figure 15.2). People who married in the decade or so after World War II are the only ones to show a substantial decrease in their divorce rate (although, as we said, the rate in recent years has come down *slightly*.) This cohort includes most of the parents of the baby-boom generation. The divorce rate of baby boomers, who were born between 1945 and 1959, certainly is high, but it looks especially dramatic when compared to the low divorce rate of their parents (Cherlin, 1981).

There are many reasons why couples get divorced. Divorced women say they wanted out of their marriage because of their husband's personality, drinking, "being out with the boys," lack of support, or infidelity or because they were having financial or sexual problems. Divorced men complain most about their wife's infidelity and her relatives. Women usually are more dissatisfied and find greater fault with their marriage than do men (Kitson & Sussman, 1983).

These problems have been with us for ages. Even so, the divorce rate increased considerably in the last 50 years. Social acceptance probably has a lot to do with it. People who have been divorced may for a time feel like failures and misfits, but they are no longer excluded from social contact as they once were. In the 1950s, if you got a divorce, people treated you like a leper, but now, in some parts of the United States, you need to be getting your fourth divorce or so to raise social eyebrows. Support groups and organizations such as Parents Without Partners have also helped to decrease the isolation that used to be such a painful part of divorce.

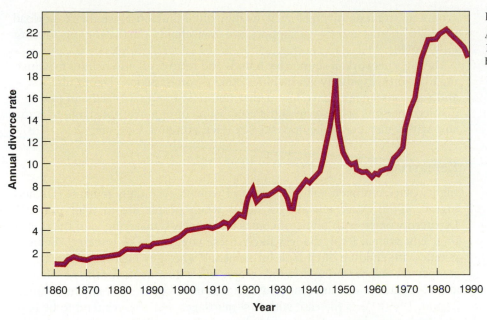

FIGURE 15.2

Annual divorce rates in the United States, 1860–1990 (SOURCE: Cherlin, 1981; U.S. Bureau of the Census, 1993)

A second reason for the jump is that in the mid-1960s, states began relaxing their divorce laws. The advent of "no fault" divorce laws has meant that couples can secure a divorce on grounds of incompatibility and do not have to identify one partner's behavior as the cause of the marital breakup.

Divorce Adjustment

Whatever the changes in social mores and laws, separation and divorce are still enormously painful for the estranged couple. Separation may actually be more stressful than divorce itself, for it is often the first public declaration of marital discord. Moreover, it marks the beginning of major life changes and legal and economic upheavals, and children, family members, and friends must be dealt with. Finally, the ambiguous status of not being really married or really single is unsettling.

Some people report that compared to separation, the divorce itself is relatively painless and that they are able to adjust reasonably well. On the whole, however, divorced people are at greater risk for psychiatric disorders, suicide, homicide, accidents, disease, morbidity, and mortality than are nondivorced people (Gove, 1973; Bloom, Hodges, Caldwell, Systra, & Cedrone, 1979). In one group of people attending a course on divorce, 44 percent reported levels of depression similar to hospitalized psychiatric patients (Dasteel, 1982). Divorced men usually show more psychiatric symptoms than do divorced women (Gove, 1973).

How people adjust to divorce depends on many variables. The person initiating the divorce has the distinct advantage of being in control, but he or she also may experience more guilt (Day & Bahr, 1986). Economic problems make adjustment more difficult, and usually the women have more economic problems than the men. It is the mother who is usually awarded custody of any children, which often makes it difficult for these women to find full-time employment, especially in a demanding career position that might require a lot of late or extra hours. In fact, of the children of divorces occurring in the 1980s, almost 50 percent spent an average of 5 years in a one-parent household (Hetherington, Stanley-Hagan, & Anderson, 1989). This can also be an

HOMOSEXUAL
A person who is sexually attracted to a member of his or her own sex.

HETEROSEXUAL
A person who is sexually attracted to a member of the opposite sex.

GAY
A homosexual man.

LESBIAN
A homosexual woman.

economic strain on divorced men, as they often must increase their workload to make enough money to support two households (Hetherington, Cox, & Cox, 1978).

Having a network of supportive friends and relatives is also helpful in adjusting to divorce, especially if it includes other divorced people. Dating also helps, and some researchers have found that the most important factor in raising a divorced person's self-esteem is the establishment of a new, satisfying relationship with a member of the opposite sex (Hetherington, Cox, and Cox, 1978).

Remarriage

Eighty percent of men and 75 percent of women eventually remarry (Hetherington, 1989). Most remarriages occur when people are in their mid-30s. Divorced women with higher incomes often delay remarrying, and the higher their educational level, the less likely these women are to remarry. Divorced people with children often look for someone who they believe will be a good stepparent. Stepparenting demands major role adjustments for the new family, and communication between spouses needs to be open and frequent (Hetherington, 1989). As is the case with first marriages, remarriages tend to be happier for husbands than for wives (Roberts & Price, 1985).

HOMOSEXUAL RELATIONSHIPS

The term **homosexual** is used to refer to people who are sexually attracted primarily to members of their own sex, while **heterosexual** refers to people who are sexually attracted primarily to members of the opposite sex. Many people find themselves somewhere on a homosexual/heterosexual continuum. However, because our society still holds many negative stereotypes about homosexuals, people may become anxious if they find themselves attracted to a member of their own sex and confused if they are sometimes attracted to a male and at other times to a female. In fact, these are very common experiences. It is important to note that the psychiatric community does not consider homosexuality to be deviant if the person finds the choice comfortable and satisfying. Rather, homosexuality is viewed merely as an alternative choice to a heterosexual lifestyle.

The term **gay** often is used to refer to homosexual men. It is thought to be derived from the sexual poems that Ralph Waldo Emerson wrote to Martin Gay when they were both undergraduates at Harvard. These were known for years among the literati as the Gay poems.

Homosexual women sometimes are referred to as **lesbians**, a word derived from the Greek isle of Lesbos, which was populated by strong and poetic women heralded by the Greek poetess Sappho. Precise numbers are hard to come by because so many lesbians and gay men are "in the closet," but current estimates are that three-quarters of lesbians have stable, couples relationships, compared to about half of gay men (Peplau, 1993).

Homosexual relationships are as diverse as heterosexual ones, but long-term homosexual relationships may actually be more egalitarian than heterosexual ones. Contrary to the notion that in a homosexual relationship one person assumes the "male" role and another the "female" role, most such relationships are patterned after a best friends/roommates model. Since both members of the couple usually work and make comparable incomes, one is not dependent on the other in the way that a traditional housewife often is dependent on her husband for financial support (Peplau, 1993).

Long-term homosexual relationships tend to be based on an egalitarian best-friend-roommate model.

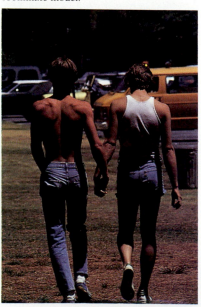

Interestingly, many sexual attitudes and desires are associated more with gender than with sexual orientation. For example, both heterosexual and homosexual men were found to be more tolerant of "one-night stands" than were either heterosexual or homosexual women. Similarly, both heterosexual and homosexual men were more desirous of younger, more physically attractive sexual partners than were either heterosexual or homosexual women (Bailey, Gaulin, Agyei, & Gladue, 1994). Similar studies conducted concerning lesbian sexual practices show that they have more in common with heterosexual women than with gay men (Schreurs, 1993).

When Erikson talked about intimacy, he spoke only of heterosexual relationships. This has led some to wonder if homosexuals can have the same kind of intimacy and mutuality that heterosexuals do. Raphella Sohier has assessed issues of mutuality and generativity in a small group of homosexual subjects. She found that these individuals not only loved each other, but also extended their caring to other people, both gay and straight. They were involved in churches and social endeavors and had active political affiliations, and one couple shared responsibility for the son of one of the partners.

In describing their mutuality, the subjects spoke of "love for each other," "shared interests," "deep respect," "complementary, not antagonistic, differences in character," and a "strong physical attraction." Sohier concluded that "homosexuals appear to express generativity in the same fashion as heterosexuals: loving and caring for children, teaching responsibilities for the next generation, and mutual caring for each other and for others outside their immediate relationship" (Sohier, 1986, p. 36).

Gay and Lesbian Parents

About one-fifth of gay men and one-third of lesbian women have had a heterosexual marriage (Harry, 1983), and about one-half of these marriages resulted in children (Bell & Weinberg, 1978). In contested custody cases, lesbian mothers win about 15 percent of the time. It is estimated that about 1.5 million lesbian mothers now live with their children (Hoeffer, 1981). The number of households headed by gay fathers is probably much smaller, since these fathers seldom get custody of their children. Some courts automatically bar homosexual parents from having custody of their children, but an increasing number of courts in many states have found that "sexual orientation is not to be a factor unless it can be demonstrated to be harmful to the child" (Gutis, 1987, p. C-1).

Children are affected by having a homosexual parent in a number of ways. After the initial surprise, children usually accept the news of a parent's homosexuality better than expected and almost always better than the spouse. Daughters usually are more accepting than sons (Maddox, 1982). The most negative reactions usually come from older adolescent boys when they learn of their mother's lesbianism (Lewis, 1977).

Almost all the studies investigating the effects of parental homosexuality on children have compared children of lesbian mothers with those of single heterosexual mothers. Few or no differences have been found in gender identification, emotional disturbances, sex role behavior, emotional adjustment, maturity, and patterns of socialization (Harris & Turner, 1985). In one study, both groups of children showed a high number of problems, but it was thought that the problems probably resulted from the fact that both groups had recently experienced parental divorce (Kirkpatrick, Smith, & Roy, 1981).

Homosexual relationships are only one of the alternative lifestyles more accepted today than they used to be. Let's look now at unmarried heterosexual cohabitation and singlehood.

COHABITATION

A living arrangement in which two unrelated adults of the opposite sex share the same household. In the past, it has implied sexual intimacy, but it does not necessarily do so today.

ANDROGYNOUS

The condition in which a single person possesses both "typically masculine" personality traits, such as assertiveness, and "typically feminine" traits, such as tenderness.

UNMARRIED HETEROSEXUAL COHABITATION

Four centuries ago, Peruvian Indians practiced unmarried heterosexual **cohabitation** to give the man's family time to assess the woman's capacity to handle both household chores and field work. Despite its long history, cohabitation has generally been held in ill repute by many Americans. In the 1950s, it was commonly called "'living in sin." In 1968, a 20-year-old student was censured by Barnard College for living off campus with her boyfriend (Danziger, 1978).

Bad reputation notwithstanding, the number of unmarried couples—two unrelated adults of the opposite sex sharing the same household—has increased more than sixfold between 1970 and 1992 and now stands at about 3.3 million (U.S. Bureau of the Census, 1993). As the numbers have increased, society as a whole has become more accepting and less likely to judge cohabitation to be morally wrong.

Five types of cohabitation relationships have been defined, and they can be placed on a continuum from "low emotional and physical involvement/minimal commitment" to "high emotional and physical involvement/maximum commitment" (Macklin, 1983, pp. 55–56):

1. **Temporary, casual, convenience relationships.** Two persons share the same living quarters because it is advantageous to do so, with interaction ranging from friendly companionship to none.
2. **Affectionate, going-together relationships.** The couple live together because they enjoy being together and will continue to live together as long as this is true.
3. **Trial marriage.** The couple live together because each member is seriously contemplating a permanent commitment and wishes to test the wisdom of it.
4. **Temporary alternative to marriage.** The couple has made a commitment to marry and will live together until it is more convenient to marry .
5. **Permanent or semipermanent alternative to marriage.** The couple are living together in a long-term committed relationship similar to marriage, but without the legal and religious sanctions.

Cohabitants Versus Married People

Cohabitants tend to be younger; in 1992, 81 percent were under 45 years old (U.S. Bureau of the Census, 1993). They generally have lower rates of religious affiliation, are more likely to live in large metropolitan areas in the West and Northeast, espouse more liberal attitudes, and engage in more unconventional behaviors (Macklin, 1983). Cohabitants perceive themselves to be more **androgynous** and less tied to traditional sex roles, but some studies have found that they still tend to handle household tasks in the traditional way—that is, the women do the housework (Stafford, Backman, & Dibona, 1977; Renwick & Lawler, 1978)!

Contrary to popular belief, cohabitants are not more likely to come from divorced homes, do not perform poorer academically, and are not less likely to want to marry eventually. They tend to be as sexually exclusive as other couples in relationships of similar length and to report similar degrees of satisfaction and problems as married couples do (Macklin, 1983). Most decide either to marry or to separate within 2 years of moving in together (Blumstein & Schwartz, 1983).

SINGLEHOOD

Single is a general term that includes people who are divorced, are widowed, or have never married. The proportion of people in the United States who are over 18 years of age and have never been married has jumped dramatically in the last two decades. In 1960, 17 percent of men and 12 percent of women had never married; by 1992, these numbers had increased to 26 percent and 19 percent, respectively (U.S. Bureau of the Census, 1993). When divorced and widowed people are added (11 percent of all men; 22 percent of all women), we see that singles now constitute nearly 40 percent of our adult population, and they form a heterogeneous group of people.

Peter Stein (1983) has categorized singles according to whether their single status is voluntary or involuntary and stable or temporary, as shown in Table 15.2. Obviously, people often move among these categories. "Ambivalents" may postpone marriage for so long that they eventually come to accept being single as their probable, although unwanted, life state. Similarly, people who have resolved never to marry may meet "Mr. or Ms. Right" and find themselves reconsidering their "firm" decision not to marry.

Much research has also supported the view that being single is hazardous to your health. In every industrialized country, premature death rates are higher for single than for married adults (Carter & Glick, 1976). Similarly, married people generally have been found to enjoy better mental health and to be happier with their lives. Single men, especially, have consistently scored lower on indices of health and well-being than have either married men and women or single women (Austrom, 1984). A central problem with this research, however, has been that most of the data were collected in nonrandom fashion from pathological populations, such as patients in state mental hospitals or prisoners. Moreover, most studies did not control for differences in education, socioeconomic status, or income.

In an attempt to tease out the contribution of marital status to health and well-being, one researcher studied 517 single and 521 married middle- to upper-middle-class adults (mean age, 35.13 years) living primarily in urban areas in Canada. He found no differences between marrieds and singles on self-reports of physical health, but the historical finding that singles are not as satisfied with their lives was again borne out. He also found that psychologi-

Table 15.2 ● A Typology of Singlehood

TYPE	VOLUNTARY	INVOLUNTARY
Temporary	Never marrieds and formerly marrieds who are postponing marriage by not actively seeking mates, but who are not opposed to the idea of marriage. (Ambivalents)	Those who have been actively seeking mates for shorter or longer periods of time, but have not yet found mates; those who were not interested in marriage or remarriage for some period of time but are now actively seeking mates. (Wistfuls)
Stable	Never marrieds and formerly marrieds who have chosen to be single; persons who for various reasons oppose the idea of marriage; religionaries. (Resolveds)	Never marrieds and formerly marrieds who wanted to marry or remarry, have not found a mate, and have more or less accepted being single as a probable life state. (Regretfuls)

Source: Stein, P. J., "Singlehood," in *Contemporary Families and Alternative Lifestyles*, edited by E. D. Macklin and R. H. Rubin. Copyright 1983 by Sage Publications. Reprinted by permission.

cal well-being was due more to the social support of friends and family than to marriage (Austrom, 1984). This is one reason single women probably get along better than single men. They tend to have richer and more intimate friendships and to turn to these friends in times of trouble. Furthermore, most single people are not particularly *unhappy* with their lives; it's just that on average, married people are happier.

WORKING

We have now looked at the traditional and nontraditional forms of establishing intimate relationships with other people and at what happens when those relationships go awry. The following remark by a well-to-do woman who had held assorted occupations reminds us, however, that love and relationships are only part of what provides us with meaning in life: "Love doesn't suffice. . . . Human beings must work to create some coherence. You do it only through love and through work. And you can only count on work." (Terkel, 1974, pp. 554–555).

So now let's look at work.

When Jennifer was 15, she wanted extra spending money, so she got a weekend job as a waitress at a restaurant where the tips were good. Initially, she enjoyed meeting customers and serving them well, and she really liked the tips. But she soon became bored and lamented, "How many times do I have to recite our list of salad dressings?" As a child, she had played "When I grow up, I'm going to be a _____," but now for the first time, she began looking around her to see what kinds of things grown-ups do for a living. She knew she didn't want to be a waitress, and suddenly her older brother's talk about college took on new relevance.

During the next couple of years, Jennifer talked with people about different careers and assessed what she liked to do and was good at doing. By the time college rolled around, she was leaning toward the sciences, but she also knew that she wanted to work with people. She spoke with a local audiologist, who helped her to secure a job at a summer camp for deaf children. This experience solidified her career decision. Thereafter, she designed her college curriculum to qualify her for graduate school in audiology. Her graduate curriculum included an intensive internship; following this, she was hired by a local hospital. She did her job well, and by 28 years of age, she had her own thriving clinical practice. By 40 years, she was well respected as a clinician, teacher, and researcher and was active in her state audiology association.

Jennifer's career path followed the five stages of occupational development first identified many years ago by Donald Super (1957, 1963) and presented in Figure 15.3. In high school, her ideas about combining sciences and working with people began to *crystallize*. In college, she took a job that helped her *specify* her career more precisely, and she *implemented* her choice by pursuing graduate work, doing an internship, and taking entry-level positions. She *stabilized* her career as a clinician, then *consolidated* it by branching out into research and teaching and by seeking active involvement in professional associations.

Many people like Jennifer have career paths that are very orderly. However, we should note that Super developed his theory during the 1950s, when men had far fewer career choices than they do today, and women had fewer still (Havighurst, 1982). The many new fields of specialization that have opened up in the last couple of decades make career choice a more complex task.

FIGURE 15.3

Super's stages of occupational development. (SOURCE: Adapted from Super, 1957, 1963)

Crystalization, ages 14–18 years: The person begins to learn about different fields and to assess in a general way how his or her skills and interests fit those fields. Broad choices, such as whether or not to go to college or whether to focus on humanities or sciences, are usually made.

Specification, ages 18–21 years: The person gets training on the job, in vocational-training programs, or in career-oriented college programs.

Implementation, ages 21–24 years: The person takes entry-level position and may continue to get more training. Job changes are frequent at this stage.

Stabilization, ages 24–35 years: The person gets established in the chosen career and develops a reputation among co-workers.

Consolidation, ages 35 years to retirement: The person advances as far as possible in the chosen profession and consolidates his or her professional identity.

College students often feel overwhelmed as they make choices that they see as irreversible. However, switching jobs is so common now that by the time most people reach 40 years of age, they will have made many job changes, some of which may necessitate major career changes.

A final problem with Super's model is that it doesn't take into account women who have children and then enter the labor market in their 30s or 40s. Many of these women start the occupational development process much later than Super's model suggests is typical. Moreover, many have to take whatever job is available and do not have the luxury of deciding what they want to do and then getting the training that will enable them to do it.

Why Do We Work?

One reason we work is that we need money to live. But in one study, when people were asked, "If by some chance you inherited enough money to live comfortably without working, do you think you would work anyway?" 80 percent said yes (Morse & Weiss, 1955). Other studies have replicated this finding with subjects ranging from the long-term unemployed to the relatively affluent (Kaplan & Tausky, 1972; Renwick & Lawler, 1978).

In addition to providing money, work helps *to define our identity.* If someone were to ask you to describe yourself, one term you would probably use is "student." When asked to describe themselves, many adults first mention their profession. The statement "I'm a doctor" conjures up different images from those we associate with "I'm a professional basketball player."

Work also helps *to structure and organize our lives,* especially if we work outside the home. Knowing that someone's going to notice if we don't show up at the office is a powerful motivator for most of us to get going in the morning. People who work at home often find they sleep later than they intend to and have a hard time settling down to business. Moreover, it's often hard for them to separate work and family life. When children bound into the office, at home, a parent may feel guilty pushing them out and saying, "Mommy (or Daddy) has to work now" (Becker, 1981).

Work enables us *to relate to other people* in ways that are very satisfying and usually not as emotionally charged as our more intimate relationships. It's fun to tackle projects with colleagues or to grouse about the boss together. People who work at home often complain about being lonely and say they miss having colleagues to talk with.

People repeatedly tell researchers they would continue to work even if they had enough money to live on comfortably.

Yet another function of work is *to keep us from getting bored*. We may have a multitude of outside interests, but rarely are they enough to keep us entertained over the long haul.

Finally, work functions *to provide a sense of worth*. It feels good to know we're making a useful contribution, and a weekly paycheck is a good reminder that someone else thinks it's useful.

So chances are that if you win the state lottery or inherit a fortune, you won't retire to a decadent life in a tropical paradise after all, but will continue to show up at work early Monday morning, just as you've always done!*

Creativity and Job Satisfaction

In his now-classic studies, H. C. Lehman (1953, 1954, 1958) identified early adulthood as a time of peak creativity. He identified key works in science, medicine, psychology, and various creative fields produced during a 200-year span and determined the ages of the contributors at the time of their major accomplishments. He found that in all fields except astronomy, people did their *most outstanding work* between ages 30 and 40 years. They may actually have done the work at even younger ages, because there is always a time lag between an initial accomplishment and its recognition. For example, Albert Einstein (1879–1955) first became known to the general public after he turned 40, becoming world famous only in his later years. But in fact, he was given the Nobel Prize in physics for work that he had completed before he was 26. By the age of 36, Einstein had essentially made all of his greatest discoveries.

Many explanations of, and objections to, Lehman's conclusions have been

---

*Okay, *late* Monday morning.

advanced. For example, older workers often get channeled into administrative positions and have less time for research. They become mentors, more concerned with fostering the development of younger people than with pursuing their own creative activities. Furthermore, other studies have not found the marked age trends of Lehman's study (Pelz & Andrews, 1966; Dennis, 1968; Cole, 1979). Older folks can take heart in the fact that Brahms was in his 40s before he wrote his first symphony, and Tolstoy was in his 50s when he wrote *War and Peace*. However, the sheer number of contributions Lehman looked at from so many different historical periods does suggest that many people's creative powers do peak in early adulthood. Or perhaps that is simply when they are the "hungriest" or most motivated.

While the highly creative people mentioned in the last paragraph probably did enjoy their jobs, most young adults generally score low on measures of job satisfaction, job involvement, and organizational commitment and high on measures of intent to leave a job (Rhodes, 1983). As we noted in Chapter 14, youths especially tend to try out different jobs to see which do and do not fit with their personalities. Another factor in high worker turnover is that better-educated people often expect interesting challenges and personal fulfillment in their careers, and young people just out of college may become rapidly disillusioned with the glaring imperfections of the real world.

An especially prevalent problem during early adulthood is **burnout**. The person gets exhausted and loses interest in what was previously a rewarding occupation, sometimes because of the long hours needed to get established in the career and sometimes because uncontrollable forces make the person feel ineffectual (Offerman & Gowing, 1990). For example, a legal-aid lawyer may skillfully handle her clients' legal problems but become discouraged when she cannot change the poverty that makes her clients miserable. Or a nurse working with terminally ill people may give his patients first-rate care but still be profoundly shaken when they die. Support from a spouse can help offset these effects and increase a person's sense of well-being as it relates to his or her job (Greenberger & O'Neil, 1993).

BURNOUT
Emotional and physical exhaustion resulting from excessive dedication to a job.

The Labor Force Today

At the turn of the century, all but a tiny part of the U.S. workforce was involved in producing goods necessary for common survival. Today, less than 40 percent of the workforce is needed to do these jobs, with the remainder working in the *service economy,* which includes jobs as diverse as cosmetologists and college professors. People also are working fewer hours than they used to. In 1900, people worked an average of 53 hours per week; by 1992, the workload had declined to 34 hours (Levitan & Johnson, 1982; U.S. Bureau of the Census, 1993).

Workers today are better educated than those in the past. In 1950, only about 33 percent of the adult population had completed high school; by 1992, 79 percent had. The composition of the labor force also has changed significantly (see Figure 15.4). The most dramatic change has been the influx of white women into the paid workforce; significant numbers of black women have always worked outside the home, although this percentage is also growing. The percentage of white men has decreased mainly because of the trend toward early retirement. For black men, however, the decrease is due more to bleak job prospects and is an expression of discouragement and despair. Primarily *older* white men have left the workforce, whereas black men of all agegroups have left (Levitan & Johnson, 1982; U.S. Bureau of the Census, 1993).

JOB
Employment in which upward advancement is limited and movement is primarily horizontal.

CAREER
Employment that consists of a series of positions that require increasingly greater mastery and responsibility and provide increasing financial return.

INTERROLE CONFLICT
The internal conflict a person feels because of the various demands of a job and family life.

Women in the Workforce.   In 1950, less than 33 percent of adult women in the United States were in the paid labor force; by 1990, this figure had jumped to almost 60 percent (see Figure 15.5). The most dramatic increase has occurred among married women—from 24 percent to 58.4 percent of the female population over 16 years of age. The overall *percentage* of working widows and divorcees has also increased somewhat, but owing to the high divorce rate, this means that the actual *number* of working women in this category has more than doubled (from less than 5 million to almost 12 million). These changes also mean that many more children now have mothers who work outside the home, and as we noted in Chapter 8, many of these children are very young. In fact, in 1975, 33 percent of women in the workforce had children at home who were under 3 years of age; by 1992, this figure had increased to 58 percent (U.S. Bureau of the Census, 1993).

Between 1975 and 1992, the percentage of women in managerial and professional positions increased significantly. Figure 15.6 shows some of the more dramatic jumps. These are the women who capture media attention because they work in nontraditional male-dominated occupations.

Despite these accomplishments, the news for working women is not all good (see At Issue). Most women still enter low-paying, female-dominated occupations, such as secretarial work, elementary school teaching, and social work, where there is little chance for upward mobility. For every $1 that men earn, women on average earn 75 cents (U.S. Bureau of the Census, 1993). This salary gap is not only a working-class phenomenon; it exists in professional positions as well.

Dual-Career, Dual-Work Families

Occupations can be classified as either jobs or careers. In a **job**, upward advancement is limited, and movement is primarily horizontal. An auto mechanic, for example, may develop greater degrees of skill at what he does,

FIGURE 15.4

Percentages of employed persons over 16 in the United States by race and sex. (SOURCE: U.S. Bureau of the Census, 1986, 1993)

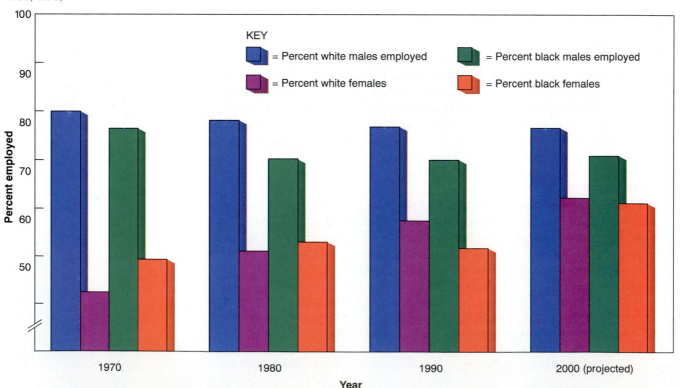

KEY
= Percent white males employed   = Percent black males employed
= Percent white females   = Percent black females

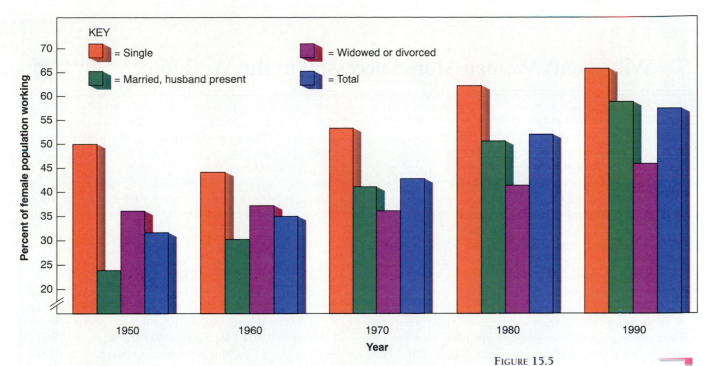

FIGURE 15.5

Percentages of U.S. women in selected categories who are employed. (SOURCE: U.S. Bureau of the Census, 1986, 1993)

but his job remains more or less the same, even if he moves from one employer to another. A **career**, on the other hand, consists of a series of positions that require increasingly greater mastery and responsibility and provide increasing financial return.

Dual-career families are those in which both spouses pursue careers, and the wife's career is as important to her identity as her husband's is to his identity. However, most families in which both spouses work are dual-work families. In these, both spouses have jobs rather than careers, and the spouse of the primary provider works mainly to supplement the family income.

As the numbers of dual-career and dual-work families have increased, researchers have begun studying **interrole conflict**, especially as it pertains to

FIGURE 15.6

Percentage of U.S. female workers in selected occupations, 1975 and 1992 (SOURCE: U.S. Department of Labor, 1976; U.S. Bureau of the Census, 1993)

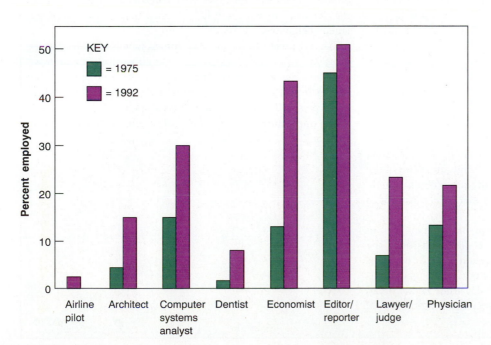

AT ISSUE

Why Aren't Women More Successful in the Workforce?

"They're not as devoted to their careers as men are." "They have to take time off if their kids get sick." "They're just working for the money and will quit as soon as they get married." These and many other reasons have been put forth to explain the failure of women to advance further in the workplace. No doubt, these factors may play a role for some women. But researchers have identified other reasons: structural factors, interpersonal factors, and cognitive biases.

A key structural factor that works against women is that in predominately male work settings, women are highly visible and are subject to pressures to perform that men, by virtue of their greater numbers, don't feel. This is especially true if there is only one token woman. This token position also is held by many blacks and members of other minority groups. Not only do token employees feel the pressures of being a visible minority, but their co-workers often feel that they are inferior employees, hired only to meet quotas (Northcraft & Martin, 1982).

Another area of concern is the "glass ceiling" (Morrison & Von Glinow, 1990). In many organizations, women who have proved their leadership ability are promoted to a level just below the top, but are allowed to go no further. The "glass ceiling" refers to being close enough to see those who work on the top floor, while still being kept one floor down. Highlighting this problem is the fact that at the beginning of this decade only 1.7 percent of the corporate officers in the top 500 U.S. corporations were women (Offerman & Gowing, 1990). The projections for the year 2000 show this percentage increasing, but slowly. The circumstances for minorities are not much better (Morrison & Von Glinow, 1990). Discrimination of this kind is a major concern, not just for reasons of justice, but because it denies organizations the talents and benefits of many potential leaders.

There are a number of interpersonal factors that are problematic for women. One is *sexual harassment*. This includes inappropriate touching, verbal insults, and outright pressure for sexual favors. One study found that 42 percent of women in the federal workforce had been harassed sexually (U.S. Merit System Protection Board, 1981). Another problematic interpersonal factor is that women seldom have mentors (Warihay, 1980). Not only are they seemingly unaware of the value of a mentor, but men seldom volunteer to mentor them. As yet, there aren't enough women in upper-level positions to guide younger women.

There might also be some cognitive biases that prevent women from getting ahead. The first is *gender discount*, the widely held notion that if a woman does it, it's not worth as much, no matter what "it" is. In one study, subjects evaluated a scholarly work. Those told it was written by a woman rated it as less competent and persuasive than did those told

it was written by a man (Goldberg, 1968). A 1985 review of the literature on gender discount concluded that (1) the tendency to devalue a competent woman appears to be more the rule than the exception; (2) competent women are most likely to be devalued when there are potential consequences for the evaluator, such as an employer's judging a prospective employee; and (3) negative evaluations are least likely when women are judged by someone who knows them well or with whom they have worked (Lott, 1985).

Another cognitive bias pertains to the way men and women view their successes and failures. When men succeed, they tend to attribute it to their innate abilities, while women tend to view their own success as the result of good luck or dogged labor. Moreover, men often attribute failure to bad luck, while women see their failures as "proving" their lack of ability (Deaux & Farris, 1977; Larwood & Gutek, 1984). It is likely that long-term discrimination in the workplace has led women to doubt and downgrade their own abilities and performance.

Finally, sex role conflict may be an issue. Like it or not, our society holds certain stereotypes about which personality traits are appropriate for men and which are appropriate for women. At the male end of the continuum are traits such as "independent," "forceful," "aggressive," "competitive," and "unemotional," all of which are usually valued in a work setting. The stereotypical "feminine" traits, however, are those such as "nurturing," "supportive," "emotional," and "accommodating" (Broverman, Vogel, Broverman, Clarkson, & Rosenkrantz, 1972). Many people believe that even the most nontraditional women experience considerable conflict when the demands of their job deviate greatly from stereotypical female behaviors.

We don't want to imply that women have not made significant strides in recent decades or that all workplaces are hostile territories for women. But it is important to recognize the barriers to further advancement that do exist for women and minorities and to try to ensure that all people have the maximum opportunity to use their professional resources as best they can.

women. This term refers to the internal conflict a woman often feels because of the many demands placed on her by her children, her spouse, and her employer. Husbands can also experience interrole conflict; but they commonly fear not meeting their boss's expectations, while women worry more about not doing enough for their family (Cooke & Rousseau, 1984).

Women in dual-work families have been found to experience significantly more interrole conflict and to be more depressed than men in these families (Keith & Schafer, 1980). Unfortunately, these women weren't compared to women in dual-career families. Another researcher found, however, that women in dual-career families did report interrole conflict, but that the conflict was offset by the financial resources, privileges, and personal growth they derived from their dual roles (Gilbert, Holahan, & Manning, 1981). It may be that the cost for women in dual-career and dual-work families is about the same, but the payoff is greater for the career women.

There are a number of factors that contribute to interrole conflict. One is simply work overload. Women whose husbands do not support their work life have a full-time job during the day and another when they get home. Another factor is finding competent, affordable, reliable day care for children, an issue we discussed at length in Chapter 8. Yet another problem is the need to mesh individual career cycles with family cycles and to deal with career issues such as geographical mobility, which is often necessary for getting ahead in high-powered careers. Finally, there is the matter of time. There is never enough of it for friends, relatives, spouses, and children, not to mention oneself.

As you might expect, interrole conflict can cause a great deal of marital discord. Fortunately, research conducted in South Africa has shed light on what factors lessen interrole conflict and make for happier homes. For women, having a supportive spouse greatly lessened their conflict and had a positive effect on the couple's relationship. If a husband did not hold fast to traditional sex role stereotypes about what a wife "ought" to do, and if he really did pitch in to do the cooking or change the baby's diapers, this decreased the wife's pressure to be all things to all people (Suchet & Barling, 1986). The critical variable in decreasing the interrole conflict of the working fathers was the men's having a "hardy personality," characterized by commitment, control, and challenge. These hardy men were actively involved in events, both at home and at work. They felt in charge of life events and not helpless in facing them. They saw stressful events as opportunities for development (Barling, 1986).

Now that we know about the value, as well as the trials and tribulations, of working, let's consider the plight of those people who, against their wishes, are not working.

Unemployment

> I'd never been fired and I'd never been unemployed. For three days I walked the streets. . . . I was demoralized. I had an inkling of how professionals my age feel when they lose their jobs and their confidence begins to sink. (Shanker, 1973, p. 29)

These words belong to Dr. John Coleman, president of Haverford College, who had just been fired not from his job at Haverford, but from his job as a porter/dishwasher. Coleman, you see, was taking an unusual sabbatical; he was working at menial jobs. "I wanted to get away from the world of words and politics and parties," he said. "As a college president . . . you forget elementary things about people. I wanted to relearn things I'd forgotten" (Shanker, 1973, p. 1). Coleman was financially secure, and his Haverford job was waiting for him, but losing a job still shattered his self-esteem, especially because the only explanation his boss gave him was, "You won't do."

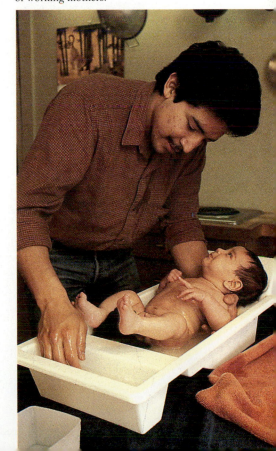

This father bathing his week-old daughter is breaking sex role stereotypes. It is the kind of behavior that lessens the interrole conflict of working mothers.

If losing a job is so devastating to someone who really still has a job as a college president, you have to wonder about the effects of unemployment on regular folks. Foremost among the negative consequences is the lack of a paycheck and the inability to feed and house oneself and one's family. Other negative consequences include the lack of a habitual time structure for the waking day. Boredom and waste of time become the rule, and people often lose their sense of time. In one study, unemployed men began averaging 10½ hours of sleep per day. The unemployed also often suffer from a lack of purpose and feel that they are on the scrapheap, not needed by anybody. If they live with employed people, they may experience such shame and self-doubt that they begin to withdraw from social relationships. Finally, unemployed people often become resigned to their plight; they adopt an "I can't do anything about it anyway" attitude (Jahoda, 1982), which then compounds the problem.

The Prevalence of Unemployment in the United States.   In 1978, Congress enacted the Full Employment and Balanced Growth Act, which targeted 4 percent as the "normal" unemployment rate. Unfortunately, the actual rate has been somewhat higher than this. In 1982 and 1983, for example, it stood at a very high 9.5 percent, or 10.72 million people. Between 1984 and 1994, however, it has ranged from 7.4 percent to 5.2 percent (8.54 and 6.53 million people, respectively).

Perhaps this chapter can best be summarized by a statement by the great writer Leo Tolstoy. Although he said it in 1856, it is equally applicable to our lives today:

> One can live magnificently in this world, if one knows how to work and how to love, to work for the person one loves and to love one's work. (Tolstoy, 1856, quoted in H. Troyat, 1967)

Finding Your One and Only

Around the world I've searched for you.
I've traveled on when hope was gone to
keep our rendezvous.
I knew somewhere, sometime, somehow
you'd look at me and I would see the
smile you're smiling now.
(From the theme from *Around the World
in 80 Days*)

The eternal romantics among us are
sure that this is the right way to find
our own true loves. More pragmatic
social scientists disagree. All that
travel, they say, really isn't necessary.

PROXIMITY

First, look to those near you. There is
strong positive correlation between
physical *proximity* and attraction. A
classic study that examined marriage
licenses found that half of the people
who applied for a license lived within
14 blocks of each other (Koller,
1953). One reason proximity is such
a critical factor is obvious: We have
to meet someone before we can
marry the person, and we're more
likely to meet people we live near or
work with.

HOMOGAMY

A second factor in mate selection is
homogamy, our tendency to choose
someone who is similar to us. Ellen
Berscheid and Elaine Walster (1978)
reviewed several research projects
and found that people who got married tended to be similar in their attitudes, physical health, attractiveness,
intelligence, educational level, family
background, religion, leisure-time
preference, and drinking and smoking habits.

The importance of homogamy was
underscored by a longitudinal study
of 164 couples, ages 20 to 35 years,
who were preparing to marry for the
first time. These couples filled out
questionnaires designed to measure

You are most likely to become intimate with
someone who lives near you, and who is
similar to you.

each partner's attitude on subjects
such as sexuality, money management, conflict resolution, leisure
activities, child rearing, and religion.
Of the 164 couples, 105 showed disagreement between the partners in a
majority of these areas. Three years
later, it was discovered that 52 of
these disagreeing couples had
delayed or canceled their wedding,
31 who married had either separated
or divorced, and 22 others said that
they were dissatisfied with their marriage. The 59 remaining couples who
had harmonious marriages had
shown much more initial agreement
on the questionnaire (Flowers &
Olson, 1986).

What, then, about the old saying
that "opposites attract"? The "opposites" who are attracted to each other
usually aren't opposite in their beliefs
and values. Rather, they may be oppo-

site in the sense that each person may
lack something that the partner can
provide. This is known as *sharing
complementary needs*. Some
researchers have argued that similarity is most important at the beginning
of a relationship, but that complementary needs are more important as
the relationship becomes a long-term
one (Kerckhoff & Davis, 1962).
Other people believe, however, that
similarity remains most important,
especially among well-adjusted married couples (Meyer & Pepper, 1977).

AUTHENTICITY

A third factor is *authenticity*. Psychologist William Swann has discovered
that when couples first begin to date,
they most like to hear praise from
their partner, regardless of how they
might view themselves. This seems
reasonable. After all, wouldn't most
people prefer to hear nice things
about themselves than something
negative?

The interesting part of Swann's
work, however, was his finding that
after marriage, people were found to
prefer honest evaluations from their
partner, including negative comments. Couples rating their level of
intimacy viewed their dating relationship as more intimate if they were
praised, but viewed their marriage as
more intimate if they received both
positive and negative feedback from
their partner (Swann et al., 1994).

It seems, then, that we want acceptance at first, but once the relationship becomes very intimate, perhaps
following marriage, we value authenticity more. Swann believes that this
can sometimes lead to trouble for
dating couples who are too honest
with each other, or conversely, marrieds who are too free with praise

and who overlook faults. Authenticity in the form of criticism while dating may seem like rejection. But total acceptance after marriage may make a partner feel, "I have faults but you don't see them—I guess you don't really know me."

FINDING A PARTNER

Some people feel that the older you get, the harder it is to find your "one and only." In 1986, the press seized on a study titled "Marriage Patterns in the United States" (Bloom & Bennett, 1985) and issued pronouncements like the following:

White, college-educated women born in the mid-'50s who are still single at 30 have only a 20% chance of marrying. By the age of 35 the odds drop to 5%. Forty-year-olds are more likely to be killed by a terrorist. (Salholz et al., 1986, p. 55)

The notion that "forty-year-olds are more likely to be killed by a terrorist" obviously is absurd, and the researchers who did the original study have stated that most of what the press has made of their study "amounts to little more than hyped-up twaddle" (Bennett & Bloom, 1986, p. 27).

It is true that there are fewer traditionally appropriate men for women of the baby-boom generation, mainly because women tend to marry men who are older than they are. For women born after 1957, the numbers get better because they are drawing on the larger pool of baby-boom men. But the researchers stress that women's greater economic and social

independence has resulted in many women *choosing* not to marry, and they lament the fact that "this positive side of the study has had a difficult time finding its way into print" (Bennett & Bloom, 1986, p. 27).

Many single people have lives consisting of a rewarding profession, a good income, intimate friends, and good ties to family. While perhaps not everybody's idea of perfect, such a life certainly can be fulfilling. Be that as it may, those single people who want to change their status would be advised to restrain the impulse to go on a worldwide search for a mate. Instead, they might start being friendlier to the eligible man or woman next door!

SUMMARY

- Passionate love is an intense emotional reaction to another person characterized by feelings of romance and excitement. It seldom lasts more than a few years. Compassionate love, however, grows deeper and more powerful as the years progress.
- Family life cycle theory does not take into account divorces, remarriages, childless couples, or intergenerational relationships, but it is useful for helping traditional families understand what may be happening within their family.
- The divorce rate of the baby-boom generation looks especially dramatic when compared with the low divorce rate of their parents.
- Both divorced men and women cite spousal infidelity as a primary reason they wanted out of their marriage.
- Divorced people are at greater risk for psychiatric disorders, suicide, homicide, accidents, disease, morbidity, and mortality than are nondivorced people.
- Long-term homosexual relationships are often more egalitarian than heterosexual relationships, and they are often patterned after a best friends/roommates model.
- Cohabitation relationships can be placed on a continuum ranging from low emotional and physical involvement and minimal commitment to high involvement and maximum commitment.
- Single people usually report lower levels of overall life satisfaction than do married people.
- According to Super's theory of occupational development, we move through the following stages in pursuing our careers: crystallization, specification, implementation, stabilization, and consolidation.
- In addition to providing money, work helps to define our identity, structure our lives, provide social contacts, and increase our sense of worth.
- Early adulthood generally is a time of peak productivity, but it is not a time of high job satisfaction. Burnout is especially prevalent among young adults.
- Women in both dual-career and dual-work families experience interrole conflict, but the payoff for women in dual-career families probably is greater.
- Unemployed people often suffer from boredom, lose their sense of time, lack purpose, experience much shame and self-doubt, and become resigned to their situation.

QUESTIONS FOR DISCUSSION

1. Think of the happiest and unhappiest relationships you know about. What factors seem to be paramount in each?

2. What factors might be responsible for women's reporting a decrease in family satisfaction from stage I to stage III in the family life cycle research?

3. To what extent is your current career path consistent with Super's stages of occupational development?

4. What do you think you would do about your work or career if you won a million dollars?

Suggestions for Further Reading

1. Bolles, R. N. (1984). *What color is your parachute? A practical manual for job-hunters and career-changers.* Berkeley, CA: Ten Speed Press.

2. Coleman, J. (1974). *Blue-collar journal.* Philadelphia: Lippincott.

3. Cowan, C. P., & Cowan, P. A. (1992). *When partners become parents.* New York: Basic Books.

4. Demick, J., Bursik, K., & DiBiase, R. (Eds.). (1993). *Parental development.* Hillsdale, NJ: Erlbaum.

5. Hall, F. S., & Hall, D. T. (1979). *The two career couple.* Reading, MA: Addison-Wesley.

6. Hayslip, B., Jr., & Panek, P. E. (1993). *Adult development & aging.* New York: HarperCollins.

7. Smelser, N. J., & Erikson, E. H. (1980). *Themes of work and love in adulthood.* Cambridge, MA: Harvard University Press.

CHAPTER 16

Middle Adulthood: Physical, Cognitive, and Personality Development

CHAPTER PREVIEW
The Midlife Turn Toward Androgyny

"These aren't the people I grew up with!" Jake said. "Mom's never home, and Dad struck up a conversation with me last night about medical ethics."

Susan just looked at him, "While you were at med school, things around here got strange. The first clue I had was last year. Mom left a note on the fridge saying, `Will be home late; don't wait dinner,' and Dad came home and cooked."

Twenty-six-year-old Jake and 22-year-old Susan were trying to make sense of the behavior of their 52-year-old father and 47-year-old mother—"Super Mom" and "The Banker," they used to call them. Susan attributed the changes to their mother's finishing law school, but Jake reminded her that this didn't account for their father's enrolling in a "Music and Imagery" workshop.

Jake and Susan agreed that their parents' behavior was odd indeed. No longer did their father work long hours and read only The Wall Street Journal. *No longer did their mother bake cookies and volunteer at the hospital. They wondered whether they should consult their family doctor.*

Jake and Susan were witnessing a frequently observed developmental process of modern middle adulthood. Their parents had begun what David Gutman has called the midlife turn toward androgyny (Gutman, 1976). Gutman meant that as men and women age, they take on personality traits usually associated with the other sex. Men become more thoughtful, more sentimental, and more nurturing, while women become more ambitious, more assertive, and more self-confident.

Some researchers think that the cause of these personality changes may be hormonal shifts of midlife (Rossi, 1980). But other people point to social and cultural factors. For example, Gutman studied agrarian societies and concluded that parenthood constitutes "a period of chronic emergency based on children's vital needs for emotional as well as physical security" (Gutman, 1976, p. 53). Traditional sex roles, in which the father is an aggressive breadwinner and the mother a nurturer, have come about, he says, because of the physical and emotional needs of children. Once children can care for themselves, "both sexes can then afford the luxury of living out the potentials and pleasures that they had to relinquish earlier in the service of their particular parental assignment" (Gutman, 1976, p. 53).

Whatever the cause, this midlife turn toward androgyny can come as a surprise to children, who tend more or less to expect their parents to "stay put." It also can be unsettling for spouses if one makes changes and the other doesn't. Imagine, for example, how upset "The Banker" might be if he continued his long working hours and narrow interests, only to arrive home to find a "don't wait dinner" note!

Obviously, the changes that middle-aged people go through require changes in their interactions with one another and with their children. In this chapter, we'll examine some of the physical, cognitive, and personality changes; then, in Chapter 17, we'll see how middle-aged people deal with their important relationships and with the world of work. For the sake of convenience, we define middle adulthood roughly as the period between 40 and 65 years of age.

LIFE BEGINS AT 40?

"The prime of life." "The empty nest." "The command generation." "The midlife crisis." At one time or another, people have used each of these phrases to try to capture some "essence" of middle age. On the one hand, people in the age-group of 40 to 65 years do have power. They are usually the ones who govern nations, anchor families, direct industry, lead citizen groups, teach the young, and take care of the old (Waring, 1978). They become better at self-reflection and feel more confident of their ability to handle the complexities of life (Neugarten, 1968). The combination of power and a more mature level of personality integration often brings with it an extremely valuable coping skill, the ability to laugh at oneself. Jokes that begin, "You know you're over 40 when . . ." abound. They're funny, however, only if told by someone over 40!

Ironically, having power brings with it a startling realization: If I'm in charge of so many things, I must be grown up! One 50-year-old woman captured the realization that she was now a full-fledged adult in this way: "You always have younger people looking to you and asking questions. . . . You don't want them to think you're a blubbering fool. . . . You try to be adequate as a model" (Neugarten, 1968, p. 95).

Still other events signal that a person has grown up. Teenage children go off to college. Elderly parents may look to their middle-aged children for emotional or financial support. When they die, their children suddenly become "the older generation." A middle-aged person's time perspective changes. Rather than calculating the years since her birth, she may wonder how many more years she will live. If she hasn't already done so, she will go to her lawyer to make a will and may be startled when her lawyer asks, "And what about the disposal of the body?" Whatever her body's shortcomings, she never before intended to "dispose" of it! Understandably, middle-aged people begin to ask how to make the most of the years remaining. A new job? A new romance? A guru? For many, but not all people, these issues precipitate an emotional upheaval rivaled only by adolescence.

Given the magnitude of these issues, it is interesting that researchers have not studied them at length. The lack of data about adult development is especially true for middle adulthood. Daniel Levinson took note of this ongoing problem nearly 20 years ago when he explained, "Adults hope that life begins at 40 but the great anxiety is that it ends there." This "pervasive dread about middle age," he says, results in researchers being unwilling to look closely at this period of life (Levinson, Darrow, Klein, Levinson, & McKee, 1978, p. ix).

Researcher Joanne Stevenson advanced a less dreary reason. She noted that "troublesome groups" such as adolescents or the elderly are studied more often. For whom are these groups troublesome? For the middle-aged! As it is the middle-aged who are in command, they dictate that *these* are the appropriate groups to study (Stevenson, 1977). It may be that the recent interest in studying middle age has come about because middle-aged people themselves are more willing to admit to the more troublesome aspects of their age. Levinson acknowledged that at age 46, he "wanted to study the transition into middle age in order to understand what I had been going through myself" (Levinson, Darrow, Klein, Levinson, & McKee, 1978, p. x).

Where Middle Age Begins

We have used the ages 40 to 65 years as the boundaries of middle adulthood. But we all know some middle-aged 30- and 70-year-old people. For this reason, it is sometimes hard to tell when middle adulthood begins and ends. A 50-year-old man suffering from a chronic illness may describe himself as "old," while a 50-year-old woman caught up in a new romance may describe herself as "young." In one of the earliest studies of middle adulthood, Bernice Neugarten found that her female subjects tended to define middle age according to events within the family, such as the launching of children into the adult world. Unmarried women often talked about families they might have had or about their relationships with their nieces and nephews. Her male subjects felt middle-aged when they received deferential treatment from younger colleagues at work, such as having younger men hold doors open for them (Neugarten, 1968).

College students and people over 60 were asked when they thought young adulthood, middle age, and old age began. The younger subjects lowered middle age to include the late 30s, while the older ones saw it as beginning in the early 40s (Drevenstedt, 1976). In one of the first studies of its kind, blue-collar workers considered middle adulthood to begin at about 35, whereas white-collar workers, especially those pursuing an executive career, said it began at 50 (Neugarten & Peterson, 1957).

As we have defined it, middle adulthood encompasses even more years than early adulthood. It also includes a very heterogeneous group of people. Those people who turned 40 years old in 1995 are actually the tail end of the

FARSIGHTED
The inability to see close objects clearly.

baby-boomers, those born within 10 years following the end of World War II. In college, they had warned the world never to trust anyone over 30, and they had provided the impetus for Kenneth Keniston's optional stage of youth (see Chapter 14). At the other end of middle adulthood are people who were children during the depression and adolescents during World War II. They tended to marry, to have children, and to settle down fairly early in life. So we obviously must be very cautious when we begin to generalize about middle adulthood.

Let's turn now to a consideration of some of the physical changes that commonly occur between ages 40 and 65 years.

PHYSICAL DEVELOPMENT IN MIDDLE ADULTHOOD

The bodies and good health we take for granted in early adulthood begin to demand more attention in middle adulthood. Charts of aging show gradual, usually insignificant decrements in functioning. But for many people, the decrements don't *feel* insignificant. Ironically, the feeling that they're getting older often prompts people to start exercising and eating better, so they may actually whip themselves into better shape than they were in during early adulthood!

Appearance

The thinning and graying of hair that starts during early adulthood continues; by age 50 years, most people have some gray hair. By the end of middle adulthood, stiff hairs have begun to appear in men's noses, ears, and eyelashes and on women's upper lips and chins (Troll, 1985).

Skin continues to lose elasticity, and more wrinkles appear. Body shape changes as the bust and chest grow smaller and the abdomen and hips grow larger. If a middle-aged person has a sedentary lifestyle and consumes as many calories as when he was younger, he must contend with the infamous middle-age spread. Women are confronted with our society's double standard about appearance: While gray hair and wrinkles are thought to make men look "distinguished," they are perceived to make women look "old." In a society as youth-conscious as ours, looking old can be quite a blow to a woman's self-esteem. This double standard may be changing somewhat, however; magazines and television advertisements have begun to feature attractive graying women as models.

As the U.S. population has begun to grow older, magazines and television advertisers are featuring attractive graying models.

The Senses

Middle-aged people often joke that their arms aren't long enough to read the newspaper. They mean that they've become **farsighted**—unable to see objects up close—and they now often need reading glasses. The good news is that people often become less nearsighted as they age and so may no longer need glasses to see objects far away. The high-frequency hearing loss begun earlier continues, but usually is not noticeable. Taste buds become less sensitive around age 50 years, and sensitivity to touch drops sharply after about age 45 years (Troll, 1985).

Strength and Endurance

In the early 1960s, Nathan Shock and his colleagues did a classic cross-sectional experiment in which they investigated the physical capacity to "do work." They measured this by having subjects lie on their backs and turn the crank of an ergometer, an apparatus that measures effort. The crank could be adjusted to turn more stiffly or more easily. The researchers measured the subjects' blood pressure, heart rate, cardiac output, oxygen consumption, and carbon dioxide production. They thereby determined the amount of "work" the men could do and have cardiac function return to normal within 2 minutes after they stopped working. Measured this way, the work rate peaked at about age 28 years, then declined by about 10 percent by age 40. The 65-year-old subjects' work rate was about 81 percent of that of the 40-year-old subjects, or 73 percent of the peak work rate. The researchers also found that strength of the dominant hand usually peaked at about age 35, then decreased very slowly; the 65-year-old men still had about 86 percent of the hand-grip strength of the 40-year-old men (Shock, 1962).

What this means is that our strength and endurance gradually decline during middle adulthood, although exercise can certainly slow the rate of decline. Dick Bass was a businessperson with relatively little mountain-climbing experience when, in his early 50s, he became the first person ever to climb the highest peaks on each of the seven continents, including Mt. Everest, the highest mountain in the world, the summit of which he reached at age 55 (Bass, Wells, & Ridgeway, 1986). Given the fitness boom of recent years, it's conceivable that the decreases that Shock found would be less drastic if he repeated the study today.

Moreover, even if people do decline a bit physically, they usually can find ways to compensate. In the words of 53-year-old jockey Willie Shoemaker, who had won some 8,500 races at the time, "I don't know if I'm as strong as I've ever been, but I'm smarter" (Callahan, 1985, p. 50).

Health Status

People entering middle adulthood can look forward to the fact that they'll become less susceptible to colds and allergies and their incidence of accidents will decrease. However, the "silent diseases" of early adulthood now become vocal as chronic illnesses make their appearance.

There are a number of chronic diseases that commonly appear in middle adulthood. Various arthritic problems often begin in the early 40s, and diabetes often begins between ages 50 and 60. Peptic ulcer, hypertension, and health problems brought on by excessive alcohol consumption also are major concerns. The adverse consequences of smoking may appear in the form of chronic bronchitis, emphysema, lung and oral cancers, and coronary artery disease (Bierman & Hazzard, 1973).

Although our response to a middle-aged person's dying usually is shock—"He was too young to die!"—the death rate for people 45 to 54 years of age is twice that for 35- to 44-year-old people. And for people aged 55 to 64 years, the rate is more than twice that of those aged 45 to 54 years. Prior to age 55 years, the leading causes of death in middle adulthood are cancer, heart disease, accidents, and liver disease. After age 55 years, heart disease assumes the leading position, followed by cancer, strokes, and accidents (U.S. Bureau of the Census, 1993).

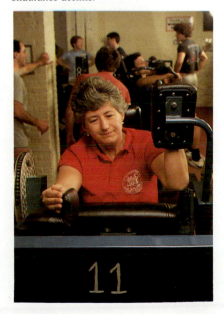

Middle-aged people learn that exercise can't completely stop the aging process, but it can slow the *rate* at which strength and endurance decline.

Stress and Health

Sometimes, a stressful experience can be strong enough, or last long enough, to result in direct physical consequences that are harmful to one's health. Stress-related illnesses often make themselves first known during middle age. Among the most common early symptoms of chronic stress are headaches from muscle tension, gastrointestinal disturbances, skin rashes and hives, dizziness, and fatigue. Chronic stress can also lead to high blood pressure, referred to as *hypertension*.

Some terrible experiences may encompass many months of exposure and later appear as chronic illness in middle age. For many, the Vietnam war was such an experience (Cusack, 1993). Over the past few years, it has come to light that approximately 15 percent of Vietnam veterans suffer from psychological problems (Kaylor, King, & King, 1987; Goldberg, True, Eisen, & Henderson, 1990). Symptoms associated with long-term stress among the vets were not found to be linked to their personalities or behavioral characteristics, but rather to their exposure to combat (Goldberg, True, Eisen, & Henderson, 1990). These symptoms, including dizziness, headaches, memory loss, anxiety, intestinal problems, depression, and nightmares, were especially prevalent among combat soldiers who had participated in atrocities, such as torture and murder of prisoners (Yager, Laufer, & Gallops, 1984; Breslau & Davis, 1987).

Measuring Susceptibility to Stress and Illness.   Is there any way to measure how much stress you may be facing from day to day? In Table 16.1, you'll see a scale for rating life changes, developed by Holmes and Rahe back in 1967. Each of these life events is assigned a value, a certain number of stress points. In their study, Holmes and Rahe found that individuals who accumulated more than 300 stress points within 1 year were two or three times as likely to suffer illnesses and other stress-related problems than were individuals who had fewer stress points. However, it is important to point out that these were only averages. Some people with many stress points remained quite healthy, while some with few stress points became ill. On the average, however, a relationship between stress and illness was found.

One interesting detail you may notice while reading the table is that some very nice things seem to be stressful. Among these often pleasant events or circumstances are marriage, gaining a new family member, a change in financial state (which could mean for the better as well as for the worse), an outstanding personal achievement, the beginning of school, family get-togethers, and even a vacation.

There are also several important points to keep in mind. First, these data are correlational and do not necessarily imply cause and effect. For example, people of lower socioeconomic status (who are also more likely to have poorer health care) lead lives in which more changes take place, often because of financial problems. Stressful changes in the lives of such people may be only correlated with poor health, not the cause of it. If so, then adding up stress points may not be a valid way to explain future problems. Similarly, the stress points should be used solely as a guideline. Although the numbers may seem highly specific, they aren't. For example, it's highly doubtful that one pregnancy, one Christmas, and four vacations would be more stressful than the death of a spouse. So read the table with an open mind.

Most research dealing with stress and illness begins with an examination of a population suffering from illness; the objective is to determine how much stress that group was under before the illness. But this kind of research can be biased, since the researchers often know ahead of time that the people they are

Table 15.1 ● Social Readjustment Rating Scale

RANK	LIFE EVENT	MEAN VALUE	RANK	LIFE EVENT	MEAN VALUE
1.	Death of spouse	100	24.	Trouble with in-laws	29
2.	Divorce	73	25.	Outstanding personal achievement	28
3.	Marital separation from mate	65	26.	Wife beginning or ceasing work outside the home	26
4.	Detention in jail or other institution	63	27.	Beginning or ceasing formal schooling	26
5.	Death of a close family member	63	28.	Major change in living conditions (e.g., building a new home, remodeling, deterioration of home or neighborhood)	25
6.	Major personal injury or illness	53			
7.	Marriage	50	29.	Revision of personal habits (e.g., dress, manners, associations)	24
8.	Being fired at work	47			
9.	Marital reconciliation with mate	45	30.	Trouble with the boss	23
10.	Retirement from work	45	31.	Major change in working hours or conditions	20
11.	Major change in the health or behavior of a family member	44	32.	Change in residence	20
			33.	Changing to a new school	20
12.	Pregnancy	40	34.	Major change in usual type and/or amount of recreation	19
13.	Sexual difficulties	39			
14.	Gaining a new family member (e.g., through birth, adoption, oldster moving in)	39	35.	Major change in church activities (e.g., a lot more or a lot less than usual)	19
15.	Major business readjustment (e.g., merger, reorganization, bankruptcy)	39	36.	Major change in social activities (e.g., clubs, dancing, movies, visiting)	18
16.	Major change in financial state (e.g., a lot worse off or a lot better off than usual)	38	37.	Taking out a mortgage for a lesser purchase (e.g., for a car, TV, freezer)	17
17.	Death of a close friend	37	38.	Major change in sleeping habits (a lot more or a lot less sleep, or change in part of day when asleep)	16
18.	Changing to a different line of work	36			
19.	Major change in the number of arguments with spouse (e.g., either a lot more or a lot less than usual regarding child rearing, personal habits)	35	39.	Major change in number of family get-togethers (e.g., a lot more or a lot less than usual)	15
20.	Taking out a mortgage or loan for a major purchase (e.g., for a home, business)	31	40.	Major change in eating habits (a lot more or a lot less food intake, or very different meal hours or surroundings)	15
21.	Foreclosure on a mortgage or loan	30	41.	Vacation	13
22.	Major change in responsibilities at work (e.g., promotion, demotion, lateral transfer)	29	42.	Christmas	12
23.	Son or daughter leaving home (e.g., marriage, attending college)	29	43.	Minor violations of the law (e.g., traffic tickets, jay-walking, disturbing the peace)	11

Source: Holmes & Rahe, 1967.

dealing with are suffering from stress-related illnesses. When time and funds permit, researchers prefer to conduct *prospective* research, in which they find a healthy population, study the subjects' stress patterns, and observe the long-term effects on health.

The largest study of this kind has been conducted by George E. Vaillant (1979). He selected 204 men who were in the sophomore class at Harvard from 1942 to 1944. For over four decades, he kept in touch with 185 of them. During these years, Vaillant and other researchers conducted many psychological and physical tests on these subjects, as well as interviews with them. Stress predictors included how often the subjects visited a psychiatrist or psycholo-

At the Vietnam Memorial in Washington, D.C., a veteran mourns his colleagues who were killed in the war. Many veterans who saw combat were especially vulnerable to stress-related illnesses years after the war ended.

gist, whether they were failing to make progress at their job, whether they were dissatisfied with their job, whether their marriage was unhappy, whether they received little vacation or recreation time, and whether they had a poor outlook on life.

The findings of this study generally support the notion that people who have the ability to cope well with stress are likely to be healthier. Of the 59 men in this study who coped well with stress and who had the best mental health, only two became extremely ill or died by the time they were 53 years of age. Of the 48 men who were found to have the worst mental health, 18 became chronically ill or died. The men in this second group had shown themselves to be less able to deal with stress. The men in both groups came from very similar backgrounds. Clearly, their ability to cope with stress was directly related to their physical health. By 1990, Vaillant could report that one of the strongest predictors of mental and physical health after age 65 was the extent of tranquilizer use before age 50 (Vaillant & Vaillant, 1990). It is assumed that those who were in need of tranquilizers were either under more stress or coping less well.

In keeping with these findings, another prospective study took almost 3,000 initially healthy subjects ages 45 to 77 and tracked them for 12 years. The results of the study showed that subjects who reported feeling the most hopeless about their lives throughout the study were four times more likely to die from heart disease than were the other subjects. The study controlled for the effects of gender, age, smoking, alcohol use, blood pressure, and other factors known to be related to heart disease (Anda et al., 1993).

Disease-Prone Personalities.   For centuries, philosophers and scientists have wondered about the role of personality in the onset of disease (Taylor, 1990). In the 1930s and 1940s, specific personality profiles were developed along with the claim that they were able to predict the likelihood of hypertension, cancer, heart disease, ulcers, arthritis, and other diseases (Dunbar, 1943; Alexander, 1950). Convincing evidence to support these claims, however, was lacking.

Yet, common sense tells us that individuals exposed to prolonged stress will differ in their vulnerability to serious disease. In 1959, researchers Meyer

Friedman and Ray Rosenman separated male personalities into two categories, **type A** and **type B**, and linked them to coronary artery disease. Men with type A personalities are intense, alert, competitive, and striving, while those with type B are relaxed, easygoing, and unpressured (Friedman & Rosenman, 1959). (see Figure 16.1).

Since that time, much research has indicated that type A males have a greater chance than do type B males of incurring heart disease (Suinn, 1977). This research implies that certain personality types are more prone to specific stress-related illnesses. In fact, the idea of type A personality and its relationship to heart disease became so well established that efforts to change personality with the hope of lessening heart disease became commonplace.

More recently, however, support for the idea of a heart attack–prone personality has not been forthcoming. The problems with the concept were brought to light when cardiologist Robert Case analyzed the personalities of 516 heart attack victims and discovered that type A's were no more likely to have heart attacks than type B's (Case, Heller, Case, & Moss, 1985). To avoid possible bias, another physician, Richard Shekelle, had conducted a prospective study with 3,110 men who had never had a heart attack. He classified their personality types according to the recognized methods of sorting type A from type B; then he waited to see what would happen. After a few years, the subjects had had a total of 129 heart attacks, divided evenly between type A's and type B's (Shekelle et al., 1985). These new findings have led some researchers to conclude that the earlier results linking type A personality to heart disease may have been due to interviewer bias or other confounding measures (Lazarus, DeLongis, Folkman & Gruen, 1985).

TYPE A

A behavior pattern characterized by ambition, aggression, competitiveness, and impatience.

TYPE B

A behavior pattern characterized by a relaxed, easygoing manner and lack of aggression and competitiveness.

---

1. **Ordinarily, how rapidly do you eat?**

   I'm usually the first one finished.
   I eat a little faster than average.
   I eat at about the same speed as most people.
   I eat more slowly than most people.

2. **When you listen to someone talking, and this person takes _too long_ to come to the point, how often do you _feel_ like hurrying the person along?**

   Frequently
   Occasionally
   Almost never

3. **If you tell your spouse or a friend that you will meet somewhere at a definite time, how often do you arrive late?**

   Once in a while
   Rarely
   I am never late

4. **How was your temper when you were younger?**

   Fiery and hard to control
   Strong but controlable
   No problem
   I almost never got angry

5. **Do you ever set deadlines or quotas for yourself at work or at home?**

   No, never
   Yes, but only in emergencies
   Yes, once a week or more

FIGURE 16.1

Sample questions that assess type A versus type B personality (SOURCE: Jenkins, Zyzanski, & Rosenman, 1979)

META-ANALYSIS

An examination of many studies that focus on one topic to discover an overall consensus. Careful attention is paid to eliminate faulty studies.

MENOPAUSE

The complete cessation of menstruation, which usually occurs during middle age. It is said to have occurred when a woman has not had a menstrual period for 12 consecutive months.

CLIMACTERIC

The 2- to 10-year period during which the biological changes involved in menopause take place.

ESTROGEN

A hormone that is produced primarily by the ovaries and is responsible for the development of female secondary sex characteristics. The adrenal glands of the male also produce some estrogen, but the hormone is found primarily in females.

HOT FLASHES

Sudden, brief sensations of heat, often accompanied by reddening of the skin. They are thought to be caused by the fluctuating levels of estrogen during the climacteric.

ATROPHY OF THE VAGINAL LINING

Thinning, loss of elasticity, drying, and itching of the vaginal walls caused by decreasing estrogen levels during the climacteric.

These findings then prompted two psychologists, Howard Friedman and Stephanie Booth-Kewley, to carefully analyze and compare 101 studies conducted between 1945 and 1984 on disease and personality. This approach is called a **meta-analysis**. Their conclusion was that there does appear to be a slight link between type A behavior and heart attack (Friedman & Booth-Kewley, 1987). But others conducting meta-analysis of these studies have come to the opposite conclusion—that type A behavior is *not* related to heart attack (Matthews, 1988). The cause of all this confusion may be that "type A" has never been clearly defined (Friedman & Booth-Kewley, 1988; Rodin & Salovey, 1989) and is often assessed differently from one study to the next.

It may well be that certain personalities make people more prone to illness in general, although perhaps not to *specific* illnesses, but further research is needed before we can say which personalities might be at higher risk.

SEXUALITY IN MIDDLE ADULTHOOD

Cultural myths about changes in the reproductive systems and sexual functioning are no doubt a major reason people dread middle age. Historically, menopausal women have been described in the most disparaging terms imaginable. Consider these words from a 1966 article in the reputable *Journal of Nervous and Mental Disorders*:

> And then, after giving "the best years of her life" to raising a family and caring for the house, she finds herself reduced by the climacteric to a shriveled shell of a woman, used up, sucked dry, de-sexed, and, by comparison with her treasured remembrances of bygone days of glory and romance, fit only for the bone heap. (Sillman, 1966, p. 166)

The man caught up in the so-called "male menopause" is thought to be depressed, hypochondriacal, and impulsive—prone to quit a job or leave a 25-year-old marriage for a 25-year-old woman. These are the myths. Let's look now at some of the realities.

Menopause means "cessation of menses." It is said to have occurred when a woman has gone 12 consecutive months without a menstrual period. The biological changes involved in menopause usually take place over a period of 2 to 5 or even 10 years, known as the **climacteric**. One of the early signs of menopause is irregular menstrual periods. These irregularities are caused by fluctuating levels of the hormone **estrogen**, which gradually decreases during the climacteric. The average age at which menopause now occurs in the United States is about 50 years (Block, Davidson, & Grambs, 1981).

Everything from backache to psychosis has been attributed to the decrease in estrogen at menopause. However, only hot flashes and atrophy of the vaginal lining are now thought to be caused by the drop in estrogen. **Hot flashes** are unexpected, brief waves of a hot, feverish sensation that vary widely in intensity, frequency, and duration. Some women experience a warm glow, while others become drenched with perspiration. Some have only a few hot flashes over many years; others have several each day. Chills frequently precede or follow a hot flash. Rarely do other people know when a woman is having a hot flash. The only thing they might notice is a slight change in the woman's coloring.

Atrophy of the vaginal lining, which is by no means as dreadful as it sounds, occurs when the lining of the vagina becomes drier, thinner, and less elastic; this may make intercourse somewhat painful. Lubricating creams can alleviate this problem, but an active sex life is said to be just as effective a treatment (Comfort, 1976).

The decreases in estrogen can usually be remedied by administration of synthetic estrogen. When first introduced, *estrogen-replacement therapy (ERT)* was heralded as a miracle cure for many symptoms of menopause. It has been shown to slow the progression of **osteoporosis**, which generally becomes more severe after menopause. It is a controversial treatment, however, because it has been found to cause cancer in test animals and to stimulate some existing breast, uterine, cervical, and vaginal cancers in women. When ERT is combined with progesterone, the risk of uterine cancer is markedly reduced (Gambrell, 1987).

Younger women who have not gone through menopause usually view the prospect as much more traumatic than women who have gone through it say it really was (Neugarten, Wood, Kraines, & Loomis, 1968; Cohen, Coburn, & Pearlman, 1980). By and large, postmenopausal women have reported that they feel better physically and that their sex lives often improve, since they no longer have to worry about getting pregnant (Cohen, Coburn, & Pearlman, 1980).

Researchers have generally found that the level of the male hormone **testosterone**, which is in part responsible for sexual desire, decreases gradually with age. However, studies have found that healthy older men had about the same level of testosterone as did younger men. Interestingly, in these older men, levels of sexual activity correlated highly with levels of testosterone (Tsitouras, Martin, & Harman, 1982; Vermeulen, 1983). Despite this optimistic finding, some very gradual hormonal changes do occur during middle adulthood, and most men notice that their testes and penis get a bit smaller (Talbert, 1977). Sperm production also decreases gradually, but many men are able to father children right into late adulthood.

The term *male menopause* has been jokingly used by the popular media to refer to the emotional and behavioral changes that some men show during middle age, and which we'll consider later in this chapter. In reality, however, the hormonal changes that men undergo are by no means as pronounced as those experienced by middle-aged women. Although stories about the male menopause may make good reading, no such physiologically based event exists.

Sexual Interest and Activity

The variability we noted earlier among adults is nowhere more evident than in their sexual interest and activity. Some people report declining interest in sex

OSTEOPOROSIS
A condition in which loss of calcium and various minerals results in bones becoming more porous and fragile.

TESTOSTERONE
A hormone that is produced primarily by the testes and is responsible for the development of male secondary sex characteristics. The adrenal glands of the female also produce some testosterone, but the hormone is found primarily in males.

cathy®   **by Cathy Guisewite**

SEXUAL IMPOTENCE
The inability to achieve and maintain an erection of sufficient duration to have intercourse.

by the time they turn 40 years old; others report an active sex life well into their 80s.

As the middle years progress, many men notice that it takes longer and requires more direct stimulation to achieve an erection, but they usually can maintain the erection longer than they could when they were younger. Orgasm may occur less frequently, contractions may be fewer and less intense, and it may take longer to achieve another erection following ejaculation. These changes may produce substantial performance anxiety, which is probably the chief cause of sexual dysfunction in middle-aged men. Life events such as job reversals or problems at home that make a man feel powerless also can lead to **sexual impotence**.

Many women find that their interest in sex increases markedly during middle adulthood. This may happen in part because androgenic hormones, which are strongly implicated in sexual desire, decrease only slightly during menopause, while estrogen, which suppresses the effects of androgens, drops significantly. Moreover, following menopause, women are free to enjoy sex without fear of pregnancy. Finally, certain personality changes, which we'll consider later in this chapter, also contribute to women's greater willingness to seek ways to meet their needs, including sexual ones.

In concluding this section, we urge you not to panic the next time you hear middle-aged people lamenting the loss of their youthful bodies. While poor health can certainly make people feel old, by and large, the negative physical changes of middle adulthood are gradual, and by no means do they fling most of us onto a bone heap!*

Let's turn now to cognitive development in middle adulthood.

---

*If you've already enjoyed your middle age, you know what we mean!

For many couples, romance and sexual activity remain high throughout middle age.

COGNITIVE DEVELOPMENT IN MIDDLE ADULTHOOD

Just as middle-aged people sometimes joke about their physical stamina, they also may joke about their mental capacities, and the jokes are funny so long as the person really knows they're not true. After all, it's convenient to invoke our aging memory when we "forget" to attend our teenage son's heavy-metal concert. But the jokes are not so funny when a person really does feel that her intellect is failing and she can't think as well as she once did.

Measuring Intelligence in Adulthood

In Chapter 14, we looked at the results of K. Warner Schaie's cross-sequential study of adult intelligence and found that the picture in young adulthood was very bright. During middle adulthood, however, some decrements begin to appear.

Slightly different patterns emerge according to whether you look at cross-sectional or longitudinal data. In general, however, verbal meaning scores increase until age 46 years, level off until age 53 years, then begin to decrease. Spatial ability and inductive reasoning begin to decline in a person's 50s. Data about numerical abilities and word fluency show erratic patterns. Cross-sectional data on numerical abilities do not show a significant decline until ages 60 to 74 years, but longitudinal data show small decreases beginning as early as 39 to 53 years. Cross-sectional data on word fluency show decreases between ages 25 and 39 years, increases from 39 to 46 years, a leveling off until 53 years, then gradual decreases again. In longitudinal data, however, decrements do not show up until ages 46 to 60 years.

These data are averages, based on the scores of many different subjects. Although the overall trend in middle adulthood is one of gradual decline, any decline before age 60 is likely to be so slight that it will have little practical importance (Schaie, 1994).

Many people think that what is really important in adult cognitive development is not the kind of intelligence measured by Schaie & Hertzog's test. What we should be looking at, they say, is how people identify important problems in their lives and how people use both reason and intuition to solve these problems.

Problem Finding and Solving

In Chapter 14, we raised the question of whether there is a stage of cognitive development beyond Piaget's stage of formal operations. One theorist who thinks there is maintains that a primary distinguishing characteristic of this postformal stage is the ability to identify relevant problems and to ask important questions about ourselves, our life's work, and the world around us. Such problem finding enables us to look at old problems in a new light and to think of creative new solutions (Arlin, 1975, 1977, 1984).

The Integration of Reason and Intuition

Our valuable problem-finding skills may cause us trouble, however, when we take traditional tests. In fact, it sometimes looks as though adults regress to earlier ways of thinking that involve too much subjectivity when they take tests. They tend to personalize the information, to analyze the many possible ways a question might be interpreted, to consider the emotional aspects

SOCIAL COGNITION
The application of cognitive principles to the social arena.

involved in the issue, and to suggest that several answers might be possible. In going beyond the information given, adults may not score as high as they would if their thinking weren't "contaminated" by all this complexity.

Many people, however, think that integrating subjectivity with reason and grappling with complexity are major strengths of adult cognition. They criticize Piaget's theory because it "assumes a progression toward a 'pure' state of reasoning, free from subjectivity and cultural contamination and totally objective in its search for truth" (Datan, Rodeheaver, & Hughes, 1987, p. 167). In mature thinking, subjective, intuitive knowledge and objective, rational knowledge not only can coexist, but also can balance and enrich each other (Labouvie-Vief, 1982, 1984, 1985).

Still, there hasn't been much research that substantiates these ideas about adult thinking. In one study, adults ages 20 to 79 years were given two types of tests—one that measured abilities typically measured by intelligence tests and another that measured practical problem-solving skills. The latter test asked subjects what they would do in situations such as being stranded in a car during a blizzard or dealing with a flooded basement. Although younger people did better on the traditional IQ tests, middle-aged people did better at solving the practical problems (Denney & Palmer, 1981).

There also is some evidence that adults' experience dealing with complex, real-life problems is correlated with their level of moral reasoning . One study found that people's ability to make moral judgments rose to its highest level during middle adulthood, and subjects stated that coping with problems ranging from everyday dealings with their children to confronting life-threatening illnesses had strongly influenced their moral reasoning (Bielby & Papalia, 1975). Moreover, another researcher found that the more spouses engage in joint household decision making, the higher their level of moral maturity (Walker, 1986).

That middle-aged adults perform better on tests of practical problem solving suggests that what Sternberg (1985) calls contextual intelligence may increase as we get older (see Chapter 10). We'll consider this possibility again in Chapter 18, when we examine cognitive development in late adulthood.

Social Cognition

Social cognition is the application of cognitive principles to the social arena. Social cognition continues to develop into adulthood, and many people believe that postformal thinking is a necessary prerequisite for this development (Sinnott, 1984).

Consider for a moment your relationship with your best friend. When you are on vacation hiking and laughing together, you feel very close to him and thank your lucky stars he's in your life. But then exam time comes, and you're studying for a difficult calculus test. Your friend wanders into your room, wanting to chat about whether he should ask out a particular young woman. "Who cares?" you think to yourself. "Can't he see I'm busy?" You wonder how you can possibly hang out with such an egocentric fellow who wants to socialize when you're under so much stress.

If you reason at a formal operational level, and if I were to ask you to describe your friendship, you might say something like, "Sometimes he's kind and considerate, and we get along well; at other times, he's really insensitive." But if you reason at a postformal level, you are much more aware of the complexity of the relationship and of the extent to which your own changing feelings and circumstances influence how you see the relationship (Datan, Rodeheaver, & Hughes, 1987). You might say something like, "When we're both relaxed and having a good time, I see our relationship as really good. But when I'm under a lot of stress and he seems oblivious to it, I never want to see him again. So basically, our friendship has its ups and downs, but on the whole, I value it and certainly intend to continue it."

In short, mature social cognition lets you know that your friendship is actually many relationships and that those relationships may even be contradictory, depending on the social circumstances and the prevailing mood of each of you. You can simultaneously hold different views of the relationship and acknowledge your own role, as well as that of your friend, in the relationship's success or failure.

Creativity

Another important aspect of adult cognitive development is creativity. Now you may be wondering whether my memory is failing and I've forgotten that I told you in Chapter 15 that creativity peaks in early adulthood. No, I haven't forgotten. The work of Lehman discussed in that chapter focused on *superior* contributions. Wayne Dennis has assessed creativity in another way by looking at the total output, not just at the superior works, of 738 male scholars, scientists, and artists who lived to be at least 80 years old. Judged this way, middle adulthood, especially the decade of the 40s, is clearly the most productive time in all fields except mathematics and chamber music (Dennis, 1966).

It is also true that artists usually peak at an earlier age than do scholars and scientists, perhaps because the latter usually need more formal education and must gather and evaluate more data before producing a work. There is a difference between hot-from-the-fire creativity and sculpted creativity (Jacques, 1965). A spontaneous overflow of powerful feelings often helps young musicians and poets (such as Mozart and Keats) create rapidly, but rarely can that pace last for long. In sculpted creativity, the initial inspiration may be intense, but the material often has to be worked and reworked before the product is finally completed. No doubt Charles Darwin had many flashes of insight and enthusiasm and often "knew" that his ideas about evolution were correct; but it took him until age 50 to gather his data, construct his argument, and finally publish *The Origin of Species* (1859).

Some studies have examined the performance of "average" human beings on tests of divergent thinking, which is a key component of creativity (see Chapter 10). However, these studies have produced mixed results. One conducted with members of adult education classes in Finland found that young adults (25 to 35 years) scored higher than did middle-aged adults (45 to 55 years) or elderly adults (65 to 75 years) (Ruth & Birren, 1985). A comparable study done in the United States, however, found that middle-aged people (40 to 60 years) scored higher than either younger people (18 to 39 years) or older people (61 to 84 years) (Jaquish & Ripple, 1981). This study further found that self-esteem was positively correlated with the creative abilities, but that doesn't tell us whether feeling good about yourself frees you to be more creative or whether being creative makes you feel good about yourself. Jennifer Sasser-Coen contends that creativity doesn't decline with increasing age; rather there is a shift away from divergent thinking and toward using one's own subjective experience to think integratively and originally (Sasser-Coen, 1993).

We have seen that middle adulthood is a dynamic time for people both physically and cognitively. Now let's turn to personality development during the middle years.

GENERATIVITY

The concern about establishing and guiding the next generation, and other forms of "care for the creatures of the world."

PERSONALITY DEVELOPMENT IN MIDDLE ADULTHOOD

Developmental Tasks of Middle Adulthood

"Mature man needs to be needed," said Erik Erikson (1950, pp. 266–267). In his scheme, this need becomes most evident in middle adulthood. The key developmental task at this stage of life, Erikson said, is the achievement of **generativity**, which is a person's concern about establishing and guiding the next generation. Generativity is not necessarily limited to having and caring for one's own children. Rather, it includes many forms of "care for the creatures of this world" (Erikson, 1950, pp. 267–268). Even institutions, such as monasteries, that forbid their members to procreate are careful to transmit their ideas to succeeding generations, and many uphold service to other people as a central value.

According to Erikson, if a person does not achieve generativity, the person feels "a pervading sense of stagnation and personal impoverishment" that may be so pronounced that it amounts to physical or psychological invalidism (Erikson, 1950, p. 267). No one would deny that the need to be needed can become burdensome at times. Far worse, however, at least in Erikson's scheme, is to renounce that need and not to teach and guide other people.

George Vaillant's research provided more objective support for Erikson's scheme in that the best adjusted of the Grant Study men (see Chapter 14) were those who, by this stage in life, enjoyed contributing to other people's lives both at home and at work. Furthermore, Vaillant proposed that a period that he called *keeping the meaning versus rigidity* might come after Erikson's stage of generativity versus stagnation and before the final stage of ego integrity versus despair.

The best adjusted of the Grant Study men tried to ensure that their culture would be carried on rather than replaced, and they had attained a degree of tranquility. The worst adjusted became rigid in their conviction that the good old days were gone forever and that only immorality, decline, and decay lay ahead for humanity. One of the well-adjusted men commented, "I don't plan on leaving any big footsteps behind, but I am becoming more insistent in my attempts to move the town to build a new hospital, support schools, and teach kids to sing" (Vaillant, 1977, p. 232).

Robert Peck (1968) expanded Erikson's theory by enumerating four major tasks essential for people in middle adulthood. First, Peck says, people must come to value wisdom over physical strength and attractiveness. Second, they must come to value people more as friends and companions and less as sex objects. Third, they must learn to shift emotional investments from one person to another, because they will experience losses as their children move away or as their parents and friends die. Finally, middle-aged people must maintain their mental flexibility and must remain open to new ideas. Failure to do so results in rigidity and lack of intellectual growth (see At Issue).

In Erikson's scheme, concern about teaching and guiding younger people is the key developmental task of middle adulthood.

The Midlife Crisis: Myth or Reality?

During the 1970s, the media picked up the term *midlife crisis* and made it part of our vocabulary. However, the term's meaning is not always clear. George Vaillant noted that the term "brings to mind some variation of the renegade minister who leaves behind four children and the congregation that loved him in order to drive off in a magenta Porsche with a 25 year old striptease artiste"

AT ISSUE

Personality Change and Stability Over Time

In the comic strip "Peanuts," Lucy has been known to offer her playmates psychological counseling. Her message is generally the same: "Your personality is formed by the time you are 6. That will be 5 cents, please." Lucy's personality theory clearly runs counter to the picture we have been painting of dynamic changes in adulthood, but perhaps we should consider it more seriously, especially since the question of personality change versus stability is one on which many researchers disagree.

For years, the bulk of the longitudinal research concluded that people's personalities remained fairly stable over time. In one study, women were found to maintain very stable scores on traits such as excitability, self-satisfaction, and cheerfulness between ages 30 and 70 years (Mussen, Honzik, & Eichorn, 1982). One longitudinal study of men from ages 20 to 60 years showed stability of traits including extroversion, openness, and neuroticism (Costa & McCrae, 1980). Many other studies have found a great deal of stability, especially in people's values, vocational interests, and temperament (Woodruff & Biren, 1972; Costa, McCrae, & Arenburg, 1980; Block, 1981; Brim & Kagan, 1980). These findings jibed with common observations, such as that achievement-oriented teenagers tend to be go-getters as adults and that children who successfully handle the problems of childhood tend to grow into competent adults. And the findings generally support older folks who tell each other, "You haven't changed a bit."

More recently, Norma Haan, Roger Millsap, and Elizabeth Hartka (1986) analyzed data from subjects tested at different intervals over a 50-year span. They looked specifically at six components of personality and found different patterns for different traits. The subjects' *self-confidence* was high during childhood, dropped significantly during adolescence, started climbing during early adulthood, but didn't again reach levels as high as in childhood until well into middle age. With regard to *assertiveness*, the sexes had different histories. For males, assertiveness scores increased markedly from childhood to adolescence, continued to increase gradually until they peaked in middle adulthood, then dropped slightly by late maturity. The females' scores peaked during early adolescence and middle adulthood also, but they were never as high as the males', and in both childhood and late maturity, the females had relatively low scores.

The *cognitively committed* scores (the extent to which subjects had an intellectual achievement orientation accompanied by innovativeness) for the females dropped sharply at early adolescence, remained low until early adulthood, then began to climb, finally surpassing the males' scores by middle adulthood. The males' scores increased steadily throughout the life span, with only a slight decrease during middle adulthood. Both sexes became a bit less *outgoing* in adolescence, then increased on this measure steadily, with females always being more outgoing than males. *Dependability* peaked for both sexes in early adulthood and remained high. Finally, *warmth* scores peaked for males in adolescence, then decreased, and didn't reach a high level again until late adulthood. Females were not particularly warm in adolescence, but by early adulthood their scores had surpassed those of the males, and their scores remained significantly higher than the males' throughout adulthood.

Haan and her colleagues drew several interesting conclusions from this research. They noted that childhood and adolescence were times of stability and systematic personality development. However, substantial changes did occur in adults right up to late adulthood, especially for women. Moreover, they maintain that the "usual supposition that personality develops in a linear and orderly fashion is plainly incorrect" (Haan, Millsap, & Hartka, 1986, p. 230). Their subjects did become increasingly and systematically committed to cognitive ways of solving problems and to being dependable and outgoing in their relationships. But the subjects' self-confidence, warmth, and assertiveness seemed to be more reactive to the hazards and opportunities of experience.

In sum, it is probably safe to say that among groups of people, some personality traits change over time, while other traits remain fairly stable, and some individuals change markedly even on characteristics for which the group as a whole is consistent. The entity we call *personality* is clearly a complex matter. A degree of consistency in personality traits enables people to count on themselves to behave in more or less predictable ways. But their personalities also are likely to undergo some changes as they deal with the developmental tasks of middle age.

(Vaillant, 1977, p. 222). In reality, few people do anything quite this colorful at any point in their lives!

Some of the strongest support for the existence of a midlife crisis comes from Daniel Levinson's research, which we began looking at in Chapter 14. Fully 80 percent of his subjects underwent enough emotional turmoil between ages 40 and 45 years to be described as going through a moderate to severe crisis. They struggled with questions such as, "What have I done with my life?" "What do I really get from and give to my wife, children, friends, work, community and self?" "What is it I truly want for myself and others?" "What have I done with my early dream and what do I want with it now?" (Levinson, Darrow, Klein, Levinson, & McKee, 1978, p. 192).

Because people in this process may be irrational, their spouses, children, boss, and parents may think that they're sick and may try to restore them to their "old selves." But in fact, the desire to question and modify our lives stems from the healthier parts of our beings. "No life structure can permit the living out of all aspects of the self," Levinson says. "In the Mid-life Transition these neglected parts of the self urgently seek expression" (Levinson, Darrow, Klein, Levinson, & McKee, 1978, p. 200).

Some of the subjects made external changes, such as undertaking divorce, remarriage, or shifts in occupation and lifestyle. Others made internal changes in social outlook, in personal values, in what they wanted to give the world, and in what they wanted to be for themselves. Those who negotiated the midlife transition successfully became more compassionate, more reflective, and more genuinely loving of themselves and of other people. Failure to do so resulted in their lives becoming "increasingly trivial or stagnant" (Levinson, 1986, p. 5).

A stable, structure-building period followed for most of those who experienced a midlife crisis. Moreover, Levinson maintains that those who did not experience a crisis during their early 40s probably would do so when they made the transition to age 50 (Levinson, 1978).

A Second Adolescence?

George Vaillant was 33 years old when he first interviewed the Grant Study men, who were then 46 years old. Alarmed by what he heard, he rushed to his 54-year-old department chairperson and exclaimed, "I don't want to grow up; these men are all so . . . so depressed" (Vaillant, 1977, p. 226). Interestingly, the Grant Study men who had the "best outcomes" later said that the period from 35 to 49 years was the happiest in their lives; the calmer period from 21 to 35 years had been the unhappiest.

What Vaillant first saw as depression among these men, he later attributed to their having reached a stage in life where they were better able and more willing to acknowledge the painful experiences of their lives. Content no longer to be "bland young men in gray flannel suits" (Vaillant, 1977, p. 217), they had, like adolescents, "once more become explorers of the world within" (Vaillant, 1977, p. 220). They often experienced some emotional turbulence owing to dissatisfaction with careers, marriages, children, themselves, and miscellaneous events of middle age. The period did require growth and change, but, Vaillant said, it was better characterized as a "transition" than as a "crisis" for most of the men.

The Empty-Nest Syndrome

While the stereotype of the man caught up in a midlife crisis is Vaillant's renegade minister in the magenta Porsche, the stereotype of the middle-aged woman is that of a depressed housewife mourning the loss of her maternal role as her children grow up and move away. This **empty-nest syndrome**, especially when combined with menopause, is reputed to be so traumatic for women that it constitutes a major crisis.

Lillian Rubin interviewed 160 middle-aged women, all of whom had children who were leaving or had left home. All these women had given up jobs for at least 10 years following the birth of a child, and a majority were homemakers. Rubin found that only one suffered the classical symptoms of the empty-nest syndrome. In fact, almost all responded to their children's leaving home "with a decided sense of relief" (Rubin, 1979, p. 15). The most ambivalent women were those closest to the transition.

Other research has supported Rubin's findings (Cohen, Coburn, & Pearlman, 1980; Fahrenberg, 1986). One group of researchers found that women experienced their most difficult and tumultuous transitions when their children were preschoolers or late adolescents. The postparental stage was characterized by "increases in life and marital satisfaction, and positive personality changes such as increased mellowing, patience, assertiveness, and expressivity" (Harris, Ellicott, & Holmes, 1986, p. 415).

It is probably safe to say that parents experience a multitude of conflicting emotions as they see their children grow older and move away from home. For women whose identity and self-esteem have come solely from their mothering role, their children's leaving home might indeed cause them to feel a profound sense of loss. And fathers who never had much time for their children may be shaken and depressed when they realize that "suddenly" their children are gone. However, there are no data that would lead us to conclude that most people suffer from anything approaching a full-blown empty-nest syndrome, just as there are no data that lead us to conclude that any kind of midlife crisis is either universal or inevitable.

Multiple Paths

While some researchers have focused on the developmental tasks of middle adulthood, and others have investigated midlife crises or transitions, yet others have looked at the different pathways people take during these years. One

EMPTY-NEST SYNDROME
Depression that parents may experience when their grown children leave home.

A child's graduating and leaving home is a major event, but relatively few parents suffer a full-blown empty-nest syndrome.

longitudinal study used as its subjects psychologically healthy women who were first interviewed in 1931–32 as part of the Oakland Growth Study. Based on their personality assessments as adolescents, some women were classified as *traditionals*, in that they were gregarious, feminine, conventional, popular, and socially skilled. Others, referred to as *independents*, were intellectual, achievement oriented, introspective, and unconventional. At age 50 years, both groups of women had more complex personalities, but their basic styles were consistent with their adolescent personalities (Livson, 1976).

The chief difference in the women's developmental paths was that at age 40 years, the independents tended to be depressed, irritable, conflicted, and out of touch with their intellectual and creative potential, while the traditionals never showed a period of such turmoil. By age 50 years, the difficulties apparently were resolved, however, and independents scored as high as traditionals on measures of happiness.

The researcher believes that the independents' unhappiness came about because they had poured their intellectual competence into child care, and when the children reached adolescence and didn't need as much care, the mothers no longer had an outlet for their intellect and creativity. By age 50 years, the women had disengaged from the mothering role and had found other outlets. The traditionals, on the other hand, seemed simply to find ways to nurture other people as their children left home, and did not experience a loss of identity (Livson, 1976). Another possible explanation is that the independents were less likely to be satisfied in a society with rigid sex roles and limited opportunities for women and that the women's movement of the 1960s and 1970s created a far more agreeable atmosphere.

In another major project, researchers studied 200 men aged 25 to 30 years and 300 men aged 38 to 48 years from a wide range of income and educational levels (Farrell & Rosenberg, 1981). They did not find evidence of a universal midlife crisis among these men, but they did find that the men tended to follow one of these four paths to middle age:

1. **The anti-hero.** The 12 percent of the men in this category were the most likely to have a midlife crisis. They were openly dissatisfied with their work and home lives and were most likely to report that they would like to "start afresh and do things over, knowing what I do now." They were the most self-reflective, the most tolerant of ambiguity, and the most able to see the "gray" side of issues.
2. **The pseudo-developed type.** This type accounted for 26 percent of the men. They reported satisfaction with their wives, children, and jobs, but a closer look revealed considerable masked depression. Moreover, while they could not acknowledge their own failings, they were quick to point out the problems of their children and often saw minorities as being devious and dangerous.
3. **The punitive-disenchanted type.** Thirty percent of the men were in this category. They were the most symptomatic and unhappy group, but rather than questioning themselves or their life choices as did the anti-heroes, they blamed external circumstances and other people for their unhappiness.
4. **The transcendent-generative type.** The 32 percent of the men in this category reported convincingly that they still found their work challenging, their marriages rewarding, and their children gratifying. They scored lowest on measures of depression, authoritarianism, and prejudice.

Which path these men followed often was related to their socioeconomic class. Professionals and middle-class executives in urban areas were the most likely to have comfortable, asymptomatic paths, while unskilled laborers showed considerable personal disorganization and psychopathology. The researchers were astounded by how few of the subjects were either willing or able to look within themselves for the source of their pain and by how many externalized their frustration and despair or sought to hide it (Farrell & Rosenberg, 1981).

The multiplicity of paths and variability in development during middle adulthood may leave you wishing for more concrete facts about what middle adulthood is *really* like. You've no doubt observed that some people have midlife crises; some don't. Some people develop serious illnesses; some remain healthy throughout the years. Significant decrements occur in some intellectual skills, but not in others—sometimes!

Perhaps it would be useful to recall a quote from our discussion of adult development in Chapter 14. In it Bernice Neugarten likened people's lives to the spreading of a fan: "The longer people live, the greater the differences between them" (Neugarten & Hall, 1980, p. 78). During the 25 years between ages 40 and 65, people experience a good deal of this kind of "spreading" in every aspect of their development. A growing appreciation of this spreading is a crowning achievement of many people during these years.

Dealing with the Stress of Life

You don't need a psychologist to tell you that it is both impossible and undesirable to lead a stress-free life. This does not necessarily mean, however, that you are doomed to suffer a multitude of stress-related health problems. Researchers have found that the ability of the body to ward off illnesses is not always directly related to *how much* stress someone is experiencing, but rather to *how well* that person copes with the stress (Locke, Furst, Heisel, & Williams, 1978).

People at any age may look for different ways to cope with stress. However, it is often during middle adulthood that they decide to take concrete, deliberate steps to deal with stress. They may reach this decision for many reasons. For example, a man's doctor may tell him that he has high blood pressure and that he should "calm down." Or a woman may decide that the demands of life are taking too great a toll and that she needs better ways to deal with these demands.

Certain things help us cope with stress. We mentioned two of them when we discussed interrole conflict in Chapter 15. The first is having a network of supportive people, and the second is having a hardy personality, characterized by feelings of control over your life, a deep commitment to events of your life, and a view of change as an exciting challenge (Kobasa, 1979, 1982; Kobasa, Maddi, & Kahn, 1982).

In recent years, many people have become interested in different stress management techniques. For example, some people learn *modified progressive relaxation*. In this approach, the person is taught deep-muscle relaxation by use of a soothing envi-ronment, deep breathing, and cycles of tensing and relaxing the muscles. Other people learn *yoga* or *meditation* and achieve similar relaxation.

One technique that has been especially successful in treating high blood pressure and migraine headaches is *biofeedback*. Patients are hooked up to a device that measures body temperature, muscle tension, blood pressure, and other physiological variables and are taught how to control these physiological responses. *Psychotherapy*, in which people talk about their problems with a trained clinician, is helpful for some people, and sometimes *medication* may be used on a temporary basis to help people deal with life stresses. The effectiveness of these techniques, however, depends a great deal on the skill and wisdom of the clinician applying them, and no approach should be viewed as a panacea (Woolfolk & Lehrer, 1984).

Many of these techniques either take time to learn or require the help of professionals. But there are some good coping strategies you can use on your own right now. First, rather than acting impulsively to rid yourself of the stress and thereby possibly making matters worse, *gather information* about what's causing the stress and what options you have to alleviate it. If you are doing well in all your pre-med courses except calculus, don't abandon pre-med before talking with your calculus teacher, your advisor, and perhaps a tutor.

Second, *trust in time*. It doesn't heal all wounds, but it helps. For example, divorce may shatter a life for a time, but within 2 years, the stress usually is significantly reduced (Hetherington, 1979).

Third, *try not to be alone too much*. When you're by yourself, you discuss personal issues with yourself too much. And you especially see the

One relaxation technique that has been proven to be useful in treating migraine headaches and high blood pressure is biofeedback.

world a lot darker if you try to solve your problems when you can't sleep at 3 A.M. Other people can keep you from becoming too introspective, and their ideas and good moods can have a relaxing and comforting effect.

Fourth, *think positively and rationally, and try to keep a sense of humor*. If you had planned to be a prima ballerina since you were 6 years old, but don't make it, you've learned that you can't trust a 6-year-old child to decide your future. What does the adult in you think you're most suited for now?

Fifth, *begin to think of yourself as a relaxed person*. Take deep breaths, and move, speak, and eat more slowly. Don't overschedule yourself and make yourself rush. If you get caught in a traffic jam, there's nothing you can do about it, so relax, listen to the radio, and take pleasure in the fact that you're not as tense and angry as most of the people around you probably are.

Finally, remember that some stress is not necessarily a bad thing. You may recall from Chapter 4 that one of our earliest stresses—the normal

oxygen deprivation that occurs as we are being born—actually strengthens our breathing apparatus. In adulthood, stress usually propels us to some much-needed action or forces us to look at the world differently, thereby contributing to our growth. In one of the Chinese languages, the characters for "stress" mean both "danger" and "opportunity." We would do well to broaden our concept in this way.

SUMMARY

- In the midlife turn toward androgyny, men often become more nurturing and emotional, while women become more assertive and ambitious.

- In middle adulthood, people often enjoy wielding power, but they also often experience the stress of being responsible for both the younger and the older generations.

- Some decrements in physical functioning do occur during middle age, but the rate of these changes often can be slowed by exercise and other lifestyle factors.

- Chronic diseases such as diabetes and hypertension often first appear during middle age.

- Prior to age 55 years, the leading causes of death in middle adulthood are cancer, heart disease, accidents, and liver diseases. After age 55 years, heart disease assumes the leading position, followed by cancer, strokes, and accidents.

- Chronic stress has been linked to a variety of illnesses, ranging from headaches and skin rashes to strokes and cancer.

- Type A people display a behavior pattern characterized by ambition, aggressiveness, and competitiveness; type B people are more relaxed and easygoing.

- Menopause is said to have occurred when a woman has gone 12 consecutive months without a menstrual period.

- Testosterone levels in men generally decrease very gradually during middle age.

- Middle-aged people show some slight decrements in intellectual functioning as measured by traditional IQ tests, but tend to do well on tests of problem-solving skills.

- Mature adult thinking is characterized by problem finding and by the integration of reason and intuition.

- Middle age is a time of peak creativity as assessed by total output, not just superior works.

- According to Erikson, the developmental task of middle adulthood is the achievement of generativity, the concern about establishing and guiding the next generation.

- Although many people undergo transitions during middle adulthood, there is no evidence to suggest that midlife crises are either universal or inevitable.

- Midlife transitions are valuable because they permit people to explore aspects of their personalities that they previously suppressed.

- Although some people do feel depressed when their children leave home, there is no evidence that the empty-nest syndrome is a widespread phenomenon.

QUESTIONS FOR DISCUSSION

1. Consider the middle-aged people you know. What evidence do you have that they might or might not be experiencing a midlife crisis?

2. What is your score on the Holmes & Rahe scale? Why do you think desired events such as vacations are included on the scale?

3. When you think about the significant works you are learning about in your other courses, which would you say represent hot-from-the-fire creativity, and which sculpted creativity?

4. How might socioeconomic status influence whether a man becomes an anti-hero, a pseudo-developed type, a punitive-disenchanted type, or a transcendent-generative type in middle adulthood?

SUGGESTIONS FOR FURTHER READING

1. Commons, M. L., Richards, F. A., & Armon, C. (Eds.). (1984). *Beyond formal operations: Late adolescent and adult cognitive development*. New York: Praeger.

2. Eichorn, D. H., Clausen, J. A., Haan, N., Honzik, M. P., & Mussen, P. H. (1981). *Present and past in middle life*. New York: Academic Press.

3. Farrell, M., & Rosenberg, S. (1981). *Men at midlife*. Boston: Auburn House.

4. Lenz, E. (1992). *Rights of passage*. Los Angeles: Lowell House.

5. Rubin, L. (1979). *Women of a certain age: The midlife search for self*. New York: Harper & Row.

6. Schulz, R., & Ewen, R. B. (1993). *Adult development and aging: Myths and emerging realities* (2nd ed.). New York: Macmillian.

CHAPTER 17

Middle Adulthood: Relationships and Occupational Development

The Twenty-Fifth High School Reunion

A few years ago, I went back home for my twenty-fifth high school reunion. The party was held at Bobby Hopewell's* 20-room mansion on the mountain overlooking our small Appalachian community. Bobby was one of our less academically inclined classmates, and our algebra teacher used to tell him, "Bobby, if you don't straighten up, you'll never amount to a hill of beans." Judging from his living quarters, Bobby apparently had straightened up.

There were other surprises as well. Sandra Landfry and Barbara Rollins horrified their teenage children by wearing their old cheerleading uniforms to the party. Susie Powell, who was given a poor prognosis when she was 4 years old, laughed radiantly about all those fund-raisers we held in high school to fight the muscular dystrophy that crippled her. But the biggest surprise was Buddy Clark, our class clown, who hadn't made it to previous reunions. A sickly child with heart problems, he hadn't been expected to live much past 20. By now, however, he had fathered 11 children, the class record, and he looked as healthy as a horse. He was miffed when we didn't elect him "Macho Man."

We passed around pictures of children, and sometimes even grandchildren, and offered appropriate commentary: "She's going to Vanderbilt next year." "I hope his rebellion is short-lived." "He's interested in math, like his dad." "They live in Houston with their mother."

Everywhere there was talk of aging parents. "Mom's health is getting worse." "Dad's arthritis slows him down." "Mom still cooks for the whole neighborhood." "Dad retired, then got a part-time job to social-

---

*Names have been changed to protect both innocent and guilty, but the rest is more or less true.

ize." And there were awkward silences when the response to an inquiry was that the parent was dead.

On the whole, we had been a bright and conscientious group, and we now had a goodly share of doctors, dentists, lawyers, teachers, businesspeople, preachers, and professors among us. The class psychologist smiled when her classmates confided that her profession had saved their marriages and sanity, especially during their children's adolescent years. We all agreed that kids today are different, and we were never as difficult as they are.

We reminisced about Miss Dillard's love of Latin and all things classical, Mr. Swafford's often unpredictable science classes, our nearly winning the state basketball championship, the marching band's trip to Washington, and the time Walter Mathis concocted such a foul-smelling brew in chemistry lab that they had to let school out for the day. Some confessed adolescent crushes, accompanied at times by wishes that those dreams might yet come true.

Our spirits were tempered by the moment of silence for deceased classmates, victims of accidents or of the Vietnam War. As we made a videotape for a classmate who was battling cancer at a local hospital, thoughts of our own mortality inevitably flashed through our minds.

The evening ended with fifties music and dancing. Some energetic classmates talked through the night and ate breakfast at the same diner where 25 years earlier we had eaten the morning after the prom.

On the whole, we seemed more thoughtful and less competitive than at previous reunions, more appreciative of what our common past had given us. The sentiments seemed more genuine, whether happiness for individual successes or empathy for the sorrow of divorces, illnesses, deaths of loved ones, job reversals, and problematic children. We vowed to return in five years, with the unspoken hope that the progression of middle age would not take too much more of a toll.

In this chapter, we'll look first at relationships in middle adulthood, including the changes that traditional families often undergo, midlife divorce, and adult children's relationships with aging parents, siblings, and friends. Then we'll turn to the variety of experiences that middle-aged people have in the world of work.

RELATIONSHIPS IN MIDDLE ADULTHOOD

Middle adulthood is characterized by multiple connections. Some researchers call people this age the *sandwich generation*, because they get caught between the demands of their growing children and those of their aging parents. In addition, most have spouses, friends, siblings, and other relatives to whom they must attend.

It's not as though these connections didn't exist earlier; most did. But they take on new significance in middle age because people's changing time perspective, plus their increased awareness of their own and other people's mortality, makes them realize how precious, and sometimes problematic, these relationships are. Let's turn now to look at some of those relationships in traditional families.

THE TRADITIONAL FAMILY

The Family Life Cycle

In Chapter 15, we began looking at the cross-sectional family life cycle research that David Olson, Hamilton McCubbin, and their colleagues (1983) conducted on intact families. You may recall that these researchers divided the family life cycle into seven stages:

I. Young married couples without children
II. Families with preschool children
III. Families with school-age children
IV. Families with adolescents in the home
V. Launching families
VI. Empty-nest families
VII. Families in retirement

While there is enormous variability in the length of time a given family spends in a particular stage, the middle adulthood years normally encompass stages IV through VI. We will use Olson and McCubbin's framework as we examine key developmental tasks, stresses, and relationships within traditional families during the parents' middle years (see Figure 17.1).

Stage IV: Families with Adolescents in the Home.   A major developmental task for stage IV families is to balance freedom with responsibility as the teenagers mature and begin to separate from the family. Moreover, if they haven't already done so, parents would be advised to develop outside interests and activities, in anticipation of their children's leaving home.

Olson and McCubbin's stage IV couples had been married an average of 19 years, and the average ages of husbands and wives were 43 and 40 years, respectively. These couples had an average of three children, and the average age of the oldest was 16 years. About one-third of the wives worked full time, and sometimes one of the spouses held both full- and part-time jobs.

As we can see in Figure 17.1, these families experienced financial pressures as more money was needed for essentials such as food and clothing. In addition, they had a hard time getting household chores done and were stressed by the children's involvement in so many outside activities. Moreover, parents reported much difficulty managing their teenage children.

GENERATION GAP
Differences in social and political values held by members of different generations, often resulting in conflict.

Not all parents and teenage children have trouble getting along. The publicity given to the so-called **generation gap** ignores the fact that many teenagers get along well with their parents and that the adolescent years are not always as fraught with conflict as we've been led to expect.

Those parents and teenagers who do experience conflict generally have many reasons for doing so. In Chapter 13, we noted how emotionally taxing it can be for adolescents to handle the demands of their changing bodies and to establish a solid sense of their own identity. Ironically, middle-aged parents often are dealing with similar issues. Their bodies are changing in unpredictable ways, and their sense of self changes as they reexamine the choices they have made thus far in their lives. It can be particularly unsettling for parents to have their children challenging their values and lifestyles at precisely the same time they themselves are doing so!

Another reason these years often are so difficult is that the parents' authority is diminishing as the stakes are getting higher. As teenagers have to deal with issues of sexuality, drugs, alcohol, and peer pressure, parents often want to be involved, but simply don't know how to approach these subjects. If parents try to offer advice, they may be greeted with, "Oh, Mother, I already know all that!"—which the parent knows may not be true. Finally, teenagers themselves are often ambivalent about what they want from their parents. At one moment, they may give parents a "take care of me" message, and at the next say, in effect, "Watch what I can do on my own."

Among Olson and McCubbin's couples, the large majority were happy and satisfied, as was the case in the previous stages. However, overall marital satis-

FIGURE 17.1

Profile of family stresses and strains in middle adulthood. The top four stressors for families in each stage are listed. (SOURCE: Adapted from Olson et al., 1983, pp. 127–129)

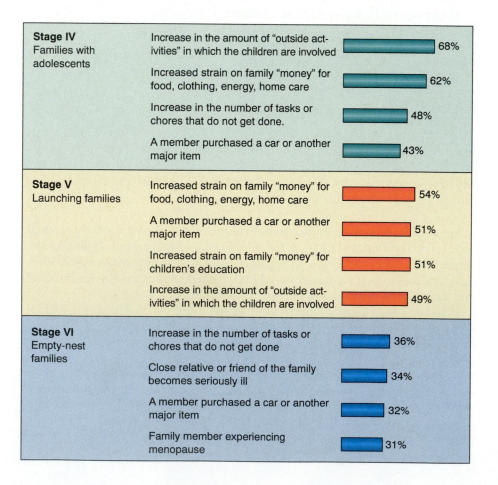

faction scores dipped slightly. Seventeen percent of the women and 15 percent of the men said they had considered divorce or separation at some point. Disagreement over how to deal with teenage children probably is a major source of contention between parents during these years. Moreover, couples often clash over financial problems, which may increase during middle adulthood.

Stage V: Launching Families.   Providing appropriate rituals and assistance to release young adults into the world and simultaneously maintaining a supportive home base are the major developmental tasks of stage V families. Most of Olson and McCubbin's couples at this stage had been married about 25 years. The average age of the husbands was 49 years, and that of the wives was 46 years. Stage V families had an average of four children, and the average age of the oldest was 23 years. Almost one-fifth of the men reported working a combination of full- and part-time jobs; only stage II men reported as high a percentage of multiple jobs.

If you are in your late teens or early 20s, your parents may be at this stage right now, so you'll know what we mean when we say that the relationship between parents and offspring is usually "in transition." Chances are that you feel under pressure to make major decisions about your education and career, and you may feel both eager and awkward about asking your parents for advice, then skeptical about what they tell you. Your parents may want to be helpful, but may seriously wonder whether they know enough about "the world today" to offer sound advice.

While many parents report intense conflict with their teenage children, others say the adolescent years are not nearly as difficult as they had anticipated.

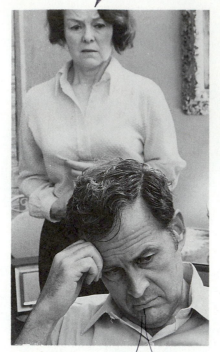

Couples' relationships often reach their lowest point as the spouses undergo personality changes in middle age and as the children begin to leave home.

The question of "Am I a child or an adult?" usually is highlighted when college students go home for holidays or vacations. Your mom may ask your opinion about the worldwide monetary system at the same time she's waiting for you to remove your socks so she can wash them. Your dad may discuss some of his office problems with you, but still wait up till you get home at night. And you find yourself both irritated by and grateful for their strange behavior. It is not a simple transition for any of you! On the whole, however, you'll probably find that your relationship with your parents improves as you move through this period, although your parents may still be caught up in conflicts with your younger siblings. In fact, some parents at this stage are increasing the size of their family (see At Issue).

In Olson and McCubbin's sample, marital satisfaction reached its lowest point during stage V. However, the percentage of spouses who had contemplated separation or divorce was about the same as for stage IV families, 18 percent of the wives and 16 percent of the husbands. These families were beset by many of the same financial and intrafamily strains as were stage IV families, and these were likely sources of the couples' problems.

Spouses also may have problems if their midlife changes are out of sync with each other or not appreciated by one another. If the wife becomes more assertive and develops a life of her own, the husband may miss his passive helpmate. If the husband becomes more emotional and sentimental, the wife may miss her strong lover. In short, we want our spouses to change, but we want to choose the direction of that change (Cohen, Coburn, & Pearlman, 1980)!

Yet another reason couples may experience trouble during these years, as reported by about 36 percent of Olson and McCubbin's stage V families, is that the serious illness of a close relative or friend causes stress. It is unfortunate but true that tragedy can pull a couple apart just at the time when they need each other most.

Stage VI: Empty-Nest Families.   The developmental tasks of stage VI families are to strengthen the marriage relationship and to maintain kin ties with older and younger generations. Olson and McCubbin's couples who no longer had children in the house had been married an average of 34 years. Average ages were 58 years for the husbands and 56 years for the wives. These families had an average of three children, and the average age of the oldest was 32 years.

Financial pressures lessened a bit at this stage, but families continued to have trouble getting everything done that needed to be done. Moreover, illness and death of friends or relatives became sources of stress for more and more families.

We have relatively few data about relationships between parents and their grown children, but the theme we've sounded so many times before certainly is true now: There is enormous variability in how parents and their adult children interact. Some children become completely independent of their parents financially soon after they leave home, while others look to their parents for help with down payments for homes, with car loans, and sometimes even with day-to-day expenses well into their adult years. Some move to other towns, marry, have children, and become self-sufficient, while others live near home and rely heavily on their parents for emotional support and help with the grandchildren.

How parents feel about these different interactions probably varies a great deal also. They may enjoy having their children and grandchildren nearby and be glad to help out when needed. However, most are pleased when they see their children able to care for themselves, because they know the time will come when they are no longer around to provide help. Moreover, what parents

AT ISSUE

Having Your First Child After 40

Only one generation ago, a couple would have been either courageous or reckless, depending on your perspective, to have considered having a first child after the wife had turned 40 years old. Some women did so, of course, but it was usually an accident, something no reasonable woman would do. Now, however, the number of women undertaking motherhood after 40 years of age is growing, and most are reasonable people who have spent their early adult years establishing careers. At midlife, they suddenly wake up to the realization that, cliché though it may be, there is more to life than work. As someone once said, no one on his or her deathbed ever spoke the words, "I wish I had spent more time at the office."

Health risks associated with late childbearing aren't as great as they once were. Middle-aged women today generally are healthier, are better educated, and have greater access to good obstetrical care than did women in the past. If an older woman starts her pregnancy healthy, her risk of physical complications is virtually the same as that of a younger woman. If, however, she has a history of certain illnesses, then the risk to her and to her baby does increase (Schrotenboer & Weiss, 1985).

Bladder and kidney infections are common during pregnancy, especially in women who have had past episodes of them. If not treated, the mother can suffer kidney damage,

The number of women undertaking pregnancy after the age of 40 is increasing.

and the baby may be born prematurely. Hypertension and diabetes also can complicate pregnancies, but both can usually be controlled successfully, so that mother and baby stay healthy.

The most common problem older pregnant women face is *gestational diabetes*, diabetes that first develops, or becomes obvious, during pregnancy. It affects 1 to 3 percent of all pregnant women in the United States and is most prevalent in older women and in those who have a family history of diabetes. It usually resolves after the delivery, but may resurface during a later pregnancy. Furthermore, one study found that 60 percent of gestational diabetics developed permanent, overt diabetes within 16 years (Schrotenboer & Weiss, 1985). There is no way of knowing whether these women would have developed diabetes anyway.

Other medical problems also increase the risk of harm to both mother and baby, so it is essential that the physician know the details of an expectant mother's medical history. But this is just as true for younger mothers as for older ones.

The risk of having a baby with some significant chromosomal abnormality such as Down syndrome also increases with maternal age, as we can see in Table 17.1. However, these odds are no lower for women who have already had children. Having your *first* child after 40 years does not increase the odds.

Amniocentesis, which we learned about in Chapter 3, can detect over 80 different diseases, primary among which are chromosomal abnormalities. Even with amniocentesis, however, parents can never be 100 percent sure that their baby will be okay, and there is in some cases about a 1 percent risk that the amniocentesis itself will cause a miscarriage. Moreover, amniocentesis is not commonly done until the fourteenth to sixteenth week of pregnancy, and while it usually only takes 1 week to get back the results, it sometimes can

Table 17.1 ● Maternal Age and Risk of Chromosomal Abnormality

AGE	RISK
15	1:455
20	1:526
25	1:476
30	1:385
35	1:179
40	1:63
45	1:18
49	1:7

Source: Schrotenboer & Weiss, 1985, p. 110.

AT ISSUE

Having Your First Child After 40, continued

take up to 3 weeks if the first sample of fluid failed to pick up any fetal cells (which is quite rare).

A newer technique known as chorionic villi sampling can sometimes be used during the first trimester of pregnancy to diagnose chromosomal abnormalities. This technique has the distinct advantage of letting prospective parents know fairly early in the pregnancy whether the baby will have certain problems. At this stage, abortion can be done on an outpatient basis and is not nearly as traumatic a physical procedure as it is during the second trimester. However, the risk of miscarriage due to chorionic villi sampling has not yet been firmly established; and there is some concern of it having been associated with limb deformities. Until this technique has been better established, most couples probably will continue to opt for amniocentesis. Also, although the results from the amniocentesis aren't available until later in the pregnancy, they can detect more problems than can the chorionic villi sampling and therefore may be worth the wait.

All this may seem to make a good case for not having a first baby after 40 years of age. But there is another side to this argument. As we noted, healthy older women are at no greater risk for problematic pregnancies than are younger women. Moreover, people who have their first child after 40 years of age usually want a child very badly. This means that the child is indeed welcomed into the world, a treasured little person right from the start. Moreover, older parents usually are more mature and more secure financially than are younger ones, and many have reached a point in their careers where they can slack off a bit and have more time for a family. Finally, for those people interested in their own growth and development, there is probably no better way to "stretch oneself" than by commitments to other people. Most older parents agree that having a child is a commitment par excellence that forces them to grow in profound and almost always positive ways.

would not take pride in introducing "our daughter, the professor" to their friends?

How do spouses relate to each other once their children leave home? This question probably would never have occurred to you had you lived at the turn of the century, because most women were widowed by the time their youngest child left home (Neugarten & Datan, 1973). Today, however, couples can expect to live together another 14 years, on the average, after their children leave (U. S. Bureau of the Census, 1993).

The key change for couples once their children leave home is that for better or worse, they begin to focus more on each other for companionship, communication, leisure-time activities, and emotional support. Among Olson and McCubbin's couples, marital satisfaction rose at this stage, and only 4 percent of the husbands and 9 percent of the wives reported ever having considered divorce or separation (Olson et al., 1983). In another study that focused on only middle-aged women, 75 percent of the subjects said that one benefit of growing older was an improved relationship with their spouses (Cohen, Coburn, & Pearlman, 1980).

The women especially valued the sense of shared history that these long-term relationships provided, and they reported far greater acceptance, companionability, and understanding. They said that their sex lives had improved, but that they and their husbands also shared an intimacy that went beyond sex. Many stated that they had developed a better perspective on the relationship and had become more accepting of its predictable patterns. They knew that sometimes they would share companionable silences with their husbands and at other times would simply have nothing to say to him. They knew that passion often gave way to comfort and familiarity, but would return again. If they seethed with rage about their marriage or were bored by its routine, they knew that these feelings, too, would pass. In short, they had become more accepting of their ambivalent feelings about their marriages, more willing to weather its storms, and better able to enjoy its rewards (Cohen, Coburn, & Pearlman, 1980).

Much current research points to the idea that marriages become more satisfying over time. But we have to consider whether this conclusion might be an artifact of the study designs. In Chapter 14, we discussed how *selective attrition* might skew research on intellectual development among adults. The same thing may be happening in research on marital satisfaction; that is, couples who don't get along may get divorced before they reach the launching or postparental stages, leaving a sample of primarily happy people.

The Nest Refilled. Bernice Neugarten maintains that the empty nest usually is not a problem when it occurs on time. However, it is a problem, she says, when it does *not* occur as expected (1979).

The departure of children from the home usually is a gradual process, with the children returning off and on for vacations or visits. However, many grown children decide they want to return home to live until they get married; with the cost of living rising in recent years, the number of these children has increased by nearly 50 percent since 1970 (Webb, 1988; U. S. Bureau of the Census, 1993).

There are often serious problems when grown children return to the nest. The children may still want nurturing and caretaking from their parents, but don't want to be asked any questions about where they're going or what they're doing. Parents may want companionship and contact with the children, but don't want to be caretakers or to give up their privacy and freedom. Spouses often argue if one wants the child at home and the other thinks he should be out on his own. Two writers who have interviewed many professionals, parents, and offspring (whom they call home-ing pigeons) offer the suggestions in Figure 17.2 for parents whose grown children want to move back home.

MIDLIFE DIVORCE

Currently, over one-fifth of all divorces in the United States occur while the spouses are in middle or late adulthood (Hayes, Stinnet, & Defrain, 1980), and the percentage is expected to rise in the future (Smyer & Hofland, 1982). Middle-aged couples point to factors such as unfulfilled goals for their marriage, sexual problems, physical disability of one spouse, infidelity, insufficient communication, and long-term disenchantment as key reasons for their desire to dissolve their marriages (Livson, 1977; Deckert & Langelier, 1978; Nadelson, Polonsky, & Mathews, 1981). Many of these couples have contemplated divorce for a long time, sometimes for as long as two decades (Hagestad & Smyer, 1982).

The launching of children often has much to do with why people finally move ahead with divorce in midlife. Once the spouses are left to interact with each other, many couples experience increased marital satisfaction. Others, however, realize they have little in common and simply don't like each other very much. The midlife feeling that time is running out often prompts people to change their living situation in an attempt to live out their later years in as pleasant a way as possible. Moreover, since their children are no longer so dependent on them, a major barrier to divorce is removed.

HOW TO LIVE WITH YOUR KIDS AFTER THE'VE LIVED SOMEPLACE ELSE

1. Be aware of the circumstances that drive grown children home.

2. Realize that home-ing pigeons sometimes need a respite from adult taske to become adults.

3. Admit you enjoyed your respite from child-rearing tasks.

4. Clear the air. Talk to your children and let them talk even if it means saying or hearing things you'd rather not.

5. Tell young adults what you expect of a grown-up child, and be prepared to wince when they tell you what they expect of a grown-up parent. Fair is fair.

6. Accommodate their needs, and, if need be, they'll accommodate yours.

7. Establish a bill of rights and be willing to pay the costs.

8. Handle your money matters as if your money matters. Give children a hand—but not your right arm. Even government aid to dependent children has its limits.

9. Don't let grown children adulterate your marriage.

10. Don't let them displace your spouse. Remember, grown children's stays are temporary.

11. If it becomes apparent that they're playing parent to the younger children at home, set the record straight. Home is still your domain. But don't referee sibling rivalry between grown children.

12. Taking in grown children can be an opportunity to strengthen the family bond. Treat them as you would beloved friends.

13. Tolerate their faults, especially the ones they inherited from you. Any stranger will appreciate their virtues. If all else fails, tell them to turn in their house keys. That's what they may need to hear to overcome their reluctance to leave. Home should be where the heart, not the hearth, is.

Midlife crises probably also precipitate many divorces. It has been said that middle age is something one first notices in one's spouse. So one way to stave off having to confront one's own middle age, especially for men, is to get a younger spouse!

Finally, midlife divorce is more socially acceptable now than it was a generation ago. The sheer numbers of middle-aged people who are divorcing means that with a little looking, newly divorced people can find others who are going through the same difficult life transition as they are.

The Effect of Divorce on Grown Children

Grown children are generally thought to weather parental divorces more easily than younger children because they are more mature and independent, can get along without steady attention from parents, and are more involved with friends and activities outside the home (Weiss, 1979). Be that as it may, parental divorces can still be traumatic events for young adults.

In one study of college students whose parents had divorced within the last 3 years, three-fifths of the young women and two-fifths of the young men reported emotional problems at some point during the divorce. The adjustment was especially difficult, they said, since it came at the time when they were already making major transitions, such as getting settled at college, making new friends, choosing a career, and forming intimate relationships. Moreover, the students felt loyalty conflicts when each parent demanded attention. They worried about their parents' current and future lives and about the increased demands that their parents might make on them. On the whole, the most resilient relationships were those between mothers and daughters. Relationships with fathers frequently deteriorated, especially for the daughters (Cooney, Sayer, Hagestad, & Klock, 1986). This study made it very clear that age alone does not insulate children against the pain and stress associated with parental divorce.

Displaced Homemakers

It is conventional wisdom now that women should develop marketable skills and not allow themselves to rely solely on their husbands for financial security, but this was not the case when many women who are now middle-aged got married. A woman who married at the age of 20 in 1960 was unlikely to entertain the thought that at age 55 she would be entering the labor force for the first time. But statistics show that that is what has happened. The percentage of middle-aged women in the U.S. labor force has risen almost 50 percent in the last 25 years and has almost doubled since 1960, from 37 percent to 70 percent (U. S. Bureau of the Census, 1993). As a result, when divorces occur or husbands die in middle adulthood, women who have devoted their lives to keeping house and raising children often find themselves in difficult circumstances, as we will see when we look at occupational development in midlife later in this chapter.

RELATIONSHIPS WITH ELDERLY PARENTS

You may be surprised to learn that a key characteristic of many middle-aged people's relationships with their elderly parents is **reciprocity** (Brubaker, 1985). Just as the older people may look to their grown children for support, companionship, and various forms of help, many middle-aged children look to their parents for the same things. As the years progress, however, the balance usually tips so that the parents actually need more from their children than they can give in return.

It is a widely held myth that children don't take care of aging parents the way they did in the "good old days," but there are virtually no data to substantiate this. One study found that 80 to 90 percent of elderly people report that they have frequent contact with their children (Brubaker, 1985). In another study, 50 percent of the subjects had seen one of their children the day of or the day before the interview, and only 13 percent of the men and 9 percent of the women had not seen at least one of their children for more than 1 month. A major reason for the lack of visits in the latter cases was that the children lived in other towns, but these children often did maintain frequent telephone contact with their parents (Shanas, 1979).

Moreover, when elderly people themselves have been asked how they feel about their relationships with their children, both nursing home residents and community-dwelling elderly have reported that they do not feel abandoned or neglected and are basically satisfied with their family relationships. Only 25 percent of the institutionalized elderly parents reported not receiving as much love and support from their children as they would like (Seelbach & Hansen, 1980).

One reason that the myth of neglect persists may be that people remember a time when most older people lived with their children. From 1937 to 1972, the percentage of older people living with their children or other relatives declined by at least one-half, but this was because most older parents neither needed nor wanted to live with their children, owing to the growth of retire-

RECIPROCITY
A mutual exchange of privileges.

The relationships of many middle-aged people with their elderly parents are characterized by reciprocity.

ment communities, savings accounts, pensions, heath care, and nursing homes. In fact, many elderly people preferred to share intimacy with their children at a distance (Streib, 1972), and this became increasingly common with the tendency to live in different communities. Since 1972, however, the percentage of parents living with grown children has remained relatively constant, at just under 10 percent (U. S. Bureau of the Census, 1993).

Another reason for the decrease in number of elderly people living with relatives is that people are living longer and suffering more chronic illnesses. Children of these elderly people often try to provide skilled nursing care—something they're not really equipped to do over a long period of time. Eventually, despite the children's best efforts, some of these parents require the care of nursing homes, resulting in their removal from the household. Unfortunately, the children often feel that they've abandoned their parents.

Researchers have estimated that at any given time, well over 5 million people in the United States are involved in parent care, most of whom are adult daughters or daughters-in-law (Brody, 1985). We might expect that as more women are employed outside the home, they will spend less time caring for aging parents. One study of noninstitutionalized elderly people and their adult children found that although employment did significantly reduce the amount of time sons devoted to assisting their older parents, it did not significantly affect the number of hours a daughter spent helping the parents. The women simply arranged their schedules so that they could continue giving the needed help (Stoller, 1983). Another study showed that children who were divorced, widowed, or remarried provided less, but not drastically less, help to their parents than did children from intact marriages (Cicirelli, 1983).

In 1982, a National Task Force on Care-Givers was established by the Older Women's League. This organization began to publicize the plight of caregivers and to lobby for legislation that would broaden unpaid leaves from a job to include time needed for care not only of newborn, adopted, or seriously ill children, but also of parents (Brozan, 1986).

RELATIONSHIPS WITH SIBLINGS

Sibling relationships are unique by virtue of sheer duration. Most people have brothers or sisters within visiting distance throughout their lives. Relationships among middle-aged siblings may be characterized by closeness, rivalry, hostility, or apathy. Rarely does closeness originate in adulthood; however, it may be enhanced by siblings moving nearer to each other geographically or by their becoming more tolerant and understanding of each other (Ross & Milgram, 1982). Difficulties may arise if one sibling changes values, lifestyle, or socioeconomic status, and the other does not.

In general, research suggests that most middle-aged adults get along well with their siblings and enjoy the relationship. However, relatively few discuss intimate subjects with each other or involve each other in important decisions about their lives (Cicirelli, 1982).

Sibling rivalry seems to lessen over time, but research has shown that some may indeed be active in the adult years (Cicirelli, 1982). In childhood, sibling rivalry often centers on issues such as intelligence, physical attractiveness, or social competence, but from childhood through adulthood, the major issue in sibling rivalry is *achievement* (Ross & Milgram, 1982). In adulthood, brothers are more likely to feel competitive with each other than they are with sisters, or than sisters are with each other (Adams, 1968).

Positive sibling relationships can be invaluable in times of crisis. For example, siblings may provide aid, companionship, and support to each other during the illness or death of a parent. However, in families where sibling rivalry is still strong and members feel much hostility toward each other, these same crises can pull the siblings further apart. Interestingly, the death of a sibling almost always enhances feelings of closeness among the remaining siblings (Ross & Milgram, 1982).

FRIENDSHIPS IN MIDDLE AGE

It would be impossible to understand friendship during middle age without also investigating the forces that lead to attraction between one person and another. All of us know some people whom we especially like. These people have a special significance for us. We look forward to seeing them, we enjoy being with them, and they make our lives happier. And we hope that other people will like us, too. This is true of any age. Developmental psychologists have examined many of the variables that affect our relationships. Let's look at some of them.

As a general rule, friendships depend on physical proximity. There's a much greater chance that we will like those people who live nearby or work closely with us if only because we will have a greater chance to interact with them.

Friendships during middle age tend to fall into one of four categories. First, friends are often neighbors, and neighbors interact because of their proximity to one another. Often, because neighbors live in the same area, they have similar income levels and may have children of the same age, thereby enabling them to share common experiences. However, proximity to another person sometimes leads to dislike as well. Not all neighbors are loved. If people have dissimilar initial attitudes, then proximity generally will not lead to friendship. The same is true if the people involved are annoying. For instance, a neighbor who lets his dog bark all night or who fills his yard with derelict automobiles is not likely to become a close friend. The people in proximity whom we dislike tend to be those who upset or disrupt our enjoyment of our immediate environment (Ebbesen, Kjos, & Konecni, 1976). As a rule, however, closeness leads to liking rather than to disliking.

The work environment provides another common ground for the formation of friendships. People who share the same work environment often bond together by working on the same project or by facing the same problems. This is especially true during middle age, when individuals may find that they have formed friendships not only with their peers at work, but also with older superiors or with younger workers under their supervision.

Shared activities, such as church, Little League, clubs, and school events, also provide fertile ground for the formation of friendships during middle age. Middle-aged couples tend to be the most active in their communities. A number of factors contribute to this. Older children are often the catalyst for their parents' involvement in the community as part of their parenting responsibilities. By middle age, adults often have more time to spend in their communities, freed to some degree from such burdens as having to spend extra hours developing a career, attending school, earning extra money, or caring for infants. Middle-aged adults are also more likely to be home owners and therefore more likely to have a vested interest in community involvement. Many adults in their later years regret the disassociation from the community that can sometimes occur once children are grown and on their own, often leading

SOCIAL EXCHANGE THEORY
A social theory of relationships that states that human interactions can best be understood by examining the costs and rewards to each person.

GAIN-LOSS THEORY
A social theory of relationships that states that we are most attracted by those who have given us the greatest net gain and are least attracted to those who have caused the greatest net loss.

to the sale of a house because "we no longer need such a big place." Important friendships are occasionally lost at that time.

The fourth category of friendships includes those bonds carried over from young adulthood or childhood. Many people manage to keep lifelong friends despite the geographical distances or differing life paths that may ensue. People very different from one another often report staying friends for life because they shared a childhood or important early experience such as school or the military. In this sense, friendships can sometimes be more like sibling relationships. Friends we made in kindergarten can often hold a special meaning for us even 50 years later.

Theories About Liking

As you have discovered, many variables can affect whether we will like someone. Researchers have attempted to integrate these findings into comprehensive theories. Lets look briefly at two major theories about liking. These are social exchange theory and gain-loss theory.

Social Exchange Theory.   The **social exchange theory** argues that people will like each other only if, in the social exchange, they both end up with a net profit in terms of what they have put into the relationship. This theory helps to explain an attraction between people with opposite needs. In such a situation, each person fills the needs of the other, and each person feels that there has been a net gain in the exchange; that is, more has been obtained from the relationship than lost (Homans, 1961; Rubin, 1973). Although the exchange theory may clarify the formation and maintenance of liking relationships, it is difficult to apply because it is not easy to define loss or gain in a relationship; these terms are subjective. Furthermore, the exchange theory is hard-pressed to deal with acts of giving when no return for the action is expected. Such altruistic behavior, engaged in without hope of compensation, would not seem to have any value in the interpersonal marketplace described by the exchange theory.

Gain-Loss Theory.   The **gain-loss theory** argues that if someone we come to know likes us more and more as time passes, we will generally like that person better than if that person had liked us from the start. Similarly, we dislike people whose evaluations of us have become more and more negative with time more than we do people who have always held us in a negative light (Aronson, 1969).

We do not know why the gain-loss effect occurs, but one possible reason is that people tend to ignore things that don't change but pay particular attention to changes. For this reason, a loss or a gain may seem more important.

Another reason may be that we often attribute the gain or loss of someone's liking or affection to our own behavior; that is, we have either won someone over or have driven someone away. If, on the other hand, the person has always liked us or has always disliked us, we usually attribute this orientation to the individual's predispositions rather than to anything we have done. If this is true, then gaining someone's regard may enhance our self-esteem, and because we associate the enhancement with that person, he or she appears more likable. The opposite would be true for someone who initially liked us but over time came to dislike us.

Finally, if someone comes to like us, it usually makes us less anxious about them. As we become less anxious, we like them more for reducing our anxiety. The opposite would be true for someone who began to dislike us more.

Midlife Occupational Development

Having served in many high-level positions and gained a reputation for leadership, common sense, and managerial skill, George Washington, at age 57 years, was named first president of the United States. Dr. Richard Alpert was approaching 40 years of age when he left his job as professor of psychology at Harvard, changed his name to Baba Ram Dass, and became a successful Indian-style mystic and guru. Corazon Aquino was 53 years old when she left her quiet suburban life in Massachusetts to return home to the Philippines to launch a successful campaign for the presidency there.

Few of us will ever become presidents or gurus. In many ways, however, the career paths of these famous people are magnified versions of common paths ordinary people take during their middle years.

Reaching the Top of a Career

Like George Washington, most people reach the peak of their expertise, power, and prestige in middle age. Corporate executives become division heads, blue-collar workers become supervisors, teachers become administrators, and so on. Exactly what constitutes the top for anyone varies according to the person's aspirations. For some people, the top may mean becoming an office manager or running their own service station, while other people may be satisfied only if they head a multinational corporation or become president of the United States. (Or, although you probably didn't list it as a career goal on your college application, you may actually be satisfied only if you become a guru.)

Some people, however, don't seek promotion; they simply enjoy getting better and better at their chosen profession. Many skilled teachers, doctors, and therapists enjoy their jobs so much that they feel they are already at the top and actually resist efforts to move them into administrative positions. Similarly, creative people such as musicians, artists, and writers may gain in prestige and respect as their skills increase, but unlike the salesperson who gets promoted to marketing manager, they work at essentially the same job throughout the years. Whatever their chosen field, many of these people are like the better-adjusted men in the Grant Study in that they strive to ensure that the values and traditions they have fought for are carried on once they are gone. Many become mentors, more concerned with fostering the development of the next generation than with advancing their own personal accomplishments. In so doing, they achieve the *generativity* that Erikson pointed to as the key developmental task of midlife (see Chapter 16).

Many factors enter into a person's becoming professionally successful. One longitudinal study found that men who in early adolescence were bright, interested in intellectual matters, ambitious, productive, dependable, and not self-indulgent were most successful in middle age. At midlife, these men were more comfortable with uncertainty, more objective, and less hostile than were their less successful colleagues (Clausen, 1981).

No doubt personality factors, motivation, and luck play key roles in many success stories. As we learned in the Chapter 15 At Issue, however, many barriers exist for women in the workplace, and the same is true for many racial and ethnic groups as well. For these people, success may come harder, regardless of their personality, drive, or luck.

Sometimes, though, a person may realize in midlife that his or her career aspirations aren't going to come true. Daniel Levinson maintains that this realization may precipitate a midlife crisis as a person asks, "Where did I go wrong?" (Levinson, Darrow, Klein, Levinson, & McKee, 1978). However, crises also may occur for those people who reach the top, only to find that success doesn't guarantee happiness (Clausen, 1981).

Research on male middle managers in their late 30s and early 40s does not support the notion that most men expect to make it to the top or that they experience great distress when they do not. Many people think that the psychological cost of senior-level positions greatly outweighs the rewards (Sofer, 1970). Even those people who do reach their early goals and could probably go further often choose not to do so.

Midlife Career Changes

Few people do what Baba Ram Dass did or adopt such interesting names, but certainly many people make major midlife career changes. Some changes are precipitated by midlife crises, but others come about simply because people find new and interesting things they want to do. For example, John Glenn became a U.S. senator at age 53 after a successful career as an astronaut and Marine Corps pilot. And Dr. A. Bartlett Giamatti was 48 years old when he left the presidency of Yale University to head the National Baseball League.

Successful doctors, lawyers, and businesspeople who choose to become farmers, laborers, bartenders, carpenters, and the like, constitute one interesting group of midlife career changers. Often, these people have accumulated some savings and don't depend solely on their new profession for their livelihood, at least not initially. They often make these changes because they are bored, burnt out, or trying to forestall the onset of aging (Sarason, 1977).

People who contemplate leaving a professional career must weigh their present income, the years spent developing their current skills, and the satisfaction (or lack thereof) of their current job against the expected gains of the new career. Social costs also must be considered. Society often invests large sums of money in training professionals, and this expenditure is lost if the skills are suddenly shelved (Stagner, 1985).

In contrast to "downwardly mobile" professionals are people who become dissatisfied working in fairly low-level, dead-end jobs. These people often decide to obtain more training so they can qualify for positions with greater challenge, decision-making opportunities, and job involvement. These people may get their training on the job, but often they go to colleges or graduate schools for their needed skills. Community colleges especially cater to the needs of this population.

A third group of people who make midcareer changes are those forced to do so as rapidly changing technologies render their jobs obsolete. For example, industrial robots now do many assembly-line jobs, thus forcing laborers to look elsewhere. At the other end of the professional spectrum, laser surgery has replaced some traditional forms of surgery, so that many physicians either must learn to use this new technology or alter their practices considerably.

Fortunately, societal acceptance of midlife career changes is growing. It seems likely that the number of people making such changes will continue to increase if our society maintains a high level of affluence and if rapid technological change and the trend toward longer life expectancy continue.

Starting a Career in Midlife

When Corazon and Begnino Aquino were living in exile in Massachusetts, Mrs. Aquino was known as "a quiet woman whose role during political discussions with friends was to serve food and drinks" (English & Witcher, 1986, p. 1). Although she was certainly well educated and was well versed in Philippine politics, it was not until after her husband was assassinated that she stepped forth to pursue a career of her own.

The ordinary Corazon Aquinos of the world usually are women who have spent their earlier years raising children and taking care of the home. As was the case with President Aquino, many women take their first career steps only after a family tragedy, such as the death of a spouse or a divorce. Others do so, however, because the demands of their families have lessened, and they themselves have become more assertive, more self-confident, and more interested in the outside world.

As you might imagine, a woman's experience entering the job market in middle age varies greatly according to whether she does so voluntarily or is forced to do so. Moreover, financial resources, personality traits, and social supports make a difference. Women with many resources often opt for more training and usually are enthusiastic workers and students (Johnson, 1986). This is important because dual-earner families are now the dominant type among two-parent families with children (Piotrkowski & Hughes, 1993). This has come about, in great part, because it is now necessary for there to be two wage earners in a household to maintain the same standard of living that one wage earner was able to provide 30 years ago.

Some women are forced into the job market against their will. Many of these are the **displaced homemakers** we mentioned earlier when we talked about midlife divorce. Those women who have been in traditional marriages, in which the husband handled the finances and the wife kept house and raised children, often feel overwhelmed when they have to cope with bills, mortgages, insurance, and repairs.

In 1978, six demonstration projects for retraining low-income displaced homemakers over 40 years of age were established throughout the United States. Research completed on the project in inner-city Boston showed remarkable early success. The women corrected their verbal and mathematical deficiencies, participated regularly in daily training and counseling sessions, and eagerly pursued job opportunities (Bernheim, 1981, cited in Giele, 1982). By 1995, hundreds of centers were providing counseling and support to displaced homemakers and helping them with practical tasks such as writing résumés, budgeting funds, developing skills for successful interviews, and making decisions about whether to pursue vocational training.

DISPLACED HOMEMAKER
A woman who has been in a traditional marriage, who has not been employed outside the home, and whose marriage has ended, leaving her without a clearly defined social role and often without marketable skills for the workplace.

JOB SATISFACTION IN MIDLIFE

In Chapter 15, we learned that early adulthood is a period of fairly low job satisfaction. But many national surveys have found that job satisfaction increases with advancing age (Opinion Research Corporation, 1980; Weaver, 1980). Older workers report that intrinsic factors, such as getting a feeling of accomplishment, exercising skills, making decisions, and turning out a quality product, are more important than extrinsic factors, such as pay and work environment (Andrisani & Miljus, 1977). Interestingly, older workers may become dissatisfied with supervision, pay, and promotions, but enjoy the work itself so much that they still have high levels of overall job satisfaction (Muchinsky, 1978).

The research findings concerning women are inconsistent, with some surveys showing increases in satisfaction and others showing decreases with age.

One reviewer speculates that job discrimination may have resulted in women's not being promoted, so that older women may feel more keenly frustrated than men in the same age-group (Stagner, 1985).

Much research on women and work has focused on the correlation between paid work and mental and physical well-being. Repeatedly, employed women have shown less depression and other physical and psychiatric symptoms than have unemployed women (Verbrugge, 1982; Waldron & Herold, 1984; Merikangas, 1985, cited in Baruch, Biener, & Barnett, 1987). One now-classic British study found that among women with no confidants who experienced stressful life events, 14 percent of the employed compared to 79 percent of the unemployed developed psychiatric symptoms (Brown, Bhrolchain, & Harris, 1975).

We should note that these are correlational data, not cause and effect. It is conceivable that healthier women seek out paid employment, not that employment improves one's health. Be that as it may, the workplace usually does offer benefits, such as challenge, control, structure, positive feedback, increased self-esteem, and valued social ties (Baruch, Biener, & Barnett, 1987).

While readily acknowledging the pluses of paid employment, we should also note that unemployed women may be at greater risk for problems because homemaking and child rearing are much more stressful jobs than people usually acknowledge. In studies of men, work that combines high psychological demands with a low level of control has been found to increase levels of stress-related hormones. These hormones, in turn, set in motion various disease processes, especially those affecting the cardiovascular and immune systems (Karasek, Schwartz, & Theorell, 1982). Interestingly, this is precisely the type of job many homemakers hold. One group of researchers describe the situation this way:

> A major component of the roles of wife, mother, and homemaker is the obligation to see to it that another person—spouse, child—is well and happy, a success in school or at work. Yet in reality one has relatively little control over the welfare and happiness of another person, and such responsibility thus exposes one to many frustrations and failures. (Baruch, Biener, & Barnett, 1987, p. 131)

There are situations in which a job is not beneficial for a woman. One study found that the women most likely to develop psychological symptoms were single mothers who worked at low-wage jobs (Gove & Hughes, 1979). If a woman has to come home to a difficult and demanding family situation, working—especially at a thankless job for low wages—may simply add to the overall drag of life (Giele, 1982).

JOB STRESSES IN MIDLIFE

Although young adults feel the stress of finding and becoming established in the job that is right for them, middle-aged people are subjected to their own set of job stresses. Imagine, for example, how someone would feel if after 20 years on the job, he had to work for a new boss who was younger and better educated than he was, but couldn't possibly know the job as well as he did. Similarly, how might a person feel if her job was taken over by a robot, or if she suddenly discovered that she had worked for many years in a segment of the economy that was no longer expanding and was therefore more susceptible to layoffs and plant closings? These situations would probably leave anyone feeling anxious and vulnerable.

Another stress that middle-aged people often encounter is discrimination. A widely held misconception is that middle-aged adults are somehow less capable, less efficient, or less productive than their younger colleagues. In one study, although a majority of chief executives of large corporations said they thought that older workers were discriminated against, they quickly added that such discrimination certainly didn't occur in their own firms (Mercer, 1981). Ironically, it is not uncommon for executives to hold negative stereotypes about "older" employees who are, believe it or not, younger than they themselves are (Stagner, 1985)!

An especially insidious effect of these negative stereotypes is that older workers may come to believe them. In this way, an unfortunate self-fulfilling prophecy may be established. Workers who feel and think they are "old" may start to behave accordingly.

Because job stress is an important variable associated with job satisfaction, which in turn can affect job performance, more and more corporations are hiring psychologists and counselors to help them address this issue (Offerman & Gowing, 1990).

JOB PERFORMANCE

When we look at how well middle-aged workers perform, the first thing we learn is how difficult it is to measure performance. In one classic study, five workers were filmed doing extremely simple jobs, such as twisting screws or bolts, stamping boxes with a rubber stamp, and packing boxes into cartons. Two industrial engineering professors and four time-study specialists, all of whom had extensive experience with performance ratings in factory settings, served as raters. These six experts could not even agree on whether the worker was working at a normal, faster than normal, or slower than normal pace (Lifson, 1953).

If supervisors are trained intensively to evaluate manual workers' performance, the agreement among raters increases substantially (Pursell, Dossett, & Latham, 1980). However, any attempts to assess intangible factors, such as morale, ability to relate to colleagues, or flexibility, probably are still subject to considerable bias. And if the raters hold negative stereotypes about older workers, you can guess that they will rate those workers lower, regardless of actual performance.

You probably will not be surprised by the conclusion drawn by scientists who have summarized the findings of research on age and performance: "Though performance slows somewhat with age, *variation among individuals increases with age.* In each older age group, a substantial number of persons perform at a level at least equal to the average level of their juniors" [emphasis added] (Meier and Kerr, 1976, p. 148).

But consider the other aspects of an employee's performance. Absenteeism, grievances, and job switching (both to other companies and within the same company) decline with age (Blumberg, 1980; Spencer & Steers, 1980). Moreover, older employees have fewer accidents than younger employees, but are usually off the job a longer time per accident (Dillingham, 1981).

Researchers have also examined the other side of the absenteeism issue—the price that workers pay for *attending* work rather than being absent from it. In some jobs, this cost of attendance is recognized. Professional airline pilots are allowed to fly only a certain number of hours per week. The work hours per week are also limited for air traffic controllers and bus drivers. And when jobs are dissatisfying, performance correlates positively with absenteeism. That is, workers who take off a few days now and then ("mental health" days) actually perform better, often enough to outweigh the costs of the time they have taken off (Staw & Oldham, 1978). Some industries have a double standard: They recognize that the top executives benefit from a few days off after a hard job, to "decompress," but any "mental health" days for the lower echelons are distinctly discouraged (Staw, 1984).

UNEMPLOYMENT

Middle-aged workers are less likely than younger workers to lose their jobs, but those who do are often devastated by the experience, especially if they have a good work history. Unemployment in midlife often is prolonged, sometimes because there is a scarcity of jobs at the appropriate level or because employers look for workers with more formal training than the middle-aged person has. In addition, unemployed middle-aged people suffer repeated blows to their self-esteem when they suspect that prospective employers are reluctant to hire them because they're perceived as being too old (Waring, 1978).

John Coleman vividly described the plight of the unemployed middle-aged worker this way:

> The Haverford alumni who lost their jobs as a result of canceled contracts or the like started out confident that there would be other choices open to them: "Actually, it's probably good for me. I was going stale there anyway." But many times they found no one rushing to hire them. Their self-esteem fell each day. By the time that they were willing to settle for a little less than they had had in income and rank, they lacked the show of confidence necessary to land on that rung. The next jobs offered them, if any, were still lower on the ladder. That took another period of time to accept. The downward spiral for those off the ladder was fast and cruel. Its effect was on their faces, in their speech, and most of all in their walks. (Coleman, 1974, p. 97)

Even after people eventually find a job, they may still experience some long-term negative effects of unemployment, especially if they have to settle for a less attractive position and lower earnings (Waring, 1978).

ADULT EDUCATION

We have already noted that many adults go back to school so that they can advance in their current careers or begin new ones. In addition, many middle-aged people simply love learning and now have the time and money to indulge themselves. Yet others enroll in classes because they're bored or because they want to meet new people.

The combination of technological change plus increases in disposable income and leisure time in recent decades have greatly increased the demand for adult education. It is estimated that about one-fourth to one-third of all adults are involved in some kind of organized and sustained learning activity every year. However, it is usually well-educated and affluent people who enroll in courses. Programs to attract rank-and-file industrial workers generally have not been effective, and adult education has barely made a dent in adult illiteracy in the United States. Middle-aged people who enter traditional college courses usually are surprised by how well they are accepted by their younger classmates and by their ability to do the work. They have generally viewed college campuses as a "youth ghetto, a place where older people have been viewed as strangers in a foreign land."

Many adults go back to school either to train for a new job or to gain new skills for their old one.

College courses are only one form of continuing education. Public schools, private industry, libraries, museums, churches and synagogues, professional associations, government agencies, and so on, offer a wide variety of learning opportunities. Short-term programs such as educational vacations, seminars, conferences, weekend colleges, and minicourses are especially popular now. Those in which the participants have the opportunity to live together on campuses or at conference centers can be especially fun and rewarding. Whether a person's interest is fiscal planning, aerobic exercise, archeology, flower arranging, Chinese literature, or whatever, the individual can almost always find an adult education course to meet his or her needs.

COMBINING LOVING AND WORKING

We saw in Chapter 15 that both loving and working are vital concerns for young adults; now we have surveyed their importance to people in midlife. Just why both are so important was demonstrated in a research project done with a large sample of women, ages 35 to 55 years. The researchers found that paid work was the single best predictor of a woman's sense of *mastery* in the world, while the best predictor of *pleasure* was a good relationship with her husband and children.

Pointing to the high mastery and pleasure scores attained by happily married, employed mothers, the researchers note that having two important arenas in life greatly decreases these women's vulnerability. Good work experiences can offset problems at home, and a good marriage can offset problems at work (Baruch, Barnett, & Rivers, 1983). Some researchers have found that men, on average, score higher than women on indices of mental health (Kessler & McRae, 1984). It may well be that men achieve these higher scores because they traditionally have been expected to function in both work and family spheres.

The lesson seems increasingly clear. The happiest people, men and women alike, are those who have and make the most of their opportunities for connectedness and attachment to other people, as well as of their opportunities for autonomous achievement.

Helping Parents Decide Where to Live

As we will see in Chapter 18, architects have begun to design housing to meet the special needs of our aging population. However, when older people simply are no longer able to live independently, their adult children are often faced with a difficult decision: Shall I have them come live with me or insist that they go to a nursing home? In making this decision, middle-aged people usually are torn between the needs and demands of their current family and those of their aging parents, and they search for a way to be fair to both.

Some families create multigeneration households to save money or to ensure that the parent isn't lonely. However, the primary impetus usually is to keep the parent out of a nursing home. Elderly fathers sometimes live with their children, but by and large, it is an ailing mother over age 75 who moves in (Mindel, 1979).

It can be simultaneously satisfying, rewarding, and stressful to have an aging parent move in. Stress often is caused by overcrowded living conditions. For example, if teenage children are accustomed to having their own rooms, they may be reluctant to double up with a sibling to make room for a grandparent. Spouses may clash, especially if one has never gotten along with the mother- or father-in-law now living in the house. Moreover, one spouse may feel neglected by the other and resent the time devoted to the parent.

Yet another stress is that the adult child must find time to tend to the needs of the parent, even though that child may already be busy with her or his own children, spouse, and job. Often, married children look to an unmarried sibling to take in the parent, even though that sibling has a job and other significant commit-

ments. Families may be stressed financially, especially if the older person has large medical bills. And the elderly person's temperament also may cause problems. Illness, depression, anger at "being a burden," and many other factors can alter a kindly grandmother's temperament and make her difficult to live with. Finally, if aging parents and their adult children have never gotten along very well, living together again will probably exacerbate the difficulties.

To help alleviate these stresses, caregivers should try to maintain normal household routines as much as possible (Mindel & Wright, 1982). If grandparents can be active and contribute to household tasks, they should be encouraged to do so.

Another way to reduce the stress is by making use of adult day-care centers. Services offered by these centers vary, but may include rehabilitative physical, occupational, and speech and hearing therapy, as well as psychosocial services such as individual and group counseling, arts and crafts, and social activities. Many also offer support groups and other services for the client's family members (Dilworth-Anderson & Hildreth, 1982). Many adult day-care centers are publicly funded, and private organizations have begun to franchise some facilities in different cities in the United States.

Yet another way to reduce the stress is to have the older person go for brief respite stays in a nursing home. Not only does this give the caregivers a break, but positive changes in the older person's memory and behavior also have been reported (Burdy, Eaton, & Bond, 1988).

Some corporations now offer their workers support groups, flextime, seminars, and handbooks on caring

for the elderly. One Connecticut corporation even pays half the cost of parent sitters who can take over for employees on evenings and weekends (Gibbs, Hull, McDowell, & Park, 1988).

In general, if the family members have a history of getting along well together and of coping effectively with stress, and if they are prepared to use community resources to help meet the needs of the older person, a multigeneration household can be a rewarding situation (Brubaker, 1985). It is never easy to decide to have a parent move in, however, and people considering doing so may find it useful to answer the questions in Figure 17.3.

If a person decides, however, that she just can't have her parent live with her, a nursing home may be the only resort. This move can be especially agonizing if the parent subtly or not so subtly says, "Don't put me in there." The percentage of families in this situation is quite small. Less than 5 percent of people over age 65 years live in either chronic-care hospitals or nursing homes. However, the financial and emotional burden on their families often is enormous, and the time needed for visits may be greater than the time that would be required if the parents lived with their children.

A parent's resistance to entering a nursing home is understandable, given the widely held notion that people will abandon them once they're there. Research indicates, however, that this notion simply is not true. In one study, nursing home residents received an average of 12 visits per month (York & Caslyn, 1977). In another study, 96 percent of the residents had been visited by family members within the last

Getting to know your *feelings* about caring for the older parent:

1. How do you feel about helping your older parents? do you owe them something just because they raised you?

2. How do you feel about old age? Do you see your parents as old?

3. What needs do your parents have, and how can you meet these needs?

Getting to know your *family:*

1. What is your relationship with your parents? Do you get along with them? Are you close to them?

2. How does your family deal with illness of financial problems? Do they come together and help one another, feel resentment, or what?

Getting to know your *situation:*

1. Will everyone have enough privacy?

2. Will you have to do any remodeling, such as installing wheelchair ramps, railings?

3. Is there enough room in your house?

4. Will there be enough money when all the resources are pooled?

Getting to know your community *resources:*

1. Does your community have a transportation program for the elderly?

2. Is there a senior center near your home?

3. Is there an adult day-care center near your home?

4. Is there a respite program at a local nursing home?

5. Are home-delivered meals available?

6. Are home health care, telephone reassurances, and housekeeping assistance available in your community?

FIGURE 17.3

Important questions for people who are considering the formation of a multigeneration household. (SOURCE: Hennon, Brubaker, & Baumann, 1983)

month, and there was no substantial decline in the number of visits during the first year in the nursing home (Spasoff et al., 1978).

When assessing what it is like to visit a relative in a nursing home, it must be said that much depends on the nursing home itself. The facilities that function best are those that recognize that visits can be painful for family members. Many of these con-sider the family to be their client and provide services to the family as a whole. This policy tends to increase family involvement with the resident and thereby enhances the resident's feelings of well-being (Montgomery, 1982).

There are some steps you can take to make these decisions less difficult. Planning ahead would no doubt be helpful. However, the possibility that an aging parent might be dependent on his child is something most people don't want to discuss unless they absolutely have to. Another step you can take is to shore up your own support system. If this is intact, then you've greatly increased your chances of weathering the storms of middle age, whatever form they might take.

Summary

- One reason teenage children cause stress for middle-aged parents is that they often challenge their parents' values and lifestyles at precisely the same time the parents themselves are doing so.
- Marital satisfaction often reaches its lowest point during the years when parents are launching their children into the adult world.
- Recent research suggests that marital satisfaction increases once children leave home, but this may be an artifact of the selective attrition of research subjects.
- When grown children return home to live, both parents and children often face serious problems.
- Currently over one-fifth of all divorces in the United States occur while the spouses are in middle or late adulthood, although the couple may have contemplated divorce for as long as two decades.
- Parental divorces are particularly stressful for college students, who are already involved in many other major life transitions.
- A key characteristic of many middle-aged people's relationships with their elderly parents is reciprocity.
- There are virtually no data to substantiate the notion that children don't care for aging parents as they did in the "good old days."
- The major issue in sibling rivalry throughout the life span is achievement.
- Most people reach the peak of their professional expertise, power, and prestige in middle adulthood.
- Some longitudinal research has found that men who in early adolescence were bright, interested in intellectual matters, ambitious, dependable, and not self-indulgent are most successful in middle age.
- People often make midlife career changes because they are bored, are burnt out, or want a more challenging job or because new technology makes their old job obsolete.
- Women with many resources find it easier to enter the job market in middle age, and some low-income, inner-city displaced homemakers also have proved to be enthusiastic students and job hunters.
- Job satisfaction generally increases as people age.
- Job performance may slow some with age, but in each older age-group, many people perform at a level at least equal to the average level of their juniors.
- About one-fourth to one-third of all adults are involved in some kind of adult education each year.
- Paid work is the best predictor of mastery among women; a good relationship with her husband and children is the best predictor of pleasure.

QUESTIONS FOR DISCUSSION

1. In Olson and McCubbin's research, marital satisfaction scores continued their downward trend in stages IV and V, although the percentage of couples who reported having considered divorce was lower than in stages II and III. What factors might account for these discrepancies?

2. How might having to make plans for the care of aging parents decrease or intensify rivalry among siblings?

3. Who are the most interesting midlife career changers you know, and what were their motives for making the changes?

4. Given what you now know about early and middle adulthood, what advice would you give a high school student about the paths to follow in relationships and career choices?

SUGGESTIONS FOR FURTHER READING

1. Baruch, G., Barnett, R., & Rivers, C. (1983). *Lifeprints*. New York: McGraw-Hill.

2. Gilbert, L. A. (1985). *Men in dual-career families: Current realities and future prospects*. Hillsdale, NJ: Erlbaum.

3. Lamb, M. E., & Sutton-Smith, B. (1982). *Sibling relationships: Their nature and significance across the lifespan*. Hillsdale, NJ: Erlbaum.

4. Schrotenboer, K., & Weiss, J. S. (1985). *Guide to pregnancy over 35*. New York: Ballantine.

LATE ADULTHOOD
(65+ Years of Age)

CHAPTER 18
Late Adulthood: Physical, Cognitive, and Personality Development

Chapter Preview: Marathon Man
Resources: The Country of Age • The Elderly: Who Are They? • Physical Development in Late Adulthood • Sexuality in Late Adulthood • Cognitive Development in Late Adulthood • Personality Development in Late Adulthood • The View from the Country of Age
Applications: Health and a Sense of Control

CHAPTER 19
Late Adulthood: Relationships and Retirement

Chapter Preview: Some Things We Never Outgrow
Resources: Relationships in Late Adulthood • The Traditional Family • Relationships with Grown Children • Relationships with Grandchildren • Relationships with Siblings • Friendships in Later Life • Widows and Widowers • Divorce in Later Life • Remarriage and Cohabitation • Elderly Singles • Retirement
Applications: Stopping Elder Abuse

CHAPTER 20
Death, Dying, and Bereavement

Chapter Preview: "We Live Too Short and Die Too Long"
Resources: The Incomprehensible and Inevitable • Death in America: A Historical Perspective • Understanding the Incomprehensible: Conceptions of Death Through the Life Span • The Psychological and Emotional Process of Dying • Caring for the Dying: The Hospice Movement • Ethical Dilemmas • The Survivors: The Cost of Commitment
Applications: Talking about Death with Children

CHAPTER 18

Late Adulthood: Physical, Cognitive, and Personality Development

CHAPTER PREVIEW
Marathon Man

In April 1993, 85-year-old John Kelley ran a portion of the 26-mile, 385-yard course of the Boston Marathon. It was the sixty-first time he had run in the race, having completed it 58 times, the last of those 58 times when he was 82 years old. He had actually won the marathon twice, in both 1935 and 1945, and came in second seven times.

Along the way, Kelley was warmly greeted by spectators, many of whom ran onto the course to shake his hand. After Kelley completed this same race at the age of 79, he had assessed his performance as follows:

> There were two or three times that I thought I wasn't going to make it. But the longer I ran, the better I felt. I was determined to get to the finish. There were people there waiting for me. . . . I feel I survived against the odds. . . . People recognized me and I just couldn't stop. (Singelais, 1987, p. 85)

Kelley gave up running complete marathons after the 1992 race, but still continued to run portions of it, being cheered by the crowd along the way. Many of those cheering Kelley on were his age-mates, full of pride that a man "our age" was still in such good shape. But the long course also took him past hospitals and nursing homes where elderly patients waged battles against a multitude of acute and chronic illnesses. No doubt many people much younger than he were oblivious to the remarkable feat of 6,000 people running over 26 miles just outside their windows.

While it is true that John Kelley is exceptional, most older people are healthy and robust and by no means in need of institutional care. Still, we do grow increasingly prone to physical decline as we age and at no time during the life cycle is the variability in functioning as great as it is during late adulthood, which we're defining roughly as age 65 years and over.

In this chapter, we'll look first at general issues about aging. Then we will turn to physical, cognitive, and personality changes that occur as

AGEISM
Prejudice and discrimination against the elderly.

people get older. In the next chapter, we'll consider relationships in late adulthood, as well as the effect of retirement and of newly found leisure time during these years.

So if you've already begun to ask, "How can I grow old like John Kelley?" this chapter may provide part of the answer. We do hope to convince you in this and the next chapter that for many people, old age can be truly "golden," and for most it is by no means as dreadful as we might imagine when we're 20!

THE COUNTRY OF AGE

• From age 71 years until his death at 89, Michelangelo served as chief architect of St Peter's Basilica in Rome.
• Anna Mary Moses was 78 years old when her fingers became too stiff to embroider, so she started painting rural scenes in oils and gained international acclaim as Grandma Moses.
• Golda Meir served as prime minister of Israel from ages 70 to 75 years, through two Middle East wars.
• Benjamin Franklin was 75 years old when he negotiated the peace settlement with England to end the American Revolutionary War (Comfort, 1976).

The accomplishments of older people can be dazzling. But those of us who haven't yet traveled in "the country of age" often become worried when we think about growing old. We read this list or cheer on John Kelley and think, "I'll never be able to do that," which may or may not be true. The strange thing is that we can readily imagine ourselves at the opposite end of the spectrum—alone, infirm, dependent, poor, reduced to a shadow of our former selves.

Part of the reason that we are so automatically pessimistic about growing old is simply a fear of the unknown. In his book *The View from 80*, writer Malcolm Cowley defines our dilemma this way: "To enter the country of age is a new experience, different from what you supposed it to be. Nobody, man or woman, knows the country until he has lived in it and has taken out his citizenship papers" (Cowley, 1980, p. 3). So we can read and do research about old age, but not really know it from the inside out until we get there.

A second reason we fear old age is that news stories often focus on issues such as elder abuse, poverty, illnesses, and right-to-die legal cases. This focus alerts us to many social problems that need attention. But we often take these data and make the erroneous assumption that old age is nothing more than a series of serious problems.

Yet a third reason for pessimism is that **ageism**, prejudice and discrimination against the elderly, permeates our youth-oriented culture. In television programs, older people, if they are seen at all, often are portrayed as comical, stubborn, eccentric, or foolish, and older women especially often are stereotyped in roles that suggest they must deny their age and stay young (Davis & Davis, 1985). Even children's fairy tales often portray older people as villainous witches, poor beggars, or village idiots. One review of 2,500 fairy tales from around the world found that only 2 percent featured older people as happy, healthy, energetic, wise, or productive (Chinen, 1986), although many such people in the real world are all these things (and few grandmothers are ever eaten by wolves!).

Maggie Kuhn, founder of the Gray Panthers, is a leader in the fight against ageism.

Our language is replete with ageist words and phrases—"coot," "dotage," "geezer," "dirty old man," "crazy old lady," "over the hill," to name just a few (Nuessel, 1982). Ageism also may be a factor when people evaluate the performance of young and old workers (see Chapter 17). For instance, poor performance by the elderly is usually attributed to internal factors such as inability, while poor performance by the young is more often attributed to external factors such as bad luck (Banziger & Drevenstedt, 1982; Lachman & McArthur, 1986).

No doubt you can think of many other ways our society expresses ageism. The dangerous effects of this prejudice include barring older people from jobs or housing, and it is extremely damaging to an older person's self-esteem. The cumulative effects of such discrimination can lead other people to regard older people as second-class citizens, unworthy of serious attention and consideration.

Combating Ageism

Older people aren't accepting ageism lying down, however. Many have begun to fight back. Maggie Kuhn's Gray Panthers and the American Association of Retired Persons keep the needs of the elderly in front of legislators, and every legislator knows that a higher percentage of people from 65 to 74 years of age vote than do people in any other age-group (Horn & Meer, 1987). In Milwaukee, a group of seniors persuaded over 280 physicians to agree to accept Medicare's fee as full payment for services rendered to the low-income elderly. In Washington State, a group of seniors taught corporations to identify isolated and vulnerable elderly customers who may need assistance. A group of retirees known as the Texas Baptist Men traveled across the state, building churches in areas that couldn't afford to build them themselves. Their wives sang in a choir known as Grandmas on Wheels ("Grass Roots," 1987).

Finally, researchers themselves have become interested in aging. In 1914, the term *geriatric* was coined from the Greek word *gera*, meaning "to age, to become, to awaken," and the fields of **geriatrics** and **gerontology** were born. The last few decades have witnessed a true awakening of interest in gerontology; by the mid-1990s nearly 10,000 articles on aging were being published annually. One of the most encouraging reports came from a Harris poll conducted in 1981. As Figure 18.1 dramatically illustrates, the public's expecta-

GERIATRICS
A branch of medicine that deals with the problems and diseases of the elderly.

GERONTOLOGY
The study of old age and aging.

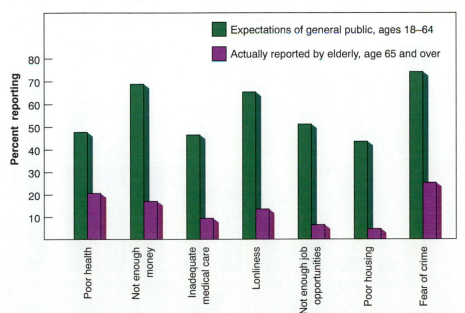

FIGURE 18.1

Problems of old age: the public's expectations and the elderly's reports. (SOURCE: Derived from Louis Harris and Associates, Inc., 1981, p. 10)

FUNCTIONAL AGE
A person's ability to perform adequately in society. It combines measures of biological, psychological, and social functioning.

tions about serious problems in old age were markedly *worse* than the problems actually reported by the elderly. We can only conclude that the citizens of the country of age know the territory far better than anyone else.

THE ELDERLY: WHO ARE THEY?

When researchers asked people to define "old age," they found the same thing we reported in Chapter 16 concerning middle age: The older the respondents, the later old age seemed to begin. People under 30 years of age set old age at 63 years, but 65-year-old people said it began at 75 years ("The Real Scoop," 1987). My 92-year-old great-uncle Leon says, "Old age starts at 100!" Increasingly, chronological age doesn't mean much. Gerontologists are more likely to consider a person's **functional age**. The concept of functional age combines the physical, psychological, and social factors that influence people's roles or attitudes.

Figure 18.2 shows the increase in the population of people over 65 years of age and illustrates dramatically the graying of America. This age-group grew from about 4 percent of the U.S. population in 1900 to about 13 percent in 1991. By 2030, when the baby-boom generation reaches late adulthood, over 20 percent of the U.S. population is expected to be over 65 years of age (U.S. Bureau of the Census, 1993). Currently, 1.5 percent of the U.S. population is over 85!

It might seem that 2030 is a long way off. But suppose you turned 20 years old in 1995. In 2030, you'll just be turning 55. So, barring unforeseen catastrophe, your chances of being alive then would be very good. As you can see in Figure 18.3, the average life expectancy of babies born in the United States has increased dramatically in recent decades.

Marital Status and Income

Women's experience of late adulthood tends to be different from that of men. In the first place, women live longer; there are now five times as many widows as widowers in the United States. Moreover, older men are almost twice as likely to be married (see Figure 18.4). As we will see in the next chapter, however, older women often deal better with singlehood than do older men because

FIGURE 18.2

Number of persons in the United States over 65 years of age (in millions), 1900 to 2030. (*Note:* Increments in years on horizontal scale are uneven.) (SOURCE: Fowles, 1986, p. 2. Based on data from U.S. Bureau of the Census)

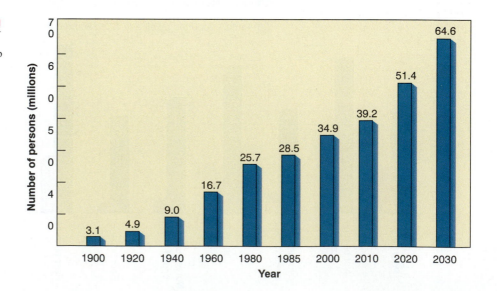

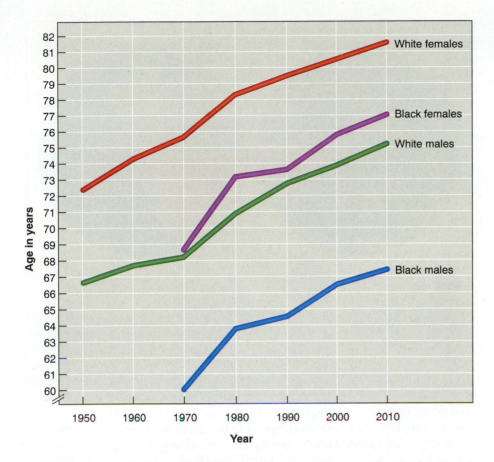

FIGURE 18.3

Average life expectancy at birth by sex and race in the U.S. population, 1950–1990, with projections for 2000 and 2010. (SOURCE: U.S. Bureau of the Census, 1993, p. 85)

they're more involved with friends and relatives and because they've developed more practical skills for daily life.

In 1991, white families headed by persons over 65 years of age reported median incomes of $31,569, while comparable black families reported median incomes of $18,807. On the positive side, about 30 percent of these latter families had incomes of $40,000 or more. Over 12.4 percent of the total population over 65 years, however, was classified as below the poverty level (U.S. Bureau of the Census, 1993). And many more are considered to be near-poor.

Living Arrangements

Most older people live in a family setting. As Figure 18.5 indicates, however, most men live with their wives, while women are more likely to live alone,

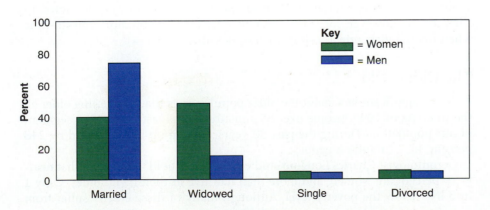

FIGURE 18.4

Marital status of persons in the United States over age 65 years, 1992 (SOURCE: U.S. Bureau of the Census, 1993, p. 45)

FIGURE 18.5

Living arrangements of persons in the United States over 65 years, 1992. (SOURCE: U.S. Bureau of the Census, 1993, p. 45)

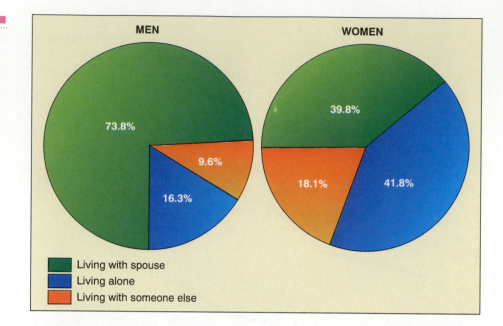

with relatives other than husbands, or with nonrelatives. Only about 5 percent of the population over 65 years of age live in nursing homes or other institutions, but this percentage varies widely with age, from 2 percent of persons aged 65 to 74 years to 23 percent of persons aged 85 or older (Fowles, 1986).

In recent years, architects have begun to design special housing to meet the needs of our aging population. Among these dwellings are *single-family houses* with features such as eye-level cabinets and closets, emergency call buttons, and modified furniture and bathroom fixtures. Another is *continuing-care communities*, where residents have independent living areas, plus restaurants, cultural events, and 24-hour nursing care on the premises. These communities usually are privately owned and are prohibitively expensive for many people.

Residents of *congregate housing* have private living quarters, but share central dining areas, transportation, housekeeping, and social services. *Mingles* are single-family homes designed specifically for two separate people ("Housing Industry," 1986).

Some older people insist on living independently, despite failing health. *Medical alert devices* operated through local hospitals can be useful in such instances. In case of an emergency, the person simply pushes a button on a pendant or wrist band, thereby alerting the hospital operator. The operator then summons emergency help. Some newer systems provide voice communication with victims who are unable to reach the telephone. As we noted in Chapter 17, however, for some older people, there eventually comes a time when living independently simply is not possible.

The Oldest Old

Another significant fact about the older population is that it is getting older all the time. As of 1995, people over 85 constituted the fastest growing segment of our population. During the past 30 years, this group has increased by 248 percent, to 3.75 million people.

Gerontologist Charles Longino studied the "oldest old" and found that nearly 70 percent are women, and more than half live in their own homes. Only 1 in 6 live below the poverty level. Although many of these elderly suffer from disabilities and serious health problems, the majority still socialize and are active.

Longino reminds us that it is unfair to say that all people over 85 are either miserable or lead wonderful lives. He does like to emphasize what he calls "youth creep: the old are getting younger all the time!" (Horn & Meer, 1987, p. 82).

Now let's consider some of the physical changes and health concerns of people aged 65 years and older.

PHYSICAL DEVELOPMENT IN LATE ADULTHOOD

How do I know my youth is all spent?
My get up and go has got up and went.
In spite of it all, I'm able to grin,
And think of the places my get up has been!
   Get Up and Go, Pete Seeger

In 1980, the Weavers, a famous quartet of folk singers, got together once again for two sold-out concerts in Carnegie Hall. Key players in the folk revival of the 1940s and 1950s, they had long raised their voices to advocate a better world. Now, with great gusto, they sang this song about the departure of their "get up and go." No one sang more enthusiastically than the ailing Lee Hays, sitting in his wheelchair. He died less than a year after the concert.

We can't deny that many of the physical changes of late adulthood are not for the better. However, refer back to Figure 18.1, which shows that only about 20 percent of the elderly said that poor health was a problem for them. Another survey found that 60 percent of noninstitutionalized people over 65 years rated their health as good to excellent, compared to 75 percent of the total population (Robey, 1982). Only about 7 percent of the elderly have physical limitations so severe that they have to restrict their activities (Branch, 1977).

Eventually, however, all people are faced with some unwanted physical changes. When that happens, there are two ways to lighten the load. First, a person can keep a sense of humor, as the Weavers did. Second, they can try to

At their 25th Anniversary Reunion Concert, The Weavers—Pete Seeger, Lee Hays, Ronnie Gilbert, and Fred Hellerman—continued to advocate a better world.

SENESCENCE
The gradual weakening of the body that begins during early adulthood and continues until death.

ORGAN RESERVE
The extra capacity of the heart, lungs, and other organs that is drawn on in times of physical or emotional stress or illness.

HOMEOSTASIS
An internal environment in which such body components as blood pressure, blood chemistry, breathing, digestion, and temperature are kept at levels optimal for the survival of the organism.

see the inevitable changes as challenges to be met, problems to be solved, rather than as curses inflicted on them that must be passively endured. In their book *Enjoy Old Age*, B. F. Skinner and Margaret Vaughan offer suggestions about how to meet many of these challenges (1983). We'll illustrate what they mean as we look at some specific changes.

Senescence, Organ Reserve, and Homeostasis

As we get older, we become increasingly aware of a process known as **senescence**, a gradual weakening of the body that usually begins sometime during early adulthood and continues until we die. Moreover, **organ reserve** begins to diminish. As we go about our daily lives, our heart, lungs, kidneys, and other organs are rarely required to function at their maximum capacity. Under stress, however, each organ in a healthy young adult body can put forth 4 to 10 times its usual effort. Imagine, for example, how much more work your heart and lungs and leg muscles have to do when you're riding a bicycle uphill, as compared to when you're lying down reading a book. This extra capacity that we can call on when we need it is known as organ reserve. Table 18.1 shows the average percentage of reserve for organs at different ages.

Organ reserve enables our bodies to maintain **homeostasis**, a relatively stable internal environment. As organ reserve gradually diminishes, it becomes harder to maintain homeostasis; if a person is unable to do so, disease and death follow. It is probably the depletion of organ reserve and the consequent inability to maintain homeostasis that causes older people to die from relatively minor illnesses such as pneumonia or the flu, which are rarely life-threatening in younger people (Fries & Crapo, 1981). As Table 18.1 indicates, however, the average percentage of reserve for some organs remains quite high well into late adulthood.

Having briefly considered the general processes that affect all areas of our functioning, let's turn now to some of the more specific changes of late adulthood.

Appearance

Artists have long been fascinated by the faces of older people, because the faces have such character. Several physiological processes combine to produce this character. By late adulthood, the skin becomes drier and thinner, and people begin to look somewhat bony and hollow, especially in their faces. Changes in skin pigmentation cause Caucasians to become paler, and brown "age spots"

Table 18.1 ● Average Percentage Remaining in Different Body Functions for Each 10 Years During the Adult Life Span

BODY FUNCTION	AGE (YEARS)					
	30	40	50	60	70	80
Cardiac output at rest	100	94	83	77	70	N.A.
Vital capacity of lungs	100	88	79	70	59	56
Nerve conduction velocity	100	99	97	94	93	89
Filtration rate of kidney	100	99	91	82	76	58
Basal metabolic rate	100	97	94	92	87	86

Source: Based on the data from Shock, 1962.

and freckles appear. The skin loses some elasticity, and this causes wrinkles. Wrinkles occur most frequently on the face because of repeated stress produced by the muscles of expression. (Frowning requires more muscles than smiling, so to minimize wrinkles, smile a lot. It can't hurt, and people will think you're either very friendly or have been up to something!)

You've probably also noticed that people get shorter and often stoop forward as they grow older. This occurs in part because the discs between the vertebrae atrophy, making the spinal column compress.

The Senses

Vision.   Most people over 65 years have some loss in vision, but fewer than 1 percent have extremely severe visual impairments (U.S. Bureau of the Census, 1993). Nearsightedness and farsightedness may gradually increase with age, and correcting them with glasses or contact lenses becomes more difficult after age 70. However, a large hand lens can be helpful for reading, and many books and periodicals are now printed in large type. Trouble adapting to changes in illumination can be offset by wearing dark glasses outdoors, then removing them as you enter a dark theater or restaurant (Skinner & Vaughan, 1983).

Glaucoma and **cataracts** are the two leading causes of blindness. If diagnosed early, glaucoma can be treated with medicine, and blindness can be prevented; only an eye test done by a doctor can identify glaucoma. Laser technology has so decreased the danger of cataract surgery that it now appears to be effective for almost everyone.

Hearing.   Approximately 20 percent of the U.S. population between ages 45 and 54 years have some hearing loss. For the 75- to 79-year age-group, this figure jumps to about 75 percent (Harris, 1975; Butler & Lewis, 1977). Men are almost twice as likely as women to have a hearing loss. Older people especially have trouble hearing high-frequency pitches, such as doorbells, or consonant sounds, such as *s, sh, ch, th,* and *f.* Thus, someone might mistake "deaf" for "death" or "fed" for "said." Impaired hearing can lead to feelings of isolation, confusion, and depression, especially when accompanied by poor eyesight.

Most hearing problems can be at least partly corrected by surgery or a hearing aid, or both. Unfortunately, many people don't get hearing tests,* and many who do refuse to wear hearing aids for fear of looking old. Many hearing aids are now so small, however, that they fit inside the ear and are easily concealed by longer hairstyles. They are wonderful devices because they allow a person to hear what he wants to hear—then he can turn the device down and tune out television commercials, argumentative colleagues, and even rowdy children! Hearing aids are not perfect, however, because they amplify background noise as well as the sounds a person wants to hear.

Other Senses.   For most people, the sense of smell is fairly keen until about age 60, and it drops off sharply after 80 (Doty, 1984). In addition, the number and sensitivity of taste buds decrease with age. Also, much of the sense of taste depends on the ability to smell. As a result of these decreases, food doesn't taste as good as it once did. If these changes are combined with poorly fitting dentures, people may lose interest in food, and their nutrition will suffer. Simply

---

*A quick and easy telephone screening test for hearing is available in the United States at no charge from Occupational Hearing Services, Inc.; it will work on any telephone of good quality. For the local test number nearest you, call 1-800-222-3277 (9A.M.–5P.M. EST, M–F).

GLAUCOMA
A disease in which a buildup of aqueous fluid causes increased pressure within the eyeball, resulting in a gradual loss of vision.

CATARACT
A clouding of the lens of the eye, which decreases the amount of light that reaches the retina.

By late adulthood the skin becomes drier and thinner. It loses elasticity, and begins to wrinkle.

HYPOTHERMIA
The condition in which body temperature drops to 95° F or lower. Confusion, stupor, and death may result.

HYPERPYREXIA
Exceptionally high body temperature, which may result in a heat stroke.

COLLAGEN
A key protein found in connective tissue and in bones throughout the body.

ATHEROSCLEROSIS
A condition in which arterial walls thicken and stiffen, and calcified fatty deposits accumulate.

MYOCARDIAL INFARCTION
A condition in which a portion of the heart muscle dies because the blood (and thus the oxygen) supply to it has been obstructed.

CEREBROVASCULAR ACCIDENT (CVA)
Sudden obstruction of blood supply to a portion of the brain or leakage of blood into the brain due to rupture of brittle vessels. May result in mild to severe brain damage, depending on the length of time the blood supply is disrupted and the area of the brain that is affected.

B CELLS
White blood cells that create antibodies that attack foreign bacteria and viruses.

T CELLS
White blood cells that help B cells to divide and to produce antibodies more efficiently.

AUTOIMMUNE RESPONSE
The tendency of the immunological system to attack some tissue or organ of the body, as if those cells were a foreign bacterium or virus.

seasoning food a bit more may perk up an appetite (Skinner & Vaughan, 1983). This must be done with care, however, in order not to alienate the elderly person's digestive system or violate any dietary restrictions.

Older people tend not to adjust to changes in temperature as well as younger people and therefore are more susceptible to both **hypothermia** (too cold) and **hyperpyrexia** (too hot). Similarly, sensitivity to touch and pressure also decreases with age.

The Cardiovascular and Respiratory Systems

As we get older, many changes occur in **collagen**, a key protein found throughout the body. For example, collagen changes in the skin is one cause of wrinkles. More serious, however, is that the collagen surrounding the heart stiffens, and a thickening of the collagen in the valves may keep the valves from closing properly. As a result, the heart muscle loses some strength and cannot pump blood as efficiently as it once did.

Arterial walls become harder, thicker, and more resistant to blood flow as their collagen content increases, and calcified fatty deposits accumulate within the arteries. This condition is known as **atherosclerosis**, and it results in a decrease of the supply of oxygenated blood that gets through to vital organs.

When the heart muscle doesn't get enough oxygen, severe chest pains known as *angina pectoris* may develop. If the blood supply is completely cut off or is too low for too long, the heart muscle is damaged; this is called a **myocardial infarction** (heart attack). As we all know, heart attacks can be fatal.

Atherosclerosis is also a major cause of **cerebrovascular accidents (CVAs)**, commonly referred to as strokes. The risk of having a stroke is increased further if the person smokes or suffers from hypertension. Strokes occur when clots form in narrowed blood vessels or travel from other parts of the cardiovascular system and cut off blood to parts of the brain or when brittle vessels crack and leak blood into the brain.

It's hard to distinguish age-related changes in the lungs from those caused by air pollution, smoking, and respiratory infections. In general, however, the lungs seem to lose some elasticity, and their capacity to inhale, hold, and exhale air decreases with age. Be that as it may, at 85 years of age, a person can still inhale in a single breath about 60 percent of what he or she could at age 25 years (Norris, Mittman, & Shock, 1964). The three major lung diseases that afflict older people are chronic bronchitis, emphysema, and lung cancer. These are aggravated by smoking and air pollution.

The Immunological System

The immunological system works by recognizing, isolating, and destroying viruses and other disease-causing microorganisms. Two key components of the immune system are white blood cells known as **B cells** and **T cells**. The former create antibodies that attack foreign bacteria and viruses. T cells are called *helper cells* because they release substances that help B cells to divide and to produce antibodies more efficiently. One reason the immunological system becomes less efficient as people age is that there is a reduction in these cells.

Many types of cancer apparently develop as the immunological system weakens. Moreover, sometimes the system mistakes one of its own body's organs for a foreign invader and attacks that organ. This can happen at any age, but such **autoimmune responses** are suspected in many diseases of the elderly. Perhaps the best-known autoimmune disease is *rheumatoid arthritis,* a chronic disease characterized by stiff, swollen, painful joints.

Health Concerns

A few years ago, my colleagues and I sat in a staff meeting, bemoaning our poor health. One had a bum knee, another had a sinus headache, two had problems with their "internal plumbing," and another had pain in his back. If you've begun to envision a roomful of elderly hypochondriacs, you've made an ageist assumption. At 39 years of age, I was the oldest person in the room!

A widely held misconception is that older people complain at length about imaginary ailments. Researchers have found that the percentage of people who are hypochondriacs is no greater among the elderly than among younger age-groups (Costa & McCrae, 1980). In fact, older people often fail to report serious symptoms because they expect poor health in old age, are depressed or otherwise cognitively impaired, fear a serious condition will be found, or fear doctors and medical procedures in general (Besdine, 1980).

When we looked at health concerns in middle age, we noted that many chronic illnesses begin to appear during those years. In late adulthood, these illnesses become much more prevalent, as we can see in Figure 18.6.

In addition to having chronic illnesses, older people often suffer from multiple disorders. Furthermore, many diseases are compounded by psychological factors. For example, depression and anxiety are sometimes **prodromal** symptoms of illnesses such as cancer and Parkinson's disease (Goodstein, 1985).

The leading causes of death for people 65 years and older are heart disease, cancer, and stroke (U.S. Bureau of the Census, 1993).

Mental Health

Another erroneous assumption about older people is that most eventually become senile. Different types of **dementia** do occur more frequently among older people, but they can occur at any age.

Alzheimer's Disease. **Alzheimer's disease** is the best known of the dementias. An early symptom of Alzheimer's is premature loss of memory, especially for recent events or familiar routines. At this stage, victims usually worry that

PRODROMAL
Precursor, or early warning.

DEMENTIA
Irreversible loss of personality and intellectual functioning caused by disease or brain damage.

ALZHEIMER'S DISEASE
A deteriorating dementia characterized by progressive loss of memory, concentration, and judgment and by personality changes. Eventually, victims are unable to recognize other people and to control body functions.

FIGURE 18.6

Selected chronic medical conditions by age, 1990. (SOURCE: U.S. Bureau of the Census, 1993, p. 135)

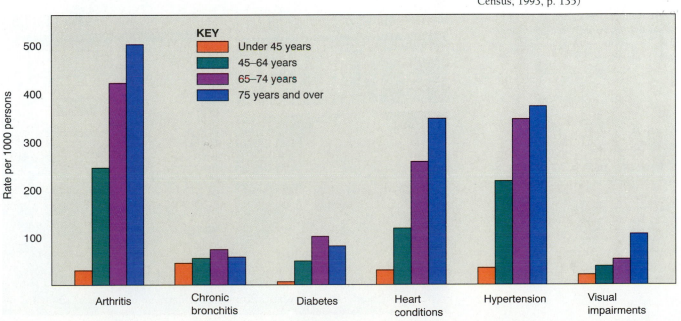

BETA-AMYLOID

A protein that forms abnormalities in the brains of some people and which may play a significant role in Alzheimer's disease.

MULTI-INFARCT DEMENTIA

Dementia that occurs as a result of one or more cerebrovascular accidents.

something is wrong and try to compensate by making lists or writing down names, addresses, or directions.

As the illness progresses, the victims become increasingly confused and show more impairments of memory, concentration, and judgment. Often, personality changes, including hostility and paranoia, become prominent. Many people begin to deny they have a problem and may talk as if they're carrying on normal routines, despite being unable to work, take care of a house, or function appropriately in social settings. As the severity of the disease increases, the victims lose their ability to recognize family members, to speak, and to understand what is said to them. Eventually, they are unable to feed and dress themselves and to control bladder and bowel functions.

Currently, Alzheimer's afflicts between 2 and 4 million Americans. Unless some form of prevention or cure is found, the number is expected to double by the year 2000, as more and more people live to advanced ages (Massachusetts Committee on Alzheimer's Disease, 1986).

No one knows for sure what causes Alzheimer's disease. Genetics may play a role in some cases, because in about one-third of cases, another first-degree relative has had the disease. The genetic factor seems to be most prevalent in those cases in which a person develops Alzheimer's disease early in life (Kokmen, 1984). Moreover, some people have a genetic propensity to form extra **beta-amyloid**, a protein that can produce abnormalities in the brain (Marx, 1992, 1993). This protein builds up in Alzheimer's patients, and slides of their brain tissue show a characteristic pattern of plaques made up of beta-amyloid (see Figure 18.7). Viruses, biochemical deficiencies, environmental toxins, and an abnormal acceleration of the aging process also are being investigated as possible causes or contributing factors (Massachusetts Committee on Alzheimer's Disease, 1986). As yet, there is no known cure; in the very near future, however, a test may be available to detect those people who are at risk for developing the disorder.

Multi-Infarct Dementias.   Another disorder most associated with aging is **multi-infarct dementia**, which occurs as a result of strokes. If someone suffers a minor stroke, his intellectual and motor functioning will probably return.

In the middle stages of Alzheimer's disease, this man is increasingly dependent on his wife for support, protection, and help with daily activities.

However, if he suffers many minor strokes over time, his course is likely to be similar to that of a victim of Alzheimer's disease.

One of the unfortunate consequences of the recent publicity about Alzheimer's disease is that people often fear that any hint of memory problems in an older person means that the person is a victim of the disease. To help clarify the issue, it has been said that Alzheimer's isn't forgetting where you left your keys; it's forgetting what keys are.

Depression.   Many highly treatable illnesses often are mistaken for dementia. Primary among these is **depression**. About 1 in 5 elderly people have an episode of significant depression at some point (Roth, 1976; Dunn & Gross, 1977; Ban, 1978). Symptoms include loss of appetite, insomnia, early morning awakening, crying, memory impairments, morbid thoughts, excessive worrying, and perhaps hypochondriasis or unusual irritability. Depression usually can be treated effectively with medication, psychotherapy, or both.

Untreated depression can be fatal in that depression greatly increases the person's risk for suicide. However, the suicide rate for people aged 65 years is about 300 per 100,000, compared to 522 per 100,000 for younger age-groups. For people aged 75 years, the rate drops to 250 per 100,000, decreasing for both males and females (U.S. Bureau of the Census, 1993). Suicide rates for elderly whites are 11 times higher than for elderly blacks (U.S. Bureau of the Census, 1993). Why this is so is unknown. In fact, the suicide rate among elderly black women is so low that it is considered a rare occurrence.

About 70 percent of suicides are thought to be directly related to the trauma of physical disability (Dunn & Gross, 1977). Older men are especially at risk during the year following the death of their wives (Jacobs & Ostfeld, 1977; Rowland, 1977).

Other Conditions.   Other conditions might also be mistaken for dementia. One is an adverse reaction to medication. Older people metabolize many med-

DEPRESSION
A mood disturbance characterized by feelings of sadness, pessimism, apathy, excessive worry, guilt, and an inability to experience pleasure. Sometimes, these feelings are accompanied by difficulty in sleeping, loss of appetite, and loss of sexual desire.

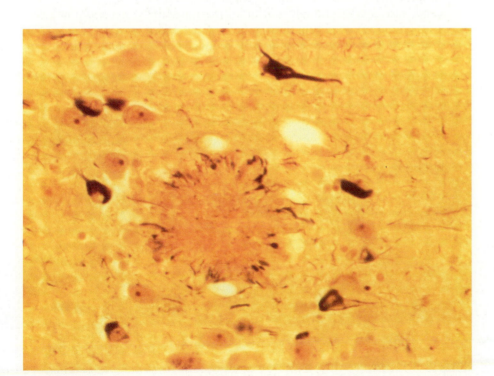

FIGURE 18.7

This photo of tissue from the brain of a 69-year-old man with Alzheimer's disease shows a classic plaque consisting of beta-anyloid protein. The plaques appear in the brains of healthy older adults, but usually to a much lesser extent than in Alzheimer's patients.

icines more slowly than younger people and may experience side effects such as disorientation and confusion. Some scientists have reported that older people suffer unpleasant side effects three to seven times more frequently than younger people (Lamy & Vestal, 1976; Butler, 1977; Van Praag, 1977). Antihypertensive (blood-pressure-lowering) medications are especially likely to cause troubling side effects. Moreover, older people often take several different medicines, and the interactions of these medicines can mimic dementia. Finally, malnutrition, dehydration, infections, metabolic disorders, alcoholism, hypothyroidism, and anemia all can produce symptoms that look like dementia (National Institute on Aging, 1980).

SEXUALITY IN LATE ADULTHOOD

"Color television sets emit rays that may adversely affect male potency." That was the shocking news that a middle-aged friend of mine heard while watching the nightly news with his 85-year-old father. He was even more shocked when, without saying a word, his father got up and moved his chair well back from the television!

My friend's reaction was similar to that of many "sexually liberated" young people when they learned that Dr. Alex Comfort, author of *The Joy of Sex*, is a gerontologist. Our society is replete with ageist attitudes about sexuality. Researchers are finding, however, that the idea that older people aren't interested in sex is a myth.

Many cultural and religious factors are involved in the development of this myth, and our research has perpetuated it. First, much early sex research focused on quantitative elements, such as frequency of intercourse, rather than on qualitative elements, such as emotional satisfaction or overall sensuality. Older people usually say, however, that quality rather than quantity of sex is most important to them (Stimson, Wase, & Stimson, 1981).

Second, early studies did not control for marital status. Data about married, unmarried, and widowed subjects were combined and reported as representative of all elderly subjects. If you look at frequency of intercourse among peo-

Romance and sensuality are by no means the sole province of the young!

ple who don't have a partner, you're going to conclude that most elderly people don't have intercourse often. But lack of frequency in this population isn't necessarily due to lack of interest. The primary reason older women give for decreased sexual activity is simply lack of a partner (Gibson, 1984).

Finally, most sex research has used cross-sectional designs that don't separate aging effects from cohort effects. We know that cultural norms and values influence sexual behavior, and they certainly influence the *reporting* of that behavior. Understandably, 50-year-old people who are products of the "sexual revolution" of the 1960s will talk more freely about their sexual experiences than will older people who, whatever their sexual feelings and behavior, often feel that *talking* about sex is taboo.

But as far back as 1926, one researcher found that 4 percent of men in their 70s were having intercourse every third day, and another 9 percent at least weekly (Comfort, 1976). In more recent times, almost 50 percent of people polled between ages 60 and 71 years reported frequent intercourse, as did 15 percent of those 78 years and older (Comfort, 1980). A 1981 study found rates of intercourse among 70- to 80-year-old people to be about the same as those Kinsey found among 40-year-old people in the 1940s (Starr & Weiner, 1981).

In one survey of older dating couples, the subjects revealed that they, like younger couples, often hid their behavior from family members because they feared disapproval. One retiree described his 64-year-old friend's covert actions as follows: "My girlfriend lives just down the hall from me . . . when she spends the night she usually brings her cordless phone . . . just in case her daughter calls" (Bulcroft & O'Conner-Roden, 1986, p. 69).

Health and Sexual Performance

Health can often affect sexual functioning in the elderly. The **prostate gland,** which secretes fluid to transport sperm, may enlarge and interfere with bladder functioning and ejaculation and may have to be partially or completely removed surgically. Uncomplicated prostate surgery may alter the sensation of ejaculation, but it rarely causes impotence. Radical surgery for prostate cancer, however, usually does cause impotence. In addition, many chronic diseases cause severe fatigue, so that a person has little energy for most activities, including sex. And, many medicines decrease sexual desire and may even cause impotence.

Health plays a crucial role in people's enjoyment of many aspects of late adulthood. If this section has made you nervous, review what earlier chapters have said about exercise, diet, alcohol, stress, and smoking. Nothing you do can guarantee that you'll never have health problems, but at least you can try to maximize your chances for a healthy old age. You also probably want to aim for an intellectually healthy old age. Let's turn now to a consideration of cognitive development in late adulthood.

COGNITIVE DEVELOPMENT IN LATE ADULTHOOD

> They tell you that you'll lose your mind when you grow older. What they don't tell you is that you won't miss it very much. (Cowley, 1980, p. 28)

So proclaimed an octogenarian lawyer at a testimonial dinner for his senior partner. It's the kind of joke that only older people with all their wits about them could make. In reality, people's fear of becoming senile often is greater than their fear of death itself. This fear may lead them to interpret ordinary memory lapses as clear evidence that senility is creeping up on them. In the

PROSTATE GLAND
A small gland that secretes fluid to transport sperm. Located at the base of a man's bladder, it may enlarge and interfere with urination and ejaculation.

words of one researcher, "A 35-year-old who forgets his hat is forgetful, but if the same thing happens to grandpa we start wondering if his mind is going" (Siegler, quoted in Meer, 1986, p. 62).

As we saw in earlier chapters, the major longitudinal research on intellectual functioning has used traditional IQ tests. After looking at how older people perform on these tests, we'll consider the issue of memory and aging. Then we'll discuss factors that may contribute to cognitive declines in later life and what can be done about them. We'll conclude with a discussion of qualitative factors in cognition in later life.

Traditional IQ Tests

In Chapters 14 and 16, we looked at what the Seattle Longitudinal Study found about changes on the Primary Mental Abilities (PMA) subtests during early and middle adulthood and found little cause for alarm. We noted then that the declines prior to age 60 years are not of sufficient magnitude to be of practical significance. However, the declines that occur between ages 60 and 80 years are large enough to cause concern, as you might surmise from Figure 18.8 (Schaie, 1994).

We remind you that Schaie's findings represent *averages* derived from many people's scores, and average scores almost always show younger adults doing better than older ones on experimental tasks. In practically every experiment, however, *some* older adults perform better than *some* younger ones. The range of intellectual functioning is quite wide, but this range is not apparent when we look only at average scores.

One intriguing finding in these data is that this decline in people older than 60 years occurs in every PMA subtest. How, then, does this square with our statement in Chapter 14 that *crystallized ability* which certainly includes verbal meaning and word fluency—increases throughout the life span? The answer seems to be that we failed to stress one important thing about the PMA—that it is a *speed-sensitive* test of intelligence, and an age-related decrease in the speed of almost all behavioral processes is the least disputed, most pervasive finding in all of aging research (Salthouse, 1994). James Birren, the noted aging researcher, has articulated this idea so forcefully that it has become known as the *Birren hypothesis*. He maintains that older adults perform as though in a condition of electrical energy "brown out." They carry out the same processes as do younger adults, but at a slower rate (Salthouse, Kausler, & Saults, 1988; Salthouse, 1994).

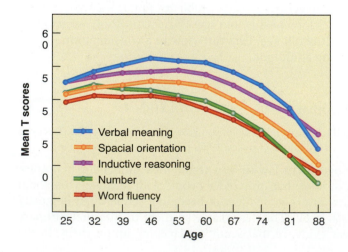

FIGURE 18.8

Longitudinal estimates of mean T scores* for single markers of the Primary Mental Abilities subtests. (A T score is a standard score used for statistical analysis.) (SOURCE: Schaie, 1994, p. 306)

Is it possible that these decrements might not show up if the subjects had more time to answer the questions? We don't know for sure, but it is tempting to speculate that much of the decline is indeed due to the slower speed at which the older adults execute the cognitive operations required by the different PMA subtests (Schaie & Hertzog, 1983). Researchers have found that older people's scores on other tests did improve substantially under "power" conditions—that is, when the time limits for answering questions were extended or eliminated (Hofland, Willis, & Baltes, 1981).

Other factors might also account for the decline in test scores in later life. One key factor is a phenomenon known as **terminal drop**. Repeatedly, researchers have found that as people approach death, their intellectual functioning declines markedly (Jarvik, 1962; Reimanis & Green, 1971; Botwinick, West, & Storandt, 1978). At least one study has found that intellectual decline predicted death better than did measures of physical health (Lieberman, 1965). Terminal drop also is found among younger subjects who are approaching death. Because older people are more likely to be nearing death, terminal decline is thought to be a major contributing factor to the decline in IQ test scores they show.

Several other factors probably also contribute to this decline in later life. We'll look at these and at what can be done about them after we consider memory in late adulthood.

Memory

Many cognitive functions, such as judgment and problem-solving ability, are vital to our well-being. However, as people age, they tend to worry most about their memory because they know that memory loss may be an early sign of serious mental problems. Researchers generally concern themselves with two types of memory systems—working memory and long-term memory.

Working Memory. Working memory, sometimes known as short-term memory, is active memory. While millions, perhaps billions, of recollections might be stored in your memory's "library," working memory deals with only

TERMINAL DROP
A decrease in intellectual functioning that occurs as people approach death.

WORKING MEMORY
An inclusive term for a number of short-term memory systems that enable individuals to hold onto recently acquired information for about 30 seconds to 4 minutes. Working memory also holds information from declarative memory that is being actively examined.

Older chess players may continue to be very skilled at the game, perhaps because speed of performance is not important.

DECLARATIVE MEMORY
The type of long-term memory containing conscious memories of facts and events that need to be "brought to mind" to become active. It is sometimes called explicit memory or fact memory. The ability to recognize a face, recall a number, or recall any verbal or sensory information requires declarative memory.

a few memories at a time. The working memory might best be thought of as the library's blackboard on which you have written your current thoughts and mental activities. In other words, working memory consists of the thoughts that you are working on at any given moment. This has led researchers to think of working memory as standing "at the crossroads between memory, attention, and perception" (Baddeley, 1992, p. 559).

One form of working memory is the memory we use between the time we look up a telephone number and the time we dial it. After about 15 to 20 seconds, the information starts to fade unless we rehearse it. We can hold about seven items (give or take a couple) in short-term memory (Miller, 1956). This memory is usually pretty efficient in older people unless the person has to manipulate the information in some way. For example, if asked to repeat a string of digits, older people perform as well as younger people; if asked to repeat the digits *backward,* however, they don't do as well (Walsh, 1983).

Long-Term Memory Systems.   Information held in working memory may be transferred into long-term memory, a virtually unlimited, permanent set of storehouses of memories. Long term memories can also be stored directly without having to first pass through a working memory. We know this from the case of Mr. K. F. and his unique amnesia following a motorcycle accident in which his working memory was nearly destroyed but his long-term memory systems were unaffected.

There are two major types of long-term memory: declarative memory and implicit memory. **Declarative memory** is sometimes called fact memory or explicit memory, because it contains conscious memories of specific facts and events. After a few weeks of processing and storage within the brain, long-term memories are believed to be permanently stored.

Declarative memories can be acquired very quickly, although they are not always reliable. For example, the experience of watching a good movie will place much information about the film into declarative memory and do it quickly (you only have to see a good film once to remember a lot of it). However, over time your recollections might fade somewhat, losing reliability, and you may even recall scenes happening differently than they really did. Memory is simply not the same as a camera.

Once older people get information into long-term memory, they seem to be able to hold it there as well as younger people. However, they often have trouble encoding the information in the first place or retrieving it later, so they usually don't perform as well as younger people on tests of long-term declarative memory.

One reason older people have trouble encoding information is that they tend not to use efficient organizational strategies. This probably has to do with their having fewer years of formal schooling, on average, than younger people in the United States. When older people are taught efficient strategies, however, their encoding improves markedly. In one experiment, for example, older people were asked to remember a 16-item list. Those people who were first told to think of 16 locations in their home, then to link each item to a location, did better than those who simply tried to memorize the list (Meer, 1986). Other examples of efficient encoding strategies include organizing by category (e.g., grouping all the states in New England), making a word out of the first letters of each item to be remembered (e.g., you go to the store to buy "mob"—milk, oranges, and bread), or simply rehearsing the material.

Retrieval is another matter. How can we tell if someone knows something if the person can't retrieve it? Have you ever "known" the answer to a game-show question, but just couldn't get it out? Then you hear the answer and say, "I knew it all the time!" You've discovered the distinction between *recall* and *recognition*, the two processes researchers examine in trying to understand how people retrieve information from declarative memory.

In tests where people memorize a list of words and then simply recall as many as they can, scores begin to decline when subjects are in their early 30s. However, if given a retrieval cue of some sort, people of all ages can remember more words, and age differences diminish (Craik, 1977). Researchers reason that the subjects had all probably encoded the information satisfactorily and that the problem was one of retrieval, since the cue that made the words more accessible increased recall.

The idea of retrieval difficulty is also supported by the fact that recognition shows much less decline with age than does recall (Schonfield & Robertson, 1966; Hultsch, 1971, 1975). If subjects are given a list of words to look at, then later shown another list and asked how many of those words were on the original list, older subjects generally do as well as younger ones.

Implicit memory, sometimes called nondeclarative memory, occurs unconsciously; that is, we don't have to bring these memories into conscious recall for them to function. Implicit memories, such as how to play the piano or ride a bicycle, are recalled almost effortlessly as we perform the activity. Similarly, professional dancers or fighters often report that they don't have to think about their next move in a certain situation; they just act. In fact, thinking about what they are doing can interfere with the action.

Unlike declarative memory, implicit memories are usually acquired slowly with practice and are very hard to forget. Although reaction time might slow with aging, there is little evidence, in the absence of obvious pathology, that implicit memories weaken with age. Like they say, once you've learned how to ride a bicycle, you never forget.

It is probably safe to conclude that when memory deficits do occur, they are most likely in declarative memory. However, memory tricks and retrieval cues (lists, for example) may jog the memory and help people compensate for whatever deficits they have.

Plasticity of Intellectual Functioning

There's probably nothing more frustrating for a student than to study hard for a test, to know the material well, and then simply to have a bad day and not do well on the test. The fact that a person's performance may vary a great deal, depending on different social, environmental, and physical conditions, is known as **intellectual plasticity**. This concept is as relevant for older people as it is for 20-year-old students.

Different conditions can affect intellectual functioning. We noted earlier that giving older people more time or teaching them more efficient strategies improves their performance. Another reason older people score low on tests is that they often feel *anxious* about being evaluated, especially if they know that speed is important and that they're being compared with college students. If they're taught to use anxiety-reducing techniques such as deep-muscle relaxation, however, their motivation, attention, and general cognitive functioning improve significantly (Zarit, Cole, & Guider, 1981; Zarit, Gallagher, & Kramer, 1981).

Lack of a stimulating environment also has a negative effect on intellectual functioning. It is interesting to note that the decline on many test scores coincides with the period typically marked by retirement. Whatever a job's drawbacks, the intellectual demands it makes may keep thought processes from getting rusty (Labouvie-Vief, 1985).

IMPLICIT MEMORY
The memory underlying cognitive, perceptual, and motor skills. Implicit memories include the unconscious expression of skills or habits and conditioning without awareness. It is sometimes called skill memory or procedural memory. Examples include activities that have become fairly automatic, such as playing the piano or riding a bicycle.

INTELLECTUAL PLASTICITY
The variability in intellectual functioning caused by different social, environmental, and physical conditions.

Lack of stimulation is especially pronounced in many nursing homes. When residents are provided with tasks that force them to think, this greatly improves their cognitive functioning. In one study, residents were asked questions that required them to search the environment and their own memories for the answers. Compared to control groups, these subjects showed marked improvement in working memory and increased involvement with their environment, and nurses rated them more aware, more active, and more self-initiating (Langer, Rodin, Beck, Weinman, & Spitzer, 1979). In another study, residents who met weekly to tell stories about themselves and their families showed improved working memory and rated themselves as healthier and happier after 3 months (Berghorn & Schafer, quoted in Meer, 1985).

Some cognitive functions other than memory can be improved. Skills that constitute fluid intelligence, which decreases over time more than crystallized intelligence, appear to be quite malleable. Cognitive training sessions aimed specifically at fluid skills such as inductive reasoning have markedly increased the performance of healthy, community-dwelling older people in both the United States and Germany (Schaie & Willis, 1986; Schaie, 1994). Similarly, subjects given practice by retaking tests and those who have more time to complete tests have significantly improved their scores on these abilities (Hofland, Willis, & Baltes, 1981).

Finally, we know that if nerve cells receive no stimulation over a long enough period, they will die. An old saying among neuroscientists is "Use it, or lose it," because a certain amount of stimulation is necessary to keep nerve cells alive (Sloviter et al., 1989). If you think you have already lost some cognitive functioning, however, getting involved in some kind of training program or simply living in a more stimulating environment is likely to prove that you're a lot smarter than you think!

Qualitative Factors in Cognition in Late Adulthood

The qualitative factors in adult cognition, which we examined in earlier chapters, continue to be significant in late adulthood. *Problem-solving skills* are of special interest to researchers who try to reconcile declines in IQ scores with the fact that most older people get along just fine in the world. In Chapter 16, we reported that in one study, middle-aged people did better than younger or older subjects on tests of practical problem-solving skills (Denney & Palmer, 1981). A more recent study found, however, that these skills may increase steadily into late adulthood. The more formal education the subjects had, the better they did on traditional, academic tests, but their ability to solve everyday problems was unrelated to their formal schooling (Cornelius & Caspi, 1987). This research demonstrates the difference between what Sternberg (1984) calls *componential intelligence,* or "school smart," and *contextual intelligence,* or "street smart" (see Chapter 10).

Other qualitative factors in later life are also important in cognition. *Dialectical thinking* may increase right into late adulthood. Young, middle-aged, and older adults, most of whom were students, were asked to solve a career dilemma in which a woman was deciding whether to enter the workforce for the first time and a hostage dilemma in which both parties presented good reasons to do what they were doing. The older subjects were better able to see all sides of the arguments and to come to a conclusion that integrated the different viewpoints and contradictory ideas (Kramer & Woodruff, 1986).

Studies of *creativity* in late adulthood have yielded contradictory results. Older people tend not to do as well as younger ones on tests of divergent thinking. Moreover, as we discussed in Chapters 15 and 16, creativity as mea-

Lack of intellectual stimulation is a major contributor to the cognitive deficits of many nursing home residents.

sured by superior works and total output peaks for most fields in early or middle adulthood. However, Wayne Dennis found that historians, inventors, and philosophers were most productive during their 60s and that they and other scholars continued to be productive into their 70s (1968). And whether or not they themselves become more creative, many older people do develop a stronger aesthetic sense, becoming more appreciative of beauty in all its forms. According to gerontologist Robert Kastenbaum,

> Aging tests the creative spirit in a way that might be compared with the ordeal of the saint. . . though few of us be saints. The triumph of the creative spirit in old age—no matter how personal and unobserved a triumph—would be cherished by a more perceptive society as perceptive people now cherish a glowing sunset at the end of a long and eventful day. (Kastenbaum, 1992, p. 304)

Finally, given all their experience and reflection, we do expect older people to develop *wisdom* (Peck, 1968; Luszki & Luszki, 1985). Interestingly, older people themselves equate wisdom not so much with age as with empathy and understanding, qualities that are by no means the sole province of the aged (Clayton & Birren, 1980). We'll consider this issue again after we examine personality development, since the acquisition of wisdom probably depends on both cognitive and personality factors.

PERSONALITY DEVELOPMENT IN LATE ADULTHOOD

Developmental Tasks of Late Adulthood

In Chapters 14 and 16, we looked at how different researchers have modified Erik Erikson's theory of psychosocial development in early and middle adulthood. For late adulthood it was Erikson himself, who lived into his 90s, who furthered the investigation into the final stage, *ego integrity versus despair*. In this task, Erikson and his wife Joan (who was in her 80s) were joined by Helen Kivnick, a clinician and researcher some 50 years younger than they. Together,

LIFE REVIEW
The process in which a person approaching death looks back over his or her life and attempts to understand its meaning.

Older people who find ways to exercise their problem-solving skills and creativity often discover they're smarter than they thought they were.

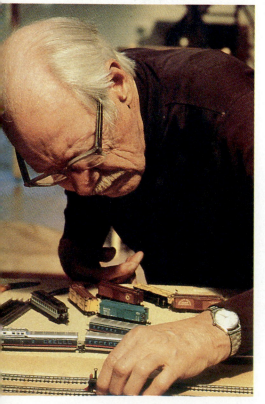

these researchers interviewed 29 octogenarians, all of whom were parents of the now-grown children in the Berkeley Guidance Study.

In that study it was found that all of these older people were, in one way or another, attempting to come to terms with their lives and the inevitability of their own death. In Erikson's scheme, this is the chief developmental task of later life. The successful outcome of this process is the achievement of ego integrity, "the acceptance of one's one and only life cycle as something that had to be and that, by necessity, permitted of no substitutions" (Erikson, 1950, p. 268). This task involves a new acceptance of our parents and ourselves, and of the fact that whatever our failings, we have lived our life as best we knew how. It also implies an acceptance of our own "inescapable death . . . which is both wholly certain and wholly unknowable" (Erikson, Erikson, & Kivnick, 1986, p. 72).

Failure to achieve ego integrity may result in our being swept away with despair as we realize that too little time is left to embark on a whole new life course. However, even people who achieve a high degree of integrity normally feel some despair at this stage of life. After all, there is always something in the past we wish we had done differently, and there is always something in the present that causes pain.

Older people have various ways to negotiate this crisis. Probably the most concise statement of the process is what gerontologist Robert Butler calls the **life review**, a normal, universal process prompted by the biological fact of approaching death. It occurs not only among older people, but also among younger people with terminal illnesses (1963). Some people silently reminisce, while others tell stories about their lives to anyone who will listen. Many make pilgrimages back to their childhood homes or go to family and class reunions. Many muse alone over scrapbooks, photo albums, and old letters, while others share these mementos with friends or family members.

Most people probably do have the capacity to come to terms with their lives and to find meaning, especially if they can share the life review process with someone who is accepting and who doesn't dismiss their reminiscence as the idle ramblings of old age. People who aren't able to find meaning may experience such anxiety, guilt, and depression that they are overcome by despair.

Other researchers have expanded on Erikson and Butler's ideas. For example, Robert Peck has enumerated three tasks that he believes are necessary for personality development in late adulthood. First, he says, people must come to terms with who they are, apart from their occupational roles. Retirement forces them to grapple with the question, "Am I a worthwhile person only insofar as I can do a full-time job; or can I be worthwhile . . . as a performer of several other roles, and also because of the person I am?" (Peck, 1968, p. 90).

The second task is to accept the inevitability of some physical decline. We must shift emphasis away from physical beauty and prowess, and direct it toward intellectual activities and relationships with other people. Finally, people must accept the inevitability of their approaching death and appreciate what will live on after they are gone—their children, their contributions to their culture, and their friendships. Some individuals, however, take a very long time to live out their lives (see At Issue).

Personality Traits, Personality Types, and Social Interaction

While Erikson, Butler, and Peck have defined developmental tasks for late adulthood, other researchers have investigated changes in specific personality traits. They have delineated different personality types in late adulthood and have sought to describe patterns of successful aging.

AT ISSUE

How Old Can We Grow?

In Vilcabamba, Ecuador, in Georgian Russia, and in the mountains of Kashmir, people have allegedly lived as long as 170 years. Needless to say, such longevity interests gerontologists. In the early 1970s, Alexander Leaf interviewed several of the aged Ecuadorians, including one man who gave his age as 122 years (Leaf, 1973). When Leaf returned to Ecuador in 1974, this gentleman had turned 134 years of age. Leaf got suspicious!

Searching for documentation to verify the ages of these elders, researchers found that many had used the birth certificates of their parents or grandparents, who had the same names as they did. However, the birth certificates also listed godparents' names, and by doing a lot of tracing and matching, the scientists eventually concluded that none of the Vilcabamba elderly was really over 96 years old (Mazess & Forman, 1979; Mazess & Mathisen, 1982).

The oldest person able to provide acceptable documentation of his age was Shigechiyo Izumi of Japan, who died on February 21, 1986, at age 120 years (Mathews, 1993). Before his death, Izumi attributed his longevity to "the daily cup of *shochu* sugar-cane liquor and keeping a simple diet" (*Time*, 1986, p. 79).*

There are many theories about why we age and eventually die. The most general is the *wear and tear theory*, which compares the human body to a machine. Ordinary stresses such as exams and jobs and rowdy children take their toll; and our bodies are assaulted by diseases, radiation, pollution, accidents, poor diets, and so on. This theory maintains that the accumulation of all these factors causes us to age and eventually just to wear out; but it doesn't explain exactly how or why these insults are so destructive (Hayflick, 1985).

Another theory holds that a *breakdown in our immunological system* causes us to age and reduces our ability to ward off fatal diseases. The immunological system, however, is influenced by other systems, especially the endocrine system, so it may be a *malfunction in the endocrine system* that causes the aging. This theory is attractive because hormones influence every part of the body, and the efficiency of the hormonal system does decline with time, but we don't know why (Hayflick, 1985).

The *cross-linkage theory* focuses on the process by which different kinds of molecules are joined together permanently, or cross-linked. This theory has been studied most frequently in regard to the collagen molecule, which, when cross-linked with other molecules, produces changes ranging from wrinkling to atherosclerosis. Many people also believe that cross-linkage occurs with DNA molecules, which carry our genetic programs, and that this damage to DNA leads to mutation or cell death (Hayflick, 1985).

Another theory is known as the *free radical theory*. Free radicals are highly unstable molecules that react with other molecules in a way that may damage cells considerably. Exposure to radiation and certain enzymes are thought to cause these reactions (Hayflick, 1985).

Proponents of the endocrine theory maintain that hormonal changes produce free radicals, cross-linkages, and autoimmunity, while many people think that free radicals are simply a special form of cross-linkage, and still other people believe that cross-linkage causes free radicals. Clearly, the theories overlap, and at this point it is impossible to distinguish chickens from eggs.

Shigechiyo Izumi (1865–1986).

*Winston Churchill once noted that if you don't drink, don't smoke, and stay away from the opposite sex, you can live to be 100, but it will seem like 200!

AT ISSUE

How Old Can We Grow? Continued

So how old *can* we grow? In an experiment that has been replicated many times, Leonard Hayflick cultured cells from a human embryo, provided them with everything necessary for growth and replication, and watched anxiously, hoping the cells would multiply forever. The cells stopped multiplying after about 50 divisions. Hayflick then cultured cells from adults and found that the older the donor, the fewer the times the cells would divide. He concluded that we are apparently genetically programmed so that our cells will divide only a limited number of times. The upper limit of the human life span, now known as the *Hayflick limit*, is about 100 to 120 years (Hayflick & Moorhead, 1961).

It should be noted that cancer cells, as well as egg and sperm cells, appear to have no limits to their division. It may be that when egg and sperm fuse at conception, they reset the genetic death clock; and cancer cells may reshuffle their genetic information in some similar way so that they never stop dividing (Hayflick, 1980).

Medical advances in genetic engineering and organ transplants may eventually provide ways of extending our life span. However, before you leap for life-prolonging techniques, remember the myth of the goddess Eos and her mortal lover Tithonus. Eos convinced Zeus to grant Tithonus eternal life, but forgot to ask for youth and health. Poor Tithonus grew old and shriveled away to nothingness, so that eventually only his voice was left (Kirkwood, 1959). So if someone offers you the chance to live forever, make sure the deal includes the opportunity to continue to be healthy and productive!

Personality Traits.   As we saw in the Chapter 16 At Issue, research about changes in personality in adulthood has yielded inconsistent findings, with some traits showing stability and others showing change. Two traits, however, almost always show an increase as people get older.

First, the midlife move toward androgyny continues into late adulthood, and life circumstances often foster its development. For example, widows often must take over chores previously done by their husbands, and these chores may require more "masculine" assertiveness. Similarly, widowers may find themselves serving as the emotional supports of their middle-aged children in times of distress, a role their deceased wives previously filled.

The second trait that usually increases in late adulthood is what Bernice Neugarten calls **interiority** (1976). This essentially means introspection, a tendency to look inward and become better acquainted with one's inner world. Although people start becoming more introspective in middle age, the life review process of old age fosters further development of this trait.

Personality Types.   One classic study has identified four major personality types. *Integrated* people were intact intellectually, had rich personalities, functioned well in the world, and were generally happy with their lives. The *armored-defended* were highly controlled, achievement-oriented people who tried to stave off aging either by maintaining previous life patterns or by conserving their energy. *Passive-dependent* people either relied on other people to keep them active or simply were extremely inactive. *Unintegrated* people functioned at a low level intellectually and emotionally and generally had difficulty getting along in the world. Overall, the more active people in this study tended to be happier, and the highest degrees of life satisfaction were found among the integrated and armored-defended types (Neugarten, Havighurst, & Tobin, 1968).

Patterns of Successful Aging.   In the 1960s, one group of theorists advanced what has come to be known as **disengagement theory**. They noted that older people retire from jobs, reduce the number of roles they play in society, decrease the number of people with whom they interact, and focus more on issues of immediate concern to them and less on the world at large. Disengagement, these researchers said, is a universal and inevitable process that elderly people welcome because it lets them face death more peacefully, knowing they have put their house in order and are no longer needed (Cumming & Henry, 1961).

As you might expect, this theory has generated more than a little controversy! Another group of theorists proposed **activity theory** as an alternative to disengagement theory. They maintained that older people have essentially the same social and psychological needs as younger people. Disengagement often does occur, they said, but when it does, it occurs contrary to the wishes of most older people (Neugarten, Havighurst, & Tobin, 1968; Lemon, Bengtson, & Peterson, 1972). Forced retirement, health problems, poverty, widowhood, and ageist notions that older people can no longer be productive members of society are responsible for their withdrawal, not age alone or the wishes of the aging. According to these theorists, successful aging involves staying actively involved with other people and with the world at large.

In general, researchers have found that most evidence supports the view that activity is related to happiness in old age. However, the sheer volume of activity may not matter so much as the particular kind of activity. Informal activities with friends and relatives were found to be related to life satisfaction in old age, but formal and solitary activities were not (Neugarten, Havighurst, & Tobin, 1968; Longino & Kart, 1982).

What seems most likely is that there are many different paths to aging, and whether or not they are considered successful depends on the personality of a given individual. One older person might consider frequent social activities to be too hectic and prefer to disengage, whereas another might be happy only if he continued to be as active as he was during middle age. Some people may be delighted that they have time for solitary activities like reading, while others prefer Gray Panther political rallies. The important thing is that society be flexible enough to support older people's wishes and not bar them from making the most of their later years.

THE VIEW FROM THE COUNTRY OF AGE

In concluding this chapter, we would like to take special note of the unique perspective that old age provides. Only from that vantage point can a person take stock of his or her entire life cycle and see how and why events unfolded, for better or worse. People see how they coped over the years with physical and intellectual challenges, with relationships and jobs, and how these combined to make them who they are.

Erikson said that during this time, "the life cycle weaves back on itself" and that people renegotiate tasks of earlier stages in new ways. If people are successful, they can integrate mature "hope, will, purpose, competence, fidelity, love, and care into a comprehensive sense of wisdom" (Erikson, Erikson, & Kivnick, 1986, pp. 55-56).

For those people interested in the life of the mind, wisdom is a much-sought-after commodity. We would do well to remember, however, that older people see empathy and understanding, not age, as the hallmarks of wisdom. A personal journey to the country of age may help us develop these qualities. But we don't have to wait until then to begin.

INTERIORITY
The increased introspection that often occurs as people grow older, especially during middle and late adulthood.

DISENGAGEMENT THEORY
A psychosocial theory that maintains that successful aging depends on the mutual and voluntary withdrawal of an older person from society and of society from the older person.

ACTIVITY THEORY
A psychosocial theory that maintains that successful aging depends on an older person's staying actively involved in society.

Health and a Sense of Control

In 1983, a joint task force of the American Medical Association and the American Nursing Association addressed the question of how to improve health care of chronically ill elderly people. One key conclusion was that having a sense of purpose and control over their lives is essential to the health of the elderly (American Medical Association/ American Nursing Association, 1983). This is a striking assertion, given how many life events assault an older person's sense of control. Increasingly, friends and family members die. An elderly man is forced to retire from his job. Well-intentioned people assist him in crossing the street, and he wonders whether he really wobbles that much. He visits doctors more frequently and often is reinforced for conforming and obedient behavior (Lorber, 1975; Wills, 1978).

If an elderly person doesn't feel in control, it may lead to stress, which is associated with undesirable physical consequences. For one thing, the body produces more catecholamines, which are associated with increased blood pressure and heart rate and with irregular heartbeat. Corticosteroid levels become elevated, and this interferes with the body's ability to regulate blood pressure and metabolize sugar, cholesterol, and other substances involved in atherosclerosis (Hanson, Larson, & Snowden, 1976; Davis et al., 1977). Moreover, the immune system may begin to weaken (Laudenslager, Ryan, Drugan, Hyson, & Maier, 1983).

Many of these changes are evident in everyday life, and dramatic results have been found in studies conducted in natural settings. One study looked at older people who were forced to move from their own deteriorating neighborhood to new, feder-ally subsidized housing. Despite better living conditions, those people forced to move had more hospitalizations, nursing home admissions, strokes, and heart problems, and they rated their health as poorer, than did a control group not forced to move (Kasl, Ostfeld, & Brody, 1980).

In another study, one group of nursing home residents were given more responsibility for daily events at the home, while a matched group were told that the staff would care for them and try to satisfy their needs. At an 18-month follow-up, the "responsible" group showed greater health improvements than did the "attention" group, and only 15 percent of the former subjects had died, compared to 30 percent of the latter (Langer & Rodin, 1976).

TAKING CONTROL

Undertaking a sensible physical exercise program is one way to guarantee increased feelings of control. We stress the word *sensible* because some older people get so enthusiastic about their new program that they do too much too quickly, injure themselves, and end up feeling even less in control.

Here are some general rules for older people contemplating an exercise program (Brody, 1986):

1. *See a doctor.* A checkup is extremely important, especially if you have been relatively sedentary, if you have a chronic health problem, or if you are taking any medicine.
2. *Take it slowly.* Start at a low, comfortable level of exertion and increase in intensity very gradually.

Undertaking a physical exercise program is one way to gain a feeling of control and improve health.

3. *Know your limits.* If you have excessive fatigue, sleep problems, or persistent muscle soreness, you are probably trying to do too much.

4. *Exercise regularly.* Try to exercise three times per week, but stop if you become ill, even if it's only a cold.

5. *Warm up first.* About 10 minutes of warm-up protects the heart, muscles, and joints from injury.

6. *Cool down afterward.* Never stop vigorous exercise abruptly, and never take a hot shower or sauna immediately after a vigorous workout.

There are other things that people can do as well. Have you ever heard of brain aerobics? Here are some recommendations (Lynch, 1986; Smart, 1986):

1. *Don't follow the same route every day.* Take different streets and notice things happening along the way.

2. *Challenge your mental abilities.* Do crossword or spatial-relations puzzles and manual-skill games.

3. *Find a social cause to support vigorously.* Doing so will please idealistic sensitivities.

4. *Write a family history.* You will enjoy doing it, and younger generations will love it.

Most of these recommendations are appropriate for virtually anyone. However, if the person does have a serious illness, it really helps to seek out information about the disease and to enroll in any available self-help courses. "The principal benefit of the course is it gives people hope," one 76-year-old graduate of an arthritis self-help course commented. "I'd expected to go down hill with my arthritis and gradually have to curtail my activities. But they give you confidence that you can decelerate the progress of the disease" (Briley, 1986, p. 43).

Certainly, there are instances when people feel excessively responsible about situations over which they have no control, and this can lead to guilt and self-blame that may find expression in poor physical health. On the whole, however, finding ways to help older people exert control in their lives almost always reaps rewards in both physical and psychological well-being. As author Betty Friedan has said,

We have to be part of change, not deny it, and pay attention to what's going on—the changes in our body and in the outside world. Men and women who deny their age are not open to change. (Friedan, 1994, p. 4)

SUMMARY

- Prejudice and discrimination against the elderly are known as ageism.
- Geriatrics is the branch of medicine concerned with diseases and problems of the elderly; gerontology is the general study of aging.
- By the year 2030, over 20 percent of the U.S. population will be over 65 years of age.
- Older men are almost twice as likely as older women to be married.
- The majority of people over 65 years of age are economically secure; however, over 12% are classified as below the poverty level.
- Senescence is the gradual weakening of the body that begins during early adulthood and continues until we die.
- Diminishing organ reserve and the consequent inability to maintain homeostasis probably accounts for older people's dying from relatively minor illnesses that are rarely life-threatening to younger people.
- Changes in collagen are implicated in processes as diverse as wrinkling and atherosclerosis.
- Glaucoma and cataracts are the two leading causes of blindness in older people.
- The immunological system works by recognizing, isolating, and destroying viruses and other disease-causing microorganisms.
- Alzheimer's disease and multi-infarct dementia are serious and chronic conditions; more treatable conditions, such as depression and side effects from medication, can mimic these dementias.
- Scores on traditional IQ tests may decrease with age because the tests are highly speed sensitive, because the subjects are anxious, or because of terminal drop.
- The most frequent age-related memory deficits occur in recall of information from long-term memory.
- Intellectual plasticity refers to the fact that a person's performance on a test may vary considerably, depending on different social, environmental, and physical conditions.
- Older subjects have been found to score higher than younger subjects on tests of practical problem-solving skills and dialectical thinking.
- The final stage in Erikson's developmental scheme is ego integrity versus despair.
- The process by which people come to terms with their lives and the inevitability of their death is known as the life review.
- Androgyny and interiority generally increase as people get older.
- Four major personality types identified among older subjects are integrated, armored-defended, passive-dependent, and unintegrated.
- Disengagement theory maintains that older people want to withdraw from social activity, while activity theory maintains that successful aging requires that people continue to be actively involved with the world.

QUESTIONS FOR FURTHER DISCUSSION

1. Think of some examples of ageism you have observed. What might be done to correct these misconceptions or injustices?

2. Think of the older people you know. What combination of physical, cognitive, and personality factors do you find in the best adjusted? In the most poorly adjusted?

3. Suppose you could live to be 500 years old and still be healthy and productive. What different lives would you want to lead? Why did you choose these lives?

4. What examples of intellectual plasticity have you encountered in your own life?

SUGGESTIONS FOR FURTHER READING

1. Cole, T. R., Van Tassel, D. D., & Kastenbaum, R. (Eds.). (1992). *Handbook of the humanities and aging*. New York: Springer.

2. Comfort, A. (1990). *Say yes to old age*. New York: Crown.

3. Erikson, E., Erikson, J., & Kivnick, H. (1986). *Vital involvement in old age*. New York: Norton.

4. Friedan, B. (1994). *Fountain of age*. New York: Simon & Schuster.

5. Hayflick, L. (1994). *How and why we age*. New York: Ballantine.

6. Skinner, B. F., & Vaughan, M. (1983). *Enjoy old age*. New York: Norton.

CHAPTER 19

Late Adulthood: Relationships and Retirement

CHAPTER PREVIEW
Some Things We Never Outgrow

Party dresses! Flirtation! Heart palpitations!

It must be an eighth-grade dance, or the junior prom, or a first fraternity party!

No. It's a singles dance at the local senior center!

If the idea of older people dating and falling in love doesn't jibe with your picture of late adulthood, you're out of step with the times. As people are living longer, are staying healthier, and are less likely to live with grown children, the ranks of dating seniors have grown significantly. Researchers interviewed dating couples, ages 60 to 92 years, in a midwestern metropolitan area and were surprised at what they found.

As is the case with younger people, the older daters regularly suffered the "sweaty-palm syndrome." They experienced a heightened sense of reality, awkwardness, problems concentrating, perspiring hands, heart palpitations, and anxiety when the loved one was away. "When you fall in love at my age there's initially a kind of 'oh, gee!' feeling," commented one 68-year-old divorcee. "It's just a little scary" (Bulcroft & O'Conner-Roden, 1986, p. 68).

Like younger people, the older people saw dating as quite distinct from friendship, and they tended to start "going steady" fairly rapidly. They often developed committed, long-term, monogamous relationships, complete with sexual involvement, although they didn't necessarily plan to get married. Also like younger daters, they were selective about what they told their families. "I have a tendency to hide his shoes when my grandchildren are coming over," commented one woman (Bulcroft & O'Conner-Roden, 1986, p. 69).

The older daters enjoyed candlelight dinners, flowers and candy, movies and dances every bit as much as younger daters. Some also reported going camping, enjoying the opera, and flying to Hawaii for the weekend. They said that physical intimacy was certainly important, but experience had taught them not to count on passionate love lasting forever. They knew the value of compassionate love and appreciated passion as "the frosting on the cake" (Bulcroft & O'Conner-Roden, 1986, p. 69).

The next time you find yourself dismissing an older couple as "cute" or believing that romance is only for the young, think twice. Has anyone ever flown with you to Hawaii for a romantic weekend?

In this chapter, we'll look first at relationships in late adulthood—the traditional family and relationships with grown children, grandchildren, siblings, and friends. Then we'll consider the effects of widowhood and divorce in later life. We'll conclude this section with a look at remarriage and at elderly singles. Following that, we'll look at how older people deal with retirement and with newly found leisure time.

RELATIONSHIPS IN LATE ADULTHOOD

Older adults today face a novel situation. Increased longevity means that relationships have the potential of lasting longer than at any other time in history. Families consist of more generations than ever before, and more members are middle-aged and older. In fact, about 1 out of 9 people over 65 years of age have a child who is also *at least* 65 years old (U. S. Bureau of the Census, 1993)!

Having more older family members who have outgrown sibling rivalries and other family conflicts and who have come to appreciate their common family heritage can make for harmonious relationships. It can also make for increased strain as the "younger" people try to care for older infirm relatives when they themselves are dealing with declining health (Aizenberg & Treas, 1985).

Another novel situation is that social peerships that have nothing to do with chronological age have sprung up. Early retirement means that younger people now deal with issues traditionally assigned to the old. The increase in adult education means that children, grandchildren, parents, and grandparents all may be students at the same time (Aizenberg & Treas, 1985). And now that romance among older people is out of the closet, grandmothers and granddaughters may shop together for their respective party dresses.

Older people try their best to adjust to these novelties. But there are few norms and guidelines for these changes, and that inevitably creates anxiety. It also creates excitement as older people try to transmit to younger people the best of the past while enjoying new ways of relating made possible by the present.

Let's look now at the traditional family in late adulthood.

THE TRADITIONAL FAMILY

In Chapters 15 and 17, we looked at the first six stages of the family life cycle as defined by David Olson, Hamilton McCubbin, and their colleagues in their cross-sectional research on intact families (1983). We now come to their seventh and final stage, families in retirement (see Figure 19.1).

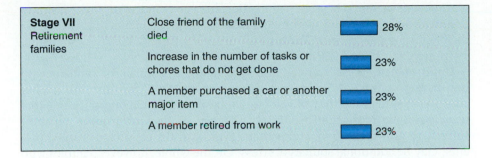

Stage VII Retirement families	Close friend of the family died	28%
	Increase in the number of tasks or chores that do not get done	23%
	A member purchased a car or another major item	23%
	A member retired from work	23%

FIGURE 19.1

Profile of family stresses and strains in late adulthood. The top four stressors are listed. (SOURCE: Adapted from Olson et al., 1983, p. 130)

Olson and McCubbin's stage VII families had been married an average of 42 years. The average ages of husbands and wives were 71 and 68 years, respectively. Families had an average of three children, and the average age of the oldest was 41 years. Although all these couples considered themselves retired, 20 percent of the men and 4 percent of the women were still employed full-time.

As might be expected, families at this stage weren't so pressured to try to get necessary chores done, but many did report financial problems, and increasingly they were confronted by the illnesses and deaths of loved ones. These couples reported high levels of marital satisfaction, with only 3 percent of the wives and none of the husbands saying they had ever considered separation or divorce.

Research reporting high levels of marital satisfaction among older couples has suffered from many methodological problems. Most studies are cross-sectional, and few distinguish between long-term marriages and remarriages. As we mentioned, selective attrition of subjects through divorce may leave only the happiest of couples to be interviewed. Furthermore, older people may be reluctant to admit that their marriages are unhappy, given how long they've spent in them.

Although these methodological problems limit the degree of confidence we can have in the findings, the research does suggest that the increase in marital satisfaction, which begins during the postparental stage, continues into old age (Miller, 1976; Anderson, Russell, & Schumm, 1983). "Golden wedding" couples, those who have been married at least 50 years, report very high levels of

Couples who celebrate fiftieth wedding anniversaries usually say their marriages are very happy.

marital satisfaction. They cite companionship, give and take, little desire to dominate each other, and working together as major elements that have made their marriages successful (Parron & Troll, 1978; Sporakowski & Hughston, 1978; Roberts, 1979–1980).

Unfortunately, these couples also experience a number of problems. Ill health may make one partner so dependent on the other that his or her self-esteem suffers and the caregiver is overburdened. The reduced income that usually follows retirement may cause financial strain. Furthermore, relationships with grown children, and perhaps even with the couple's own aged parents, may be additional sources of stress. On the whole, however, couples who have a history of working together and supporting each other usually are able to weather these storms and perhaps even to strengthen their own relationships because of them.

RELATIONSHIPS WITH GROWN CHILDREN

As we noted in Chapter 17, contrary to popular belief, older people generally do not want to live with their children. Moreover, most adult children provide every bit as much care and support to their aging parents as in the "good old days," and most older people do not feel abandoned.

About 80 percent of people 65 years and older have living children (Shanas, 1979a, 1979b, 1980), and about 90 percent of these have frequent contact with the children (Brubaker, 1985). About 75 percent of noninstitutionalized elderly parents live within 30 minutes of at least one of their children (Shanas, 1979a, 1979b, 1980).

Merely having contact with sons and daughters does not guarantee happiness and well-being in old age (Glenn & McLanahan, 1981; Lee & Ellithorpe, 1982). In fact, some research has found that those people who are most involved with their families have the lowest morale (Troll, 1985). This does not necessarily mean that you and your parents would be happier if you stayed away from one another! Before you decide never to have children or to abandon your family, remember that ill health often makes older people more dependent and thereby increases contact with family members. So it is more likely the poor health, not just the family involvement, that decreases morale.

Increasingly, researchers have begun to look at the *quality* of relationships, rather than at the frequency of contact, between the elderly and their adult children. If parents and children share interests and values and agree on child-rearing practices, treatment of siblings, intergenerational get-togethers, and religious commitments, they are likely to enjoy each other's company (Aldous, Klaus, & Klein, 1985). Disagreements on such matters can understandably cause problems. If parents are angered by their daughter's divorce, dislike her new husband, and disapprove of how she's raising their grandchildren, chances are they're not going to enjoy her visits.

The increased mobility in our society has resulted in many grown children being separated from their parents, often by long distances. In one study, almost one-half of the elderly parents had at least one child living over 150 miles away, and one-third had a child over 500 miles away (Schooler, 1979). Daughters and sons with more money and education tend to move farther away, and they often make their moves in early adulthood (Cicirelli, 1981). Although these parents and children visit less frequently, they usually stay in fairly close touch by telephone and mail. The content of these contacts is probably less important than the fact that they occur. Emotional ties certainly can be maintained despite geographical distance (Litwak et al., 1981), and brief letters or telephone conversations can convey a broad range of feelings. Probably the hardest part of living far away is that it is more difficult for parents and their children to assess each other's needs. This can lead to unrealistic worries and feelings of guilt that "I ought to be doing more for them, but what?"

When older people have to go live with one of their children, it is usually necessitated by the parent's failing health. Reactions among the elderly can vary, but most feel grateful for having someone to care for them, sad and angry about needing the care, and distressed about leaving their own homes. Most of all, parents usually worry about being a burden and want to contribute whatever they can to the household. One researcher told how his grandfather insisted on making the family breakfast and doing the dishes every morning. As "Grandpa Engstrom" got older, his family tried to retire him from his role because "his cataracts made the source of ingredients for the daily breakfast an increasing source of surprise!" (Bengtson, 1985, p. 20).

RELATIONSHIPS WITH GRANDCHILDREN

Our culture tends to romanticize grandparenting. We say that it provides older people with a sense of immortality and younger people with a tie to the past, which, in many cases, it does. However, this stereotype overlooks the fact that grandparents are an extremely heterogeneous group of people, and the experience of being a grandparent can mean many different things. "I could break my daughter's neck for having this baby," commented one 29-year-old grandmother (that's right, 29!). "I just got a new boyfriend. Now he will think I'm too old" (Burton, 1985, p. 1).

As with many major life experiences, we feel better about becoming grandparents if we do so "on time." And while we normally think of grandparenting as an experience of late adulthood, on the average, women now become grandmothers at age 50 years, and men become grandfathers at 52 years (Troll, 1983).

Grandchildren often provide grandparents with a sense of immortality.

AT ISSUE

Are Age Wars on the Horizon?

Age Wars: The Coming Battle Between Young and Old. *Futurist* magazine

The Coming Conflict as We Soak the Young to Enrich the Old *The Washington Post*

Headlines like these suggest that conflict between the generations is brewing on a far greater scale than during the Vietnam War protests of the 1960s. Back then, differences in social and political values pitted the generations against each other; but some people argue that in the future, economic pressures are going to pit them against each other in something akin to generational warfare (Carlson, 1987).

ECONOMIC PRESSURES

In 1984, Samuel Preston, chairman of the University of Pennsylvania's sociology department, made a highly controversial speech about "intergenerational inequity"—the idea that older people benefit more from government spending, while young workers, new families starting out, and children get short-changed. Preston pointed out that the poverty rate for children had soared, reaching 21 percent in 1985. Meanwhile, the poverty rate for older people had declined, leveling off at about 13 percent (Carlson, 1987). As of 1991, these percentages were esentially unchanged (U. S. Bureau of the Census, 1993).

Preston argued that the deteriorating situation of children could be understood only in light of the fact that our national priorities are now dictated by our aging population. The elderly vote in large numbers, he said, but children can't vote. They must rely on the political power of their parents, and increasingly one parent is missing. Only 38 percent of voters now live with a child. As a result, Preston maintained, more of our resources go to the elderly at the expense of children. It remains an appalling and shameful fact that in the richest nation on this planet, 1 out of every 5 children live in poverty. This has led some people to conclude that Americans don't like children very much, unless they are their own. Moreover, we will reap the tragedy of this neglect in a single generation when these children add to the crime rate and continue the cycle of poverty with their own children.

Preston's position has gained some support, as people point to the fact that Social Security payments have jumped 46 percent in real terms since 1970. Social Security and Medicare now account for almost 30 percent of federal expenditures, and these programs are the largest nondefense item in the national budget (U. S. Bureau of the Census, 1993). Younger workers have to pay high payroll taxes to support the Social Security and Medicare systems, goes the argument, but these workers may not get a fair return on their money when they retire in the next century (Carlson, 1987).

CORRECTING THE INEQUITIES

A rather extreme way to correct these inequities was proposed by Richard Lamm, former governor of Colorado, when he questioned whether the large sums of money spent on extraordinary medical procedures to prolong the lives of the elderly might not be better spent on needy children. Other people, however, have vehemently attacked the idea that there is a causal relationship between the improved plight of the elderly and the deteriorated circumstances of children. "That's like saying that government spends a lot on the elderly and nothing to control acid rain, so old folks must be the cause of acid rain," declared Senator Dave Durenberger (Carlson, 1987, p. 36).

A national survey of 2,000 people ages 21 years and older found little evidence of intergenerational tension (The Daniel Yankelovich Group, Inc., 1987). In fact, mutual respect and concern among the generations were abundantly evident. The elderly were seen as a group needing and deserving assistance, and this perception was most widely held by the youngest groups surveyed. Conversely, older people expressed even more concern than the young themselves for the struggles faced by young families—a lackluster economy, prohibitive housing costs, and pressures on two-earner couples. People of all ages expressed a wish to assist children living in poverty. Most people believed that both the energy of the young and the experience of the elderly are needed to solve the country's problems. Only 13 percent believed that older workers should retire early to make room for the young.

When tensions did exist, they were due more to social-class divisions than to age. Low-income, poorly educated people were more likely to harbor resentments against groups such as the elderly, whom they perceived to be better off or better cared for than themselves. The researchers stressed, however, that on most measures, lower-income people showed greater commitment to family responsibility than did the other groups. The researchers speculated that the anti-elderly sentiment might have come about because these people feared they would not have enough resources to take care of their own immediate families.

Finally, although older people were less inclined than other groups to favor more funding for education, the vast majority of all age-groups agreed that funding should be continued for Medicare and that more should be done for children living in poverty and for the homeless. In short, there was strong evidence that people of different generations were searching for ways to continue to care for one another and virtually no support for the idea that intergenerational warfare was looming on the horizon.

Types of Grandparents

A classic study done in the 1960s described the following types of grandparents (Neugarten & Weinstein, 1964):

1. *The formal grandparent:* a grandparent who is not involved in the daily care of the grandchildren, although he or she might occasionally baby-sit
2. *The fun seeker:* a grandparent who is essentially a playmate
3. *The surrogate parent:* a grandparent who has a great deal of caretaking responsibility, often because the grandchildren's parents both work or are otherwise unavailable
4. *The reservoir of family wisdom:* a grandparent who is the family authority figure, whose knowledge is valued and respected
5. *The distant figure:* a grandparent who has little contact with the grandchildren other than perhaps on holidays and birthdays

Benefits that Grandparents Provide and Derive

Despite their heterogeneity, grandparents often do perform some common functions. By simply being there, they serve as family *stabilizers*. They provide a buffer against their own children's feelings of mortality, and contact between mothers and grandmothers often increases the mother's warmth and sense of competence as a parent (Abernathy, 1973; Hagestad, 1985). In addition, older grandparents especially may foster family *cohesion*, as their birthdays and holidays provide convenient excuses for family members to get together.

Another common function is that of family *watchdog*. In this role, aging parents usually don't play an active part in their children's and grandchildren's lives. Rather, they stand on the sidelines keeping watch. When a crisis such as a divorce or serious illness occurs, they rush to the rescue, providing both emotional and practical support (Troll, 1983).

The experience of grandparenting varies greatly from one person to another. Some studies have found little relationship between grandparenting and life satisfaction (Blau, 1973; Wood & Robertson, 1976). Others have found that grandchildren provide grandparents with feelings of creativity, accomplishment, and competence, as well as a reconfirmation of their own identity, and a sense of immortality (Timberlake, 1980).

Helen Kivnick, who worked with the Eriksons on their project on old age, maintains that grandparenting facilitates personality development in late adulthood. It provides opportunities, she says, for older people to rework the tasks and come to age-appropriate balances for psychosocial tensions of earlier developmental stages. For example, mutual love and security between grandparents and grandchildren may enable grandparents to establish a new balance between intimacy and isolation. Dealing with issues of authority and responsibility may help them achieve a new balance between generativity and stagnation (Kivnick, 1981, 1985).

To some extent, grandparents might spoil the grandchildren, but this is typically part of our romanticized view of grandparents. However, grandparents do buy a large portion of the expensive toys and clothing sold in "grandmother boutiques" in upscale department stores. Moreover, many offer practical financial help. For example, Duquesne University enables alumni to prepay discounted tuition for children, many of whom are nowhere near college age. Over 10 percent of those people taking advantage of the program have been paying for grandchildren (Deutsch, 1986). Moreover, even grandparents of modest means have been known to maintain that their grandchildren can do no wrong, and parents often complain that their children are impossible to live with after a grandparent's visit.

The Effects of Divorce

Ties between maternal grandparents and grandchildren usually are strengthened following a divorce because the mother typically gets custody of the children, and she often needs practical help from her parents. However, ties with paternal grandparents usually are weakened (Furstenberg, Nord, Peterson, & Zill, 1983).

In some bitter divorces, the custodial parent may forbid the ex-spouse's parents from seeing their grandchildren at all. It has been estimated that grandparents have filed as many as 50,000 lawsuits because of this. Some grandparents have actually sought custody, but most have merely sought the right to visit, to send letters and birthday cards, and to receive an occasional picture of their grandchildren.

Most states now have laws granting grandparents the right to petition to visit their grandchildren. If these laws have to be invoked, however, family relations have probably deteriorated so much that the grandchildren may feel disloyal to their parent if they enjoy a court-won visit with their grandparents (Demkovich, 1986).

RELATIONSHIPS WITH SIBLINGS

Most older people have at least one living sibling, and this relationship is likely to be the longest-lasting one of their lives (Cicirelli, 1980; Scott, 1983). Older siblings usually visit each other several times a year, although the frequency tends to decrease as they age (Cicirelli, 1982).

In one study, siblings ages 70 to 92 years reported a stronger sense of family unity and saw each other as friends and confidants more often than did younger ones. A few reported that feelings of closeness first developed during adulthood. However, memories of shared childhood experiences, which may have emerged as the brothers and sisters conducted their individual life reviews, often drew the siblings closer together (Ross & Milgram, 1982).

Sibling relationships usually are the longest-lasting relationships of a person's life.

In time of need, older siblings often turn to each other, especially if a spouse or an adult child is not available. Sisters have been found to be more influential than brothers in their family systems. They often provide emotional support for the brothers, which seems to help buffer the men against the strain of aging, and they prod their sisters to stay active and in touch with the world at large (Cicirelli, 1977).

When a sibling dies, the surviving brothers and sisters are inevitably reminded of their own mortality, especially if the deceased is not the oldest (Brubaker, 1985). As we mentioned in Chapter 17, such a death almost always brings the surviving siblings closer together, as they realize that they have only a limited amount of time left to mend fences and share lives (Ross & Milgram, 1982).

FRIENDSHIPS IN LATER LIFE

We noted earlier that having children and grandchildren does not guarantee happiness and well-being in old age (Glenn & McLanahan, 1981; Lee & Ellithorpe, 1982; Keith, 1983). However, satisfaction and happiness in later life are consistently associated with having friends (Davidson & Cotter, 1982). Friends provide us with acceptance, support, and companionship, which are as vital to our sense of self-worth in late adulthood as they are when we are younger (Roberto & Scott, 1986). Although we share a gene pool and family heritage with our siblings, we may share more interests with our friends and trust them more as confidants.

Older women usually have a wider circle of friends than do older men, who rely mainly on their wives for support and companionship. Older men, however, report more cross-sexed friendships. The women say there just aren't many men around with whom to be friends, and they worry about what their friends will think. When asked how often her male friend visited her, one woman replied, "I don't let him in my apartment. It wouldn't be proper. People would talk" (Adams, 1985, p. 607). She was right about the last point. Some women at the local senior center told researchers that this woman was "fast" and was "always running around!"

Let's turn now to the event that most frequently disrupts family relationships in later life—the death of a spouse.

WIDOWS AND WIDOWERS

On their scale of stressful life events, Holmes and Rahe assigned the most points to death of a spouse. Although we normally think of this as an event of late adulthood, about one-half of all married women are widowed by their mid-50s (Balkwell, 1981). At all age levels, widows greatly outnumber widowers. By 1992, in the group of people aged 65 years and older, there were more than 8.6 million widows in the United States, compared to only 1.9 million widowers (U.S. Bureau of the Census, 1993).

Sometimes, widowhood comes unexpectedly, as when the spouse dies in a car accident or of a sudden heart attack. Sometimes it is anticipated, as when it comes after an increasingly debilitating illness that may have dominated the couple's life for many years. In most cases, however, the spouse has been ill for quite some time, but the illness has not been immediately life-threatening. The possibility of death may have been considered, but when it actually occurs, it is still quite a shock (Bowling & Cartwright, 1982). Reactions of the surviving spouse vary greatly, depending on the nature of the marital relationship, the circumstances leading up to the death, and the coping resources of the survivor. Most people usually go through some fairly predictable stages as they try to adjust to their loss; we'll look at these in Chapter 20.

Widows and widowers are not necessarily isolated. Immediately after the death, friends and relatives rally around, offering both practical and emotional support. As time goes on, people return to their regular routines, and the bereaved are expected to carry on by themselves, and some may become isolated then. However, many widows actually have more social interactions with friends, neighbors, and family members than they had while their husbands were alive. This is especially true for healthier, better-educated widows with higher incomes (Lopata, 1973; 1979; Atchley, 1975).

When decreases in social participation occur, they usually come 5 or more years after the spouse's death, and they are due more to factors such as poverty and poor health, than to widowhood alone (Harvey & Bahr, 1974). In one large British study, one-half of the widowed people who lived alone said that loneliness was a major problem for them (Bowling & Cartwright, 1982).

Older widowers tend to be better off financially than widows, and their remarriage rate is about 20 per 1,000, compared to 2 per 1000 for widows (Glick, 1979). Moreover, they tend not to express as much emotional difficulty adjusting to the loss of their spouse (Bowling & Cartwright, 1982). But, by other measures, widowers seem to have a harder time adjusting to the loss than do widows. They often find dealing with practical demands, such as cooking and housekeeping, extremely difficult. Moreover, although social involvement usually increases for widows, it often does not change significantly for widowers. One study found that only 39 percent of widowers, compared to 68 percent of widows, reported a great deal of satisfaction from their family lives (Hyman, 1983). And whereas groups such as Widows to Widows provide emotional support and concrete help to widows seeking to establish a new life, support groups and role models for widowers are practically nonexistent (Brubaker, 1985).

Divorce in Later Life

Most people do not get divorced in late adulthood. Most couples apparently figure that since they've made it this far, they'll stay together no matter what. Current estimates are that about 3 percent of men and 4 percent of women over 65 years of age are divorced and have not remarried, but data on the age at which these people got divorced are not available (U.S. Bureau of the Census, 1993).

The little research that exists on older divorced men and women suggests that they are markedly less happy and more pessimistic about life than are their married or widowed counterparts. Older widows have been found to have lower incomes than older divorcees, but the latter expressed more dissatisfaction with their financial situation. Divorced men expressed even more dissatisfaction with their finances than did either group of women (Hyman, 1983).

Divorced men also were extremely isolated, much more so than divorced women. They were more likely to socialize at bars or taverns than were married or widowed people or divorced women, and they reported less satisfaction with family life and friendships (Hyman, 1983). Another study found higher rates of mental illness and death for older divorced people, men and women alike (Uhlenberg & Myers, 1981).

REMARRIAGE AND COHABITATION

As we saw in our Chapter Preview, romance can sweep us off our feet at virtually any age. Some older people are reluctant to remarry, however, because they fear having to take care of a new spouse, a role that many of them have only recently relinquished with their prior spouse.

Although the number of people over 65 who remarry is relatively small (around 3 or 4 percent of the population remarries after age 65), at least two studies have found that these marriages tend to be very happy indeed. Most of the subjects had been widowed and had known each other during their previous marriages. Many said that companionship was a primary reason they chose to remarry. The happiest couples tended to have their friends' approval for the marriage, had adequate money and satisfactory housing, and had adjusted well to the demands and changes of aging (McKain, 1972; Vinick, 1978).

During the 1970s, elderly cohabitation received a fair bit of media attention. Many people reasoned that it made economic sense to live together rather than remarry, because Social Security benefits and sometimes pensions were more favorable if a person was not married. In 1970, about 22 percent of the cohabitants in the United States were 65 years of age and older. For reasons that are unclear, however, this percentage decreased to 5 percent by 1992, and the absolute numbers also decreased by about 12,000 (U.S. Bureau of the Census, 1993).

ELDERLY SINGLES

The proportion of older men and women who have never married has declined dramatically in recent years. Between 1970 and 1992, there was a 64 percent drop in the proportion of never-married men over 65 years of age and a 45 percent decline in women of that age (U.S. Department of Commerce, 1983; U.S. Bureau of the Census, 1993). Part of this decrease may be due to the removal, for the most part, of the stigma elderly couples once encountered when dating and marrying.

Not much research has been done on elderly singles. One study reported that its 22 subjects were lifelong isolates (Gubrium, 1975). However, more recent studies have found that many elderly singles have rich social networks (Rubinstein, 1987). In general, elderly singles tend to be independent and to express considerable satisfaction with their lives.

Let's turn now to the subject of retirement and to the many different activities people find to fill their leisure time.

RETIREMENT

Retirement on a large scale is a twentieth-century phenomenon. At the turn of the century, two-thirds of all men 65 years and older were still working, compared to about one-third in the early 1990s. Moreover, very few of those who did not work had enough money to retire comfortably. They quit working only because of poor health or because employers felt that they were too old to be productive (Parnes & Less, 1985a).

In 1935, the U.S. Congress passed the Social Security Act, which set the "normal" retirement age at 65 years. Today, Social Security provides retirement benefits for over 90 percent of the labor force. People can begin collecting ben-

Some of the happiest later-life marriages are between people who have been friends for many years.

Some people become idle when they retire and have too much time on their hands.

efits at age 62 years, or even earlier if they are completely disabled. In addition, private employers now provide pensions for about one-half of all wage and salary workers, and they often encourage older people to retire early to make room for less expensive younger employees. The net result of these social changes has been a move toward early retirement. Almost half of the men in the labor force retire by age 62 years (Parnes & Less, 1985a).

Interestingly, many social forces are now putting pressure in the opposite direction from the trend toward early retirement. Older employees who want to keep working have challenged mandatory retirement at age 65 years, and many companies have moved the age limit to 70 years.

The Decision to Retire

There are many different reasons people choose to retire. On the positive side, having enough money to live comfortably as a result of pensions, Social Security, and savings is a strong inducement to retire. People often want to spend more time with their families or are eager to pursue certain activities. On the negative side, poor health forces many people to retire, often against their wishes.

The occupation itself also plays a key role. Men in high-status, white-collar occupations tend to retire later than those in blue-collar occupations (Hardy, 1985). It is understandable that blue-collar workers might *choose* early retirement, because many of their jobs involve mundane tasks and heavy physical labor that gets harder as they get older (Hayward & Hardy, 1985). However, these workers usually do not have as much control over the retirement decision as do white-collar workers. Some are forced to retire, even though they *need* to continue working for financial reasons or *want* to continue working to feel productive.

Just as high school students must plan for college, so workers need to plan for retirement. Some companies offer retirement-planning seminars, but these usually are for white-collar workers, who probably need them less than blue-collar workers do. Anyone who is considering retiring should give careful thought to the questions in Table 19.1.

Table 19.1 ● Is Retirement For You?

1. Can you afford to retire? (Most retirement planners say that people need 80 percent of their preretirement income to maintain their accustomed standard of living.)
2. Do you dislike what you are doing now?
3. Do you have a consuming hobby or avocation you'd like to put more time into?
4. Will your health let you enjoy retirement?
5. Is your spouse completely in favor of your retiring?
6. Do you feel you've reached a plateau in your job?
7. Will you enjoy your other activities as much as you now enjoy your job?
8. After being retired awhile, would you have much to offer a prospective employer?
9. Would you be able to get up to speed as fast as a rival candidate who is working?
10. Could you set up an appealing, viable business at home?

- People who respond with a definite "yes" to all or nearly all the questions will probably do well when they retire.
- People who respond several times with "I'm not sure" probably should consult a retirement counselor and reconsider all aspects of the decision carefully.
- People who respond with a definite "no" to almost all the first seven questions and with "yes" to the last three are likely to find themselves among the ranks of retirees who return to work.

Source: Adapted from Bell, 1986.

Experiencing and Adapting to Retirement

Retirement means different things to different people. Researchers once interviewed subjects 1 month prior to, and 6 to 8 months following, retirement. They identified four major ways their subjects experienced and adapted to retirement (Hornstein & Wapner, 1985).

Some people experienced retirement as a *transition to old age*. It was a time to wind down, decrease activities, and settle into a quiet and more limited lifestyle. They wanted to rest, to reflect, and to put their lives in order, and they quietly accepted the end of their lives as working people. They were attuned to the inevitability of death and had a sense that the future was shrinking.

In marked contrast to these subjects, other people saw retirement as a *new beginning*, a time of revitalization, enthusiasm, and increased energy. These people saw the future as an expanding universe, filled with opportunities for them to do the things they had always wanted to do. They tended to deny the aging process and did not identify with "old people" or even with "retirees."

For the third group, retirement meant *continuation*. These people simply kept on doing what they had been doing, although in a less pressured, more satisfying way. For some subjects, this meant switching from full- to part-time work or being self-employed rather than working for a company. For other people, it meant focusing on activities other than work. One man, for example, retired from his job as a technician to devote more time to his role as town treasurer and community spokesperson.

The final group experienced retirement as an *imposed disruption*, the loss of a highly valued activity. Most of these people so identified with their jobs that when they stopped working, they felt they'd lost part of themselves. Some of them tried new activities and established new routines, but these never quite provided a real sense of accomplishment, and these retirees continued to experience an underlying sense of frustration.

These categories must be viewed as preliminary because they are based on a small sample of workers. However, they provide a beginning for conceptualizing the different ways people feel and adjust during the first few months of this major life transition.

Retirement Satisfaction

As is the case with perception of old age in general, people who are still working view retirement much more negatively than do those who have already
retired, as we can see in Table 19.2. Forty percent of people in this survey
reported that retirement was better than they had anticipated. Other studies
have reported that most retirees are happy and would choose to retire at the
same age if they had to do it over again (Parnes & Less, 1985a).

As we've seen, whether the decision is made voluntarily or involuntarily
plays a major role in how people react, at least initially. Being forced out of a
job because someone thinks you're too old or because your health is failing can
be a major psychological trauma. Fortunately, less than one-half of all retire-
ments are in any sense involuntary (Parnes & Nestel, 1981).

Good health and adequate finances are key factors in retirement satisfaction, as are feelings of self-worth, the development and maintenance of stable
relationships, and a sense of purposeful activity. Furthermore, different
retirees may look for different things. Rural retirees, for example, said that
high-quality relationships, frequent aid from confidants and relatives, and
involvement in organizations greatly aided their adjustment to retirement
(Dorfman, Kohout, & Heckert, 1985), while college professors pointed to
continued involvement in selected professional activities (Conner, Dorfman,
& Tompkins, 1985).

The Effect of Retirement on Marriage.   The stereotype of the disastrous
retirement is that of an aimless man following his wife around, asking her what
he can do next. With more and more women working outside the home, however, husbands may not have anyone to follow around—many retire before
their wives do.

As is the case when children leave home, retirement highlights both the positive and negative aspects of a couple's relationship. In one study of over 200
middle-class couples, the subjects placed a high value on intimacy and family
ties and said that retirement gave them the freedom to enjoy each other (Atchley & Miller, 1983). In general, the marital relationship is strengthened when
the spouse helps the retiree feel good about him- or herself and about the decision to retire. If the spouse conveys the message that the retiree is in the way
or is unproductive, however, then the marriage is likely to suffer (Ade-Ridder
& Brubaker, 1983).

Women who expect their retired husbands to help with the housework may
be disappointed. Although wives sometimes organize their activities around
their husband's new schedule, couples usually simply continue the patterns
established before retirement (Keating & Cole, 1980). Wives generally keep on
cooking, cleaning, and doing other "inside" tasks, while husbands typically are

Table 19.2 ● Problems of Retirement

PROBLEM	PERCENT OF WORKERS ANTICIPATING PROBLEM	PERCENT OF RETIREES REPORTING PROBLEM
Money	66	25
Loneliness	33	22
Boredom	33	19
Cutting back on extras	32	15

Source: "Is Retirement Really So Bad?" 1987.

responsible for "outside" activities such as gardening and taking out the garbage (Szinovacz, 1980).

Retirement Activities

The Working Retired. In 1986, newspapers across the United States carried stories about 79-year-old Rear Admiral Grace Hopper, standing on the deck of the USS *Constitution,* ending her tenure as the nation's oldest active-duty naval officer. Less than 1 month later, those same newspapers announced Rear Admiral Hopper's employment as a senior consultant to a major computer company. She had retired once before in 1967, but it didn't last then either! ("Computer Admiral," 1986; Cushman, 1986).

Many people deal with retirement in the same way as Rear Admiral Hopper—they go back to either full- or part-time jobs. In the 15-year National Longitudinal Surveys (NLS) of older men, 1 out of 7 men ages 62 to 74 years had never retired, and 30 percent of these vowed they never would (Parnes, 1985). Other surveys have found that as many as one-third of the retired men work at some point during their retirement (Beck, 1985).

In the NLS sample, college graduates were the ones most likely to keep working, but the second largest group consisted of men who had not completed high school. Most of the men enjoyed above-average health, although about one-fourth reported substantial or severe health problems. Chief occupations represented were agriculture, finance, and miscellaneous services, and a large proportion of the men were self-employed (Parnes & Less, 1985b).

Many corporations are now recruiting retirees because these people have valued skills, are stable employees, and relate better to older customers. The McDonald's Corporation, for example, has instituted a McMasters program for prospective employees aged 55 years and older, and Corning Glass Works hires retirees for short-term projects (American Association of Retired Persons, 1987). Senior job fairs are held in many cities, and many seniors organizations offer employment services.

Some people choose not to retire because work defines their identity.

Some people keep working even though they could retire comfortably because work *defines their identity*. "Acting is my life," commented 72-year-old actress Mary Martin shortly before she died. "Why was I given talent if not to use it as long as I can?" Some people keep working because they *enjoy what they do*. At 66 years of age, the late Isaac Asimov, who had written over 300 science fact and fiction books, stated that for the last 30 years, he had been "on one long vacation," writing only about things that interested him. Yet other people work to satisfy a *creative drive*. Dr. Linus Pauling, winner of Nobel prizes for peace and chemistry, at 85 years of age stated, "I keep working because there is always the chance that I will think of something new."

Some people keep working because there are *still goals to accomplish*. At 86 years of age, U.S. Representative Claude Pepper was working to increase health coverage and to protect the elderly against abuse. "I want to get that done in the time I have left," he commented. For still other people, work provides *emotional rewards*; indeed, some even see it as the mainspring of life. At 71 years of age, Dr. Jonas Salk, discoverer of the Salk polio vaccine, commented, "We are, or should be, constantly revitalized by what we do, which is why looking forward to retirement and seeking to do nothing can be fatal" (Lobsenz, 1986, pp. 16–17). In 1993, Salk's new vaccine for AIDS underwent testing. Although in 1994 the vaccine was shown not to be successful, the effort did provide valuable information that might eventually yield an effective vaccine.

Paid work, however, is clearly not for everyone. Some prefer to offer their services free of charge.

Volunteer Work.   In the past, volunteer work usually was done by young and middle-aged homemakers. Today, with so many of these women in the paid labor force, organizations often look to retirees to perform vital volunteer jobs. Almost 38 percent of all people over 50 years of age do some kind of volunteer work (U.S. Bureau of the Census, 1993). Some of them seek jobs that teach them new skills, while others find positions where they can share the expertise they've developed over the years.

In recent years, many organizations that match older volunteers with jobs have been established. For example, the Service Corps of Retired Executives (SCORE) provides consultants for small-business operators, while the National Executive Service Corps provides consultants to nonprofit organizations. Volunteers Intervening for Equity trains older people to be advocates with different social agencies on behalf of people needing help ("Volunteering Comes of Age," 1987). The American Association of Retired Persons operates a Volunteer Talent Bank that matches volunteers with jobs within AARP and other organizations. Sixty percent of its registrants are men, and they range in age from 50 to 90 years (Brodsky, 1987).

Volunteers repeatedly stress that they gain as much as they give. "If it weren't for volunteer activities, I'd have gone out of my mind after my husband died," commented one woman. "But soon I was back guiding tours" (Brodsky, 1987, p. 46). Not only that, but she also soon received training to work with other recently widowed women. Besides providing an opportunity to contribute to other people, volunteer work fulfills personal needs, leads to substantial growth, and sometimes even serves as a training ground for a new career.

Education.   In June of 1987, George Gibson, Jr., 88 years of age, received his high school diploma in Mount Vernon, New York. Having dropped out of school 76 years earlier, Gibson had returned to get his diploma in order to receive credit for college courses he had been auditing (McGeary, 1987).

For many people, the wish to continue learning never ceases, and increasingly retirees are appearing on college campuses. Many colleges offer reduced tuition to older people, and some even waive tuition entirely in courses where space is available (Dietz, 1986). In fact, some programs are especially designed for older people. In 1975, five New Hampshire colleges began the Elderhostel program, which has grown into a nationwide nonprofit organization offering older people the chance to live on college campuses and take up to three non-credit courses at a time. Elderhostels offer a diverse selection of courses, including creative writing, history, ethnic issues, opera, and solar energy. The student body also is quite diverse. In terms of educational background, some students never attended high school, while others hold advanced degrees.

Comparable programs have sprung up in many other countries as well. At three major universities in Israel, for example, not only do the older students enjoy learning, but many do volunteer jobs such as translating materials from foreign languages into Hebrew, teaching Hebrew to students who are immigrants, and reading to blind students (Glanz & Tabory, 1985).

Virtually all the programs provide a nonpressured environment, opportunities for class participation, a structure appropriate to the social needs of the students, and a gradual introduction of new information (Peacock & Talley, 1985).

Leisure Competence.   So far we've presented a multitude of ways retirees can stay busy. But what about those people who just want to relax? Overworked young and middle-aged people long for the day when they'll be free to do nothing, and retirement certainly should provide opportunities for *rest and restoration*. After all, pausing to recoup energy is essential for physical and mental

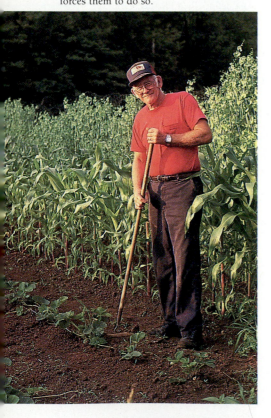

Many farmers retire only when their health forces them to do so.

health at any age. Used well, the retiree's newly found leisure time also can provide *spiritual renewal*. This might mean making or renewing religious commitment, getting to know oneself better, developing trust in oneself and other people, or gaining a heightened awareness of other people and the world at large. Leisure time also may allow for *self-realization*, which usually involves some degree of meaningful activity. Finally, it should provide a chance for *entertainment* (Peacock & Talley, 1985).

Working, volunteering, learning, and relaxing—all these activities have an important place in a retiree's life. Without the first three, however, it is unlikely that any amount of traveling, watching television, playing golf, or cheering on favorite athletes will be ultimately satisfying. In the words of Alex Comfort, "You can read and play shuffleboard just so long!" (Comfort, 1976, p. 179).

Stopping Elder Abuse

A 74-year-old New Jersey woman was beaten and raped by her son-in-law. Her daughter threatened her with the loss of her home if she told anyone.

A bedridden woman in her 70s lay in her own waste for several months, covered with maggots. She was found by a protective services worker only a few hours before she died. (Fisher, 1985, p. 24)

Stories like these outrage, but no longer surprise, us. Out of the research on family violence that began in the 1960s came the realization that it is not only children and wives who are abused, but elderly people as well (Rathbone-McCuan & Goodstein, 1985).

CATEGORIES OF ELDER ABUSE

In 1981, the Congressional Select Committee on Aging delineated six categories of elder abuse (Giordano & Giordano, 1984):

1. *Physical abuse:* violence resulting in bodily harm or mental distress. This includes assaults, denial of rights, sexual abuse, restrictions on freedom of movement, and murder.
2. *Negligence:* the breach of duty or carelessness that results in injury or the violation of rights
3. *Financial exploitation:* the theft or conversion of money or objects of value belonging to an elderly person by a relative or caretaker, which is accomplished by force or misrepresentation
4. *Psychological abuse:* the provoking of the fear of violence or isolation, including name calling, other verbal assaults, or threats of placement in a nursing home
5. *Violations of rights:* the breach of rights that are guaranteed to all citizens by the Constitution, by federal statutes, by federal courts, and by state laws

6. *Self-neglect:* self-inflicted physical harm and the failure to take care of personal needs. It stems from the elderly person's diminished physical or mental abilities and is brought on by the attitudes and behavior of relatives.

THE PREVALENCE OF ELDER ABUSE

We don't have precise data on the prevalence of elder abuse. Relatively few states have mandatory reporting laws, and even in those that do, victims often are too ashamed or frightened to report abuse or they don't know to whom they should report it. A random sample survey of over 2,000 community-dwelling elderly persons in the Boston metropolitan area found a prevalence rate of overall maltreatment of 32 elderly persons per 1,000. This translates to an estimated 701,000 to 1,093,560 people nationwide (Pillemer & Finkelhor, 1988). Other estimates have ranged as high as 2.5 million people (Pedrick-Cornell & Gelles, 1982).

Most researchers have reported that the most common victims are severely impaired women, aged 75 years and over, white, widowed, and living with relatives (Giordano & Giordano, 1984). However, the Boston survey found that men were twice as likely to be abused as women (Pillemer & Finkelhor, 1988). Older men were at greater risk than older women because they were more likely to be living with someone. However, older women were more likely to be seriously abused and were more likely to come to the attention of protective agencies (Pillemer & Finkelhor, 1988).

One study found that adult daughters were the perpetrators twice as frequently as any other type of relative, followed by sons, granddaugh-

ters, husbands, and siblings, usually sisters (Lau & Kosberg, 1978). In another study, spouses were shown to be more likely to engage in violence than other relatives (Pillemer & Suitor, 1992).

Nursing home owners and staff members may also be abusers. In 1985, a Texas prosecutor filed murder charges against the managers of a nursing home for failing to buy medical supplies ordered by physicians and for neglecting the residents so badly that many died (Fisher, 1985).

THE MOTIVATION TO ABUSE

Many theories have been advanced to explain elder abuse. In some cases violence has been accepted behavior in a family for many years. One researcher found that 1 in 400 children who were reared nonviolently attacked their parents later on, compared to 1 in 2 who were treated violently by their parents (Steinmetz, 1978).

Another theory is that abusers have certain personality traits, such as the inability to make appropriate judgments (O'Rourke, 1981), or that they suffer from severe psychopathology or alcoholism, which predisposes them to behave abusively (Wolf, Godkin, & Pillemer, 1984). Related to this is the notion that some children carry their adolescent conflicts with their parents into adulthood and then act them out in violence toward the parents (Lau & Kosberg, 1978; Block & Sinnott, 1979).

Excessive stress on caregivers may also lead to abuse. In one study, caregivers reported spending an average of 24 hours per week providing physical and psychological assistance to frail elderly relatives. Two-thirds were exhausted and anxious and said that their own health had deteriorated

(O'Rourke, 1981). The situation is exacerbated if the family is experiencing other stresses, such as economic problems, alcoholism, or other medical problems (Legal Research and Services for the Elderly, 1979), and if the elderly themselves are unusually demanding or provoking.

Finally, ageism certainly can play a significant role. Negative attitudes about the elderly dehumanize these people, making it easier for an abuser to victimize the elderly without feeling remorse (Giordano & Giordano, 1984).

PREVENTING ELDER ABUSE

Both the victim and the abuser need considerable services. Sometimes, the victim needs emergency medical attention and perhaps removal from the home. If a family is involved, all members may need services that support and enhance the caregiving role and decrease their stress. These services might include home nursing care, home-delivered meals, home visitation programs, day care, overnight respite care, education, and counseling. More comprehensive state and national policies aimed at identifying, reporting, and treating elder abuse also are needed. For older people themselves to avoid becoming victims, researchers offer the advice detailed in Table 19.3.

Table 19.3 ● How to Avoid Being a Victim

1. Plan for the possibility of disability by seeking out an attorney, possibly one who specializes in probate law, who can advise you about powers of attorney, guardianships or conservatorships, natural death acts, and "living wills."
2. Consider nominating coconservators or coguardians so more than one person knows your affairs and can take action if something goes wrong in the administration of your assets or personal care.
3. Make a will and revise it annually, but do not revise it lightly.
4. Be wary about deeding or willing your house or other assets to anyone who promises to keep you out of a nursing home or care for you at home if you become disabled.
5. Be careful when asked to sign anything. Have someone you trust review the document.
6. Be sure you are thoroughly familiar with your financial status and know how to handle your assets.
7. Arrange for direct deposit of your Social Security check or any other regular payments.
8. Do not rely solely on family for your social life or for health care. Cultivate friends of all ages so there are always people around who are concerned about you.
9. If an adult child, particularly one who has led a troubled life, wants to return home to live, think it over carefully. Be especially careful if your family has a history of violence or drug or alcohol abuse.
10. If you are alienated from family or friends, make peace to the extent possible. It is a healing thing to do, and it creates a climate of concern for you.

Source: Winter, 1986b, p. 56.

SUMMARY

- Older adults today often simultaneously belong to families with many generations and to social peerships that have nothing to do with chronological age.
- A key stress reported by many older couples is the illness and death of loved ones.
- Most people over 65 years of age have frequent contact with their children, but such contact does not guarantee happiness and well-being.
- Adult children who live far away from home usually stay in fairly close touch with their parents via letters and telephone calls.
- Types of grandparents include the formal grandparent, the fun seeker, the surrogate parent, the reservoir of wisdom, and the distant figure.
- Grandparents often serve as family stabilizers and watchdogs and foster family cohesion.
- Most older people have at least one living sibling, and the siblings usually visit each other several times a year.
- Friends may provide more happiness than do relatives, and they may serve as more trusted confidants.
- Widowers usually have more money and are more likely to remarry than widows, but they often have a harder time dealing with the practical demands of daily life, such as cooking.
- Older divorced people tend to be more pessimistic about life than their married or widowed counterparts.
- Later-life remarriages tend to be very happy.
- The little research on older people who have never married suggests that these people tend to be independent and satisfied with life.
- Early retirement has become commonplace because money from Social Security and pensions is available and because employers often prefer less costly younger employees.
- People often retire because they can afford to do so, they want to spend more time with their families or on other activities, or their health is too poor to keep working.
- People may experience retirement as a transition to old age, as a new beginning, as a continuation of what they've been doing, or as an imposed disruption.
- Deciding voluntarily to retire and having good health and adequate money are key factors in retirement satisfaction.
- Many people keep working beyond retirement age because work defines their identity, they enjoy what they do, work satisfies a creative drive and provides emotional rewards, and they still have goals to accomplish.
- Almost 38 percent of all people over 50 do some kind of volunteer work.
- Increasingly, college and universities are designing programs for older students.
- If used well, retirement can provide rest and restoration, spiritual renewal, self-realization, and entertainment.

QUESTIONS FOR DISCUSSION

1. How would your grandparents be classified according to the four classic types presented in this chapter? If you did not know your grandparents, what type do you think you are likely to be?

2. What might be some of the reasons that older divorced people are markedly less happy and more pessimistic than either older widowed people or people who have never married?

3. If you were designing a retirement-planning seminar for blue-collar workers, what would you include in the curriculum?

4. What physical, cognitive, and personality factors might contribute to someone's experiencing retirement in each of the four ways reported—as a transition to old age, as a new beginning, as a continuation of what the person's been doing, or as an imposed disruption?

SUGGESTIONS FOR FURTHER READING

1. Brubaker, T. H. (Ed.). (1990). *Family relationships in later life* (2nd ed.). Newbury Park, CA: Sage.

2. Cicirelli, V. G. (1982). *Sibling relationships: Their nature and significance across the lifespan.* Hillsdale, NJ: Erlbaum.

3. Downs, H. (1994). *Fifty to forever.* Nashville: Nelson.

4. Havel, Z., Ehrlich, P., & Hubbard, R. W. (Eds.). (1990). *The vulnerable aged: People, services, and policies.* New York: Springer.

5. Hess, B. B., & Markson, E. W. (1991). *Growing old in America* (4th ed.). New Brunswick, NJ: Transaction Publishers.

6. LeShan, E. (1994). *I want more of everything.* New York: New Market Press.

7. Parnes, H. S., Crowley, J. E., Haurin, R. J., Less, L. J., Morgan, W. R., Mott, F. L., & Nestel, G. (1985). *Retirement among American men.* Lexington, MA: Lexington Books.

CHAPTER 20

Death, Dying, and Bereavement

CHAPTER PREVIEW
"We Live Too Short and Die Too Long"

On the morning of March 29, 1994, Dr. Paul Spangler laced up his track shoes and headed out for a run. Although Spangler was 95 years old, his training schedule called for running about 7 miles a day three days a week. On odd days, he would lift weights and swim half a mile (Folkart, 1994). This morning would prove to be different, however. He collapsed and died not far from his home.

Spangler wasn't a lifelong athlete like John Kelley, whom we met in Chapter 18. He didn't take up running until the age of 67, when he became aware that all his friends and relatives were slowly succumbing to coronary heart disease; he determined that he wasn't ready to go just yet. He didn't run his first marathon until 1977, at the age of 78. He ran his last in 1991, when he completed the New York City Marathon at the age of 93. Along the way he met gerontologist Walter Bortz, who wrote the book We Live Too Short and Die Too Long *(1992), about staying fit in the older years. Bortz said of Spangler's death: "The fact that he died running is so supremely wonderful. Paul would always say, I'm the proof of what Bortz said. . . . Paul certainly didn't live too short or die too long, so he fulfilled my very best design" (Folkart, 1994, p. 20).*

Many of us who have contemplated our own inevitable death have hoped for such a sudden and "appropriate" end as Spangler's. Yet such a death is rare. Some of us live way too brief a time, such as children or young adults who die of accident or disease, while others of us die over too long a time, losing our health and well-being early from lack of conditioning or chronic disease and then continuing to exist for years rather than truly live. And many of us who try to do all the "right" things to prolong the length and quality of our lives are cheated by genes or circumstance into an early or drawn-out death.

Very few people die in an ideal way—suddenly, following a full and long life. Most die in ways far from this ideal. Most of us don't even die at home or in the presence of those we love. According to Dr. Sherwin Nuland, author of the book How We Die *(1993),*

> Nowadays, very few of us actually witness the deaths of those we love. Not many people die at home anymore, and those who do are usually the victims of drawn-out diseases or chronic degenerative conditions in which drugging and narcosis effectively hide the biological events that are occurring. Of the approximately 80 percent of Americans who die in a hospital, almost all are in large part concealed, or at least the details of the final approach to mortality are concealed, from those who have been closest to them in life. (Nuland, 1993, p. 8)

The Book of Ecclesiastes reminds us that there is "a time to be born, and a time to die," and on some level we know that this is true. As we've noted about other major life events, death is, if not easier, at least more comprehensible if it occurs "on time" and if it comes first to great-grandparents, then to grandparents, and so on down the generational ladder.

In this chapter, we will first examine common emotional responses to death and our society's changing awareness of death. Following that, we'll examine conceptions of death throughout the life span, the psychological and emotional experiences people often undergo when dying, innovations in caring for the dying, and relevant ethical dilemmas. We'll conclude the chapter with a discussion of how people survive and adjust to the loss of a loved one.

The Incomprehensible and Inevitable

Death is unique among human experiences: Not only does it end our earthly life, but it alone is "both wholly certain and wholly unknowable" (Erikson, Erikson, & Kivnick, 1986, p. 72). We may learn about the physiology of dying or about psychological reactions of grieving, but the totality of death itself is ultimately incomprehensible. For centuries, poets, philosophers, and religious leaders have tried to explain death, but they, too, have run up against the limits of the human intellect.

Dealing with something both incomprehensible and inevitable naturally generates powerful feelings, and those feelings vary, depending on our particular life circumstances. Some people feel defiant about death, while others welcome death as a blessed relief from suffering. Some feel sorrow and anger, others feel resentment and resignation, and yet others may actually feel joy (Hinton, 1967). However, many writers not bound by rules of scientific investigation would agree that most people do fear death. Jean Jacques Rousseau, whom we met in Chapter 1, expressed it this way: "He who pretends to look on death without fear lies. All men are afraid of dying, this is the great law of sentient beings, without which the entire human species would be destroyed" (Rousseau, 1960, pp. 131–132).

Certainly, there are some good reasons to fear both death and the process of dying. Among the fears expressed by terminally ill people are the following (Kassoff, 1984):

- Fear of the unknown
- Fear of loneliness, isolation, separation, and abandonment
- Fear of loss of the body and loss of self
- Fear of loss of self-control and loss of courage if the process goes on too long
- Fear of insanity
- Fear of emotional and physical pain
- Fear of loss of identity
- Fear of loss of power over one's destiny
- Fear of dependency and of being a nuisance

With all these possibilities, it is probably safe to assume that at one time or another, almost everyone feels some fear about death and dying. And as the quote by Rousseau suggests, this fear propels us to attend to self-preservation and to master dangers that threaten us. Ironically, however, we can't function if we are constantly mindful of the fear of death. So, to get on with life, we must accept the fear as normal and valuable, then suppress it, knowing that it will return to be dealt with and suppressed once again (Becker, 1973).

Interestingly, older people do not necessarily fear death more, even though they are closer to it. Research suggests that on average, older people generally report lower death anxiety, while middle-aged people express the greatest death anxiety (Bengtson, Cuellar, & Ragan, 1977). In one study, married women with children had the highest death anxiety, and lower anxiety was positively correlated with both advancing age and higher education (Cole, 1978–1979). Among women 60 to 85 years old, feeling a sense of purpose in life seemed greatly to reduce death anxiety (Quinn & Reznikoff, 1985).

One intriguing study found that terminally ill patients whose *physicians* had high death anxiety were hospitalized an average of 5 days longer before dying than were patients whose physicians had medium or low death anxiety. When the physicians' total caseloads were considered, however, physicians who had higher death anxiety did not have patients with significantly lower death rates (Schulz & Aderman, 1978–1979).

We'll leave open for now the question of what these data might mean. Once we've examined other issues related to death and dying, we can make more informed decisions about the significance and applicability of these findings to our own lives.

DEATH IN AMERICA: A HISTORICAL PERSPECTIVE

Lengthening the Life Span

Well into the twentieth century, death was an all-too-familiar part of American life. Death of infants and young children was common, many women died in childbirth, and otherwise healthy adults succumbed to contagious diseases. People died at home and were laid out and buried by family members. It is doubtful that most people felt comfortable with death, but death certainly was no stranger to them. This is still the way death occurs and is handled throughout most of the Third World.

As the century progressed, the widespread use of vaccinations and antibiotics virtually eliminated killers such as smallpox, typhoid, diphtheria, cholera, and bubonic plague. People began to live longer. Those who became seriously ill were taken to hospitals, where respirators and other new technology kept them alive while doctors tried a variety of new treatments. When the treatments didn't work and people died, these people were surrounded more often by machines and medical specialists than by family and friends.

Denial of Death

Having fewer direct contacts with death allowed Americans to develop a somewhat death-denying society. The British historian Arnold Toynbee went so far as to say that for Americans, death is "un-American," inconsistent with the "earthly paradise" hoped for in "the American way of life" (Toynbee, 1968, p. 131). In all fairness, Americans were not alone in their tendency to deny death. Most nations with advanced medical care did so as well.

On a practical level, denial of death was expressed in a number of ways. Discussions of death were deemed "morbid," and the topic of death often was scrupulously avoided, especially in conversations with dying people. Children were excluded from funerals and were told stories about "grandmother's going on a long journey." Dead people were handed over to morticians who embalmed "the body," made it "look natural," laid it out in an expensive coffin, and presided over the funeral and the "disposal."

You may have noticed that we used the past tense to describe these actions. But to some extent, they are still common today. The incomprehensibility of death, coupled with our need to suppress the fear of death in order to carry on with life, probably will always push us toward denying death. However, a switch in our attitude toward death and dying began to occur in the 1960s. In 1970, Edwin Shneidman, who taught courses on death and dying at Harvard, stated that "the age of death" had been ushered in. "In the Western world," he wrote, "we are probably more death-oriented today than we have been since the days of the Black Plague in the 14th Century" (Shneidman, 1970, p. 37).

In brief, Shneidman meant that like it or not, people had begun to think about death in a way they had avoided for the last few decades. Nightly news programs carried vivid and horrifying images of people dying in Vietnam, and

A tragic consequence of some attempts to prolong life by means of sophisticated technology is that many people die surrounded by machines and medical specialists rather than by friends and family.

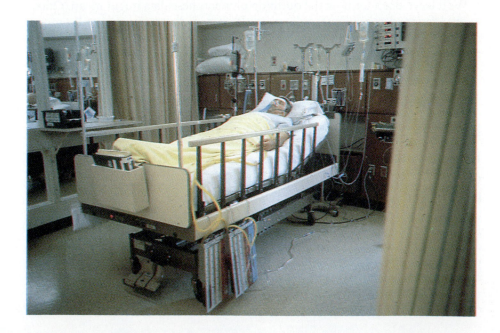

young men watched intently as draft lottery numbers were drawn. Suddenly, although the war was being fought "over there," death was happening "to us." At the same time, people were becoming increasingly aware of the possibility of nuclear annihilation of the human race. And our new and miraculous life-sustaining technology had begun to force us to face many ethical, medical, and legal problems concerning the "artificial" maintenance of life, such as when efforts to sustain life should end.

Also during the 1960s, a "**thanatology** boom" began. In 1966, thanatologists Richard Kalish and Robert Kastenbaum began to publish a newsletter on death and dying, which by 1970 had evolved into the journal *Omega*. In 1969, Elisabeth Kübler-Ross published *On Death and Dying*; based on interviews with dying patients, the book rapidly became a best-seller. On college campuses, courses on death and dying were heavily subscribed; Shneidman had expected 20 students for his course, but 200 showed up! Researchers began to look at different aspects of death, dying, and grief, and groups to aid the bereaved sprung up across the country (Leviton, 1977).

The interest in thanatology continues today, and as more people have become involved in death education courses, the topic of death has become less taboo. It probably is not accurate to say that we, as a society, are becoming comfortable with death. Rather, like our ancestors, we're just becoming more willing to acknowledge that death is a fact of life and to be accepting of our discomfort.

Let's turn now to some of the issues researchers have been grappling with over the last few decades.

THANATOLOGY
The study of death and dying.

UNDERSTANDING THE INCOMPREHENSIBLE: CONCEPTIONS OF DEATH THROUGH THE LIFE SPAN

Death-related matters have a way of capturing our attention early on in our lives. The fact that we can never completely comprehend the totality of death on either an emotional or a cognitive level doesn't stop us from trying.

Researchers have defined a cognitively mature, adult concept of death as one acknowledging that (1) death is irreversible and final, (2) death represents the end of life, and (3) all living things die (Speece & Brent, 1984). Although some people may take issue with this definition, developmental researchers have focused mainly on how we think about these concepts as we grow up. As we will see, even without a fully mature capacity to think about these issues, infants and toddlers do react to death-related matters. Adults who readily accept these concepts intellectually continue to grow in their emotional and cognitive understanding of death as they age.

As we examine the research on how people of different ages view death, don't forget that we're presenting general tendencies and that there are enormous differences among individuals. One researcher maintains that many different views of death probably are present at all stages of our development and that how someone says he or she views death reflects "intellectual and social experiences and psychological concerns and circumstances at the time the question is asked" (Bluebond-Langner, 1977, p. 51).

Infants and Toddlers

> A 16-month-old boy . . . became alarmed when adult feet began to tread down a garden path right toward a fuzzy caterpillar he had been watching. The foot did come down (unwittingly) upon the caterpillar. The boy studied its residue intently. Finally he said: "No more!" (Kastenbaum, 1977, p. 27)

No one would argue that infants and toddlers have a sophisticated intellectual understanding of death, or of anything else, for that matter. However, as the vignette suggests, many young children clearly do have an awareness of some death-related matters. Primary among these is probably the threat of separation and abandonment (Kastenbaum, 1974; Bluebond-Langner, 1977).

When someone dies, infants can sense that things are different. Daily routines change, new people are in the house, and the sadness and anxiety of caretakers often is tangible. As a result, infants may show changes in sleeping and eating patterns and may become easily upset and more difficult to comfort (Schaefer & Lyons, 1986). Children who have begun to walk and talk may ask questions about what is happening or may express their concerns through play activities.

Early Childhood (3–5 Years)

The classic research on how children conceptualize death was conducted in Hungary shortly after World War II, when Maria Nagy interviewed children 3 to 10 years of age (1948, 1959). Nagy found that children less than 5 years old were very curious about death but that they generally saw it as temporary and reversible. They thought that a dead person might return at any time to carry on life as usual. Gerald Koocher, who later examined children's concepts of death according to the children's levels of cognitive development, pursued the question of how a person might return from the dead. His preoperational children (see Chapter 6) readily provided concrete suggestions: "Keep them warm" or "Give them hot food" (Koocher, 1973, p. 373).

Nagy's children at this stage usually thought that dead people do essentially the same things as living people, but maybe not as well. "If he is dead he feels too," commented one 6-year-old child who was moving toward the next stage. "If he is dead he feels a tiny little bit. When he is quite dead he no longer feels anything" (Nagy, 1959, p. 85).

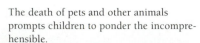

The death of pets and other animals prompts children to ponder the incomprehensible.

Middle Childhood (5–9 Years)

Nagy's children between ages 5 and 9 years came to believe that death is final and permanent, but they did not see it as inevitable. Moreover, they often personified death. "Death is a skeleton. It is so strong it can overturn a ship," commented one 9-year-old child. "Death can't be seen. Death is in a hidden place. It hides in an island" (Nagy, 1959, p. 89).

During these years, the children gradually realized that they themselves *could* die, but felt that they did not necessarily *have* to. Their general reasoning was that older people are more likely to die because they can't run fast enough or hide from death the way younger, smaller people can (Kastenbaum, 1967).

Koocher's concrete operational children did not personify death the way Nagy's children did. However, Koocher did note that as the children moved from preoperations to concrete operations, they began to observe the experiences of other people as they thought about their own death. When asked, "When will you die?" one 6-year-old boy said that he would live to be 21. He then paused and asked the examiner his age. When the examiner answered, "twenty-four," the boy then replied, "Well, I'm gonna live to be twenty-five" (Koocher, 1973, p. 374).

Late Childhood (9–10 Years)

By about age 9 or 10 years, Nagy's children understood that death is not only final, but also inevitable and universal. In keeping with their increasing understanding of their life circumstances, children at this stage may be quite concerned about how a death would affect their family's emotional and financial security, and they may show more anger, guilt, and grief than do children at earlier stages (Schaefer & Lyons, 1986).

When Children Die

Many researchers have duplicated Nagy's findings (Jackson, 1965; Kliman, 1968; Cook, 1973; Melear, 1973; Zeligs, 1974); but others have taken issue with them. A major challenge has come from Myra Bluebond-Langner's research with terminally ill children. As you might suspect, dying children have a very different perspective on death than do healthy children:

> "I thought you would understand," pleaded the pediatrician, trying to get on with the procedure. "You once told me you wanted to be a doctor."
>
> "I'm not going to be anything!" the 6-year-old screamed, and threw a syringe at her.
>
> Understanding the boy's message, the doctor quietly replied, "OK, OK." But a nurse persisted: "What *are* you going to be?"
>
> "A ghost," the boy said, and turned away from them. (Bluebond-Langner, 1978, p. 194)

Bluebond-Langner found that regardless of what parents and doctors told the children, the children acquired information about their disease (in this case, leukemia); as they did so, they redefined their self-concept, as we can see in Table 20.1. Bluebond-Langner further maintained that not only did these children (ages 18 months to 14 years) come to know they were dying, but they also understood that death is final, irreversible, and inevitable. She concluded that age and intellectual ability were not significant in a child's understanding of death. What was significant, she said, was the child's ability to integrate and synthesize information, and this was related more to experience than to anything else (Bluebond-Langner, 1977, 1978).

Adolescence

By adolescence, most people believe that death is irreversible and final, that it is the end of life, and that all living things die. However, many romanticize it and assume an attitude of "it won't happen to me." When combined with the cultural expectation that young men must "prove" their masculine prowess, this attitude leads many teenagers to take chances with their lives. For example, they may drive recklessly, use drugs and alcohol, and take unnecessary risks in athletics (Kastenbaum, 1977).

Table 20.1 ● The Acquisition of Knowledge and the Changing Self-Concept of Terminally Ill Children

ACQUISITION OF INFORMATION				
1	2	3	4	5
"It" is serious illness	Names of drugs and side effects	Purposes of treatments and procedures	Disease as a series of relapses and remissions (− death)	Diseases as a series of relapses and remissions (+ death)
DEVELOPMENT OF SELF-CONCEPT				
Seriously ill	Seriously ill and will get better	Always ill and will get better	Always ill and will never get better	Dying

Source: Bluebond-Langner, pp. 166, 169.

Teenagers and young adults may hold a mature concept of death, but still on some level believe "it can't happen to me."

Given the growing interest in ideas and abstractions that comes with formal operational thinking, adolescents also might be expected to engage in philosophical and religious discussions about death. Many certainly do so. Instructors in death education courses also have found that many teenagers want to talk about specific people who have died, apparently because they have never had an opportunity to talk about these emotion-laden matters before (McLendon, 1979).

Early Adulthood

As we noted in Chapter 14, the period we call early adulthood covers many years, from age 18 to 40 years. It is understandable that a person's thinking about death would undergo changes during these years. Most college-aged people probably hold ideas about death similar to those of adolescents, and risk-taking behavior continues to be common. However, as young people take on more adult roles—make commitments to a career, marriage, and parenthood, for example—awareness of their obligations to other people often leads them to view death more soberly. Most probably don't expect to die anytime soon, but many still buy life insurance to provide for their families "just in case."

If young adults do have to face their own death, they are often enraged that their lives are ending, just at the time that "real life" is getting under way. The anger may be directed at hospital staff members, and this may cause special problems, because many staff members themselves are young adults who are already having a hard time dealing with the death of someone their own age (Kastenbaum, 1977).

Middle Adulthood

In Chapter 16, we talked about how our time perspective changes in middle age, leading us to think not so much about how long we *have* lived as about how much longer we *will* live (Neugarten, 1967). Many factors are involved in this change, not the least of which is the death of a parent, which most people must deal with during middle age. Writer Ben Hecht described the effect of such a loss this way:

> I can recall the hour in which I lost my immortality, in which I tried on my shroud for the first time and saw how it became me. . . . The knowledge of my dying came to me when my mother died. . . . I went and returned dry-eyed from the burial, but I brought death back with me. I had been to the edge of the world and looked over its last foot of territory into nothingness. (Hecht, quoted in Kastenbaum, 1977, p. 19)

No doubt Hecht had long held a "mature" concept of death. But personal experiences with death, which usually increase during middle age, combined perhaps with declining health or the loss of youthful dreams, radically alter how we think and feel about death. Kastenbaum goes so far as to speculate that "perhaps a person does not become fully adult until death has been recognized as an authentic companion to life" (Kastenbaum, 1977, p. 19).

Late Adulthood

Older people would have to live in a state of high denial not to think about death, for it is during this time that "the familiar phrase 'till death us do part' becomes a sharp-edged, insistent theme" (Kastenbaum, 1977, p. 40). Increasingly, friends and relatives die, so that the longer people live, the more intimate companions they lose. Moreover, declining health leads the older person to worry simultaneously about becoming a burden and about being abandoned.

As we noted earlier, the fact that older people are increasingly acquainted with death does not necessarily lead them to fear it more (Munnichs, 1966; Bengston, Cuellar, & Ragan, 1977). Nor does it lead them to think or talk about it incessantly. In fact, obsession with death is most likely to occur when people are *not* able to talk about it. Given a sympathetic ear, most people probably can achieve the ego integrity Erikson saw as the developmental task of late adulthood, to accept their "one and only life cycle" (Erikson, 1950, p. 268), and to meet death with an acceptance that younger people often find hard to imagine.

Let's turn now to the psychological and emotional reactions that people often experience as they approach death.

THE PSYCHOLOGICAL AND EMOTIONAL PROCESS OF DYING

In the fall of 1965, students at the Chicago Theological Seminary were instructed to write a paper on "crisis in human life." Having decided that dying is the biggest crisis people ever face, four students approached Dr. Elisabeth Kübler-Ross, who was on the staff of a leading local hospital, for help with their project. The group decided that the best way to gather data about dying was to talk with terminally ill patients. Eventually, the group interviewed over 200 patients, and Kübler-Ross identified five stages the patients passed through in the process of dying.

Stage I: Denial and Isolation

"No, not me, it cannot be true." This was the initial reaction of most patients. One woman was convinced that her X-ray examination and pathology reports had been mixed up with someone else's. Denial usually was a temporary defense, and it was replaced by partial acceptance. But even when the patients moved to another stage, they often reverted to partial denial in order to enjoy life in the time they had left.

Stage II: Anger

Once denial was broken through and the patients realized, "Oh, yes, it is me, it was not a mistake," the next question was an angry "Why me?" (Kübler-Ross, 1969, p. 50). Many expressed rage, envy of the healthy, and resentment. Wherever they looked, they found grievances, and they often displaced their anger onto doctors, nurses, family members, and God. When staff and family reacted with anger or avoidance, the anger of the patients intensified.

Stage III: Bargaining

"If God did not respond to my angry pleas, maybe he'll listen if I ask nicely." This was the premise people worked from in the third stage. Patients often made bargains with God, and many kept these bargains secret. The bargains usually were an attempt to postpone the inevitable, and they often contained a self-imposed deadline: "I'll be ready to go if I can just do _____ one more time."

Stage IV: Depression

Denial, anger, and bargaining eventually gave way to a sense of great loss. Kübler-Ross found two types of depression at this stage. The first was caused

HOSPICE
A program of palliative and supportive services that provides physical, psychological, social, and spiritual care for terminally ill people and their families.

PALLIATIVE
Serving to reduce pain and suffering.

by losses such as body disfigurement or the inability to work or to care for children. Talking about these losses and tending to whatever could be done—for example, placement of children with a caring relative—usually helped to alleviate this type of depression.

The second type of depression was the "preparatory grief" that these dying people experienced as they prepared for the final separation from this world. This was usually a silent depression, best treated by "a touch of a hand, a stroking of the hair, or just a silent sitting together" (Kübler-Ross, 1969, p. 87).

Stage V: Acceptance

By this stage, Kübler-Ross's patients contemplated their approaching death with quiet expectation. It was a time almost void of feeling. The patients' interest in the world around them diminished, they preferred only short visits, and they valued silent communication over "noisy" words. Such moments were gratifying for visitors, as they illustrated that "dying is not such a frightening, horrible thing that so many want to avoid" (Kübler-Ross, 1969, p. 114).

Kübler-Ross is widely respected because her pioneering work has helped clarify the multitude of emotions and behaviors dying people often exhibit. Unfortunately, many people have taken her stage theory as gospel and have tried to fit all dying people into it. As you know by now, it's hard to make "all people," especially adults, fit anything.

Some people do not go through the stages in any particular order, and many never enter some stages at all (Shneidman, 1973). Some people experience denial and anger throughout the illness (Pattison, 1977), while others mainly experience depression (Hinton, 1967). In one study of cancer patients, anger was most prevalent among those whose illnesses terminated quickly (Achte & Vauhkonen, 1971). Some age differences have been identified, with younger people being more prone to denial and anger, and older people being more accepting (Pattison, 1977). In short, the individual differences we've noted so many times before are certainly apparent as people approach dying. There simply is no single "right way" to do it.

Perhaps the most dangerous effect of an uncritical acceptance of Kübler-Ross's stage theory is that it can lead staff and family members to discount a person's legitimate complaints. Many things happen in hospitals that would make anyone angry. An insensitive staff member, however, may dismiss a patient's complaints as simply being "part of the anger stage."

CARING FOR THE DYING: THE HOSPICE MOVEMENT

Modern hospitals are well equipped to treat people who have acute, curable illnesses or emergency situations, and caregivers feel successful when their patients get well and carry on with their lives. Dying people pose a major challenge to this system. Doctors may try to avoid them, and nurses may respond more slowly to their signal calls (Glasser & Strauss, 1965). An attempt to provide a more humane atmosphere for dying people is being made by those involved in the **hospice** movement.

A hospice is a program of **palliative** and supportive services that provides physical, psychological, social, and spiritual care for terminally ill people and their families. Analgesics are used to alleviate suffering, and patients and family members are allowed to talk freely about their feelings about dying. Hospice workers try to bring family members into as much of the caregiving as possible, and they try to ensure that people will be surrounded by their loved ones during the final stage of illness (Gray-Toft & Anderson, 1984, p. 110).

Hospice care of some type has existed for centuries, but the U.S. hospice movement usually traces its origins to St. Christopher's Hospice, which Dr. Cicely Saunders founded in England in 1967. The first hospice was established in the United States in 1974 in New Haven, Connecticut. Today, hospice services may take place in autonomous institutions, or they may be part of hospital services or home-care or day-care programs.

Hospice work is very difficult. Helping people die is emotionally and psychologically draining, and it simply cannot be done by a single person. A staff of chaplains, social workers, physicians, nurses, volunteers, and psychologists is needed. Moreover, the administrator of the program must be sensitive to the enormous demands the work makes on the staff (Gray-Toft & Anderson, 1983). Burnout can be avoided if the staff members are mature, if they have hobbies and interests outside of work, if they have adequate time off from their jobs, and if they are supportive of one another.

ETHICAL DILEMMAS

Defining Death

"You are dead when a physician says you are dead" (Metz, 1983, p. 49). So it has been throughout much of history. Obviously, this is not a precise definition of death, but it does make you want to stay on the good side of your physician.

Only a few decades ago, defining death was not a difficult task. If a person stopped breathing and his heart stopped beating, he was considered dead. However, over the last few decades, an increasing number of people who were "dead" in this sense of the word have been resuscitated by means of **cardiopulmonary resuscitation** (CPR) or **defibrillation**. Many such people regained consciousness, their heart and lungs spontaneously functioning again. Yet others have been kept alive by means of artificial respiration, kidney dialysis, or other complex or mechanically augmented techniques. Some regained consciousness and some did not.

Many legal and ethical dilemmas have resulted from the use of life-prolonging technology. Is a person dead or alive, for example, if he is breathing only because he is attached to a respirator? This situation has given rise to the idea that biological death is a *process*, not a moment, and has led to the identification of three types of death—clinical, brain, and cellular death (Schulz, 1978).

Clinical Death. **Clinical death** occurs when spontaneous breathing and heartbeat stop. This is the traditional definition of death, and it is usually not hard to determine whether a person meets these criteria, although sometimes it is necessary to insert a catheter into the heart to know for certain that blood is no longer being pumped. (Some people have recovered after being pronounced clinically dead because the heart made no discernable sound, although it continued to pump enough blood to keep the person alive.) If given prompt emergency treatment (even sometimes as much as an hour after being pronounced dead), many clinically dead people, such as heart attack victims, may be revived to carry on normal lives.

Brain Death.   If a clinically dead person's brain is deprived of oxygen for as little as 4 to 6 minutes, brain cells begin to die. The *cortex*, which controls vol-

BRAIN DEATH

The condition in which the cells of the cortex and midbrain, but not the brain stem, cease to function, and the person lapses into an irreversible coma. To be declared brain dead, a person must meet specific criteria: lack of spontaneous movements, lack of reflex activity, lack of responsiveness, a flat electroencephalogram, and a certain duration of the condition.

CELLULAR DEATH

The condition in which a given organ, because of widespread death of cells, cannot be returned to a functional state, regardless of extraordinary intervention.

LIVING WILL

A document that a person constructs while mentally competent, specifying what treatment the person wants carried out if he or she is seriously ill and unconscious or otherwise mentally incompetent.

BEREAVEMENT

The state or condition of being deprived of a loved person or object, especially by death.

untary action, thought, and memory, dies first, followed by the *midbrain*, which controls reflexes. The *brain stem*, which controls respiration and heartbeat, dies last. If the cortex and midbrain die but the brain stem is spared, the person lapses into an irreversible coma in which she can breathe unaided. If fed through a feeding tube inserted through the nose or directly into the stomach, she can avoid clinical death for years (Schulz, 1978). But is such a person truly "alive"? The prevailing opinion is that she has experienced **brain death**, but not clinical death. In 1968, criteria were established by the Harvard Ad Hoc Committee to Examine the Definition of Brain Death. Their criteria for brain death are presented in Figure 20.1.

Cellular Death.   Different body organs die at different rates. An organ is said to have undergone **cellular death** if no intervention could return it to a functional state (Schulz, 1978). Kidneys, lungs, and other organs of a person who is brain dead but clinically alive may be functioning well. They could be transplanted into someone else's body and thereby prolong the latter person's life, although it would mean clinical death for the brain-dead person.

A fundamental question for many people is whether such transplantation procedures are ethical. Should life, whatever its condition, be preserved at all costs? Should the heart be removed from the chest of a brain-dead 20-year-old man and transplanted into a 50-year-old woman who would die without it? You say yes, but how can you be *absolutely sure* that the 20-year-old man will never recover? Who is to make these decisions? The doctor? Family members?

Many people now make **living wills** in which they specify what treatment they want carried out if they are seriously ill and unconscious or otherwise mentally incompetent. A sample living will is distributed by an organization known as Concern for Dying; it is presented in Figure 20.2.

THE SURVIVORS: THE COST OF COMMITMENT

Between the Christian and Buddhist Memorial Day Services, I was standing by the graves across from the Japanese monument. A Caucasian woman was placing flowers on a nearby grave. A Japanese-American woman was standing close to her apparently waiting for the Buddhist service to begin. She was looking intently at the gravesite where the Caucasian woman was kneeling. As the woman stood up, the Nisei lady softly said to her, "It looks like a new grave." Obviously appreciating the concern shown her, the Caucasian put her arm around the Japanese and said with tears in her eyes, "Yes,

FIGURE 20.1

Key elements of the Harvard criteria for the diagnosis of brain death. (SOURCE: Adapted from Report of the Ad Hoc Committee of the Harvard Medical School to Examine the Definition of Brain Death, 1968)

1. ***Unreceptivity and unresponsivity***—The person shows no awareness of, and is completely unresponsive to, externally applied stimuli, no matter hoe painful.

2. ***No movements or breathing***—Failure to make any spontaneous movements for at least 1 hour, or to breathe for 3 minutes when taken off a respirator.

3. ***No reflexes***—Reflex actions, such as swallowing, yawning, or the pupils' contracting in response to bright light, cannot be detected.

4. ***A flat electroencephalogram (EEG)***—No brain waves can be elicited, even in the presence of a loud noise or it the person is pinched.

Before brain death can be definitively diagnosed, all these tests have to be repeated at least 24 hours later with no change. Moreover, hypothermia and a drug overdose, which can produce symptoms similar to brain death, must be ruled out.

FIGURE 20.2

A sample living will. (SOURCE: "The Living Will" reprinted with permission from Concern for Dying)

TO MY FAMILY, MY PHYSICIAN, MY LAWYER,
AND ALL OTHERS WHOM IT MAY CONCERN

Death is as much a reality as birth, maturity and old age—it is the one certainty of life. If the time comes when I can no longer take part in decisions for my own future, let this statement stand as an expression of my wishes and directions, while I am still of sound mind.

If at such a time the situation should arise in which there is no reasonable expectation of my recovery from extreme physical or mental disability, I direct that I be allowed to die and not be kept alive by medications, artificial means or "heroic measures." I do, however, ask that medication be mercifully administered to me to alleviate suffering even though this may shorten my remaining life.

This statement is made after careful consideration and in accordance with my strong convictions and beliefs. I want the wishes and directions here expressed carried out to the extent permitted by law. Insofar as they are not legally enforceable, I hope that those to whom this Will is addressed will regard themselves as morally bound by these provisions.

my husband died three weeks ago." They stood there for a few minutes, together, looking at the grave. (Kalish & Reynolds, 1981, p. 191)

The only way to avoid grief is never to care about anyone or anything. Collin Murray Parkes, the noted bereavement researcher, describes our dilemma this way: "The pain of grief is just as much a part of life as the joy of love; it is, perhaps, the price we pay for love, the cost of commitment" (Parkes, 1986, p. 26). So if we are going to care, we also eventually will be faced with bereavement, mourning, and grief.

Bereavement, Mourning, and Grief

Bereavement is the state or condition of having lost someone by death. However, bereavement also follows other significant losses that produce major life changes. For example, people who are forced to flee their homelands or who lose a part of their bodies may be said to be bereaved.

Funerals and other mourning rituals honor the deceased and help the bereaved express their grief.

AT ISSUE

The Right to Die

Many people believe that if a person is hopelessly ill or brain dead, there are times when helping that person to die quickly is the most merciful thing to do. This is the position taken by people who advocate **euthanasia** (from the Greek *euthanatos*, meaning "easy death"), or mercy killing. *Active euthanasia* occurs when someone deliberately does something to shorten the life of the sufferer. But because of legal sanctions against assisted suicide or murder, people often are reluctant to help the terminally ill end their lives.

According to Dr. Sherwin Nuland

A decision to end life must be as defensible to those whose respect we seek as it is to ourselves. Only when that criterion has been satisfied should anyone consider the finality of death. Against such a standard, the suicide of Percy Bridgman was close to being irreproachable. Bridgman was a Harvard professor whose studies in high pressure physics won him a Nobel Prize in 1946. At the age of seventy-nine and in the final stages of cancer, he continued to work until he could no longer do so. Living at his summer home in Randolph, New Hampshire, he completed the index to a seven-volume collection of his scientific works, sent it off to the Harvard University Press, and then shot himself on August 20, 1961, leaving a suicide note in which he summed up a controversy that has since embroiled an entire world of medical ethics: "It is not decent for society to make a man do this to himself. Probably, this is the last day I will be able to do it myself." (Nuland, 1993, p. 152)

The ethical and moral questions involved in the decision to take the life of someone who is terminally ill or incapacitated cannot be answered with any certainty. In 1985, for example, 75-year-old Roswell Gilbert deliberately shot and killed his 73-year-old wife, who was suffering from Alzheimer's disease and osteoporosis. He defended his actions by saying, "I just could not allow my lovely lady of 51 years to descend into a hell of suffering and degradation" (Marx, 1987, p. 32). Although some courts have acquitted perpetrators of active euthanasia, the court found Gilbert guilty of first-degree murder and sentenced him to 25 years in prison (Marx, 1987).

A more common form of euthanasia is *passive euthanasia*, in which treatment is withheld or withdrawn so that the person will die more quickly than if treatment were administered. For example, a physician may decide not to try aggressively to resuscitate a terminally ill patient who experiences heart failure.

The country that has taken the lead in active, *voluntary euthanasia* is the Netherlands, even though euthanasia is still illegal there. It is estimated that Dutch physicians carry out 8,000 to 10,000 "mercy deaths" every year. The unofficial conditions that must be met include that the request be initiated by a fully conscious patient who is experiencing unbearable suffering and whose family agrees with the request. Then a second physician must concur that there is no hope of the patient's recovering (Clines, 1986; Painton, 1987).

During the last few years, an American physician, Dr. Jack Kevorkian, has raised the issue to national attention by providing means that allow others to easily commit suicide. Dr. Kevorkian admits that administering lethal drugs into a vein is the preferred way to die; but this is not practical when the physician is forbidden to administer such treatments, for the patient cannot easily place a needle into his or her own vein. Instead, Dr. Kevorkian brings a mask and hose connected to tanks of carbon monoxide to the home of the suffering, dying individual and verbally instructs the individual in the use of the device for suicide.

As you might imagine, this has created a great deal of controversy. Some people feel that this is kindness; others feel it is murder. In response to Dr. Kevorkian's efforts, the state of Michigan passed a law forbidding assisted suicide. However, in 1993 this law was overturned by the higher court as unconstitutional.

There is some evidence that assisted suicide and voluntary, passive euthanasia have been growing in acceptance. Numerous polls have found that respondents believe that doctors should not use extraordinary techniques to preserve a person's life if the person asked them not to. This was true 10 years ago as well (Schmeck, 1986). At that time, a presidential commission studying ethical problems in medicine concluded that doctors could give pain-relieving drugs, even if the drugs were likely to shorten a patient's life, if the sole purpose of giving the drugs was to alleviate pain (Schmeck, 1983).

Many difficult ethical questions remain, however. No one would argue that people do not have the right to a "good" or "easy" death. But the issues involved in defining and securing a good death take us out of the realms of medicine and psychology and plunge us headlong into matters of ethics, philosophy and religion.

The culturally prescribed behaviors that bereaved people are expected to perform to honor the deceased are known as **mourning**. The Irish wake and Jewish shiva are both mourning rituals, as are customs such as funerals, wearing black, wailing and keening, refusing social invitations, and flying flags at half-mast. As our society has decreased use of these rituals and as people have been encouraged to "keep a stiff upper lip," thanatologists have become concerned that not giving adequate expression to grief may have potentially harmful consequences.

Grief is the emotional suffering people feel when they lose a loved one. Uncomplicated grief usually proceeds through fairly predictable phases (Schulz, 1978). The *initial* phase, which continues for a few weeks after the death, is characterized at first by shock and disbelief. The bereaved person feels numb, dazed, empty, and confused. Soon these feelings give way to enormous sadness and free-floating anxiety. Bereaved persons may not be able to stop crying and may fear that they are losing their mind.

Also during this phase, many physical symptoms may appear, such as an empty feeling in the abdomen, shortness of breath, tightness in the throat, and muscle aches and weakness (Lindemann, 1944). Other common symptoms are insomnia, loss of appetite, irritability, lethargy, headaches, and menstrual irregularities. In some cases, the bereaved person may exhibit some of the symptoms that caused the loved one's death (Schulz, 1978).

The *intermediate* phase, which generally lasts about a year, is characterized by feelings of tremendous loneliness and three distinct behavior patterns. First, bereaved people are obsessed by the death and repeatedly review scenes associated with it. They often berate themselves with "if only" thoughts: "If only I had made him stay with us," "If only I had taken her to the doctor sooner," and so on. Unaware of how much grief work must be done, friends and family members may encourage the bereaved person to "get on with life," and this only intensifies the feelings of loneliness.

Second, bereaved people search for meaning in the death. One woman expressed this search by saying, "Why, why, why, why was it him? What did he do? But I just have no answer. I don't know, I ask myself every day" (Glick, Weiss, & Parkes, 1974, p. 131).

Finally, bereaved people feel an impulse to search for the deceased. "I can't help looking for him everywhere," commented one widow (Parkes, 1986, p. 64). Activities that the survivor regularly shared with the deceased and places that the deceased frequented may especially evoke searching behaviors. Survivors may feel that the deceased is actually present, or they may imagine that they see the deceased. Interestingly, searching for the lost loved one has been observed among lower animals, including the jackdaw, goose, domestic dog, orangutan, and chimpanzee (Bowlby, 1961).

By the beginning of the second year after the death, these behaviors usually have decreased. Around this time, bereaved people usually feel more in control of their lives, and the *recovery* phase begins. Usually, bereaved people make a conscious decision to go forward with life, and they begin to seek out more social encounters and to experience themselves as stronger and more capable. They take pride in having survived a devastating event and in the new daily living skills that they may have been forced to acquire (Schulz, 1978).

Bereavement researchers do frequently see the pattern just described, especially if the death is expected and the bereaved person has experienced **anticipatory grief** prior to the actual death. This is true for widows and widowers (Schulz, 1978), as well as for parents who have lost children (Rando, 1983). If the death is sudden and unexpected, however, or if there are other complicating factors, then grief may be more intense and long-lasting. One study found

EUTHANASIA
The act or practice of killing people who are hopelessly sick or injured, for reasons of mercy.

MOURNING
Culturally prescribed behaviors that bereaved people are expected to perform to honor the deceased.

GRIEF
Emotional suffering caused by bereavement.

ANTICIPATORY GRIEF
Emotional suffering caused by an impending loss.

that family members who lost loved ones as a result of sudden, traumatic accidents experienced marked depression and anxiety and were unable to resolve their loss as much as 4 to 7 years after the death. The researchers concluded that "our data clearly indicate that, following the traumatic loss of one's spouse or child, lasting distress is not a sign of individual coping failure but, rather, a common response to the situation" (Lehman, Wortman, & Williams, 1987, p. 229). This is an especially chilling thought, given that in the United States alone, sudden traumatic accidents claim about 90,000 victims annually (U. S. Brueau of the Census, 1993).

Widows and widowers whose spouses have died unexpectedly are less likely to remarry than are those who anticipated their spouse's death. The survivors apparently do not want to risk unanticipated loss again and have become somewhat phobic toward marriage (Schulz, 1978).

Another factor that may complicate the grief process is the person's having died from a cause that carries a social stigma, such as suicide, acquired immune deficiency syndrome (AIDS), or drug overdose. Therapists who work with families of AIDS victims, for example, find these families' problems to be different from, and more severe than, those of other families. Some people, they note, are shocked to learn that their loved one has been leading a secret life. Almost all have to deal with the strain of having the young die before the old. The partner of the victim often is terrified that he or she, too, is infected with the virus and will die. And for many survivors, the sense of isolation can be almost unbearable. In one case, only the mother went in for counseling after her daughter and 2-year-old grandson died of AIDS. The daughter had been married to a drug dealer; since her death, no one else in the family would even mention her name (Walker, 1987).

Health Status of the Bereaved

In 1657, the causes of death in London were listed as follows (Parkes, 1986, p. 34):

Flox and small pox	835
Found dead in the streets, etc.	9
French pox	25
Gout	8
Griefe	10
Griping and plague in the guts	446
Hang'd and made away 'emselves	24

Notice that the fifth item on the list is grief. In fact, after the death of a spouse, it is not uncommon for the remaining partner to become seriously ill or to die within 2 years. The rate of illness and death is much higher among survivors than among similar individuals of the same age who have not suffered the loss of a loved one (Glick, Weiss, & Parkes, 1974; Parkes, 1986). Thus, in one sense, they may have died from grief. One study found a 63 percent increase in the number of times widows consulted their family physicians in the 6 months after bereavement, compared to the 6 months prior to bereavement. Most visits were for psychological symptoms clearly attributable to grief, but many others were for physical problems, especially arthritis and rheumatism (Parkes, 1986).

One possible mechanism for the increased illness and mortality of bereaved people was identified by Steven J. Schleifer and his colleagues at the Mount

Sinai School of Medicine in New York. These researchers examined the white blood cell count, which is a gauge of the effectiveness of the immune system (see Chapter 18), of six men who were married to women dying of cancer. The average age of the men was 65 years. Within 10 months, all their wives had died. As the wives became increasingly sick, the husbands' white blood cell counts became lower and lower and were "markedly depressed after bereavement" (Greenberg, 1980, p. 335).

Widows seem to be most at risk during the first 3 months of bereavement, while widowers are at increased risk during the entire first year (Mellstrom, Nilsson, Oden, Rundgren, & Svanborg, 1982). One study found that the increased mortality among widowers often was due to suicide, cirrhosis of the liver, and heart attacks. The researchers noted that these types of deaths have clear clinical antecedents—depression, alcoholism, and cardiovascular disease, respectively. Identification of people with these illnesses could alert doctors to the fact that these people are at high risk when bereaved and could allow them to provide early intervention (Osterweis, Solomon, & Green, 1984).

One proposed intervention is remarriage. Widowers who remarry have been found to have a substantially lower mortality rate than either unmarried widowers or even married men in the control group. It is hard to know just how to interpret this latter finding (Helsing, Comstock, & Szklo, 1982)!

"A time to be born, and a time to die," and much life to be lived in between. As older people reminisce with friends, they may recall many of the developmental milestones we have examined: a toddler's first step; a child's playing with friends; a teenager's first love; a young woman's launching a career; a middle-aged man's taking command of his world. Older people, no doubt, also recall the pain and sorrow of losses and life's reversals. But the hope is that as they come to die, they can look back with pride and can say with Bertrand Russell, "This has been my life. I have found it worth living, and would gladly live it again if the chance were offered me" (Russell, 1951, p. 4).

APPLICATIONS

Talking About Death with Children

I can talk to them about sex or drinking or drugs . . . just about anything. But when it comes to talking about death, forget it. (Schaefer & Lyons, 1986, p. 3)

People find it especially difficult to talk to children about death. Parents are understandably reluctant to worry children or put them through unnecessary pain. Allowing a child to see a dead body may be too traumatic, they reason, because the child is "just too young to understand." Moreover, parents often are confronted with this issue at a time when they themselves are upset, exhausted, and confused. Almost always, parents simply don't know what to say.

Excluding children from mourning rituals and offering no explanations about what has occurred or why so many adults are upset if everything is "fine" can make children feel alienated from the family. Furthermore, children will use whatever information they can get to explain what's happening, and their fantasies usually are far more frightening than the truth would be (Kellerman, 1981). "I kept thinking that since they wouldn't let me come to see her, how horrible she must look!" one man commented, recalling the death of his grandmother when he was a child (Schaefer & Lyons, 1986, p. 6).

Children also are prone to assume that they have caused the family's distress and to feel guilt and anxiety as a result. This is especially true in cases where, say, a boy has told his sister, "I wish you were dead," a not uncommon sentiment among siblings, and the sister subsequently dies. The boy is quite likely to feel that his thoughts may have, in some magical way, contributed to his sister's death—that he has, in fact, been granted his wish. Such feelings are

likely to cause terrible guilt and anguish.

People may give various explanations to children when someone has died. Some of these, such as equating death with sleep or a journey, may cause unintended problems. The problem with telling children that "grandmother has just gone to sleep" is that, since grandmother doesn't wake up, the children themselves may develop a pathological dread of sleeping. They may struggle to stay awake, fearing that they, too, may go to sleep and not wake up. American author Mark Twain blamed such a statement on his lifelong battle with insomnia. When he was a child, he had been told that a family member who had died had, "gone to sleep forever." From that time on, he couldn't get it out of his head that he, too, might sleep "forever." That dread followed him into adulthood, keeping him awake many a night.

Similarly, telling children that "mother has gone on a long journey" can generate feelings of abandonment, especially if their mother left without even saying goodbye. Moreover, they will expect their mother to return, and they will know that having so many adults upset about mother's "journey" just doesn't make sense.

Another common explanation given to children is that "God took Daddy because your father was so good that God wanted him for himself." Children may become resentful of a God who takes their parent away, and may begin to think, "But God loves me too; maybe I'll be the next one God takes away" (Grollman, 1987, p. 5).

EXPLAINING DEATH TO CHILDREN

We need to tell the simple truth in a way the child can understand. We can assume that the children already

Talking about death in a manner appropriate to a child's age and cognitive development helps decrease frightening fantasies and alleviate guilt.

have some notions about death, and it is helpful to know what these are. Obviously, the way we would talk with a 3-year-old child is different from the way we would explain death to an 8-year-old child. In *How Do We Tell the Children?*, Dan Schaefer and Christine Lyons (1986) offer excellent, concrete suggestions about how to talk about death to children of different ages. In general, certain guidelines are useful to keep in mind.

First, the child needs to know why everyone is so sad and to understand that he didn't cause the sadness. The conversation might begin with comments such as "Mommy and Daddy are sad because . . ." or "This is how we feel when someone dies" (Schaefer & Lyons, 1986, p. 119).

Second, the child needs to know what "dead" means. The adult might offer explanations such as these:

• The person's body has stopped working and won't work anymore.
• The body won't do any of the things it used to do: It won't talk, walk, move, see, or hear; none of the parts work.
• The person won't feel any of the feelings she used to feel, such as sad, mad, happy, hurt, hot, or cold.

• The person will not eat, drink, or go to the bathroom anymore.

When the child asks questions, the adult can then refer back to these explanations. For example, if the child asks something like, "Why can't they fix him?" the adult might say, "Once the body stops working, it can't start again" (Schaefer & Lyons, 1986, p. 120).

It will probably upset children greatly to be told that bodies stop working and can't start again, and children need to be able to express their fears in words and play. They also need to know that caring adults are there to keep them safe and to listen. When a nursery school child died of cancer, teachers found that the little girl's 3-year-old classmates repeatedly asked questions such as, "Did she die because she fell while we were playing?" "Is cancer like getting a cold?" and "Why didn't the doctors help her?" They became increasingly interested in playing "hospital," and although in the past the "doctors" had always made the "babies" better, sometimes the "doctors" no longer were able to do so. Discussions of the children's feelings about their playmate's death contin-

ued sporadically throughout the school year. The teachers concluded that "what could have been ignored or become a frightening experience became instead a time of growing for adults as well as children" (Pohlman, 1984, p. 133).

Discussing death with children in an appropriate and sensitive manner can greatly reduce the confusion the children usually feel when someone they know dies. Although no child should be forced to participate in funeral rituals or discussions if he or she clearly doesn't want to, researchers have found that those children who do participate have a significantly greater cognitive understanding of death. Trying to shelter children may limit their ability to learn through practical experience about this extremely important life cycle event and may lead them to fear excessively the unknown of death, rather than to begin to accept death as an integral part of life (Weber & Fournier, 1985).

SUMMARY

- On average, older people generally report low death anxiety, while middle-aged people express the greatest death anxiety.
- To some degree, America is still a death-denying society. However, the thanatology boom of recent years has resulted in people's being more willing to discuss death and dying.
- Developmental researchers have defined a cognitively mature, adult concept of death as one that acknowledges that death is inevitable, irreversible, and the end of life.
- Different views of death may be present at all stages of our development.
- Among the children that Maria Nagy interviewed, those under 5 years of age saw death as temporary and reversible, while those 5 to 9 years of age thought it was final and permanent, but not inevitable.
- Myra Bluebond-Langner maintains that a child's life experience is most significant in how he or she conceptualizes death.
- Even people who hold the mature concept of death continue to grow in their understanding of death.
- According to Kübler-Ross's theory, dying people pass through the following stages: denial and isolation, anger, bargaining, depression, and acceptance.
- A major problem with the uncritical acceptance of Kübler-Ross's stages is that it may lead people to discount a dying person's legitimate complaints.
- Hospice programs provide mainly palliative care.
- Clinical death occurs when spontaneous breathing and heartbeat stop.
- To be considered brain dead, a person must meet the criteria set forth by the Harvard Ad Hoc Committee to Examine the Definition of Brain Death.
- If no intervention could return an organ to a functional state, the organ is said to have undergone cellular death.
- Living wills allow people to specify what treatment they want if they are seriously ill but unconscious or otherwise mentally incompetent.
- Mercy killing is also known as euthanasia. Active euthanasia occurs when someone deliberately does something to shorten a person's life. Passive euthanasia occurs when treatment is withheld so that the person will die more quickly. Voluntary euthanasia occurs when a competent person's request to be allowed to die is met.
- Bereavement is the state of having lost someone by death. Mourning is the behaviors that bereaved people perform to honor the deceased. Grief is the emotional suffering that people feel when they lose a loved one.
- The grief process often is complicated if the death is sudden and unexpected or if the person dies from a cause that carries a social stigma.

QUESTIONS FOR DISCUSSION

1. What factors might lead some physicians to have higher death anxiety than others do? Would you prefer your physician to have high or low death anxiety? Why?

2. By what criteria might active euthanasia be distinguished from first-degree murder?

3. Suppose a close friend of yours lost a loved one. What kind of support do you think he would need from you at each phase of the grief process?

4. Comedian Woody Allen once quipped, "I'm not afraid to die. I just don't want to be there when it happens." Can you think of other instances in which humor has been used to deal with the fear of dying? When might this humor be appropriate, and when inappropriate?

SUGGESTIONS FOR FURTHER READING

1. Dickenson, D., & Johnson, M. (Eds.). (1993). *Death, dying, and bereavement*. London: Sage.

2. Fitzgerald, H. (1994). *The mourning handbook*. New York: Simon & Schuster.

3. Kübler-Ross, E. (1969). *On death and dying*. New York: Macmillan.

4. Nuland, S. B. (1993). *How we die: Reflections on life's final chapter*. New York: Knopf.

5. Schaefer, D., & Lyons, C. (1986). *How do we tell the children?* New York: Newmarket Press.

FOR DISCUSSION

Even Though the Beer Commercial Said You Only Go Around Once, What Would Happen if Your Exact Biochemical Combination Occurred Again?

You are alive and conscious. You see, hear, and feel. You exist. You are you and not somebody else; you are unique. You "reside" in your body; others "reside" in theirs. The reason that so many different people exist in the world is probably that there are so many different biochemical combinations that can result in a human being. Perhaps you are you because you possess a particular biochemical combination, and others are different because they possess different combinations.

If the universe does not end but continues to be active indefinitely, and some physicists and mathematicians, such as Stephen Hawking and Roger Penrose, believe it may (Hawking, 1988), it might be only a matter of time before somewhere out among the trillions upon trillions of stars and worlds, your biochemical combination comes up again by chance. Although you'd have no memory of the past (memories are a function of experience), *you* would be alive again, seeing, hearing, feeling—conscious, perhaps as a sentient being beginning a life once again.

Your biochemical combination already has occurred once in this universe; you are proof of that. What's to say that in an active, everlasting universe it can't happen again? Is there some rule that says that once a particular combination of chemistry has occurred, it can never be repeated? Such a rule, by our current understanding of biochemistry, seems a bit far-fetched. To many, the alternative appears more likely. Roger Penrose has said that once we die, we are probably born again as somebody else (Hawking, 1989). This Oxford mathematician, whom many consider one of the world's finest intellects, says it with a straight face. He is serious.

"You only go around once" may be a more far-fetched notion than "You keep going around"! Our view of one life may be shortsighted. Death may be a beginning rather than an end, or it may be something else. The point is not to jump to conclusions. Unfortunately, in the case of "after-death phenomena," reliable scientific evidence simply doesn't exist. It would seem, then, that we shouldn't make any assumptions, including the one that "you only go around once." For all any of us know, our own death may not even "exist" for us because we can never perceive it. We may have only life after life, with new bodies and erased memories to begin each one. Then again, maybe we do go around only once—or maybe only beer drinkers do. What do you think?

GLOSSARY

Accepting-rejecting Dimension One of two major dimensions used by Baumrind to describe parenting; denotes the degree of affection within the parent-child relationship.

Accommodation Piaget's term for the process in which people adjust or change their understanding to incorporate aspects of an experience not currently represented in the cognitive structures.

Activity Theory A psychosocial theory that maintains that successful aging depends on an older person's staying actively involved in society.

Adaptation A term used by Piaget to describe the mechanism through which an organism develops by adjusting to changes; such adjustment occurs through the processes of assimilation and accommodation.

Adoption Design A research design used for sorting the influence of nurture from nature. Genetically related individuals who are reared apart or genetically unrelated individuals who are reared together are studied.

Ageism Prejudice and discrimination against the elderly.

AIDS (acquired immune deficiency syndrome) A human retrovirus type HIV, which can be transmitted sexually through the exchange of bodily fluids or by shared needle use among infected IV (intravenous) drug abusers. The disease may also be passed by infusion of unscreened blood or blood products. Once the disease process occurs, the immune system fails and death follows. The virus may infect an unborn child by crossing the placental barrier of an infected mother.

Allele Any of a group of possible mutational forms of a gene.

Altruism Behavior that benefits someone other than the actor, with little or no apparent benefit for the actor.

Alzheimer's Disease A deteriorating dementia characterized by progressive loss of memory, concentration, and judgment and by personality changes. Eventually, victims are unable to recognize other people and to control body functions.

Amenorrhea The absence of the menstrual period from any cause other than pregnancy or menopause.

Amniocentesis A medical procedure wherein fetal cells are removed from the amniotic sac by use of a syringe at about the sixteenth week of pregnancy. The technique is used to screen for genetic and chromosomal disorders.

Anal Stage According to Freud, the second psychosexual stage, during which bowel control is achieved and pleasure is focused on the functions of elimination.

Androgynous The condition in which a single person possesses both "typically masculine" personality traits, such as assertiveness, and "typically feminine" traits, such as tenderness.

Animistic Thinking A kind of thinking common in preconceptual children in which inanimate objects, especially those that move or appear to move, are believed to be alive.

Anticipatory Grief Emotional suffering caused by an impending loss.

Antisocial Behavior Behavior that shows little or no concern for other people and little sense of right or wrong.

Anxious/avoidant Attachment A form of attachment observed by Ainsworth in which children do not approach—but rather actively avoid—their returning mothers.

Anxious/resistant Attachment A form of attachment observed by Ainsworth in which children approach their returning mothers, cry to be picked up, and then struggle to be free. Their behavior is ambivalent; they appear to wish to approach and avoid their mothers simultaneously.

Artificial Intelligence A computer simulation of human cognitive ability and performance.

Assimilation Piaget's term for the act of taking in information and perceptions in a way that is compatible with the person's current understanding of the world.

Associated Play According to Parten's classification, the type of play in which children play and share with others.

Atherosclerosis A condition in which arterial walls thicken and stiffen, and calcified fatty deposits accumulate.

Atrophy of the Vaginal Lining Thinning, loss of elasticity, drying, and itching of the vaginal walls caused by decreasing estrogen levels during the climacteric.

Attachment An especially close affectional bond formed between living creatures.

Authoritarian Parents Parents who put forward a strict set of rules and require unquestioned obedience to them. They are both demanding and hostile. Authoritarian parents often use physical punishment to enforce their rules, and reasoned discussion with the child is rare.

Authoritative Parents Parents who set strict standards, but who are also warm and willing to explain their reasoning to their children.

Autoimmune Response The tendency of the immunological system to attack some tissue or organ of the body, as if those cells were a foreign bacterium or virus.

Autosome Any chromosome that is not a sex chromosome.

B Cells White blood cells that create antibodies that attack foreign bacteria and viruses.

Baby Biography A relatively informal naturalistic observation of an infant's routines and behavior.

Behavior Modification A set of procedures for changing human behavior, especially by using behavior therapy and operant conditioning techniques.

Behavioral Genetics The interdisciplinary science that focuses on the relationship of nature and nurture, that is, on the interaction of what is inherited and what is acquired and how that interaction affects behavior.

Behaviorism The school of psychology that views learning as the most important aspect of an organism's development. Behaviorists objectively measure behavior and the way in which stimulus-response relationships are formed.

Bereavement The state or condition of being deprived of a loved person or object, especially by death.

Beta Amyloid A protein that forms abnormalities in the brains of some people and which may play a significant role in Alzheimer's disease.

Birth The passage of a child from the uterus to outside the mother's body.

Blastocyst A stage of development during the period of the ovum when the embryo consists of one or several layers of cells around a central cavity, forming a hollow sphere.

Brain Death The condition in which the cells of the cortex and midbrain, but not the brain stem, cease to function, and the person lapses into an irreversible coma. To be declared brain dead, a person must meet specific criteria: lack of spontaneous movements, lack of reflex activity, lack of responsiveness, a flat electroencephalogram, and a certain duration of the condition.

Breech Birth A vaginal delivery during which the buttocks or feet of the fetus appear first.

Burnout Emotional and physical exhaustion resulting from excessive dedication to a job.

Cardiopulmonary Resuscitation (CPR) A technique by which a person who has stopped breathing and whose heart has stopped beating may be revived. It involves a combination of mouth-to-mouth resuscitation and pressure applied to the chest at regular intervals.

Career Employment that consists of a series of positions that require increasingly greater mastery and responsibility and provide increasing financial return.

Caretaker Speech A speech pattern used in addressing others who are obviously less competent in their speech than the speaker. Universally applied, caretaker speech is characterized by short, simple sentences, simple vocabulary, a relatively high-pitched voice, and exaggerated inflections. It should not be confused with baby talk, which refers only to the simplification of individual words, such as saying "wa-wa" for water.

Carrier In genetics, an organism that carries a particular trait in its genes and, while not expressing that trait itself, is able to pass on the trait to its offspring.

Case Study An intensive study of a single case, with all available data, test results, and opinions about that individual; Usually done in more depth than are group studies.

Cataract A clouding of the lens of the eye, which decreases the amount of light that reaches the retina.

Catharsis In psychoanalytic theory, elimination of a complex by bringing it to consciousness and allowing it to be expressed. Also, any emotional release resulting from a buildup of internal tensions.

Cellular Death The condition in which a given organ, because of widespread death of cells, cannot be returned to a functional state, regardless of extraordinary intervention.

Cerebrovascular Accident (CVA) Sudden obstruction of blood supply to a portion of the brain or leakage of blood into the brain due to rupture of brittle vessels. May result in mild to severe brain damage, depending on the length of time the blood supply is disrupted and the area of the brain that is affected.

Cervix The opening between the vagina and the uterus in the female animal.

Cesarean Section A surgical incision through the abdominal wall and uterus, performed to extract a fetus.

Child Neglect Failure by parents, caregivers, or other people responsible for children's welfare to provide reasonable and prudent standards of care for children in their charge, which thereby threatens the child's well-being.

Child Abuse Behavior by parents, caregivers, or other people responsible for children's welfare that, through malice or negligence, results in psychological or physical injury to a child.

Chorionic Villi Sampling A technique in which a few cells are removed from the chorionic sac that surrounds the fetus via the use of a plastic catheter inserted through the vagina. The cells may then be examined for chromosomal or genetic disorders.

Chromosome A thread-shaped body that is contained within the nucleus of a cell and that determines those characteristics that will be passed on to the offspring of an organism. Chromosomes carry the genes; humans have 23 pairs of chromosomes.

Chronological Age (CA) A concept developed by Alfred Binet that was subsequently incorporated in the formula IQ = mental age/chronological age X 100. The chronological age of a person is his or her actual age.

Circular Reactions A behavior sequence described by Piaget that occurs during the sensorimotor period of development. There are three kinds of circular reactions: primary, secondary, and tertiary.

Classical Conditioning An experimental learning procedure in which a stimulus that normally evokes a given reflex is continually associated with a stimulus that does not usually evoke that reflex, with the result that the latter stimulus will eventually evoke the reflex when presented by itself.

Climacteric   The 2- to 10-year period during which the biological changes involved in menopause take place.

Clinical Death   The cessation of spontaneous breathing and heartbeat.

Codominance   Situation in which heterozygous alleles consist of two dominant genes. In such instances, both genes are expressed.

Cohabitation   A living arrangement in which two unrelated adults of the opposite sex share the same household. In the past, it has implied sexual intimacy, but it does not necessarily do so today.

Cohort   A group of people, all of whom possess a common demographic characteristic; for example, a group of people born at approximately the same time.

Cohort Sequential Design   A research design in which both longitudinal and cross-sectional data are gathered and compared. It allows researchers to separate changes due to aging from those due to cohort differences, the practice effect, or selective attrition.

Collagen   A key protein found in connective tissue and in bones throughout the body.

Compassionate Love   A feeling of closeness to and companionship with another person that grows stronger over time.

Componential Intelligence   From Sternberg's triarchic theory of intelligence, that aspect of intelligence encompassing the cognitive problem-solving and information-processing skills measured by most IQ tests.

Concept   An abstract idea based on grouping objects by common properties.

Conception   The moment at which the sperm penetrates the ovum and the ovum becomes impervious to the entry of other sperm.

Concrete Operations   A set of logical operations listed by Piaget as indicative of the third period of cognitive development, occurring roughly between the ages of 6 and 11. Such operations are logical, but still tied to the physical world and physical actions.

Conditioned Stimulus   In classical conditioning, a previously neutral stimulus that, through pairing with an unconditioned stimulus, acquires the ability to produce a similar response.

Cononical Stage   A stage of language acquisition that typically occurs between the ages of 7 and 10 months and is typified by an increase in babbling and the production of cononical syllables (made of consonant and vowel sounds of certain intensities). Duplicated sequences such as "dadada" or "mamama" also mark this stage.

Conservation   The principle that quantities such as mass, weight, and volume remain constant regardless of changes in the appearance of these quantities and that such changes in appearance can be undone, thereby regaining the original state by reversing any operations that had been performed. The concept of conservation encompasses the concepts of identity, decentration and reversibility.

Contextual Intelligence   From Sternberg's triarchic theory of intelligence, that aspect of intelligence encompassing the ability of the individual to adapt to his or her environment or culture.

Contraction Stage   A stage of language acquisition that typically occurs between the ages of 10 and 14 months. It is so named because during this time, infants begin to narrow their phoneme production to the phonemes common to the language to which they are exposed. During this stage, infants also acquire the pacing and rhythm of their language.

Control   In a controlled study, experimental or research conditions are arranged deliberately so that observed effects can be traced directly to one or more known variables. The control is similar to the experimental subject but is not exposed to the variable.

Conventional Level   According to Kohlberg, the level of moral development in which the individual strives to maintain the expectations of family, group, or nation, regardless of the consequences.

Convergent Production   In Guilford's model of intelligence, a type of thinking in which an individual searches through his or her knowledge and uses all that can be found to converge on one correct answer.

Cooperation   Working together toward a common end or purpose.

Cooperative Play   According to Parten's classification, the type of play in which children play structured games with other children according to rules.

Correlation   A relationship between two variables.

Creativity   The ability to originate something new and appropriate by transcending common thought constraints.

Creole   A mixture of language that develops when groups speaking different languages have prolonged contact. Typically, the basic vocabulary of the dominant language is combined with the grammar of a subordinate language, creating an admixture (a mingling within a mixture) of words and grammar that becomes in itself a new subordinate and creolized language.

Crisis Nursery   A place where parents may leave infants and young children for a short time until the parents are better able to deal with their stress and the danger of abuse is thus lessened.

Critical Period   A specific time in an organism's development when certain experiences will have an effect, and after which the effect can no longer be obtained through exposure to the experience.

Cross-sectional Approach   A research strategy in which investigators examine subjects of different ages simultaneously to study the relationships between age, experience, and behavior.

Cross-cultural Research   Research in which different cultures are evaluated on different behavioral dimensions, such as attachment, emotional development, or intellectual development. Its primary purpose is to isolate and distinguish the effects and influences of culture from those of other variables.

Cross-modal Transfer   A recognition of an object as familiar when perceived with a sense other than that previously used when exposed to the object.

Crystallized Intelligence   Stored information about oneself and the world.

Culture-fair Test   A test that is supposed to be free of cultural biases, usually constructed so that language differences and other cultural effects are minimized.

Cytomegalovirus A common virus to which a majority of American women have been exposed at some time in their lives. An active infection in a pregnant woman may cause harm to the unborn child.

Decentration In Piagetian theory, the cognitive ability to break out of the frame of thought that causes one to focus on only one aspect of a changing situation.

Declarative Memory The type of long-term memory containing conscious memories of facts and events that need to be "brought to mind" to become active. It is sometimes called explicit memory or fact memory. The ability to recognize a face, recall a number, or recall any verbal or sensory information requires declarative memory.

Defibrillation The administration of an electrical shock to the heart that causes all myocardial cells to fire simultaneously. This technique i used to terminate *fibrillation*, a condition in which the cells have ceased to fire in concert and the heart has therefore ceased to function as a pump.

Dementia Irreversible loss of personality and intellectual functioning caused by disease or brain damage.

Deoxyribonucleic Acid (DNA) A chemical constituent of cell nuclei, consisting of two long chains of alternating phosphate and deoxyribose units twisted into a double helix and joined by bonds between the complementary bases of adenine, thymine, cytosine, and guanine. It is the substance that enables cells to copy themselves.

Dependent Variable In an experiment, the variable that may change as a result of changes in the independent variable.

Depression A mood disturbance characterized by feelings of sadness, pessimism, apathy, excessive worry, guilt, and an inability to experience pleasure. Sometimes, these feelings are accompanied by difficulty in sleeping, loss of appetite, and loss of sexual desire.

Developmental Psychology The study of age-related differences in behavior. It is a branch of psychology. Psychology is the study of behavior and mental processes.

Dialectical Thinking Thinking characterized by an understanding of the advantages and disadvantages of any idea or course of action.

Differential Reproduction A mechanism by which organisms with favorable traits tend to reproduce in greater numbers than those with less favorable traits, resulting in an increase in favored traits in later generations.

Discrete Emotions Theory A view of emotional development that has as its central premise that all basic emotions are present and functional in newborns or very shortly after birth.

Disengagement Theory A psychosocial theory that maintains that successful aging depends on the mutual and voluntary withdrawal of an older person from society and of society from the older person.

Displaced Homemakers Women who have been in traditional marriages, who have not been employed outside the home, and whose marriages have ended, leaving them without a clearly defined social role and often without marketable skills for the workplace.

Distinctive Feature Gibson's term for that portion of an object that can be discriminated from other portions.

Divergent Production In Guilford's model of intelligence, a type of thinking in which a person searches for multiple ideas or solutions to a problem. It is characteristic of the creative thought process.

Diversification In evolution, the great range of individual differences in each species from which natural forces may select.

Dominant In genetics, describing a gene whose characteristics are expressed while suppressing the characteristics controlled by the other corresponding gene for that trait.

Double Recessive A condition in which both allelic pairs for a given trait are recessive, and no dominant allelic gene is present to override them. In this case, the recessive trait will be expressed.

Down Syndrome A chromosomal abnormality that manifests itself in such features as a thick tongue, extra eyelid folds, and heart deformities, as well as deficient intelligence. It is caused by a trisomy of the twenty-first chromosome pair or by a translocation of part of a third chromosome 21 onto another chromosome.

Duo A two-word utterance made by children during the two-word stage.

Dysmenorrhea Painful menstruation.

Electra Complex According to Freud, the female form of the Oedipus complex; the desire of a girl to possess her father sexually.

Embryo The unborn child from the time of attachment to the uterine wall until the formation of bone (approximately 2-8 weeks from conception).

Empathy An insightful awareness and ability to share the emotions, thoughts, and behavior of another person.

Empirical Relying or based solely on experiments or objective observation.

Empty-nest Syndrome Depression that parents may experience when their grown children leave home.

Encode In memory, the process of organizing a stimulus input into an acceptable form for storage.

Endometriosis A pathological condition in which bits of the endometrial lining of the uterus invade the body cavity and periodically bleed during a woman's monthly cycle. The disorder is found more often in women over 30 years of age and may interfere with fertility by producing scar tissue that can damage or block the fallopian tubes.

Environmental Theories Theories that attempt to predict or explain behavior based primarily on a person's learning and past experience.

Epigenetic Theories Theories that emphasize the interaction between the environment and a person's genetic inheritance.

Equilibrium Term used by Piaget to describe a hypothetical innate drive that forces a person to actively pursue cognitive adaptation. In this view, children have a natural inclination toward cognitive development.

Erogenous Zones According to psychoanalytic theory, physically defined areas of the body from which the greatest psychosexual gratification is obtained. Different areas are predominant during different stages of psychosexual development.

Estrogen A hormone that is produced primarily by the ovaries and is responsible for the development of female secondary sex characteristics. The adrenal glands of the male also produce some estrogen, but the hormone is found primarily in females.

Ethology The study of human and animal behavior from a biological point of view, characterized by the study of animals in their natural environments.

Eugenics The science of improving the genetic characteristics of humans through breeding; term coined by Sir Francis Galton.

Euthanasia The act or practice of killing people who are hopelessly sick or injured, for reasons of mercy.

Evolution The process by which plants or animals change from earlier existing forms. Darwin understood evolution to occur primarily through the processes of diversification and natural selection.

Expansion An enlargement, increase, or extension of initial research.

Expansion Stage A stage of language acquisition that typically occurs between the ages of 4 and 7 months. During this stage, infants produce many new sounds and rapidly expand the number of phonemes they use, giving rise to babbling.

Experience-dependent System A neural model of the central nervous system that pictures the CNS as containing structures that are flexible and prepared to incorporate information that is unique to each individual member of a species. The portion of the CNS that is not experience-expectant.

Experience-expectant System A neural model of the central nervous system that pictures the CNS as containing structures that are prepared, or "prewired," to rapidly respond to, or make sense of, experiences that are common to all members of the species. The portion of the CNS that is not experience-dependent.

Experiential Intelligence From Sternberg's triarchic theory of intelligence, that aspect of intelligence encompassing the ability to take a newly learned skill and make it routine.

Experiment A test made to demonstrate the validity of some hypothesis or to determine the predictability of a theory. Variables are manipulated during the test. Any changes are contrasted with those of a control that has not been exposed to the variables of interest.

Exploration-play-application Sequence An ethological term describing the function of play as a bridge between the cautious exploration of the unfamiliar and its eventual application for useful purposes.

Factor Load The weight, or emphasis, given to any factor or ability.

Factor Analysis A statistical procedure aimed at discovering the constituent traits within a complex system such as personality or intelligence. The method enables the investigator to compute the minimum number of factors required to account for intercorrelations in test scores.

Fallopian Tubes The pair of slender ducts leading from the uterus to the region of the ovaries in the female reproductive system.

Fantasy Play Play in which an object, person, or situation becomes a target for fantasy and is not treated as what it actually is.

Farsighted The inability to see close objects clearly.

Fast Mapping The ability of children to rapidly narrow down the correct meaning of a word.

Fetal Alcohol Syndrome A disorder suffered by some infants whose mothers ingested alcohol during the prenatal period. It is characterized by facial, limb, or organ defects and reduced physical size and intellectual ability.

Fetus The unborn child from the first formation of bone (approximately the eighth week after conception) until the time of birth.

Fluid Intelligence The innate ability to learn and understand information and to solve problems.

Foreclosure The failure of an adolescent to explore and discover a self-identity; the unquestioning acceptance and adoption of the identity demanded by parents or other important adults.

Fragile X Syndrome A sex-linked inherited chromosomal disorder that produces moderate retardation among males who inherit the fragile X chromosome. After Down syndrome, it is the most common biological cause of retardation.

Friendships Close emotional ties formed with another person through mutual preference for interaction, skill at complementary and reciprocal peer play, and shared positive affect.

Functional Age A person's ability to perform adequately in society. It combines measures of biological, psychological, and social functioning.

Gain-loss Theory A social theory of relationships that states that we are most attracted by those who have given us the greatest net gain and are least attracted to those who have caused the greatest net loss.

Gamete Male or female germ cell containing one-half the number of chromosomes found in the other cells of the body.

Gay A homosexual man.

Gender Schema Theory The theory developed by Sandra Bem that explains how cognitive advances help the child to organize and integrate the information that he or she has learned about his or her sex.

Gender Role The behaviors associated with one sex or the other.

Gender Constancy The realization that one's sex is determined by unchanging criteria and is unaffected by one's activities or behavior; usually develops in children by the age of 6 or 7 years.

Gender-role Identification The degree to which a child adopts the gender role of a particular model.

Gene The smallest functional unit for the transmission of a hereditary trait; a section of genetic code.

Generation Gap Differences in social and political values held by members of different generations, often resulting in conflict.

Generativity The concern about establishing and guiding the next generation, and other forms of "care for the creatures of the world."

Genetic Imprinting The process whereby identical sections of the same chromosome will yield different phenotypic outcomes, depending on whether the chromosome was inherited from the mother or the father.

Genetic Counseling   Services provided to prospective parents that include detailed analysis of genetic inheritance and the possibilities or prospects of the occurrence of genetic disorders in offspring.

Genital Stage   In psychoanalytic theory, the final stage of psychosexual development, characterized by the expression of heterosexual desires.

Genotype   The characteristics that an individual has inherited and may transmit to descendants, regardless of whether the individual manifests these characteristics.

Geriatrics   A branch of medicine that deals with the problems and diseases of the elderly.

Gerontology   The study of old age and aging.

Glaucoma   A disease in which a buildup of aqueous fluid causes increased pressure within the eyeball, resulting in a gradual loss of vision.

Gooing Stage   A stage of language acquisition that typically occurs between the ages of 2 and 4 months. During this stage, infants combine the quasi vowels from the phonation stage with harder sounds that are precursors of consonants.

Grammar   A set of rules that determines how sounds may be put together to make words and how words may be put together to make sentences.

Grammatical Morphemes   Words or parts of words that help add meaning to a sentence. Grammatical morphemes are acquired by children generally between the ages of 2 1/2 and 5 years. Conjunctions, prepositions, suffixes, and prefixes are examples of grammatical morphemes. Morphemes are the smallest language units to have meaning and cannot be broken down into smaller meaningful units.

Grief   Emotional suffering caused by bereavement.

Growth Spurt   The time during puberty in which an adolescent's growth undergoes a marked acceleration.

Habituation   A process whereby an organism ceases to respond to a stimulus that is repeatedly presented.

Herpes   A disease caused by a number of viruses that can attack the skin or mucous membranes. Genital herpes is difficult to treat and can harm an infant born to a mother whose herpes is in an active stage.

Heterosexual   A person who is sexually attracted to a member of the opposite sex.

Heterozygous   Describing alleles of a gene pair that are different.

Hierarchy of Motives   A theory of motivation developed by Maslow in which more basic needs must first be met before needs of a higher order can come into play.

Holophrase   A possible semantic statement made by children in the one-word stage when they utter single words. A holophrase is a single-word "sentence," that is, a one-word utterance that may be interpreted to contain the semantic content of a phrase.

Homeostasis   An internal environment in which such body components as blood pressure, blood chemistry, breathing, diges-

tion, and temperature are kept at levels optimal for the survival of the organism.

Homosexual   A person who is sexually attracted to a member of his or her own sex.

Homozygous   Describing alleles of a gene pair that are identical.

Horizontal Decalage   Term used by Piaget to describe the onset and order of different conservation abilities.

Hospice   A program of palliative and supportive services that provides physical, psychological, social, and spiritual care for terminally ill people and their families.

Hot Flashes   Sudden, brief sensations of heat, often accompanied by reddening of the skin. They are thought to be caused by the fluctuating levels of estrogen during the climacteric.

Human Genome   All the genes on all 46 human chromosomes.

Humanistic Theory   A school of psychology that emphasizes the uniqueness of the individual and the search for self-actualization.

Hyperpyrexia   Exceptionally high body temperature, which may result in a heat stroke.

Hypothermia   The condition in which body temperature drops to 95 degrees Fahrenheit or lower. Confusion, stupor, and death may result.

Ideational Fluency   A term used by Michael Wallach to describe an individual's ability to produce many ideas. Ideational fluency is sometimes used as a measure of creativity.

Identity   The concept that two objects will remain identical in some elemental way even though one of the objects may have its appearance altered in some dramatic way. In Piagetian theory, children achieve a deep understanding of identity during the period of concrete operations.

Identity Diffusion   A problem faced by adolescents who find themselves committed to few goals or values and who are apathetic about searching for their own identity.

Implicit Memory   The memory associated with recall of muscular or glandular responses that have been conditioned. Implicit memories are acquired slowly with practice. This type of memory is required to recall the skills necessary for object manipulation and learned physical activity. It is sometimes called skill or motor memory.

Imprinting   As used by ethologists, a species-specific bonding that occurs within a limited period early in the life of the organism and that is relatively unmodifiable thereafter.

Independent Variable   In an experiment, the variable that is manipulated or treated to see what effect differences in it will have on the variables considered to be dependent on it.

Induction   A disciplinary technique in which caregivers try to show the child the reasoning behind the discipline.

Information-processing Approach   A cognitive approach to the understanding of intellectual development that relies on the computer as a model. Researchers using this approach are concerned with the storage, processing, and retrieval mechanisms involved in cognition.

Intellectual Plasticity   The variability in intellectual functioning caused by different social, environmental, and physical conditions.

Intelligence Quotient (IQ)   A quotient derived from the formula MA/CA × 100, where MA is mental age and CA is chronological age. The intelligence quotient was devised by German psychologist L. William Stern and introduced in the United States by Lewis Terman.

Intelligence   A general term for a person's abilities in a wide range of tasks, including vocabulary, numbers, problem solving, and concepts. It may also include the ability to profit from experience, to learn new information, and to adjust to new situations.

Interiority   The increased introspection that often occurs as people grow older, especially during middle and late adulthood.

Internal Working Model   The memories on which people can draw that help to determine the consequences that may result from actions in a given situation.

Interobserver Reliability   The degree of agreement or disagreement between two or more observers who make simultaneous observations of a single event.

Interrole Conflict   The internal conflict a person feels because of the various demands of a job and family life.

Intraorganismic Perspective   The theory, first espoused by Bowlby, that infants possess innate mechanisms that foster and promote the development of attachment. Such mechanisms are believed to have been naturally selected, as they have survival value.

Job   Employment in which upward advancement is limited and movement is primarily horizontal.

Joint Custody   An arrangement in which more than one person shares legal custody of a child.

Karyotype   A photomicrograph of chromosomes in a standard array.

Kibbutz   An Israeli farm or collective where children are often reared in groups and receive nurturance and guidance from many different adults and older children.

Labor   The physical efforts of childbirth; parturition.

Language Acquisition Device (LAD)   As hypothesized by Noam Chomsky, a neural structure inborn in every healthy individual that is preprogrammed with the underlying rules of a universal form of grammar. Once children are exposed to a particular language, they select from the complete set of rules with which they were born only those rules required by the language they will be speaking. Most psychologists and linguists find the idea interesting, but agree that proof of such a device is doubtful because of the difficulties involved in demonstrating its existence.

Latency stage   In psychoanalytic theory, the fourth psychosexual stage, occurring between the phallic stage and puberty, during which sexual drives and feelings become lessened or nonexistent.

Law of Effect   Thorndike's principle that responses associated with pleasant consequences tend to be repeated, while those associated with discomforting consequences tend to be eliminated.

Learned Helplessness   Giving up even though success is possible because of previous experience with situations in which success was impossible.

Learning   A relatively permanent change in behavior as a result of experience.

Lesbian   A homosexual woman.

Life Structure   The underlying pattern of a person's life at a given time.

Life Review   The process in which a person approaching death looks back over his or her life and attempts to understand its meaning.

Lightening   The rotation of the fetus into a head-downward position prior to birth.

Linear Development   Development that progresses steadily and continuously (as would a straight line). In this process, each development is dependent on those that came before.

Living Will   A document that a person constructs while mentally competent, specifying what treatment the person wants carried out if he or she is seriously ill and unconscious or otherwise mentally incompetent.

Longitudinal Approach   A research study design in which investigators follow an individual through time, taking measurements at periodic intervals.

Looming   A technique to measure depth perception in infants and animals. A target, usually a bull's-eye, is rushed toward a seated subject's face. Head retraction is taken as a sign that the subject expects collision—an indication of depth perception, as the subject must be assuming that the object is coming nearer.

Love Withdrawal   A disciplinary technique in which caregivers express disapproval by ignoring, isolating, or expressing lack of love for the child.

Magnetic Resonance Imaging (MRI)   A technique that makes internal body structures clearly visible. It uses radio waves to excite atoms in the body, and the excitations, monitored by a huge magnet, are interpreted by a computer to produce a composite picture.

Maturation   A genetically programmed biological plan of development that is relatively independent of experience. Maturation is highly correlated with, and dependent on, the growth and development of the nervous system.

Mechanistic-functional Approach   An approach to the understanding of cognitive development that takes the machine as its metaphor. Environmental influences on cognitive development are considered major, since machines don't change from within but must be added to from without.

Meiosis   The process of cell division in sexually reproducing organisms that reduces the number of chromosomes in reproductive cells, leading to the production of gametes.

Memory   The complex mental function of recalling what has been learned or experienced.

Menarche   The first occurrence of menstruation.

Menopause   The complete cessation of menstruation, which usually occurs during middle age. It is said to have occurred when a woman has not had a menstrual period for 12 consecutive months.

Mental Age (MA)   A concept developed by Alfred Binet that was subsequently incorporated into the formula IQ = mental age/chronological age × 100. The mental age of a person is derived by comparing his or her score with the average scores of others within specific age groups.

Mentor   A more experienced person in a work setting who provides guidance, support, and advice about career development to a less experienced person.

Meta-emotion   One's knowledge about one's own emotions.

Meta-analysis   An examination of many studies that focus on one topic, in order to discover an overall consensus. Careful attention is paid to eliminate faulty studies.

Metacognition   All the skills and abilities that encompass one's knowledge and understanding about one's own cognitive and thinking abilities; what one knows about one's own cognition and thinking processes.

Metamemory   Knowledge of how best to use one's memory.

Model   In social learning theory, anyone who demonstrates a behavior that other people observe.

Modifier Genes   Genes that act on other genes and modify the latter's effects.

Molecule   A distinct chemical unit or group of atoms that have joined together.

Monosomy   A single unpaired chromosome that is located where there should be a pair of chromosomes.

Morals   The attitudes and beliefs that people hold that help them to determine what is right or wrong.

Moratorium   The time during which an adolescent is searching for an identity.

Mourning   Culturally prescribed behaviors that bereaved people are expected to perform to honor the deceased.

Multi-infarct Dementia   Dementia that occurs as a result of one or more cerebrovascular accidents.

Multisomy   A chromosomal abnormality in which more than one additional chromosome is associated with a chromosome pair.

Mutation   Any heritable alteration of the genes or chromosomes of an organism.

Myelin Sheath   A white fatty covering on neural fibers that serves to channel and increase the transmission speed of impulses along those fibers.

Myocardial Infarction   A condition in which a portion of the heart muscle dies because the blood (and thus the oxygen) supply to it has been obstructed.

Naming   A development of early childhood in which the child begins pointing out objects and calling them by name. It is considered a special development because it appears to be intrinsically reinforcing and satisfying to humans and seems to occur only in our species.

Natural Selection   The process, first suggested by Darwin, through which those individuals of a species best adapted to their environment have a better chance of passing on their genes to the next generation than do those not as well adapted.

Naturalist   A person who studies natural history, especially zoology and botany.

Nature   In developmental research, the hereditary component of an organism's development.

Nearsightedness   The inability to see distant objects clearly.

Negative Identity   A development among some adolescents in which the identity adopted is the opposite of what parents and society desired or expected.

Neonate   A newborn infant.

Nucleus   A central body within a living cell that contains the cell's hereditary material and controls its metabolism, growth, and reproduction.

Nurture   In developmental research, the environmental component of an organism's development.

Object Permanence   Term used by Piaget to refer to the individual's realization that objects continue to exist even though they are not presently sensed.

Oedipus Complex   A Freudian term representing the sexual attachment of a boy to his mother. This desire is repressed and disguised in various ways. The child expresses jealousy and hatred of his father because the father can have relations with the mother that the son is denied.

One-word Stage   The universal stage in language development in which children's speech is limited to single words.

Onlooker Play   According to Parten's classification, the type of play in which the child watches other children play but does not participate.

Operant Conditioning   Skinner's term for changes in behavior that occur as a result of consequences that reinforce or punish emitted responses. They are, in turn, shaped by further environmental experiences.

Oral Stage   According to Freud, the first psychosexual stage, in which pleasure is focused on the mouth and oral cavity.

Organ Reserve   The extra capacity of the heart, lungs, and other organs that is drawn on in times of physical or emotional stress or illness.

Organismic-structural Approach   An approach to the understanding of cognitive development that takes as its metaphor the growing biological organism. Environmental influences on cognitive development are considered minor, with only extreme environmental forces having any appreciable effect on biological structure or development.

Osteoporosis   A condition in which loss of calcium and various minerals results in bones becoming more porous and fragile.

Palliative   Serving to reduce pain and suffering.

Parallel Play   According to Parten's classification, the type of play children engage in when they play alongside other children but do not participate directly with the other children.

Parents Anonymous   An organization to help parents who abuse their children make constructive changes in their responses; uses the same intensive contact and principles as Alcoholics Anonymous.

Passionate Love   An intense emotional reaction to another person characterized by feelings of romance and excitement.

Peer Groups   Groups that develop their own set of values and goals and establish durable social relationships. Generally, each member has a specified role or status.

Peers Equals; developmentally, people who interact at about the same behavioral level, regardless of age.

Period of the Embryo Time from the attachment of the zygote to the uterine wall until the first formation of solid bone in the embryo, from about 2 to 8 weeks following conception.

Period of the Fetus Time from the first formation of bone in the embryo until birth, generally from 8 weeks following conception until birth.

Period of the Ovum Time from conception until the zygote is first attached within the uterus, about 2 weeks following conception.

Permissive-demanding Dimension One of two major dimensions used by Baumrind to describe parenting; denotes the degree of parental permissiveness.

Personality The organization of relatively enduring characteristics unique to an individual, as revealed by the individual's interaction with his or her environment.

Phallic Stage According to Freud, the third psychosexual stage, during which the child manipulates and explores his or her genitals and experiences a strong attraction for the parent of the opposite sex.

Phenotype The observable characteristics of an organism due to inheritance.

Phenylketonuria (PKU) A genetic disorder marked by an inability to oxidize properly the amino acid phenylalanine. If this disorder is not controlled by proper diet, permanent damage is caused to the developing child's central nervous system.

Phonation Stage A stage of language acquisition that develops between birth and 2 months of age. During this stage, infants often make comfort sounds composed of quasi vowels.

Phoneme Constancy A perceptual ability that develops in infancy in which a phoneme, although spoken or pronounced differently by different individuals, is perceived as a single entity regardless of speaker.

Phonemes The smallest units of speech that can affect meaning. For instance, the only difference between mat and bat is the phoneme sounds m and b. These two sounds are phonemes because they affect meaning; a mat is certainly not a bat. Phonemes are typically composed of phones. Some languages use more phonemes than others.

Phones The smallest units of vocalized sound that do not affect meaning but can be discriminated. (Derived from the Greek word phone, meaning "voice" or "sound.") Phones are often responsible for regional and foreign accents. For example, someone from Boston might pronounce the word car differently than someone from Dallas.

Phonology The study of how sounds (phonemes and phones) are put together to make words.

Phrenology A system for identifying types of people by examining their physical features, especially the configuration of the skull.

Pidgin A simplified form of speech typically derived from a mixture of two or more languages. It has as its basis a rudimentary form of grammar and vocabulary and is generally used for communication between people speaking different languages.

Placenta A vascular, membranous organ that develops during pregnancy, lining the uterine wall and partially enveloping the fetus. The placenta is attached to the fetus by the umbilical cord.

Play Pleasurable activity engaged in for its own sake, with means emphasized rather than ends. Play usually is not engaged in as a serious activity and is flexible, in that it varies in form or context.

Population Pyramid A graphic depiction of the number of individuals within given age ranges. Each age range is stacked from the youngest to oldest; in the normal population, the graph typically forms a pyramid shape.

Post-formal Operational Thought A type of thinking that may develop in late adolescence or adulthood. No widely accepted definition yet exists; in general, characteristics include an ability to understand relativity, contradiction, and subjectivity, and to integrate these into decision making.

Postconventional Level According to Kohlberg, the level of moral development characterized by self-chosen ethical principles that are comprehensive, universal, and consistent.

Power Assertion A disciplinary technique in which caregivers use physical punishment, removal of privileges, or the threat of these actions.

Practice Effect The improvement in performance that comes about from doing a task more than once.

Precision The accuracy of predictions made from a theory.

Preconcepts A Piagetian term describing immature concepts held by children in the preoperational stage.

Preconventional Level According to Kohlberg, a level of moral development in which good or bad is determined by the physical or hedonistic consequences of obeying or disobeying the rules.

Premature Infant An infant who weighs less than 5.5 pounds at birth and who was carried less than 37 weeks.

Presbycusis The progressive, age-related decrease in the ability to hear high-frequency tones.

Primary Circular Reactions Simple repetitive acts that center on the infant's own body, such as thumb sucking or foot grasping; characteristic of the second stage of the sensorimotor period.

Probabilistic Epigenesis Literally, the direction in which growth will probably go. In cognitive development theory, the term is used to describe the stages of cognitive development that typically occur during the development of most individuals, but not necessarily in the development of all individuals.

Prodromal Precursor, or early warning.

Prosocial Behavior Behavior that benefits other people and society.

Prostate Gland A small gland that secretes fluid to transport sperm. Located at the base of a man's bladder, it may enlarge and interfere with urination and ejaculation.

Psychoanalytic Theory The school of psychological thought founded by Freud that emphasizes the study of unconscious mental processes and psychosexual development. As a therapy, psychoanalysis seeks to bring unconscious desires into consciousness and to resolve conflicts that usually date back to early childhood experiences.

Psychological Maltreatment   Mistreatment of children in a psychological way, as distinguished from physical abuse or neglect; includes verbal abuse, failure to provide warmth or love, and belittlement or berating.

Psychosexual Stages   Five stages of human development postulated by Freud. All but the latency stage are centered about the stimulation of erogenous zones. The erogenous stages—oral, anal, phallic, and genital—are predominant at different times.

Psychosocial Stages   Stages of ego development as formulated by Erikson, incorporating both sexual and social aspects.

Puberty   The stage of maturation in which the individual becomes physiologically capable of sexual reproduction.

Punishment   An aversive stimulus consequence that has the effect of decreasing the strength of an emitted response.

Pupil   The dark circular opening in the center of the eye that helps to regulate the amount of light entering the eye.

Raspberry   In foodstuffs: a rather tasty fruit; a type of berry. In social discourse: an explosive sound caused by the rapid expulsion of air from the mouth. The expelled air vigorously vibrates the lips (especially the lower lip), which have been deliberately placed in a configuration so as to make contact with and surround the protruded tongue. Considered unrequired in most social circumstances.

Reality Play   Play devoid of fantasy or in which fantasy is an insignificant part; essentially, play in which an object or situation is treated as what it actually is.

Recessive   In genetics, describing a gene whose characteristics are not expressed when paired with a dominant gene.

Reciprocity   A mutual exchange of privileges.

Reflex Exercise   Piagetian description of the first stage of the sensorimotor period, during which the infant's reflexes become smoother and more coordinated.

Reflexes   Simple innate responses to an eliciting stimulus.

Rehearsal   Repetitive review of learned material undertaken to facilitate later recall.

Reinforcement   An event that strengthens the response that preceded it. Operant conditioning is a process by which a response is reinforced.

Replication   Repetition of an experiment to enhance the reliability of the results.

Reversibility   The concept that actions that affect objects, if reversed in sequence, will return the objects to their original state. In Piagetian theory, the ability to understand reversibility is obtained during concrete operations.

Role Confusion   A consequence of the failure to establish a sense of identity during Erikson's fifth psychosocial stage. Without a sense of identity, the individual will be confused about his or her role in society and will find it difficult to form a life philosophy or create a stable base on which to build a career or have a family.

Rubella   A viral infection, commonly known as German measles, that may have a serious effect on an unborn child, especially if contracted by the mother during the first trimester.

Saltatory Growth   Literally, growth by leaping. Growth that occurs in "spurts" or sudden leaps.

Scheme   The comprehensions that an infant, child, or adult has about different aspects of his or her world at any given moment in time. Piaget believed that children develop schematic outlines (or maps) of what the world is like and maintain these outlines in their memories.

Script   In cognitive study, one's knowledge of the appropriate events that should occur in a particular social setting and of how one might carry them out. This includes knowledge of who is expected to do what to whom as well as when, where, and why. A script would include the typical behaviors expected of a person going to a restaurant or movie.

Secondary Circular Reactions   Circular reactions characteristic of the third stage of the sensorimotor period, in which the child reaches out to manipulate objects discovered in the environment.

Secular Trend   The tendency during the last century for children to mature and grow taller at a younger age.

Secure Attachment   Most common form of attachment observed by Ainsworth. Securely attached children respond happily to their mother's return, greet her, and stay near her for a while.

Selective Attention   The process of discriminating one stimulus from multiple stimuli and attending to it.

Selective Attrition   The tendency of people who do not perform well in a given situation (for example, college, a job, a research project) to leave that situation.

Self-actualization   Maslow's term for an individual's constant striving to realize full potential.

Self-in-relation Theory   A theory in which the goal of personality development is a deepening capacity for competence in relationships, in contrast to theories that emphasize autonomy, self-reliance, and separation from other people.

Senescence   The gradual weakening of the body that begins during early adulthood and continues until death.

Sensitive Period   A time during which a particular organism is most sensitive to the effect of certain stimuli.

Separation Anxiety   The anxiety over the possible loss of anyone to whom a person has become attached.

Sequential Design   A research design that combines elements of different time-dependent research approaches to control for biases that might be introduced when any single approach is used alone.

Sex Chromosomes   In humans, those chromosomes responsible for producing the sex of the child, the X and Y chromosomes.

Sex-linked Disorder   A hereditary disorder controlled by a gene carried on the sex-determining chromosome. Color blindness is an example.

Sex Typing   The process whereby an individual incorporates the behaviors, traits, and attitudes appropriate to his or her biological sex or the sex assigned at birth.

Sexual Impotence   The inability to achieve and maintain an erection of sufficient duration to have intercourse.

Sexually Transmitted Diseases (STDs)   Diseases that are primarily transmitted through sexual intercourse.

Shoulder Presentation   During birth, the presentation of the shoulder first, rather than the head.

Slow Virus   A virus that may take years to produce symptoms. Slow viruses have been implicated in some forms of mental retardation.

Social Learning   Learning by observing the actions of other people.

Social Referencing   The use of emotional signals or cues from others as a guide for one's own behavior in ambiguous situations.

Social Fantasy Play   Play in which one pretends to be someone else or adopts a role other than one's own; common to children age 5 years or older.

Social Role Taking   The act of taking or understanding the perspective of another.

Social Cognition   The application of cognitive principles to the social arena.

Social Exchange Theory   A social theory of relationships that states that human interactions can best be understood by examining the costs and rewards to each person.

Solitary Play   According to Parten's classification, the type of play children engage in when they play by themselves.

Spoonerism   An unintentional transposition of sounds in a sentence, as in, "People in glass houses shouldn't stow thrones." Named for the English clergyman William A. Spooner (1844-1930), who was well known for such errors.

Stranger Anxiety   A fear of unfamiliar individuals that most infants develop when they are about 6 months of age.

Survey   A method of collecting data through interviews and questionnaires.

Syncretic Reasoning   A type of reasoning used by preconceptual children, in which objects are classified according to a limited and changing set of criteria.

Syntax   The body of linguistic rules that makes it possible to relate a series of words in a sentence to the underlying meaning of that sentence; that is, the rules governing word order in a language (sentence structure).

T Cells   White blood cells that help B cells to divide and to produce antibodies more efficiently.

Telegraphic Speech   Pattern of speech that develops during and following the two-word stage, in which English-speaking children rely on a grammar of strict word order to convey their meaning and do not use conjunctions, prepositions, or other function words.

Temperament Theory   Any theory of human development that places an emphasis on the enduring and stable aspects of personality, which are generally considered to be constitutional in nature, that is, due to the biogenetics of the individual.

Teratogens   Substances capable of producing fetal abnormalities, such as alcohol and tobacco.

Terminal Drop   A decrease in intellectual functioning that occurs as people approach death.

Tertiary Circular Reactions   Circular reactions characteristic of the fifth stage of the sensorimotor period, in which the child actively experiments with things to discover how various actions affect an object or outcome.

Testosterone   A hormone that is produced primarily by the testes and is responsible for the development of male secondary sex characteristics. The adrenal glands of the female also produce some testosterone, but the hormone is found primarily in males.

Thanatology   The study of death and dying.

Theory   A system of rules or assumptions used to predict or explain phenomena.

Time-lag Design   A research design in which different groups of people are measured on a characteristic or behavior when they are the same age; for example, one group of 2-year-old children are measured in one year, another group of 2-year-old children are measured in a subsequent year, and so on.

Toxoplasmosis   A disease of humans, dogs, cats, and certain other mammals, caused by a parasitic microorganism that affects the nervous system. The disorder is especially damaging to an embryo or fetus.

Transductive Reasoning   A type of reasoning used by preconceptual children, in which inferences are drawn about the relationship between two objects based on a single attribute.

Trisomy   A chromosomal abnormality in which a third chromosome occurs on a chromosome pair.

Trophoblast   The outer layer of cells by which the fertilized ovum is attached to the uterine wall and through which the embryo receives its nourishment.

Twin Design   A research design used for sorting the influence of nurture from nature. A characteristic or behavior is compared between identical twins; then the same characteristic or behavior is compared between fraternal twins.

Two-word Stage   The universal stage of language development in which children's expressions are limited to two-word utterances.

Type A   A behavior pattern characterized by ambition, aggression, competitiveness, and impatience.

Type B   A behavior pattern characterized by a relaxed, easygoing manner and lack of aggression and competitiveness.

Umbilical Cord   The flexible, cordlike structure connecting the fetus at the navel with the placenta. This cord contains the blood vessels that nourish the fetus and remove its wastes.

Unconditioned Stimulus   The stimulus that normally evokes an unconditioned response, such as the food that originally caused Pavlov's dogs to respond with salivation.

Validity   The capacity of an instrument to measure what it purports to measure.

Visual Cliff   An apparatus constructed to study depth perception in humans and other animals. It consists of a center board resting on a glass table. On one side of the board, a checkered surface is visible directly beneath the glass; on the other side, the surface is several feet below the glass, thus giving the impression of a drop-off.

Working Memory   An inclusive term for a number of short-term memory systems that enable individuals to hold onto recently acquired information for about 30 seconds to 4 minutes. Working memory also holds information from declarative memory that is being actively examined.

Youth A stage of development that some people go through following adolescence and prior to assuming full responsibilities of adulthood.

Zone of Proximal Development In Vygotsky's cognitive theory, any or all activities that a child is almost able to perform, or is able to perform with a little help.

Zygote The fertilized ovum that results from the union of a sperm and an egg.

REFERENCES

Abel, E. L. (1984). Prenatal effects of alcohol. *Drug and Alcohol Dependence, 14*, 1-10.

Abelson, R. P. (1981). Psychological status of the script concept. *American Psychologist, 36*, 715-729.

Abernathy, V. (1973). Social network and response to the maternal role. *International Journal of Sociology and the Family, 3*, 86-92.

Abramovitch, R., Corter, C., Pepler, D. J., & Stanhope, L. (1986). Sibling and peer interaction: A final follow-up and a comparison. *Child Development, 57*, 217-229.

Abramovitch, R., Pepler, D., & Corter, C. (1982). Patterns of sibling interaction among preschool-age children. In M. E. Lamb & B. Sutton-Smith (Eds.), *Sibling relationships: Their nature and significance across the lifespan* (pp. 61-86). Hillsdale, NJ: Erlbaum.

Achte, K. A., & Vauhkonen, M. L. (1971). Cancer and the psyche. *Omega, 2*, 45-46.

Acredolo, L. P. (1978). Development of spatial orientation in infancy. *Developmental Psychology, 14*, 224-234.

Acredolo, L. P., & Hake, J. L. (1982). Infant perception. In B. B. Wolman (Ed.), *Handbook of developmental psychology* (pp. 244-283). Englewood Cliffs, NJ: Prentice-Hall.

Adams, B. N. (1968). *Kinship in an urban setting.* Chicago: Markham.

Adams, G. R. (1977). Physical attractiveness, personality, and social reactions to peer pressure. *Journal of Psychology, 96*, 287-296.

Adams, G. R., & Jones, R. M. (1981). Imaginary audience behavior: A validation study. *Journal of Early Adolescence, 1*, 1-10.

Adams, R. G. (1985). People would talk: Normative barriers to cross-sex friendships for elderly women. *The Gerontologist, 25*, 605-611.

Ade-Ridder, L., & Brubaker, T. H. (1983). The quality of long-term marriages. In T. H. Brubaker (Ed.), *Family relationships in later life* (pp. 21-30). Beverly Hills, CA: Sage.

Adler, I., & Kandel, D. B. (1982). A cross-cultural comparison of sociopsychological factors in alcohol use among adolescents in Israel, France, and the United States. *Journal of Youth and Adolescence, 11*, 89-113.

Adler, J., & Carey, J. (1980, February 25). The science of love. *Newsweek,* pp. 89-90.

Adler, J., Katz, S., & Jackson, T. (1985, March 25). A teen-pregnancy epidemic. *Newsweek,* p. 90.

Ahlgren, A. (1983). Sex differences in the correlates of cooperative and competitive school attitudes. *Developmental Psychology, 19*, 881-888.

Ainsworth, M. D. S. (1973). The development of infant-mother attachment. In B. Caldwell & H. Ricciuti (Eds.), *Review of child development research* (Vol. 3). Chicago, Il: Univ. of Chicago Press.

Ainsworth, M. D. S., Blehar, M., Waters, E., & Wall, S. (1978). *Strange-situation behavior of one-year-olds: Its relation to mother-infant interaction in the first year and to qualitative differences in the infant-mother attachment relationship.* Hillsdale, NJ: Erlbaum.

Aizenberg, R., & Treas, J. (1985). The family in late life: Psychosocial and demographic considerations. In J. E. Birren & K. W. Schaie (Eds.), *Handbook of the psychology of aging* (2nd ed., pp. 169-189). New York: Van Nostrand Reinhold.

Akiyama, M. M. (1985). Denials in young children from a cross-linguistic perspective. *Child Development, 56*, 95-102.

Aldous, J. (1978). *Family careers.* New York: Wiley.

Aldous, J., Klaus, E., & Klein, D. M. (1985). The understanding heart: Aging parents and their favorite children. *Child Development, 56*, 303-316.

Alexander, F. (1950). *Psychosomatic medicine.* New York: Norton.

Alexander, K. L., & Entwisle, D. R. (1988). Achievement in the first 2 years of school: Patterns and processes. *Monographs of the Society for Research in Child Development, 53*(2, Serial No. 218).

Alley, T. R. (1981). Head shape and the perception of cuteness. *Developmental Psychology, 17*, 650-654.

Allman, W. F. (1986, May). Mindworks. *Science 86,* pp. 23-31.

Altenor, A., Kay, E., & Richter, M. (1977). The generality of learned helplessness in the rat. *Learning & Motivation, 8*, 54-61.

Altus, W. D. (1967). Birth order and its sequelae. *International Journal of Psychiatry, 3*, 23-36.

American Association of Retired Persons. (1987, January). The job market beckons retirees. *AARP News Bulletin,* p. 2.

American Medical Association/American Nursing Association. (1983). *The improvement of health care of the aged chronically ill.* (Joint Task Force Report). Kansas City, MO: American Nursing Assoc.

Amsterdam, B. (1972). Mirror self-image reactions before age two. *Developmental Psychology, 5*, 297-305.

Anda, R., Williamson, D., Jones, D., Macera, C., Eaker, E., Glassman, A., & Marks, J. (1993). Depressed affect, hopelessness, and the risk of ischemic heart disease in a cohort of U. S. adults. *Epidemiology, 4*, 285-294.

Anderson, D. R., Lorch, E. P., Field, D. E., Collins, P. A., & Nathan, J. G. (1986). Television viewing at home: Age trends in visual attention and time with TV. *Child Development, 57*, 1024-1033.

Anderson, L. D. (1939). The predictive value of infant tests in relation to intelligence at 5 years. *Child Development, 10*, 203-212.

Anderson, S. A., Russell, C. S., & Schumm, W. R. (1983). Perceived marital quality and family life cycle categories: A further analysis. *Journal of Marriage and the Family, 45*, 127-139.

Andersson, B. (1992). Effects of day-care on cognitive and socioemotional competence of thirteen-year-old Swedish schoolchildren. *Child Development, 63*, 20-36.

Andreasen, N. C., Flaum, M., Swayze, H., O'Leary, D. S., Alliger, R., Cohen, G., Ehrhardt, J., & Yuh, W. T. C. (1993). Intelligence and brain structure in normal individuals. *American Journal of Psychiatry, 150*, 130-134.

Andrisani, P. J., & Miljus, R. C. (1977). Individual differences in preferences for intrinsic vs. extrinsic aspects of work. *Journal of Vocational Behavior, 11*, 14-30.

Anisfeld, E., Casper, V., Nozyce, M., & Cunningham, N. (1990). Does infant carrying promote attachment? An experimental study of the effects of increased physical contact on the development of attachment. *Child Development, 61*, 1617-1627.

Antell, S. E., Caron, A. J., & Myers, R. S. (1985). Perception of relational invariants by newborns. *Developmental Psychology, 21*, 942-948.

Apgar, V. (1953). A proposal for a new method of evaluation of the newborn infant. *Current Researches in Anesthesia and Analgesia, 32*, 260-267.

Apgar, V., Holaday, D. A., James, L. S., Weisbrot, I. M., & Berrien, C. (1958). Evaluation of the newborn infant{m-second report. *Journal of the American Medical Association, 168*, 1985-1988.

Argyle, M. (187). *The psychology of happiness*. London: Methuen.

Aries, P. (1962). *Centuries of childhood: A social history of family life* (R. Baldick, Trans.). New York: Alfred A. Knopf. (Original work published 1960)

Arlin, P. K. (1975). Cognitive development in adulthood: A fifth stage? *Developmental Psychology, 11*, 602-606.

Arlin, P. K. (1977). Piagetian operations in problem finding. *Developmental Psychology, 13*, 297-298.

Arlin, P. K. (1984). Adolescent and adult thought: A structural interpretation. In M. L. Commons, F. A. Richards, & C. Armon (Eds.), *Beyond formal operations: Late adolescent and adult cognitive development* (pp. 258-271).

Aronson, E. (1969). Some antecedents of interpersonal attraction. In W. J. Arnold & D. Levine (Eds.), *Nebraska symposium on motivation*. Lincoln, Nebraska: Univ. of Nebraska Press.

Ascione, F. R., & Sanok, R. L. (1982). The role of peer and adult models in facilitating and inhibiting children's prosocial behavior. *Genetic Psychology Monographs, 106*, 239-259.

Ashton, P. T. (1975). Cross-cultural Piagetian research: An experimental perspective. *Harvard Educational Review, 45*, 475-506.

Atchley, R. C. (1975). Dimensions of widowhood in later life. *The Gerontologist, 15*, 176-178.

Atchley, R. C., & Miller, S. J. (1983). Types of elderly couples. In T. H. Brubaker (Ed.), *Family relationships in later life* (pp. 77-90). Beverly Hills, CA: Sage.

Atwell, A. E., Moore, U. S., Nielsen, E., & Levite, Z. (1984). Effects of joint custody on children. *Bulletin of the American Academy of Psychiatry & the Law, 12*, 149-157.

Au, T. K., & Glusman, M. (1990). The principle of mutual exclusivity in word learning: To honor or not to honor? *Child Development, 61*, 1474-1490.

Au, T. K., & Laframboise, D. E. (1990). Acquiring color names via linguistic contrast: The influence of contrasting terms. *Child Development, 61*, 1808-1823.

Austrom, D. R. (1984). *The consequences of being single*. New York: Peter Lang Pub.

Azrin, N. H., & Foxx, R. M. (1974). *Toilet training in less than a day*. New York: Simon & Schuster.

Azrin, N. H., & Lindsley, O. R. (1956). The reinforcement of cooperation between children. *Journal of Abnormal and Social Psychology, 52*, 100-102.

Bachman, J. G., O'Malley, P. M., & Johnston, J. (1978). *Adolescence to adulthood: Change and stability in the lives of young men*. Ann Arbor, MI: Institute for Social Research.

Baddeley, A. (1992). Working memory. *Science, 255*, 556-559.

Baer, D. M., & Wright, J. C. (1974). Developmental psychology. *Annual Review of Psychology, 25*, 1-82.

Baerends, G. P. (1976). A model of the functional organization of incubation behavior. In G. P. Baerends, & R. H. Drent (Eds.), *The Herring Gull and its Egg. Behaviour Supplement. 17*, 261-310.

Bahrick, L. E. (1988). Intermodal learning in infancy: Learning on the basis of two kinds of invariant relations in audible and visible events. *Child Development, 59*, 197-209.

Bailey, J. M., Gaulin, S., Agyei, Y., & Gladue, B. A. (1994). Effects of gender and sexual orientation on evolutionarily relevant aspects of human mating psychology. *Journal of Personality and Social Psychology, 66*, 1081-1093.

Bailey, R. H. (1975). *The role of the brain*. New York: Time-Life Books.

Baillargeon, R. (1987). Object permanence in 3 1/2- and 4 1/2-month-old infants. *Developmental Psychology, 23*, 655-664.

Baillargeon, R., & DeVos, J. (1991). Object permanence in young infants: Further evidence. *Child Development, 62*, 1227-1246.

Baldwin, A. L. (1949). The effect of home environment on nursery school behavior. *Child Development, 20*, 49-61.

Baldwin, D. A., & Markman, E. M. (1989). Establishing word-object relations: A first step. *Child Development, 60*, 381-398.

Baldwin, J. M. (1894). *The development of the child and of the race*. New York: MacMillan.

Bales, J. (1986, May). What works: Consensus report gets good marks from researchers. *APA Monitor*, p. 13.

Balkwell, C. (1981). Transition to widowhood: A review of the literature. *Family Relations, 30*, 117-127.

Ball, W., & Dibble, A. (1980). Perceived movement in the visual crib. *Journal of Genetic Psychology, 137*, 191-198.

Ban, P. L., & Lewis, M. (1974). Mothers and fathers, girls and boys: Attachment behavior in the one-year-old. *Merrill-Palmer Quarterly, 20*, 195-204.

Ban, T. A. (1978). The treatment of depressed geriatric patients. *American Journal of Psychotherapy, 32*, 93-104.

Bandura, A. (1965). Influence of models' reinforcement contingencies on the acquisition of imitative responses. *Journal of Personality and Social Psychology, 1*, 589-595.

Bandura, A. (1978). The self system in reciprocal determinism. *American Psychologist, 33*, 344-358.

Bandura, A., & Menlove, F. L. (1968). Factors determining vicarious extinction of avoidance behavior through symbolic modeling. *Journal of Personality and Social Psychology, 8*, 99-108.

Bandura, A., Ross, D., & Ross, S. A. (1963). A comparative test of the status envy, social power, and secondary reinforcement theories of identificatory learning. *Journal of Abnormal and Social Psychology, 67*, 527-534.

Bandura, A., Ross, D., & Ross, S. A. (1963). Imitation of film-mediated aggressive models. *Journal of Abnormal and Social Psychology, 66*, 3-11.

Banziger, G., & Drevenstedt, J. (1982). Achievement attributions by young and old judges as a function of perceived age of stimulus person. *Journal of Gerontology, 37*, 468-474.

Bar-Tal, D., Raviv, A., & Goldberg, M. (1982). Helping behavior among preschool children: An observational study. *Child Development, 53*, 396-402.

Barclay, A. M., & Haber, R. N. (1965). The relation of aggressive to sexual motivation. *Journal of Personality, 33*, 462-475.

Barglow, P., Vaughn, B. E., & Molitor, N. (1987). Effects of maternal absence due to employment on the quality of infant-mother attachment in a low-risk sample. *Child Development, 58,* 945-954.

Barling, J. (1986). Interrole conflict and marital functioning amongst employed fathers. *Journal of Occupational Behavior, 7,* 1-8.

Barnes, D. M. (1989). "Fragile X" syndrome and its puzzling genetics. *Science, 243,* 171-172.

Barnett, K., Darcie, G., Holland, C. J., & Kobasigawa, A. (1982). Children's cognitions about effective helping. *Developmental Psychology, 18,* 267-277.

Barnett, M. A., Howard, J. A., Melton, E. M., & Dino, G. A. (1982). Effect of inducing sadness about self or other on helping behavior in high- and low-empathic children. *Child Development, 53,* 920-923.

Barnett, M. A., King, L. M., & Howard, J. A. (1979). Inducing affect about self or other: Effects on generosity in children. *Developmental Psychology, 15,* 164-167.

Barr, H. M., Streissguth, A. P., Darby, B. L., & Sampson, P. D. (1990). Prenatal exposure to alcohol, caffeine, tobacco, and aspirin: Effects on fine and gross motor performance in 4-year-old children. *Developmental Psychology, 26,* 339-348.

Baruch, G., Barnett, R., & Rivers, C. (1983). *Lifeprints.* New York: McGraw-Hill.

Baruch, G. K., Biener, L., & Barnett, R. C. (1987). Women and gender in research on work and family stress. *American Psychologist, 42,* 130-136.

Bass, D., Wells, F., & Ridgeway, R. (1986). *Seven summits.* New York: Warner Books.

Bates, E., Camaioni, L., & Volterra, V. (1975). The acquisition of performatives prior to speech. *Merrill-Palmer Quarterly, 21,* 205-226.

Bates, E., MacWhinney, B., Caselli, C., Devescovi, A., Natale, F., & Venza, V. (1984). A cross-linguistic study of the development of sentence interpretation strategies. *Child Development, 55,* 341-354.

Bateson, M. C. (1975). Mother infant exchanges: The epigenesis of conversational interaction. *Annals of the New York Academy of Sciences, 263,* 101-113.

Bauer, P. J. (1993). Memory for gender-consistent and gender-inconsistent event sequences by twenty-five-month-old children. *Child Development, 64,* 285-297.

Bauer, P. J., & Mandler, J. M. (1992). Putting the horse before the cart: The use of temporal order in recall of events by one-year-old children. *Developmental Psychology, 28,* 441-452.

Baumrind, D. (1967). Child care practices anteceding three patterns of preschool behavior. *Genetic Psychology Monographs, 75,* 43-88.

Baumrind, D. (1971). Current patterns of parental authority. *Developmental Psychology, 4*(1, Pt. 2), 1-103.

Baumrind, D. (1980). New directions in socialization research. *American Psychologist, 35,* 639-652.

Baumrind, D. (1991). The influence of parenting style on adolescent competence and substance use. *Journal of Early Adolescence, 11,* 56-95.

Baydar, N., & Brooks-Gunn, J. (1991). Effects of maternal employment and child-care arrangements on preschoolers' cognitive and behavioral outcomes: Evidence from the children of the National Longitudinal Survey of Youth. *Developmental Psychology, 27,* 932-945.

Bayer, A. E. (1966). Birth order and college attendance. *Journal of Marriage and the Family, 28,* 480-484.

Bayley, N. (1968). Behavioral correlates of mental growth: Birth to thirty-six years. *American Psychologist, 23,* 1-17.

Bayley, N. (1969). *Manual for the Bayley Scales of Infant Development.* New York: Psychological Corporation.

Beaconsfield, P., Birdwood, G., & Beaconsfield, R. (1980). The placenta. *Scientific American, 243*(2), 94-102.

Beck, S. H. (1985). Determinants of labor force activity among retired men *Research on Aging, 7,* 251-280.

Becker, E. (1973). *The denial of death.* New York: The Free Press.

Becker, F. D. (1981). *Workspace: Creating environments in organizations.* New York: Praeger.

Becker, W. C. (1964). Consequences of different kinds of parental discipline. In M. L. Hoffman (Ed.), *Review of child development research* (Vol. 1). New York: Russell Sage Foundation.

Belenky, M. F., Clinchy, B. M., Goldberger, N. R., & Tarule, J. M. (1986). *Women's ways of knowing: The development of self, voice and mind.* New York: Basic Books, Inc.

Bell, A., & Weinberg, M. (1978). *Homosexualities.* New York: Simon & Schuster.

Bell, R. (1986, October-November). Is retirement for you? *Modern Maturity,* pp. 43-45.

Bell, R. Q. (1979). Parent, child, and reciprocal influences. *American Psychologist, 34,* 821-826.

Bell, S. M. (1970). The development of the concept of object as related to infant-mother attachment. *Child Development, 41,* 291-311.

Bellanti, J. A. (1984). Prevention of food allergies. *Annals of Allergy, 53,* 683-688.

Bellinger, D., Leviton, A., Waternaux, C., Needleman, H., & Rabinowitz, M. (1987). Longitudinal analyses of prenatal and postnatal lead exposure and early cognitive development. *New England Journal of Medicine, 316,* 1037-1043.

Belmont, L., & Marolla, F. A. (1973). Birth order, family size, and intelligence. *Science, 182,* 1096-1101.

Belsky, J. (1986). Infant day care: A cause for concern. *Zero to Three, 7*(1), 1-7.

Belsky, J. (1988). The "effects" of infant day care reconsidered. *Early Childhood Research Quarterly, 3,* 235-272.

Belsky, J., & Braungart, J. M. (1991). Are insecure-avoidant infants with extensive day-care experience less stressed by and more independent in the strange situation? *Child Development, 62,* 567-571.

Belsky, J., Gilstrap, B., & Rovine, M. (1984). The Pennsylvania Infant and Family Development Project, I: Stability and change in mother-infant and father-infant interaction in a family setting at one, three, and nine months. *Child Development, 55,* 692-705.

Belsky, J., & Most, R. K. (1981). From exploration to play: A cross-sectional study of infant free play behavior. *Developmental Psychology, 17,* 630-639.

Belsky, J., & Steinberg, L. D. (1978). The effects of day care: A critical review. *Child Development, 49,* 929-949.

Belsky, J., Steinberg, L., & Draper, P. (1991). Childhood experience, interpersonal development, and reproductive strategy: An evolutionary theory of socialization. *Child Development, 62,* 647-670.

Bem, S. L. (1981). Gender schema theory: A cognitive account of sex typing. *Psychological Review, 88,* 354-364.

Bem, S. L. (1989). Genital knowledge and gender constancy in preschool children. *Child Development, 60,* 649-662.

Benedict, H. (1979). Early lexical development: Comprehension and production. *Journal of Child Language, 6,* 183-200.

Bengtson, V. L. (1985). Diversity and symbolism in grandparental roles. In V. L. Bergtson & J. F. Robertson (Eds.), *Grandparenthood* (pp. 11-25). Beverly Hills: Sage Publications.

Bengtson, V. L., Cuellar, J. B., & Ragan, P. K. (1977). Stratum contrasts and similarities in attitudes toward death. *Journal of Gerontology, 32,* 76-88.

Bennett, N. G., & Bloom, D. E. (1986, December 13). Why fewer American women marry. *New York Times,* p. 27.

Berbaum, M. L., Markus, G. B., & Zajonc, R. B. (1982). A closer look at Galbraith's "closer look". *Developmental Psychology, 18,* 181-191.

Berbaum, M. L., & Moreland, R. L. (1985). Intellectual development within transracial adoptive families: Retesting the confluence model. *Child Development, 56,* 207-216.

Berbaum, M. L., Moreland, R. L., & Zajonc, R. B. (1986). Contentions over the confluence model: A reply to Price, Walsh, and Vilburg. *Psychological Bulletin, 100,* 270-274.

Berg, W. K., & Berg, K. M. (1979). Psychophysiological development in infancy: State, sensory function, and attention. In J. Osofsky (Ed.), *Handbook of infant development* (pp. 283-343). New York: Wiley Interscience.

Berk, L. (1986, May). Private speech. *Psychology Today*, pp. 35-39.

Berkeley Planning Associates. (1977, December). *Evaluation of child abuse and neglect demonstration projects 1974-1977: Vol. II. Final Report*. Berkeley, Calif.: Author. (NTIS No. PB-278 439).

Berko, J. (1958). The child's learning of English morphology. *Word, 14*, 150-177.

Berndt, T. J., & Bulleit, T. N. (1985). Effects of sibling relationships on preschoolers' behavior at home and at school. *Developmental Psychology, 21*, 761-767.

Berndt, T. J., Hawkins, J. A., & Hoyle, S. G. (1986). Changes in friendship during a school year: Effects on children's and adolescents' impressions of friendship and sharing with friends. *Child Development, 57*, 1284-1297.

Berndt, T. J., & Perry, T. B. (1986). Children's perceptions of friendship as supportive relationships. *Developmental Psychology, 22*, 640-648.

Berreby, D. (1992 April). Kids, creoles, and the coconuts. *Discover*, pp. 44-53.

Berscheid, E. (1983). Emotion. In H. H. Kelley et al. (Eds.), *Close relationships* (pp. 110-168). New York: W. H. Freeman.

Berscheid, E., & Walster, E. H. (1978). *Interpersonal attraction*. Reading, Mass.: Addison-Wesley.

Besdine, R. W. (1980). Geriatric medicine: An overview. *Annual Review of Gerontology & Geriatrics, 1*, 135-153.

Bianchi, B. D., & Bakeman, R. (1983). Patterns of sex typing in an open school. In M. B. Liss (Ed.), *Social and cognitive skills: Sex roles and children's play* (pp. 219-233). New York: Academic Press.

Bielby, D. D., & Papalia, D. E. (1975). Moral development and perceptual role taking egocentrism: Their development and interrelationship across the life span. *International Journal of Aging and Human Development, 6*, 293-308.

Bierman, E. L., & Hazzard, W. R. (1973). Adulthood, especially the middle years. In D. W. Smith, & E. L. Bierman (Eds.), *The biologic ages of man: From conception through old age* (pp. 154-170). Philadelphia: W. B. Saunders.

Birch, H. G. (1945). The role of motivational factors in insightful problem-solving. *Journal of Comparative Psychology, 38*, 295-317.

Birch, H. G., & Gussow, J. D. (1970). *Disadvantaged children: Health, nutrition and school failure*. New York: Grune & Stratton.

Birnbaum, J. A. (1975). Life patterns and self-esteem in gifted family oriented and career committed women. In M. S. Mednick, S. S. Tangri, & L. W. Hoffman (Eds.), *Women and achievement*. Washington, D.C.: Hemisphere.

Birnholz, J. C., & Benacerraf, B. R. (1983). The development of human fetal hearing. *Science, 222*, 516-518.

Birns, B., & Sternglanz, S. H. (1983). Sex-role socialization: Looking back and looking ahead. In M. B. Liss (Ed.), *Social and cognitive skills: Sex roles and children's play* (pp. 235-251). New York: Academic Press.

Bitterman, M. E. (1969). Thorndike and the problem of animal intelligence. *American Psychologist, 24*, 444-453.

Bixenstine, V. E., DeCorte, M. S., & Bixenstine, B. A. (1976). Conformity to peer-sponsored misconduct at four grade levels. *Developmental Psychology, 12*, 226-236.

Black, B., & Hazen, N. L. (1990). Social status and patterns of communication in acquainted and unacquainted preschool children. *Developmental Psychology, 26*, 379-387.

Blake, J. (1989). Number of Siblings and educational attainment. *Science, 245*, 32-36.

Blasi, A., & Hoeffel, E. C. (1974). Adolescence and formal operations. *Human Development, 17*, 344-363.

Blau, Z. S. (1973). *Old age in a changing society*. New York: Franklin Watts.

Blewitt, P. (1983). Dog versus collie: Vocabulary in speech to young children. *Developmental Psychology, 19*, 602-609.

Block, J. (1981). Some enduring and consequential structures in personality. In A. I. Rabin, J. Aronoff, A. M. Barclay, & R. A. Zucker (Eds.), *Further explorations in personality* (pp. 27-43). New York: Wiley.

Block, J. (1982). Assimilation, accommodation, and the dynamics of personality development. *Child Development, 53*, 281-295.

Block, J. H., Block, J., & Gjerde, P. F. (1986). The personality of children prior to divorce: A prospective study. *Child Development, 57*, 827-840.

Block, M. R., & Sinnott, J. D. (Eds.). (1979). *The battered elder syndrome: An exploratory study*. Unpublished manuscript, University of Maryland Center on Aging, College Park, Maryland.

Block, M. R., Davidson, J. L., & Grambs, J. D. (1981). *Women over forty*. New York: Springer.

Bloom, B. L., Hodges, W. F., Caldwell, R. A., Systra, L., & Cedrone, A. R. (1977). Marital separation: A community survey. *Journal of Divorce, 1*(1), 7-19.

Bloom, B. S. (1964). *Stability and change in human characteristics*. New York: Wiley.

Bloom, D. E., & Bennett, N. G. (1985, April). *Marriage patterns in the United States*. Unpublished paper, originally presented at the 1984 annual meeting of the Population Association of America.

Bloom, L., & Capatides, J. B. (1987). Expression of affect and the emergence of language. *Child Development, 58*, 1513-1522.

Bluebond-Langner, M. (1977). Meanings of death to children. In H. Feifel (Ed.), *New meanings of death* (pp. 47-66). New York: McGraw-Hill Book Company.

Bluebond-Langner, M. (1978). *The private worlds of dying children*. Princeton: Princeton Univ. Press.

Blumberg, M. (1980). Job switching in autonomous work groups: An exploratory study in a Pennsylvania coal mine. *Academy of Management Journal, 23*, 287-306.

Blumstein, P., & Schwartz, P. (1983). *American couples: Money, work, sex*. New York: Morrow.

Bock, K. (1990). Structure in language: Creating form in talk. *American Psychologist, 45*, 1221-1236.

Boggiano, A. K., Klinger, C. A., & Main, D. S. (1986). Enhancing interest in peer interaction: A developmental analysis. *Child Development, 57*, 852-861.

Bortz, W. M., II. (1992). *We live too short and die too long*. New York: Bantam Books.

Botwinick, J., West, R., & Storandt, M. (1978). Predicting death from behavioral test performance. *Journal of Gerontology, 33*, 755-762.

Bouchard, T. J., Jr., Lykken, D. T., McGue, M., Segal, N. L., & Tellegen, A. (1990). Sources of human psychological differences: The Minnesota study of twins reared apart. *Science, 250*, 223-228.

Bouchard, T. J., Jr., Lykken, D. T., McGue, M., Segal, N. L., & Tellegen, A. (1991). Response to Dudley. *Science, 252*, 191-192.

Bouchard, T. J., Jr., & McGue, M. (1981). Familial studies of intelligence: A review. *Science, 212*, 1055-1059.

Bower, B. (1985, April 27). Caution: Emotions at play. *Science News*, pp. 266-267.

Bower, B. (1988, August 27). Retardation: The eyes have it. *Science News*, p. 140.

Bower, B. (1989a, August 19). Teenagers reap broad benefits from "authoritative" parents. *Science News*, pp. 117-118.

Bower, B. (1989b, May 27). Kids talk about the "good pill." *Science News*, p. 332.

Bower, T. G. R. (1979). *Human development*. San Francisco: W. H. Freeman.

Bower, T. G. R., Broughton, J. M., & Moore, M. K. (1970). Infant response to approaching objects: An indicator of response to distal variables. *Perception and Psychophysics, 9*, 193-196.

Bowlby, J. (1958). The nature of the child's tie to his mother. *International Journal of Psycho-Analysis, 39*, 350-373.

Bowlby, J. (1961). Processes of mourning. *International Journal of Psychoanalysis, 44*, 317.

Bowlby, J. (1969). *Attachment and loss* (Vol. 1). New York: Basic Books.

Bowlby, J. (1973). *Separation and loss*. New York: Basic Books.

Bowlby, J. (1982a). Attachment and loss: Retrospect and prospect. *American Journal of Orthopsychiatry, 52*, 664-678.

REFERENCES

Bowlby, J. (1982b). *Attachment and loss: Vol. 1. Attachment* (2nd ed.). New York: Basic Books.

Bowling, A., & Cartwright, A. (1982). *Life after a death: A study of the elderly widowed.* London: Tavistock Publications.

Boxer, A. M., Gershenson, H. P., & Offer, D. (1984). Historical time and social change in adolescent experience. *New Directions for Mental Health Services,* No. 22, 83-95.

Brackbill, Y. (1958). Extinction of the smiling response in infants as a function of reinforcement schedule. *Child Development, 29,* 115-124.

Braine, M. D. S. (1963). The ontogeny of English phrase structure: The first phase. *Language, 39*(1), 1-13.

Branch, L. G. (1977). *Understanding the health and social service needs of people over age 65.* Boston: Center for Survey Research of the University of Massachusetts and the Joint Center for Urban Studies of MIT and Harvard University.

Brand, C. (1987). Intelligence testing: Bryter still and bryter? *Nature, 328,* 110.

Braungart, J. M., Plomin, R., DeFries, J. C., & Fulker, D. W. (1992). Genetic influence on tester-rated infant temperament as assessed by Bayley's Infant Behavior Record: Nonadoptive and adoptive siblings and twins. *Developmental Psychology, 28,* 40-47.

Brazelton, T. B. (1973). *Neonatal behavioral assessment scale.* Philadelphia, PA: Lippincott.

Brazelton, T. B., Koslowski, B., & Main, H. (1974). The origins of reciprocity: The early infant-mother interaction. In M. Lewis, & L. A. Rosenblum (Eds.), *The effect of the infant on its caregiver* (pp. 49-76). New York: Wiley-Interscience.

Breslau, N., & Davis, G. C. (1987). Posttraumatic stress disorder: The etiologic specificity of wartime stressors. *American Journal of Psychiatry, 144,* 578-583.

Bretherton, I. (1985). Attachment theory: Retrospect and prospect. *Monographs of the Society for Research in Child Development, 50*(1-2, Serial No. 209), 3-35.

Briley, M. J. (1986, August-September). Taking command of arthritis. *Modern Maturity,* pp. 41-45.

Brim, O. G., & Kagan, J. (Eds.). (1980). *Constancy and change in human development.* Cambridge, Mass.: Harvard University Press.

Brittain, C. V. (1963). Adolescent choices and parent-peer cross-pressures. *American Sociological Review, 28,* 385-391.

Brodsky, R. (1987, April-May). As much to gain as to give. *Modern Maturity,* pp. 46-50.

Brody, E. M. (1985). Parent care as a normative family stress. *The Gerontologist, 25,* 19-29.

Brody, G. H., Stoneman, Z., MacKinnon, C. E., & MacKinnon, R. (1985). Role relationships and behavior between preschool-aged and school-aged sibling pairs. *Developmental Psychology, 21,* 124-129.

Brody, J. E. (1986, June 11). Personal health. *New York Times,* p. C14.

Brodzinsky, D. M., Singer, L. M., & Braff, A. M. (1984). Children's understanding of adoption. *Child Development, 55,* 869-878.

Broman, S. H., Nichols, P. L., & Kennedy, W. A. (1975). *Preschool IQ: Prenatal and early developmental correlates.* Hillsdale, NJ: Lawrence Erlbaum.

Bronfenbrenner, U., Alvarez, W. F., & Henderson, C. R. (1984). Working and watching: Maternal employment status and parents' perceptions of their three-year-old children. *Child Development, 55,* 1362-1378.

Bronson, W. C. (1985). Growth in the organization of behavior over the second year of life. *Developmental Psychology, 21,* 108-117.

Brooks-Gunn, J., Burrow, C., & Warren, M. P. (1988). Attitudes toward eating and body weight in different groups of female adolescent athletes. *International Journal of Eating Disorders, 7*(6).

Brooks-Gunn, J., & Lewis, M. (1975). *Mirror-image stimulation and self-recognition in infancy.* Paper presented at the meeting of the Society for Research in Child Development, Denver, Colorado.

Brooks-Gunn, J., & Lewis, M. (1981). Infant social perception: Responses to pictures of parents and strangers. *Developmental Psychology, 17,* 647-649.

Broverman, I. K., Vogel, S. R., Broverman, D. M., Clarkson, F. E., & Rosenkrantz, P. S. (1972). Sex-role stereotypes: A current appraisal. *Journal of Social Issues, 28*(2), 59-77.

Brown, B. B., Clasen, D. R., & Eicher, S. A. (1986). Perceptions of peer pressure, peer conformity dispositions, and self-reported behavior among adolescents. *Developmental Psychology, 22,* 521-530.

Brown, B. B., Eicher, S. A., & Petrie, S. (1986). The importance of peer group ("crowd") affiliation in adolescence. *Journal of Adolescence, 9,* 73-96.

Brown, B. B., Lohr, M. J., & McClenahan, E. L. (1986). Early adolescents' perceptions of peer pressure. *Journal of Early Adolescence, 6,* 139-154.

Brown, E. W. (1988). Study of injury mechanisms in youth sports. In E. W. Brown & C. F. Branta (Eds.), *Competitive sports for children and youth: An overview of research and issues* (pp. 107-113). Champaign, IL: Human Kinetics.

Brown G. W., Bhrolchain, M. N., & Harris, T. (1975). Social class and psychiatric disturbance among women in an urban population. *Sociology, 9,* 225-254.

Brown, J. B. (1984). Examination of grammatical morphemes in the language of hard-of-hearing children. *Volta Review, 86,* 229-238.

Brown, R. (1973). *The first language: The early stages.* Cambridge, Mass.: Harvard Univ. Press.

Brownell, C. A., & Carriger, M. S. (1990). Changes in cooperation and self-other differentiation during the second year. *Child Development, 61,* 1164-1174.

Brozan, N. (1986, November 13). Infirm relatives' care: A new women's issue. *New York Times,* pp. C1, C6.

Brubaker, T. H. (1985). *Later life families.* Beverly Hills, CA: Sage Publications.

Brumberg, J. J. (1985). "Fasting girls": Reflections on writing the history of anorexia nervosa. In A. B. Smuts & J. W. Hagen (Eds.), History and research in child development. *Monographs of the Society for Research in Child Development 50*(4-5, Serial No. 211), 93-104.

Bruner, J. S. (1983). *Child's talk.* New York: Norton.

Brunk, M. A., & Henggeler, S. W. (1984). Child influences on adult controls: An experimental investigation. *Developmental Psychology, 20,* 1074-1081.

Bryan, J. H. (1970). Children's reactions to helpers: Their money isn't where their mouths are. In J. Macaulay, & L. Berkowitz (Eds.), *Altruism and helping behavior* (pp. 61-73). New York: Academic Press.

Bryan, J. H. (1975). Children's cooperation and helping behaviors. In E. M. Hetherington (Ed.), *Review of child development research* (Vol. 5). Chicago, IL: Univ. of Chicago Press.

Buchanan, C. M., Eccles, J. S., & Becker, J. B. (1992). Are adolescents the victims of raging hormones: Evidence for activational effects of hormones on moods and behavior at adolescence. *Psychological Bulletin, 111,* 62-107.

Buckley, N., Siegel, L. S., & Ness, S. (1979). Egocentrism, empathy, and altruistic behavior in young children. *Developmental Psychology, 15,* 329-330.

Buckley, W. E., Yesalis, C. E., III., Friedl, K. E., Anderson, W. A., Streit, A. L., & Wright, J. E. (1988). Estimated prevalence of anabolic steroid use among male high school seniors. *Journal of the American Medical Association, 260,* 3441-3445.

Buhrmester, D., & Furman, W. (1987). The development of companionship and intimacy. *Child Development, 58,* 1101-1113.

Buhrmester, D., & Furman, W. (1990). Perceptions of sibling relationships during middle childhood and adolescence. *Child Development, 61,* 1387-1398.

Bulcroft, K., & O'Conner-Roden, M. (1986, June). Never too late. *Psychology Today,* pp. 66-69.

Bullen, B. A., Skrinar, G. S., Beitins, I. Z., von Mering, G., Turnbull, B. A., & McArthur, J. W. (1985). Induction of menstrual disorders by strenuous exercise in untrained women. *New England Journal of Medicine, 312,* 1349-1353.

Bullock, M. (1985). Animism in childhood thinking: A new look at an old question. *Developmental Psychology, 21,* 217-225.

Bullough, V. L. (1981). Age at menarche: A misunderstanding. *Science, 213,* 365-366.

Burchinal, M., Lee, M., & Ramey, C. (1989). Type of day-care and preschool intellectual development in disadvantaged children. *Child Development, 60,* 128-137.

Burton, L. M. (1985). *Early and on-time grandmotherhood in multigenerational black families.* Unpublished doctoral dissertation, University of Southern California, Los Angeles.

Bushnell, E. W., Shaw, L., & Strauss, D. (1985). Relationship between visual and tactual exploration by 6-month-olds. *Developmental Psychology, 21,* 591-600.

Butler, R. N. (1963). The life review: An interpretation of reminiscence in the aged. *Psychiatry, 26,* 65-76.

Butler, R. N. (1977). Pharmacological interventions of the aging process. *Advances in Experimental Medical Biology, 97,* 231-241.

Butler, R. N., & Lewis, M. (1977). *Aging and mental health.* St. Louis, MO: Mosby.

Cahan, S., & Cohen, N. (1989). Age versus schooling effects on intelligence development. *Child Development, 60,* 1239-1249.

Cairns, R. B., Cairns, B. D., & Neckerman, H. J. (1989). Early school dropout: Configurations and determinants. *Child Development, 60,* 1437-1452.

Caldera, Y. M., Huston, A. C., & O'Brien, M. (1989). Social interactions and play patterns of parents and toddlers with feminine, masculine, and neutral toys. *Child Development, 60,* 70-76.

Callahan, T. (1985, March 18). To be simply the best. *Time,* pp. 50-51.

Campbell, T. (1982). *Formal cues and content difficulty as determinants of children's cognitive processing of televised educational messages.* Unpublished doctoral dissertation, University of Kansas.

Campos, J. J., Barrett, K. G., Lamb, M. E., Stenberg, C., & Goldsmith, H. H. (1983). Socioemotional development. In M. M. Haith & J. J. Campos (Eds.), Infancy and developmental psychology. In P. H. Mussen (Gen. Ed.), *Handbook of child psychology.* New York: Wiley.

Campos, J. J., Hiatt, S., Ramsay, D., Henderson, C., & Svejda, M. (1978). The emergence of fear on the visual cliff. In M. Lewis, & L. A. Rosenblum (Eds.), *The development of affect* (pp. 149-182). New York: Plenum Press.

Carey, S. (1985). *Conceptual change in childhood.* Cambridge, MA: MIT/Bradford.

Carey, S., & Bartlett, E. (1978). Acquiring a single new word. *Papers and Reports on Child Language Development* (Department of Linguistics, Stanford University), *15,* 17-29.

Carey, W. B., & McDevitt, S. C. (1978). Stability and change in individual temperament diagnoses from infancy to early childhood. *Journal of the American Academy of Child Psychiatry, 17,* 331-337.

Carlson, E. (1987, February-March). The phoney war. *Modern Maturity,* pp. 34-46.

Carlson, V., Cicchetti, D., Barnett, D., & Braunwald, K. (1989). Disorganized/disoriented attachment relationships in maltreated infants. *Developmental Psychology, 25,* 525-531.

Caron, R. F., Caron, A. J., & Myers, R. S. (1982). Abstraction of invariant face expressions in infancy. *Child Development, 53,* 1008-1015.

Carr, M., Kurtz, B. E., Schneider, W., Turner, L. A., & Borkowski, J. G. (1989). Strategy acquisition and transfer among American and German children: Environmental influences on metacognitive development. *Developmental Psychology, 25,* 765-771.

Carroll, J. L., & Rest, J. R. (1982). Moral development. In B. B. Wolman (Ed.), *Handbook of developmental psychology* (pp. 434-467). Englewood Cliffs, NJ: Prentice-Hall.

Carter, H., & Glick, P. C. (1976). *Marriage and divorce.* Cambridge, Mass.: Harvard University Press.

Case, R. (1985). *Intellectual development.* Orlando, FL: Academic Press.

Case, R. B., Heller, S. S., Case, N. B., & Moss, A. J. (1985). Type A behavior and survivial after acute myocardial infarction. *New England Journal of Medicine, 312,* 737-741.

Casper, R. C. (1984). Hypothalamic dysfunction and symptoms of anorexia nervosa. *Psychiatry Clinica of North America, 7,* 201-213.

Cassidy, J., & Asher, S. R. (1992). Loneliness and peer relations in young children. *Child Development, 63,* 350-365.

Casto, G., & Mastropieri, M. A. (1986). The efficacy of early intervention programs: A meta-analysis. *Exceptional Children, 52,* 417-424.

Cattell, P. (1966). *The measurement of intelligence of infants and young children.* New York: Psychological Corporation.

Ceci, S. J. (1991). How much does schooling influence general intelligence and its cognitive components? A reassessment of the evidence. *Developmental Psychology, 27,* 703-722.

Chapman, M., & Zahn-Waxler, C. (1981). *Young children's compliance and noncompliance to parental discipline in a natural setting.* Unpublished manuscript.

Chapman, M., Zahn-Waxler, C., Cooperman, G., & Iannotti, R. (1987). Empathy and responsibility in the motivation of children's helping. *Developmental Psychology, 23,* 140-145.

Chazan, S. E. (1981). Development of object permanence as a correlate of dimensions of maternal care. *Developmental Psychology, 17,* 79-81.

Cherlin, A. J. (1981). *Marriage, divorce, and remarriage.* Cambridge, MA: Harvard Univ. Press.

Cherlin, A. J., Furstenberg, F. F., Chase-Lansdale, P. L., & Kiernan, K. E. (1991). Longitudinal studies of effects of divorce on children in Great Britain and the United States. *Science, 252,* 1386-1389.

Cherry, F. F., & Eaton, E. L. (1977). Physical and cognitive development in children of low-income mothers working in the child's early years. *Child Development, 48,* 158-166.

Chess, S., & Thomas, A. (1982). Infant bonding: Mystique and reality. *American Journal of Orthopsychiatry, 52,* 213-222.

Chess, S., & Thomas, A. (1986b). Developmental issues. In S. Chess & A. Thomas (Eds.), *Annual progress in child psychiatry and child development* (pp. 21-26). New York: Brunner/Mazel.

Chess, S., & Thomas, A. (Eds.). (1986a). Cross-cultural temperament studies. In S. Chess & A. Thomas (Eds.), *Annual progress in child psychiatry and child development* (pp. 353-354). New York: Brunner/Mazel.

Chevalier-Skolnikoff, S. (1979). Kids. *Animal Kingdom, 82*(3), 11-18.

Cheyne, J. A., & Rubin, K. H. (1983). Playful precursors of problem solving in preschoolers. *Developmental Psychology, 19,* 577-584.

Chi, M. T. (1978). Knowledge structures and memory development. In R. S. Siegler (Ed.), *Children's thinking: What develops?* Hillsdale, NJ: Erlbaum.

Childers, J. S., Durham, T. W., Bolen, L. M., & Taylor, L. H. (1985). A predictive validity study of the Kaufman Assessment Battery for Children with the California Achievement Test. *Psychology in the Schools, 22,* 29-33.

Chinen, A. B. (1986). Elder tales revisited: Forms of transcendence in later life. *Journal of Transpersonal Psychology, 18,* 171-192.

Chodorow, N. (1974). Family structure and feminine personality. In M. Z. Rosaldo & L. Lamphere (Eds.), *Women, culture, and society* (pp. 43-66). Stanford: Stanford Univ. Press.

Chodorow, N. (1978). *The reproduction of mothering.* Berkeley: Univ. of California Press.

Chomsky, N. (1957). *Syntactic structures.* The Hague: Mouton.

Chugani, H. T., & Phelps, M. E. (1986). Maturational changes in cerebral function in infants determined by 18FDG positron emission tomography. *Science, 231,* 840-843.

Chumlea, W. M. (1982). Physical growth in adolescence. In B. B. Wolman (Ed.), *Handbook of developmental psychology* (pp. 471-485). Englewood Cliffs, NJ: Prentice-Hall.

Cicirelli, V. G. (1977). Relationship of siblings to the elderly person's feelings and concerns. *Journal of Gerontology, 32,* 317-322.

REFERENCES

Cicirelli, V. G. (1980). Sibling relationships in adulthood: A life span perspective. In L. W. Poon (Ed.), *Aging in the 1980s: Psychological issues* (pp. 455-462). Washington, DC: Am. Psychological Association.

Cicirelli, V. G. (1981). *Helping elderly parents: The role of adult children.* Boston: Auburn House.

Cicirelli, V. G. (1982). Sibling influence throughout the lifespan. In M. E. Lamb & B. Sutton-Smith (Eds.), *Sibling relationships: Their nature and significance across the lifespan* (pp. 267-284). Hillsdale, NJ: Erlbaum.

Cicirelli, V. G. (1983). A comparison of helping behaviors to elderly parents of adult children with intact and disrupted marriages. *The Gerontologist, 23,* 619-625.

Clark, H. H., & Clark, E. V. (1977). *Psychology and language: An introduction to psycholinguistics.* New York: Harcourt Brace.

Clarke-Stewart, K. A. (1977, March). *The father's impact on mother and child.* Paper presented at the biennial meeting of the Society for Research in Child Development, New Orleans, Louisiana.

Clarke-Stewart, K. A., & Hevey, C. M. (1981). Longitudinal relations in repeated observations of mother-child interaction from 1 to 2 1/2 years. *Developmental Psychology, 17,* 127-145.

Clarkson, M. G., & Berg, W. K. (1983). Cardiac orienting and vowel discrimination in newborns: Crucial stimulus parameters. *Child Development, 54,* 162-171.

Clarren, S. K., & Smith, D. W. (1978). The fetal alcohol syndrome. *New England Journal of Medicine, 298,* 1063-1067.

Clary, E. G., & Miller, J. (1986). Socialization and situational influences on sustained altruism. *Child Development, 57,* 1358-1369.

Clausen, J. A. (1981). Men's occupational careers in the middle years. In D. H. Eichorn, J. A. Clausen, N. Haan, M. P. Honzik, & P. Mussen (Eds.), *Present and past in middle life* (pp. 321-351). New York: Academic Press.

Clayton, V., & Birren, J. E. (1980). Age and wisdom across the life-span: Theoretical perspectives. In P. B. Baltes & O. G. Brim, Jr. (Eds.), *Life-span development and behavior* (Vol. 1). New York: Academic Press.

Clifton, R. K., Gwiazda, J., Bauer, J. A., Clarkson, M. G., & Held, R. M. (1988). Growth in head size during infancy: Implications for sound localization. *Developmental Psychology, 24,* 477-483.

Clifton, R., Perris, E., & Bullinger, A. (1991). Infants' perception of auditory space. *Developmental Psychology, 27,* 187-197.

Clines, F. X. (1986, October 31). Dutch are quietly taking the lead in euthanasia. *New York Times,* p. A4.

Clopton, W. (1973). Personality and career change. *Industrial Gerontology, 17,* 9-17.

Coburn, J. (1974). Sterilization regulations: Debate not quelled by HEW document. *Science, 183,* 935-939.

Cohen, J. Z., Coburn, K. L., & Pearlman, J. C. (1980). *Hitting our stride: Good news about women in their middle years.* New York: Delacorte Press.

Cohen, S. (1971). Peers as modeling and normative influences in the development of aggression. *Psychological Reports, 28,* 995-998.

Cohen, S. (1988). Psychosocial models of the role of social support in the etiology of physical disease. *Health Psychology, 7,* 269-297.

Cohen, S. E., & Parmelee, A. H. (1983). Prediction of five-year Stanford-Binet scores in preterm infants. *Child Development, 54,* 1242-1253.

Cohn, D. A. (1990). Child-mother attachment of six-year-olds and social competence at school. *Child Development, 61,* 152-162.

Coie, J. D., Dodge, K. A., Terry, R., & Wright, V. (1991). The role of aggression in peer relations: An analysis of aggression episodes in boys' play groups. *Child Development, 62,* 812-826.

Coie, J. D., & Kupersmidt, J. B. (1983). A behavioral analysis of emerging social status in boys' groups. *Child Development, 54,* 1400-1416.

Colby, A., Kohlberg, L., Gibbs, J., & Lieberman, M. (1983). A longitudinal study of moral judgment. *Monographs of the Society for Research in Child Development, 48*(1-2, Serial No. 200).

Cole, M. A. (1978-79). Sex and marital status differences in death anxiety. *Omega, 9,* 139-147.

Cole, M., Gay, J., Glick, J., & Sharp, D. (1971). *The cultural context of learning and thinking.* New York: Basic Books.

Cole, S. (1979). Age and scientific performance. *American Journal of Sociology, 84,* 958-977.

Coleman, J. R. (1974). *Blue collar journal: A college president's sabbatical.* Philadelphia: J. B. Lippincott.

Coles, C. D., Smith, I., Fernhoff, P. M., & Falek, A. (1985). Neonatal neurobehavioral characteristics as correlates of maternal alcohol use during gestation. *Alcoholism, 9,* 454-460.

Collard, R. R. (1968). Social and play responses of first-born and later-born infants in an unfamiliar situation. *Child Development, 39,* 325-334.

Collins, W. A. (1984). Introduction. In W. A. Collins (Ed.), *Development during middle childhood: The years from six to twelve* (pp. 1-23). Washington, DC: National Academy Press.

Comfort, A. (1976). *A good age.* New York: Crown.

Comfort, A. (1980). Sexuality in later life. In J. E. Birren & J. Renner (Eds.), *Handbook of mental health and aging.* Englewood Cliffs, NJ: Prentice-Hall.

Commons, M. L., Richards, F. A., & Kuhn, D. (1982). Systematic and metasystematic reasoning: A case for levels of reasoning beyond Piaget's stage of formal operations. *Child Development, 53,* 1058-1069.

Computer admiral in new job at 79. (1986, September 3). *Boston Herald,* p. 36.

Comstock, M. L. C. (1973). Effects of perceived parental behavior on self-esteem and adjustment. *Dissertation Abstracts, 34,* 465B.

Conner, K. A., Dorfman, L. T., & Tompkins, J. B. (1985). Life satisfaction of retired professors: The contributions of work, health, income, and length of retirement. *Educational Gerontology, 11,* 337-347.

Connolly, J. A., & Doyle, A. (1984). Relation of social fantasy play to social competence in preschoolers. *Developmental Psychology, 20,* 797-806.

Connolly, J., Doyle, A., & Ceschin, F. (1983). Forms and functions of social fantasy play in preschoolers. In M. B. Liss (Ed.), *Social and cognitive skills: Sex roles and children's play* (pp. 71-92). New York: Academic Press.

Cook, S. (1973). *Children and dying: An exploration and a selective professional bibliography.* New York: Health Sciences.

Cooke, R. A., & Rousseau, D. M. (1984). Stress and strain from family roles and work-role expectations. *Journal of Applied Psychology, 69,* 252-260.

Cooney, T. M., Sayer, M. A., Hagestad, G. O., & Klock, R. (1986). Parental divorce in young adulthood: Some preliminary findings. *American Journal of Orthopsychiatry, 56,* 470-477.

Cooper, C. R. (1977, March). *Collaboration in children: Dyadic interaction skills in problem solving.* Paper presented at the meeting of the Society for Research in Child Development, New Orleans, Louisiana.

Coopersmith, S. (1967). *The antecedents of self-esteem.* San Francisco: W. H. Freeman.

Cornelius, S. W., & Caspi, A. (1987). Everyday problem solving in adulthood and old age. *Psychology and Aging, 2,* 144-153.

Cornell, E. H., & Heth, C. D. (1983). Spatial cognition: Gathering strategies used by preschool children. *Journal of Experimental Child Psychology, 35,* 93-110.

Cornell, E. H., Heth, C. D., Broda, L. S., & Butterfield, V. (1987). Spatial matching in 1 1/2- to 4 1/2- year-old children. *Developmental Psychology, 23,* 499-508.

Correa, P., Pickle, L. W., Fontham, E., Lin, Y., & Haenszel, W. (1983). Passive smoking and lung cancer. *Lancet, 2*(8350), 595-597.

Costa, P. T., Jr., & McCrae, R. R. (1980). Still stable after all these years: Personality as a key to some issues in adulthood and old age. In P. B. Baltes, & O. G. Bria (Eds.), *Life-span development and behavior* (Vol. 3, pp. 65-102). New York: Academic Press.

Costa, P. T., Jr., McCrae, R. R., & Arenberg, D. (1980). Enduring dispositions in adult males. *Journal of Personality and Social Psychology, 38,* 793-800.

Coveney, J. (1985). Is breast milk the best food for all infants? *Human Nutrition and Applied Nutrition, 39,* 179-188.

Cowan, C. T., & Cowan, P. A. (1987). Men's involvement in parenthood: Identifying the antecedents and understanding the barriers. In P. Berman, & F. A. Pedersen (Eds.), *Fathers' transitions to parenthood.* Hillsdale, NJ: Erlbaum.

Cowart, B. J. (1981). Development of taste perception in humans: Sensitivity and preference throughout the lifespan. *Psychological Bulletin, 90,* 43-73.

Cowley, M. (1980). *The view from 80.* New York: The Viking Press.

Craik, F. I. M. (1977). Age differences in human memory. In J. E. Birren & K. W. Schaie (Eds.), *Handbook of the psychology of aging.* New York: Van Nostrand Reinhold.

Crain-Thoreson, C., & Dale, P. S. (1992). Do early talkers become early readers? Linguistic precocity, preschool language, and emergent literacy. *Developmental Psychology, 28,* 421-429.

Cravens, H. (1992). A scientific project locked in time: The Terman genetic studies of genius, 1920s-1950s. *American Psychologist, 47,* 183-189.

Cronbach, L. J. (1970). *Essentials of psychological testing.* New York: Harper.

Cronbach, L. J. (1975). Five decades of public controversy over mental testing. *American Psychologist, 30,* 1-14.

Crouter, A. C., MacDermid, S. M., McHale, S. M., & Perry-Jenkins, M. (1990). Parental monitoring and preceptions of children's school performance and conduct in dual- and single-earner families. *Developmental Psychology, 26,* 649-657.

Crowell, J. A., & Feldman, S. S. (1991). Mothers' working models of attachment relationships and mother and child behavior during separation and return. *Developmental Psychology, 27,* 597-605.

Crowell, J. A., & Feldman, S. S. (1988). Mothers' internal models of relationships and children's behavioral and developmental status: A study of mother-child interaction. *Child Development, 59,* 1273-1285.

Cumming, E., & Henry, W. E. (1961). *Growing old.* New York: Basic Books.

Curtis, R. L. (1975). Adolescent orientations toward parents and peers: Variations by sex, age, and socioeconomic status. *Adolescence, 10,* 483-494.

Cusack, J. R. (1993). The wounds of war. *American Journal of Psychiatry, 150,* 997-999.

Cushman, J. H. (1986, August 14). Admiral Hopper's farewell. *New York Times,* p. 86.

Daffos, F., Forestier, F., Capella-Pavlovsky, M., Thulliez, P., Aufrant, C., Valenti, D., & Cox, W. L. (1988). Prenatal management of 746 pregnancies at risk for congenital toxoplasmosis. *New England Journal of Medicine, 318,* 271-275.

Daniel Yankelovich Group, Inc., The (1987, April). *Intergenerational tension in 1987: Real or imagined.* Washington, DC: Author.

Daniels, D., Dunn, J., Furstenberg, F. F., & Plomin, R. (1985). Environmental differences within the family and adjustment differences within pairs of adolescent siblings. *Child Development, 56,* 764-774.

Dannemiller, J. L., & Stephens, B. R. (1988). A critical test of infant pattern preference models. *Child Development, 59,* 210-216.

Danner, F. W., & Day, M. C. (1977). Eliciting formal operations. *Child Development, 48,* 1600-1606.

Danziger, C. (1978). *Unmarried heterosexual cohabitation.* San Francisco: R & E Research Associates.

Darwin, C. (1967). *The expression of the emotions in man and animals.* Chicago: Univ. of Chicago Press. (Original work published 1872)

Dasen, P. (1975). Concrete operational development in three cultures. *Journal of Cross-cultural Psychology, 6,* 156-172.

Dasen, P., & Heron, A. (1981). Cross-cultural tests of Piaget's theory. In H. C. Triandis & A. Heron (Eds.), *Handbook of cross-cultural psychology: Vol. 4. Developmental psychology* (pp. 295-341). Boston: Allyn & Bacon.

Dasteel, J. C. (1982). Stress reactions to marital dissolution as experienced by adults attending courses on divorce. *Journal of Divorce, 5(3),* 37-47.

Datan, N., Rodeheaver, D., & Hughes, F. (1987). Adult development and aging. *Annual Review of Psychology, 38,* 153-180.

Davidson, L. E., Rosenberg, M. L., Mercy, J. A., Franklin, J., & Simmons, J. T. (1989). An epidemiologic study of risk factors in two teenage suicide clusters. *Journal of the American Medical Association, 262,* 2687-2692.

Davidson, W. B., & Cotter, P. R. (1982). Adjustment to aging and relationships with offspring. *Psychological Reports, 50,* 731-738.

Davis, D. J., Cahan, S., & Bashi, J. (1977). Birth order and intellectual development: The confluence model in the light of cross-cultural evidence. *Science, 196,* 1470-1472.

Davis, E. A. (1937). *The development of linguistic skills in twins, single twins with siblings, and only children from age 5 to 10 years.* Minneapolis: University of Minnesota Press, Institute of Child Welfare Series, No. 14.

Davis, H., Porter, J. W., Livingstone, J., Herrmann, T., MacFadden, L., & Levine, S. (1977). Pituitary-adrenal activity and leverpress shock escape behavior. *Physiological Psychology, 5,* 280-284.

Davis, R., & Davis, J. (1985). *TV's image of the elderly.* Lexington, MA: Lexington Books.

Day, R. D., & Bahr, S. J. (1986). Income changes following divorce and remarriage. *Journal of Divorce, 9(3),* 75-88.

De Lisi, R., & Stauldt, J. (1980). Individual differences in college students' performance on formal operation tasks. *Journal of Applied Developmental Psychology, 1,* 201-208.

Dean, A. L., Malik, M. M., Richards, W., & Stringer, S. A. (1986). Effects of parental maltreatment on children's conceptions of interpersonal relationships. *Developmental Psychology, 22,* 617-626.

Deaux, K., & Farris, E. (1977). Attributing causes for one's own performance: The effects of sex, norms, and outcome. *Journal of Research in Personality, 11,* 59-72.

deBoysson-Bardies, B., Sagart, L., & Durand, C. (1984). Discernible differences in the babbling of infants according to target language. *Journal of Child Language, 11,* 1-15.

DeCasper, A. J., & Fifer, W. P. (1980). Of human bonding: Newborns prefer their mothers' voices. *Science, 208,* 1174-1176.

Deckert, P., & Langelier, R. (1978). The late-divorce phenomenon: The causes and impact of ending 20-year-old or longer marriages. *Journal of Divorce, 1,* 381-390.

DeLoache, J. S., Cassidy, D. J., & Brown, A. L. (1985). Precursors of mnemonic strategies in very young children's memory. *Child Development, 56,* 125-137.

DeMeis, D. K., Hock, E., & McBride, S. L. (1986). The balance of employment and motherhood: Longitudinal study of mothers' feelings about separation from their first-born infants. *Developmental Psychology, 22,* 627-632.

Demitrack, M. A., Kalogeras, K. T., Altemus, M., Pigott, T. A., Listwak, S. J., & Gold, P. W. (1992). Plasma and cerebrospinal fluid measures of arginine vasopressin secretion in patients with bulimia nervosa and in healthy subjects. *Journal of Clinical Endocrinology, 74,* 1277-1283.

Demkovich, L. (1986, April-May). The forgotten people. *Modern Maturity,* pp. 34-39.

Denney, N. W., & Palmer, A. M. (1981). Adult age differences on traditional and practical problem solving measures. *Journal of Gerontology, 36,* 323-328.

Dennis, W. (1966). Creative production between the ages of 20 and 80 years. *Journal of Gerontology, 21,* 1-8.

Dennis, W. (1968). Creative productivity between the ages of 20 and 80 years. In B. L. Neugarten (Ed.), *Middle age and aging* (pp. 106-114). Chicago: Univ. of Chicago Press.

Deutsch, C. (1986, May 29). Grandparents maintain ties to grandchildren by helping them financially. *The Chattanooga Times,* pp. 2-6.

deVilliers, J. G., & deVilliers, P. A. (1973). A cross-sectional study of the acquisition of grammatical morphemes in child speech. *Journal of Psycholinguistic Research, 2,* 267-278.

deVries, M. W. (1984). Temperament and infant mortality among the Masai of East Africa. *The American Journal of Psychiatry, 141,* 1189-1194.

Diamond, A. (1985). Development of the ability to use recall to guide action, as indicated by infants' performance on AB. *Child Development, 56,* 868-883.

Diamond, J. (1990, December). War babies. *Discover,* pp. 70-75.

Diaz, J., & Samson, H. H. (1980). Impaired brain growth in neonatal rats exposed to ethanol. *Science, 208,* 751-753.

Diaz, R. M., & Berndt, T. J. (1982). Children's knowledge of a best friend: Fact or fancy? *Developmental Psychology, 18,* 787-794.

Dickerson, R. E. (1978). Chemical evolution and the origin of life. *Scientific American, 239*(3), 70-86.

Dickinson, D. K. (1984). First impressions: Children's knowledge of words gained from a single exposure. *Applied Psycholinguistics, 5,* 359-373.

Dickstein, S., Thompson, R. A., Estes, D., Malkin, C., & Lamb, M. E. (1984). Social referencing and the security of attachment. *Infant Behavior and Development, 7,* 507-516.

Diener, C. I., & Dweck, C. S. (1980). An analysis of learned helplessness: II. The processing of success. *Journal of Personality & Social Psychology, 39,* 940-952.

Dietz, J. (1986, September 24). Qualified elders can attend state colleges for free. *Boston Globe,* p. 43.

Dietz, W. H., Jr., & Gortmaker, S. L. (1985). Do we fatten our children at the television set? Obesity and television viewing in children and adolescents. *Pediatrics, 75,* 807-812.

DiLalla, L. F., Thompson, L. A., Plomin, R., Phillips, K., Fagan, J. F., III., Haith, M. M., Cyphers, L. H., & Fulker, D. W. (1990). Infant predictors of preschool and adult IQ: A study of infant twins and their parents. *Developmental Psychology, 26,* 759-769.

Dillingham, A. E. (1981). Age and workplace injuries. *Aging and Work, 4,* 1-10.

Dilworth-Anderson, P., & Hildreth, G. J. (1982). Administrators perspectives on involving the family in providing day care services for the elderly. *Family Relations, 31*(3), 343-348.

Dion, K. K. (1973). Young children's stereotyping of facial attractiveness. *Developmental Psychology, 9,* 183-188.

Dishion, T. J., Patterson, G. R., Stoolmiller, M., & Skinner, M. L. (1991). Family, school, and behavioral antecedents to early adolescent involvement with antisocial peers. *Developmental Psychology, 27,* 172-180.

Dodge, K. A., Bates, J. E., & Pettit, G. S. (1990). Mechanisms in the cycle of violence. *Science, 250,* 1678-1683.

Dodge, K. A., Coie, J. D., & Brakke, N. P. (1982). Behavior patterns of socially rejected and neglected preadolescents: The roles of social approach and aggression. *Journal of Abnormal Child Psychology, 10,* 389-410.

Dodge, K. A., Coie, J. D., Pettit, G. S., & Price, J. M. (1990). Peer status and aggression in boys' groups: Developmental and contextual analyses. *Child Development, 61,* 1289-1309.

Dodson, F., & Alexander, A. (1986). *Your child: Birth to age 6.* New York: Simon & Schuster.

Dolgin, K. G., & Behrend, D. A. (1984). Children's knowledge about animates and inanimates. *Child Development, 55,* 1646-1650.

Donovan, W. L., Leavitt, L. A., & Balling, J. D. (1978). Maternal physiological response to infant signals. *Psychophysiology, 15,* 68-74.

Dorfman, L. T., Kohout, F. J., & Heckert, D. A. (1985). Retirement satisfaction in the rural elderly. *Research on Aging, 7,* 577-599.

Doty, R. L. (1984). Smell identification ability: Changes with age. *Science, 226,* 1441-1443.

Douglas, J. H., & Miller, J. A. (1977, September 10). Record breaking women. *Science News,* pp. 172-174.

Douvan, E., & Adelson, J. (1966). *The adolescent experience.* New York: Wiley.

Doyle, A. B., Doehring, P., Tessier, O., de Lorimier, S., & Shapiro, S. (1992). Transitions in children's play: A sequential analysis of states preceding and following social pretense. *Developmental Psychology, 28,* 137-144.

Drevenstedt, J. (1976). Perceptions of onsets of young adulthood, middle age, and old age. *Journal of Gerontology, 31,* 53-57.

Dudley, R. M. (1991). IQ and heredity. *Science, 252,* 191.

Dumbach, A. E., & Newborn, J. (1986). *Shattering the German night: The story of the white rose.* Boston: Little, Brown.

Dunbar, F. (1943). *Psychosomatic diagnosis.* New York: Hoeber.

Dunn, G. C., & Gross, D. (1977). Treatment of depression in the medically ill geriatric patient: A case report. *American Journal of Psychiatry, 134,* 448-450.

Dunn, J. (1983). Sibling relationships in early childhood. *Child Development, 54,* 787-811.

Dunn, J. (1984). *Sisters and brothers.* London: Fontana.

Dunn, J., & Kendrick, C. (1982a). Siblings and their mothers: Developing relationships within the family. In M. E. Lamb & B. Sutton-Smith (Eds.), *Sibling relationships: Their nature and significance across the life-span* (pp. 39-60). Hillsdale, NJ: Erlbaum.

Dunn, J., & Kendrick, C. (1982b). *Siblings: Love, envy, and understanding.* Cambridge, MA: Harvard University Press.

Dunn, J., & Munn, P. (1985). Becoming a family member: Family conflict and the development of social understanding in the second year. *Child Development, 56,* 480-492.

Durkheim, E. (1925). *Moral education.* New York: Free Press.

Duvall, E. (1977). *Marriage and family development* (5th ed.). Philadelphia: Lippincott.

Duyme, M. (1988). School success and social class: An adoption study. *Developmental Psychology, 24,* 203-209.

Dweck, C. S. (1975). The role of expectations and attributions in the alleviation of learned helplessness. *Journal of Personality and Social Psychology, 31,* 674-685.

Dweck, C. S. (1986). Motivational processes affecting learning. *American Psychologist, 41,* 1040-1048.

Dweck, C. S., & Reppucci, N. D. (1973). Learned helplessness and reinforcement responsibility in children. *Journal of Personality and Social Psychology, 25,* 109-116.

Dyment, P. G. (1988). Social and medical issues in youth sports. In E. W. Brown & C. F. Branta (Eds.), *Competitive sports for children and youth: An overview of research and issues* (pp. 273-277). Champaign, IL: Human Kinetics.

East, P. L., & Rook, K. S. (1992). Compensatory patterns of support among children's peer relationships: A test using school friends, nonschool friends, and siblings. *Developmental Psychology, 28,* 163-172.

Easterbrooks, M. A., & Goldberg, W. A. (1985). Effects of early maternal employment on toddlers, mothers, and fathers. *Developmental Psychology, 21,* 774-783.

Eaton, W. O., Chipperfield, J. C., & Singbeil, C. E. (1989). Birth order and activity level in children. *Developmental Psychology, 25,* 668-672.

Ebbesen, E. B., Kjos, G. L., & Konecni, V. J. (1976). Spatial ecology: Its effects on the choice of friends and enemies. *Journal of Experimental Social Psychology, 12,* 505-518.

Eckerman, C. O., Whatley, J. L., & Kutz, S. L. (1975). Growth of social play with peers during the second year of life. *Developmental Psychology, 11,* 42-49.

Egeland, B., Jacobvitz, D., & Sroufe, L. A. (1988). Breaking the cycle of abuse. *Child Development, 59,* 1080-1088.

Eichorn, D. H., Clausen, J. A., Haan, N., Honzik, M. P., & Mussen, P. H. (Eds.). (1981). *Present and past in middle life.* New York: Academic Press.

Eimas, P. D. (1985). The perception of speech in early infancy. *Scientific American, 252*(1), 46-52.

Eisenberg-Berg, N., & Lennon, R. (1980). Altruism and the assessment of empathy in the preschool years. *Child Development, 51,* 552-557.

Eisenberg, R. B., & Marmarou, A. (1981). Behavioral reactions of newborns to speech-like sounds and their implications for developmental studies. *Infant Mental Health Journal, 2,* 129-138.

Eisert, D. C., & Kahle, L. R. (1982). Self-evaluation and social comparison of physical and role change during adolescence: A longitudinal analysis. *Child Development, 53,* 98-104.

Elder, G. H., Jr. (1986). Military times and turning points in men's lives. *Developmental Psychology, 22,* 233-245.

Elder, G. H., Jr., Nguyen, T. V., & Caspi, A. (1985). Linking family hardship to children's lives. *Child Development, 56,* 361-375.

Elkind, D. (1967). Egocentrism in adolescence. *Child Development, 38,* 1025-1034.

Elkind, D. (1971). *A sympathetic understanding of the child six to sixteen.* Boston: Allyn & Bacon.

Elkind, D. (1978). *The child's reality: Three developmental themes.* Hillsdale, NJ: Erlbaum.

Elkind, D., & Bowen, R. (1979). Imaginary audience behavior in children and adolescents. *Developmental Psychology, 15,* 38-44.

Elkind, D., Barocas, R., & Johnsen, P. (1969). Concept production in children and adolescents. *Human Development, 12,* 10-21.

Ellis, P. L. (1982). Empathy a factor in antisocial behavior. *Journal of Abnormal Child Psychology, 10,* 123-124.

Emery, R. B. (1989). Family violence. *American Psychologist, 44,* 321-328.

Emmerich, W., & Goldman, K. S. (1972). Boy-girl identity task (technical report). In V. Shipman (Ed.), *Disadvantaged children and their first school experiences* (Technical Report PR-72-20). Educational Testing Service.

Endler, N. S., Rushton, J. P., & Roediger, H. L. (1978). Productivity and scholarly impact (citations) of British, Canadian, and U.S. Departments of psychology (1975). *American Psychologist, 33,* 1064-1082.

Engen, T., Lipsitt, L. P., & Peck, M. B. (1974). Ability of newborn infants to discriminate sapid substances. *Developmental Psychology, 10,* 741-744.

English, B., & Witcher, G. (1986, September 20). A neighbor returns as a president. *The Boston Globe,* pp. 1, 6.

Enright, R. D., Lapsley, D. K., & Shukla, D. G. (1979). Adolescent egocentrism in early and late adolescence. *Adolescence, 14,* 687-695.

Epps, E. G., & Smith, S. F. (1984). School and children: The middle childhood years. In W. A. Collins (Ed.), *Development during middle childhood: The years from six to twelve* (pp. 283-334). Washington, DC: National Academy Press.

Erikson, E. H. (1950). *Childhood and society.* New York: W. W. Norton.

Erikson, E. H. (1968). *Identity, youth, and crisis.* New York: Norton.

Erikson, E. H., Erikson, J. M., & Kivnick, H. Q. (1986). *Vital involvement in old age.* New York: W. W. Norton & Company.

Eriksson, M., Catz, C. S., & Yaffe, S. J. (1973). Drugs and pregnancy. In H. Osofsky (Ed.), *Clinical obstetrics and gynecology: High risk pregnancy with emphases upon maternal and fetal well being* (pp. 192-224). New York: Harper & Row.

Ernst, C., & Angst, J. (1983). *Birth order: Its influence on personality.* New York: Springer-Verlag.

Eron, L. D., Huesmann, L. R., Brice, P., Fischer, P., & Mermelstein, R. (1983). Age trends in the development of aggression, sex typing, and related television habits. *Developmental Psychology, 19,* 71-77.

Erwin, E. (1980). Psychoanalytic therapy. *American Psychologist, 35,* 435-443.

Estrada, P., Arsenio, W. F., Hess, R. D., & Holloway, S. D. (1987). Affective quality of the mother-child relationship: Longitudinal consequences for children's school-relevant cognitive functioning. *Developmental Psychology, 23,* 210-215.

Etaugh, C. (1980). Effects of nonmaternal care on children. *American Psychologist, 35,* 309-319.

Evans, H. J., Fletcher, J., Torrance, M., & Hargreave, T. B. (1981). Sperm abnormalities and cigarette smoking. *The Lancet, I*(8221), 627-629.

Fabricius, W. V., & Wellman, H. M. (1983). Children's understanding of retrieval cue utilization. *Developmental Psychology, 19,* 15-21.

Fackelmann, K. A. (1991, July 6). Simple shield against birth defects? *Science News,* p. 141.

Fagen, J. W. (1984). Infants' long-term memory for stimulus color. *Developmental Psychology, 20,* 435-440.

Fagot, B. I., Leinbach, M. D., & O'Boyle, C. (1992). Gender labeling, gender stereotyping, and parenting behaviors. *Developmental Psychology, 28,* 225-230.

Fahrenberg, B. (1986). Coping with the "empty nest situation" as a developmental task of the aging woman: A literature review. *Zeitschrift fur Gerontologie, 19*(5), 323-335.

Falbo, T. (1981). Relationships between birth category, achievement, and interpersonal orientation. *Journal of Personality and Social Psychology, 41,* 121-131.

Fantz, R. L. (1961). The origin of form perception. *Scientific American, 204,* 66-72.

Fantz, R. L., Ordy, J. M., & Udelf, M. S. (1962). Maturation of pattern vision in infants during the first six months. *Journal of Comparative and Physiological Psychology, 55,* 907-917.

Farran, D. C., & Ramey, C. T. (1977). Infant day care and attachment behaviors toward mothers and teachers. *Child Development, 48,* 1112-1116.

Farrell, M., & Rosenberg, S. (1981). *Men at midlife.* Boston: Auburn House.

Faust, M. S. (1977). Somatic development of adolescent girls. *Monographs of the Society for Research in Child Development, 42*(1, Serial No. 169).

Federation CECOS, Schwartz, D., & Mayaux, B. A. (1982). Female fecundity as a function of age. *New England Journal of Medicine, 306,* 404-406.

Fehr, L. A. (1976). J. Piaget and S. Claus: Psychology makes strange bedfellows. *Psychological Reports, 39,* 740-742.

Feldman, D. H. (1984). A follow-up of subjects scoring above 180 IQ in Terman's "Genetic Studies of Genius." *Exceptional Children, 50,* 518-523.

Ferguson, T. J., & Rule, B. G. (1982). Influence of inferential set, outcome intent, and outcome severity on children's moral judgments. *Developmental Psychology, 18,* 843-851.

Fernald, A., & Mazzie, C. (1991). Prosody and focus in speech to infants and adults. *Developmental Psychology, 27,* 209-221.

Field, T., De Stefano, L., & Koewler, J. H., III. (1982). Fantasy play of toddlers and preschoolers. *Developmental Psychology, 18,* 503-508.

Field, T. M. (1991a). Young children's adaptations to repeated separations from their mothers. *Child Development, 62,* 539-547.

Field, T. M. (1991b). Quality infant day-care and grade school behavior and performance. *Child Development, 62,* 863-870.

Field, T. M., Schanberg, S. M., Scafidi, F., Bauer, C. R., Vega-Lahr, N., Garcia, R., Nystrom, J., & Kuhn, C. M. (1986). Tactile/kinesthetic stimulation effects on preterm neonates. *Pediatrics, 77,* 654-658.

Filsinger, E. E., & Anderson, C. C. (1982). Social class and self-esteem in late adolescence: Dissonant context or self-efficacy? *Developmental Psychology, 18,* 380-384.

Finkelstein, N. W., & Haskins, R. (1983). Kindergarten children prefer same-color peers. *Child Development, 54,* 502-508.

Finlay, D., & Ivinskis, A. (1984). Cardiac and visual responses to moving stimuli presented either successively or simultaneously to the central and peripheral visual fields in 4-month-olds. *Developmental Psychology, 20,* 29-36.

Finlayson, D. F., & Loughran, J. L. (1976). Pupils' perceptions in high and low delinquency schools. *Educational Research, 18,* 138-145.

Fischer, K. W. (1983). Illuminating the processes of moral development. *Monographs of the Society for Research in Child Development, 48*(1-2, Serial No. 200), 97-107.

Fischer, K. W., Hand, H. H., & Russell, S. (1984). The development of abstractions in adolescence and adulthood. In M. Commons, F. A. Richards, & C. Armon (Eds.), *Beyond formal operations* (pp. 43-73). New York: Praeger.

Fischer, K. W., Hand, H. H., Watson, M. W., Van Parys, M., & Tucker, J. (1986). Putting the child into socialization: The development of social categories in the preschool years. In L. G. Katz (Ed.), *Current topics in early childhood education* (Vol. 6). Norwood, NJ: Ablex.

Fischer, K. W., & Silvern, L. (1985). Stages and individual differences in cognitive development. *Annual Review of Psychology, 36,* 613-648.

REFERENCES

Fishbein, H. D. (1976). *Evolution, development, and children's learning.* Pacific Palisades, Calif.: Goodyear Publishing.

Fisher, K. (1985, December). Experts probe who, what, whys of elderly abuse. *APA Monitor*, pp. 24, 26.

Fitzgerald, H. E., & Brackbill, Y. (1976). Classical conditioning in infancy: Development and constraints. *Psychological Bulletin, 83*, 353-376.

Flavell, J. H. (1963). *The developmental psychology of Jean Piaget.* Princeton, NJ: Van Nostrand.

Flavell, J. H. (1970). Concept development. In P. H. Mussen (Ed.), *Carmichael's manual of child psychology* (3rd ed.). New York: Wiley.

Flavell, J. H. (1977). *Cognitive development.* Englewood Cliffs, NJ: Prentice-Hall.

Flavell, J. H. (1986, January). Really and truly. *Psychology Today*, pp. 38-44.

Flavell, J. H., Beach, D. R., & Chinsky, J. M. (1966). Spontaneous verbal rehearsal in a memory task as a function of age. *Child Development, 37*, 283-299.

Flynn, J. R. (1987). Massive IQ gains in 14 nations: What IQ tests really measure. *Psychological Bulletin, 101*, 171-191.

Folkart, B. A. (1994, April 2). Dr. Paul Spangler, 95; health advocate started running at 67. *Los Angeles Times*, p. 20.

Fowers, B. J., & Olson, D. (1986). Predicting marital success with PRE-PARE: A predictive validity study. *Journal of Marital and Family Therapy, 12*, 403-413.

Fowler, R. C., Rich, C. L., & Young, D. (1986). San Diego suicide study: II. Substance abuse in young cases. *Archives of General Psychiatry, 43*, 962-965.

Fowles, D. G. (1986). *A profile of older Americans, 1986.* Washington, DC: American Association of Retired Persons.

Fox, B. H. (1981). Psychosocial factors and the immune system in human cancer. In R. Ader (Ed.), *Psychoneuroimmunology* (pp. 103-157). New York: Academic Press.

Fox, J., Manitowabi, D., & Ward, J. A. (1984). An Indian community with a high suicide rate—5 years after. *Canadian Journal of Psychiatry, 29*, 425-427.

Fox, N. A. (1991). If it's not left, it's right: Electroencephalograph asymmetry and the development of emotion. *American Psychologist, 46*, 863-872.

Fozard, J. L., Wolf, E., Bell, B., McFarland, A., & Podosky, S. (1977). Visual perception and communication. In J. E. Birren & K. W. Schaie (Eds.), *Handbook of the psychology of aging* (pp. 497-534). New York: Van Nostrand Reinhold.

Frankenburg, W. K., & Dodds, J. B. (1967). The Denver Developmental Screening Test. *Journal of Pediatrics, 71*, 181-191.

Freiberg, P. (1991, April). More high school seniors say "no." The *APA Monitor*, pp. 28-29.

Freud, S. (1964). An outline of psychoanalysis. In J. Strachey (Ed.), *The standard edition of the complete psychological works* (Vol. 23). (Originally published, 1940). London: Hogarth Press.

Friedan, B. (1994, March 20). How to live longer, better, wiser. *Parade Magazine*, pp. 4-6.

Friedman, H. S., & Booth-Kewley, S. (1987). The "disease-prone personality": A meta-analytic view of the construct. *American Psychologist, 42*, 539-555.

Friedman, M., & Rosenman, R. H. (1959). Association of specific overt behavior pattern with blood and cardiovascular findings. *Journal of the American Medical Association, 169*, 1286-1296.

Friedrich, L. K., & Stein, A. H. (1973). Aggressive and prosocial television programs and the natural behavior of preschool children. *Monographs of the Society for Research in Child Development, 38*(4, Serial No. 151).

Friedrich, L. K., Stein, A. H., & Sussman, E. (1975). *The effects of prosocial television and environmental conditions on preschool children.* Paper presented at the meeting of the American Psychological Association, Chicago, Illinois.

Fries, J. F., & Crapo, L. M. (1981). *Vitality and aging.* San Francisco: W. H. Freeman.

Frisch, R. E. (1988). Fatness and fertility. *Scientific American, 258*(3), 88-95.

Frodi, A., Bridges, L., & Grolnick, W. (1985). Correlates of mastery-related behavior: A short-term longitudinal study of infants in their second year. *Child Development, 56*, 1291-1298.

Frodi, A., Lamb, M. E., Hwang, C. P., & Frodi, M. (1982). Father-mother-infant interaction in traditional and nontraditional Swedish families: A longitudinal study. *Alternative Lifestyles, 4*, 6-13.

Frodi, A., Lamb, M. E., Hwang, C. P., & Frodi, M. (1982). Father-mother-infant interaction in traditional and nontraditional Swedish families: A longitudinal study. *Alternative Lifestyles, 4*, 6-13.

Froming, W. J., Allen, L., & Jensen, R. (1985). Altruism, role-taking, and self-awareness: The acquisition of norms governing altruistic behavior. *Child Development, 56*, 1223-1228.

Fuchs, F. (1980). Genetic amniocentesis. *Scientific American, 242*(6), 47-53.

Furchtgott, E. (1984). Replicate, again and again. *American Psychologist, 39*, 1315-1316.

Furman, L. N., & Walden, T. A. (1990). Effect of script knowledge on preschool children's communicative interactions. *Developmental Psychology, 26*, 227-233.

Furman, W. (1987). Acquaintanceship in middle childhood. *Developmental Psychology, 23*, 563-570.

Furman, W., & Bierman, K. L. (1983). Developmental changes in young children's conceptions of friendship. *Child Development, 54*, 549-556.

Furstenberg, F. F., Jr., Nord, C. W., Peterson, J. L., & Zill, N. (1983). The life course of children of divorce: Marital disruption and parental contact. *American Sociological Review, 48*, 656-668.

Gagne, R. M. (1970). *The conditions of learning* (2nd ed.). New York: Holt, Rinehart & Winston.

Galbraith, R. C. (1982). Sibling spacing and intellectual development: A closer look at the confluence models. *Developmental Psychology, 18*, 151-173.

Gallup, G. G. (1977). Self-recognition in primates. *American Psychologist, 32*, 329-338.

Gambrell, R. D., Jr. (1987). Use of progestogen therapy. *American Journal of Obstetrics & Gynecology, 156*, 1304-1313.

Gardner, H. (1983). *Frames of mind: The theory of multiple intelligences.* New York: Basic Books.

Garelik, G. (1985, October). Are the progeny prodigies? *Discover*, pp. 45-57; 78-84.

Garmon, L. (1981, January 31). As it was in the beginning. *Science News*, pp. 72-74.

Garn, S. M. (1980). Human growth. *Annual Review of Anthropology, 9*, 275-292.

Garrison, E. G. (1987). Psychological maltreatment of children: An emerging focus for inquiry and concern. *American Psychologist, 42*, 157-159.

Gelman, R., & Baillargeon, R. (1983). A review of some Piagetian concepts. In J. H. Flavell & E. M. Markman (Eds.), Ph. H. Mussen (Series Ed.), *Handbook of child psychology: Vol. 3. Cognitive development* (pp. 167-230). New York: Wiley.

Geracioti, T. D., Jr., & Liddle, R. A. (1988). Impaired cholecystokinin secretion in bulimia nervosa. *New England Journal of Medicine, 319*, 683-688.

Gerbner, G., Gross, L., Morgan, M., & Signorielli, N. (1980). The "mainstreaming" of America: Violence profile No. 11. *Journal of Communication, 30*(3), 10-29.

Gerken, L., Landau, B., & Remez, R. E. (1990). Function morphemes in young children's speech perception and production. *Developmental Psychology, 26*, 204-216.

Gewirtz, J. A. (1961). A learning analysis of the effects of normal stimulation, privation, and deprivation on the acquisition of social motivation and attachment. In B. H. Foss (Ed.), *Determinants of infant behaviour* (pp. 213-298). London: Methuen.

Ghiselli, E. E. (1966). *The validity of occupational aptitude tests.* New York: Wiley.

Gibbs, J. C. (1979). Kohlberg's moral stage theory: A Piagetian revision. *Human Development, 22,* 89-112.

Gibbs, N. R., Hull, J. D., McDowell, J., & Park, J. (1988, February 22). Grays on the go. *Time,* pp. 66-75.

Gibson, E. J., & Walk, R. D. (1960). The "visual cliff." *Scientific American, 202*(4), 64-71.

Gibson, M. J. (1984). Sexuality in later life. *Ageing International, 11,* 8-13.

Giebenhain, J. E., & O'Dell, S. L. (1984). Evaluation of a parent-training manual for reducing children's fear of the dark. *Journal of Applied Behavior Analysis, 17,* 121-125.

Giele, J. Z. (1982). *Women in the middle years: Current knowledge and directions for research and policy.* New York: John Wiley & Sons, Inc.

Gilbert, L. A., Holahan, C., & Manning, L. (1981). Coping and conflict between professional and maternal roles. *Family Relations, 30,* 419-426.

Gilligan, C. (1982). *In a different voice.* Cambridge, MA: Harvard University Press.

Gillin, F. D., Reiner, D. S., & Wang, C. (1983). Human milk kills parasitic intestinal protozoa. *Science, 221,* 1290-1292.

Giordano, N. H., & Giordano, J. A. (1984). Elder abuse: A review of the literature. *Social Work, 29,* 232-236.

Glanz, D., & Tabory, E. (1985). Higher education and retirement: The Israeli experience. *Educational Gerontology, 11,* 101-111.

Glasser, B., & Strauss, A. (1965). *Awareness of dying.* Chicago: Aldine.

Gleitman, L. R., & Wanner, E. (1984). Current issues in language learning. In M. H. Bornstein & M. E. Lamb (Eds.), *Developmental psychology: An advanced textbook* (pp. 181-240). Hillsdale, NJ: Erlbaum.

Glenn, N. D., & McLanahan, S. (1981). The effects of offspring on the psychological well-being of older adults. *Journal of Marriage & the Family, 43,* 409-421.

Glick, I. O., Weiss, R. S., & Parkes, C. M. (1974). *The first year of bereavement.* New York: Wiley-Interscience.

Glick, J. (1975). Cognitive development in cross-cultural perspective. In F. D. Horowitz (Ed.), *Review of child development research* (Vol. 4). Chicago, IL: Univ. of Chicago Press.

Glick, P. C. (1979). The future marital status and living arrangements of the elderly. *The Gerontologist, 19,* 301-309.

Gnepp, J., & Gould, M. E. (1985). The development of personalized inferences: Understanding other people's emotional reactions in light of their prior experiences. *Child Development, 56,* 1455-1464.

Gold, M. S., Pottash, A. L. C., Sweeney, D. R., Martin, D. M., & Davies, R. K. (1980). Further evidence of hypothalamic-pituitary dysfunction in anorexia nervosa. *American Journal of Psychiatry, 137,* 101-102.

Goldberg, J., True, W. R., Eisen, S. A., & Henderson, W. G. (1990). A twin study of the effects of the Vietnam War on posttraumatic stress disorder. *Journal of the American Medical Association, 263,* 1227-1232.

Goldberg, P. (1968). Are women prejudiced against women? *Trans-action, 5*(5), 28-30.

Goldsmith, H. H. (1983). Genetic influences on personality from infancy to adulthood. *Child Development, 54,* 331-355.

Goldsmith, H. H., Buss, A. H., Plomin, R., Rothbart, M. K., Thomas, A., Chess, S., Hinde, R. A., & McCall, R. B. (1987). Roundtable: What is temperament? Four approaches. *Child Development, 58,* 505-529.

Goldstein, H. (1984). Effects of modeling and corrected practice on generative language learning of preschool children. *Hearing Disorders, 49,* 389-398.

Goleman, D. (1980, February). 1,528 little geniuses and how they grew. *Psychology Today,* pp. 28-53.

Goodstein, R. K. (1985). Common clinical problems in the elderly: Camouflaged by ageism and atypical presentation. *Psychiatric Annals, 15,* 299-312.

Gottfried, A. E., & Gottfried, A. W. (Eds.). (1988). *Maternal employment and children's development.* New York: Plenum.

Gottlieb, G. (1983). The psychobiological approach to developmental issues. In M. M. Haith, & J. J. Campos (Eds.), *Handbook of child psychology* (Vol. 2, pp. 1-26). New York: Wiley.

Gottman, J. M. (1983). How children become friends. *Monographs of the Society for Research in Child Development, 48*(3, Serial No. 201).

Gould, M. S., & Shaffer, D. (1986). The impact of suicide in television movies. *The New England Journal of Medicine, 315,* 690-694.

Gould, S. J. (1981). *The mismeasure of man.* New York: Norton.

Gould, S. J., & Lewontin, R. C. (1979). The spandrels of San Marco and the Panglossian paradigm: A critique of the adaptationist programme. In J. M. Smith, & R. Halliday (Eds.), *The evolution of adaptation by natural selection* (pp. 581-598). London: Roy. Soc. London.

Gove, W. F. (1973). Sex, marital status, and morality. *American Journal of Sociology, 79,* 45-67.

Gove, W. R., & Hughes, M. (1979). Possible causes of the apparent sex differences in physical health: An empirical investigation. *American Sociological Review, 44,* 126-146.

Grant, C. L., & Fodor, I. G. (1986). Adolescent attitudes toward body image and anorexic behavior. *Adolescence, 21,* 269-281.

Grass roots can grow at any age. (1987, April-May). *Modern Maturity,* p. 17.

Gravett, M., Rogers, C. S., & Thompson, L. (1987). Child care decisions among female heads of households with school-age children. *Early Childhood Research Quarterly, 2,* 67-81.

Gray, S. W., & Ruttle, K. (1980). The family-oriented home visiting program: A longitudinal study. *Genetic Psychology Monographs, 102,* 299-316.

Gray-Toft, P., & Anderson, J. G. (1983). Hospice Care: A better way of caring of the living. In A. H. Kutscher, S. C. Klagsbrun, R. J. Torpie, R. DeBellis, M. S. Hale, & M. Tallmer (Eds.), *Hospice U.S.A.* (pp. 109-125). New York: Columbia University Press.

Gray, W. M., & Hudson, L. M. (1984). Formal operations and the imaginary audience. *Developmental Psychology, 20,* 619-627.

Green, F. P., & Schneider, F. W. (1974). Age differences in the behavior of boys on three measures of altruism. *Child Development, 45,* 248-251.

Green, J. A., Gustafson, G. E., & West, M. J. (1980). Effects of infant development on mother-infant interactions. *Child Development, 51,* 199-207.

Greenbaum, C. W., & Landau, R. (1982). The infant's exposure to talk by familiar people: Mothers, fathers and siblings in different environments. In M. Lewiis & L. Rosenblum (Eds.), *The social network of the developing infant.* New York: Plenum.

Greenberg, J. (1977, July 30). The brain and emotions. *Science News,* pp. 74-75.

Greenberg, J. (1980, May 10). Ape talk: More than "pigeon" English? *Science News,* pp. 298-300.

Greenberg, J. (1980, May 24). Stressing the immune system. *Science News,* p. 335.

Greenberg, J. W., & Davidson, H. H. (1972). Home background and school achievement of black urban ghetto children. *American Journal of Orthopsychiatry, 42,* 803-810.

Greenberg, R. A., Haley, N. J., Etzel, R. A., & Loda, F. A. (1984). Measuring the exposure of infants to tobacco smoke: Nicotine and cotinine in urine and saliva. *New England Journal of Medicine, 310,* 1075-1078.

Greenberger, E., & O'Neil, R. (1993). Spouse, parent, worker: Role commitments and role-related experiences in the construction of adults' well-being. *Developmental Psychology, 29,* 181-197.

Greenman, G. W. (1963). Visual behavior of newborn infants. In A. J. Solnit, & S. A. Provence (Eds.), *Modern perspectives in child development.* New York: Internl. Universities Press.

Greenough, W. T., Black, J. E., & Wallace, C. S. (1987). Experience and brain development. *Child Development, 58,* 539-559.

Greer, D., Potts, R., Wright, J. C., & Huston, A. C. (1982). The effects of television commercial form and commercial placement on children's social behavior and attention. *Child Development, 53,* 611-619.

Grief, J. B. (1980). Fathers, children and joint custody. *Annual Progress in Child Psychiatry and Child Development, 1980,* 292-304.

Grieser, D. L., & Kuhl, P. K. (1988). Maternal speech to infants in a tonal language: Support for universal prosodic features in motherese. *Developmental Psychology, 24,* 14-20.

Griffiths, R. (1954). *The abilities of babies.* London: University of London Press.

Grilo, C. M., & Pogue-Geile, M. F. (1991). The nature of environmental influences on weight and obesity: A behavior genetic analysis. *Psychological Bulletin, 110,* 520-537.

Grollman, E. A. (1987, June). Explaining death to children and to ourselves. *The Harvard Medical School Mental Health Letter,* pp. 5-6.

Gronseth, E. (1975). Work-sharing families: Adaptations of pioneering families with husband and wife in part-time employment. *Acta Sociologica, 18,* 202-221.

Gross-Isseroff, R., Dillon, K. A., Israeli, M., & Biegon, A. (1990). Regionally selective increases in mu opoid receptor density in the brains of suicide victims. *Brain Research, 530,* 312-316.

Grotevant, H. D., & Cooper, C. R. (1985). Patterns of interaction in family relationships and the development of identity exploration in adolescence. *Child Development, 56,* 415-428.

Grotevant, M. D., Scarr, S., & Weinberg, R. A. (1975, March). *Intellectual development in family constellations with adopted and natural children: A test of the Zajonc and Markus model.* Paper presented at the meeting of the Society for Research in Child Development, New Orleans.

Gubrium, F. F. (1975). Being single in old age. *International Journal of Aging & Human Development, 6,* 29-41.

Guidubaldi, J., & Perry, J. D. (1985). Divorce and mental health sequelae for children: A two-year follow-up of a nationwide sample. *Journal of the American Academy of Child Psychiatry, 24,* 531-537.

Guilford, J. P. (1982). Cognitive psychology's ambiguities: Some suggested remedies. *Psychological Review, 89,* 48-59.

Guilford, J. P. (1983). Transformation abilities or functions. *Journal of Creative Behavior, 17,* 75-83.

Gunderson, V. M., Rose, S. A., & Grant-Webster, K. S. (1990). Cross-modal transfer in high- and low-risk infant pigtailed macaque monkeys. *Developmental Psychology, 26,* 576-581.

Gunnar, M. R., Senior, K., & Hartup, W. W. (1984). Peer presence and the exploratory behavior of eighteen and thirty-month-old children. *Child Development, 55,* 1103-1109.

Gustafson, G. E. (1984). Effects of the ability to locomote on infants' social and exploratory behaviors: An experimental study. *Developmental Psychology, 20,* 397-405.

Gutis, P. S. (1987, January 21). Homosexual parents winning some custody cases. *The New York Times,* pp. C-1 & C-16.

Gutman, D. (1976). Individual adaptation in the middle years: Developmental issues in the masculine mid-life crisis. *Journal of Geriatric Psychiatry, 9,* 41-59.

Gzesh, S. M., & Surber, C. F. (1985). Visual perspective-taking skills in children. *Child Development, 56,* 1204-1213.

Haan, N., Millsap, R., & Hartka, E. (1986). As time goes by: Change and stability in personality over fifty years. *Psychology and Aging, 1,* 220-232.

Haan, N., Smith, M. B., & Block, J. (1968). Moral reasoning of young adults: Political-social behavior, family background, and personality correlates. *Journal of Personality and Social Psychology, 10,* 183-201.

Hagestad, G. O. (1985). Continuity and connectedness. In V. L. Bengtson & J. F. Robertson (Eds.), *Grandparenthood* (pp. 31-48). Beverly Hills: Sage Publishing Inc.

Hagestad, G. O., & Smyer, M. A. (1982). Dissolving long-term relationships: Patterns of divorcing in middle age. In S. Duck (Ed.), *Personal relationships 4: Dissolving personal relationships* (pp. 155-188). London: Academic Press.

Haith, M. M. (1966). The response of the human newborn to visual movement. *Journal of Experimental Child Psychology, 3,* 235-243.

Hakuta, K. (1982). Interaction between particles and word order in the comprehension and production of simple sentences in Japanese children. *Developmental Psychology, 18,* 62-76.

Halford, G. S., & Boyle, F. M. (1985). Do young children understand conservation of number? *Child Development, 56,* 165-176.

Hall, E. (1983, June). A conversation with Erik Erikson. *Psychology Today,* pp. 22-30.

Hall, E. G., & Lee, A. M. (1984). Sex differences in motor performance of young children: Fact or fiction? *Sex Roles, 10,* 217-230.

Hall, G. S. (1904). *Adolescence* (Vols 1 and 2). New York: Appleton-Century-Crofts.

Hall, G. S. (1922). *Senescence.* New York: Appleton-Century-Crofts.

Hampson, R. B. (1981). Helping behavior in children: Addressing the interaction of a person-situation model. *Developmental Review, 1,* 93-112.

Haney, W. (1981). Validity, vaudeville, and values: A short history of social concerns over standardized testing. *American Psychologist, 36,* 1021-1034.

Hanson, J. D., Larson, M. E., & Snowden, C. T. (1976). The effects of control over high intensity noise on plasma cortisol levels in rhesus monkeys. *Behavioral Biology, 16,* 333-340.

Harding, C. G., & Golinkoff, R. M. (1979). The origins of intentional vocalizations in prelinguistic infants. *Child Development, 50,* 33-40.

Harlow, H. F., & Suomi, S. J. (1970). The nature of love—simplified. *American Psychologist, 25,* 161-168.

Harris, G., Thomas, A., & Booth, D. A. (1990). Development of salt taste in infancy. *Developmental Psychology, 26,* 534-538.

Harris, L. (1975). *The myth and reality of aging in America.* Washington, DC: National Counsel on Aging.

Harris, Louis, & Associates, Inc. (1981). *Aging in the eighties: America in transition.* Washington, DC: National Council on Aging, 1981.

Harris, M. B., & Turner, P. H. (1985). Gay and lesbian parents. *Journal of Homosexuality, 12*(2), 101-113.

Harris, R. L., Ellicott, A. M., & Holmes, D. S. (1986). The timing of psychosocial transitions and changes in women's lives: An examination of women aged 45 to 60. *Journal of Personality and Social Psychology, 51,* 409-416.

Harry, J. (1983). Gay male and lesbian relationships. In E. Macklin & R. Rubin (Eds.), *Contemporary families and alternative lifestyles: Handbook on research and theory* (pp. 216-234). Beverly Hills, CA: Sage.

Hart, S. N., & Brassard, M. R. (1987). A major threat to children's mental health: Psychological maltreatment. *American Psychologist, 42,* 160-165.

Harter, S., & Monsour, A. (1992). Developmental analysis of conflict caused by opposing attributes in the adolescent self-portrait. *Developmental Psychology, 28,* 251-260.

Hartshorne, H., May, M. A., & Maller, J. B. (1929). *Studies in the nature of character: II. Studies in service and self-control.* New York: Macmillan.

Hartup, W. W. (1970). Peer interaction and social organization. In P. H. Mussen (Ed.), *Carmichael's manual of child psychology* (3rd ed., Vol. 1, pp. 361-456). New York: Wiley.

Hartup, W. W. (1983). Peer relations. In P. H. Mussen (Ed.), *Handbook of child psychology* (4th ed., Vol. IV, pp. 103-196). New York: Wiley.

Harvard Medical School, Ad Hoc Committee of the Harvard Medical School to Examine the Definition of Brain Death. (1968). A definition of irreversible coma. *Journal of the American Medical Association, 205,* 337-340.

Harvey, C. D., & Bahr, H. (1974). Widowhood, morale, and affiliation. *Journal of Marriage & the Family, 36,* 97-106.

Harvey, M. A. S., McRorie, M. M., & Smith, D. W. (1981). Suggested limits to the use of the hot tub and sauna by pregnant women. *Canadian Medical Association Journal, 125,* 50-53.

Haskins, R., Schwartz, J. B., Akin, J. S., & Dobelstein, A. W. (1985). How much support can absent fathers pay? *Policy Studies Journal, 14,* 201-222.

Hasselhorn, M. (1992). Task dependency and the role of category typicality and metamemory in the development of an organizational strategy. *Child Development, 63,* 202-214.

Havighurst, R. J. (1982). The world of work. In B. B. Wolman (Ed.), *Handbook of developmental psychology* (pp. 771-787). Englewood Cliffs, NJ: Prentice-Hall.

Haviland, J. M., & Lelwica, M. (1987). The induced affect response: 10-week-old infants' responses to three emotion expressions. *Developmental Psychology, 23*, 97-104.

Hawking, S. (1988). *A brief history of time*. New York: Bantam.

Hawkins, J. D., Catalano, R. F., & Miller, J. Y. (1992). Risk and protective factors for alcohol and other drug problems in adolescence and early adulthood: Implications for substance abuse prevention. *Psychological Bulletin, 112*, 64-105.

Hayes, M. P., Stinnett, N., & Defrain, J. (1980). Learning about marriage from the divorced. *Journal of Divorce, 4*, 23-29.

Hayflick, L. (1980). The cell biology of human aging. *Scientific American, 242*(1), 58-65.

Hayflick, L. (1985). Theories of biological aging. *Experimental Gerontology, 20*, 145-159.

Hayflick, L., & Moorhead, P. S. (1961). The serial cultivation of human diploid cell strains. *Experimental Cell Research, 25*, 585-621.

Hayward, M. D., & Hardy, M. A. (1985). Early retirement processes among older men. *Research on Aging, 7*, 491-515.

Haywood, K. M. (1986). *Life span motor development*. Champaign, IL: Human Kinetics.

Heath, C. W. (1945). *What people are*. Cambridge, MA: Harvard University Press.

Heibeck, T. H., & Markman, E. M. (1987). Word learning in children: An examination of fast mapping. *Child Development, 58*, 1021-1034.

Heinonen, O. P., Slone, D., Shapiro, S., Gaetana, L. F., Hartz, S. C., Mitchell, A. A., Monson, R. R., Rosenberg, L., Siskind, V., & Kaufman, D. W. (1977). *Birth defects and drugs in pregnancy*. Littleton, Mass.: PSG Publications.

Helsing, K. J., Comstock, G. W., & Szklo, M. (1982). Causes of death in a widowed population. *American Journal of Epidemiology, 116*, 524-532.

Helson, R., & Crutchfield, R. S. (1970). Mathematicians: The creative researcher and the average Ph.D. *Journal of Consulting and Clinical Psychology, 34*, 250-257.

Hennessy, M. J., Dixon, S. D., & Simon, S. R. (1984). The development of gait: A study in African children ages one to five. *Child Development, 55*, 844-853.

Hennon, C. B., Brubaker, T. H., & Baumann, S. A. (1983). Your aging parent: Deciding whether to live together (*Cooperative Extension Service Bulletin B324S*). Madison: University of Wisconsin Extension.

Hernandez, D. J. (1988). Demographic trends and the living arrangements of children. In E. M. Hetherington & J. D. Arasteh (Eds.), *Impact of divorce, single parenting, and stepparenting on children* (pp. 3-22). Hillsdale, NJ: Erlbaum.

Herndon, B. K., & Carpenter, M. D. (1982). Sex differences in cooperative and competitive attitudes in a Northeastern school. *Psychological Reports, 50*, 768-770.

Hetherington, E. M. (1979). Divorce: A child's perspective. *American Psychologist, 34*, 851-858.

Hetherington, E. M. (1989). Coping with family transitions: Winners, losers, and survivors. *Child Development, 60*, 1-14.

Hetherington, E. M., Clingempeel, W. G., Anderson, E. R., Deal, J. E., Hagan, M. S., Hollier, E. A., Lindner, M. S., & Maccoby, E. E. (1992). Coping with marital transitions. *Monographs of the Society for Research in Child Development, 57*(2-3, Serial No. 227).

Hetherington, E. M., Cox, M., & Cox, R. (1979). Play and social interaction in children following divorce. *Journal of Social Issues, 35*(4), 26-49.

Hetherington, E. M., Cox, M., & Cox, R. (1978). The aftermath of divorce. In J. H. Stevens, Jr., & M. Matthews (Eds.), *Mother-child, father-child relations* (pp. 149-176). Washington, D.C.: National Association for the Education of Young Children.

Hetherington, E. M., Stanley-Hagan, M., & Anderson, E. R. (1989). Marital transitions: A child's perspective. *American Psychologist, 44*, 303-312.

Hillel, M., & Henry, C. (1976). *Of pure blood* (E. Mossbacher, Trans.). New York: McGraw-Hill. (Original work published 1975)

Himmelberger, D. U., Brown, B. W., Jr., & Cohen, E. N. (1978). Cigarette smoking during pregnancy and the occurrence of spontaneous abortion and congenital abnormality. *American Journal of Epidemiology, 108*, 470-479.

Hinde, R. A. (1991). When is an evolutionary approach useful? *Child Development, 62*, 671-675.

Hinde, R. A., Stevenson-Hinde, J., & Tamplin, A. (1985). Characteristics of 3- to 4-year-olds assessed at home and their interactions in preschool. *Developmental Psychology, 21*, 130-140.

Hindley, C. B., Filliozat, A. M., Klackenberg, G., Nicolet-Meister, D., & Sand, E. A. (1966). Differences in age of walking for five European longitudinal samples. *Human Biology, 38*, 364-379.

Hinton, J. (1967). *Dying*. Baltimore: Penguin Books.

Hock, E. (1978). Working and nonworking mothers with infants: Perceptions of their careers, their infants' needs, and satisfaction with mothering. *Developmental Psychology, 14*, 37-43.

Hock, E., & DeMeis, D. K. (1990). Depression in mothers of infants: The role of maternal employment. *Developmental Psychology, 26*, 285-291.

Hoeffer, B. (1981). Children's acquisition of sex role behavior in lesbian-mother families. *American Journal of Orthopsychiatry, 51*, 536-543.

Hoffman, L. W. (1989). Effects of maternal employment in the two-parent family. *American Psychologist, 44*, 283-292.

Hoffman, M. L. (1970). Moral development. In P. H. Mussen (Ed.), *Carmichael's manual of child psychology* (3rd ed., Vol. 2, pp. 261-360). New York: Wiley.

Hoffman, M. L. (1977). Personality and social development. In M. R. Rosenzweig, & L. W. Porter (Eds.), *Annual review of psychology* (Vol. 28). Palo Alto, CA: Annual Reviews, Inc.

Hoffman, M. L. (1979). Development of moral thought, feeling, and behavior. *American Psychologist, 34*, 958-966.

Hoffner, C., & Cantor, J. (1985). Developmental differences in responses to a television character's appearance and behavior. *Developmental Psychology, 21*, 1065-1074.

Hofland, B. F., Willis, S. L., & Baltes, P. B. (1981). Fluid intelligence performance in the elderly: Intraindividual variability and conditions of assessment. *Journal of Educational Psychology, 73*, 573-586.

Hojat, M. (1982). Loneliness as a function of parent-child and peer relations. *Journal of Psychology, 112*, 129-133.

Holden, C. (1986, October). The rational optimist. *Psychology Today*, pp. 55-60.

Holden, C. (1986). Youth suicide: New research focuses on a growing social problem. *Science, 233*, 839-841.

Holden, C. (1991). On the trail of genes for IQ. *Science, 253*, 1352.

Holmes, T. H., & Rahe, R. H. (1967). The Social Readjustment Rating Scale. *Journal of Psychosomatic Research, 11*, 213-218.

Homans, G. C. (1961). *Social behavior: Its elementary forms*. New York: Harcourt Brace & World.

Hook, S. (Ed.). (1960). *Psychoanalysis, scientific method and philosophy*. New York: Grove.

Horn, J. (1986). Intellectual ability concepts. In R. J. Sternberg (Ed.), *Advances in the psychology of human intelligence* (Vol. 3, pp. 35-77). Hillsdale, NJ: Erlbaum.

Horn, J. C., & Meer, J. (1987, May). The vintage years. *Psychology Today*, pp. 77-90.

Horn, J. L. (1982). The aging of human abilities. In B. B. Wolman (Ed.), *Handbook of developmental psychology* (pp. 847-870). Englewood Cliffs, NJ: Prentice-Hall.

Horn, J. L., & Cattell, R. B. (1966). Refinement and test of the theory of fluid and crystalized general intelligences. *Journal of Educational Psychology, 57*, 253-270.

Horn, J. L., & Cattell, R. B. (1967). Age differences in fluid and crystallized intelligence. *Acta Psychologica, 26*, 107-129.

Horn, J. L., & Donaldson, G. Y. (1980). Cognitive development in adulthood. In D. G. Brim, Jr. & J. Kagan (Eds.), *Constancy and change in human development* (pp. 445-529). Cambridge, MA: Harvard University Press.

Horn, J. M. (1983). The Texas Adoption Project: Adopted children and their intellectual resemblance to biological and adoptive parents. *Child Development, 54,* 268-275.

Horn, J. M. (1985). Bias? Indeed! *Child Development, 56,* 779-780.

Horner, M. S. (1968). *Sex differences in achievement motivation and performance in competitive and noncompetitive situations.* (Doctoral dissertation, University of Michigan, 1968). (University Microfilms No. 6912135)

Horney, K. (1939). *New ways in psychoanalysis.* New York: Norton.

Hornstein, G. A., & Wapner, S. (1985). Modes of experiencing and adapting to retirement. *International Journal of Aging & Human Development, 21,* 291-315.

Horowitz, F. D. (1992). John B. Watson's legacy: Learning and environment. *Developmental Psychology, 28,* 360-367.

Horwitz, S. M., Klerman, L. V., Kuo, H. S., & Jekel, J. F. (1991). Intergenerational transmission of school-age parenthood. *Family Planning Perspectives, 23,* 168-172, 177.

Housing industry aims at elders. (1986, June-July). *Modern Maturity,* p. 14.

Hoving, K. L., Hamm, N., & Galvin, P. (1969). Social influence as a function of stimulus ambiguity at three age levels. *Developmental Psychology, 1,* 631-636.

Howard, F. M., & Hill, J. M. (1979). Drugs in pregnancy. *Obstetrical and Gynecological Survey, 34,* 643-653.

Howard, J. A., & Barnett, M. A. (1981). Arousal of empathy and subsequent generosity in young children. *Journal of Genetic Psychology, 138,* 307-308.

Howes, C. (1983). Patterns of friendship. *Child Development, 54,* 1041-1053.

Howes, C. (1985). Sharing fantasy: Social pretend play in toddlers. *Child Development, 56,* 1253-1258.

Howes, C. (1990). Can the age of entry into child care and the quality of child care predict adjustment in kindergarten? *Developmental Psychology, 26,* 292-303.

Howes, C., Phillips, D. A., & Whitebook, M. (1992). Thresholds of quality: Implications for the social development of children in center-based child care. *Child Development, 63,* 449-460.

Howes, C., Unger, O., & Seidner, L. B. (1989). Social pretend play in toddlers: Parallels with social play and with solitary pretend. *Child Development, 60,* 77-84.

Hudson, J. (1990). Constructive processing in children's event memory. *Developmental Psychology, 26,* 180-187.

Hudson, L. M., Forman, E. A., & Brion-Meisels, S. (1982). Role taking as a predictor of prosocial behavior in cross-age tutors. *Child Development, 53,* 1320-1329.

Huebner, A., & Garrod, A. (1991). Equilibration and the learning paradox. *Human Development, 34,* 261-272.

Huel, G., Everson, R. B., & Menger, I. (1984). Increased hair cadmium in newborns of women occupationally exposed to heavy metals. *Environmental Research, 35,* 115-121.

Huesmann, L. R., Lagerspetz, K., & Eron, L. D. (1984). Intervening variables in the TV violence-aggression relation: Evidence from two countries. *Developmental Psychology, 20,* 746-775.

Hultsch, D. F. (1971). Adult age differences in free classification and free recall. *Developmental Psychology, 4,* 338-342.

Hultsch, D. F. (1975). Adult age differences in retrieval: Trace-dependent and cue-dependent forgetting. *Developmental Psychology, 11,* 197-201.

Humphreys, L. G., Rich, S. A., & Davey, T. C. (1985). A Piagetian test of general intelligence. *Developmental Psychology, 21,* 872-877.

Hunziker, U. A., & Barr, R. G. (1986). Increased carrying reduces infant crying: A randomized controlled trial. *Pediatrics, 77,* 641-648.

Huston, A. C., & Wright, J. C. (1982). Effects of communication media on children. In C. B. Kopp, & J. B. Krakow (Eds.), *The child: Development in a social context.* Boston: Addison-Wesley.

Huston, A. C., Wright, J. C., Rice, M. L., Kerkman, D., & St. Peters, M. (1990). Development of television viewing patterns in early childhood: A longitudinal investigation. *Developmental Psychology, 26,* 409-420.

Hutt, S. J., Hutt, C., Lenard, H. G., Bernuth, H. V., & Muntjewerff, W. J. (1968). Auditory responsivity in the human neonate. *Nature, 218,* 888-890.

Hyman, H. H. (1983). *Of time and widowhood: Nationwide studies of enduring effects.* Durham, NC: Duke University Press.

Hymel, S. (1986). Interpretations of peer behavior: Affective bias in childhood and adolescence. *Child Development, 57,* 431-445.

Hymel, S., Rubin, K. H., Rowden, L., & LeMare, L. (1990). Children's peer relationships: Longtudinal prediction of internalizing and externalizing problems from middle to late childhood. *Child Development, 61,* 2004-2021.

Iannotti, R. J. (1978). Effect of role-taking experiences on role taking, empathy, altruism, and aggression. *Developmental Psychology, 14,* 119-124.

Inhelder, B., & Piaget, J. (1958). *The growth of logical thinking from childhood to adolescence.* New York: Basic Books.

IQ Myth, The. (1975). New York: CBS News.

Irwin, M. H., & McLaughlin, D. H. (1970). Ability and preference in category sorting by Mano schoolchildren and adults. *Journal of Social Psychology, 82,* 15-24.

Irwin, M. H., Schafer, G. N., & Feiden, C. P. (1974). Emic and unfamiliar category sorting of Mano farmers and U.S. undergraduates. *Journal of Cross-Cultural Psychology, 5,* 407-423.

Is retirement really so bad? (1987, February-March). *Modern Maturity,* p. 15.

Isabella, R. A., & Belsky, J. (1991). Interactional synchrony and the origins of infant-mother attachment: A replication study. *Child Development, 62,* 373-384.

Isabella, R. A., Belsky, J., & von Eye, A. (1989). The origins of infant-mother attachment: An examination of interactional synchrony during the infant's first year. *Developmental Psychology, 25,* 12-21.

Isen, A. M., Horn, N., & Rosenhan, D. L. (1973). Effects of success and failure on children's generosity. *Journal of Personality and Social Psychology, 27,* 239-247.

Izard, C. E., Porges, S. W., Simons, R. F., Haynes, O. M., Hyde, C., Parisi, M., & Cohen, B. (1991). Infant cardiac activity: Developmental changes and relations with attachment. *Developmental Psychology, 27,* 432-439.

Jacklin, C. N. (1989). Female and male: Issues of gender. *American Psychologist, 44,* 127-133.

Jacklin, C. N., & Maccoby, E. E. (1983). Issues of gender differentiation in normal development. In M. D. Levine, W. B. Carey, A. C. Crocker, & R. T. Gross (Eds.), *Developmental-behavioral pediatrics.* Philadelphia: W. B. Saunders.

Jackson, C. M. (1929). Some aspects of form and growth. In W. J. Robbins, S. Brody, A. F. Hogan, C. M. Jackson, & C. W. Greed (Eds.), *Growth.* New Haven, CT: Yale University Press.

Jackson, E. N. (1965). *Telling a child about death.* New York: Channel Press.

Jackson, P. W., & Messick, D. (1968). Creativity. In P. London & D. Rosenhan (Eds.), *Foundations of abnormal psychology.* New York: Holt.

Jacobs, J. (1971). *Adolescent suicide.* New York: Wiley.

Jacobs, S., & Ostfeld, A. (1977). An epidemiological review of the mortality of bereavement. *Psychosomatic Medicine, 39,* 344-357.

Jacobsen, T., Edelstein, W., & Hofmann, V. (1994). A longitudinal study of the relation between representations of attachment in childhood and cognitive functioning in childhood and adolescence. *Developmental Psychology, 30,* 112-124.

Jacobson, J. L., Boersma, D. C., Fields, R. B., & Olson, K. L. (1983). Paralinguistic features of adult speech to infants and small children. *Child Development, 54,* 436-442.

Jacobson, J. L., & Wille, D. E. (1984). Influence of attachment and separation experience on separation distress at 18 months. *Developmental Psychology, 20,* 477-484.

Jacques, E. (1965). Death and the mid-life crisis. *International Journal of Psychoanalysis, 46,* 502-514.

Jahoda, M. (1982). *Employment and unemployment: A social-psychological analysis.* Cambridge: Cambridge Univ. Press.

James, W. (1910). *The principles of psychology* (Vol. 2). New York: Holt.

Jaquish, G. A., & Ripple, R. E. (1981). Cognitive creative abilities and self-esteem across the adult life-span. *Human Development, 24,* 110-119.

Jarvik, L. F. (1962). Biological differences in intellectual functioning. *Vita Humana, 5,* 195-203.

Jelliffe, D. B., & Jelliffe, E. F. P. (1977). Current concepts in nutrition: "Breast is best": Modern meanings. *New England Journal of Medicine, 297,* 912-915.

Jensen, A. R. (1969). How much can we boost IQ and scholastic achievement? *Harvard Educational Review, 39,* 1-123.

Joffe, L. S. (1980). *The relation between mother-infant attachment and compliance with maternal commands and prohibitions.* Unpublished doctoral dissertation, University of Minnesota.

Joffe, L. S., & Vaughn, B. E. (1982). Infant-mother attachment: Theory, assessment, and implications for development. In B. B. Wolman (Ed.), *Handbook of developmental psychology* (pp. 190-207). Englewood Cliffs, NJ: Prentice-Hall.

Johnson, C., & Flach, A. (1985). Family characteristics of 105 patients with bulimia. *American Journal of Psychiatry, 142,* 1321-1324.

Johnson, S. (1986, October 2). Women over 40 choosing law. *New York Times,* pp. C1, C6.

Johnston, J. R., Kline, M., & Tschann, J. M. (1989). Ongoing postdivorce conflict: Effects on children of joint custody and frequent access. *American Journal of Orthopsychiatry, 59,* 576-592.

Johnston, L. D., Bachman, J. G., & O'Malley, P. M. (1992, January 15). Most forms of drug use decline among American high school and college students. Ann Arbor, Michigan: University of Michigan News and Information Services.

Kagan, J. (1966). Reflection-impulsivity: The generality and dynamics of conceptual tempo. *Journal of Abnormal Psychology, 71,* 17-24.

Kagan, J. (1973). What is intelligence? *Social Policy, 4*(1), 88-94.

Kagan, J., Arcus, D., Snidman, N., Feng, W. Y., Hendler, J., & Greene, S. (1994). Reactivity in infants: A cross-national comparison. *Developmental Psychology, 30,* 342-345.

Kagan, J., & Moss, H. A. (1962). *Birth to maturity.* New York: Wiley.

Kagan, J., Reznick, J. S., & Gibbons, J. (1989). Inhibited and unhibited types of children. *Child Development, 60,* 838-845.

Kagan, J., & Snidman, N. (1991). Temperamental factors in human development. *American Psychologist, 46,* 856-862.

Kagan, S., & Madsen, M. C. (1971). Cooperation and competition of Mexican, Mexican-American, and Anglo-American children of two ages and four instructional sets. *Developmental Psychology, 5,* 32-39.

Kahn, P. H., Jr. (1992). Children's obligatory and discretionary moral judgments. *Child Development, 63,* 416-430.

Kail, R., & Hagen, J. W. (1982). Memory in childhood. In B. B. Wolman (Ed.), *Handbook of developmental psychology.* Englewood Cliffs, NJ: Prentice-Hall.

Kajino, T., McIntyre, J. A., Faulk, W. P., Cai, D. S., & Billington, W. D. (1988). Antibodies to trophoblast in normal pregnant and secondary aborting women. Journal of Reproductive *Immunology, 14,* 267-282.

Kalish, R. A., & Reynolds, D. K. (1981). *Perspectives on death and dying series: Death and ethnicity: A psychocultural study.* Farmingdale, NY: Baywood Publishing Co. Inc.

Kalnins, I. V., & Bruner, J. S. (1973). The coordination of visual observation and instrumental behavior in early infancy. *Perception, 2,* 307-314.

Kalter, N., & Plunkett, J. W. (1984). Children's perceptions of the causes and consequences of divorce. *Journal of the American Academy of Child Psychiatry, 23,* 326-334.

Kandel, D. B., & Raveis, V. H. (1989). Cessation of illicit drug use in young adulthood. *Archives of General Psychiatry, 46,* 109-116.

Kanfer, F. H., Karoly, P., & Newman, A. (1975). Reduction of children's fear of the dark by competence-related and situational threat-related verbal cues. *Journal of Consulting & Clinical Psychology, 43,* 251-258.

Kaplan, H. R., & Tausky, C. (1972). Work and welfare cadillac: The function of and commitment to work among the hard-care unemployed. *Social Problems, 19,* 469-483.

Karasek, R. W., Schwartz, J., & Theorell, T. (1982). *Job characteristics, occupation, and coronary heart disease* (Contract No. R-01-OH00906). Cleveland, OH: National Institute of Occupational Safety & Health.

Kasl, S. V., Ostfeld, A. M., & Brody, G. M. (1980). Effects of "involuntary" relocation on the health and behavior of the elderly. In S. G. Haynes & M. Feinleib (Eds.), *Second Conference on the Epidemiology of Aging.* Department of Health and Human Services, NIH Publication No. 80-969. Washington, DC: U.S. Govt. Printing Office.

Kassoff, D. B. (1984). Psychotherapeutic approaches and techniques in treatment of the terminally ill patient (1950-1975). In M. Tallmer, E. R. Prichard, A. H. Kutscher, R. DeBellis, M. S. Hale, & I. K. Goldberg (Eds.), *The life threatened elderly* (pp. 132-145). New York: Columbia University Press.

Kastenbaum, R. (1967). The child's understanding of death: How does it develop? In E. A. Grollman (Ed.), *Explaining death to children* (pp. 89-108). Boston: Beacon Press.

Kastenbaum, R. (1974). Childhood: The kingdom where creatures die. *Journal of Clinical Child Psychology, 3,* 11-14.

Kastenbaum, R. (1977). Death and development through the lifespan. In H. Feifel (Ed.), *New meanings of death* (pp. 17-45). New York: McGraw-Hill Book Company.

Kastenbaum, R. (1992). The creative process: A life-span approach. In T. R. Cole, D. D. Van Tassel, & Kastenbaum, R. (Eds.), *Handbook of the humanities and aging* (pp. 285-306). New York: Springer.

Katz, P. A., & Walsh, P. V. (1991). Modification of children's gender-stereotyped behavior. *Child Development, 62,* 338-351.

Katz, V. L., Jenkins, T., Haley, L., & Bowes, W. A. Jr. (1991). Catecholamine levels in pregnant physicians and nurses: A pilot study of stress and pregnancy. *Obstetrics & Gynecology, 77,* 338-342.

Kaufman, D. R., & Richardson, B. L. (1982). *Achievement and women: Challenging the assumptions.* New York: Free Press.

Kaufman, M. H., & O'Shea, K. S. (1978). Induction of monozygotic twinning in the mouse. *Nature, 276,* 707-708.

Kaylor, J. A., King, D. W., & King. L. A. (1987). Psychological effects of military service in Vietnam: A meta-analysis. *Psychological Bulletin, 102,* 257-271.

Keating, N. C., & Cole, P. (1980). What do I do with him 24 hours a day? Changes in the housewife role after retirement. *The Gerontologist, 20,* 84-89.

Keil, F. C. (1981). Constraints on knowledge and cognitive development. *Psychological Review, 88,* 197-227.

Keith, P. M. (1983). A comparison of the resources of parents and childless men and women in very old age. *Family Relations, 32,* 403-409.

Keith, P. M., & Schafer, R. B. (1980). Role strain and depression in two-job families. *Family Relations, 29,* 483-488.

Keller, H., & Scholmerich, A. (1987). Infant vocalizations and parental reactions during the first 4 months of life. *Developmental Psychology, 23,* 62-67.

Kellerman, J. (1981). *Helping the fearful child.* New York: Warner Books.

Kelley, H. H. (1983). Love and commitment. In H. H. Kelley et al. (Eds.), *Close relationships* (pp. 265-314). New York: W. H. Freeman.

Kempe, C. H., Silverman, F., Steele, B., Droegemueller, W., & Silver, H. (1962). The battered child syndrome. *Journal of the American Medical Association, 181,* 17-24.

Keniston, K. (1968). *Young radicals: Notes on committed youth.* New York: Harcourt, Brace, & World.

Keniston, K. (1970). Youth: A "new" stage of life. *The American Scholar, 39,* 631-654.

Keniston, K. (1983, June). Remembering Erikson at Harvard. *Psychology Today*, p. 29.

Kennedy, W. A. (1969). A follow-up normative study of Negro intelligence and achievement. *Monographs of the Society for Research in Child Development*, 34(2, Serial No. 126).

Kennell, J. H., Jerauld, R., Wolfe, H., Chesler, D., Kreger, N. C., McAlpine, W., Steffa, N., & Klaus, M. H. (1974). Maternal behavior one year after early and extended post-partum contact. *Developmental Medicine and Child Neurology, 16*, 172-179.

Kennell, J. H., & Klaus, M. H. (1984). Mother-infant bonding: Weighing the evidence. *Developmental Review, 4*, 275-282.

Kennell, J. H., Voos, D. K., & Klaus, M. H. (1979). Parent-infant bonding. In J. Osofsky (Ed.), *Handbook of infant development* (pp. 786-798). New York: Wiley Interscience.

Kerckhoff, A. C., & Davis, K. E. (1962). Value consensus and need complementarity in mate selection. *American Sociological Review, 27*, 295-303.

Kermoian, R., & Campos, J. J. (1988). Locomotor experience: A facilitator of spatial cognitive development. *Child Development, 59*, 908-917.

Kessler, R. C., & McRae, J. A. (1984). A note on the relationship of sex and marital status to psychological distress. *Research in Community and Mental Health, 4*, 109-130.

Khan, A. U. (1988). Heterogeneity of suicidal adolescents. In S. Chess, A. Thomas, & M. E. Hertzig (Eds.), *Annual progress in child psychiatry and child development* (pp. 675-686). New York: Brunner/Mazel.

Khan, L. M. L., & James, S. L. (1983). Grammatical morpheme development in three language disordered children. *Journal of Childhood Communication Disorders, 6*, 85-100.

Kinsey, A. C., Pomeroy, W. B., & Martin, C. E. (1948). *Sexual behavior in the human male*. Philadelphia: Saunders.

Kinsey, A. C., Pomeroy, W. B., Martin, C. E., & Gebhard, P. H. (1953). *Sexual behavior in the human female*. Philadelphia: Saunders.

Kirkpatrick, M., Smith, C., & Roy, R. (1981). Lesbian mothers and their children: A comparative survey. *American Journal of Orthopsychiatry, 51*, 545-551.

Kirkwood, G. M. (1959). *A short guide to classical mythology*. New York: Holt, Rinehart, & Winston.

Kitson, G. C., & Sussman, M. B. (1983). Marital complaints, demographic characteristics, and symptoms of mental distress in divorce. *Journal of Marriage and the Family, 45*, 87-101.

Kivnick, H. Q. (1981). Grandparenthood and the mental health of grandparents. *Aging & Society, 1*(3), 365-391.

Kivnick, H. Q. (1985). Intergenerational relations: Personal meaning in the life cycle. *Contributions to Human Development, 14*, 93-102.

Klaus, M. H., & Kennell, J. H. (1976). *Maternal-infant bonding*. St. Louis: Mosby.

Klaus, M. H., Jerauld, R., Kreger, N. C., McAlpine, W., Steffa, M., & Kennell, J. H. (1972). Maternal attachment: Importance of the first postpartum days. *New England Journal of Medicine, 286*, 460-463.

Klein, P. S. (1984). Behavior of Israeli mothers toward infants in relation to infants' perceived temperament. *Child Development, 55*, 1212-1218.

Kliman, G. (1968). *Psychological emergences of childhood*. New York: Grune & Stratton.

Klink, F., Jungblut, J. R., Oberheuser, F., & Siegers, C. P. (1983). Cadmium- und Bleikonzen-trationen im Fruchtwasser von rauchenden und nicht-rauchenden Gravida. [Cadmium and lead concentrations in the amniotic fluid of pregnant smokers and non-smokers.] *Geburtshilfe Fraunheilkd, 43*, 695-698.

Klinnert, M. D., Emde, R. N., Butterfield, P., & Campos, J. J. (1986). Social referencing: The infant's use of emotional signals from a friendly adult with mother present. *Developmental Psychology, 22*, 427-432.

Knight, G. P., Kagan, S., & Buriel, R. (1981). Confounding effects of individualism in children's cooperation-competition social motive measures. *Motivation and Emotion, 5*, 167-178.

Knight, G. P., Kagan, S., & Buriel, R. (1982). Perceived parental practices and prosocial development. *Journal of Genetic Psychology, 141*, 57-65.

Kobasa, S. C. (1979). Stressful life events, personality, and health: An inquiry into hardiness. *Journal of Personality and Social Psychology, 37*, 1-11.

Kobasa, S. C. (1982). Commitment and coping in stress resistance among lawyers. *Journal of Personality and Social Psychology, 42*, 707-717.

Kobasa, S. C., Maddi, S. R., & Kahn, S. (1982). Hardiness and health: A prospective study. *Journal of Personality and Social Psychology, 42*, 168-177.

Koch, H. L. (1955). The relation of certain family constellation characteristics and the attitudes of children toward adults. *Child Development, 26*, 13-40.

Kogan, N., & Pankove, E. (1972). Creative ability over a five-year span. *Child Development, 43*, 427-442.

Kohlberg, L. (1966). A cognitive-developmental analysis of children's sex-role concepts and attitudes. In E. E. Maccoby (Ed.), *The development of sex differences* (pp. 81-173). Stanford, Calif.: Stanford Univ. Press.

Kohlberg, L., & Gilligan, C. (1971). The adolescent as a philosopher: The discovery of the self in a postconventional world. *Daedalus, 100*, 1051-1086.

Kohlberg, L., Levine, C., & Hewer, A. (1983). Moral stages: A current formulation and a response to critics. *Contributions to Human Development* (Vol. 12). Basel: Karger.

Kohlberg, L., Yaeger, J., & Hjertholm, E. (1968). Private speech: Four studies and a review of theories. *Child Development, 39*, 691-736.

Kokmen, E. (1984). Dementia—Alzheimer type. *Mayo Clinic Proceedings, 59*, 35-42.

Kolata, G. (1984). Studying learning in the womb. *Science, 225*, 302-303.

Kolata, G. (1986). Obese children: A growing problem. *Science, 232*, 20-21.

Koller, M. R. (1953). Residential and occupational propinquity. In R. F. Winch & R. McGinnis (Eds.), *Marriage and the family*. New York: Holt, Rinehart & Winston.

Koocher, G. P. (1973). Childhood, death, and cognitive development. *Developmental Psychology, 9*, 369-375.

Koops, B. L., Morgan, L. J., & Battaglia, F. C. (1982). Neonatal mortality risk in relation to birth weight and gestational age: Update. *Journal of Pediatrics, 101*, 969-977.

Kopp, C. B. (1982). Antecedents of self-regulation: A developmental perspective. *Developmental Psychology, 18*, 199-214.

Kopp, C. B., & Kalar, S. R. (1989). Risk in infancy. *American Psychologist, 44*, 224-230.

Korbin, J. (1977). Anthropological contributions to the study of child abuse. *International Child Welfare Review*, No. 35, 23-31.

Korn, S. J., & Gannon, S. (1983). Temperament, cultural variation and behavior disorder in preschool children. *Child Psychiatry and Human Development, 13*, 203-212.

Korner, A. F., Hutchinson, C. A., Koperski, J. A., Kraemer, H. C., & Schneider, P. A. (1981). Stability of individual differences of neonatal motor and crying patterns. *Child Development, 52*, 83-90.

Kotelchuck, M. (1976). The infant's relationship to the father: Experimental evidence. In M. E. Lamb (Ed.), *The role of the father in child development*. New York: Wiley.

Kramer, D. A. (1983). Post-formal operations? A need for further conceptualization. *Human Development, 26*, 91-105.

Kramer, D. A., & Woodruff, D. S. (1986). Relativistic and dialectical thought in three adult age-groups. *Human Development, 29*, 280-290.

Kramer, M. S. (1981). Do breast-feeding and delayed introduction of solid foods protect against subsequent obesity? *Journal of Pediatrics, 98*, 883-887.

Krieger, W. G. (1976). Infant influences and the parent sex by child sex interaction in the socialization process. *JSAS Catalogue of Selected Documents in Psychology, 6*(1), 36 (Ms. No. 1234).

Kruse, J. (1984). Alcohol use during pregnancy. *American Family Physician, 29*, 199-203.

Kubler-Ross, E. (1969). *On death and dying*. New York: Macmillan Publishing Co.

Kuczynski, L. (1984). Socialization goals and mother-child interaction: Strategies for long-term and short-term compliance. *Developmental Psychology, 20,* 1061-1073.

Kuczynski, L., Kochanska, G., Radke-Yarrow, M., & Girnius-Brown, O. (1987). A developmental interpretation of children's noncompliance. *Developmental Psychology, 23,* 799-806.

Kuhlen, R. G., & Arnold, M. (1944). Age differences in religious beliefs and problems during adolescence. *Journal of Genetic Psychology, 65,* 291-300.

Kuhn, D. (1984). Cognitive development. In M. H. Bornstein, & M. E. Lamb (Eds.), *Developmental psychology: An advanced textbook* (pp. 133-180). Hillsdale, NJ: Lawrence Erlbaum.

Kuhn, D., Langer, J., Kohlberg, L., & Haan, N. S. (1977). The development of formal operations in logical and moral judgment. *Genetic Psychology Monographs, 95,* 97-188.

Kurdek, L. A. (1978). Perspective-taking as the cognitive basis of children's moral development: A review of the literature. *Merrill-Palmer Quarterly, 24,* 3-28.

Kurtines, W., & Greif, E. B. (1974). The development of moral thought: Review and evaluation of Kohlberg's approach. *Psychological Bulletin, 81,* 453-470.

Labouvie-Vief, G. (1982). Dynamic development and mature autonomy: A theoretical prologue. *Human Development, 25,* 161-191.

Labouvie-Vief, G. (1984). Logic and self-regulation from youth to maturity. In M. L. Commons, F. A. Richards, & C. Armon (Eds.), *Beyond formal operations: Late adolescent and adult cognitive development* (pp. 158-179). New York: Praeger.

Labouvie-Vief, G. (1985). Intelligence and cognition. In J. E. Birren & K. W. Schaie (Eds.), *Handbook of the psychology of aging* (2nd ed., pp. 500-530). New York: Van Nostrand Reinhold.

Lachman, M. E., & McArthur, L. Z. (1986). Adulthood age differences in causal attributions for cognitive, physical, and social performance. *Psychology & Aging, 1,* 127-132.

Ladd, G. W. (1990). Having friends, keeping friends, making friends, and being liked by peers in the classroom: Predictors of children's early school adjustment? *Child Development, 61,* 1081-1100.

Ladd, G. W., & Emerson, E. S. (1984). Shared knowledge in children's friendships. *Developmental Psychology, 20,* 932-940.

Ladd, G. W., Lange, G., & Stremmel, A. (1983). Personal and situational influences on children's helping behavior: Factors that mediate compliant helping. *Child Development, 54,* 488-501.

Lagercrantz, H., & Slotkin, T. A. (1986). The "stress" of being born. *Scientific American, 254*(4), 100-107.

Lamb, M. E. (1978). The father's role in the infant's social world. In J. H. Stevens, & M. Mathews (Eds.), *Mother/child, father/child relationships.* Washington, DC: National Association for the Education of Young Children.

Lamb, M. E. (1979). Paternal influences and the father's role. *American Psychologist, 34,* 938-943.

Lamb, M. E. (1984). Social and emotional development in infancy. In M. H. Bornstein & M. E. Lamb (Eds.), *Developmental psychology: An advanced textbook* (pp. 241-277). Hillsdale, NJ: Erlbaum.

Lamb, M. E., & Elster, A. B. (1985). Adolescent mother-infant-father relationships. *Developmental Psychology, 21,* 768-773.

Lamb, M. E., & Sternberg, K. J. (1990). Do we really know how day care affects children? *Journal of Applied Developmental Psychology, 11,* 351-379.

Lamb, M. E., Thompson, R. A., Gardner, W. P., Charnov, E. L., & Estes, D. (1984). Security of infantile attachment as assessed in the "strange situation": Its study and biological interpretation. *The Behavioral and Brain Sciences, 7,* 127-171.

Lamper, C., & Eisdorfer, C. (1971). Prestimulus activity level and responsivity in the neonate. *Child Development, 42,* 465-473.

Lampl, M., Veldhuis, J. D., & Johnson, M. L. (1992). Saltation and stasis: A model of human growth. *Science, 258,* 801-803.

Lamy, P. P., & Vestal, R. (1976). Drug prescribing for the elderly. *Hospital Practice, 11,* 111-118.

Landers, S. (1990, April). Sex, condom use up among teenage boys. *The APA Monitor,* p. 25.

Landrum, R. (1986). The veterans. In M. Viorst (Ed.), *Making a difference: The Peace Corps at twenty-five* (pp. 87-96). New York: Weidenfeld & Nicolson.

Lange, G., & Pierce, S. H. (1992). Memory-strategy learning and maintenance in preschool children. *Developmental Psychology, 28,* 453-462.

Langer, E. J., & Rodin, J. (1976). The effects of choice and enhanced personal responsibility for the aged: A field experiment in an institutional setting. *Journal of Personality & Social Psychology, 34,* 191-198.

Langer, E. J., Rodin, J., Beck, P., Weinman, C., & Spitzer, L. (1979). Environmental determinants of memory improvement in late adulthood. *Journal of Personality & Social Psychology, 37,* 2003-2013.

Langlois, J. H., & Downs, A. C. (1980). Mothers, fathers, and peers as socialization agents of sex-typed play behaviors in young children. *Child Development, 51,* 1237-1247.

Langlois, J. H., Ritter, J. M., Roggman, L. A., & Vaughn, L. S. (1991). Facial diversity and infant preferences for attractive faces. *Developmental Psychology, 27,* 79-84.

Langlois, J. H., & Styczynski, L. (1979). The effects of physical attractiveness on the behavioral attributions and peer preferences in acquainted children. *International Journal of Behavioral Development, 2,* 325-341.

Larwood, L., & Gutek, B. A. (1984). Women at work in the U.S.A. In M. J. Davidson & C. L. Cooper (Eds.), *Working women: An international survey* (pp. 237-267). New York: Wiley.

Lasagna, L. (1969). Special subjects in human experimentation. *Daedlus, 98,* 449-462.

Lau, E., & Kosberg, J. (1978, November). *Abuse of the elderly by informal care providers: Practice and research issues.* Paper presented at the annual meeting of the Gerontological Society, Dallas, Texas.

Laudenslager, M. L., Ryan, S. M., Drugan, R. C., Hyson, R. L., & Maier, S. F. (1983). Coping and immunosuppression: Inescapable but not escapable shock suppresses lymphocyte proliferation. *Science, 221,* 568-570.

Lazar, I., & Darlington, R. (1982). Lasting effects of early education: A report from the Consortium for Longitudinal Studies. *Monographs of the Society for Research in Child Development, 47*(2-3, Serial No. 195).

Lazarus, R. S., Delongis, A., Folkman, S., & Gruen, R. (1985). Stress and adaptational outcomes; The problem of confounded measures. *American Psychologist, 40,* 770-779.

Leaf, A. (1973). Getting old. *Scientific American, 229*(3), 44-52.

Lee, C. L. (1973, August). *Social encounters of infants: The beginnings of popularity.* Paper presented at the meeting of the International Society for the Study of Behavioral Development, Ann Arbor, Michigan.

Lee, C. L., & Bates, J. E. (1985). Mother-child interaction at age two years and perceived difficult temperament. *Child Development, 56,* 1314-1325.

Lee, G. R., & Ellithorpe, E. (1982). Intergenerational exchange and subjective well-being among the elderly. *Journal of Marriage & the Family, 44,* 217-224.

Lee, V. E., Brooks-Gunn, J., Schnur, E., & Liaw, F. (1990). Are Head Start effects sustained? A longitudinal follow-up comparison of disadvantaged children attending Head Start, no preschool, and other preschool programs. *Child Development, 61,* 495-507.

Lefrancois, G. R. (1983). *Of children* (4th ed.). Belmont, CA: Wadsworth.

Legal Research and Services for the Elderly. (1979). *Elder abuse in Massachusetts: A survey of professionals and paraprofessionals.* Unpublished manuscript, Boston, Massachusetts.

Legerstee, M., Corter, C., & Kineapple, K. (1990). Hand, arm, and facial actions of young infants to a social and nonsocial stimulus. *Child Development, 61,* 774-784.

Lehman, D. R., Mortman, C. B., & Williams, A. F. (1987). Long-term effects of losing a spouse or child in a motor vehicle crash. *Journal of Personality & Social Psychology, 52*, 218-231.

Lehman, H. C. (1953). *Age and achievement*. Princeton, NJ: Princeton Univ. Press.

Lehman, H. C. (1954). Men's creative production rate at different ages and in different countries. *Scientific Monthly, 78*, 321-326.

Lehman, H. C. (1958). The influence of longevity upon curves showing man's creative production rate at successive age levels. *Journal of Gerontology, 13*, 187-191.

Lemon, B. W., Bengtson, V. L., & Peterson, J. A. (1972). An exploration of the activity theory of aging: Activity types and life satisfaction among in-movers to a retirement community. *Journal of Gerontology, 27*, 511-523.

Lempert, H. (1984). Topic as starting point for syntax. *Monographs of the Society for Research in Child Development, 49*(5, Serial No. 208).

Lempert, H. (1989). Animacy constraints on preschool children's acquisition of syntax. *Child Development, 60*, 237-245.

Leo, J. (1986, February 24). Could suicide be contagious? *Time*, p. 59.

Lerman, H. (1986). *A mote in Freud's eye: From psychoanalysis to the psychology of women*. New York: Springer.

Lerner, J. V. (1984). The import of temperament for psychosocial functioning: Tests of a goodness of fit model. *Merrill-Palmer Quarterly, 30*, 177-188.

Lerner, R. M., & Weinstock, A. (1972). Note on the generation gap. *Psychological Reports, 31*, 457-458.

Lerner, R. M., Palermo, M., Spiro, A., & Nesselroade, J. R. (1982). Assessing the dimensions of temperamental individuality across the life span: The Dimensions of Temperament Survey (DOTS). *Child Development, 53*, 149-159.

Lester, B. M., & Dreher, M. (1989). Effects of marijuana use during pregnancy. *Child Development, 60*, 765-771.

Lester, B. M., Corwin, M. J., Sepkoski, C., Seifer, R., Peucker, M., McLaughlin, S., & Golub, H. L. (1991). Neurobehavioral syndromes in cocaine-exposed newborn infants. *Child Development, 62*, 694-705.

Levine, L. E. (1983). Mine: Self-definition in 2-year-old boys. *Developmental Psychology, 19*, 544-549.

Levinson, D. J. (1986). A conception of adult development. *American Psychologist, 41*, 3-13.

Levinson, D. J., Darrow, C. N., Klein, E. B., Levinson, M. H., & McKee, B. (1978). *The seasons of a man's life*. New York: Knopf.

Levitan, S. A., & Johnson, C. M. (1982). *Second thoughts on work*. Kalamazoo, Michigan: W. E. Upjohn Institute for Employment Research.

Leviton, D. (1977). Death education. In H. Feifel (Ed.), *New meanings of death* (pp. 253-272). New York: McGraw-Hill Book Company.

Levitt, M. J., Weber, R. A., Clark, M. C., & McDonnell, P. (1985). Reciprocity of exchange in toddler sharing behavior. *Developmental Psychology, 21*, 122-123.

Lewis, K. (1977, September 6). Lesbian mother survey results. Boston: *Gay Community News*, p. 7.

Lewkowicz, D. J. (1988). Sensory dominance in infants: 1. Six-month-old infants' response to auditory-visual compounds. *Developmental Psychology, 24*, 155-171.

Lewontin, R. C., Rose, S., & Kamin, L. J. (1984). *Not in our genes*. New York: Pantheon Books.

Lieberman, M. A. (1965). Psychological correlates of impending death: Some preliminary observations. *Journal of Gerontology, 20*, 181-190.

Lieberman, P., Crelin, E. S., & Klatt, D. H. (1972). Phonetic ability and related anatomy of the newborn and adult human, Neanderthal man, and the chimpanzee. *American Anthropologist, 74*, 287-307.

Liebert, R. M., & Sprafkin, J. (1988). *The early window: Effects of television on children and youth* (3rd ed.). New York: Pergamon Press.

Liebert, R. M., Poulos, R. W., & Marmor, G. S. (1977). *Developmental psychology*. Englewood Cliffs, NJ: Prentice-Hall.

Liebert, R. M., Sprafkin, J. N., & Poulos, R. W. (1975). Selling cooperation to children. In W. S. Hale (Ed.), *Proceedings of the 20th Annual Conference of the Advertising Research Foundation* (pp. 54-57). New York: Advertising Research Foundation, Inc.

Lifson, K. A. (1953). Errors in time-study judgments of industrial work pace. *Psychological Monographs, 67*(5, whole no. 355)

Lindemann, E. (1944). The symptomatology and management of acute grief. *American Journal of Psychiatry, 101*, 141-148.

Lingle, K. M., & Lingle, J. H. (1981). Effects of selected object characteristics on object-permanence test performance. *Child Development, 52*, 367-369.

Linney, J. A., & Seidman, E. (1989). The future of schooling. *American Psychologist, 44*, 336-340.

Lipscomb, T. J., Larrieu, J. A., McAllister, H. A., & Bregman, N. J. (1982). Modeling and children's generosity: A developmental perspective. *Merrill-Palmer Quarterly, 28*, 275-282.

Lipsitt, L. P., & Levy, N. (1959). Electrotactual threshold in the neonate. *Child Development, 30*, 547-554.

Litwak, E., Dono, J., Falbe, C., Kulis, S., Marullo, S., & Sherman, R. (1981). *The modified extended family, social networks, and research continuities in aging* (Pre-print series). New York: Center for the Social Sciences at Columbia University.

Lively, W. J., & Bromley, D. B. (1973). *Person perception in childhood and adolescence*. New York: John Wiley & Sons.

Livson, F. B. (1976). Patterns of personality development in middle-aged women: A longitudinal study. *International Journal of Aging and Human Development, 7*, 107-115.

Livson, F. B. (1977). Coming out of the closet: Marriage and other crises of middle age. In L. E. Troll, J. Israel, & K. Israel (Eds.), *Looking ahead*. Englewood Cliffs, NJ: Prentice-Hall.

Lobel, M., Dunkel-Schetter, C., & Scrimshaw, S. C. (1992). Prenatal maternal stress and prematurity: A prospective study of socioeconomically disadvantaged women. *Health Psychology, 11*, 32-40.

Lobsenz, N. M. (1986, September 14). Why do we keep working? *Parade Magazine*, pp. 16-17.

Locke, S. E., Furst, M. W., Heisel, J. S., & Williams, R. M. (1978, April). *The influence of stress on the immune response*. Paper presented at the Annual Meeting of the American Psychosomatic Society, Washington, DC.

Loehlin, J. C., Horn, J. M., & Willerman, L. (1989). Modeling IQ change: Evidence from the Texas Adoption Project. *Child Development, 60*, 993-1004.

Loizos, C. (1967). Play behavior in higher primates: A review. In D. Morris (Ed.), *Primate ethology*. London: Weidenfeld & Nicholson.

Longino, C. F., & Kart, C. S. (1982). Explicating activity theory: A formal replication. *Journal of Gerontology, 37*, 713-722.

Looft, W. R. (1971). Egocentrism and social interaction in adolescence. *Adolescence, 6*(24), 485-494.

Lopata, H. Z. (1973). *Widowhood in an American city*. Cambridge, MA: Schenkman.

Lopata, H. Z. (1979). *Women as widows*. New York: Elsevier.

Lorber, J. (1975). Good patients and problem patients: Conformity and deviance in a general hospital. *Journal of Health & Social Behavior, 16*, 213-225.

Lorenz, K. (1937). Uber die Bildung des Instinkbegriffes. *Naturwissenschaften, 25*, 289-300, 307-318, 324-331.

Lorenz, K. (1943). Die angeborenen Formen moglicher Erfahrung. *Z. Tierpsychologie, 5*, 235-409.

Lott, B. (1985). The devaluation of women's competence. *Journal of Social Issues, 41*(4), 43-60.

Lovett, S. B., & Flavell, J. H. (1990). Understanding and remembering: Children's knowledge about the differential effects of strategy and task variables on comprehension and memorization. *Child Development, 61*, 1842-1858.

Lowrey, G. H. (1978). *Growth and development of children* (7th ed.). Chicago: Year Book.

Lozoff, B. (1983). Birth and "bonding" in non-industrial societies. *Developmental Medicine and Child Neurology, 25,* 595-600.

Lucas, B. (1977). Nutrition and the adolescent. In P. L. Pipes (Ed.), *Nutrition in infancy and childhood* (pp. 132-144). St. Louis: Mosby.

Luszki, M., & Luszki, W. (1985). Advantages of growing older. *Journal of the American Geriatric Society, 33,* 216-217.

Lyle, J., & Hoffman, H. R. (1972). Children's use of television and other media. In E. A. Rubinstein, G. A. Comstock, & J. P. Murray (Eds.), *Television and social behavior, Vol. 4, television in day-to-day life: Patterns of use.* Washington, DC: U.S. Government Printing Office.

Lynch, D. (1986, June-July). Brain aerobics. *Modern Maturity,* (Au: please supply pub. info).

Lystad, M. H. (1975). Violence at home: A review of the literature. *American Journal of Orthopsychiatry, 45,* 328-345.

Lytton, H. (1980). *Parent-child interaction: The socialization process observed in twin and singleton families.* New York: Plenum.

Lytton, H., Conway, D., & Suave, R. (1977). The impact of twinship on parent-child interaction. *Journal of Personality and Social Psychology, 35,* 97-107.

Maccoby, E. E. (1988). Gender as a social category. *Developmental Psychology, 24,* 755-765.

Maccoby, E. E. (1991). Different reproductive strategies in males and females. *Child Development, 62,* 676-681.

Maccoby, E. E., & Martin, J. A. (1983). Socialization in the context of the family: Parent-child interaction. In P. H. Mussen (Ed.), *Handbook of child psychology* (4th ed., Vol. IV, pp. 1-101). New York: Wiley.

Macklin, E. D. (1983). Nonmarital heterosexual cohabitation: An overview. In E. D. Macklin & R. H. Rubin (Eds.), *Contemporary families and alternative lifestyles* (pp. 49-74). Beverly Hills, CA: Sage Publications.

Mactutus, C. F., & Fechter, L. D. (1984). Prenatal exposure to carbon monoxide: Learning and memory deficits. *Science, 223,* 409-411.

MacWhinney, B. (1978). The acquisition of morphophonology. *Monographs of the Society for Research in Child Development, 43*(1-2, Serial No. 174).

Maddox, B. (1982, February). Homosexual parents. *Psychology Today,* pp. 62-69.

Madsen, M. C. (1971). Developmental and cross-cultural differences in the cooperative and competitive behavior of young children. *Journal of Cross-Cultural Psychology, 2,* 365-371.

Madsen, M. C., & Lancy, D. F. (1981). Cooperative and competitive behavior. Experiments related to ethnic identity and urbanization in Papua New Guinea. *Journal of Cross-Cultural Psychology, 12,* 389-408.

Madsen, M. C., & Shapira, A. (1970). Cooperative and competitive behavior of urban Afro-American, Anglo-American, Mexican-American, and Mexican village children. *Developmental Psychology, 3,* 16-20.

Main, M., & George, C. (1985). Responses of abused and disadvantaged toddlers to distress in agemates: A study in the day care setting. *Developmental Psychology, 21,* 407-412.

Main, M., Kaplan, N., & Cassidy, J. (1985). Security in infancy, childhood, and adulthood: A move to the level of representation. *Monographs of the Society for Research in Child Development, 50*(209, Serial No. 209), 66-104.

Main, M., & Weston, D. R. (1982). Avoidance of the attachment figure in infancy: Descriptions and interpretations. In C. M. Parkes & J. Stevenson-Hinde (Eds.), *The place of attachment in human behavior* (pp. 31-59). New York: Basic Books.

Malina, R. M. (1978). Growth of muscle tissue and muscle mass. In F. Falkner, & J. M. Tanner (Eds.), *Human growth* (Vol. 2). New York: Plenum.

Malina, R. M. (1979). Secular changes in growth, maturation, and physical performance. *Exercise and Sport Science Reviews, 6,* 203-255.

Manicas, P. T., & Secord, P. F. (1983). Implications for psychology of the new philosophy of science. *American Psychologist, 38,* 399-413.

Marano, H. (1979, October 29). Breast or bottle: New evidence in an old debate. *New York Magazine,* pp. 56-60.

Marcus, G. F., Pinker, S., Ullman, M., Hollander, M., Rosen, T. J., & Xu, F. (1992). Overregularization in language acquisition. Monographs of the Society for Research in *Child Development, 57*(4, Serial No. 228).

Marcus, R. F., Telleen, S., & Roke, E. J. (1979). Relation between cooperation and empathy in young children. *Developmental Psychology, 15,* 346-347.

Marks, I. M. (1969). *Fears and phobias.* New York: Academic Press.

Markus, H. J., & Nurius, P. S. (1984). Self-understanding and self-regulation in middle childhood. In W. A. Collins (Ed.), *Development during middle childhood: The years from six to twelve* (pp. 147-183). Washington, DC: National Academy Press.

Martens, R. (1988). Helping children become independent, responsible adults through sports. In E. W. Brown & C. F. Branta (Eds.), *Competitive sports for children and youth: An overview of research and issues* (pp. 297-307). Champaign, IL: Human Kinetics.

Martin, B. (1975). Parent-child relations. In F. D. Horowitz (Ed.), *Review of child development research* (Vol. 4). Chicago: Univ. of Chicago Press.

Martin, C. L., & Little, J. K. (1990). The relation of gender understanding to children's sex-typed preferences and gender stereotypes. *Child Development, 61,* 1427-1439.

Martorano, S. C. (1977). A developmental analysis of performance on Piaget's formal operations tasks. *Developmental Psychology, 13,* 666-672.

Marx, J. (1992). Boring in on Beta-amyloid's role in Alzheimer's. *Science, 255,* 688-689.

Marx, J. (1993). Alzheimer's pathology begins to yield its secrets. *Science, 259,* 457-458.

Marx, L. (1987, January 12). The agony did not end for Roswell Gilbert, who killed his wife to give her peace. *People Weekly,* pp. 30-36.

Massachusetts Committee on Alzheimer's Disease. (1986). *Final report of the special committee established to make an investigation and study relative to "Alzheimer's disease."*

Masten, A. S. (1986). Humor and competence in school-aged children. *Child Development, 57,* 461-473.

Matheny, A. P., Jr., Riese, M. L., & Wilson, R. S. (1985). Rudiments of infant temperament: Newborn to 9 months. *Developmental Psychology, 21,* 486-494.

Mathews, P. (1993). *The Guinness book of world records.* New York: Bantam Books.

Matthews, K. A., (1988). Coronary heart disease and type A behaviors: Update on and alternative to the Booth-Kewley and Friedman (1987) quantitative review. *Psychological Bulletin, 104,* 373-380.

Maurer, D., & Salapatek, P. (1976). Developmental changes in the scanning of faces by young infants. *Child Development, 47,* 523-527.

Mayr, E. (1982). *The growth of biological thought.* Cambridge, MA: Belknap Press.

Mazess, R. B., & Forman, S. H. (1979). Longevity and age exaggeration in Vilcabamba, Ecuador. *Journal of Gerontology, 34,* 94-98.

Mazess, R. B., & Mathisen, R. W. (1982). Lack of unusual longevity in Vilcabamba, Ecuador. *Human Biology, 54,* 517-524.

Maziade, M., Caperaa, P., Laplante, B., Boudreault, M., Thivierge, J., Cote, R., & Boutin, P. (1985). Value of difficult temperament among 7-year-olds in the general population for predicting psychiatric diagnosis at age 12. *American Journal of Psychiatry, 142,* 943-946.

Maziade, M., Cote, R., Boutin, P., Bernier, H., & Thivierge, J. (1988). Temperament and intellectual development: A longitudinal study from infancy to four years. In S. Chess, A. Thomas, & M. E. Hertzig (Eds.), *Annual progress in child psychiatry and child development* (pp. 335-349). New York: Brunner/Mazel.

McCall, J. N., & Johnson, O. G. (1972). The independence of intelligence from family size and birth order. *Journal of Genetic Psychology, 121,* 207-213.

McCall, R. (1978). Challenges to a science of developmental psychology. In S. Chess & A. Thomas (Eds.), *Annual progress in child psychiatry and child development* (pp. 3-23). New York: Brunner/Mazel.

McCall, R. B. (1984). Developmental changes in mental performance: The effect of the birth of a sibling. *Child Development, 55,* 1317-1321.

REFERENCES

McCartney, K. (1984). Effect of quality of day care environment on children's language development. *Developmental Psychology, 20,* 244-260.

McClelland, D. C. (1973). Testing for competence rather than for "intelligence." *American Psychologist, 28,* 1-14.

McClure, G. M. G. (1986). Recent changes in suicide among adolescents in England and Wales. *Journal of Adolescence, 9,* 135-143.

McCoy, C. L., & Masters, J. C. (1985). The development of children's strategies for the social control of emotion. *Child Development, 56,* 1214-1222.

McGeary, P. (1987, June 20). Names and faces. *The Boston Globe,* p. 2.

McGowan, R. J., Johnson, D. L., & Maxwell, S. E. (1981). Relations between infant behavior ratings and concurrent and subsequent mental test scores. *Developmental Psychology, 17,* 542-553.

McGraw, M. B. (1940). Neural maturation as exemplified in achievement of bladder control. *Journal of Paediatrics, 16,* 580-590.

McGue, M., Bacon, S., & Lykken, D. T. (1993). Personality stability and change in early adulthood: A behavioral genetic analysis. *Developmental Psychology, 29,* 96-109.

McHale, S. M., & Huston, T. L. (1984). Men and women as parents: Sex role orientations, employment, and parental roles with infants. *Child Development, 55,* 1349-1361.

McKain, W. C. (1972). A new look at older marriages. *The Family Coordinator, 21,* 61-69.

McKean, K. (1985, October). Intelligence: New ways to measure the wisdom of man. *Discover,* pp. 25-41.

McKinney, J. P., & Moore, D. (1982). Attitudes and values during adolescence. In B. B. Wolman (Ed.), *Handbook of developmental psychology* (pp. 549-558). Englewood Cliffs, NJ: Prentice-Hall.

McLendon, G. H. (1979). One teacher's experience with death education for adults. *Death Education, 3,* 57-66.

McNally, S., Eisenberg, N., & Harris, J. D. (1991). Consistency and change in maternal child-rearing practices and values: A longitudinal study. *Child Development, 62,* 190-198.

Mead, M. (1928). *Coming of age in Samoa.* New York: Morrow.

Mech, E. V. (1973). Adoption: A policy perspective. In B. Caldwell & H. Ricciuti (Eds.), *Review of child development research* (Vol. 3). Chicago: Univ. of Chicago Press.

Meer, J. (1985, August). Alone but not neglected. *Psychology Today,* p. 11.

Meer, J. (1986, June). The reason of age. *Psychology Today,* pp. 60-64.

Meier, E. L., & Kerr, E. A. (1976). Capabilities of middle-aged and older workers: A survey of the literature. *Industrial Gerontology, 3,* 147-156.

Melear, J. D. (1973). Children's conceptions of death. *Journal of Genetic Psychology, 123,* 359-360.

Mellstrom, D., Nilsson, A., Oden, A., Rungren, A., & Svanborg, A. (1982). Mortality among the widowed in Sweden. *Scandinavian Journal of Social Medicine, 10,* 33-41.

Melton, G. B., & Davidson, H. A. (1987). Child protection and society: When should the State intervene? *American Psychologist, 42,* 172-175.

Meltzoff, A. N. (1988a). Infant imitation after a 1-week delay: Long-term memory for novel acts and multiple stimuli. *Developmental Psychology, 24,* 470-476.

Meltzoff, A. N. (1988b). Infant imitation and memory: Nine-month-olds in immediate and deferred tests. *Child Development, 59,* 217-225.

Meltzoff, A. N. (1988c). Imitation of televised models by infants. *Child Development, 59,* 1221-1229.

Mendelson, M. J., & Ferland, M. B. (1982). Auditory-visual transfer in four-month-old. *Child Development, 53,* 1022-1027.

Mercer, W. M. (1981). *Employer attitudes: Implications of an aging work force.* New York: William M. Mercer, Inc.

Meredith, D. (1985, June). Mom, dad and the kids. *Psychology Today,* pp. 62-67.

Mervis, C. B., & Johnson, K. E. (1991). Acquisition of the plural morpheme: A case study. *Developmental Psychology, 27,* 222-235.

Messer, D. J., McCarthy, M. E., McQuiston, S., MacTurk, R. H., Yarrow, L. J., & Vietze, P. M. (1986). Relation between mastery behavior in infancy and competence in early childhood. *Developmental Psychology, 22,* 366-372.

Metz, R. A. (1983). A right to die? In A. H. Kutscher, S. C. Klagsbrun, R. J. Torpie, R. Debellis, M. S. Hale, & M. Tallmer (Eds.), *Hospice U.S.A.* (pp. 47-76). New York: Columbia University Press.

Meyer, J. P., & Pepper, S. (1977). Need compatibility and marital adjustment in young married couples. *Journal of Personality & Social Psychology, 35,* 331-342.

Meyer, W. J., & Dusek, J. B. (1979). *Child psychology.* Lexington, Mass.: Heath.

Meyers, A. F., Sampson, A. E., Weitzman, M., Rogers, B. L., & Kayne, H. (1989). School breakfast program and school performance. *American Journal of Diseases in Children, 143,* 1234-1239.

Michael, W. B. (1977). Cognitive and affective components of creativity in mathematics and the physical sciences. In J. C. Stanley, W. C. George, & C. H. Solano (Eds.), *The gifted and creative: A fifty-year perspective.* Baltimore, MD: Johns Hopkins Univ. Press.

Micheli, L. J. (1988). The incidence of injuries in children's sports: A medical perspective. In E. W. Brown & C. F. Branta (Eds.), *Competitive sports for children and youth: An overview of research and issues* (pp. 280-284). Champaign, IL: Human Kinetics.

Michie, S. (1985). Development of absolute and relative concepts of number in preschool children. *Developmental Psychology, 21,* 247-252.

Miller, G. A. (1956). The magical number seven, plus or minus two: Some limits on our capacity to process information. *Psychological Review, 63,* 81-97.

Miller, G. A., & Gildea, P. M. (1987). How children learn words. *Scientific American, 257*(3), 94-99.

Miller, J. A. (1981, October 31). Update on Tay-Sachs screening. *Science News,* p. 282.

Miller, J. A. (1983, February 26). Wiretap on the nervous system. *Science News,* pp. 140-143.

Miller, J. A. (1985, November 9). Carving out the nervous system. *Science News,* p. 297.

Miller, J. A., & Greenberg, J. (1985, June 15). Preschool day care: Which type is best? *Science News,* p. 376.

Miller, J. B. (1976). *Toward a new psychology of women.* Boston: Beacon Press.

Miller, L. B., & Dyer, J. L. (1975). Four preschool programs: Their dimensions and effects. *Monographs of the Society for Research in Child Development, 40*(5-6, Serial No. 162).

Miller, P. H. (1989). *Theories of developmental psychology* (2nd ed.). New York: W. H. Freeman.

Miller, R. L., Brickman, P., & Bolen, D. (1975). Attribution versus persuasion as a means for modifying behavior. *Journal of Personality and Social Psychology, 31,* 430-441.

Miller, S. A. (1986). Certainty and necessity in the understanding of Piagetian concepts. *Developmental Psychology, 22,* 3-18.

Miller, W. C., Lindeman, A. K., Wallace, J., & Niederpruem, M. (1990). Diet composition, energy intake, and exercise in relation to body fat in men and women. *American Journal of Clinical Nutrition, 52,* 426-430.

Mills, J. L., Graubard, B. I., Harley, E. E., Rhoads, G. G., & Berendes, H. W. (1984). Maternal alcohol consumption and birth weight. *Journal of the American Medical Association, 252,* 1875-1879.

Mindel, C. H. (1979). Multigenerational family households: Recent trends and implications for the future. *The Gerontologist, 19,* 456-463.

Mindel, C. H., & Wright, R. (1982). Satisfaction in multigenerational households. *Journal of Gerontology, 37,* 483-489.

Minton, C., Kagan, J., & Levine, J. A. (1971). Maternal control and obedience in the two-year-old. *Child Development, 42,* 1873-1894.

Mischel, W. (1979). On the interface of cognition and personality. *American Psychologist, 34,* 740-754.

Mischel, W., & Ebbesen, E. B. (1970). Attention in delay of gratification. *Journal of Personality and Social Psychology, 16,* 329-337.

Mischel, W., & Mischel, H. N. (1979, March). *The development of children's knowledge of self-control.* Paper presented at the meeting of the Society for Research in Child Development, San Francisco.

Mishkin, M., & Appenzeller, T. (1987). The anatomy of memory. *Scientific American, 256*(6), 80-89.

Mistry, J. J., & Lange, G. W. (1985). Children's organization and recall of information in scripted narratives. *Child Development, 56,* 953-961.

Mitchell, A. M. (1975). Experimentation on minors: Whatever happened to Prince v. Massachusetts? *Duquesne Law Review, 13,* 919-936.

Mohs, M. (1982, September). I.Q. *Discover,* pp. 18-24.

Molfese, D. L., Molfese, V. J., & Carrell, P. L. (1982). Early language development. In B. B. Wolman (Ed.), *Handbook of developmental psychology* (pp. 301-322). Englewood Cliffs, NJ: Prentice-Hall.

Molfese, D. L., Morse, P. A., & Peters, C. J. (1990). Auditory evoked responses to names for different objects: Cross-modal processing as a basis for infant language acquisition. *Developmental Psychology, 26,* 780-795.

Monsaas, J. A., & Engelhard, G., Jr. (1990). Home environment and the competitiveness of highly accomplished individuals in four talent fields. *Developmental Psychology, 26,* 264-268.

Montgomery, R. J. (1982). Impact of institutional care policies on family integration. *The Gerontologist, 22,* 54-58.

Moore, B. S., Underwood, B., & Rosenhan, D. L. (1973). Affect and altruism. *Developmental Psychology, 8,* 99-104.

Moore, N. V., Evertson, C. M., & Brophy, J. E. (1974). Solitary play: Some functional considerations. *Developmental Psychology, 10,* 830-834.

Moorehouse, M. J. (1991). Linking maternal employment patterns to mother-child activities and children's school competence. *Developmental Psychology, 27,* 295-303.

Morell, P., & Norton, W. T. (1980). Myelin. *Scientific American, 242*(5), 88-118.

Morgan, M., & Gross, L. (1982). Television and educational achievement. In D. Pearl, L. Bouthilet, & J. Lazar (Eds.), *Television and behavior: Ten years of scientific progress and implications for the eighties* (Vol. 2). Washington, DC: U.S. Government Printing Office.

Morrison, A. M., & Von Glinow, M. A. (1990). Women and minorities in management. *American Psychologist, 45,* 200-208.

Morrongiello, B. A. (1988). Infants' localization of sounds along the horizontal axis: Estimates of minimum audible angle. *Developmental Psychology, 24,* 8-13.

Morrongiello, B. A., Fenwick, K. D., & Chance, G. (1990). Sound localization acuity in very young infants: An observer-based testing procedure. *Developmental Psychology, 26,* 75-84.

Morse, N. C., & Weiss, R. S. (1955). The function and meaning of work and the job. *American Sociological Review, 20,* 191-198.

Moskowitz, B. A. (1978). The acquisition of language. *Scientific American, 239*(5), 92-108.

Motley, M. T. (1985). Slips of the tongue. *Scientific American, 253*(3), 116-127.

Muchinsky, P. M. (1978). Age and job facet satisfaction: A conceptual reconsideration. *Aging and Work, 1,* 175-179.

Mueller, E., & Brenner, J. (1977). The origins of social skills and interaction among playgroup toddlers. *Child Development, 48,* 854-861.

Mueller, E., & Lucas, T. (1975). A developmental analysis of peer interaction among toddlers. In M. Lewis, & L. Rosenblum (Eds.), *Friendship and peer relations.* New York: Wiley.

Mueller, E., & Rich, A. (1976). Clustering and socially-directed behaviors in a playgroup of 1-yr-old boys. *Journal of Child Psychology and Psychiatry, 17,* 315-322.

Mueller, E., & Vandell, D. (1977). Infant-infant interaction. In J. Osofsky (Ed.), *Handbook of infant development.* New York: Wiley Interscience.

Muir, D., & Field, J. (1979). Newborn infants orient to sounds. *Child Development, 50,* 431- 436.

Munnichs, J. M. A. (1966). *Old age and finitude.* Basel, Switzerland: S. Karger.

Munroe, R. H., Shimmin, H. S., & Munroe, R. L. (1984). Gender understanding and sex role preference in four cultures. *Developmental Psychology, 20,* 673-682.

Murphy, D. M. (1985). Fears in preschool-age children. *Child Care Quarterly, 14*(3), 171-189.

Mussen, P., Honzik, M. P., & Eichorn, D. H. (1982). Early adult antecedents of life satisfaction at age 70. *Journal of Gerontology, 37,* 316-322.

Muuss, R. E. (1986). Adolescent eating disorder: Bulimia. *Adolescence, 21,* 257-267.

Myles-Worsley, M., Cromer, C. C., & Dodd, D. H. (1986). Children's preschool script reconstruction: Reliance on general knowledge as memory fades. *Developmental Psychology, 22,* 22-30.

Nadelson, C. C., Polonsky, D. C., & Mathews, M. A. (1981). Marriage problems and marital therapy in the middle-aged. In J. G. Howells (Ed.), *Modern perspectives in the psychiatry of middle age.* New York: Bruner/Mazel.

Naeye, R. L., Ladis, B., & Drage, J. S. (1976). Sudden infant death syndrome: A prospective study. *American Journal of Diseases of Children, 130,* 1207-1210.

Nagy, M. H. (1948). The child's theories concerning death. *Journal of Genetic Psychology, 73,* 3-27.

Nagy, M. H. (1959). The child's view of death. In H. Feifel (Ed.), *The meaning of death.* New York: McGraw-Hill.

Nash, J. (1978). *Developmental psychology: A psychobiological approach.* Englewood Cliffs, NJ: Prentice-Hall.

National Center for Health Statistics. (1980). *Basic data on hearing levels of adults.* U.S. Department of Health, Education, and Welfare. Vital and Health Statistics, Series 11, No. 215.

National Institute on Aging. (1980). *Sexuality: Myth or madness.* Washington, DC: U.S. Govt. Printing Office.

Nelson, L., & Madsen, M. C. (1969). Cooperation and competition in four-year-olds as a function of reward contingency and subculture. *Developmental Psychology, 1,* 340-344.

Neugarten, B. L. (1967). The awareness of middle age. In R. Owen (Ed.), *Middle age.* London: BBC.

Neugarten, B. L. (1968). The awareness of middle age. In B. L. Neugarten (Ed.), *Middle age and aging* (pp. 93-98). Chicago: Univ. of Chicago Press.

Neugarten, B. L. (1976). Adaptation and the life cycle. *Counseling Psychologist, 6,* 16-20.

Neugarten, B. L. (1979). Time, age, and the life cycle. *American Journal of Psychiatry, 136,* 887-894.

Neugarten, B. L., & Datan, N. (1973). Sociological perspectives on the life cycle. In P. Baltes & K. W. Schaie (Eds.), *Life-span developmental psychology: Personality and socialization.* New York: Academic Press.

Neugarten, B. L., & Hall, E. (1980, April). Acting one's age: New rules for old. *Psychology Today,* pp. 66-80.

Neugarten, B. L., Havighurst, R. J., & Tobin, S. S. (1968). Personality and patterns of aging. In B. L. Neugarten (Ed.), *Middle age and aging* (pp. 173-180). Chicago: Univ. of Chicago Press.

Neugarten, B. L., & Neugarten, D. A. (1987, May). The changing meanings of age. *Psychology Today,* pp. 29-33.

Neugarten, B. L., & Peterson, W. A. (1957). A study of the American age-grade system. *Proceedings of the Fourth Congress of the International Association of Gerontology, 3,* 497-502.

Neugarten, B. L., & Weinstein, K. (1964). The changing American grandparent. *Journal of Marriage and the Family, 26,* 199-205.

Neugarten, B. L., Wood, V., Kraines, R. J., & Loomis, B. (1968). Women's attitudes toward the menopause. In B. L. Neugarten (Ed.), *Middle age and aging* (pp. 195-200). Chicago: Univ. of Chicago Press.

Newberger, E. H., & Bourne, R. (1978). The medicalization and legalization of child abuse. *American Journal of Orthopsychiatry, 48,* 593-607.

Newcomb, A. F., & Brady, J. E. (1982). Mutuality in boys' friendship relations. *Child Development, 53,* 392-395.

Newell, A., Shaw, J. C., & Simon, H. A. (1958). Elements of a theory of human problem solving. *Psychological Review, 65,* 151-166.

Newman, B. M. (1982). Mid-life development. In B. B. Wolman (Ed.), *Handbook of developmental psychology* (pp. 617-635). Englewood Cliffs, NJ: Prentice-Hall.

Newman, P. R. (1982). The peer group. In B. B. Wolman (Ed.), *Handbook of developmental psychology* (pp. 526-536). Englewood Cliffs, NJ: Prentice-Hall.

Niemark, E. D. (1982). Adolescent thought: Transition to formal operations. In B. B. Wolman (Ed.), *Handbook of developmental psychology* (pp. 486-502). Englewood Cliffs, NJ: Prentice-Hall.

Nisan, M. (1984). Distributive justice and social norms. *Child Development, 55*, 1020-1029.

Nisan, M., & Koriat, A. (1984). The effect of cognitive restructuring on delay of gratification. *Child Development, 55*, 492-503.

Niswander, K. R., & Gordon, M. (Eds.). (1972). *The collaborative perinatal study of the National Institute of Neurological Diseases and Stroke: The women and their pregnancies.* Washington, DC: U.S. Government Printing Office.

Nock, S. L. (1982). The life-cycle approach to family analysis. In B. Wolman (Ed.), *Handbook of developmental psychology.* Englewood Cliffs, NJ: Prentice-Hall.

Norris, A., Mittman, C., & Shock, N. W. (1964). Lung function in relation to age: Changes in ventilation with age. In L. Cander & J. H. Moyer (Eds.), *Aging of the lungs.* New York: Grune & Stratton.

Northcraft, G. B., & Martin, J. (1982). Double jeopardy: Resistance to affirmative action from potential beneficiaries. In B. A. Gutek (Ed.), *Sex role stereotyping and affirmative action policy.* Los Angeles: Institute for Industrial Relations, University of California.

Nottelmann, E. D., & Welsh, C. J. (1986). The long and the short of physical stature in early adolescence. *Journal of Early Adolescence, 6*, 15-27.

Nuessel, F. H., Jr. (1982). The language of ageism. *The Gerontologist, 22*, 273-276.

Nuland, S. B. (1994). *How we die: Reflections on life's final chapter.* New York: Alfred A. Knopf.

O'Connor, M., & Cuevas, J. (1982). The relationship of children's prosocial behavior to social responsibility, prosocial reasoning, and personality. *Journal of Genetic Psychology, 140*, 33-45.

O'Connor, M. J., Cohen, S., & Parmelee, A. H. (1984). Infant auditory discrimination in preterm and full-term infants as a predictor of 5-year intelligence. *Developmental Psychology, 20*, 159-165.

O'Rourke, M. (1981, March). *Elder abuse: The state of the art.* Paper presented at the national conference on the abuse of older persons, Boston, Massachusetts.

Offer, D., Ostrov, E., & Howard, K. I. (1981). *The adolescent: A psychological self-portrait.* New York: Basic Books.

Offermann, L. R., & Gowing, M. K. (1990). Organizations of the future: Changes and challenges. *American Psychologist, 45*, 95-108.

Oldershaw, L., Walters, G. C., & Hall, D. K. (1986). Control strategies and noncompliance in abusive mother-child dyads: An observational study. *Child Development, 57*, 722-732.

Olejnik, A. B. (1976). The effects of reward-deservedness on children's sharing. *Child Development, 47*, 380-385.

Oliver, J. E., & Taylor, A. (1971). Five generations of ill-treated children in one family pedigree. *British Journal of Psychiatry, 119*, 473-480.

Oller, D. K., & Eilers, R. E. (1988). The role of audition in infant babbling. *Child Development, 59*, 441-449.

Olson, D. H., McCubbin, H. I., Barnes, H. L., Larson, A. S., Muxen, M. J., & Wilson, M. A. (1983). *Families: What makes them work.* Beverly Hills: Sage Publications.

One solution to teen pregnancies. (1979, April 21). *Science News*, p. 264.

Opinion Research Corporation (1980). *Strategic planning for human resources: 1981 and beyond.* Princeton, NJ: Opinion Research Corp.

Osherson, D. N., & Markman, E. (1974-75). Language and the ability to evaluate contradictions and tautologies. *Cognition, 3*(3), 213-226.

Osterweis, M., Solomon, F., & Green, M. (1984). *Bereavement: Reactions, consequences and care.* Washington, DC: National Academy Press.

Owen, D. (1985). *None of the above: Behind the myth of scholastic aptitude.* Boston: Houghton Mifflin.

Packard, V. (1977). *The people shapers.* Boston: Little, Brown.

Painton, F. (1987, August 31). Tolerance finally finds its limits. *Time*, pp. 28-29.

Palisin, H. (1986). Preschool temperament and performance on achievement tests. *Developmental Psychology, 22*, 766-770.

Palkovitz, R. (1980). Predictors of involvement in first-time fathers. *Dissertation Abstracts International, 40*, 3603B-3604B. (University Microfilms No. 8105035)

Palkovitz, R. (1984). Parental attitudes and fathers' interactions with their 5-month-old infants. *Developmental Psychology, 20*, 1054-1060.

Palti, H., Mansbach, I., Pridan, H., Adler, B., & Palti, Z. (1984). Episodes of illness in breast-fed and bottle-fed infants in Jerusalem. *Journal of Medical Sciences, 20*, 395-399.

Paludi, M. A., & Fankell-Hauser, J. (1986). An idiographic approach to the study of women's achievement striving. *Psychology of Women Quarterly, 10*, 89-100.

Palumbo, F. M., & Dietz, W. H. (1985). Children's television: Its effects on nutrition and cognitive development. *Pediatr. Ann., 14*, 793-801.

Park, K. A., & Waters, E. (1989). Security of attachment and preschool friendships. *Child Development, 60*, 1076-1081.

Parke, R. D., & Collmer, C. W. (1975). Child abuse: An interdisciplinary analysis. In E. M. Hetherington (Ed.), *Review of child development research* (Vol. 5). Chicago: Univ. of Chicago Press.

Parke, R. D., & O'Leary, S. E. (1976). Father-mother,-infant interaction in the newborn period: Some findings, some observations and some unresolved issues. In K. F. Riegel, & J. A. Meacham (Eds.), *The developing individual in a changing world: Vol. 2. Social and environmental issues.* Chicago: Aldine.

Parke, R. D., & Tinsley, B. R. (1981). The father's role in infancy: Determinants of involvement in caregiving and play. In M. E. Lamb (Ed.), *The role of the father in child development* (2nd ed., pp. 429-457). New York: Wiley-Interscience.

Parkes, C. M. (1986). *Bereavement* (2nd ed.). London: Tavistock Publications.

Parkhurst, J. T., & Asher, S. R. (1992). Peer rejection in middle school: Subgroup differences in behavior, loneliness, and interpersonal concerns. *Developmental Psychology, 28*, 231-241.

Parmelee, A. H., Jr. (1986). Children's illnesses: Their beneficial effects on behavioral development. *Child Development, 57*, 1-10.

Parnes, H. S., & Less, L. J. (1985a). Shunning retirement: The experience of full-time workers. In H. S. Parnes, J. E. Crowley, R. J. Haurin, L. J. Less, W. R. Morgan, F. L. Mott, & G. Nestel (Eds.), *Retirement among American men.* Lexington, MA: Lexington Books.

Parnes, H. S., & Less, L. J. (1985b). Introduction and overview. In H. S. Parnes, J. E. Crowley, R. J. Haurin, L. J. Less, W. R. Morgan, F. L. Mott, & G. Nestel (Eds.), *Retirement among American men.* Lexington, MA: Lexington Books.

Parnes, H. S., & Nestel, G. (1981). The retirement experience. In H. S. Parnes (Ed.), *Work and retirement: A longitudinal study of men.* Cambridge, MA: MIT Press.

Parron, E. M., & Troll, L. E. (1978). Golden wedding couples: Effects of retirement on intimacy in long-standing marriages. *Alternative Lifestyles, 1*, 447-464.

Parten, M. (1932). Social play among preschool children. *Journal of Abnormal and Social Psychology, 27*, 243-269.

Patrusky, B. (1981, May). How do cells know what to become? *Science 81*, p. 104.

Patterson, D. (1987). The causes of Down Syndrome. *Scientific American, 257*(2), 52-60.

Pattison, E. M. (1977). The experience of dying. In E. M. Pattison (Ed.), *The experience of dying* (pp. 43-60). Englewood Cliffs, NJ: Prentice-Hall/Spectrum.

Paul, D. B. (1991). Enthusiastic claims. *Science, 252*, 142-143.

Peacock, E. W., & Talley, W. M. (1985). Developing leisure competence: A goal for late adulthood. *Educational Gerontology, 11*, 261-276.

Pearl, D., Bouthilet, L., & Lazar, J. (Eds.). (1982). *Television and behavior: Ten years of scientific progress and implications for the eighties* (Vols. 1 & 2). Washington, DC: U.S. Government Printing Office.

Pearl, R. (1985). Children's understanding of others' need for help: Effects of problem explicitness and type. *Child Development, 56,* 735-745.

Pearson, J. L., Hunter, A. G., Ensminger, M. E., & Kellam, S. G. (1990). Black grandmothers in multigenerational households: Diversity in family structure and parenting involvement in the Woodlawn community. *Child Development, 61,* 434-442.

Peck, R. C. (1968). Psychological developments in the second half of life. In B. L. Neugarten (Ed.), *Middle age and aging* (pp. 88-92). Chicago: Univ. of Chicago Press.

Pedersen, E., Faucher, T. A., & Eaton, W. W. (1978). A new perspective on the effects of first grade teachers on children's subsequent adult status. *Harvard Educational Review, 48,* 1-31.

Pederson, D. R., Moran, G., Sitko, C., Campbell, K., Ghesquire, K., & Acton, H. (1990). Maternal sensitivity and the security of infant-mother attachment: A Q-sort study. *Child Development, 61,* 1974-1983.

Pederson, D. R., Rook-Green, A., & Elder, J. L. (1981). The role of action in the development of pretend play in young children. *Developmental Psychology, 17,* 756-759.

Pederson, F. A., Anderson, B. T., & Cain, R. L. (1977). *An approach to understanding linkages between the parent-infant and spouse relationships.* Paper presented at the Society for Research in Child Development, New Orleans, Louisiana.

Pedlow, R., Sanson, A., Prior, M., & Oberklaid, F. (1993). Stability of maternally reported temperament from infancy to 8 years. *Developmental Psychology, 29,* 998-1007.

Pedrick-Cornell, C., & Gelles, R. J. (1982). Elder abuse: The status of current knowledge. *Family Relations, 31,* 457-465.

Pelz, D. C., & Andrews, F. M. (1966). *Scientists in organizations.* New York: John Wiley & Sons.

Pence, A. R., & Goelman, H. (1987). Silent partners: Parents of children in three types of day care. *Early Childhood Research Quarterly, 2,* 103-118.

Peplau, A. (1993). Lesbian and gay relationships. In L. D. Garnets & D. C. Kimmel (Eds.), *Psychological perspectives on lesbian and gay male experiences* (pp. 395-419). New York: Columbia University Press.

Pepler, D. J., & Ross, H. S. (1981). The effects of play on convergent and divergent problem solving. *Child Development, 52,* 1202-1210.

Perris, E. E., Myers, N. A., & Clifton, R. K. (1990). Long-term memory for a single infancy experience. *Child Development, 61,* 1796-1807.

Perry, W. G., Jr. (1970). *Forms of intellectual and ethical development in the college years.* New York: Holt, Rinehart & Winston.

Peters-Martin, P., & Wachs, T. D. (1984). A longitudinal study of temperament and its correlates in the first 12 months. *Infant Behavior and Development, 7,* 285-298.

Petersen, A. C. (1979). Female pubertal development. In M. Sugar (Ed.), *Female adolescent development.* New York: Brunner/Mazel.

Petersen, A. C., & Taylor, B. (1980). The biological approach to adolescence. In J. Adelson (Ed.), *Handbook of adolescent psychology.* New York: Wiley.

Peterson, L. (1982). An alternative perspective to norm-based explanations of modeling and children's generosity. *Merrill-Palmer Quarterly, 28,* 283-290.

Peterson, L. (1983). Influence of age, task competence, and responsibility focus on children's altruism. *Developmental Psychology, 19,* 141-148.

Petitto, L. A., & Marentette, P. F. (1991). Babbling in the manual mode: Evidence for the ontogeny of language. *Science, 251,* 1493-1496.

Phear, W. P., et al. (1983). An empirical study of custody agreements: Joint versus sole legal custody. *Journal of Psychiatry and the Law, 11,* 419-441.

Phillips, D. A. (1987). Socialization of perceived academic competence among highly competent children. *Child Development, 58,* 1308-1320.

Phillips, D., McCartney, K., & Scarr, S. (1987). Child-care quality and children's social development. *Developmental Psychology, 23,* 537-543.

Phillips, D. P. (1977). Motor vehicle fatalities increase just after publicized suicide stories. *Science, 196,* 1464-1465.

Phillips, D. P., & Carstensen, L. L. (1986). Clustering of teenage suicides after television news stories about suicide. *New England Journal of Medicine, 315,* 685-689.

Phillips, D. P., & Paight, D. J. (1987). The impact of televised movies about suicide: A replicative study. *New England Journal of Medicine, 317,* 809-811.

Phillips, J. L. (1969). *The origins of intellect: Piaget's theory.* San Francisco: W. H. Freeman.

Piaget, J. (1932). *The moral judgment of the child.* New York: Harcourt Brace.

Piaget, J. (1952). *The origins of intelligence in children.* New York: Int'l. Universities Press.

Piaget, J. (1960). *The child's conception of the world.* London: Routledge.

Piaget J. (1964). Development and learning. In R. E. Ripple, & V. N. Rockcastle (Eds.), *Piaget rediscovered* (pp. 7-20). Ithaca, NY: Cornell School of Education Press.

Piaget, J. (1967). *Six psychological studies.* New York: Random House.

Piaget, J. (1970). Piaget's theory. In P. H. Mussen (Ed.), *Carmichael's manual of child psychology* (Vol. 1, 3rd ed.). New York: John Wiley.

Piaget, J., & Inhelder, B. (1969). *The psychology of the child.* (H. Weaver, Trans.). New York: Basic Books. (Original work published 1967)

Pick, H. L., & Pick, A. D. (1970). Sensory and perceptual development. In P. H. Mussen (Ed.), *Carmichael's manual of child psychology* (3rd ed., Vol. 1, pp. 773-847). New York: Wiley.

Pillemer, K., & Finkelhor, D. (1988). The prevalence of elder abuse: A random sample survey. *The Gerontologist,* in press.

Pillemer, K., & Suitor, J. J. (1992). Violence and violent feelings: What causes them among family caregivers? *Journals of Gerontology, 47,* S165-S172.

Pines, M. (1966). *Revolution in learning: The years from birth to six.* New York: Harper & Row.

Piotrkowski, C. S., & Hughes, D. (1993). Dual-earner families in context: Managing family and work systems. In F. Walsh (Ed.), *Normal family processes* (pp. 185-207). New York: Guilford Press.

Pipp, S., & Harmon, R. J. (1987). Attachment as regulation: A commentary. *Child Development, 58,* 648-652.

Plattner, G., Renner, W., Went, J., Beaudett, L., & Viau, G. (1983). Determination of ultrasound scan in the 2nd and 3rd trimesters. *Obstetrics & Gynecology, 61,* 454-458.

Pleck, E. (1987). *The making of social policy against family violence from colonial times to the present.* New York: Oxford University Press.

Plomin, R., McClearn, G. E., Pedersen, N. L., Nesselroade, J. R., & Bergeman, C. S. (1988). Genetic influence on childhood family environment perceived retrospectively from the last half of the life span. *Developmental Psychology, 24,* 738-745.

Pohlman, J. C. (1984). Illness and death of a peer in a group of three-year-olds. *Death Education, 8,* 123-136.

Pope, A. W., Bierman, K. L., & Mumma, G. H. (1991). Aggression, hyperactivity, and inattention-immaturity: Behavior dimensions associated with peer rejection in elementary school boys. *Developmental Psychology, 27,* 663-671.

Powell, D. (1977, March). *The coordination of preschool socialization: Parent and caregiver relationships in day care settings.* Paper presented at the meeting of the Society for Research in Child Development, New Orleans, LA.

Powell, D. (1978). The interpersonal relationship between parents and caregivers in day care settings. *American Journal of Orthopsychiatry, 48,* 680-689.

Power, M. J., Alderson, M. R., Phillipson, C. M., Schoenberg, E., & Morris, J. N. (1967, October 19). Delinquent schools? *New Society,* pp. 542-543.

Power, T. G. (1981). Sex-typing in infancy: The role of the father. *Infant Mental Health Journal, 2,* 226-240.

Power, T. G., & Chapieski, M. L. (1986). Childrearing and impulse control in toddlers: A naturalistic investigation. *Developmental Psychology, 22,* 271-275.

Powers, S. I., Hauser, S. T., Schwartz, J. M., Noam, G. G., & Jacobson, A. M. (1983). Adolescent ego development and family interaction: A structural-developmental perspective. In H. D. Grotevant, & C. R. Cooper (Eds.),

Adolescent development in the family: New directions for child development (pp. 5-25). San Francisco: Jossey-Bass.

Pratt, K. C. (1954). The neonate. In L. Carmichael (Ed.), *Manual of child psychology* (2nd ed., pp. 215-291). New York: Wiley.

Price, J. O., Elias, S., Wachtel, S. S., Klinger, K., Dockter, M., Tharapel, A., Shulman, L. P., Phillips, O. P., Meyers, C. M., & Shook, D. (1991). Prenatal diagnosis with fetal cells isolated from maternal blood by multiparameter flow cytometry. *American Journal of Obstetrics & Gynecology, 165,* 1731-1737.

Price-Williams, D., Gordon, W., & Ramirez, M. (1969). Skill and conservation: A study of pottery-making children. *Developmental Psychology, 1,* 769.

Pugliese, M. T., Lifshitz, F., Grad, G., Fort, P., & Marks-Katz, M. (1983). Fear of obesity. *New England Journal of Medicine, 309,* 513-518.

Pursell, E. D., Dossett, D. L., & Latham, G. P. (1980). Obtaining valid predictors by minimizing rating errors in the criterion. *Personnel Psychology, 33,* 91-96.

Putallaz, M. (1983). Predicting children's sociometric status from their behavior. *Child Development, 54,* 1417-1426.

Quinn, P. K., & Reznikoff, M. (1985). The relationship between death anxiety and the subjective experience of time in the elderly. *International Journal of Aging and Human Development, 21,* 197-210.

Radin, N., & Harold-Goldsmith, R. (1989). The involvement of selected unemployed and employed men with their children. *Child Development, 60,* 454-459.

Radke-Yarrow, M., Zahn-Waxler, C., & Chapman, M. (1983). Children's prosocial dispositions and behavior. In P. H. Mussen (Ed.), *Handbook of child psychology* (4th ed., Vol. IV, pp. 469-545). New York: Wiley.

Radziszewska, B., & Rogoff, B. (1991). Children's guided participation in planning imaginary errands with skilled adult or peer partners. *Developmental Psychology, 27,* 381-389.

Ralt, D., Goldenberg, M., Fetterolf, P., Thompson, D., Dor, J., Mashiach, S., Garbers, D. L., & Eisenbach, M. (1991). Sperm attraction to a follicular factor(s) correlates with human egg fertilizability. *Proceedings of the National Academy of Science USA, 88,* 2840-2844.

Ramey, C. (1982). Commentary by Craig T. Ramey. *Monographs of the Society for Research in Child Development, 47*(2-3, Serial No. 195), 142-151.

Rando, T. A. (1983). An investigation of grief and adaptation in parents whose children have died from cancer. *Journal of Pediatric Psychology, 8,* 3-20.

Rathbone-McCuan, E., & Goodstein, R. K. (1985). Elder abuse: Clinical considerations. *Psychiatric Annals, 15,* 331-339.

Ratner, N. B., & Pye, C. (1984). Higher pitch in BT is not universal: Acoustic evidence from Quiche Mayan. *Journal of Child Language, 11,* 515-522.

Real scoop on aging, The. (1987, February-March). *Modern Maturity,* p. 17.

Reaves, J. Y., & Roberts, A. (1983). The effect of type of information on children's attraction to peers. *Child Development, 54,* 1024-1031.

Reed, G. L., & Leiderman, P. H. (1983). Is imprinting an appropriate model for human infant attachment? *International Journal of Behavioral Development, 6,* 51-69.

Reese, H. W., & Lipsitt, L. P. (1970). *Experimental child psychology.* New York: Academic Press.

Reese, H. W., & Overton, W. F. (1970). Models of development and theories of development. In L. R. Goulet, & P. B. Baltes (Eds.), *Life-span developmental psychology: Research and theory* (pp. 115-145). New York: Academic Press.

Reimanis, G., & Green, R. (1971). Imminence of death and intellectual decrement in the aging. *Developmental Psychology, 5,* 270-272.

Reis, H. T. (1990). The role of intimacy in interpersonal relations. *Journal of Social and Clinical Psychology, 9,* 15-30.

Reis, H. T., Lin, Y., Bennett, M. E., & Nezlek, J. B. (1993). Change and consistency in social participation during early adulthood. *Developmental Psychology, 29,* 633-645.

Reis, H. T., & Shaver, P. (1988). Intimacy as an interpersonal process. In S. Duck (Ed.), *Handbook of personal relationships* (pp. 367-389). New York: Wiley.

Reiss, I. L. (1976). *Family systems in America* (2nd ed.). Hinsdale, IL: Dryden Press.

Reiss, I. L. (1980). *Family systems in America.* New York: Holt, Rinehart, & Winston.

Renwick, P. A., & Lawler, E. E. (1978, May). What you really want from your job. *Psychology Today,* pp. 53-65, 118.

Rest, J. (1968). *Developmental hierarchy in preference and comprehension of moral judgment.* Unpublished doctoral dissertation, University of Chicago.

Restak, R. M. (1982, January/February). Newborn knowledge. *Science 82,* pp. 58-65.

Reston, J. (1975, March 14). Proxmire on love. *New York Times,* p. 39.

Reynolds, B. A., & Weiss, S. (1992). Generation of neurons and astrocytes from isolated cells of the adult mammalian central nervous system. *Science, 255,* 1707-1710.

Reynolds, D., & Murgatroyd, S. (1977). The sociology of schooling and the absent pupil: The school as a factor in the generation of truancy. In H. C. M. Carroll (Ed.), *Absenteeism in South Wales: Studies of pupils, their homes and their secondary schools.* Swansea: Univ. of Swansea, Faculty of Educ.

Reynolds, D., Jones, D., & St Leger, S. (1976, July 29). Schools do make a difference. *New Society,* pp. 223-225.

Rheingold, H. L. (1982). Little children's participation in the work of adults, a nascent prosocial behavior. *Child Development, 53,* 114-125.

Rheingold, H. L., Cook, K. V., & Kolowitz, V. (1987). Commands activate the behavior and pleasure of 2-year-old children. *Developmental Psychology, 23,* 146-151.

Rheingold, H. L., & Eckerman, C. O. (1970). The infant separates himself from his mother. *Science, 168,* 78-83.

Rheingold, H. L., Gewirtz, J. L., & Ross, H. W. (1959). Social conditioning of vocalizations in the infant. *Journal of Comparative and Physiological Psychology, 52,* 68-73.

Rhodes, S. R. (1983). Age-related differences in work attitudes and behavior: A review and conceptual analysis. *Psychological Bulletin, 93,* 328-367.

Rice, M. L., Huston, A. C., Truglio, R., & Wright, J. (1990). Words from "Sesame Street": Learning vocabulary while viewing. *Developmental Psychology, 26,* 421-428.

Rice, M. L., & Woodsmall, L. (1988). Lessons from television: Children's word learning when viewing. *Child Development, 59,* 420-429.

Rich, C. L., Sherman, M., & Fowler, R. C. (1990). San Diego Suicide Study: The adolescents. *Adolescence, 25,* 855-865.

Richards, M. H., Boxer, A. M., Petersen, A. C., & Albrecht, R. (1990). Relation of weight to body image in pubertal girls and boys from two communities. *Developmental Psychology, 26,* 313-321.

Richards, M. P. M., Dunn, J. F., & Antonis, B. (1977). Caretaking in the first year of life: The role of fathers' and mothers' social isolation. *Child Care, Health and Development, 3,* 23-26.

Riegel, K. F. (1973). Dialectic operations: The final period of cognitive development. *Human Development, 16,* 346-370.

Riegel, K. F. (1975). Adult life crisis: A dialectical interpretation of development. In N. Datan & L. H. Ginsberg (Eds.), *Lifespan developmental psychology: Normative life crisis.* New York: Academic Press.

Riese, M. L. (1987). Temperament stability between the neonatal period and 24 months. *Developmental Psychology, 23,* 216-222.

Ritts, R. E. (1968). A physician's view of informed consent in human experimentation. *Fordham Law Review, 36,* 631-638.

Roberto, K. A., & Scott, J. P. (1986). Friendships of older men and women: Exchange patterns and satisfaction. *Psychology and Aging, 1,* 103-109.

Roberts, K. (1988). Retrieval of a basic-level category in prelinguistic infants. *Developmental Psychology, 24,* 21-27.

Roberts, L. (1989). Genome mapping goal now in reach. *Science, 244,* 424-425.

Roberts, T. W., & Price, S. J. (1985). A systems analysis of the remarriage process: Implications for the clinician. *Journal of Divorce, 9,* 1-25.

Roberts, W. L. (1979-80). Significant elements in the relationship of long-married couples. *International Journal of Aging and Human Development, 10*, 265-272.

Roberts, W. L. (1986). Nonlinear models of development: An example from the socialization of competence. *Child Development, 57*, 1166-1178.

Robey, B. (1982). Older Americans. *American Demographics, 4*, 40-41.

Roche, A. F., & Davila, G. H. (1972). Late adolescent growth in stature. *Pediatrics, 50*, 874-880.

Roche, J. P. (1986). Premarital sex: Attitudes and behavior by dating stage. *Adolescence, 21*, 107-121.

Rodin, J., & Salovey, P. (1989). Health psychology. *Annual Review of Psychology, 40*, 533-579.

Rogoff, B., & Waddell, K. J. (1982). Memory for information organized in a scene by children from two cultures. *Child Development, 53*, 1224-1228.

Rohner, R. P., & Pettengill, S. M. (1985). Perceived parental acceptance-rejection and parental control among Korean adolescents. *Child Development, 56*, 524-528.

Rohner, R. P., & Rohner, E. C. (1981). Parental acceptance-rejection and parental control: Cross-cultural codes. *Ethnology, 20*, 245-260.

Rondal, J. A. (1985). *Adult-child interaction and the process of language acquisition*. New York: Praeger.

Roopnarine, J. L. (1981). Peer play interaction in a mixed-age preschool setting. *Journal of General Psychology, 104*, 161-166.

Roopnarine, J. L., & Johnson, J. E. (1984). Socialization in a mixed-age experimental program. *Developmental Psychology, 20*, 828-832.

Roscissano, L., & Yatchmink, Y. (1983). Language skill and interactive patterns in prematurely born toddlers. *Child Development, 54*, 1229-1241.

Rose, R. J., & Ditto, W. B. (1983). A developmental-genetic analysis of common fears from early adolescence to early adulthood. *Child Development, 54*, 361-368.

Rose, S. A., Feldman, J. F., & Wallace, I. F. (1988). Individual differences in infants' information processing: Reliability, Stability, and Prediction. *Child Development, 59*, 1177-1197.

Rose, S. A., Gottfried, A. W., & Bridger, W. H. (1981). Cross-modal transfer in 6-month-old infants. *Developmental psychology, 17*, 661-669.

Rosenberg, M. (1979). *Conceiving the self*. New York: Basic Books.

Rosenblum, L. A., & Harlow, H. F. (1963). Approach-avoidance conflict in the mother surrogate situation. *Psychological Reports, 12*, 83-85.

Rosenkrantz, A. L. (1978). A note on adolescent suicide: Incidence, dynamics and some suggestions for treatment. Adolescence, *13*, 209-214.

Rosenthal, M. K. (1982). Vocal dialogues in the neonatal period. *Developmental Psychology, 18*, 17-21.

Ross, H. G., & Milgram, J. I. (1982). Important variables in adult sibling relationships: A qualititative study. In M. E. Lamb & B. Sutton-Smith (Eds.), *Sibling relationships: Their nature and significance across the lifespan* (pp. 225-249). Hillsdale, NJ: Erlbaum.

Ross, H. S., & Goldman, B. M. (1976). Establishing new social relations in infancy. In T. Alloway, L. Krames, & P. Pliner (Eds.), *Advances in communication and affect* (Vol. 4). New York: Plenum.

Rossi, A. S. (1980). Aging and parenthood in the middle years. In P. B. Baltes & O. G. Brim, Jr. (Eds.), *Lifespan development and behavior* (vol. 3). New York: Academic Press.

Roth, M. (1976). The psychiatric disorders of later life. *Psychiatric Annals, 6*, 57-101.

Rothbart, M. K. (1986). Longitudinal observation of infant temperament. *Developmental Psychology, 22*, 356-365.

Rother, L. (1987, January 4). Women gain degrees, but not tenure. *The New York Times*, p. 9.

Rotheram-Borus, M. J., Koopman, C., Haignere, C., & Davies, M. (1991). Reducing HIV sexual risk behaviors among runaway adolescents. *Journal of the American Medical Association, 266*, 1237-1241.

Roupp, R., Travers, J., Glantz, F., Coelen, C., Bache, W. L., O'Neil, C., & Singer, J. (1979). *Children at the center: Final report of the National Day Care Study* (Vol. 1). Cambridge, MA: Abt Books.

Rousseau, J. J. (1960). *Julie; or, the new Eloise* (R. Pomeau, Ed.). Paris: Garnier Freres.

Rovee, C. K. (1972). Olfactory cross-adaptation and facilitation in human neonates. *Journal of Experimental Child Psychology, 13*, 368-381.

Rovee, C. K., Cohen, R. Y., & Shlapack, W. (1975). Life-span stability in olfactory sensitivity. *Developmental Psychology, 11*, 311-318.

Rovee-Collier, C., Schechter, A., Shyi, G. C.-W., & Shields, P. (1992). Perceptual identification of contextual attributes and infant memory retrieval. *Developmental Psychology, 28*, 307-318.

Rowe, D. C., & Plomin, R. (1981). The importance of nonshared (E1) environmental influences in behavioral development. *Developmental Psychology, 17*, 517-531.

Rubenstein, J., & Howes, C. (1976). The effects of peers on toddler interaction with mother and toys. *Child Development, 47*, 597-605.

Rubin, K. H., Fein, G. G., & Vandenberg, B. (1983). Play. In E. M. Hetherington (Ed.), *Handbook of child psychology* (4th ed., Vol. IV, pp. 693-774). New York: Wiley.

Rubin, K. H., Maioni, T. L., & Hornung, M. (1976). Free play behaviors in middle- and lower-class preschoolers: Parten and Piaget revisited. *Child Development, 47*, 414-419.

Rubin, L. (1979). *Women of a certain age*. New York: Harper & Row.

Rubin, Z. (1973). *Liking and loving: An invitation to social psychology*. New York: Holt, Rinehart & Winston.

Rubinson, L., & de Rubertis, L. (1991). Trends in sexual attitudes and behaviors of a college population over a 15-year period. *Journal of Sex Education & Therapy, 17*, 32-41.

Rubinstein, E. A. (1983). Television and behavior: Research conclusions of the 1982 NIMH report and their policy implications. *American Psychologist, 38*, 820-825.

Rubinstein, R. L. (1987). Never married elderly as a social type: Re-evaluating some images. *The Gerontologist, 27*(1), 108-113.

Ruff, H. A. (1980). The development of perception and recognition of objects. *Child Development, 51*, 981-992.

Rushton, J. P., & Sorrentino, R. M. (Eds.). (1981). *Altruism and helping behavior: Social, personality, and developmental perspectives*. Hillsdale, NJ: Erlbaum.

Russell, B. (1951). *The autobiography of Bertrand Russell* (vol. 1). Boston: Little, Brown, & Company.

Russell, G. (1980, July 15-17). *Fathers as caregivers: Possible antecedents and consequences*. Papers presented to a study group on "The Role of the Father in Child Development, Social Policy and the Law," University of Haifa, Haifa, Israel.

Ruth, J. E., & Birren, J. E. (1985). Creativity in adulthood and old age: Relations to intelligence sex and mode of testing. *International Journal of Behavioral Development, 8*, 99-109.

Rutter, M. (1983). School effects on pupil progress: Research findings and policy implications. *Child Development, 54*, 1-29.

Rutter, M., & Maughan, B., Mortimore, P., Ouston, J., & Smith, A. (1979). *Fifteen thousand hours: Secondary schools and their effects on children*. Cambridge, MA: Harvard University Press.

Sagar, H. A., Schofield, J. W., & Snyder, H. N. (1983). Race and gender barriers: Preadolescent peer behavior in academic classrooms. *Child Development, 54*, 1032-1040.

Sagi, A., & Hoffman, M. L. (1976). Empathic distress in the newborn. *Developmental Psychology, 12*, 175-176.

Sagi, A., Van IJzendoorn, M. H., & Koren-Karie, N. (1991). Primary appraisal of the strange situation: A cross-cultural analysis of preseparation episodes. *Developmental Psychology, 27*, 587-596.

Sagotsky, G., Wood-Schneider, M., & Konop, M. (1981). Learning to cooperate: Effects of modeling and direct instruction. *Child Development, 52*, 1037-1042.

Sainsbury, P., Jenkins, J., & Levey, A. (1980). The social correlates of suicide in Europe. In R. T. D. Farmer, & S. R. Hirsch (Eds.), *The suicide syndrome* (pp. 38-53). London: Croom Helm.

Salholz, E., Michael, R., Starr, M., Doherty, S., Abramson, P., & Wingert, P. (1986, June 2). Too late for prince charming? *Newsweek*, pp. 54-61.

Salthouse, T. A., (1994). The nature of the influence of speed on adult age differences in cognition. *Developmental Psychology, 30,* 240-259.

Salthouse, T. A., Kausler, D., & Saults, J. S. (1988). Investigation of student status, background variables, and feasibility of standard tasks in cognitive aging research. *Psychology and Aging, 3*(1), 29-37.

Saltzstein, H. D. (1983). Critical issues in Kohlberg's theory of moral reasoning. *Monographs of the Society for Research in Child Development, 48*(1-2, Serial No. 200), 108-119.

Sampson, E. E. (1962). Birth order, need achievement, and conformity. *Journal of Abnormal and Social Psychology, 64,* 155-159.

Sandburg, C. (1954). *Abraham Lincoln: The prairie years and the war years* (1 vol. ed.). New York: Harcourt Brace Jovanovich.

Sanson, A., Prior, M., & Kyrios, M. (1990). Contamination of measures in temperament research. *Merrill-Palmer Quarterly, 36,* 179-192.

Santrock, J. W., & Tracy, R. L. (1978). Effects of children's family structure status on the development of stereotypes by teachers. *Journal of Educational Psychology, 70,* 754-757.

Sapienza, C. (1990). Parental imprinting of genes. *Scientific American, 263*(4), 52-60.

Sarason, S. B. (1977). *Work, aging, and social change: Professionals and the life-one career imperative.* New York: The Free Press.

Sarason, S. B., & Klaber, M. (1985). The school as a social situation. *Annual Review of Psychology, 36,* 115-140.

Sarlo, G., Jason, L. A., & Lonak, C. (1988). Parents' strategies for limiting children's television viewing. *Psychological Reports, 63,* 435-438.

Sasser-Coen, J. R. (1993). Qualitative changes in creativity in the second half of life: A life-span developmental perspective. *Journal of Creative Behavior, 27,* 18-27.

Savage-Rumbaugh, S., Sevcik, R. A., & Hopkins, W. D. (1988). Symbolic cross-modal transfer in two species of chimpanzees. *Child Development, 59,* 617-625.

Savin-Williams, R. C. (1979). Dominance hierarchies in groups of early adolescents. *Child Development, 50,* 923-935.

Savin-Williams, R. C., & Demo, D. H. (1984). Developmental change and stability in adolescent self-concept. *Developmental Psychology, 20,* 1100-1110.

Saxe, G. B. (1988). The mathematics of child street vendors. *Child Development, 59,* 1415-1425.

Scanlan, T. K., & Lewthwaite, R. (1988). From stress to enjoyment: Parental and coach influences on young participants. In E. W. Brown & C. F. Branta (Eds.), *Competitive sports for children and youth: An overview of research and issues* (pp. 41-48). Champaign, IL: Human Kinetics.

Scarr, S., & Grajek, S. (1982). Similarities and differences among siblings. In M. E. Lamb, & B. Sutton-Smith (Eds.), *Sibling relationships: Their nature and significance across the lifespan.* Hillsdale, NJ: Erlbaum.

Scarr, S., & McCartney, K. (1988). Far from home: An experimental evaluation of the mother-child home program in Bermuda. *Child Development, 59,* 531-543.

Scarr, S., & Weinberg, R. A. (1976). IQ test performance of black children adopted by white families. *American Psychologist, 31,* 726-739.

Scarr, S., Phillips, D., & McCartney, K. (1989). Working mothers and their families. *American Psychologist, 44,* 1402-1409.

Schacter, D. L., Moscovitch, M., Tulving, E., McLachlan, D. R., & Freedman, M. (1986). Mnemonic precedence in amnesic patients: An analogue of the AB error in infants? *Child Development, 57,* 816-823.

Schaefer, D., & Lyons, C. (1986). *How do we tell the children?* New York: Newmarket Press.

Schaefer, E. S. (1959). A circumplex model for maternal behavior. *Journal of Abnormal and Social Psychology, 59,* 226-235.

Schaffer, H. R., & Emerson, P. E. (1964). The development of social attachments in infancy. *Monographs of the Society for Research in Child Development,* (3, Serial No. 94).

Schaie, K. W. (1983). *Longitudinal studies of adult psychological development.* New York: The Guilford Press.

Schaie, K. W. (1994). The course of adult intellectual development. *American Psychologist, 49,* 304-313.

Schaie, K. W., & Hertzog, C. (1982). Longitudinal methods. In B. B. Wolman (Ed.), *Handbook of developmental psychology* (pp. 91-115). Englewood Cliffs, NJ: Prentice-Hall.

Schaie, K. W., & Hertzog, C. (1983). Fourteen-year cohort sequential analyses of adult intellectual development. *Developmental Psychology, 19,* 531-543.

Schaie, K. W., & Willis, S. L. (1986). Can decline in adult intellectual functioning be reversed? *Developmental Psychology, 22,* 223-232.

Schiff, M., Duyme, M., Dumaret, A., & Tomkiewicz, S. (1982). How much could we boost scholastic achievement and IQ scores? A direct answer from a French adoption study. *Cognition, 12,* 165-196.

Schiller, P. H. (1957). Innate motor action as a basis of learning. In S. H. Schiller (Ed.), *Instinctive behavior.* New York: Int'l. Universities Press.

Schmeck, H. M., Jr. (1983, March 22). U.S. panel calls for patients' right to end life. *New York Times,* pp. A-1, C-7.

Schmeck, H. M., Jr. (1986, December). 90% in poll back patients' right to die. *New York Times,* p. C-10.

Schmemann, S. (1986, October 10). Kasparov makes a key move, and the fans sense a victory. *New York Times,* pp. 1, 42.

Schmidt, H. J., & Beauchamp, G. K. (1988). Adult-like odor preferences and aversions in three-year-old children. *Child Development, 59,* 1136-1143.

Schofield, J. W., & Francis, W. D. (1982). An observational study of peer interaction in racially mixed "accelerated" classrooms. *Journal of Educational Psychology, 74,* 722-732.

Schofield, J. W., & Whitley, B. E., Jr. (1983). Peer nomination vs. rating scale measurement of children's peer preferences. *Social Psychology Quarterly, 46,* 242-251.

Schonfield, D., & Robertson, B. A. (1966). Memory storage and aging. *Canadian Journal of Psychology, 20,* 228-236.

Schooler, K. K. (1979). *National senior citizens survey.* Ann Arbor, MI: Inter-University Consortium for Political Social Research.

Schreurs, K. M. G. (1993). Sexuality in lesbian couples: The importance of gender. *Annual Review of Sex Research, 4,* 49-66.

Schrotenboer, K., & Weiss, J. (1985). *Guide to pregnancy over 35.* New York: Ballantine Books.

Schultz, R. (1978). *The psychology of death, dying, and bereavement.* Reading, MA: Addison-Wesley.

Schultz, R., & Aderman, D. (1978-79). Physician's death anxiety and patient outcomes. *Omega, 9,* 327-332.

Schulz, R., & Ewen, R. B. (1993). *Adult development and aging: Myths and emerging realities* (2nd ed.). New York: McMillan.

Schwartz, H. (1978). Abraham Lincoln and cardiac decompensation: A preliminary report. *Western Journal of Medicine, 128*(2), 174-177.

Schweinhart, L. J., & Weikart, D. P. (1985). Evidence that good early childhood programs work. *Phi Delta Kappan, 66,* 545-551.

Schweinhart, L. J., & Weikart, D. P. (1986). What do we know so far? A review of the Head Start Synthesis Project. *Young Children, 41,* 49-55.

Scoe, H. F. (1933). Bladder control in infancy and early childhood. *University of Iowa Studies in Child Welfare, V,* No. 4.

Sears, R. R., Maccoby, E. E., & Levin, H. (1957). *Patterns of childrearing.* Evanston, IL: Row, Peterson.

Seefeldt, V. (1982). The changing image of youth sports in the 1980s. In R. A. Magill, M. J. Ash, & F. L. Smoll (Eds.), *Children in sport* (pp. 16-26). Champaign, IL: Human Kinetics.

Seelbach, W. C., & Hansen, C. J. (1980). Satisfaction with family relations among the elderly. *Family Relations, 29,* 91-96.

Segal, N. L. (1985). Monozygotic and dizygotic twins: A comparative analysis of mental ability profiles. *Child Development, 56,* 1051-1058.

Seitz, V., Rosenbaum, L. K., & Apfel, N. H. (1985). Effects of family support intervention: A ten-year follow-up. *Child Development, 56,* 376-391.

Seligman, M. E. P., & Maier, S. F. (1967). Failure to escape traumatic shock. *Journal of Experimental Psychology, 74,* 1-9.

Selman, R. (1980). *The growth of interpersonal understanding: Developmental and clinical analyses.* New York: Academic Press.

Selman, R. L., Schorin, M. Z., Stone, C. R., & Phelps, E. (1983). A naturalistic study of children's social understanding. *Developmental Psychology, 19,* 81-102.

Serbin, L. A., & Sprafkin, C. (1986). The salience of gender and the process of sex typing in three- to seven-year-old children. *Child Development, 57,* 1188-1199.

Service. R. F. (1994). Closing in on human and mouse maps. *Science, 264,* 1404.

Sevinc, M., & Turner, C. (1976). Language and the latent structure of cognitive development. *International Journal of Psychology, 11,* 231-250.

Shaffran, R., & Decarie, T. G. (1973). *Short term stability of infants' responses to strangers.* Paper presented at the meeting of the Society for Research in Child Development, Philadelphia, Pennsylvania.

Shanas, E. (1979a). The family as a social support system in old age. *The Gerontologist, 19,* 169-174.

Shanas, E. (1979b). Social myth as hypothesis: The case of the family relations of old people. *The Gerontologist, 19,* 3-9.

Shanas, E. (1980). Older people and their families: The new pioneers. *Journal of Marriage and the Family, 42,* 9-15.

Shanker, I. (1973, June 10). College head's sabbatical: Two months at menial jobs. *New York Times,* pp. 1, 29.

Shapira, A., & Madsen, M. C. (1974). Between- and within-group cooperation and competition among kibbutz and nonkibbutz children. *Developmental Psychology, 10,* 140-145.

Sharabany, R., & Bar-Tal, D. (1982). Theories of the development of altruism: Review, comparison and integration. *International Journal of Behavioral Development, 5,* 49-80.

Shaver, J. P., & Strong, W. (1976). *Facing value decisions: Rationale-building for teachers.* Belmont, CA: Wadsworth.

Shedler, J., & Block, J. (1990). Adolescent drug use and psychological health. *American Psychologist, 45,* 612-630.

Shekelle, R. B., Hulley, S. B., Neaton, J. D., Billings, J. H., Borhani, N. O., Gerace, T. A., Jacobs, D. R., Lasser, N. L., Mittlemark, M. B., & Stamler, J. (1985). The MRFIT behavior pattern study. II. Type A behavior and incidence of coronary heart disease. *American Journal of Epidemiology, 122,* 559-570.

Sherman, M., & Sherman, I. C. (1925). Sensori-motor responses in infants. *Journal of Comparative Psychology, 5,* 53-68.

Sheslow, D. V., Bondy, A. S., & Nelson, R. O. (1982). A comparison of graduated exposure, verbal coping skills, and their combination in the treatment of children's fear of the dark. *Child & Family Behavior Therapy, 4*(2-3), 33-45.

Shigetomi, C. C., Hartmann, D. P., & Gelfand, D. M. (1981). Sex differences in children's altruistic behavior and reputations for helpfulness. *Developmental Psychology, 17,* 434-437.

Shirley, M. M. (1931). *The first two years. A study of twenty-five babies (Vol. I). Postural and locomotor development.* Minneapolis, Minn.: Univ. of Minnesota Press.

Shneidman, E. (1970, August). The enemy. *Psychology Today,* pp. 37-66.

Shneidman, E. (1973). *Death of men.* New York: Quadrangle.

Shock, N. W. (1962). The physiology of aging. *Scientific American, 206*(1), 100-110.

Shock, N. W. (1985). Longitudinal studies of aging in humans. In C. E. Finch & E. L. Schneider (Eds.), *Handbook of the biology of aging* (2nd ed.). New York: Van Nostrand Reinhold Co.

Shonkoff, J. P. (1984). The biological substrate and physical health in middle childhood. In W. A. Collins (Ed.), *Development during middle child-

hood: The years from six to twelve* (pp. 24-69). Washington, DC: National Academy Press.

Short, R. V. (1984). Breast feeding. *Scientific American, 250*(4), 35-41.

Shweder, R. A. (1981). What's there to negotiate? Some questions for Youniss. *Merrill-Palmer Quarterly, 27,* 405-412.

Siegel, O. (1982). Personality development in adolescence. In B. B. Wolman (Ed.), *Handbook of developmental psychology* (pp. 537-548). Englewood Cliffs, NJ: Prentice-Hall.

Siegler, R. S., & Liebert, R. M. (1975). Acquisition of formal scientific reasoning by 10- and 13-year-olds: Designing a factorial experiment. *Developmental Psychology, 11,* 401-402.

Siegler, R. S., & Richards, D. D. (1982). The development of intelligence. In R. J. Sternberg (Ed.), *Handbook of human intelligence* (pp. 897-971). Cambridge, Engl.: Cambridge Univ. Press.

Silber, S. J. (1980). *How to get pregnant.* New York: Charles Scribner's Sons.

Silberner, J. (1985, October 12). Herpes babies. *Science News,* p. 232.

Sillman, L. R. (1966). Femininity and paranoidism. *The Journal of Nervous and Mental Disease, 143,* 163-170.

Siman, M. L. (1977). Application of a new model of peer group influence to naturally existing adolescent friendship groups. *Child Development, 48,* 270-274.

Simister, N. E., & Mostov, K. E. (1989). An Fc receptor structurally related to MHC class I antigens. *Nature, 337,* 184-187.

Simons, R. L., Lorenz, F. O., Conger, R. D., & Wu, C. (1992). Support from spouse as mediator and moderator of the disruptive influence of economic strain on parenting. *Child Development, 63,* 1282-1301.

Simons, R. L., Whitbeck, L. B., Conger, R. D., & Chyi-In, W. (1991). Intergenerational transmission of harsh parenting. *Developmental Psychology, 27,* 159-171.

Sinclair, A. H., Berta, P., Palmer, M. S., Hawkins, J. R., Griffiths, B. L., Smith, M. J., Foster, J. W., Frischauf, A. M., Lovell-Badge, R., & Goodfellow, P. N. (1990). A gene from the human sex-determining region encodes a protein with homology to a conserved DNA-binding motif. *Nature, 346,* 240-244.

Singelais, N. (1987, April 21). Two for two. *The Boston Globe,* p. 85.

Singer, D. G. (1982). Television and the developing imagination of the child. In D. Pearl, L. Bouthilet, & J. Lazar (Eds.), *Television and behavior: Ten years of scientific progress and implications for the eighties* (Vol. 2). Washington, DC: U.S. Government Printing Office.

Singer, D. G. (1983). A time to reexamine the role of television in our lives. *American Psychologist, 38,* 815-816.

Singer, J. L., & Singer, D. G. (1974). *Fostering imaginative play in preschool children: Effects of television viewing and direct adult modeling.* Paper presented at the meeting of the American Psychological Association, New Orleans, Louisiana.

Singer, J. L., & Singer, D. G. (1976). Fostering creativity in children: Can TV stimulate imaginative play? *Journal of Communication, 26*(3), 74-80.

Singer, J. L., & Singer, D. G. (1983a). Psychologists look at television: Cognitive, developmental, personality, and social policy implications. *American Psychologist, 38,* 826-834.

Singer, J. L., & Singer, D. G. (1983b). Implications of childhood television viewing for cognition, imagination, and emotion. In J. Bryant, & D. R. Anderson (Eds.), *Children's understanding of television: Research on attention and comprehension.* New York: Academic Press.

Singer, L. M., Brodzinsky, D. M., Ramsay, D., Steir, M., & Waters, E. (1985). Mother-infant attachment in adoptive families. *Child Development, 56,* 1543-1551.

Sinnott, E. W., Dunn, L. C., & Dobzhansky, T. (1958). *Principles of genetics.* New York: McGraw-Hill.

Sinnott, J. D. (1984). Reasoning: The relativistic stage. In M. L. Commons, F. A. Richards, & C. Armon (Eds.), *Beyond formal operations: Late adolescent and adult cognitive development* (pp. 158-179). New York: Praeger.

Sirignano, S. W., & Lachman, M. E. (1985). Personality change during the transition to parenthood: The role of perceived infant temperament. *Developmental Psychology, 21,* 558-567.

REFERENCES

Siwolop, S., & Mohs, M. (1985, February). The war on Down Syndrome. *Discover*, pp. 67-73.

Skeels, H. M., Updegraff, R., Wellman, B. L., & Williams, H. M. (1938). A study of environmental stimulation: An orphanage preschool project. *University of Iowa Studies in Child Welfare, 15*(4).

Skinner, B. F. (1969). *Contingencies of reinforcement.* New York: Appleton-Century-Croft.

Skinner, B. F., & Vaughan, M. E. (1983). *Enjoy old age.* New York: Norton.

Slater, A., Morison, V., & Rose, D. (1983). Perception of shape by the new-born baby. *British Journal of Developmental Psychology, 1*, 135-142.

Slobin, D. I. (1966). The acquisition of Russian as a native language. In F. Smith, & G. Miller (Eds.), *The genesis of language* (pp. 129-148). Cambridge, Mass.: MIT Press.

Sloviter, R. S., Valiquette, G., Abrams, G. M., Ronk, E. C., Sollas, A. L., Paul, L. A., & Neubort, S. (1989). Selective loss of hippocampal granule cells in the mature rat brain after adrenalectomy. *Science, 243*, 535-538.

Smart, W. (1986, August 31). Keeping your brain in shape. *The Boston Globe*, pp. 89-92.

Smith, B. A., Fillion, T. J., & Blass, E. M. (1990). Orally mediated sources of calming in 1- to 3-day-old human infants. *Developmental Psychology, 26*, 731-737.

Smith, P. B., & Pederson, D. R. (1988). Maternal sensitivity and patterns of infant-mother attachment. *Child Development, 59*, 1097-1101.

Smith, P. K., & Vollstedt, R. (1985). On defining play: An empirical study of the relationship between play and various play criteria. *Child Development, 56*, 1042-1050.

Smolucha, F. (1988). An introduction to Vygotsky's theory of social-cognitive development. Unpublished manuscript.

Smyer, M. A., & Hofland, B. F. (1982). Divorce and family support in later life: Emerging concerns. *Journal of Family Issues, 3*, 61-77.

Snarey, J. R., Reimer, J., & Kohlberg, L. (1985). Development of social-moral reasoning among kibbutz adolescents: A longitudinal cross-cultural study. *Developmental Psychology, 21*, 3-17.

Snow, C. E. (1972). Mothers' speech to children learning language. *Child Development, 43*, 549-565.

Snyderman, M., & Rothman, S. (1987). Survey of expert opinion on intelligence and aptitude testing. *American Psychologist, 42*, 137-144.

Sofer, C. (1970). *Men in mid-career: A study of British managers and technical specialists.* London: Cambridge Univ. Press.

Sohier, R. (1986). Homosexual mutuality: Variation on a theme by Erik Erikson. *Journal of Homosexuality, 12*, 25-38.

Sokol, R. J., Miller, S. I., & Reed, G. (1980). Alcohol abuse during pregnancy: An epidemiologic study. *Alcoholism, 4*, 135-145.

Sommerville, C. J. (1982). *The rise and fall of childhood.* Beverly Hills, CA: Sage Publications.

Sontag, L. W., & Wallace, R. F. (1935). The effect of cigarette smoking during pregnancy upon the fetal heart rate. *American Journal of Obstetrics and Gynecology, 29*, 77-83.

Sorce, J. F., Emde, R. N., Campos, J., & Klinnert, M. D. (1985). Maternal emotional signaling: Its effect on the visual cliff behavior of 1-year-olds. *Developmental Psychology, 21*, 195-200.

Sorensen, R. C. (1973). *Adolescent sexuality in contemporary America.* New York: World.

Sosa, R., Kennell, J., Klaus, M., Robertson, S., & Urrutia, J. (1980). The effect of a supportive companion on perinatal problems, length of labor, and mother-infant interaction. *New England Journal of Medicine, 303*, 597-600.

Sowell, C. (1986, June-July). Starting over. *Modern Maturity*, pp. 64-69.

Spalding, D. A. (1873). Instinct, with original observations on young animals. *Macmillan's Magazine, 27*, 282-293. Reprinted in *British Journal of Animal Behaviour* (1954), 2, 2-11.

Spasoff, R. A., Kraus, A. S., Beattie, E. J., Holden, D. E., Lawson, J. S., Rodenburg, M., & Woodcock, G. M. (1978). A longitudinal study of elderly residents of long-stay institutions: I. Early response to institutional care. *The Gerontologist, 18*, 281-292.

Spearman, C. (1927). *The abilities of man.* New York: Macmillan.

Speece, M., & Brent, S. B. (1984). Children's understanding of death: A review of three components of a death concept. *Child Development, 55*, 1671-1686.

Spencer, D. G., & Steers, R. M. (1980). The influence of personal factors and perceived work experiences on employee turnover and absenteeism. *Academy of Management Journal, 23*, 567-572.

Spinetta, J. J., & Rigler, D. (1972). The child-abusing parent: A psychological review. *Psychological Bulletin, 77*, 296-304.

Sporakowski, M. J., & Hughston, G. A. (1978). Prescriptions for happy marriage: Adjustments and satisfactions of couples married for 50 or more years. *Family Coordinator, 27*, 321-327.

Sprunger, L. W., Boyce, W. T., & Gaines, J. A. (1985). Family-infant congruence: Routines and rhythmicity in family adaptations to a young infant. *Child Development, 56*, 564-572.

Sroufe, L. A. (1979). Socioemotional development. In J. Osofsky (Ed.), *Handbook of infant development* (pp. 462-516). New York: Wiley Interscience.

Sroufe, L. A. (1983). Individual patterns of adaptation from infancy to preschool. In M. Perlmutter (Ed.), *Minnesota Symposium in Child Psychology* (Vol. 16). Hillsdale, NJ: Erlbaum.

St. Peters, M., Fitch, M., Huston, A. C., Wright, J. C., & Eakins, D. J. (1991). Television and families: What do young children watch with their parents? *Child Development, 62*, 1409-1423.

Stafford, R., Backman, E., & Dibona, P. (1977). The division of labor among cohabitating and married couples. *Journal of Marriage and the Family, 39*, 43-57.

Stagner, R. (1985). Aging in industry. In J. E. Birren & K. W. Schaie (Eds.), *Handbook of the psychology of aging* (2nd ed.). New York: Van Nostrand Reinhold Co.

Stagno, S., Reynolds, D. W., Huang, E., Thames, S. D., Smith, R. J., & Alford, C. A. (1977). Congenital cytomegalovirus infection: Occurrence in an immune population. *New England Journal of Medicine, 296*, 1254-1258.

Stallings, J. (1975). Implementation and child effects of teaching practices in Follow Through classrooms. *Monographs of the Society for Research in Child Development, 40*(7-8, Serial No. 163).

Starr, B. D., & Weiner, M. B. (1981). *The Starr-Weiner report on sex and sexuality in the mature years.* New York: Stein & Day.

Starr, R. H. (1979). Child abuse. *American Psychologist, 34*, 872-878.

Staub, E. (1971). The use of role playing and induction in children's learning of helping and sharing behavior. *Child Development, 42*, 805-816.

Staub, E. (1978). *Positive social behavior and morality.* New York: Academic Press.

Staw, B. M. (1984). Organizational behavior: A review and reformulation of the field's outcome variables. *Annual Review of Psychology, 35*, 627-666.

Staw, B. M., & Oldham, G. R. (1978). Reconsidering our dependent variables: A critique and empirical study. *Academy of Management Journal, 21*, 539-559.

Stebbins, G. L., & Ayala, F. J. (1985). The evolution of Darwinism. *Scientific American, 253*(1), 72-82.

Stechler, G., & Halton, A. (1982). Prenatal influences on human development. In B. B. Wolman (Ed.), *Handbook of developmental psychology* (pp. 175-189). Englewood Cliffs, NJ: Prentice-Hall.

Steckol, K. F., & Leonard, L. B. (1981). Sensorimotor development and the use of prelinguistic performatives. *Journal of Speech and Hearing Research, 24*, 262-268.

Stein, A. H. (1973). The effects of maternal employment and educational attainment on the sex-typed attributes of college females. *Social Behavior and Personality, 1*, 111-114.

Stein, A. H., & Friedrich, L. K. (1972). Television content and young children's behavior. In J. P. Murray, E. A. Rubinstein, & G. A. Comstock (Eds.), *Television and social behavior, Vol. 2: Television and social learning.* Washington, DC: U.S. Government Printing Office.

Stein, P. J. (1983). Singlehood. In E. D. Macklin & R. H. Rubin (Eds.), *Contemporary families and alternative lifestyles* (pp. 27-47). Beverly Hills: Sage Publications.

Steinberg, L. (1986). Latchkey children and susceptibility to peer pressure: An ecological analysis. *Developmental Psychology, 22,* 433-439.

Steinberg, L., & Dornbusch, S. M. (1991). Negative correlates of part-time employment during adolescence: Replication and elaboration. *Developmental Psychology, 27,* 304-313.

Steinberg, L., Elmen, J. D., & Mounts, N. S. (1989). Authoritative parenting, psychosocial maturity, and academic success among adolescents. *Child Development, 60,* 1424-1426.

Steiner, G. A. (1963). *The people look at television.* New York: Knopf.

Steiner, J. E. (1977). Facial expressions of the neonate infant indicating the hedonics of food-related chemical stimuli. In J. M. Weiffenbach (Ed.), *Taste and development: The genesis of sweet preference.* Washington, D.C.: U.S. Government Printing Office.

Steiner, J. E., & Finnegan, L. (1975). Innate discriminative facial expression to food related odorants in the neonate infant. *Israel Journal of Medical Sciences, 11,* 858-859.

Steinmetz, S. K. (1978, July-August). Battered parents. *Society,* pp. 54-55.

Sternberg, R. J. (1984). *Beyond IQ: A triarchic theory of human intelligence.* New York: Cambridge Univ. Press.

Sternberg, R. J. (1985). Human intelligence: The model is the message. *Science, 230,* 1111-1118.

Sternberg, R. J. (1986). *Intelligence applied.* San Diego, CA: Harcourt Brace.

Stevenson, J. S. (1977). *Issues and crisis during middlescence.* New York: Appleton-Century-Crofts.

Stewart, R. B., Mobley, L. A., Van Tuyl, S. S., & Salvador, M. A. (1987). The firstborn's adjustment to the birth of a sibling: A longitudinal assessment. *Child Development, 58,* 341-355.

Stimson, A., Wase, J., & Stimson, J. (1981, June). Sexuality and self-esteem among the aged. *Research on Aging,* pp. 228-239.

Stith, S. M., & Davis, A. J. (1984). Employed mothers and family day-care substitute caregivers: A comparative analysis of infant care. *Child Development, 55,* 1340-1348.

Stocker, C., Dunn, J., & Plomin, R. (1989). Sibling relationships: Links with child temperament, maternal behavior, and family structure. *Child Development, 60,* 715-727.

Stoller, E. P. (1983). Parental caregiving by adult children. *Journal of Marriage and the Family, 45,* 851-858.

Stoller, R. J. (1985). *Presentations of gender.* New Haven: Yale Univ. Press.

Streissguth, A. P. (1977). Maternal alcoholism and the outcome of pregnancy. In M. Greenwealth (Ed.), *Alcohol problems in women and children.* New York: Grune & Stratton.

Streissguth, A. P., Aase, J. M., Clarren, S. K., Randels, S. P., LaDue, R. A., & Smith, D. F. (1991). Fetal alcohol syndrome in adolescents and adults. *Journal of the American Medical Association, 265,* 1961-1967.

Streissguth, A. P., Barr, H. M., & Martin, D. C. (1983). Maternal alcohol use and neonatal habituation assessed with the Brazelton Scale. *Child Development, 54,* 1109-1118.

Streissguth, A. P., Barr, H. M., Sampson, P. D., Darby, B. L., & Martin, D. C. (1989). IQ at age 4 in relation to maternal alcohol use and smoking during pregnancy. *Developmental Psychology, 25,* 3-11.

Subramanian, S. K. (1990). *Problems in intervention: The crisis of teenage pregnancy.* Paper presented at the meeting of the Society for the Study of Social Problems.

Suchet, M., & Barling, J. (1986). Employed mothers. Interrole conflict, spouse support, and marital functioning. *Journal of Occupational Behavior, 7,* 167-178.

Sugarman, S. (1977). A description of communicative development in the prelanguage child. In I. Markova (Ed.), *The social context of language.* London: Wiley.

Suinn, R. M. (1977). Type A behavior pattern. In R. B. Williams, Jr. & W. D. Gentry (Eds.), *Behavioral approaches to medical treatment* (pp. 55-56). Cambridge, Mass.: Ballinger.

Sulik, K. K., Johnston, M. C., & Webb, M. A. (1981). Fetal alcohol syndrome: Embryogenesis in mouse model. *Science, 214,* 936-938.

Sullivan-Bolyai, J., Hull, H. F., Wilson, C., & Corey, L. (1983). Neonatal herpes simplex virus infection in King County, Washington: Increasing incidence and epidemiologic correlates. *Journal of the American Medical Association, 250,* 3059-3062.

Sullivan, S. A., & Birch, L. (1990). Pass the sugar, pass the salt: Experience dictates preference. *Developmental Psychology, 26,* 546-551.

Super, D. E. (1957). *The psychology of careers.* New York: Harper & Row.

Super, D. E. (1963). *Career development: Self-concept theory.* New York: College Entrance Examination Board.

Surber, C. F. (1982). Separable effects of motives, consequences, and presentation order on children's moral judgments. *Developmental Psychology, 18,* 257-266.

Surrey, J. L. (1985). *Self-in-relation: A theory of women's development.* Work in Progress. Wellesley College, Wellesley, Massachusetts.

Sussman, N. (1976). Sex and sexuality in history. In B. J. Sadock, H. I. Kaplan, & A. M. Freedman (Eds.), *The sexual experience.* Baltimore, MD: Williams & Wilkins.

Suttie, I. D. (1935). *The origins of love and hate.* London: Kegan Paul.

Sutton-Smith, B. (1981). *A history of children's play: The New Zealand Playground 1840-1950.* Univ. of Penn. Press.

Sutton-Smith, B. (1985, October). The child at play. *Psychology Today,* pp. 64-65.

Swedo, S. E., Rettew, D. C., Kuppenheimer, M., Lum, D., Dolan, S., & Goldberger, E. (1991). Can adolescent suicide attempters be distinguished from at-risk adolescents? *Pediatrics, 88,* 620-629.

Sylva, K., Bruner, J., & Genova, P. (1976). The role of play in the problem solving of children 3-5 years old. In J. S. Bruner, A. Jolly, & K. Sylva (Eds.), *Play.* New York: Basic Books.

Szinovacz, M. E. (1980). Female retirement: Effects on spousal roles and marital adjustment. *Journal of Family Issues, 1,* 423-440.

Tager, I. B., Weiss, S. T., Munoz, A., Rosner, B., & Speizer, F. E. (1983). Longitudinal study of the effects of maternal smoking on pulmonary function in children. *New England Journal of Medicine, 309,* 699-703.

Talbert, G. B. (1977). Aging of the reproductive system. In C. E. Finch & L. Hayflick (Eds.), *The handbook of the biology of aging.* New York: Van Nostrand Reinhold Co.

Tanner, J. M. (1962). *Growth at adolescence* (2nd ed.). Oxford: Blackwell.

Tanner, J. M. (1968). Earlier maturation in man. *Scientific American, 218*(1), 21-27.

Tanner, J. M. (1969). Growth and endocrinology in the adolescent. In L. I. Gardner (Ed.), *Endocrine and genetic diseases of childhood.* Philadelphia, PA: Saunders.

Tanner, J. M. (1978). *Foetus introduction to man: Physical growth from conception to maturity.* London: Open Books.

Tanner, J. M., Whitehouse, R. H., & Takaishi, M. (1966). Standards from birth to maturity for height, weight, height velocity and weight velocity: British children, 1965. *Archives of Disease in Childhood, 41,* 454-471; 613-635.

Taylor, M., & Gelman, S. A. (1989). Incorporating new words into the lexicon: Preliminary evidence for language hierarchies in two-year-old children. *Child Development, 60,* 625-636.

Taylor, S. E. (1990). Health psychology: The science and the field. *American Psychologist, 45,* 40-50.

Terkel, S. (1974). *Working.* New York: Aron Books.

Terman, L. M. (1925). Mental and physical traits of a thousand gifted children. In L. M. Terman (Ed.), *Genetic studies of genius.* Stanford: Stanford University Press.

Terman, L. M. (1954). Scientists and nonscientists in a group of 800 gifted men. *Psychological Monographs, 68*(7), 1-44.

Terman, L. M., & Oden, M. H. (1947). *Genetic studies of genius* (vol. 4). Stanford, CA: Stanford Univ. Press.

Terman, L. M., & Oden, M. H. (1959). *Genetic studies of genius* (vol. 5). Stanford, CA: Stanford Univ. Press.

Tessman, L. H. (1978). *Children of parting parents.* New York: Aronson.

Teti, D. M., & Ablard, K. E. (1989). Security of attachment and infant-sibling relationships: A laboratory study. *Child Development, 60,* 1519-1528.

Thomas, A., Chess, S., & Birch, H. (1968). *Temperament and behavior disorders in children.* New York: New York Univ. Press.

Thomas, A., Chess, S., & Birch, H. G. (1970). The origin of personality. *Scientific American, 223*(2), 102-109.

Thomas, D. G., Campos, J. J., Shucard, D. W., Ramsay, D. S., & Shucard, J. (1981). Semantic comprehension in infancy: A signal detection analysis. *Child Development, 52,* 798-803.

Thomas, L. (1982, March). On altruism. *Discover,* pp. 58-59.

Thompson, L. A., Fagan, J. F., & Fulker, D. W. (1991). Longitudinal prediction of specific cognitive abilities from infant novelty preference. *Child Development, 62,* 530-538.

Thompson, R. A. (1988). The effects of infant day care through the prism of attachment theory: A critical appraisal. *Early Childhood Research Quarterly, 3,* 273-282.

Thompson, S. K. (1975). Gender labels and early sex role development. *Child Development, 46,* 339-347.

Thorndike, E. L. (1905). *The elements of psychology.* New York: Seiler.

Thurstone, L. L. (1938). Primary mental abilities. *Psychometric Monographs, 1.*

Timberlake, E. M. (1980). The value of grandchildren to grandmothers. *Journal of Gerontological Social Work, 3,* 63-76.

Time. (1986, March 3). Died; Shigechiyo Izumi. P. 79.

Timiras, P. S. (1972). *Developmental physiology and aging.* New York: Macmillan.

Torrance, E. P., & Wu, T. (1981). A comparative longitudinal study of the adult creative achievements of elementary school children identified as highly intelligent and as highly creative. *Creative Child and Adult Quarterly, 6,* 71-76.

Tower, R. B., Singer, D. G., Singer, J. L., & Biggs, A. (1979). Differential effects of television programming on preschoolers' cognition, imagination, and social play. *American Journal of Orthopsychiatry, 49,* 265-281.

Toynbee, A. (1968). Changing attitudes toward death in the modern Western world. In A. Toynbee, A. K. Mant, N. Smart, J. Hinton, S. Yudkin, E. Rhode, R. Haywood, & H. H. Price (Eds.), *Man's concern with death* (pp. 122-132). New York: McGraw-Hill.

Traupmann, J., & Hatfield, E. (1981). Love and its effect on mental and physical health. In R. W. Fogel, E. Hatfield, S. B. Kiesler, & E. Shanas (Eds.), *Aging: Stability and change in the family.* New York: Academic Press.

Trehub, S. E., Schneider, B. A., Morrongiello, B. A., & Thorpe, L. A. (1988). Auditory sensitivity in school-age children. *Journal of Experimental Child Psychology, 46,* 273-285.

Trickett, P. K., & Kuczynski, L. (1986). Children's misbehaviors and parental discipline strategies in abusive and nonabusive families. *Developmental Psychology, 22,* 115-123.

Troll, L. E. (1983). Grandparents: The family watchdogs. In T. A. Brubaker (Ed.), *Family relationships in later life* (pp. 63-74). Beverly Hills: Sage Publishing Company.

Troll, L. E. (1985). The contingencies of grandparenting. In V. L. Bengtson & J. F. Robertson (Eds.), *Grandparenthood* (pp. 135-149). Beverly Hills: Sage Publishing Co.

Tronick, E. Z., Morelli, G. A., & Ivey, P. K. (1992). The Efe forager infant and toddler's pattern of social relationships: Multiple and simultaneous. *Developmental Psychology, 28,* 568-577.

Trotter, R. J. (1983, August). Baby face. *Psychology Today,* pp. 14-20.

Trotter, R. J. (1987, May). You've come a long way, baby. *Psychology Today,* pp. 34-45.

Troyat, H. (1967). *Tolstoy.* New York: Doubleday.

Tsitouras, P. D., Martin, C. E., & Harman, S. M. (1982). Relationship of serum testosterone to sexual activity in healthy elderly men. *Journal of Gerontology, 37,* 288-293.

Tunmer, W. E. (1985). The acquisition of the sentient-nonsentient distinction and its relationship to causal reasoning and social cognition. *Child Development, 56,* 989-1000.

Turkington, C. (1986, November). Down syndrome child is frequently educable. *APA Monitor,* p. 22.

Turner, G., Brookwell, R., Daniel, A., Selikowitz, M., & Zilibowitz, M. (1980). Heterozygous expression of X-linked mental retardation and X-chromosome marker fra(X)(q27). *New England Journal of Medicine, 303,* 662-664.

Turner, P. J. (1991). Relations between attachment, gender, and behavior with peers in preschool. *Child Development, 62,* 1475-1488.

U.S. Bureau of the Census. (1984). Projections of the population of the United States by age, sex, and race: 1983 to 2080. *Current Population Reports,* Series P-25, No. 952. Washington, DC: U.S. Govt. Printing Office.

U.S. Bureau of the Census. (1986). *Statistical abstract of the United States: 1987* (107th ed.). Washington, DC: U.S. Govt. Printing Office.

U.S. Bureau of the Census. (1993). *Statistical abstract of the United States: 1994* (114th ed.). Washington, DC: U. S. Govt. Printing Office.

U.S. Department of Commerce. (1983). Marital status and living arrangements: March, 1982. U.S. Bureau of the Census, *Current Population Reports,* Series P-20, No. 380. Washington, DC: U.S. Govt. Printing Office.

U.S. Department of Labor, Bureau of Labor Statistics. (1976). *Employment and earnings.* Washington, DC: U.S. Dept. of Labor.

U.S. Merit Systems Protection Board. (1981). *Sexual harrassment in the federal workplace: Is it a problem?* Washington, DC: U.S. Govt. Printing Office.

Uhlenberg, P., & Myers, M. A. (1981). Divorce and the elderly. *The Gerontologist, 21,* 276-282.

United States Adivsory Board on Child Abuse and Neglect. (1990). *Child abuse and neglect: Critical first steps in response to a national emergency* (stock no. 017-092-00104-5). Washington, DC: U. S. Government Printing Office, Congressional Sales Office.

Vaillant, G. E. (1977). *Adaptation to life.* Boston: Little, Brown, & Company.

Vaillant, G. E. (1979). Natural history of male psychologic health: Effects of mental health on physical health. *New England Journal of Medicine, 301,* 1249-1254.

Vaillant, G. E., & Vaillant, C. O. (1990). Natural history of male psychological health, XII: 45-year study of predictors of successful aging at age 65. *American Journal of Psychiatry, 147,* 31-37.

Valdez-Menchaca, M. C., & Whitehurst, G. J. (1988). The effects of incidental teaching on vocabulary acquisition by young children. *Child Development, 59,* 1451-1459.

Valencia, R. R. (1985). Predicting academic achievement in Mexican-American children using the Kaufman Assessment Battery for children. *Educational and Psychological Research, 5,* 11-17.

van Doorninck, W. J., Caldwell, B. M., Wright, C., & Frankenburg, W. K. (1981). The relationship between twelve-month home stimulation and school achievement. *Child Development, 52,* 1080-1083.

Van IJzendoorn, M. H., & Kroonenberg, P. M. (1988). Cross-cultural patterns of attachment: A meta-analysis of the strange situation. *Child Development, 59,* 147-156.

Van Praag, H. M. (1977). Psychotropic drugs in the aged. *Comprehensive Psychiatry, 18,* 429-442.

Vandenberg, B. (1978). Play and development from an ethological perspective. *American Psychologist, 33,* 724-738.

Vandenberg, B. (1981). Environmental and cognitive factors in social play. *Journal of Experimental Child Psychology, 31,* 169-175.

Vandenberg, B. (1984). Developmental features of exploration. *Developmental Psychology, 20,* 3-8.

Vandiver, R. (1972). *Sources and interrelation of premarital sexual standards and general liberality conservatism.* Unpublished doctoral dissertation, Southern Illinois University.

Vaughn, B. E., & Langlois, J. H. (1983). Physical attractiveness as a correlate of peer status and social competence in preschool children. *Developmental Psychology, 19*, 561-567.

Vaughn, B. E., Kopp, C. B., & Krakow, J. B. (1984). The emergence and consolidation of self-control from eighteen to thirty months of age: Normative trends and individual differences. *Child Development, 55*, 990-1004.

Verbrugge, L. M. (1982). Women's social roles and health. In P. Berman & E. Ramey (Eds.), *Women: A developmental perspective* (pp. 49-78). Bethesda, MD: Nat'l Institute of Health.

Vermeulen, A. (1983). Androgen secretion after age 50 in both sexes. *Hormone Research, 18*, 37-42.

Vernon, P. E. (1965). Ability factors and environmental influences. *American Psychologist, 20*, 723-733.

Vinick, B. H. (1978). Remarriage in old age. *Journal of Geriatric Psychiatry, 11*, 75-77.

Vitz, P. C. (1990). The use of stories in moral development: New psychological reasons for an old education method. *American Psychologist, 45*, 709-720.

Vollrath, D., Foote, S., Hilton, A., Brown, L. G., Beer-Romero, P., Bogan, J. S., & Page, D. C. (1992). The human Y chromosome: A 43-interval map based on naturally occurring deletions. *Science, 258*, 52-59.

Volunteering comes of age. (1987, March). *Modern Maturity*, pp. 16-17.

Vondracek, F. W., & Lerner, R. M. (1982). Vocational role development in adolescence. In B. B. Wolman (Ed.), *Handbook of developmental psychology* (pp. 602-614). Englewood Cliffs, NJ: Prentice-Hall.

Vuchinich, S., Hetherington, E. M., Vuchinich, R. A., & Clingempeel, W. G. (1991). Parent-child interaction and gender differences in early adolescents' adaptation to stepfamilies. *Developmental Psychology, 27,* 618-626.

Vygotsky, L. S. (1962). *Thought and language* (E. Hanfmann & G. Vakar, Trans.). Cambridge: Massachusetts Institute of Technology. (Original work published 1934).

Waldhauser, F., Weiszenbacher, G., Frisch, H., Zeitlhuber, U., Waldhauser, M., & Wurtman, R. J. (1984). Fall in nocturnal serum melatonin during prepuberty and pubescence. *Lancet, 1*(8373), 362-365.

Waldron, I., & Herold, J. (1984, March). *Employment, attitudes toward employment, and women's health.* Paper presented at the meeting of the Society of Behavior Medicine, Philadelphia Pennsylvania.

Walker, E., & Emory, E. (1985). Commentary: Interpretive bias and behavioral genetic research. *Child Development, 56*, 775-778.

Walker, L. A. (1987, June 21). What comforts AIDS families? *New York Times Magazine*, pp. 16-78.

Walker, L. J. (1986). Experiential and cognitive sources of moral development in adulthood. *Human Development, 29*, 113-124.

Walker, L. J., & Taylor, J. H. (1991b). Stage transitions in moral reasoning: A longitudinal study of developmental processes. *Developmental Psychology, 27*, 330-337.

Walker, L. J., & Taylor, J. H. (1991a). Family interactions and the development of moral reasoning. *Child Development, 62*, 264-283.

Walker, L. J., de Vries, B., & Trevethan, S. D. (1987). Moral stages and moral orientations in real-life and hypothetical dilemmas. *Child Development, 58*, 842-858.

Walker, L. J., de Vries, B., & Bichard, S. L. (1984). The hierarchical nature of stages of moral development. *Developmental Psychology, 20*, 960-966.

Wallach, M. A. (1970). Creativity. In P. H. Mussen (Ed.), *Carmichael's manual of child psychology* (3rd ed., pp. 1211-1272). New York: Wiley.

Wallach, M. A., & Wing, C. W. (1969). *The talented student: A validation of the creativity-intelligence distinction.* New York: Holt.

Wallerstein, J. S. (1984a). Children of divorce: Preliminary report of a ten-year follow-up of young children. *American Journal of Orthopsychiatry, 54*, 444-458.

Wallerstein, J. S. (1984b). Children of divorce: The psychological tasks of the child. *Annual Progress in Child Psychiatry and Child Development, 1984*, 263-280.

Wallerstein, J. S. (1985). Effect of divorce on children. *The Harvard Medical School Mental Health Letter, 2*(3), 8.

Wallerstein, J. S., & Kelly, J. B. (1975). The effects of parental divorce: Experiences of the preschool child. *Journal of the American Academy of Child Psychiatry, 14*, 600-616.

Wallerstein, J. S., & Kelly, J. B. (1976). The effects of parental divorce: Experiences of the child in later latency. *American Journal of Orthopsychiatry, 46*, 256-269.

Wallerstein, J. S., & Kelly, J. B. (1981). *Surviving the breakup: How children and parents cope with divorce.* New York: Basic Books.

Wallis, C., Booth, C., Ludtke, M., & Taylor, E. (1985, December 9). Children having children. *Time*, pp. 78-90.

Wallis, C., Hull, J. D., Ludtke, M., & Taylor, E. (1987, June 22). The child-care dilemma. *Time*, pp. 54-60.

Wallis, C., & Ludtke, M. (1987, June 22). Is day care bad for babies? *Time*, p. 63.

Walsh, D. A. (1983). Age differences in learning and memory. In D. S. Woodruff & J. E. Birren (Eds.), *Aging: Scientific perspectives and social issues* (pp. 149-177). Monterey, CA: Brooks/Cole.

Walster, E., & Walster, G. W. (1978). *A new look at love.* Reading, MA: Addison-Wesley.

Warihay, P. D. (1980). The climb to the top: Is the network the route for women? *Personnel Administrator, 25*, 55-60.

Waring, J. (1978). *The middle years: A multidisciplinary view.* New York: Academy for Ed. Develop.

Warren, M. P. (1980). The effects of exercise on pubertal progression and reproductive function in girls. *Journal of Clinical Endocrinology and Metabolism, 51*, 1150-1157.

Waters, E., Wippman, J., & Sroufe, L. A. (1979). Attachment, positive affect, and competence in the peer group: Two studies in construct validation. *Child Development, 50*, 821-829.

Watson, J. B. (1928). *Psychological care of the infant and child.* New York: Norton.

Watson, J. D., & Crick, F. H. C. (1953). Molecular structure of nucleic acids: A structure for deoxyribose nucleic acid. *Nature, 171*, 737-738.

Weaver, C. N. (1980). Job satisfaction in the United States in the 1970's. *Journal of Applied Psychology, 65*, 364-367.

Webb, M. (1988, February 1). Back to the nest. *New York*, pp. 25-33.

Weber, G. (1971). *Inner city children can be taught to read: Four successful schools.* Washington, D.C.: Council for Basic Education, Occasional Paper no. 18.

Weber, J. A., & Fournier, D. G. (1985). Family support and a child's adjustment to death. *Family Relations, 34*, 43-49.

Wehren, A., & De Lisi, R. (1983). The development of gender understanding: Judgments and explanations. *Child Development, 54*, 1568-1578.

Weinberg, R. A. (1989). Intelligence and IQ. *American Psychologist, 44*, 98-104.

Weinstock, A., & Lerner, R. M. (1972). Attitudes of late adolescents and their parents toward contemporary issues. *Psychological Reports, 30*, 239-244.

Weisfeld, G. E. (1982). The nature-nurture issue and the integrating concept of function. In B. B. Wolman (Ed.), *Handbook of developmental psychology* (pp. 208-229). Englewood Cliffs, NJ: Prentice-Hall.

Weisler, A., & McCall, R. B. (1976). Exploration and play. *American Psychologist, 31*, 144-152.

Weisner, T. S., & Wilson-Mitchell, J. E. (1990). Nonconventional family life-styles and sex typing in six-year-olds. *Child Development, 61*, 1915-1933.

Weiss, R. (1989, January 21). Predisposition and prejudice. *Science News*, pp. 40-42.

Weiss, R. S. (1979). Growing up a little faster: The experience of growing up in a single-parent household. *Journal of Social Issues, 35*, 97-111.

REFERENCES

Weist, R. M. (1983). The word order myth. *Journal of Child Language, 10,* 97-106.

Wells, G. (1985). Preschool literacy-related activities and success in school. In D. R. Olson, N. Torrance, & A. Hildyard (Eds.), *Literacy, language, and learning: The nature and consequences of reading and writing* (pp. 229-255). New York: Cambridge University Press.

Wertheimer, M. (1961). Psycho-motor coordination of auditory-visual space at birth. *Science, 134,* 1692.

West, J. R., Hodges, C. A., & Black, A. C., Jr. (1981). Prenatal exposure to ethanol alters the organization of hippocampal mossy fibers in rats. *Science, 211,* 957-958.

West, M. J., & Rheingold, H. L. (1978). Infant stimulation of maternal instruction. *Infant Behavior and Development, 1,* 205-215.

White, B. L. (1975). Critical influences in the origins of competence. *Merrill-Palmer Quarterly, 21,* 243-266.

Whitehurst, G. J. (1982). Language development. In B. B. Wolman (Ed.), *Handbook of developmental psychology* (pp. 367-386). Englewood Cliffs, NJ: Prentice-Hall.

Whitehurst, G. J., Falco, F. L., Lonigan, C. J., Fischel, J. E., DeBaryshe, B. D., Valdez-Menchaca, M. C., & Caulfield, M. (1988). Accelerating language development through picture book reading. *Developmental Psychology, 24,* 552-559.

Whiting, B. B., & Whiting, J. W. M. (1975). *Children of six cultures: A psychocultural analysis.* Cambridge, Mass.: Harvard Univ. Press.

Wilcox, A. J., Weinberg, C. R., O'Connor, J. F., Baird, D. D., Schlatterer, J. P., Canfield, R. E., Armstrong, E. G., & Nisula, B. C. (1988). Incidence of early loss of pregnancy. *New England Journal of Medicine, 319,* 189-194.

Wilentz, A., Gorman, C., & Hull, J. (1987, March 23). Teen suicide. *Time,* pp. 12-13.

Will, J. A., Self, P. A., & Datan, N. (1976). Maternal behavior and perceived sex of infant. *American Journal of Orthopsychiatry, 46,* 135-139.

Willerman, L., Schultz, R., Rutledge, J. N., & Bigler, E. D. (1991). In vivo brain size and intelligence. *Intelligence, 15,* 223-228.

Williams, D. A., & King, P. (1980a, December 22). It really is a head start. *Newsweek,* p. 54.

Williams, T. M. (Ed.). (1986). *The impact of television: A natural experiment in three communities.* Orlando, FL: Academic Press, Inc.

Wills, T. A. (1978). Perceptions of clients by professional helpers. *Psychological Bulletin, 85,* 968-1000.

Wilson, E. O. (1975). *Sociobiology.* Cambridge, Mass.: Belknap Press.

Wilson, R. S. (1983). The Louisville Twin Study: Developmental synchronies in behavior. *Child Development, 54,* 298-316.

Winter, A. (1986a, August-September). What should I do? *Modern Maturity,* pp. 82-89.

Winter, A. (1986b, October-November). The shame of elder abuse. *Modern Maturity,* pp. 50-57.

Wolf, R., Godkin, M., & Pillemer, K. (1984, December). *Elder abuse and neglect: Final report from three model projects.* University of Massachusetts Medical Center: University Center on Aging.

Wolock, I., & Horowitz, B. (1984). Child maltreatment as a social problem: The neglect of neglect. *American Journal of Orthopsychiatry, 54,* 530-543.

Wood, V., & Robertson, J. F. (1976). The significance of grandparenthood. In J. Gubrium (Ed.), *Time, roles, and self in old age.* New York: Behavioral Publications.

Woodhead, M. (1988). When psychology informs public policy: The case of early childhood intervention. *American Psychologist, 43,* 443-454.

Woodruff, D. S., & Birren, J. E. (1972). Age changes and cohort differences in personality. *Developmental Psychology, 6,* 252-259.

Woods, M. B. (1972). The unsupervised child of the working mother. *Developmental Psychology, 6,* 14-25.

Woolfolk, R. L., & Lehrer, P. M. (1984). Clinical stress reduction: An overview. In R. L. Woolfolk & P. M. Lehrer (Eds.), *Principles and practice of stress management* (pp. 1-11). New York: Guilford Press.

Wright, H. F. (1967). *Recording and analyzing child behavior.* New York: Harper & Row.

Wroblewski, R., & Huston, A. C. (1987). Televised occupational stereotypes and their effects on early adolescents: Are they changing? *Journal of Early Adolescence, 7,* 283-297.

Yager, T., Laufer, R., & Gallops, M. (1984). Some problems associated with war experience in men of the Vietnam generation. *Archives of General Psychiatry, 41,* 327-333.

Yang, R. K., & Douthitt, T. C. (1974). Newborn responses to threshold tactile stimulation. *Child Development, 45,* 237-242.

Yarrow, M. R., & Waxler, C. (1977, March). Paper presented at the meeting of the Society for Research in Child Development, New Orleans, Louisiana.

Yarrow, M. R., Campbell, J. D., & Burton, R. (1968). *Child rearing, an inquiry into research and methods.* San Francisco: Jossey-Bass.

Yates, B. T., & Mischel, W. (1979). Young children's preferred attentional strategies for delaying gratification. *Journal of Personality and Social Psychology, 37,* 286-300.

Yogman, M., Dixon, S., Tronick, E., & Brazelton, T. B. (1976, April). *Development of infant social interaction with fathers.* Paper presented at the meeting of the Eastern Psychological Association, New York.

York, J. L., & Caslyn, R. J. (1977). Family involvement in nursing homes. *The Gerontologist, 17,* 500-505.

Youngblade, L. M., & Belsky, J. (1992). Parent-child antecedents of 5-year-olds' close friendships: A longitudinal analysis. *Developmental Psychology, 28,* 700-713.

Youngstrom, N. (1991, October). Warning: Teens at risk for AIDS. The *APA Monitor,* pp. 38-39.

Zahn-Waxler, C., Radke-Yarrow, M., Wagner, E., & Chapman, M. (1992). Development of concern for others. *Developmental Psychology, 28,* 126-136.

Zajonc, R. B. (1986). The decline and rise of scholastic aptitude scores: A prediction derived from the confluence model. *American Psychologist, 41,* 862-867.

Zajonc, R. B., & Markus, G. B. (1975). Birth order and intellectual development. *Psychological Review, 82,* 74-88.

Zarbatany, L., Hartmann, D. P., Gelfand, D. M., & Vinciguerra, P. (1985). Gender differences in altruistic reputation: Are they artifactual? *Developmental Psychology, 21,* 97-101.

Zarbatany, L., Hartmann, D. P., & Rankin, D. B. (1990). The psychological functions of preadolescent peer activities. *Child Development, 61,* 1067-1080.

Zarit, S. H., Cole, K. D., & Guider, R. L. (1981). Memory training strategies and subjective complaints of memory in the aged. *The Gerontologist, 21,* 158-164.

Zarit, S. H., Gallagher, D., & Kramer, N. (1981). Memory training in the community aged: Effects on depression, memory complaint, and memory performance. *Educational Gerontology, 6,* 11-27.

Zeligs, R. (1974). *Children's experience with death.* Springfield, IL: Charles C. Thomas.

Zigler, E., & Turner, P. (1982). Parents and day care workers: A failed partnership? In E. Zigler, & E. Gordon (Eds.), *Day care: Scientific and social policy issues.* Boston, MA: Auburn House.

SUBJECT INDEX*

Acknowledgments

Page 5, Fig. 1.1, REPRINTED FROM PSYCHOLOGY TODAY MAGAZINE. Copyright © 1987 American Psychological Association.

Page 34, Fig. 2.3, From "Thorndike and the Problem of Animal Intelligence," by M. E. Bitterman. In *American Psychologist,* 1969, Vol. 24, p. 445. Copyright 1969 by the American Psychological Association. Reprinted by permission of the author.

Page 93, Fig. 4.3, From "Neonatal Mortality Risk in Relation to Birth Weight . . . Update," by B. L. Koops, L. J. Morgan, & F. C. Battaglia. In *Journal of Pediatrics,* 1982, 101, p. 962. Reprinted by permission of the C. V. Mosby Company and B. L. Koops.

Page 95, Table 4.1, From "Evaluation of the Newborn Infant—Second Report," by V. Apgar, D. A. Holaday, L. S. James, I. M. Weisbort, & C. Berrien. In *Journal of the American Medical Association,* Vol. 168, p. 1988. Copyright 1958, American Medical Association. Reprinted by permission.

Page 103, Fig. 4.6, From "A Critical Test of Infant Pattern Preference Models," by J. L. Dannemiller and B. R. Stephens. In *Child Development,* 1988, Vol. 59, p. 212. © The Society for Research in Child Development. Reprinted by permission.

Page 119, Table 5.1, From "The Origin of Personality," by Alexander Thomas, Stella Chess, and Herbert G. Birch. Copyright © 1970 by Scientific American, Inc. All rights reserved.

Page 135, Table 5.5, Adapted from "Socioemotional development," by L. Alan Sroufe. In J. Osofsky (Ed.), *Handbook of infant development,* 1979, p. 473. Reprinted by permission of John Wiley & Sons, Inc.

Page 159, Figures 6.2 and 6.3, From "Object Permanence in 3½–4½-month Old Infants," by Renee Baillargeon. In *Developmental Psychology,* 1987, Vol. 23, p. 656. Copyright 1987 by the American Psychological Association. Reprinted by permission.

Page 183, Fig. 7.1, From "Retrieval of a Basic-Level Category in Prelinguistic Infants," by Kenneth Roberts. In *Developmental Psychology,* 1988, Vol. 24, p. 23. Copyright 1988 by the American Psychological Association. Reprinted by permission.

Page 186, Fig. 7.2, From "The Acquisition of Language," by Breyne Arlene Moskowitz. Copyright © 1978 by Scientific American, Inc. All rights reserved.

Page 188, Table 7.2, From PSYCHOLOGY AND LANGUAGE by Herbert H. Clark and Eve V. Clark © 1977 by Harcourt Brace Jovanovich, Inc. Reprinted by permission of the publisher.

Page 189, Fig. 7.3, From WORD, Vol. 14 (1958), page 154, reprinted by permission of Johnson Reprint Corporation.

Page 190, Table 7.3, From Gover J. Whitehurst "Language Development" in HANDBOOK OF DEVELOPMENTAL PSYCHOLOGY, Wolman et al, eds., © 1982, p. 371. Reprinted by permission of Prentice-Hall, Inc., Englewood Cliffs, New Jersey.

Page 207, Fig. 8.2, From "A Circumplex Model for Maternal Behavior," by E. S. Schaefer. In *Journal of Abnormal and Social Psychology,* 1959, Vol. 59, pp. 226–235. Copyright 1959 by the American Psychological Association. Reprinted by permission of the author.

Page 218, Fig. 8.3, From "Growth of Social Play with Peers During the Second Year of Life," by C. O. Eckerman, J. L. Whatley, & S. L. Kutz. In *Developmental Psychology,* 1975, Vol. 11, p. 47. Copyright 1975 by the American Psychological Association. Reprinted by permission of the author.

Page 221, Table 8.1, From "How Children Become Friends," by J. M. Gottman. In *Monographs of the Society for Research in Child Development,* 48, 1983, pp. 27, 53–54. © The Society for Research in Child Development, Inc. Reprinted by permission.

Page 222, Table 8.2, From "How Children Become Friends," by J. M. Gottman. In *Monographs of the Society for Research in Child Development,* 48, 1983, pp. 54–55. © The Society for Research in Child Development, Inc. Reprinted by permission.

Page 238, Fig. 9.2, From OF CHILDREN, Fourth Edition, by Guy R. Lefrancois. © 1983, 1980 by Wadsworth, Inc. Reprinted by permission of the publisher.

Page 244, Table 9.1, Dilemma and pro and con answers reprinted from Developmental Hierarchy in Preference and Comprehension of Moral Judgment, by James Rest, Unpublished doctoral dissertation, 1968. Reprinted by permission of the author.

Page 277, Fig. 10.3, Sample item A5 from the Raven STANDARD PROGRESSIVE MATRICES is reproduced by permission of J. C. Raven Limited.

Page 280, Fig. 10.4, From *Stability and Change in Human Characteristics,* by B. S. Bloom. Reprinted by permission of Benjamin S. Bloom.

Page 305, Fig. 11.2, From *Disadvantaged Children: Health, Nutrition and School Failure,* by H. G. Birch & J. D. Gussow, 1970, p. 268. Reprinted by permission of Grune & Stratton, Inc.

Page 311, Fig. 11.3, From "Developmental Differences in Responses to a Television Character's

Appearance and Behavior," by C. Hoffner, & J. Cantor. In *Developmental Psychology*, 1985, Vol. 21, p. 1067. Copyright 1985 by the American Psychological Association. Reprinted by permission of the authors.

Page 319, Fig. 12.1, Adapted from "Growth and Endocrinology in the Adolescent," by J. M. Tanner. In L. I. Gardner (Ed.), *Endocrine and Genetic Diseases of Childhood*, 1969. Adapted by permission of W. B. Saunders Co. and Dr. J. M. Tanner.

Page 321, Fig. 12.2, From "Standards From Birth to Maturity for Height, Weight, Height Velocity and Weight Velocity: British Children 1965," by J. M. Tanner, R. H. Whitehouse, and M. Takaishi. In *Archives of Disease in Childhood*, 1966, 41, 454–471; 613–635. Reprinted by permission.

Page 322, Fig. 12.3, From J. M. Tanner, 1962, *Growth at Adolescence*; data from Jones, 1949. By permission of Blackwell Scientific Publications and J. M. Tanner.

Page 329, Fig. 12.5, From "Adolescence and Formal Operations," by A. Blasi & E. C. Hoeffel. In *Human Development*, 1974, 17, p. 345. Reprinted by permission of S. Karger AG, Basel, Switzerland.

Page 350, Table 13.2, From "Premarital Sex: Attitudes and Behavior by Dating Stage," by John P. Roche. In *Adolescence*, 1986, 21(No. 81), p. 110. Reprinted by permission.

Page 351, quotation. Copyright 1985, Time Inc. All rights reserved. Reprinted by permission from TIME.

Page 365, Fig. 14.2, From SRA Primary Mental Abilities, Ages 11–17. Form AM. Copyright 1948 by L. L. Thurstone and Thelma Gwinn Thurstone. Reprinted by permission of the publisher, Science Research Associates, Inc.

Page 367, Fig. 14.4, From "The Course of Adult Intellectual Development," by K. Warner Schaie. In *American Psychologist*, Vol. 49, p. 308. Copyright 1994 by the American Psychological Association. Reprinted by permission.

Page 368, Fig. 14.5, From "Cognitive Development in Adulthood," by J. L. Horn & G. Y. Donaldson. In O. G. Brim & J. Kagan (Eds.), *Constancy and Change in Human Development*, pp. 469, 471. Reprinted by permission of Harvard University Press and J. L. Horn.

Page 371, Fig. 14.64, From "A Longitudinal Study of Moral Judgment," by A. Colby, L. Kohlberg, J. Gibbs, & M. Lieberman. In *Monographs of the Society for Research in Child Development*, Volume 48 (1-2,Serial No. 200), P. 46. Copyright The Society for Research in Child Development. Reprinted by permission.

Page 377, Fig. 14.7, From *The Seasons of a Man's Life*, p. 57, by D. J. Levinson, C. N. Darrow, & E. B. Klein. Copyright 1978 by Alfred A. Knopf, Inc. Adapted by permission of Alfred A. Knopf and Daniel J. Levinson.

Page 401, Table 15.2, From Peter J. Stein, "Singlehood," p. 31 in *Contemporary Families and Alternative Lifestyles*, edited by E. D. Macklin & R. H. Rubin (Eds.). Copyright © 1983 by Sage Publications. Reprinted by permission of Sage Publications, Inc., and Peter J. Stein.

Page 423, Table 16.1, Reprinted with permission from the *Journal of Psychosomatic Research*, Volume 11, T. H. Holmes & R. H. Rahe, "The Social Readjustment Rating Scale," Copyright 1967, Pergamon Journals, Ltd.

Page 425, Fig. 16.1, From Jenkins Activity Survey. Copyright © 1978 by The Psychological Corporation. Reproduced by permission. All rights reserved.

Page 427, cartoon, From CATHY by Cathy Guisewite. © 1986 Universal Press Syndicate. Reprinted with permission.

Page 452, Fig. 17.2, Reprinted from THE NOT-SO-EMPTY NEST copyright 1981 by Phyllis Feuerstein and Carol Roberts by permission of New Century Publishers, Inc., Piscataway, New Jersey.

Page 474, Fig. 18.2, Copyright (1988) American Association of Retired Persons, Reprinted with Permission.

Page 486, Fig. 18.8, From "The Course of Adult Intellectual Development," by K. Warner Schaie. In *American Psychologist*, Vol. 49, p. 306. Copyright 1994 by the American Psychological Association. Reprinted by permission.

Page 529, Table 20.1, From Myra Bluebond-Langner, *The Private Worlds of Dying Children*. Copyright © 1978 Princeton University Press. Figures, pp. 166–169, reprinted with permission of Princeton University Press.

Page 535, Fig. 20.2, Reprinted with permission of Concern for Dying, 250 West 57th Street, New York, NY 10107; (212) 246-6962.

Photo Credits